A CARLYLE READER

*Selections from the Writings of
Thomas Carlyle*

EDITED BY G. B. TENNYSON

*Professor of English Literature
University of California, Los Angeles*

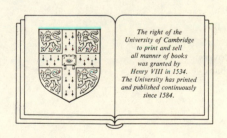

The right of the
University of Cambridge
to print and sell
all manner of books
was granted by
Henry VIII in 1534.
The University has printed
and published continuously
since 1584.

CAMBRIDGE UNIVERSITY PRESS

*Cambridge
London   New York   New Rochelle
Melbourne   Sydney*

Published by the Press Syndicate of the University of Cambridge
The Pitt Building, Trumpington Street, Cambridge CB2 1RP
32 East 57th Street, New York, NY 10022, USA
296 Beaconsfield Parade, Middle Park, Melbourne 3206, Australia

© Random House, Inc. 1969
© Cambridge University Press 1984

First published by Random House 1969
First published by Cambridge University Press 1984

Printed in Malta by Interprint Ltd.

Library of Congress Catalog Card number: 83–21024

British Library Cataloguing in Publication Data

Carlyle, Thomas
A Carlyle reader.
I. Title   II. Tennyson, G. B.
828'.808   PR4434

ISBN 0 521 26238 0 hard covers
ISBN 0 521 27873 2 paperback

FOR CAM AND HOLLY,
AGAIN

Preface

The study of the great Victorian writers of nonfictional prose has long been hampered by the unavailability of modern texts, forcing a direct confrontation by the student with the daunting ranks of nineteenth-century volumes on the library shelf. Desirable as such a confrontation is as an ultimate goal, for the uninitiated it more often results in sounding retreat than advance, especially when the author is Thomas Carlyle, whose works occupy thirty volumes in the standard edition, to say nothing of the letters and uncollected writings. The present selection from Carlyle's works is designed to lessen the shock of the initial encounter and to ease the way for later, fuller study by making available in a single volume a representative selection from his vast output. Since Carlyle is himself the pattern and type of the great Victorian prose writer, acquaintance with his work through this volume may also encourage the study of Victorian prose generally and of those authors who followed in Carlyle's wake.

Without pretending to be exhaustive, the present volume seeks nevertheless to be representative. The selections here offered are designed to show both the range and the depth of Carlyle's work and to give something of a picture of the man himself. Thus there are selections from all periods and types of Carlyle's writing, with the greatest emphasis on the work of the first part of his career. His best-known work, *Sartor Resartus*, is printed in its entirety, as are several of the early seminal essays that mark out the territory that Carlyle was to explore for the rest of his literary life; and substantial selections from *The French Revolution* are included. For the later period, whole chapters, essays, and sections are presented from works up to the end of Carlyle's life. Throughout, there are selections from his correspondence and from other personal writings (such as his Journal, never before anthologized, his poetry, and the *Reminiscences*), which give a developing picture of Carlyle the man and the writer.

The selections here presented should lend themselves to readings for various purposes, from the classroom to the private study. The follower of Carlyle's ideas has here a concentrated gathering of his views on virtually every important subject he treated; the student of Carlyle's distinctive literary style has *Sartor Resartus* and other works in Carlyle's most characteristic and celebrated vein; the reader of Carlyle as historian, biographer, essayist, literary or social critic, will find all these areas well represented; and the student of biography can see Carlyle's life through the correspondence and headnotes and the chronological presentation of his writings as he moved from unknown Scotsman to public man of letters. And, since the arrangement is developmental, one can follow all of these aspects of Carlyle as they unfolded.

The selections have also been chosen to interest modern readers who are gradually discovering, or rediscovering, Carlyle. These readers have here an opportunity to grasp the qualities of style and belief that made Carlyle such an exciting writer for his Victorian contemporaries and a quarry of ideas for writers as various as Ruskin, Emerson, Arnold, William Morris, and Shaw. Modern readers can also see the many ways in which Carlyle is still strikingly alive and vital and in which he continues to speak to issues of contemporary relevance.

In compiling the original form of this volume I was greatly aided by Ellen Cole and staff at UCLA who prepared the manuscript. I am grateful to Wayne H. Phelps and to my wife, Elizabeth J. Tennyson, for vigilant proofreading. For the present appearance of this volume I am especially indebted to Andrew Brown of the Cambridge University Press.

G.B.T.

Los Angeles, California
July, 1983

Contents

Introduction

BY G. B. TENNYSON

In his early years Thomas Carlyle was known as a mystic and a radical, in his later years as the Sage of Chelsea, and after his death by other less charitable terms. Emerson likened him to a great cathedral bell which society rang from time to time to temper its jollity. The society in question, that of Victoria's England, had at first rejected the strange writings of the rude prophet but ended by showering him with honors. In his seventieth year the students of Edinburgh University gave him more than twice the number of votes they gave Benjamin Disraeli in the election to Rector of the University; five years later, the British crown offered him the Grand Cross of Bath and a pension. He accepted the rectorship and declined the royal offer. In our own time Carlyle survives as a staple of the study of Victorian life and literature and as the creator of the most inventive and dynamic of English prose styles.

Carlyle's posthumous reputation has not always been steady. After his death in 1881 there was a decade or so of reminiscences and biographies by those who had known him, but the tone of much that was written about him in the last years of the nineteenth century became increasingly personal and spiteful. Petty revelations of domestic infelicity between Thomas and Jane Carlyle sustained interest for a time in the two as individuals and provoked charges and countercharges, but all the while Carlyle's literary reputation was sinking lower and lower. There was an irony in the biographical obsessions of the late Victorians, for Carlyle had stoutly insisted that he never wanted his biography written and he had refused requests to write an autobiography. He wanted his message to ring clear, but instead the literary public found itself debating aspects of Carlyle's personal life. The result of the tempest is summed up by Samuel Butler's remark that

"It was very good of God to let Carlyle and Mrs. Carlyle marry one another and so make only two people miserable instead of four, besides being very amusing." On such a note the interest in Thomas Carlyle died away.

Carlyle's reputation might have recovered in a few years but there were other hindrances. He had gained his early fame as a translator and interpreter of German literature and thought; toward the end of his life he was honored for his intellectual services to Germany by the Prussian Order of Merit, an order established by Frederick the Great. The First World War was not calculated to enhance the position of Germanophiles in England, nor in the aftermath was there much interest left in anything Victorian. Carlyle lost on both counts. The ominous rise of Nazism in the 1930s and the eruption of the Second World War cast a further blight on anyone who had exalted things German. It is regrettable, but perhaps understandable, that critics did not distinguish between Carlyle's enthusiasm for Goethe, Schiller, and German romanticism and the perversion of his later writings by overzealous German readers. Meanwhile Carlyle's thirty volumes languished on the shelf. However, *Sartor Resartus* and a few other works remained steadily in print, able to exert their power and fascination only upon graduate students obliged to read them.

Today the situation is different. No one who hopes to understand the nineteenth century in England can dispense with Carlyle. We meet him everywhere. Dickens admired his works this side of idolatry. John Ruskin never ceased to consider him the Master. John Stuart Mill was for years an intimate friend. Thackeray, Tennyson, Browning, Emerson, William Morris, not to mention lesser figures like J. A. Froude, John Sterling, Richard Monckton Milnes, and Thomas Arnold of Rugby, were in varying degrees admirers or even worshipers of Carlyle's wisdom. When in old age Carlyle delivered his inaugural address at Edinburgh, the unanimous verdict of the audience and soon of all Britain was expressed by John Tyndall's telegram to Jane: "A perfect triumph." Today, the fact that Carlyle was immensely popular and influential in Victorian England is, or should be, less a cause for condescension from our age than a matter of absorbing intellectual and literary interest. How did the man Lytton Strachey described as "not an English gentleman" but a "Scotch peasant" become the most influential writer of his age? And why is he now appealing in his own right to a new generation of readers? To these questions the following pages are addressed.

I

Thomas Carlyle was born on December 4, 1795 in Ecclefechan in the Annandale section of Dumfriesshire, Scotland, the first of nine children (eight of whom survived) of James Carlyle, a stonemason, and Margaret Aitken Carlyle, his second wife. The Carlyles were of humble origin, although they could trace their ancestry to the Lords Carlyle of Torthorwald, and the name was a distinguished one in Cumberland, Durham, and lowland Scotland. The James Carlyles, however, were far removed from all that. They were stern Calvinists in religion, adhering to the Burgher sect which dissented from the Kirk of Scotland on the grounds that it was too lax. The impact of this early Calvinism on Carlyle has been exhaustively studied and almost everything he ever did has been attributed to it. However overdone such interpretations may be, it is certain that Carlyle's character was strongly influenced by the piety, severity, and frugality of his family. He even attributed aspects of his famous style to his father, although in this case it was to his father's exuberant manner of speech. Carlyle's mother was a woman of the purest Scottish Calvinist cast, but also kind and gentle. Her continual concern in letters was for Tom's religion. She always reminded him to read a chapter of the Bible every day. Once when he was in his twenties she wrote asking if he had read the Bible through. "If you have," she added, "read it again." Carlyle's own character displayed much of the dogmatism and irascibility of his father but also a good portion of the kindness and spiritual sweetness of his mother. As a boy he was argumentative and opinionated, but lacking in social graces. His early school years attest to the problems such a combination can produce.

In 1806, after some education in the village school, Carlyle was sent to Annan Academy where he remained for three years. There he first saw Edward Irving, a young man several years his senior and Annan's prize graduate, now a student at Edinburgh University. He was to become Carlyle's closest friend. In 1809, when he was not quite fourteen, Carlyle walked the hundred miles to Edinburgh to enroll at the University to study for the ministry. He remained there five years, but his faith had begun to waver by the time he returned to Annan Academy in 1814 as a teacher of mathematics. He had been depressed by the aridity of intellectual and spiritual life in Edinburgh and assailed by doubts of his own fitness for the ministry. He remained at Annan teaching mathematics for two years, but he enjoyed neither the post at Annan nor the profession of teaching. In 1816 he accepted a post at the Burgh school in Kirkcaldy, near Edinburgh, which made him a neighbor and a kind of rival of Edward Irving who was teaching in a newer school in the same town. But nonetheless they became fast friends. They spent weekends in long walks (thirty miles a day was not uncommon for them) and in endless discussions of philosophical, literary, and social matters. Irving continued to be Carlyle's senior in virtually all things, especially in manners and elegance. Moreover, Irving had completed his ministerial studies and, as an ordained clergyman of the Scottish Kirk, his sermons were bringing him some attention. Some of Carlyle's later famous style he attributed also to Edward Irving. Carlyle, however, had abandoned entirely any ministerial hopes of his own, for he had come to doubt the truth of traditional Christianity. His failure to enter the ministry was a great disappointment to his parents but they never reproached him for it. Despite his loss of faith, the two years in Kirkcaldy with the friendship of Irving were in many ways the happiest years of Carlyle's life. Certainly they were the most intellectually rewarding up to that time. During the Kirkcaldy years Carlyle also experienced his first love.

The lady was Margaret Gordon, afterwards Lady Bannerman. There was no real possibility of a match because of social differences, but years later when they met by chance in Hyde Park, Carlyle and Margaret recognized each other with something of the old ardor, for in Carlyle's words "her *eyes* (but that was all) said to me almost touchingly, 'Yes, yes, that is you!' "

Kirkcaldy and teaching were not for Carlyle. Irving left in 1819 for Edinburgh, then later for a higher post in Glasgow, and finally to London for what was to become a notorious career as a preacher. Carlyle left for Edinburgh too. There he eked out a living, first by writing translations and scientific articles, then later by contributing biographical and historical articles to the *Edinburgh Encyclopaedia.* For a time he studied law, but soon gave that up as unprofitable. The momentous event of the early Edinburgh years was Carlyle's study of German. He had read Mme. de Staël's *De l'Allemagne* and had taken up the study of mineralogy, a science dominated by Germans. But his study of German led far beyond these things. In German romantic literature Carlyle found spiritual treasure beyond the dreams of avarice. He was deeply affected by Goethe, Schiller, and others, especially by their transcendentalism and mysticism. For more than a decade the Germans were to be Carlyle's intellectual mentors, and he was to enjoy his first literary success as the British evangel of the gospel according to the Germans. Twelve years later in *Sartor Resartus* Carlyle was to sum it up by writing "Close thy *Byron,* Open thy *Goethe.*" But all that was far from clear to the young Carlyle, for while he was exploring the new world opened to him by the Germans he was also suffering from what he called "dyspepsia," chronic indigestion, which was to plague him for the rest of his life, and he was still uncertain of his own goals. Nor did he have at this time any human companionship equal to the Kirkcaldy years.

Carlyle's lack of companionship was partially remedied in 1821 when he met Jane Baillie Welsh of Haddington, a student of Irving's from the years before Kirkcaldy, now a young woman of twenty. Jane Welsh was by all odds the fairest young lady of the town, wellborn, beautiful, alert, and vivacious. Carlyle courted her for five years before they were married in 1826. Earlier she had entertained hopes of marrying Irving, but that was not to be. The Carlyle marriage that later became the subject of intense biographical conflict was launched from a lengthy-enough courtship, much of it carried on by correspondence, with Carlyle as a kind of advanced tutor. It is clear from the love letters that the courtship had chiefly the obstacles of money and social position (both lacking on Carlyle's side) to be overcome, but also that these two sharp-witted and strong-willed individuals found fitting mates in each other.

Some time after Carlyle met and began to court Jane Welsh there occurred to him the experience he referred to later as his "conversion" (in *Sartor* the "Spiritual Newbirth"), an experience of mystic communion with a transcendent reality. It was to form the basis for his whole outlook on life for it gave him the positive belief in God and the transcendent world that colors everything he wrote. If G. K. Chesterton is correct in speaking of the "profound security of Carlyle's sense of the unity of the Cosmos," that security surely rests in the experience Carlyle had, probably in the summer of 1822, in Leith Walk in Edinburgh on the way to the strand between Leith and Portobello. Mystic experiences are by their nature incommunicable and unverifiable. Carlyle's is no less so than that of other mystics. Yet the authority such experiences carry for those who have them transcends any other authority whatsoever and is sufficient for the most profound belief. So with Carlyle's experience.

All of these events of Carlyle's early years—from schooldays at Annan to the Newbirth in Leith Walk—are frequently said to be described in the biographical section of *Sartor Resartus* (Book II). This is true but not in any literal sense. Symbolically the biography of Teufelsdröckh uses the background of Carlyle's own experiences to delineate characteristic experiences of the age, and Teufelsdröckh's growth and development up to the Everlasting Yea do parallel in outline Carlyle's own to the mid-1820s. The Spiritual Newbirth Teufelsdröckh experiences in the Rue de L'Enfer is perhaps as persuasive a description of Carlyle's conversion as any. But on balance we must take Teufelsdröckh's biography as far as it touches Carlyle's own life as just what Carlyle called it, "symbolical myth."

Carlyle needed the remaining years of the 1820s to work out his convictions and to gain a livelihood. For a time he was private tutor to the sons of Mr. and Mrs. Charles Buller. He continued writing and energetically made translations from the German. His first book was his translation of Goethe's *Wilhelm Meister's Apprenticeship,* published in 1824. It initiated Carlyle's correspondence with Goethe, which lasted until Goethe's death in 1832. In 1825 Carlyle published his *Life of Schiller.* After his marriage in 1826 he and Jane resided for a time in Edinburgh and in 1827 Carlyle placed his first article in the prestigious *Edinburgh Review.* It was an article on Jean Paul Friedrich Richter (known in Germany simply as Jean Paul) and its publication marks the true turning of the tide for Carlyle as a man of letters, although he continued in virtual poverty for many additional years and himself hardly recognized at the time that he was now properly launched. The year 1827 also saw the publication of the four volumes of *German Romance* containing translations from the German of authors like Goethe, Jean Paul Richter, Ludwig Tieck, and E. T. A. Hoffmann. It also contained *Wilhelm Meister's Travels,* thus completing the first and still the finest translation in English of Goethe's great novel.

In 1828 the Carlyles moved to Craigenputtock, an isolated farm owned by Jane Welsh's family in the mountains of southern Scotland. There they lived for six years, the witty sociable Jane and the intense Thomas, with few visits away and fewer visitors. There was an occasional trip to Edinburgh, one to London, and visits with family, but in the main life at Craigenputtock (the name means "crag of the hawks") was uncommonly tranquil. It was Carlyle's Wilderness. It was a period in which he worked out in thought and written word his understanding of the world and it may be said to have completed his conversion. At Craigenputtock Carlyle produced a considerable body of essays on literary and social matters. They appeared in such publications as the *Edinburgh Review,* the *Foreign Review,* the *Foreign Quarterly Review,* and *Fraser's Magazine,* and they covered such authors and topics as Jean Paul Richter, Goethe, Schiller, Novalis, Burns, Samuel Johnson, German playwrights, and early German literature. He also wrote those pregnant essays about society and history, "Signs of the Times," "On History," and "Characteristics" that are still regarded as fundamental to an understanding of Victorian ideas. All of this material was published anonymously as was then the practice in literary journals, but Carlyle did become known to the literary and publishing world as a man of great parts, if a bit mystical and radical. As testimony of his fame we have the pilgrimage of the young Ralph Waldo Emerson to remote Craigenputtock to meet the author of those arresting articles on German literature he had encountered across the Atlantic. He came with a letter of introduction from John Stuart Mill whom Carlyle had gotten to know as a result of the publication of "Characteristics." Mill was to be a close friend for many years until their ideas drove them irreconcilably apart.

It was during the middle Craigenputtock years, in 1830 and 1831, that Carlyle wrote what has since come to be his best known work, *Sartor Resartus.* His trials in finding a publisher for it were largely a result of its heterodoxy in style and opinion. When he was unsuccessful in 1831 in marketing the manuscript he brought it back to Craigenputtock and turned to other things, more essays on German literature, essays on Diderot, on biography, on Boswell's Johnson. He tried again with more success to publish *Sartor* in 1833. This time it was accepted for serial publication in *Fraser's Magazine* where it ran from November 1833 to August 1834. In this case authorial anonymity may have been a blessing because *Sartor* was ill-received by the reading public, even the public of so unconventional a magazine as *Fraser's,* noted for its humor and its irreverence. Still, the publication of *Sartor* marks an important date in Carlyle's career. In 1834 he and Jane moved from Craigenputtock to Chelsea, London, and a new era began in their lives.

The Carlyles were to live in London, at number 5, Great Cheyne Row, from 1834 to their deaths, Jane in 1866, Thomas in 1881. There were frequent trips back to Scotland, trips by Carlyle to Ireland and Germany, but the basic pattern was set for the rest of their lives. The early years in London offered almost as many financial and social difficulties as the early years in Edinburgh, except that Carlyle now had a firmer grip on life and he had Jane at his side. He confronted his London difficulties with courage and something approaching good cheer.

Apart from the publication of *Sartor* in 1833-1834, the main events of the early London years are the death of Edward Irving and the writing and publication of *The French Revolution*. Irving's preaching in London had taken a bizarre turn. He was at first a great success; the fashionable flocked to his Caledonian Chapel in Hatton Garden. But he became obsessed with strange notions of the second coming of Christ and he encouraged glossolalia, the "gift of tongues," among his followers. His triumph turned to scandal. He was convicted of heresy and removed from the Kirk of Scotland even before the Carlyles moved to London. But still he pressed on. A new church (the Catholic Apostolic, commonly known as Irvingite) was founded with Irving as "First Angel" but with virtually no control of the group. He was through. He died of exhaustion and despair on a trip to Scotland in 1834. Jane remarked, "If Irving had married me, the tongues would never have been heard."

The writing of *The French Revolution* occupied Carlyle for a good portion of the early London years. Despite the appalling calamity of the destruction of the manuscript of the first volume, Carlyle managed to complete and publish the work in 1837. With the publication of *The French Revolution* Carlyle became a public figure. The magnificence of his rhetoric in that book overwhelmed contemporary readers. Here was at last a Sage and Prophet, a role not only relished by Carlyle but, what is often overlooked, much desired by the Victorian public.

The interest that attaches to Carlyle personally from 1840 on is the interest in a public figure, a man who knew all the literary and social luminaries of his day, a man who was increasingly respected by his countrymen, although, as he claimed, also totally ignored. By now Carlyle had largely abandoned German literature and turned to social questions. A steady stream of books, articles, and pamphlets, appraising the society of his day, excoriating the lazy and the selfish, and advancing heterodox views on leadership and government, issued from his pen. His essays of the twenties and thirties were collected in four volumes in 1839. *Sartor Resartus* was published in book form in England (1838 and again in 1840). He wrote a book about Chartism (1839), a labor movement seeking a wider extension of the franchise. He gave four series of public lectures on such topics as European literature and modern revolutions. One of these was published as *On Heroes and Hero-Worship* (1841). He re-created the middle ages in contrast to contemporary society in *Past and Present* (1843). Singlehanded, he undertook to rescue the memory of the detested Oliver Cromwell in *Oliver Cromwell's Letters and Speeches* (1845). These works of Carlyle's middle years found an ever growing audience, especially among the young. Many later eminent Victorians first came under Carlyle's spell at the universities in the thirties and forties, the years that Carlyle came into his full prophethood.

At home the Carlyles entertained a steady stream of illustrious visitors. Men of letters, Continental radicals, ladies of society, all called on the Sage of Chelsea. In the 1840s and 1850s the Carlyles were much in the company of Lord and Lady Ashburton, social leaders who gathered about them a circle of literary and intellectual celebrities, chief of whom was Carlyle himself. The relationship between Carlyle and Lady Ashburton, although sexually beyond reproach, caused Jane considerable anguish, for Jane was herself a woman of sparkling wit whose ability to preside over a circle of friends was equal to Lady Ashburton's. Much of the criticism of Carlyle after his death was based on the "revelation" of Jane's distress over his constant association with Lady Harriet, along with the suspicion that in marrying Carlyle, Jane Welsh had buried a not inconsiderable literary talent of her own. There is truth on all sides. Jane was legitimately distressed; she was also neurotic and jealous. Still, she maintained to the end a vivacity and charm and an unshakable loyalty to Carlyle that make her one of the most appealing of great Victorian ladies. For his part Carlyle was self-centered and neglectful, also gruff and demanding, but always deeply devoted to Jane. Through his efforts we have the *Letters and Memorials of Jane Welsh Carlyle* wherein much of her charm is enshrined.

After 1850 Carlyle wrote fewer works, but his industry did not flag until some time after Jane's death. In 1850 he issued *Latter-Day Pamphlets,* a scorching attack on democracy, political economy, and much else that Carlyle considered to be modern cant. In 1851 he published *The Life of John Sterling,* a biography of one of his close friends. From then on he devoted himself to the study and writing of the history of Frederick the Great. He later called it his Thirteen Years' War. Sequestered in his soundproof room, for he was pathologically sensitive to noise, Carlyle consumed mountains of material in a search for the facts of Frederick's life. He made two trips to Germany gathering materials. And at last, from 1858 to 1865, the volumes appeared, finally numbering six in all.

Jane Welsh Carlyle lived to see the completion of *Frederick the Great.* She had declared *Sartor Resartus* to be "a work of genius" thirty-five years before when no one would publish it. Now she declared *Frederick* to be Carlyle's finest work. It is unquestionably his longest. That has impeded modern reading of it, but it did not discourage Victorians. They greeted the work with great acclaim. The same year in which the last volume of *Frederick* appeared, Carlyle was elected Rector of Edinburgh University. In the following year, just after his triumphant inaugural speech, while he was still in Scotland, Jane Welsh Carlyle died in her carriage in Hyde Park. Carlyle came home to Chelsea to live on in the same house for fifteen more years.

The grief that assailed Carlyle upon the death of Jane is frequently taken as a sign of weakness, but it is even more a sign of the deep bonds between them. Carlyle was an irascible and dogmatic man, no more so than in his later years, but he was also deeply devoted to Jane and given to frequent acts of kindness and gentleness. Jane was neurotic and hypochondriac, but also a woman of irrepressible spirit and gaiety, a perfect counterpoint to Carlyle's gloom. After Jane's death, Carlyle, ever the compulsive writer, set down his *Reminiscences*. With astonishing clarity the man of more than seventy years recalled incidents of half a century before and he produced a remarkable memoir of a remarkable woman. To this he added reminiscences of others such as Edward Irving, Wordsworth, and Sir Francis Jeffrey that are among his finest pieces of writing. He also took the occasion of the Second Reform Bill in 1867 to issue his final thunderblast against democracy in "Shooting Niagara: and After?" Though alarmist in tone, "Shooting Niagara" remains an eloquent and potent critique of democratic dogma.

In his later years Carlyle was granted public honors—an audience with the Queen, the receipt of the Prussian Order of Merit for his work on Frederick the Great, the offer of a knighthood and a pension from the Crown—but his life style remained unchanged. His right hand suffered from palsy after about 1872 so that he was obliged to dictate all his correspondence. In this way, too, he wrote a piece on John Knox and his last book, *The Early Kings of Norway* (1875). In 1875 when he was eighty, he was honored with a gold medallion from a host of admirers including virtually all the literary and intellectual leaders of the day and with a testimonial that he had in his life comported himself as the "Hero as Man of Letters." He outlived most of his earlier associates such as Mill, Dickens, Mazzini, and even his younger brothers John and Alick. On February 5, 1881, Thomas Carlyle died in London. By his own wish refusing burial in Westminster Abbey, he was buried near his father and mother in Ecclefechan churchyard.

II

What Carlyle had to say and the way he said it are very closely linked, almost inseparably, and critics have frequently come to grief by attempting to treat the style as a mere appendage to a philosophy. When the task proves impossible to execute, they usually protest that Carlyle lacks system. System, of course, is a thing Carlyle consciously avoided. He can be faulted if you choose for his avoidance of system, but he should not be taxed with a failure to do what he sought not to do. For purposes of elucidation, however, it is possible to talk about Carlyle's ideas and his style in sequence. In so doing we must not suppose we are discussing a philosophical system. It is rather in Carlyle's case an insight and a philosophical stance. We can first examine Carlyle's governing ideas, with reference to *Sartor Resartus* (which is available in this volume in its entirety); then we can look at the manner in which Carlyle presents his ideas.

If Carlyle avoided system he nevertheless rested his views on certain fundamental ideas. The foremost of these, from which the rest flow, is Carlyle's conviction of the transcendent reality of God. His awareness of God's existence and power came from the transfiguring experience in Leith Walk. As religious mystics rest their case in an ineffable communion with the divine, so Carlyle's understanding of the world came to rest on his personal experience of the Open Secret, the Divine Idea of the World—that there is an animating spiritual life in the universe. It would be easy to underestimate the importance of what this meant for Carlyle. It was not acceptance from unreflecting habit or custom; it was not belief in God because it was easier than not believing. Carlyle had in fact been raised in such a belief and had rejected it. Nor did his experience alter his convictions about organized Christianity, or in any clearly orthodox sense make him a Christian at all. For Carlyle the awareness of a transcendent reality was as much a burden as a joy. It was for him awesome. It meant not only the rejection of every kind of mechanistic or materialistic theory of life—theories which he had already found tending toward unbelief and despair—but the affirmation that a whole and organic life was sustained by God's will and subject to his judgment. It set him against the tenor of his own society, made him an opponent of the *Zeitgeist* or spirit of the age, which he correctly diagnosed as moving toward irreligion, skepticism, liberalism, and democracy. It was Carlyle's obligation and honor to carry his message to a society that had lost sight of it. Like the Old Testament prophets Carlyle was obliged by the very terms of his understanding of the world to call his countrymen back to fundamental realities.

It is not entirely helpful to term Carlyle's faith vitalism—the doctrine of an ongoing vital spiritual principle—as has often been done, for vitalism is a trifle vague. What becomes vitalism in Shaw or Bergson is still in Carlyle a fervent theism. True, he says of God to Sterling, "Wer darf ihn NENNEN?" (who dare name him?), but he also says in *Sartor* "Or what is Nature? Ha! why do I not name thee GOD? Art not thou the 'Living Garment of God'? O Heavens, is it, in very deed, HE, then, that ever speaks through thee; that lives and loves in thee, that lives and loves in me?" And later, "Love not Pleasure; love God. This is the *Everlasting* YEA, wherein all contradiction is solved; wherein who so walks and works, it is well with him." Carlyle's God is not so much the Life Force as it is the omnipotent, omniscient creator of Hebrew and Christian tradition.

If then the fundamental reality of the world is the existence of God, what follows? For Carlyle it was that man must first come to recognize the truth of that basic proposition. (When Margaret Fuller announced that she accepted the universe, Carlyle rumbled, "You'd better!") At one time recognition of the truth of God was facilitated by organized religion, but no more; hence Carlyle's disinterest in churches except as their waning power may aid perception of the truth. In the nineteenth century, Carlyle thought the poets and men of letters had the deeper insight; they were the prophets who could make men see the reality of God. Once the truth is perceived man must order his own life so as to make his world a reflection in its sphere of the order and harmony that God desires for the whole world ("Be no longer a Chaos," says Teufelsdröckh). Thus we have the persistent reference to rebirth, reformation, renewal, which also draw on the Christian message. For all his appeals to governing classes or whole societies, Carlyle's first appeal is to the individual. Reformation begins at home. Hence his contempt for palliative measures to correct social evils by adjustment of this or that special interest (although no man was more conscious of the growing power of special interest groups).

In what direction should man reform himself, one may well ask. In accordance with the age-old concepts of truth, justice, and mercy. The way to do so was by curbing the sin of pride, first of the seven deadly sins. It is pride that leads to Mammon-worship or greed, pride that issues in social injustice, pride that maintains in power a do-nothing aristocracy blind to the needs of the people, pride that denies man's littleness in the face of the immensity of God and eternity. Pride stood behind the materialism of the age, which Carlyle taught men like Ruskin and Matthew Arnold to abhor. Today the attack on materialism is still a rallying cry for moralists. Carlyle went even further than suggesting a quiet acceptance of time-tested values. He spoke, rather, in a characteristically nineteenth-century way, of God's *laws,* the avoidance of which was death. Ignore these laws at your peril, Carlyle said; they *will* be enforced, do what you may.

From Carlyle's understanding of the majesty and glory of God come the so-called Calvinist corollaries, beliefs which Calvinism expresses in more theological terms and which Carlyle made vivid by his language and fervor. These and other beliefs are also frequently analyzed in terms of German idealist philosophy which affected Carlyle powerfully through Goethe, Fichte, Novalis, Kant, and Schelling. Carlyle's achievement was to make an imaginative amalgamation of German idealism with traditional Christianity of a Calvinist cast, including perhaps some ideas all his own, and to express it in terms not theological but heavily Biblical. We cannot trace sources here. It is enough to note what the principal subordinate ideas are: there is the doctrine of Work ("Work while it is called Today; for the Night cometh, wherein no man can work"); the doctrine of Duty ("Do the Duty which lies nearest thee"); the doctrine of Renunciation, or *Entsagen,* and "Worship of Sorrow" ("It is only with Renunciation [*Entsagen*] that Life, properly speaking, can be said to begin"); the doctrine of Reverence ("Know that there is in man a quite indestructible Reverence for whatsoever holds of Heaven"); the doctrine of the Hero ("Great Men are the inspired . . . Text of that divine Book of Revelation, whereof a Chapter is completed from epoch to epoch, and by some named HISTORY"); and the doctrine of Silence ("Speech is of Time, Silence is of Eternity"). There is, too, a consuming hatred of cant and sham, a commitment to truth so passionate as to be át times rude, but such is ever the price of strong belief.

All of Carlyle's conceptions, then, are infused with his conviction of the divine plan and harmony of the universe; of the illusory nature, opposing the actual fact of existence, of the world and the flesh, and of time and space; and of a dualism of matter and spirit that is also hierarchical, for the spirit holds first place over matter and matter is to be so deployed as to fulfill spirit. Because of his sense of the divine unity of the cosmos, Carlyle was extremely sensitive to the interrelations of things. Today the merest editorial scribbler can point to the interlocking connections between economics and health or education and social success and so on, but Carlyle was one of the first to make these connections clear ("It is a mathematic fact that the casting of this pebble from my hand alters the center of gravity of the Universe!").

All of this may sound redolent of the pulpit and of course it was. Carlyle was a "prophet new inspired" with an ancient message. But he was also a trenchant social observer. Some of his best known doctrines are applications of his understanding of life to the contemporary social scene. For those who cannot share Carlyle's convictions about the ultimate nature of reality, there is nevertheless an abundance of ideas regarding specific social ills that Carlyle's insights made him uniquely qualified to see. In his own day he was as widely known for his attacks on social abuses as for his exhortations about transcendent reality. And today, even for those for whom God is dead, Carlyle's social doctrine still contains many points with which they could agree. First of all, Carlyle more than any man before him perceived the changes being wrought by the Industrial Revolution. The romantics had sensed it all and withdrawn. Carlyle fronted the demon in the very capital of England. He was in the forefront of those who cried out against abuses of laissez-faire economics. John Stuart Mill ultimately broke his friendship with Carlyle over the issues of liberty and democracy, not economics, but the friendship must have been sorely tried as he read Carlyle's biting invective against the "Goddess Utilitaria" and political economy. Carlyle cried out that conscience and belief could not tolerate the exploitation of masses of human beings working in bestial conditions and living in unparalleled squalor. It must be owned that it is hard to attack mechanistic materialism on mechanistic grounds. All one can say is that it works or it does not. Carlyle, however, had other grounds from which to mount his attack on the dominant philosophy of liberalism. It was inhuman and it was also ungodly; it reduced life to mere profit and loss; men became machines; justice vanished in the face of calculation; Mammon- or money-worship replaced genuine worship of a higher reality. But in fact, as Teufelsdröckh said, "Soul is *not* synonymous with Stomach." John Henry Newman said that his whole life had been a battle against liberalism, which he defined as the "Anti-dogmatic Principle." Though neither would have acknowledged it, Carlyle and Newman were battling on the same side in this crusade, and it is no longer so clear as it was to nineteenth-century liberals that their arguments have no merit. It is an irony that Carlyle should be remembered for his support of a strong leader and forgotten for his passionate outcries against the exploitation of men.

Nor could the Tories take comfort from Carlyle. Carlyle's view of the world, while it encompassed hierarchy, insisted upon a just hierarchy. Carlyle could and did say, to the annoyance of many, that men were not equal in endowments, thus not equal in judgment, thus not suited to a government that decides issues on a mere count of heads; but that did not stop him from saying at the same time that the existing stratification of society, was another instance of old clothes now out at elbow. The aristocracy, especially in Carlyle's earlier writings, was "going gracefully idle in Mayfair." It was not giving leadership because it was an aristocracy by historical accident, not an aristocracy of virtue and talent. Carlyle paraded the lesson of eighteenth-century France for the benefit of the English "game-preserving" aristocracy. Later he came to see greater virtues in the existing aristocracy, although perhaps not so many as his detractors have claimed. It was not so much in later years that Carlyle approved of the aristocracy as that he disapproved of democracy, which was in his view another way of saying mob rule.

If in his attack on democracy Carlyle underestimated his countrymen and his American cousins (though some would say he did *not*), his critique of democracy and the modern world might make instructive reading today in those quarters that imagine that democracy and the vote will usher in the millennium. As a prophet Carlyle foresaw a process lasting some centuries before the upheavals would be done, before the old order would yield and a truly viable new order be established. The upheavals have occurred, or are occurring; whether the new order is in the offing only another prophet could say. Carlyle's ideas on these matters are somewhat contradictory in any case. He was on the one hand a revolutionary who in word and thought assaulted tradition and complacency, but on the other hand he was morally a traditionalist who drew on the established body of Christian teaching to call his contemporaries back to right reason. The truth is that Carlyle gives little comfort today to professional liberals or conservatives as he gave little comfort in his own day to Whigs and Tories. He was above all a moralist and a God-intoxicated man. One reason perhaps that he failed to found a political movement is that his appeal must in the first instance be to the individual. It is not a call for political action but a call for personal reformation. "Sinner, Repent" is a better watchword for Carlyle than "To Arms." There are thus obvious shortcomings: Carlyle calls for religion and rejects all existing churches; he seeks social justice but does not show us the vehicle for achieving it. Still, his insights and criticisms have left us a body of powerful literature.

There is yet another aspect of Carlyle that appears strikingly modern—his speculative side. Carlyle peered into many a dark recess of mind and society. He explored the forces that animate men and groups. He had moreover a profound and still valid insight into the nature of symbols and the nature of belief. And he was fiercely independent, kowtowing to no group, captive of no ideology—a rebel to the end. Only now are these aspects of Carlyle's genius being recognized. They are bound to bring him more and more serious attention.

Equipped as he was with conviction and supreme literary gifts, Carlyle saw truths that many overlooked and he made other men see what he saw. His warnings that mankind stands permanently over the pit of hell are not unlike warnings heard today that the veneer of civilization is nowhere very thick. But Carlyle says it better. Since with Carlyle manner is matter, it is necessary to look at *how* he expressed his message.

III

Carlyle's passionately held convictions demanded and got for their expression an equally passionate style. It is the style that first attracts or repels readers of Carlyle and it is the style (taken to include the whole literary dimension) that has secured Carlyle a place in literary history. In the nineteenth century many critics objected to Carlyle's radical departure from Johnsonian English. Such a charge would be curious today when we praise a Joyce or an Eliot for liberating contemporary English from the Victorian stylistic straight jacket. The fact is that Carlyle performed the same service for nineteenth-century prose at a time when eighteenth-century models had begun to weigh heavy. The eighteenth-century aim of balance, gravity, and composure hardly suited Carlyle's worldview. He explains his stylistic idiosyncrasies in his reply (printed in this volume) to John Sterling's criticisms; but the modern reader will want to press beyond that explanation to understand the extraordinary style known as Carlylese.

Carlyle's is above all else an emphatic style. It seems positively to avoid composure and balance. The adjectives

that have been applied to it run toward such words as tumultuous, wild, energetic, passionate, vital, electric, thundering.
All these suggest movement, and Caryle's style is always
in motion. It seems to stem directly from his worldview. We
may say that the emphasis comes from Carlyle's conviction
that God *is*; the movement from his conviction that God
lives.

It is a style that owes much to vivid conversation (Carlyle
himself was a formidable talker), to pulpit oratory (here
Irving's "Old English Puritan Style," as Carlyle called it, may
have contributed), to German example (Jean Paul Richter
is the most frequently cited), to the Bible, to poetry, and to
a kind of rhetoric that we might call the prophetic mode.
There are, beyond this, specific devices, or even tricks of
style that may at first strike the reader's attention—the use
of the second person familiar, capitalizations, italics, inver-
sions, exclamations. These are all of interest but not of the
essence. They are all aspects of that emphasis and movement
that lies at the heart of Carlyle's style.

It is now almost a commonplace of Carlyle criticism to
quote Carlyle himself on Jean Paul Richter's style as a commentary on his own, but the procedure is still extremely
instructive, for Carlyle in writing of Richter was obviously
writing with a strong fellow-feeling for an unorthodox stylist
very like himself:

He is a phenomenon from the very surface; he presents himself
with a professed and determined singularity; his language itself
is a stone of stumbling to the critic; to critics of the grammarian
species, an unpardonable, often an insuperable, rock of offence.
Not that he is ignorant of grammar, or disdains the science of
spelling and parsing; but he exercises both in a certain latitu-
dinarian spirit; deals with astonishing liberality in parentheses,
dashes, and subsidiary clauses; invents hundreds of new words,
alters old ones, or, by hyphen, chains and pairs and packs them
together into most jarring combination; in short, produces sentences of the most heterogeneous, lumbering, interminable kind.
Figures without limit; indeed, the whole is one tissue of metaphors, and similes, and allusions to all the provinces of Earth,

Sea and Air; interlaced with epigrammatic breaks, vehement bursts, or sardonic turns, interjections, quips, puns, and even oaths! A perfect Indian jungle it seems; a boundless, unparalleled imbroglio; nothing on all sides but darkness, dissonance, confusion worse confounded!

Except that the description is so brilliantly executed it sounds like the verdict of many critics and readers on Carlyle's own style. However, there is a sense in which such descriptions do not do it justice. They suggest chaos, confusion. Carlyle was more discerning as a literary critic than many critics of Carlyle, for his treatment of Richter's prose goes on to suggest that there is much more there than "Rhapsody and Affectation": "There are rays of the keenest truth, nay steady pillars of scientific light rising through this chaos: Is it in fact a chaos; or may it be that our eyes are of finite, not of infinite vision, and have only missed the plan?" Again, we can apply these sentiments to Carlyle as well, for Carlyle generally worked out his pieces with a surer grasp than the catalogue of idiosyncrasies would suggest. This is true on the syntactic as well as on the structural level. Space does not permit a thorough study of Carlyle's method but the main outlines can be set forth so that the reader can approach his work with greater confidence and sympathy.

Structurally Carlyle's works are usually organized around certain dominant ideas, frequently expressed in a metaphor, such as that of the Clothes Philosophy or that of the contrast between past and present. Carlyle's verbal inventiveness is so enormous that he is capable of generating variations on his underlying theme to a point approaching infinity, but once the central idea is grasped, the variations can be perceived as expansions and intensifications rather than as sources of confusion or diversion. Even Carlyle's many structural digressions usually serve a central organizing principle. The fact that Carlyle habitually uses quotation (frequently self-quotation from his own works or statements), for example, may be seen as his way of looking at an idea or proposition through prismatic glasses. Each angle of vision reveals new dimensions and is a reflection of the life that animates the whole universe. The device of quotation or editorial commentary on a text, that incessant switching back and forth to and from works within works, also dramatizes and heightens what might otherwise remain dry and abstract.

On the narrower stylistic level of sentences and words, we can cite some of the characteristic features to be found virtually everywhere in Carlyle. His sentence structure is loose, even exploded, as though a power from within had dispersed the conventional sentence order. Carlyle does deal in parallelisms and periodic sentences, but with a twist. The traditional periodic sentence, in which the full meaning of the sentence is not clear until the end, is a device for rounding off the statement, making a self-sufficient whole of it. Carlyle's periodic sentences come to completeness at the end for the very different purpose of carrying the reader forward. Indeed, often at the end the reader has arrived at a point hardly foreseen at the beginning. The sentence has not so much been rounded as launched. Other aspects of the same forward drive are found in Carlyle's ellipses, his abrupt shifts, his compounds and hyphenations, and his exclamations. Still another is his frequent use of metaphor, which has already been touched on in terms of larger structure. The smaller metaphors and images are spin-offs of the larger, though some have a life of their own from book to book, such as Carlyle's menagerie of animal images that crow and growl and gibber on page after page. John Holloway speaks of Carlyle's constructions as "The Ocean rolling round the Islet," whereby all things in the world are shown to have consequences and interrelations far beyond an ordinary imagination. All things in Carlyle ultimately lead to everything else; we see heaven in a grain of sand.

The sense of interrelationships is also created by the allusiveness of Carlyle's style. Whatever the deficiencies of Carlyle's education—and he himself was the most unsparing critic of the educational system that produced him—they were more than made up by his own voracious reading. This, coupled with an exceptional memory, gave Carlyle the equipment for a style that refers, now dartingly, now exhaustively, to everything in the universe. Literature, economics, mythology, history, language, philosophy, religion—all are levied upon to provide Carlyle with a superabundance of allusion that packs his writing with a density and plenitude unparalleled in any other prose writer. The pulsating movement carries the reader on, even if he should encounter an unfamiliar allusion, and it leads him to another and yet another. One of them is bound to find an echo.

Carlyle also uses devices such as paradox ("Fire-baptism," for example, or the "Death-Birth" of society). The use of paradox extends to whole statements and ideas. It is most often reminiscent of certain religious truths: man must die in order to be reborn, for example. Into the same category fall exaggeration and hyperbole, devices designed to startle the reader into awareness, often of what lies right under his nose. There are further devices that we can no more than catalogue: Carlyle is fond of Germanisms in word and syntax. Thus he not only compounds in a manner similar to German (where a greater freedom in compounding exists than in English), but he likes to invert word order for emphasis, creating sometimes a German rather than an English sentence pattern. He is also given to suppression of parts of speech, omission of articles and the like. He relies far more than most authors do on exclamation and the imperative mode and direct address. He is also extremely fond of the present tense, and his histories very quickly move the reader into the presence of the action by this means. But then Carlyle said that prophecy is a new form of history.

On the level of individual words, Carlyle must be credited with an amazing inventiveness. His compounds ("Flesh-Garment," "World-Phoenix") are celebrated if not notorious. He also created new words in other ways. More than half the coinages of words ending in *-dom* in the first forty years of the nineteenth century have been credited to Carlyle. He was astonishingly productive of nouns ending in *-hood, -ity, -ness,* and *-ship,* but he also created new adjectives, adverbs, and verbs. His strong negative feelings resulted in a mass of new words through negative prefixes: *un-, in-, non-,* and *dis-.* In this use of words, Carlyle is carrying through on another level the same principles he follows in syntax and structure.

While the normal words of English have been broken up and rearranged with prefixes and suffixes added where they were not before and compounds yoked by violence, the effect still is to make the reader see connections not seen before and to call him back to fundamentals. The reader must participate in the raid on the storehouse of language to see for the first time the treasures that lie hidden—the Divine Idea of the World which is clear to the poet or prophet "because the 'open secret' is no longer a secret to him, and he knows that the Universe is *full* of goodness; that whatever has being has beauty." Thus Carlyle habitually traces etymologies of words, reminding the reader of the metaphorical basis of words, calling him back to the "true" meaning of a word or expression. But even on the level of individual words, Carlyle is at once radical and conservative. It would be hard to find another writer whose worldview permeates his work so totally.

With all of this originality to give wonder and delight to the reader, Carlyle's humor seems an added attraction. He looked askance at any man whose laugh was not something like as hearty as his own, and his own laugh was a great, body-shaking roar. Humor in Carlyle is, of course, a subject that transcends narrow considerations of style and one that could occupy far more space than is available here. We may note in quick review, however, Carlyle's use of satire, irony, grotesque exaggeration, bathos, and sheer verbal highjinks. Many a ponderous passage is relieved by a sudden shift in tone, the introduction of a similar but ridiculous idea, or the shift in perspective from the sublime to the ridiculous. And many passages of satire or invective, biting though they are, are sustained by exuberant fun, just as some of Carlyle's acerb criticisms (as when he called the *Idylls of the King* "superb lollipoppery") are also full of merriment. This vast phantasmagoria of life, as Carlyle might say, extends from the highest to the lowest, from the Godhead to a Pickelherring farce.

The fantastic and elaborate language structures, the imaginative and far-reaching style, are described by Lytton Strachey as the "endless glare of that aurora borealis," and the "roar and rattle of that inexhaustible artillery," and by R. H. Hutton's reference to a "spiritual volcano." If Coleridge can boast the deepest and most circumambient style in the nineteenth century, Newman the subtlest and most urbane, and Ruskin the most pictorial and artistic, Carlyle surely can claim the mightiest and most stirring. It is no small distinction. Great prose, like great poetry, can truly ravish the soul. That is what Carlyle does at his best.

Of course only a blind partisan would maintain that Carlyle never nods. There are times when exhortation becomes harangue, when the deep-toned voice turns strident, or when conviction changes to bigotry. There are times when we see the great guns being rolled into place to demolish a flea. What is remarkable in the thirty volumes of Carlyle's work is that these occasions are as few as they are. A moralist and dogmatist cannot please all indefinitely. Sooner or later the reader's own notions are disturbed, and sooner or later the moralist himself grows impatient with the fact that the world changes only in the same old ways. The Sage of Chelsea was not the most patient of men when it came to the world's follies, and we cannot say he always held his temper.

If, like all of us, Carlyle has his weaknesses, he has also his countervailing strengths. He was a man and writer of uncompromising integrity. Both as an unknown and as a prominent literary figure Carlyle stood for principle not expediency. For all his gruff exterior and abrasive manner he had great sympathy for his fellow man, especially for the downtrodden. From Carlyle, and the public conscience he awakened, stem many of our own deepest social concerns. From him stems much of our awareness of the state of modern life. Whether writing of slums and poorhouses or of Parliament and aristocratic society, Carlyle published his findings with regard only for what he saw as the truth. He discerned the nature of the stresses the new industrial society was producing and he defined problems we have yet to solve. An age as tolerant as our own can certainly find a place for an uncompromising critic of society, even when he occasionally criticizes some of our own cherished myths and pieties.

More than being an acute observer, however, Carlyle was an opponent of hypocrisy and cant and injustice who never let the mere show of things, the surface of the symbol, obscure the animating beliefs underneath. Nor was he restrained by old forms or established patterns: he delighted in breaking new ground, in thought as well as in style. *Sartor Resartus* still defies category, as do his essays, histories, and other highly individual works; for through them Carlyle sought to see into the heart of things, from the meaning of history to the structure of society to the darkest promptings of the psyche. But the quality that finally raises Carlyle's work above the level of historical interest alone is the sweep and power of his literary gifts. If others saw some of the things Carlyle did, none equalled his power to convey them in words. In his own day Carlyle was highly regarded as a philosopher with an idiosyncratic style; today he is highly regarded as a stylist with an idiosyncratic philosophy. However we place our emphasis, we can find in Carlyle a man and writer of exceptional vision and force whose works contend manfully with the perplexities and mysteries of the human condition.

Selected Bibliography

I. WORKS BY THOMAS CARLYLE,
CORRESPONDENCE, NOTEWORTHY EDITIONS

Works. Edited by H. D. Traill. Centenary Edition. 30 vols. London: Chapman and Hall, 1896-1901. [The standard edition.]

Correspondence between Goethe and Carlyle. Edited by Charles Eliot Norton. London: Macmillan, 1887.

Correspondence of Emerson and Carlyle. Edited by Joseph Slater. New York: Columbia University Press, 1963.

Early Letters of Thomas Carlyle, 1814-1826. Edited by Charles Eliot Norton. 2 vols. London: Macmillan, 1886.

Last Words of Thomas Carlyle. London: Longmans, Green, 1892.

Letters of Thomas Carlyle, 1826-1836. Edited by Charles Eliot Norton. 2 vols. London: Macmillan, 1888.

Letters of Thomas Carlyle to John Stuart Mill, John Sterling and Robert Browning. Edited by Alexander Carlyle. New York: Stokes, 1923.

Love Letters of Thomas Carlyle and Jane Welsh. Edited by Alexander Carlyle. 2 vols. London: The Bodley Head, 1909.

New Letters of Thomas Carlyle. Edited by Alexander Carlyle. London: The Bodley Head, 1904.

On Heroes and Hero-Worship and the Heroic in History. Edited by Archibald MacMechan. Boston: Ginn, 1902.

Past and Present. Edited by A. M. D. Hughes. Oxford: The Clarendon Press, 1918.

Reminiscences. Edited by Charles Eliot Norton. 2 vols. London: Macmillan, 1887.

Sartor Resartus. Edited by Charles Frederick Harrold. New York: Odyssey, 1937.

Sartor Resartus. Edited by Archibald MacMechan. Boston: Ginn, 1896.

Two Notebooks of Thomas Carlyle; from 23rd March 1822 to 16th May 1832. Edited by Charles Eliot Norton. New York: The Grolier Club, 1898.

II. CRITICAL AND BIOGRAPHICAL WORKS
ABOUT THOMAS CARLYLE

Allingham, William. *A Diary*. Edited by H. Allingham and D. Radford. London: Macmillan, 1907.

Burdett, Osbert. *The Two Carlyles*. Boston: Houghton, Mifflin, 1931.

Calder, Grace J. *The Writing of Past and Present*. New Haven, Conn.: Yale University Press, 1949.

Carlyle, Jane Welsh. *Letters and Memorials*. Edited by James Anthony Froude. 3 vols. London: Longmans, Green, 1883.
————. *New Letters and Memorials*. Edited by Alexander Carlyle. 2 vols. London: The Bodley Head, 1903.

Cazamian, Louis. *Carlyle*. Translated by E. K. Brown. New York: Macmillan, 1932.

Craig, R. S. *The Making of Carlyle*. New York: Lane, 1909.

DeLaura, David J. "Arnold and Carlyle," *PMLA*, LXXIX (1964), 104-129.

Duffy, Sir Charles Gavan. *Conversations with Carlyle*. New York: Scribner's, 1892.

Dyer, Isaac Watson. *A Bibliography of Thomas Carlyle's Writings and Ana*. Portland, Me.: Southworth Press, 1928.

Froude, James Anthony. *Thomas Carlyle: A History of the First Forty Years of His Life, 1795-1835*. 2 vols. London: Longmans, Green, 1882.
————. *Thomas Carlyle: A History of His Life in London, 1834-1881*. 2 vols. London: Longmans, Green, 1884.

Harrold, Charles Frederick. *Carlyle and German Thought, 1819-1834*. New Haven, Conn.: Yale University Press, 1934.

Holloway, John: *The Victorian Sage: Studies in Argument*. London: Macmillan, 1953.

Holme, Thea. *The Carlyles at Home*. London: Oxford, 1965.

Johnson, W. S. *Thomas Carlyle: A Study of His Literary Apprenticeship, 1814-1831*. New Haven, Conn.: Yale University Press, 1911.

Kraeger, Heinrich. "Carlyles Stellung zur deutschen Sprache und Literatur," *Anglia*, XXII (1899), 145-343.

Larkin, Henry. *Carlyle and the Open Secret of His Life*. London: Kegan, Paul, 1886.

La Valley, Albert J. *Carlyle and the Idea of the Modern*. New Haven, Conn.: Yale University Press, 1968.

Lehman, B. H. *Carlyle's Theory of the Hero*. Durham, N. C.: Duke University Press, 1928.

Levine, George. "*Sartor Resartus* and the Balance of Fiction," *Victorian Studies*, VIII (1964), 131-160.

Mämpel, Arthur. *Thomas Carlyle als Künstler*. Bochum-Langendreer: Pöppinghaus, 1935.

Moore, Carlisle. "The Persistence of Carlyle's 'Everlasting Yea,'" *Modern Philology*, LIV (1957), 187-196.

————. "*Sartor Resartus* and the Problem of Carlyle's 'Conversion,'" *PMLA*, LXX (1955), 662-681.

————. "Thomas Carlyle and Fiction: 1822-1834," in *Nineteenth Century Studies*. Edited by H. Davis. Ithaca, N. Y.: Cornell University Press, 1940.

Neff, Emery. *Carlyle*. New York: Norton, 1932.

————. *Carlyle and Mill: Mystic and Utilitarian*. New York: Columbia University Press, 1924.

Perry, Bliss. *Thomas Carlyle*. Indianapolis, Ind.: Bobbs-Merrill, 1915.

Ralli, Augustus. *A Guide to Carlyle*. 2 vols. Boston: Small, Maynard, 1922.

Roellinger, Francis X. "The Early Development of Carlyle's Style," *PMLA*, LXXII (1957), 936-951.

Sanders, Charles Richard. "The Byron Closed in *Sartor Resartus*," *Studies in Romanticism*, III (1964), 77-108.

————. *Coleridge and the Broad Church Movement*. Durham, N. C.: Duke University Press, 1942.

————. "The Victorian Rembrandt: Carlyle's Portraits of His Contemporaries," *Bulletin of the John Rylands Library*, XXXIX (1957), 521-527.

Shine, Hill. *Carlyle and the Saint-Simonians*. Baltimore, Md.: Johns Hopkins University Press, 1941.

————. *Carlyle's Early Reading to 1834*. Lexington, Ky.: University of Kentucky Libraries, 1953.

————. *Carlyle's Unfinished History of German Literature*. Lexington, Ky.: University of Kentucky Press, 1951.

Smeed, J. W. "Thomas Carlyle and Jean Paul Richter," *Comparative Literature*, XVI (1964), 226-253.

Strachey, Lytton. *Portraits in Miniature*. New York: Harcourt, Brace, 1931.

Symons, Julian. *Thomas Carlyle: The Life and Ideas of a Prophet*. London: Gollancz, 1952.

Tennyson, G. B. "Carlyle's Poetry to 1840: A Checklist and Discussion, a New Attribution, and Six Unpublished Poems," *Victorian Poetry*, I (1963), 161-181.

————. *Sartor Called Resartus: The Genesis, Structure and Style of Thomas Carlyle's First Major Work*. Princeton, N. J.: Princeton University Press, 1965.

Wellek, René. *Confrontations: Studies in the Intellectual and Literary Relations between Germany, England and the United States during the Nineteenth Century*. Princeton, N. J.: Princeton University Press, 1965.

Wilson, David Alec. *Life of Thomas Carlyle*. 6 vols. London: Kegan, Paul, 1923-1934.

RECENT PUBLICATIONS

The Collected Letters of Thomas and Jane Welsh Carlyle. Edited by C. R. Sanders, K. J. Fielding, et al. Durham, N.C.: Duke University Press, 1971–continuing (40 vols. projected).

Two Reminiscences of Thomas Carlyle. Edited by John Clubbe. Durham, N.C.: Duke University Press, 1974.

Works. Reissue of Centenary Edition, 30 vols., with new introduction by G. B. Tennyson. New York: AMS Press, 1980.

Campbell, Ian. *Thomas Carlyle*. London: Hamish Hamilton, 1974.

Clubbe, John, ed. *Carlyle and His Contemporaries*. Durham, N.C.: Duke University Press, 1976.

Drescher, Horst, ed. *Thomas Carlyle 1981*. Bern and Frankfurt: Peter Lang Verlag, 1983.

Fielding, K. J. and Rodger L. Tarr, eds. *Carlyle Past and Present*. London: Vision Press, 1976.

Goldberg, Michael. *Carlyle and Dickens*. Athens, Ga.: University of Georgia Press, 1972.

Kaplan, Fred. *Thomas Carlyle, A Biography*. Ithaca, N.Y.: Cornell University Press, and Cambridge: Cambridge University Press, 1983.

Rosenberg, Philip. *The Seventh Hero*. Cambridge, Ma.: Harvard University Press, 1974.

Seigel, Jules Paul, ed. *Thomas Carlyle: The Critical Heritage*. New York: Barnes & Noble, 1971

Tarr, Rodger L., ed. *Thomas Carlyle: A Bibliography of English-language Criticism, 1824–1974*. Charlottesville, Va.: University Press of Virginia, 1976.

Tennyson, G. B. "The Carlyles," in *Victorian Prose: A Guide to Research*. Edited by David J. DeLaura. New York: Modern Language Association of America, 1973.

————. "Carlyle: Beginning with the Word," in *The Victorian Experience: The Prose Writers*. Edited by Richard A. Levine. Athens, O.: Ohio University Press, 1982.

Chronology

1795	Thomas Carlyle born, December 4, at Ecclefechan, Annandale, Scotland.
1801	Jane Baillie Welsh born, July 14, at Haddington, East Lothian, Scotland.
1806-1809	Carlyle attends Annan Academy.
1808	Carlyle first sees Edward Irving at Annan Academy.
1809-1814	Attends Edinburgh University.
1814	Returns to Annan Academy as mathematics tutor.
1816-1818	Begins teaching in Burgh school in Kirkcaldy. Meets Margaret Gordon. Friendship with Irving.
1819	Moves to Edinburgh. Begins study of German.
1820-1823	Contributes articles to *Edinburgh Encyclopaedia.*
1821	Meets Jane Baillie Welsh in Haddington.
1822	Tutors Charles and Arthur Buller.
1823	"Life of Schiller" published in *London Magazine.*
1824	Translation of *Wilhelm Meister's Apprenticeship* published. Travels to London and Paris.
1825	*The Life of Schiller* published in book form.
1826	Marries Jane Baillie Welsh, October 17; they move to 21 Comley Bank, Edinburgh.
1827	"Jean Paul Friedrich Richter" published in June, Carlyle's first contribution to *Edinburgh Review*. *German Romance* published, 4 vols.
1828	Carlyles move to Craigenputtock. "Burns" published in *Edinburgh Review*. Articles on German literature published in *Foreign Review*.
1829	"Signs of the Times" published in *Edinburgh Review*. Articles on German literature published in *Foreign Review*.
1830	"On History" published in *Fraser's Magazine*. Begins

Sartor Resartus. Articles on German literature published in *Foreign Review* and *Fraser's Magazine*.

1831   *Sartor Resartus* completed. "Characteristics" published in *Edinburgh Review*. Travels to London. Meets John Stuart Mill.

1832   Death of James Carlyle, Carlyle's father, January 22.

1833   Emerson visits Craigenputtock. *Sartor Resartus* begins in *Fraser's*.

1834   Carlyles move to London, 5 Great Cheyne Row, Chelsea. Death of Edward Irving.

1835   First volume of *French Revolution* destroyed by Mill's servant. Meets John Sterling.

1836   *Sartor Resartus* published in book form in Boston.

1837   *The French Revolution* completed and published.

1838   *Sartor Resartus* published in book form in England.

1839   *Critical and Miscellaneous Essays* published, 4 vols. *Chartism* published.

1840   Gives lecture series on heroes and hero-worship.

1841   *On Heroes and Hero-Worship* published.

1842   Meets Mr. and Mrs. Baring (afterwards Lord and Lady Ashburton).

1843   *Past and Present* published.

1844   Death of John Sterling.

1845   *Oliver Cromwell's Letters and Speeches, with Elucidations* published, 2 vols.

1846   Carlyle visits Ireland.

1847   Emerson visits Carlyles in London.

1850   *Latter-Day Pamphlets* published.

1851   *The Life of John Sterling* published.

1852   Begins work on *Frederick the Great*; tours Germany.

1853   Death of Margaret Aitken Carlyle, Carlyle's mother, December 25.

1856-1858 First collected edition of Carlyle's works published.

1858   First two volumes of *History of Frederick the Great* published. Second visit to Germany.

1863   Third volume of *History of Frederick the Great* published.

1864   Fourth volume of *History of Frederick the Great* published.

1865   Fifth and sixth volumes of *History of Frederick the Great* published.

1866   Inaugural address as Rector of Edinburgh University, April 2. Death of Jane Welsh Carlyle, April 21. Begins writing *Reminiscences*.

1867   "Shooting Niagara: and After?" published in *Macmillan's*.

1869   Audience with Queen Victoria.

1874   Receives Prussian Order of Merit.

1875   *The Early Kings of Norway* and *The Portraits of John Knox* published.

1879   Death of John Carlyle, Carlyle's brother.

1881   Death of Thomas Carlyle, February 4; burial in Ecclefechan churchyard. *Reminiscences* published.

Textual Note

Except for correspondence, *Reminiscences*, and extracts from Carlyle's journal, the text throughout is that of the Centenary Edition of Carlyle's *Works*, edited by H. D. Traill, in thirty volumes, London, 1896-1901. Carlyle's spelling and punctuation have been retained throughout. Misprints have been silently corrected. The text for the *Reminiscences* is taken from the edition by Charles Eliot Norton, in two volumes, London and New York, 1887. The selections from Carlyle's journal are taken from *Two Notebooks of Thomas Carlyle*, edited by Charles Eliot Norton, New York, 1898. The texts for the letters are: *Love Letters of Thomas Carlyle and Jane Welsh*, edited by Alexander Carlyle, in two volumes, London, 1909; *Correspondence between Goethe and Carlyle*, edited by Charles Eliot Norton, London, 1887; *Letters of Thomas Carlyle, 1826-1836*, edited by Charles Eliot Norton, in two volumes, London, 1888; *Letters of Thomas Carlyle to John Stuart Mill, John Sterling and Robert Browning*, edited by Alexander Carlyle, New York, 1923; and *New Letters of Thomas Carlyle*, edited by Alexander Carlyle, London, 1904. The text for the letter to Emerson is taken from *Correspondence of Emerson and Carlyle*, edited by Joseph Slater, New York, 1964.

A CARLYLE READER

Selections from the Writings of Thomas Carlyle

LETTERS TO JANE WELSH

1823-1825

[Thomas Carlyle met Jane Baillie Welsh in 1821 through his friend and her tutor Edward Irving. A brilliant, witty, intellectually alert woman, Jane was known as the "Flower of Haddington." Her line could claim direct descent from John Knox, the sixteenth-century Scottish Reformer. Jane was generally regarded as a highly desirable catch. She herself was ambitious as well as beautiful, and she chose Carlyle in part because she recognized his brilliance and knew he would one day be a great man. Their courtship lasted five years (they were married in October 1826), during which time they exchanged numerous letters marked on both sides by sensitivity, wit, passion, and frequently high seriousness. The selections that follow show Carlyle's attitude toward Jane as well as some of his early literary and social interests.]

FROM A LETTER
TO JANE WELSH, *Haddington*

3 Moray Street [Edinburgh], 6 April 1823

. . . "Angry at you!" My dear Jane, I was never angry at you in my life, and do believe I shall never be seriously so. I cannot understand what sort of clay the man is made of that could be angry at you: I would have him drummed out of Earth as an interloper and a counterfeit. My worst feeling towards you is pain at seeing you uncomfortable, and anxiety lest you may spoil your future happiness. Even on this subject I have no serious fears; but there is no end to one's scruples and suspicions. Formerly, I used to feel afflicted at your contemptuousness and want of constancy in your emotions; now I am turned to the other extreme, and begin to dread that you are growing too serious. In fact I think I have noticed in you of late a tendency to contemplative melancholy, and what they term a romantic turn of mind—not the romance which milliners experience when they think of becoming actresses or running off with young grocers; but that sickness of noble hearts, that deep and sad feeling of the nothingness of the world, which is apt to arise from too exclusive a pursuit of things high and spiritual, and too great an isolation from the every day interests and enjoyments of life. I fear there *is* some truth in this. If so, my dear Jane, let me entreat you with the earnest voice of affec-

3

tion to guard against the approaches of this black demon, which has poisoned the existence of so many men of genius, and converted the world which they might have enlightened and adorned into a prison-house which they have deformed and disgraced. It is an evil of the first magnitude—the want of which almost compensates to the *servum pecus* for all their other wants. Fight against such thoughts, and fly when you cannot conquer. There is no efficient remedy but mingling ourselves as much as possible in the solid living concerns of our fellow-creatures: these shadows disappear when we come forth from the cell of our own meditations into the cheerful light of day. You may feel that the people about you are frivolous and shallow and unworthy of your sympathies; no doubt they are so; but still they are our brethren, and it is the inflexible law of nature, that *whoever withdraws from them is miserable*.

As to your literary hopes, entertain them confidently! There is to me no better symptom of what is in you than your despair of getting it expressed. Cannot write! My dear Pupil, you have no idea of what a task it is to everyone, when it is taken up in that solemn way. Did you never hear of Rousseau lying in his bed and painfully wrenching every syllable of his *Nouvelle Héloïse* from the obscure complexities of his imagination. He composed every sentence of it, on an average, *five times over*; and often when he took up the pen, the whole concern was vanished quite away! John James [Rousseau] is my only comfort when I sit down to write. I could frequently swear that I am the greatest dunce in creation: the cooking of a paragraph is little better than the labour of the Goldmaker; I sweat and toil and keep tedious vigil, and at last there runs out from the tortured melting-pot an ingot—of solid pewter. There is no help but patient diligence, and *that will conquer everything*. Never waver, my own Jane! I shall yet "stand a-tiptoe!" at your name. Not write! I declare if I had known nothing of you but your Letters, I should have pronounced you to be already an excellent writer. Depend upon it, this is nothing but your taste outgrowing your practice. Had you been born a Peer's daughter, and lived among literary men, and seen things to exercise your powers of observation, the world would ere this have been admiring the sagacious humour of your remarks and the graceful vigour of your descriptions. As it is, you have only to begin and go on: time will make all possible, all easy. Why did you give up that Essay on Friendship? *For my sake,* resume it and finish it! Never mind how bad, how execrable it may seem, go thro' with it. The next will be better, and the next, and the next; you will approach at each trial nearer the Perfection which no one ever reached. If I knew you fairly on the way, I should feel quite easy: your reading is going on as it ought; there wants only that you should write also. Begin this Essay again, if you love me!

Goethe lies waiting for your arrival. You make a right distinction about Goethe: he is a great genius and *does not make you cry.* His feelings are various as the hues of Earth and Sky, but his intellect is the Sun which illuminates and overrules them all. He does not yield himself to his emotions, but uses them rather as things for his judgement to scrutinize and apply to purpose. I think Goethe the only living model of a great writer. The Germans say there have been *three* geniuses in the world since it began—Homer, Shakespeare and Goethe! This of course is shooting on the wing; but after all abatements, their countryman is a glorious fellow. It is one of my finest day-dreams to see him ere I die . . .

[The excerpt from the following letter is concerned chiefly with Edward Irving, who was enjoying an enormous success in London as a preacher. Compare this selection with the essay "Death of Edward Irving" and the selection from the *Reminiscences.*]

FROM A LETTER
TO JANE WELSH, *Haddington*

Mainhill [Dumfries], 10 August 1823
. . . Have you actually "admonished" the great Centre of Attraction? If not, wait for two months, and you will see his "raven locks and eagle eye" as you have done of old, and may admonish him by word of mouth. I was at Annan; and found *the* Argument for Judgment to Come, in a clear type, just arrived, and news that Irving himself was returning soon to the North—to be married! The Lady is Miss Martin of Kirkcaldy—so said his Mother. On the whole I am sorry that Irving's preaching has taken such a turn. It had been much better, if without the gross pleasure of being a newspaper Lion and a season's wonder, he had gradually become, what he must ultimately pass for, a preacher of first-rate abilities, of great eloquence and great absurdity, with a head fertile above all others in sense and nonsense, and a heart of the most honest and kindly sort. As it is, our friend

incurs the risk of many vagaries and disasters, and at best the certainty of much disquietude. His path is steadfast and manly, in general only when he has to encounter opposition and misfortune; when fed with flatteries and prosperity, his progress soon changes into "ground and lofty tumbling," accompanied with all the hazards and confusion that usually attend this species of movement. With three newspapers to praise him and three to blame, with about six Peers and six dozen Right Honourables introduced to him every Sunday, tickets issuing for his church as if it were a theatre, and all the devout old women of the Capital treating him with comfits and adulation, I know that ere now he is "striking the stars with his sublime head:" well if he do not break his shins among the rough places of the ground! I wish we saw him safely down again, and walking as other men walk. The comfort is he has a true heart and genuine talents; so I conclude that after infinite flounderings and pitchings in the mud he will at last settle much about his true place, just as if this uproar had never taken place. For the rest, if he does not write to his friends, the reason is, not that he has ceased to love them, but that his mind is full of tangible interests continually before his face. With him at any time the present is worth twenty times the past and the future; and such a present as this he never witnessed before. I could wager any money that he thinks of you and me very often, tho' he never writes to either; and that he longs above all to know what we do think of his monstrous flourishing of drums and trumpets in which he lives and moves. I have meant to write to him very frequently for almost three months; but I know not well how to effect it. He will be talking about "the Lord," and twenty other things, which he himself only wishes to believe, and which to one that knows and loves him are truly painful to hear. See that you do not think unkindly of him; for except myself, there is scarcely a man in the world that feels more true concern for you.

Happy Irving that is fitted with a task that he loves and is equal to! He entertains no doubt that he is battering to its base the fortress of the Alien, and lies down every night to dream of planting the old true blue Presbyterian flag upon the summit of the ruins. When shall you and I make an onslaught upon the empire of Dulness and bring back *spolia opima* to dedicate to one another? Some day yet, I swear it! Let us fear nothing; but believe that diligence will conquer every difficulty, and act on that belief.—Heaven grant I may get a Letter from you ere I go. My solitary ride will otherwise be full of vague and unpleasant speculations. At all events you will not keep me waiting at Kinnaird. Tell me what are your purposes and proceedings, your hopes and fears. I send you all the crudities that enter my head: are we two not *friends forever*? I will also see you soon tho' I should ride from Dunkeld for that special purpose. God bless you, Jane! I am ever yours,

T. Carlyle.

[In 1824 Carlyle had gone to London to supervise the publication of his first book, *The Life of Schiller*. In the following letter he reports to Jane on London literary figures and on Edward Irving.]

FROM A LETTER
TO JANE WELSH, *Haddington*

Pentonville [London], 20 December 1824

My Dearest,—These booksellers are certainly a consequence of the Fall of Adam; they were sent into the world for our sins. I expected ere this to have been cherishing myself with your answer to my Letter; you are unpleasantly awaiting the arrival of the promised parcel; and I must keep my patience for another week and a half. Rascally, drivelling, two-footed things that they are! Three weeks ago I hurried off the packet in the greatest haste; Jack writes that it has not come; I go to ask about it; and find it—quietly reposing on its shelf in Fleet-street! They were sorry; they had not understood; they were *very* sorry.—So I brought it home with me, and here it lies expecting some more trustworthy conveyance. By good luck I have got a Council-office frank; and I hope this Letter will reach you on Friday-night. The rest will follow in due season; there was nothing but a sorry copy of Molière's Plays, which I got for you in Paris; they may come as slowly as they like. But do not, I pray you, delay to write, the moment you get this, if you have not already written: I am immeasurably anxious to hear from you. A whole month has passed without a word.

In the aspect of my own affairs there is scarcely any change since I wrote last. The printing of *Schiller* proceeds with somewhat less tardiness than I dreaded: today I got the seventh sheet; so that almost a third part of the work is already off my hands. It is going to make a handsome enough Book; rather larger than a volume of *Meister,* and somewhat in the same style. A certain Mr. *Bull,* one of Irving's *geniuses,* is engraving a portrait for it. I long to have the pitiful affair put past me, that I may be able to quit the tumults of the *Wen* (so Cobbett calls it), and establish myself somewhere more to my wishes and wants. My future movements are still as undecided as ever; only here I ought not to be, longer than I cannot help it. If there be sleep and quiet and free air to be had on Earth, I will have them; if there are not, I will reconcile myself the best way I can to do without them; but not till I have found that there are not. The Translation of Schiller has made advances towards being realized: indeed the first Letter I had written on the subject, I find still lying among these unhappy books, and only send it off with this. Patience! Patience! A little time will settle all. If I can get no suitable arrangement made for this, I will abandon it, and take to something better. The very sparrow earns for itself a livelihood, beneath the eaves of the cottage: if I the illustrious Mr. Thomas Carlyle cannot, then let me be sent to the Australian Continent directly. Faint-hearted mortal! These scribblers round thee are a mere *canaille*: struggle thro' ten thousand of them, or go to pot—as thou deservest.

Irving advises me to stay in London; partly with a friendly feeling, partly with a half-selfish one, for he would fain keep me near him. Among all his followers there is none whose intercourse can satisfy him; any other than him it would go far to disgust. Great part of them are blockheads, a few fools; there is no rightly intellectual man among them. Then he speculates and speculates, and would rather have me contradict him rationally, at least now and then he would, than gape at him with the vacant stare of children viewing "the Grand Turk's Palace with his Guards—all alive." He advises me, not knowing what he says. He himself has the nerves of a buffalo; and forgets that I have not. His philosophy with me is like a gill of ditch-water thrown into the crater of Mount Aetna; a million gallons of it would avail me nothing. I receive his nostrums with a smile: he at length despairs of ever seeing me converted.

On the whole, however, he is among the best fellows in London; by far the best that I have met with. Thomas Campbell has a far clearer judgement, infinitely more taste and refinement; but there is no living well of thought or feeling in him; his head is a shop not a manufactory; and for his heart, it is dry as a Greenock *kipper*. I saw him for the second time, the other night; I viewed him more clearly and in a kindlier light, but scarcely altered my opinion of him. He is not so much a man, as the Editor of a Magazine: his life is that of an exotic; he exists in London, as most Scotchmen do, like a shrub disrooted, and stuck into a bottle of water. Poor Campbell! There were good things in him too: but Fate has pressed too heavy on him, or he has resisted it too weakly. His poetic vein is failing or run out; he has a Port-Glasgow Wife, and their only son is in a state of idiocy. I sympathized with him; I could have loved him but he has forgot the way to love.—Little Procter here has set up house on the strength of his writing faculties, with his Wife, a Daughter of the "Noble Lady." He is a good-natured man, lively and ingenious; but essentially a small.—Coleridge is sunk inextricably in the depths of putrescent indolence. Southey and Wordsworth have retired far from the din of this monstrous City. So has Thomas Moore. Whom have we left? . . .

Such is the "Literary World" of London; indisputably the poorest part of its population at present. Among the other classes of people, I have met with several whom I like considerably, and whose company still continues to afford me pleasure. The Montagus I see perhaps once a-week: the husband is a wiseacre, with an obliging heart; the lady has the most cultivated taste (in pictures, and players, and attitudes and forms) of any person I remember; in her own sphere of observation, she is quick-sighted as a lynx; she delights to be among geniuses and lions, and *has* a touch of kindness for one in her heart, tho' she shows it very much as if it were *all* counterfeit. You may draw on her for any quantity of *flattery* you like, and of any degree of fineness. Irving she treats with it by the hogshead; me by the dram-glass, in a stolen way, having almost turned my stomach with excessive doses of it at first. If there is an eccentric virtuoso, a crack-brained philosopher in London, you will hear of him at that house; a man of true sense is a *specie* whom I have scarcely ever met with there. Yet they are kind and good, and as the world goes very superior people: I talk with them in a careless, far-off, superficial way, for an hour or two with great ease and enjoyment of its kind. The Stracheys are a better tho' less speculative family: I *wish* the lady had been possessed of any philosophy or true culture, I should have admired and loved her much, for she is in truth a noble-minded woman. . . .

But I must not kill you with my talk. One little piece of news; and thou shalt have a respite. The other twilight, the lackey of one Lord Bentinck came with a lackey's knock to the door, and delivered me a little blue parcel, requiring for it a receipt under my hand. I opened it somewhat eagerly, and found two small pamphlets with ornamental covers, and—a letter from—Goethe! Conceive my satisfaction: it was almost like a message from Fairy Land; I could scarcely think that *this was* the real hand and signature of that mysterious personage, whose name had floated thro' my fancy, like a sort of spell, since boyhood; whose thoughts had come to me in maturer years with almost the impressiveness of revelations. But what says the Letter? Kind nothings, in a simple patriarchal style, extremely to my taste. I will copy it, for it is in a character that you cannot read; and send it to you with the original, which you are to keep as the most precious of your literary relics. Only the last line and the signature are in Goethe's hand: I understand he constantly employs an amanuensis. Do you transcribe my copy, and your own translation of it, into the blank leaf of that German paper, before you lay it by; that the same sheet may contain some traces of him whom I most venerate and her whom I most love in this strangest of all possible worlds. . . .

[The following letter refers to Jane as "Ruth" in reference to the steadfastness of the Biblical Ruth. It was written a year before their marriage.]

FROM A LETTER
TO JANE WELSH, *Templand*

Hoddam Hill [Dumfries], 10 August 1825

My dearest little Ruth!—I owe you many thanks for your kindness of heart, for your true unflinching love of me, unworthy as I am "by destiny or by my own deserving" of such bounties. Your faith in me is great, greater than I ever can fulfil, or pay with due gratitude. So we are *not* to part! O my Darling, how could we ever part? Do we not love each other? Does not your fervid trembling spirit cleave to mine as to its pillar of hope in the darkness and tempests of life? Are not my arms about you, is not my breast your pillow? If you love me with the whole strength of that noble heart, it *were* unwise in you to leave me. No, we will never part, betide what may!

In truth, I believe, I should not be so generous with my offers to that effect, were it not for some secret persuasion that they had little chance to be accepted. I feel as if there were no sacrifice which I could not make to see, still more to cause, your happiness; but sacrifices in idea, and sacrifices in deed are different matters; and this would in truth be a sacrifice of almost all that still binds me to the world by any tie of hope, that still tinges my sky with a streak of dawn amid the gloom that overshadows me. Who knows, too, but we may still be happy? In calm hours, hope has not yet forsaken me; for we are still in the land of the living which is the place of hope, and more perverse destinies than ours have changed to smoothness and serenity. The evil is deep and dark, but it is *one*, and I see it clearly. If this accursed burden of disease were cast away, nine-tenths of my faults and incapacities would pass away with it. Life might still lie round me like a huge quarry; but I should have my strength to labour in it, and form its shapeless masses into an edifice. Nay, perhaps, this same deathlike cold eclipse under which my youth has passed away in heaviness and woe, might not be without its uses in my future fortunes, tho' I have stormed at it as the blackest most unmingled curse with which the wrath of Heaven could have visited me. "Ye shall become perfect thro' sufferings," says the Scripture, and Experience is beginning to show me the truth of the maxim. Thou, too, my Darling, hast thy share! Repine not at it, Jane; it is the lot of all mortals; the curse of fools, but sometimes also the blessing of the wise. How wild are our wishes, how frantic our schemes of happiness when we first enter on the world! Our hearts encircled in the delusions of vanity and self-love, we think the Universe was made for us alone; we glory in the strength of our gifts, in the pride of our place; and forget that the fairest ornament of our being is "the quality of mercy," the still, meek, humble Love that dwells in the inmost shrine of our nature, and cannot come to light till Selfishness in all its cunning forms is banished out of us, till affliction and neglect and disappointment have sternly taught us that self is a foundation of sand, that we, even the mighty *we,* are a poor and feeble and most unimportant fraction in the general sum of existence. Fools writhe and wriggle and rebel at this; their life is a little waspish battle against all mankind for refusing to take part with them; and their little dole of reputation and sensation, wasting more and more into a shred, is annihilated at the end of a few beggarly years, and they leave the Earth without ever feeling that the spirit of man is a child of Heaven, and has thoughts and aims in which self and its interests are lost from the eye, as the Eagle is swallowed up in the brightness of the sun, to which it soars. Let *us* be wise, let us admit this painful but medicinal conviction, and meekly learn the lesson which it teaches us. O Jane! Why should we murmur? Are we not rich in better things than silver or gold, or the vain babble of stupid men? We have found each other, and our hearts are one, our beings are one; for we love each other with a love not grounded on deception but on *truth*, and no force can part us, or rob us of that blessing! Heavenly affection! Heavenly trust of soul to soul! This *can* soften all afflictions, if it is genuine and lasting, as it is in noble hearts. The summer sunshine of joy is not its chosen place; it burns with its clearest light in the dark winter of sorrow; when heart is pressed to heart, and one has no hope but in the other, no care but for the other. Do you know this as it is? Do you dare to front it, not decked in the stage-light of the imagination, but in the squalid repulsiveness of the actual world? Then, my little Ruth, thou art a heroine, and I would not give thee for a kingdom!

It is thus I change from week to week, and from day to day! Heaven knows I have no wish to deceive you; but to show you all that is in me, all my feelings and fantasies as I view the brightest or the darkest side of our fortunes. By and by you will learn what manner of man I am. As yet I sometimes scarcely know *myself*. . . .

Selections from Carlyle's Journal

1 8 2 5 - 1 8 3 2

[The following passages are taken from Carlyle's early journal which covers the years 1822-1832. The whole work was published in 1898 under the title *Two Note Books of Thomas Carlyle,* edited by Charles Eliot Norton. For the most part, Carlyle's entries refer to his writing plans or problems and his intellectual interests; there are relatively few entries of a highly personal nature. But the journal contains many interesting reflections on topics central to Carlyle's thought. Some of the passages appear later in modified form in *Sartor Resartus.* Lines between entries are Carlyle's own marks separating entries made on or near the same date; three asterisks between entries mark off selections chosen for this edition.]

21st September, 1825. Hoddam Hill. . . . Since the last line was written, what a wandering to and fro, how many sad vicissitudes of despicable suffering and inaction have I undergone! This little book and the desk that carries it have passed a summer and winter in London, since I last opened it; and I their foolish owner have roamed about the brick-built Babylon, the sooty Brummagem, and Paris the Vanity-fair of our modern world! My mood of mind is changed: is it improved? *Weiss nicht.* This stagnation is not peace, or it is the peace of Galgacus' Romans: *ubi solitudinem faciunt pacem appellant.* How difficult it is to free one's mind from *cant*; how very seldom are the principles we act on clear to our own reason! Of the great nostrums "forgetfulness of self" and "humbling of vanity," it were better therefore to say nothing: in my speech concerning them I overcharge the impression they have made on me, for my Conscience like my sense of Pain or Pleasure has grown dull, and I secretly desire to compensate for laxity of *feeling* by intenseness of *describing.* How much of these great nostrums *is* the product of necessity? *Am* I like a sorry hack *content* to feed on heather while rich clover seems to lie around it at a little distance, *because* in struggling to break the tether it has almost hanged itself? O that I *could* "go out of the body to philosophize!" That I could even feel as of old the glory and magnificence of things till my own little *me* (*mein kleines Ich*) were swallowed up and lost in them! (partly cant!) But I cannot, I cannot! Shall I ever more? *Gott weiss.* At present I am but an *abgerissenes Glied,* a limb torn off from the family of Man, excluded from activity, with Pain for my companion, and Hope that comes to all rarely visiting me, and what is stranger rarely desired with vehemence! Unhappy man in whom the body has gained mastery over the soul! Inverse Sensualist, not drawn into the rank of beasts by pleasure, but driven into it by pain! Hush! Hush! Perhaps this *is* the Truce which weary Nature has conquered for herself to re-collect her scattered strength! Perhaps like an Eagle (or a Goose) she *will* "mew her mighty youth and fly against the sun, or at least fish paddocks with equanimity, like other birds of a similar feather; and no more lie among the pots, winged, maimed and plucked, doing nothing but chirp like a chicken in the coop for the livelong day. "Jook and let the jaw gae by," my pretty Sir: when this solitude becomes intolerable to you, it will be time enough to quit it for the dreary blank which society and the bitterest activity have hitherto afforded you. You deserve considerable pity Mr. C.; and likewise considerable contempt. Heaven be your comforter my worthy Sir, you are in a promising condition at this present; sinking to the bottom, yet laid down to sleep; Destruction brandishing his sword above you, and you quietly desiring him to take your life but spare your rest! *Gott hilf Ihnen!*

* * *

[February 1829] Above all things, I should like *to know England*, the essence of social life in this same little Island of ours. But how? No one that I speak to can throw light on it; not he that has worked and lived in the midst of it for half a century. The blind following the blind! Yet each cries out: What a glorious sunshine we have! The "old Literature" only half contents me: it is ore and not metal. I have not even a *history* of the country, half precise enough. With Scotland, it is little better. To me there is nothing poetical in Scotland, but its Religion. Perhaps because I *know* nothing else so well. England with its old Chivalry, Art and "creature comfort" looks beautiful, but only as a cloud-country, the distinctive features of which are all melted into one gay sunny mass of hues. After all, we are a world "within ourselves;" a "self-contained house."

The English have never had an Artist, except in Poetry; no Musician, no Painter; Purcell (was he a native?) and Hogarth are not exceptions, or only such as confirm the rule.

He who would understand England must understand her Church, for that is half of the whole matter. Am I not conscious of *prejudice* on that side? Does not the very sight of a shovel-hat in some degree indispose me to the wearer thereof? shut up my heart against him? This must be looked into: without love there is no knowledge.

Do I not also partly hate the Aristocracy of Scotland? I fear, I do, tho' under cover. This too should be remedied. —On the whole, I know little of the Scottish Gentlemen; and more than enough of the Scottish *Gigman.*—All are not mere rent-gatherers and game-preservers.

Have the Scottish Gentry *lost* their national character of late years, and become mere danglers in the train of the wealthier English? Scott has seen certain characters among them; of which I hitherto have not heard of any existing specimen.

Is the true Scotchman the Peasant and Yeoman; chiefly the former?

Shall we actually go and *ride* thro' England to see it? Mail-coaches are a mere mockery.

A national character, that is, the description of one, tends to realize itself, as some prophecies have produced their own fulfillment. Tell a man that he is brave, and you help him to become so. The "national character" hangs like a pattern in every head; each sensibly or insensibly shapes himself thereby, and feels pleased when he can in any measure realize it.

Is the characteristic strength of England its Love of Jus-

tice, its deep-seated, universally-active sense of Fair Play?
—On many points it seems to be a very stupid people; but
seldom a hide-bound, bigoted, altogether unmanageable
and unaddressable people.

The Scotch have more enthusiasm and more consideration; that is, at once, more sail and ballast: they seem to
have a *deeper* and *richer* character as a nation.—The old
Scottish music, our Songs etc., are a highly distinctive
feature.

Must see Southey's *Book of the Church,* Tytler's *History
of Scotland.* Also Sir W. Scott's *Tales of a Grandfather.*

Read *Novalis Schriften* for the second time some weeks
ago, and wrote a Review of them. A strange, mystic, unfathomable book; but full of matter for most earnest meditation. What is to become (next) of the world and the
sciences thereof? Rather, what is to become of *thee* and thy
science? Thou longest to *act* among thy fellow men, and
canst (yet) scarcely *breathe* among them.

Friedrich Schlegel dead at Dresden on the 9th of January! Poor Schlegel what toilsome *seeking* was thine: thou
knowest now whether thou hadst *found*—or thou carest
not for knowing!

What am I to say of *Voltaire?* (His *name* has stood at
the top of a sheet for three days, and no other word!) Writing is a dreadful Labor; yet not so dreadful as Idleness.

Every living man is a visible mystery: he walks between
two Eternities and two Infinitudes (said already!)—Were
we not blind as moles we should value our Humanity at *x,*
and our Ranks, Influence etc. (the trappings of our Humanity), at *o.* Say, I am a man; and you say all: whether
King or Tinker is a mere appendix.—("very true, Mr. Carlyle, but then"—we must believe *Truth* and practice Error?)—

—Pray that your eyes be opened, that you may *see* what
is before them! The whole world is built as it were, on Light
and Glory; only that our *spiritual* eye must discern it: to
the bodily eye Self is as a perpetual *blinder,* and we see
nothing but darkness and contradiction.

* * *

March (perhaps 1st.) [1830]. I am occupied writing a *History of German Literature* (save the mark!) which will nowise fashion itself into any shape in my hands. Few men have attempted a compilation under such circumstances: no Books, continual disappointments from Bookagents, etc. etc. But what boots complaining? Bear a hand, and let us do our best; the strongest can do no better.

Does it seem hard to thee that thou shouldst toil, in dullness, sickness, isolation? Whose lot is not even this? Toil, then, *et tais-toi.*

Either I am degenerating into a *caput mortuum,* and shall never think another reasonable thought; or some new and deeper view of the world is about to arise in me. Pray Heaven, the latter! It is dreadful to live without *vision:* where there is no light the people perish.—

With considerable sincerity I can pray at this moment: Grant me, O Father, enough of wisdom to live well, prosperity to live happily (easily) grant me or not, as Thou Seest best.—A poor faint *prayer,* as such, yet surely a kind of wish; as indeed it has generally been with me: and now a kind of comfort to feel it still in my otherwise too withered heart.—

I am a "dismembered limb"; and feel it again too deeply. Was I ever other? Stand to it tightly, man; and do thy utmost. Thou hast little or no hold on the world; promotion will never reach thee; nor true fellowship with any active body of men: but hast thou not still a hold on Thyself? *Ja, beym Himmel!*—

Religion, as Novalis hints, *is* a social thing. Without a Church there can be little or no Religion. The action of mind on mind is mystical, infinite; Religion, worship can hardly (perhaps not at all) support itself without this aid. The derivation of *Schwärmerey* indicates some notion of this in the Germans. To *schwärmen* (to be enthusiastic) means, says Coleridge, to *swarm,* to crowd together, and excite one another.—

What is the English of all quarrels that have been, are, or can be between man and man? Simply this: Sir you are taking more than your share of Pleasure in this world, something from *my* share; and by the gods, you shall not; nay I will fight you rather. Alas! and the whole lot to be divided in such a beggarly account of empty boxes; truly a "feast of shells," not eggs, for the yolks have all been blown out of them! Not enough to fill half a stomach, and the whole human species famishing to be at them! Better we should say to our Brother: Take it, poor fellow, take that larger share, which I reckon mine, and which thou so wantest: take it with a blessing: would to Heaven I had but enough for thee!—This is the Moral of the Christian Religion: how easy to write, how *hard* to practice! (Suggested itself one wet evening, on the Trailtrow moss, as I came from Annan, in 1825; or perhaps I only mentioned it to Jack then, as a thing I had lately seen.—I love to be particular.)

I have now almost done with the Germans. Having seized their opinions, I must turn me to inquire *how* true are they? That truth is in them, no lover of Truth will doubt: but how much? And after all, one needs an intellectual Scheme (or ground plan of the Universe) drawn with one's own instruments.—

I think I have got rid of Materialism: Matter no longer seems to me so ancient, so unsubduable, so *certain* and palpable as Mind. *I* am mind: whether matter or not I know not—and care not.—Mighty glimpses into the spiritual Universe I have sometimes had (about the true nature of Religion, the possibility, after all, of "supernatural" (really natural) influences etc., etc.): would they could but stay with me, and ripen into a perfect view!

Miracle? What is a Miracle? Can there be a thing more miraculous than any other thing? I myself am a standing wonder. It is "the inspiration of the Almighty that giveth us understanding."—

What is poetry? Do I really love Poetry? I sometimes fancy almost, not. The jingle of maudlin persons, with their mere (even genuine) "sensibility" is unspeakably fatiguing to me. My greatly most delightful reading is, where some Goethe musically *teaches* me. Nay, *any* fact, relating especially to man, is still valuable and pleasing.—

My Memory, which was one of the best, has failed sadly of late years, (principally the last two): yet not so much by defect in the faculty, I should say, as by want of earnestness in using it. I *attend* to few things as I was wont: few things have any interest for me; I live in a sort of waking dream.

Doubtful it is in the highest degree, whether ever I shall make men hear my voice to any purpose or not. Certain only that I shall be a *failure* if I do not, and unhappy: nay unhappy enough (that is with suffering enough) even if I do. My own talent I cannot in the remotest attempt at estimating. Something superior often does seem to be in me, and hitherto the world has been very kind; but *many* things inferior also; so that I can strike no balance.—Hang it, *try*; and leave this *Grübeln*!

What we have done is the only mirror that can show us what we *are*.

* * *

September 7th [1830]. Yesterday I received tidings that my project of cutting up that thrice-wretched *Hist[ory of] G[erman] Literature* into Review Articles, and so realizing *something* for my Year's work, will not take effect. The "Course of Providence" (nay sometimes I almost feel that there *is* such a thing even for *me*) seems guiding my steps into new regions; the question is coming more and more towards a decision: Canst thou, there as thou art, accomplish aught good and true, or art thou to die miserably as a vain Pretender? It is above a year since I wrote one sentence that came from the right place; since I did one action that seemed to be really worthy. The want of money is a comparatively insignificant affair: were I doing well otherwise, I could most readily consent to go destitute and suffer all sorts of things. On the whole I am a—But tush!—

The Moral Nature of a man is not a composite factitious concern, but lies in the very heart of his being, as his very Self of Selves. The first alleviation to irremediable Pain is some conviction that it has been merited; that it comes from the All-Just, from God.—

What am I but a sort of Ghost? Men rise as Apparitions from the bosom of Night, and after grinning, squeaking, gibbering some space, return thither. The earth they stand on is Bottomless; the vault of their sky is Infinitude; the Life-*Time* is encompassed with Eternity. O wonder! And they buy cattle or seats in Parliament, and drink coarser or finer fermented liquors, as if all this were a City that had foundations.

———

I have strange glimpses of the power of spiritual Union, of Association among men of like object. Therein lies the true Element of Religion: it is a truly supernatural climate. All wondrous things, from a Pennenden Heath, or Penny-a-week Purgatory Society, to the foundation of a Christianity, or the (now obsolete) exercise of magic, take their rise here. Men work godlike miracles thereby, and the horridest abominations. *Society* is a wonder of wonder; and Politics (in the right sense, far, very far from the common one) *is* the noblest Science.

Cor ne edito! Up and be doing! Hast thou not the strangest grandest of all talents committed to thee; namely *Life* itself? O Heaven! And it is momently rusting and wasting, if thou use it not. Up and be doing; and pray (if thou but can) to the Unseen Author of all thy Strength to guide thee and aid thee; to give thee if not Victory and Possession, unwearied Activity and *Entsagen.*—

Is not every Thought properly an Inspiration? Or how is one thing more *inspired* than another? Much is in this.—

* * *

September (about the 28th) [1830]. . . . I am going to write—Nonsense. It is on "Clothes." Heaven be my comforter!—

It was a wise regulation which ordained that certain days and times should be set apart for Seclusion and Meditation; whether as *Fasts* or not may reasonably admit of doubt, the business being "to get *out* of the Body to philosophize." But, on the whole, there is a deep significance in Silence. Were a man forced for a length of time but to hold his peace, it were in most cases an incalculable benefit to his insight. Thought works in Silence; so does Virtue. One might erect statues to Silence. I sometimes think it were good for *me,* who after all cannot err much in loquacity here, did I impose on myself at set times, the duty—of not speaking for a day. What folly would one avoid, did the tongue lie quiet till the mind had finished, and were calling for utterance. Not only our good Thoughts but our good Purposes also are frittered asunder and dissipated by unseasonable speaking of them. *Words,* the strangest product of our nature, are also the most potent. Beware of speaking. Speech is human, Silence is divine; yet also brutish and dead; therefore we must learn *both* arts, they are both difficult. Flower-roots *hidden* under soil; Bees working in Darkness, etc. The soul too in Silence.—Let not thy left hand know what thy right hand doeth. Indeed, Secrecy is the element of all Goodness; every Virtue, every Beauty is *mysterious.* I hardly understand even the surface of this.—

Written a strange piece "On Clothes;" know not what will come of it. October 28th, 1830.

* * *

27th [September, 1831]. . . . Is all Education properly an *unfolding;* does all Knowledge already exist in the mind. And Education only uncover it? There is something in this: but not what is here (so ill) expressed.

Vision of *all* the suits of "Clothes" you have ever worn!—

* * *

October 10th [1831]. . . . Meanwhile *what* were the true duty of Man; were it to stand utterly aloof from Politics (not ephemeral only, for that of course, but generally from all speculation about social systems, etc. etc.); or is not perhaps the very want of this time, an infinite want of Governors, of Knowledge how to govern itself?—Canst *thou* in any measure spread abroad Reverence over the hearts of men? That were a far higher task than *any* other. Is it to be done by Art; or are men's minds as yet shut to Art, and open only at best to oratory; not fit for a Meister, but only for a better and better *Teufelsdreck; Denk' und schweig!*

The stupidity I labor under is extreme. All dislocated, prostrated, obfuscated; cannot even speak, much less write. What a dogged piece of toil lies before me, before I get afoot again! Set doggedly to it then.

When Goethe and Schiller say or insinuate that Art is higher than Religion, do they mean perhaps this: That whereas Religion represents (what is the essence of Truth for men) the Good as *infinitely* (the word is emphatic) different from the Evil, but sets them in a state of hostility (as in Heaven and Hell),—Art likewise admits and inculcates this quite infinite difference; but *without* hostility, with peacefulness; like the difference of two Poles which *can-*

not coalesce, yet do not quarrel, nay should not quarrel for both are essential to the whole? In this way is Goethe's morality to be considered as a *higher* (apart from its comprehensiveness, nay universality) than has hitherto been promulgated? *Sehr einseitig!* Yet perhaps there is a glimpse of the truth here.

* * *

22nd October [1831]. . . . In a better time this huge monster of a city [London] will contract itself into some third part of its present bulk. The Landed People have almost no business here except incidentally; they should be *governing* in their respective districts; not here flaunting and flirting. Were the quite superfluous population of London shipped off, it would shrink to the third part of its bulk, and be still large enough.

Potatoes (one penny per lb.) are exactly *ten* times the price they are in Annandale. (Of their quality I say nothing.) So is it in all things, in a less or greater ratio: so many mortals living together hamper and hinder one another in innumerable ways.

How men are hurried here; how they are haunted and terrifically chased into double quick speed; so that in self-defense they *must not* stay to look at one another! Miserable is the scandal mongery and evil idle speaking of the country population: more frightful still the total ignorance and mutual heedlessness of these poor souls in populous city pent. "Each passes on, quick transient; regarding not the other or his woes." Each must button himself together, and take no thought (not even for *evil*) of his neighbor. There in their little cells divided by partitions of brick or board, they sit strangers, unknowing, unknown; like Passengers in some huge Ship, each within his own cabin: Alas! and the Ship is Life, and the voyage is from Eternity to Eternity!

Everywhere there is the most crying want of *Government*, a true all-ruining anarchy: no one has any *knowledge* of London in which he lives; it is a huge aggregate of little systems, each of which is again a small Anarchy, the members of which do not *work* together but *scramble* against each other.

The Soul, what can properly be called the Soul, lies dead in the bosom of man; starting out only in mad ghastly Nightwalkings (e.g. "the gift of tongues"): Ignorance eclipses all things with its owlet wings; man walks he knows not whither; walks and wanders till he walk into the jaws of Death, and is there devoured.—Nevertheless, *God is in it:* here, even here, is the Revelation of the Infinite in the Finite; a majestic Poem (tragic, comic, or epic), couldst thou but read it and recite it! Watch it then; study it, catch the secret of it, and proclaim the same in such accent as is given thee.—Alas! the spirit is willing, but the flesh is weak.

* * *

November 2nd [1831]. How few people speak for Truth's sake, even in its humblest modes! I return from Enfield, where I have seen Lamb etc., etc. Not one of that class will tell you a straightforward story, or even a credible one, about any matter under the sun. All must be perked up into epigrammatic contrasts, startling exaggerations, claptraps that will get a plaudit from the galleries! I have heard a hundred anecdotes about W. Hazlitt (for example); yet cannot, by never so much crossquestioning even, form to myself the smallest notion of how it really stood with him.—Wearisome, inexpressibly wearisome to me is that sort of clatter: it is not walking (to the end of time you would never advance, for these persons indeed have no WHITHER); it is not bounding and frisking in graceful natural joy; it is dancing—a St. Vitus dance. Heighho!—

Charles Lamb I sincerely believe to be in some considerable degree *insane*. A more painful, rickety, gasping, staggering, stammering Tom fool I do not know. He is witty by denying truisms, and abjuring good manners. His speech wriggles hither and thither with an incessant painful fluctuation; not an opinion in it or a fact or even a phrase that you can thank him for: more like a convulsion fit than natural systole and diastole.—Besides he is now a confirmed shameless drunkard; *asks* vehemently for gin-and-water in strangers' houses; tipples till he is utterly mad, and is only not thrown out of doors because he is too much despised to taking such trouble with him. Poor Lamb! Poor England where such a despicable abortion is named genius!—He said: There are just two things I regret in English History; first that Guy Fawkes's Plot did not take effect (there would have been so glorious an *explosion*); second, that the Royalists did not hang Milton (then we might have laughed at them) : etc. etc. *Armer Teufel!*

* * *

Friday, 23rd December [1831]. Finished the *Characteristics,* about a week ago; baddish, with a certain beginning of deeper insight in it.

Reading the Corn Law Rhymes. "Ballaam's Ass has not only stopt, but begins to *speak!*"

Byron we call "a Dandy of Sorrows, and acquainted with grief." That is a brief definition of him.

13th January 1832. *London still.*—Have spent nearly three weeks in reading Croker's Boswell's Johnson; on which I have now (and had) some purpose of writing an Essay. I mean to try whether I cannot get into a more *currente calamo* style of writing; for magazines and the like, it were far more suitable: whether also for me and my objects? The *Characteristics* was written with almost intolerable difficulty, and is ill written, I fear no one will understand it. We shall see in a week or two, for it is coming out.—

* *' *

London, Monday, April 2, 1832 [from the *London Times*].

"These papers announce a death which may almost be considered an event in politics as well as in literature,— the celebrated GOETHE died at Weimar on the 22d ult. He expired, without any apparent suffering, in his armchair, having a few minutes previously called for paper for the purpose of writing, and expressed his delight at the arrival of spring. He had, however, for the last two years enjoyed little of his usual health, and had fallen off greatly in personal appearance. We believe that he had passed his 82d year. All Europe knows the literary era of Germany which commenced with this distinguished man, which ends with him, and which may be considered as identified with his personal history."

This came to me at Dumfries, on my first return thither. I had written to Weimar, asking for a Letter to welcome me home; and *this* was it. My Letter would never reach its *address:* the great and good Friend was no longer *there;* had departed some seven days before.—Craigenputtock, 19th April, 1832.

* * *

Sunday morning [April 22, 1832]. Yesterday quite down-pressed, over-powered (with bodily obstruction chiefly) and worthless, or next to that. Did no work, that can be shown; tho' I rather zealously attempted it. Again endeavour! Times *will* mend.

The whole thing I want to write seems lying in my mind; but I *cannot get my eye on it.* The Machine is lazy, languid; the motive Principle cannot conquer the inertia.

A question arises, whether there ought to be, in a perfect society, *any* class of purely speculative men? Whether all men should not be of active employment and habitude; their speculation only growing out of their activity, and incidental thereto?—

The grand Pulpit is now the Press; the true Church (as I have said twenty times of late) is the Guild of Authors. How these *two* Churches and Pulpits (the velvet-cushion one and the metal-type one) are to adjust their mutual relations and cognate workings: this is a problem which some centuries may be taken up in solving. It is the deepest thing to be solved in these days.

Every man that writes is writing a new Bible; or a new Apocrypha; to last for a week, or for a thousand years: he that convinces a man and sets him working is the doer of a *miracle.* [Strange language this: but it is as in the immigration of the Northmen, or any other great world-revolution, *two* languages must get *jumbled together,* and old words get new meanings; all things for a time being confused enough.]

Ought any writing to be transacted with such intense difficulty. Does not the True always flow *lightly* from the lips and pen? I am not clear in this matter; which is a deeply practical one with me. Consider the following also:

The *True* indeed flows lightly; but how stands it with the *mixture* of True and Untrue (or Unknown), wherein the latter element has to be continually eliminated, and elaborated, or rejected?—

One thing, at all events, is plain: Take not *too* much care about thy writing, or about aught else that belongs to thee. Know that it is intrinsically *trivial* (as thyself art) and will *soon* perish,—let vanity whisper what she may. Quick, then; thro' with it! Learn to do it *honestly* (learn what that means); *perfectly* thou wilt never do it.

Time flies; while thou balancest a sentence, thou art nearer the *final* Period.

Cast thy thought forth (so soon as thou hast *thought* it) with some fearlessness: let it sink into the great mass of Action (under which rolls Eternity!): let it sink there, since such was its allotment. *Dissolved* (what we call Dead), the *Life* of it will still go on working there. *Deny* THYSELF; whatsoever is *thyself,* consider it as nothing.

This, however, I must say for myself: It is seldom or never the Phraseology, but always the Insight, that fails me, and retards me.

On, then; on! why stand describing how thou *shouldst* move; forward, and move, in *any* way.

* * *

[May 1832]. The only Reform is in *thyself*. Know this O Politician, and be moderately political.

For me I have never yet done any one political act; not so much as the signing of a petition. My case is this: I comport myself wholly like an alien; like a man who is not in his own country; whose own country lies perhaps a century or two distant. When the time comes, should it ever come, that I can do *any good* in such a coming forward, then let me not hang back. Meanwhile pay thy taxes to his Majesty and the rest, so long as they can force thee; the instant they can*not* force thee, that instant cease to pay. This has been my political principle for many a year. The passing or the failing of innumerable Reform Bills might not alter it much: money is paid to him who does a service worth money; obedience is due to him who governs: to him who wears the governor's *mask,* the *mask* of obedience,—as to the ass in lion's skin (who in any case could kick)—while you are near him.—

And now a truce to Politics. All this I have written down, this Wednesday, May 16th, 1832 years: knowing that it is trivial; also that some day even transitory phrases will have meaning.

Reminiscence. Two nights before leaving London I went down to the House of Commons with W. Fraser, who however could not get admittance for himself and me; a thing I partly rejoiced at. We went to a Club house in St. James, the first and only one I was ever in. Waited also afterwards a while in the Lobby of the "House": while here saw Macaulay (Thomas Babington) come out, and buy two oranges; a sign, Fraser said, that he was going to speak; which accordingly next day showed that he had done. Macaulay, whom I noted strictly, is a short squat thickset man of vulgar but resolute energetic appearance. Fair-complexioned, keen gray eyes, a large cylindrical head set close down between two strong round shoulders; the brow broad and fast-receding, the crown flat—perhaps it was baldish. Inclines already to corpulence, tho' I suppose he is not five-and-thirty, of which age or a somewhat higher he wore the air. The globular will one day be his shape, if he continue. I likened him, in my own mind, to a managing Iron-master (I know not well why); with vigorous talent for that or some such business (on what *scale* fortune may order); with little look of talent for anything higher. He is the young man of most force at present before the world. Successful he may be to great lengths, or not at all, according as the times turn: meanwhile, the limits of his worth are discernible enough. Great things lie not in him. It is a fatal circumstance that he rests satisfied with being a *Critic*, feels not the want of any force belonging to himself wherewith he might *do* somewhat; has yet attained to no *belief*, and apparently is not wretched for not having any. The moral nature of the man I take to be intrinsically common; hence, if no otherwise, were his intellectual nature marked as common also. He may be heard of, and loudly; but what is being heard of? Whosoever beats a drum is heard of. Let us hope too that M. will gain better insight, a clear, manly foundation, and be what he might be: "a man among clothes-screens." . . .

But here, my paper being done, let me close. Joy and sorrow; irreparable losses; toils fruitless or fruitful: a share of all lies noted in this little Tome. Onwards we are going, ever onwards: Eternity alone can give back what Time daily takes away. I am Fatherless now, (thank God, not yet Motherless): be all that remains the dearer. Improve, cherish, laudably work with whatever Time gives and leaves. *Gedenke zu leben*! Farewell ye loved ones! I have still *zu leben*.

Poems

[Carlyle wrote very few poems and most of those were written in the years before 1840. Some of the poems were published in *Fraser's Magazine* (of those below only "Cui Bono" was so published, in 1830); others appeared for the first time in the *Miscellanies* (1839) and were dated as having been written between 1823-1833. Only one of Carlyle's poems enjoyed any substantial popularity. It is the poem titled "Today," and it was frequently anthologized in the nineteenth century.]

CUI BONO

What is Hope? A smiling rainbow
  Children follow through the wet;
'Tis not here, still yonder, yonder:
  Never urchin found it yet.

What is Life? A thawing iceboard
  On a sea with sunny shore;—
Gay we sail; it melts beneath us;
  We are sunk, and seen no more.

What is Man? A foolish baby,
  Vainly strives, and fights, and frets;
Demanding all, deserving nothing;—
  One small grave is what he gets.

TODAY

So here hath been dawning
Another blue Day:
Think wilt thou let it
Slip useless away.

Out of Eternity
This new Day is born;
Into Eternity,
At night, will return.

Behold it aforetime
No eye ever did:
So soon it forever
From all eyes is hid.

Here hath been dawning
Another blue Day:
Think wilt thou let it
Slip useless away.

FORTUNA

The wind blows east, the wind blows west,
And the frost falls and the rain:
A weary heart went thankful to rest.
And must rise to toil again, 'gain
And must rise to toil again.

The wind blows east, the wind blows west,
And there comes good luck and bad;
The thriftiest man is the cheerfulest;
'Tis a thriftless thing to be sad, sad,
'Tis a thriftless thing to be sad.

The wind blows east, the wind blows west;
Ye shall know a tree by its fruit:
This world, they say, is worst to the best;—
But a dastard has evil to boot, boot,
But a dastard has evil to boot.

The wind blows east, the wind blows west;
What skills it to mourn or to talk?
A journey I have, and far ere I rest;
I must bundle my wallets and walk, walk,
I must bundle my wallets and walk.

The wind does blow as it lists alway;
Canst thou change this world to thy mind?
The world will wander its own wise way;
I also will wander mine, mine,
I also will wander mine.

Signs of the Times

1 8 2 9

[One of the enduring preoccupations of the nineteenth century was the effort to assess the spirit of the age (a term that provided both Hazlitt and John Stuart Mill with essay titles). Carlyle's first important contribution to the discussion, published in the June 1829 *Edinburgh Review,* is also the first of his essays to deal directly with social rather than literary matters. Like the literary essays, this one purports to be a review of some recently published works. The three works in question are: *Anticipation: or, an Hundred Years Hence*; *The Rise, Progress, and Present State of Public Opinion in Great Britain*; and *The Last Days, or Discourses on These Our Times,* all published in London in 1829. The third of these was by Edward Irving. In this essay, as in "Characteristics," Carlyle endeavors to penetrate to the underlying nature of the age, which he deems to be mechanical. The result is one of the seminal essays of the nineteenth century that introduces issues destined to be debated throughout the age and beyond. Carlyle titled his essay after Christ's words in Matthew, 16:3, "O ye hypocrites, ye can discern the face of the sky; but can ye not discern the signs of the times?"]

It is no very good symptom either of nations or individuals, that they deal much in vaticination. Happy men are full of the present, for its bounty suffices them; and wise men also, for its duties engage them. Our grand business undoubtedly is, not to *see* what lies dimly at a distance, but to *do* what lies clearly at hand.

> Know'st thou *Yesterday,* its aim and reason;
> Work'st thou well *Today,* for worthy things?
> Calmly wait the *Morrow's* hidden season,
> Need'st not fear what hap soe'er it brings.

But man's 'large discourse of reason' *will* look 'before and after'; and, impatient of the 'ignorant present time,' will indulge in anticipation far more than profits him. Seldom can the unhappy be persuaded that the evil of the day is sufficient for it; and the ambitious will not be content with present splendour, but paints yet more glorious triumphs, on the cloud-curtain of the future.

The case, however, is still worse with nations. For here

the prophets are not one, but many; and each incites and confirms the other; so that the fatidical fury spreads wider and wider, till at last even Saul must join in it. For there is still a real magic in the action and reaction of minds on one another. The casual deliration of a few becomes, by this mysterious reverberation, the frenzy of many; men lose the use, not only of their understandings, but of their bodily senses; while the most obdurate unbelieving hearts melt, like the rest, in the furnace where all are cast as victims and as fuel. It is grievous to think, that this noble omnipotence of Sympathy has been so rarely the Aaron's-rod of Truth and Virtue, and so often the Enchanter's-rod of Wickedness and Folly! No solitary miscreant, scarcely any solitary maniac, would venture on such actions and imaginations, as large communities of sane men have, in such circumstances, entertained as sound wisdom. Witness long scenes of the French Revolution, in these late times! Levity is no protection against such visitations, nor the utmost earnestness of character. The New-England Puritan burns witches, wrestles for months with the horrors of Satan's invisible world, and all ghastly phantasms, the daily and hourly precursors of the Last Day; then suddenly bethinks him that he is frantic, weeps bitterly, prays contritely, and the history of that gloomy season lies behind him like a frightful dream.

Old England too has had her share of such frenzies and panics; though happily, like other old maladies, they have grown milder of late: and since the days of Titus Oates have mostly passed without loss of men's lives; or indeed without much other loss than that of reason, for the time, in the sufferers. In this mitigated form, however, the distemper is of pretty regular recurrence; and may be reckoned on at intervals, like other natural visitations; so that reasonable men deal with it, as the Londoners do with their fogs,—go cautiously out into the groping crowd, and patiently carry lanterns at noon; knowing, by a well-grounded faith, that the sun is still in existence, and will one day reappear. How often have we heard, for the last fifty years, that the country was wrecked, and fast sinking; whereas, up to this date, the country is entire and afloat! The 'State in Danger' is a condition of things, which we have witnessed a hundred times; and as for the Church, it has seldom been out of 'danger' since we can remember it.

All men are aware that the present is a crisis of this sort;

and why it has become so. The repeal of the Test Acts, and
then of the Catholic disabilities, has struck many of their
admirers with an indescribable astonishment. Those things
seemed fixed and immovable; deep as the foundations of the
world; and lo, in a moment they have vanished, and their
place knows them no more! Our worthy friends mistook
the slumbering Leviathan for an island; often as they had
been assured, that Intolerance was, and could be nothing
but a Monster; and so, mooring under the lee, they had an-
chored comfortably in his scaly rind, thinking to take good
cheer; as for some space they did. But now their Leviathan
has suddenly dived under; and they can no longer be fastened in the stream of time; but must drift forward on it,
even like the rest of the world: no very appalling fate, we
think, could they but understand it; which, however, they
will not yet, for a season. Their little island is gone; sunk
deep amid confused eddies; and what is left worth caring
for in the universe? What is it to them that the great continents of the earth are still standing; and the polestar and
all our loadstars, in the heavens, still shining and eternal?
Their cherished little haven is gone, and they will not be
comforted! And therefore, day after day, in all manner of
periodical or perennial publications, the most lugubrious
predictions are sent forth. The King has virtually abdicated;
the Church is a widow, without jointure; public principle is
gone; private honesty is going; society, in short, is fast falling in pieces; and a time of unmixed evil is come on us.

At such a period, it was to be expected that the rage of
prophecy should be more than usually excited. Accordingly,
the Millennarians have come forth on the right hand, and
the Millites on the left. The Fifth-monarchy men prophesy
from the Bible, and the Utilitarians from Bentham. The
one announces that the last of the seals is to be opened,
positively, in the year 1860; and the other assures us that
'the greatest-happiness principle' is to make a heaven of
earth, in a still shorter time. We know these symptoms too
well, to think it necessary or safe to interfere with them.
Time and the hours will bring relief to all parties. The
grand encourager of Delphic or other noises is—the Echo.
Left to themselves, they will the sooner dissipate, and die
away in space.

Meanwhile, we too admit that the present is an important time; as all present time necessarily is. The poorest Day

that passes over us is the conflux of two Eternities; it is made up of currents that issue from the remotest Past, and flow onwards into the remotest Future. We were wise indeed, could we discern truly the signs of our own time; and by knowledge of its wants and advantages, wisely adjust our own position in it. Let us, instead of gazing idly into the obscure distance, look calmly around us, for a little, on the perplexed scene where we stand. Perhaps, on a more serious inspection, something of its perplexity will disappear, some of its distinctive characters and deeper tendencies more clearly reveal themselves; whereby our own relations to it, our own true aims and endeavours in it, may also become clearer.

Were we required to characterise this age of ours by any single epithet, we should be tempted to call it, not an Heroical, Devotional, Philosophical, or Moral Age, but, above all others, the Mechanical Age. It is the Age of Machinery, in every outward and inward sense of that word; the age which, with its whole undivided might, forwards, teaches and practises the great art of adapting means to ends. Nothing is now done directly, or by hand; all is by rule and calculated contrivance. For the simplest operation, some helps and accompaniments, some cunning abbreviating process is in readiness. Our old modes of exertion are all discredited, and thrown aside. On every hand, the living artisan is driven from his workshop, to make room for a speedier, inanimate one. The shuttle drops from the fingers of the weaver, and falls into iron fingers that ply it faster. The sailor furls his sail, and lays down his oar; and bids a strong, unwearied servant, on vaporous wings, bear him through the waters. Men have crossed oceans by steam; the Birmingham Fire-king has visited the fabulous East; and the genius of the Cape, were there any Camoens now to sing it, has again been alarmed, and with far stranger thunders than Gamas. There is no end to machinery. Even the horse is stripped of his harness, and finds a fleet fire-horse yoked in his stead. Nay, we have an artist that hatches chickens by steam; the very brood-hen is to be superseded! For all earthly, and for some unearthly purposes, we have machines and mechanic furtherances; for mincing our cabbages; for casting us into magnetic sleep. We remove mountains, and make seas our smooth highway; nothing can resist us. We war with rude Nature; and, by our resistless engines, come off always victorious, and loaded with spoils.

What wonderful accessions have thus been made, and are still making, to the physical power of mankind; how much better fed, clothed, lodged and, in all outward respects, accommodated men now are, or might be, by a given quantity of labour, is a grateful reflection which forces itself on every one. What changes, too, this addition of power is introducing into the Social System; how wealth has more and more increased, and at the same time gathered itself more and more into masses, strangely altering the old relations, and increasing the distance between the rich and the poor, will be a question for Political Economists, and a much more complex and important one than any they have yet engaged with.

But leaving these matters for the present, let us observe how the mechanical genius of our time has diffused itself into quite other provinces. Not the external and physical alone is now managed by machinery, but the internal and spiritual also. Here too nothing follows its spontaneous course, nothing is left to be accomplished by old natural methods. Everything has its cunningly devised implements, its preëstablished apparatus; it is not done by hand, but by machinery. Thus we have machines for Education: Lancastrian machines; Hamiltonian machines; monitors, maps and emblems. Instruction, that mysterious communing of Wisdom with Ignorance, is no longer an indefinable tentative process, requiring a study of individual aptitudes, and a perpetual variation of means and methods, to attain the same end; but a secure, universal, straightforward business, to be conducted in the gross, by proper mechanism, with such intellect as comes to hand. Then, we have Religious machines, of all imaginable varieties; the Bible-Society, professing a far higher and heavenly structure, is found, on inquiry, to be altogether an earthly contrivance: supported by collection of moneys, by fomenting of vanities, by puffing, intrigue and chicane; a machine for converting the Heathen. It is the same in all other departments. Has any man, or any society of men, a truth to speak, a piece of spiritual work to do; they can nowise proceed at once and with the mere natural organs, but must first call a public meeting, appoint committees, issue prospectuses, eat a public dinner; in a word, construct or borrow machinery, wherewith to speak it and do it. Without machinery they were hopeless, helpless; a colony of Hindoo weavers squatting in the heart of Lancashire. Mark, too, how every machine must have its moving power, in some of the great currents of society; every little sect among us, Unitarians, Utilitarians, Anabaptists, Phrenologists, must have its Periodical, its monthly or quarterly Magazine;—hanging out, like its windmill, into the *popularis aura,* to grind meal for the society.

With individuals, in like manner, natural strength avails little. No individual now hopes to accomplish the poorest enterprise single-handed and without mechanical aids; he must make interest with some existing corporation, and till his field with their oxen. In these days, more emphatically than ever, 'to live, signifies to unite with a party, or to make one.' Philosophy, Science, Art, Literature, all depend on machinery. No Newton, by silent meditation, now discovers the system of the world from the falling of an apple; but some quite other than Newton stands in his Museum, his Scientific Institution, and behind whole batteries of retorts, digesters, and galvanic piles imperatively 'interrogates Nature,'—who, however, shows no haste to answer. In defect of Raphaels, and Angelos, and Mozarts, we have Royal Academies of Painting, Sculpture, Music; whereby the languishing spirit of Art may be strengthened, as by the more generous diet of a Public Kitchen. Literature, too, has its Paternoster-row mechanism, its Trade-dinners, its Editorial conclaves, and huge subterranean, puffing bellows; so that books are not only printed, but, in a great measure, written and sold, by machinery.

National culture, spiritual benefit of all sorts, is under the same management. No Queen Christina, in these times, needs to send for her Descartes; no King Frederick for his Voltaire, and painfully nourish him with pensions and flattery: any sovereign of taste, who wishes to enlighten his people, has only to impose a new tax, and with the proceeds establish Philosophic Institutes. Hence the Royal and Imperial Societies, the Bibliothèques, Glypothèques, Technothèques, which front us in all capital cities; like so many well-finished hives, to which it is expected the stray agencies of Wisdom will swarm of their own accord, and hive and make honey. In like manner, among ourselves, when it is thought that religion is declining, we have only to vote half-a-million's worth of bricks and mortar, and build new churches. In Ireland it seems they have gone still farther, having actually established a 'Penny-a-week Purgatory-Society'! Thus does the Genius of Mechanism stand by to help us in all difficulties and emergencies, and with his iron back bears all our burdens.

These things, which we state lightly enough here, are yet of deep import, and indicate a mighty change in our whole manner of existence. For the same habit regulates not our modes of action alone, but our modes of thought and feeling. Men are grown mechanical in head and in heart, as well as in hand. They have lost faith in individual endeavour, and in natural force, of any kind. Not for internal perfection, but for external combinations and arrangements, for institutions, constitutions,—for Mechanism of one sort or other, do they hope and struggle. Their whole efforts, attachments, opinions, turn on mechanism, and are of a mechanical character.

We may trace this tendency in all the great manifestations of our time; in its intellectual aspect, the studies it most favours and its manner of conducting them; in its practical aspects, its politics, arts, religion, morals; in the whole sources, and throughout the whole currents, of its spiritual, no less than its material activity.

Consider, for example, the state of Science generally, in Europe, at this period. It is admitted, on all sides, that the Metaphysical and Moral Sciences are falling into decay, while the Physical are engrossing, every day, more respect and attention. In most of the European nations there is now no such thing as a Science of Mind; only more or less advancement in the general science, or the special sciences, of matter. The French were the first to desert Metaphysics; and though they have lately affected to revive their school, it has yet no signs of vitality. The land of Malebranche, Pascal, Descartes and Fénelon, has now only its Cousins and Villemains; while, in the department of Physics, it reckons far other names. Among ourselves, the Philosophy of Mind, after a rickety infancy, which never reached the vigour of manhood, fell suddenly into decay, languished and finally died out, with its last amiable cultivator, Professor Stewart. In no nation but Germany has any decisive effort been made in psychological science; not to speak of any decisive result. The science of the age, in short, is physical, chemical, physiological; in all shapes mechanical. Our favourite Mathematics, the highly prized exponent of all these other sciences, has also become more and more mechanical. Excellence in what is called its higher departments depends less on natural genius than on acquired expertness in wielding its machinery. Without undervaluing the wonderful results which a Lagrange or Laplace educes by means of it, we may remark, that their calculus, differential and integral, is little else than a more cunningly-constructed arithmetical mill; where the factors being put in, are, as it were, ground into the true product, under cover, and without other effort on our part than steady turning of the handle. We have more Mathematics than ever; but less Mathesis. Archimedes and Plato could not have read the *Mécanique Céleste*; but neither would the whole French Institute see aught in that saying, 'God geometrises!' but a sentimental rodomontade.

Nay, our whole Metaphysics itself, from Locke's time downwards, has been physical; not a spiritual philosophy, but a material one. The singular estimation in which his Essay was so long held as a scientific work (an estimation grounded, indeed, on the estimable character of the man) will one day be thought a curious indication of the spirit of these times. His whole doctrine is mechanical, in its aim and origin, in its method and its results. It is not a philosophy of the mind: it is a mere discussion concerning the origin of our consciousness, or ideas, or whatever else they are called; a genetic history of what we see *in* the mind. The grand secrets of Necessity and Freewill, of the Mind's vital or non-vital dependence on Matter, of our mysterious relations to Time and Space, to God, to the Universe, are not, in the faintest degree touched on in these inquiries; and seem not to have the smallest connexion with them.

The last class of our Scotch Metaphysicians had a dim notion that much of this was wrong; but they knew not how to right it. The school of Reid had also from the first taken a mechanical course, not seeing any other. The singular conclusions at which Hume, setting out from their admitted premises, was arriving, brought this school into being; they let loose Instinct, as an undiscriminating bandog, to guard them against these conclusions;—they tugged lustily at the logical chain by which Hume was so coldly towing them and the world into bottomless abysses of Atheism and Fatalism. But the chain somehow snapped between them; and the issue has been that nobody now cares about either,—any more than about Hartley's, Darwin's, or Priestley's contemporaneous doings in England. Hartley's vibrations and vibratiuncles, one would think, were material and mechanical enough; but our Continental neighbours have gone still farther. One of their philosophers has lately discovered, that 'as the liver secretes bile, so does the brain secrete thought'; which astonishing discovery Dr. Cabanis, more lately still, in his *Rapports du Physique et du Morale de l'Homme,* has pushed into its minutest developments.

The metaphysical philosophy of this last inquirer is certainly no shadowy or unsubstantial one. He fairly lays open our moral structure with his dissecting-knives and real metal probes; and exhibits it to the inspection of mankind, by Leuwenhoek microscopes, and inflation with the anatomical blowpipe. Thought, he is inclined to hold, is still secreted by the brain; but then Poetry and Religion (and it is really worth knowing) are 'a product of the smaller intestines'! We have the greatest admiration for this learned doctor: with what scientific stoicism he walks through the land of wonders, unwondering; like a wise man through some huge, gaudy, imposing Vauxhall, whose fire-works, cascades and symphonies, the vulgar may enjoy and believe in,—but where he finds nothing real but the saltpetre, pasteboard and catgut. His book may be regarded as the ultimatum of mechanical metaphysics in our time; a remarkable realisation of what in Martinus Scriblerus was still only an idea, that 'as the jack had a meat-roasting quality, so had the body a thinking quality,'—upon the strength of which the Nurembergers were to build a wood-and-leather man, 'who should reason as well as most country parsons.' Vaucanson did indeed make a wooden duck, that seemed to eat and digest; but that bold scheme of the Nurembergers remained for a more modern virtuoso.

This condition of the two great departments of knowledge,—the outward, cultivated exclusively on mechanical principles; the inward, finally abandoned, because, cultivated on such principles, it is found to yield no result,— sufficiently indicates the intellectual bias of our time, its all-pervading disposition towards that line of inquiry. In fact, an inward persuasion has long been diffusing itself, and now and then even comes to utterance, That, except the external, there are no true sciences; that to the inward world (if there be any) our only conceivable road is through the outward; that, in short, what cannot be investigated and understood mechanically, cannot be investigated and understood at all. We advert the more particularly to these intellectual propensities, as to prominent symptoms of our age, because Opinion is at all times doubly related to Action, first as cause, then as effect; and the speculative tendency of any age will therefore give us, on the whole, the best indications of its practical tendency.

Nowhere, for example, is the deep, almost exclusive faith we have in Mechanism more visible than in the Politics of this time. Civil government does by its nature include much that is mechanical, and must be treated accordingly. We term it indeed, in ordinary language, the Machine of Society, and talk of it as the grand working wheel from which all private machines must derive, or to which they must adapt, their movements. Considered merely as a metaphor, all this is well enough; but here, as in so many other cases, the 'foam hardens itself into a shell,' and the shadow we have wantonly evoked stands terrible before us and will not depart at our bidding. Government includes much also that is not mechanical, and cannot be treated mechanically; of which latter truth, as appears to us, the political speculations and exertions of our time are taking less and less cognisance.

Nay, in the very outset, we might note the mighty interest taken in *mere political arrangements,* as itself the sign of a mechanical age. The whole discontent of Europe takes this direction. The deep, strong cry of all civilised nations,— a cry which, every one now sees, must and will be answered, is: Give us a reform of Government! A good structure of legislation, a proper check upon the executive, a wise arrangement of the judiciary, is *all* that is wanting for human happiness. The Philosopher of this age is not a Socrates, a Plato, a Hooker, or Taylor, who inculcates on men the necessity and infinite worth of moral goodness, the great truth that our happiness depends on the mind which is within us, and not on the circumstances which are without us; but a Smith, a De Lolme, a Bentham, who chiefly inculcates the reverse of this,—that our happiness depends entirely on external circumstances; nay, that the strength and dignity of the mind within us is itself the creature and consequence of these. Were the laws, the government, in good order, all were well with us; the rest would care for itself! Dissentients from this opinion, expressed or implied, are now rarely to be met with; widely and angrily as men differ in its application, the principle is admitted by all.

Equally mechanical, and of equal simplicity, are the methods proposed by both parties for completing or securing this all-sufficient perfection of arrangement. It is no longer the moral, religious, spiritual condition of the people that is our concern, but their physical, practical, economical condition, as regulated by public laws. Thus is the Body-politic more than ever worshipped and tendered; but the Soul-politic less than ever. Love of country, in any high or generous sense, in any other than an almost animal sense, or mere habit, has little importance attached to it in such reforms, or in the opposition shown them. Men are to be guided only by their self-interests. Good government is a good balancing of these; and, except a keen eye and appetite for self-interest, requires no virtue in any quarter. To both parties it is emphatically a machine: to the discontented, a 'taxing-machine'; to the contented, a 'machine for securing property.' Its duties and its faults are not those of a father, but of an active parish-constable.

Thus it is by the mere condition of the machine, by preserving it untouched, or else by reconstructing it, and oiling it anew, that man's salvation as a social being is to be ensured and indefinitely promoted. Contrive the fabric of law aright, and without farther effort on your part, that divine spirit of Freedom, which all hearts venerate and long for, will of herself come to inhabit it; and under her healing wings every noxious influence will wither, every good and salutary one more and more expand. Nay, so devoted are we to this principle, and at the same time so curiously mechanical, that a new trade, specially grounded on it, has arisen among us, under the name of 'Codification,' or codemaking in the abstract; whereby any people, for a reasonable consideration, may be accommodated with a patent code;— more easily than curious individuals with patent breeches, for the people does *not* need to be measured first.

To us who live in the midst of all this, and see continually the faith, hope and practice of every one founded on Mechanism of one kind or other, it is apt to seem quite natural, and as if it could never have been otherwise. Nevertheless, if we recollect or reflect a little, we shall find both that it has been, and might again be otherwise. The domain of Mechanism,—meaning thereby political, ecclesiastical or other outward establishments,—was once considered as embracing, and we are persuaded can at any time embrace, but a limited portion of man's interests, and by no means the highest portion.

To speak a little pedantically, there is a science of *Dynamics* in man's fortunes and nature, as well as of *Mechanics*. There is a science which treats of, and practically addresses, the primary, unmodified forces and energies of man, the mysterious springs of Love, and Fear, and Wonder, of Enthusiasm, Poetry, Religion, all which have a truly vital and *infinite* character; as well as a science which practically addresses the finite, modified developments of these, when they take the shape of immediate 'motives,' as hope of reward, or as fear of punishment.

Now it is certain, that in former times the wise men, the enlightened lovers of their kind, who appeared generally as Moralists, Poets or Priests, did, without neglecting the Mechanical province, deal chiefly with the Dynamical; applying themselves chiefly to regulate, increase and purify the inward primary powers of man; and fancying that herein lay the main difficulty, and the best service they could undertake. But a wide difference is manifest in our age. For the wise men, who now appear as Political Philosophers, deal exclusively with the Mechanical province; and occupying themselves in counting-up and estimating men's motives, strive by curious checking and balancing, and other adjustments ·of Profit and Loss, to guide them to their true advantage: while, unfortunately, those same 'motives' are so innumerable, and so variable in every individual, that no really useful conclusion can ever be drawn from their enumeration. But though Mechanism, wisely contrived, has done much for man in a social and moral point of view, we cannot be persuaded that it has ever been the chief source of his worth or happiness. Consider the great elements of human enjoyment, the attainments and possessions that exalt man's life to its present height, and see what part of these he owes to institutions, to Mechanism of any kind; and what to the instinctive, unbounded force, which Nature herself lent him, and still continues to him. Shall we say, for example, that Science and Art are indebted principally to the founders of Schools and Universities? Did not Science originate rather, and gain advancement, in the obscure closets of the Roger Bacons, Keplers, Newtons; in the workshops of the Fausts and the Watts; wherever, and in what guise soever Nature, from the first times downwards, had sent a gifted spirit upon the earth? Again, were Homer and Shakspeare members of any beneficed guild, or made Poets by means of it? Were Painting and Sculpture created by forethought, brought into the world by institutions for that end? No; Science and Art have, from first to last, been the free gift of Nature; an unsolicited, unexpected gift; often even a fatal one. These things rose up, as it were, by spontaneous growth, in the free soil and sunshine of Nature. They were not planted or grafted, nor even greatly multiplied or improved by the culture or manuring of institutions. Generally speaking, they have derived only partial help from these; often enough have suffered damage. They made constitutions for themselves. They originated in the Dynamical nature of man, not in his Mechanical nature.

Or, to take an infinitely higher instance, that of the Christian Religion, which, under every theory of it, in the believing or unbelieving mind, must ever be regarded as the crowning glory, or rather the life and soul, of our whole modern culture: How did Christianity arise and spread abroad among men? Was it by institutions, and establishments and well-arranged systems of mechanism? Not so; on the contrary, in all past and existing institutions for those ends, its divine spirit has invariably been found to languish and decay. It arose in the mystic deeps of man's soul; and was spread abroad by the 'preaching of the word,' by simple, altogether natural and individual efforts; and flew, like hallowed fire, from heart to heart, till all were purified and illuminated by it; and its heavenly light shone, as it still shines, and (as sun or star) will ever shine, through the whole dark destinies of man. Here again was no Mechanism; man's highest attainment was accomplished Dynamically, not Mechanically.

Nay, we will venture to say, that no high attainment, not even any far-extending movement among men, was ever accomplished otherwise. Strange as it may seem, if we read History with any degree of thoughtfulness, we shall find that the checks and balances of Profit and Loss have never been the grand agents with men; that they have never been roused into deep, thorough, all-pervading efforts by any computable prospect of Profit and Loss, for any visible, finite object; but always for some invisible and infinite one. The Crusades took their rise in Religion; their visible object was, commercially speaking, worth nothing. It was the boundless Invisible world that was laid bare in the imaginations of those men; and in its burning light, the visible shrunk as a scroll. Not mechanical, nor produced by mechanical means, was this vast movement. No dining at Freemasons' Tavern, with the other long train of modern machinery; no cunning reconciliation of 'vested interests,' was required here: only the passionate voice of one man, the rapt soul looking through the eyes of one man; and rugged, steel-clad Europe trembled beneath his words, and followed him whither he listed. In later ages it was still the same. The Reformation had an invisible, mystic and ideal aim; the result was indeed to be embodied in external things; but its spirit, its worth, was internal, invisible, infinite. Our English Revolution too originated in Religion. Men did battle, in those old days, not for Purse-sake, but for Conscience-sake. Nay, in our own days, it is no way different. The French Revolution itself had something higher in it than cheap bread and a Habeas-corpus act. Here too was an Idea; a Dynamic, not a Mechanic force. It was a struggle, though a blind and at last an insane one, for the infinite, divine nature of Right, of Freedom, of Country.

Thus does man, in every age, vindicate, consciously or unconsciously, his celestial birthright. Thus does Nature hold on her wondrous, unquestionable course; and all our systems and theories are but so many froth-eddies or sandbanks, which from time to time she casts up, and washes away. When we can drain the Ocean into mill-ponds, and bottle-up the Force of Gravity, to be sold by retail, in gas jars; then may we hope to comprehend the infinitudes of man's soul under formulas of Profit and Loss; and rule over this too, as over a patent engine, by checks, and valves, and balances.

Nay, even with regard to Government itself, can it be necessary to remind any one that Freedom, without which indeed all spiritual life is impossible, depends on infinitely more complex influences than either the extension or the curtailment of the 'democratic interest'? Who is there that, 'taking the high *priori* road,' shall point out what these influences are; what deep, subtle, inextricably entangled influences they have been and may be? For man is not the creature and product of Mechanism; but, in a far truer sense, its creator and producer: it is the noble People that makes the noble Government; rather than conversely. On the whole, Institutions are much; but they are not all. The freest and highest spirits of the world have often been found under strange outward circumstances: Saint Paul and his brother Apostles were politically slaves; Epictetus was personally one. Again, forget the influences of Chivalry and Religion, and ask: What countries produced Columbus and Las Casas? Or, descending from virtue and heroism to mere energy and spiritual talent: Cortes, Pizarro, Alba, Ximenes? The Spaniards of the sixteenth century were indisputably the noblest nation of Europe: yet they had the Inquisition and Philip II. They have the same government at this day; and are the lowest nation. The Dutch too have retained their old constitution; but no Siege of Leyden, no William the Silent, not even an Egmont or De Witt any longer appears among them. With ourselves also, where much has changed, effect has nowise followed cause as it should have done: two centuries ago, the Commons Speaker addressed Queen Elizabeth on bended knees, happy that the virago's foot did not even smite him; yet the people were then governed, not by a Castlereagh, but by a Burghley; they had their Shakspeare and Philip Sidney, where we have our Sheridan Knowles and Beau Brummel.

These and the like facts are so familiar, the truths which they preach so obvious, and have in all past times been so universally believed and acted on, that we should almost feel ashamed for repeating them; were it not that, on every hand, the memory of them seems to have passed away, or at best died into a faint tradition, of no value as a practical principle. To judge by the loud clamour of our Constitution-builders, Statists, Economists, directors, creators, reformers of Public Societies; in a word, all manner of Mechanists, from the Cartwright up to the Code-maker; and by the nearly total silence of all Preachers and Teachers who should give a voice to Poetry, Religion and Morality, we might fancy either that man's Dynamical nature was, to all spiritual intents, extinct, or else so perfected that nothing more was to be made of it by the old means; and henceforth only in his Mechanical contrivances did any hope exist for him.

To define the limits of these two departments of man's activity, which work into one another, and by means of one another, so intricately and inseparably, were by its nature an impossible attempt. Their relative importance, even to the wisest mind, will vary in different times, according to the special wants and dispositions of those times. Meanwhile, it seems clear enough that only in the right coördination of the two, and the vigorous forwarding of *both,* does our true line of action lie. Undue cultivation of the inward or Dynamical province leads to idle, visionary, impracticable courses, and, especially in rude eras, to Superstition and Fanaticism, with their long train of baleful and well-known evils. Undue cultivation of the outward, again, though less immediately prejudicial, and even for the time productive of many palpable benefits, must, in the long-run, by destroying Moral Force, which is the parent of all other Force, prove not less certainly, and perhaps still more hopelessly, pernicious. This, we take it, is the grand characteristic of our age. By our skill in Mechanism, it has come to pass, that in the management of external things we excel all other ages; while in whatever respects the pure moral nature, in true dignity of soul and character, we are perhaps inferior to most civilised ages.

In fact, if we look deeper, we shall find that this faith in Mechanism has now struck its roots down into man's most intimate, primary sources of conviction; and is thence sending up, over his whole life and activity, innumerable stems,—fruit-bearing and poison-bearing. The truth is, men have lost their belief in the Invisible, and believe, and hope, and work only in the Visible; or, to speak it in other words: This is not a Religious age. Only the material, the immediately practical, not the divine and spiritual, is important to us. The infinite, absolute character of Virtue has passed into a finite, conditional one; it is no longer a worship of the Beautiful and Good; but a calculation of the Profitable. Worship, indeed, in any sense, is not recognised among us, or is mechanically explained into Fear of pain, or Hope of pleasure. Our true Deity is Mechanism. It has subdued external Nature for us, and we think it will do all other things. We are Giants in physical power: in a deeper than metaphorical sense, we are Titans, that strive, by heaping mountain on mountain, to conquer Heaven also.

The strong Mechanical character, so visible in the spiritual pursuits and methods of this age, may be traced much farther into the condition and prevailing disposition of our spiritual nature itself. Consider, for example, the general fashion of Intellect in this era. Intellect, the power man has of knowing and believing, is now nearly synonymous with Logic, or the mere power of arranging and communicating. Its implement is not Meditation, but Argument. 'Cause and effect' is almost the only category under which we look at, and work with, all Nature. Our first question with regard to any object is not, What is it? but, How is it? We are no longer instinctively driven to apprehend, and lay to heart, what is Good and Lovely, but rather to inquire, as onlookers, how it is produced, whence it comes, whither it goes. Our favourite Philosophers have no love and no hatred; they stand among us not to do, nor to create anything, but as a sort of Logic-mills, to grind out the true causes and effects of all that is done and created. To the eye of a Smith, a Hume or a Constant, all is well that works quietly. An Order of Ignatius Loyola, a Presbyterianism of John Knox, a Wickliffe or a Henry the Eighth, are simply so many mechanical phenomena, caused or causing.

The *Euphuist* of our day differs much from his pleasant predecessors. An intellectual dapperling of these times boasts chiefly of his irresistible perspicacity, his 'dwelling in the daylight of truth,' and so forth; which, on examination, turns out to be a dwelling in the *rush*-light of 'closet-logic,' and a deep unconsciousness that there is any other light to dwell in or any other objects to survey with it. Wonder, indeed, is, on all hands, dying out: it is the sign of uncultivation to wonder. Speak to any small man of a high, majestic Reformation, of a high majestic Luther; and forthwith he sets about 'accounting' for it; how the 'circumstances of the time' called for such a character, and found him, we suppose, standing girt and road-ready, to do its errand; how the 'circumstances of the time' created, fashioned, floated him quietly along into the result; how, in short, this small man, had he been there, could have performed the like himself! For it is the 'force of circumstances' that does everything; the force of one man can do nothing. Now all this is grounded on little more than a metaphor. We figure Society as a 'Machine,' and that mind is opposed to mind, as body is to body; whereby two, or at most ten, little minds must be stronger than one great mind. Notable absurdity! For the plain truth, very plain, we think is, that minds are opposed to minds in quite a different way; and *one* man that has a higher Wisdom, a hitherto unknown spiritual Truth in him, is stronger, not than ten men that have it not, or than ten thousand, but than *all* men that have it not; and stands among them with a quite ethereal, angelic power, as with a sword out of Heaven's own armory, sky-tempered, which no buckler, and no tower of brass, will finally withstand.

But to us, in these times, such considerations rarely occur. We enjoy, we see nothing by direct vision; but only by reflection, and in anatomical dismemberment. Like Sir Hudibras, for every Why we must have a Wherefore. We have our little *theory* on all human and divine things. Poetry, the workings of genius itself, which in all times, with one or another meaning, has been called Inspiration, and held to be mysterious and inscrutable, is no longer without its scientific exposition. The building of the lofty rhyme is like any other masonry or bricklaying: we have theories of its rise, height, decline and fall,—which latter, it would seem, is now near, among all people. Of our 'Theories of Taste,' as they are called, wherein the deep, infinite, unspeakable Love of Wisdom and Beauty, which dwells in all men, is 'explained,' made mechanically visible, from 'Association' and the like, why should we say anything? Hume has written us a 'Natural History of Religion'; in which one Natural History all the rest are included. Strangely too does the general feeling coincide with Hume's in this wonderful problem; for whether his 'Natural History' be the right one or not, that Religion must have a Natural History, all of us, cleric and laic, seem to be agreed. He indeed regards it as a Disease, we again as Health; so far there is a difference; but in our first principle we are at one.

To what extent theological Unbelief, we mean intellectual dissent from the Church, in its view of Holy Writ, prevails at this day, would be a highly important, were it not, under any circumstances, an almost impossible inquiry. But the Unbelief, which is of a still more fundamental character, every man may see prevailing, with scarcely any but the faintest contradiction, all around him; even in the Pulpit itself. Religion in most countries, more or less in every country, is no longer what it was, and should be,—a thousand-voiced psalm from the heart of Man to his invisible Father, the fountain of all Goodness, Beauty, Truth, and revealed in every revelation of these; but for the most part, a wise prudential feeling grounded on mere calculation; a matter, as all others now are, of Expediency and Utility; whereby some smaller quantum of earthly enjoyment may be exchanged for a far larger quantum of celestial enjoyment. Thus Religion too is Profit, a working for wages; not Reverence, but vulgar Hope or Fear. Many, we know, very many we hope, are still religious in a far different sense; were it not so, our case were too desperate: but to witness that such is the temper of the times, we take any calm observant man, who agrees or disagrees in our feeling on the matter, and ask him whether our *view* of it is not in general well-founded.

Literature too, if we consider it, gives similar testimony. At no former era has Literature, the printed communication of Thought, been of such importance as it is now. We often hear that the Church is in danger; and truly so it is, —in a danger it seems not to know of: for, with its tithes in the most perfect safety, its functions are becoming more and more superseded. The true Church of England, at this moment, lies in the Editors of its Newspapers. These preach to the people daily, weekly; admonishing kings themselves; advising peace or war, with an authority which only the first Reformers, and a long-past class of Popes, were possessed of; inflicting moral censure; imparting moral encouragement, consolation, edification; in all ways diligently 'administering the Discipline of the Church.' It may be said too, that in private disposition the new Preachers somewhat resemble the Mendicant Friars of old times: outwardly full of holy zeal; inwardly not without stratagem, and hunger for terrestrial things. But omitting this class, and the boundless host of watery personages who pipe, as they are able, on so many scrannel straws, let us look at the higher regions of Literature, where, if anywhere, the pure melodies of Poesy and Wisdom should be heard. Of natural talent there is no deficiency: one or two richly-endowed individuals even give us a superiority in this respect. But what is the song they sing? Is it a tone of the Memnon Statue, breathing music as the *light* first touches it? A 'liquid wisdom,' disclosing to our sense the deep, infinite harmonies of Nature and

man's soul? Alas, no! It is not a matin or vesper hymn to
the Spirit of Beauty, but a fierce clashing of cymbals, and
shouting of multitudes, as children pass through the fire to
Moloch! Poetry itself has no eye for the Invisible. Beauty
is no longer the god it worships, but some brute image of
Strength; which we may call an idol, for true Strength is
one and the same with Beauty, and its worship also is a
hymn. The meek, silent Light can mould, create and purify
all Nature; but the loud Whirlwind, the sign and product of
Disunion, of Weakness, passes on, and is forgotten. How
widely this veneration for the physically Strongest has
spread itself through Literature, any one may judge who
reads either criticism or poem. We praise a work, not as
'true,' but as 'strong'; our highest praise is that it has 'affected' us, has 'terrified' us. All this, it has been well observed, is the 'maximum of the Barbarous,' the symptom,
not of vigorous refinement, but of luxurious corruption. It
speaks much, too, for men's indestructible love of truth, that
nothing of this kind will abide with them; that even the
talent of a Byron cannot permanently seduce us into idol-
worship; that he too, with all his wild siren charming, already begins to be disregarded and forgotten.

Again, with respect to our Moral condition: here also he
who runs may read that the same physical, mechanical influences are everywhere busy. For the 'superior morality,'
of which we hear so much, we too would desire to
be thankful: at the same time, it were but blindness to deny
that this 'superior morality' is properly rather an 'inferior
criminality,' produced not by greater love of Virtue, but by
greater perfection of Police; and of that far subtler and
stronger Police, called Public Opinion. This last watches over
us with its Argus eyes more keenly than ever; but the 'inward eye' seems heavy with sleep. Of any belief in invisible,
divine things, we find as few traces in our Morality as elsewhere. It is by tangible, material considerations that we
are guided, not by inward and spiritual. Self-denial, the
parent of all virtue, in any true sense of that word, has perhaps seldom been rarer: so rare is it, that the most, even in
their abstract speculations, regard its existence as a chimera.
Virtue is Pleasure, is Profit; no celestial, but an earthly
thing. Virtuous men, Philanthropists, Martyrs are happy
accidents; their 'taste' lies the right way! In all senses, we
worship and follow after Power; which may be called a

physical pursuit. No man now loves Truth, as Truth must be loved, with an infinite love; but only with a finite love, and as it were *par amours*. Nay, properly speaking, he does not *believe* and know it, but only *'thinks'* it, and that 'there is every probability!' He preaches it aloud, and rushes courageously forth with it,—if there is a multitude huzzaing at his back; yet ever keeps looking over his shoulder, and the instant the huzzaing languishes, he too stops short.

In fact, what morality we have takes the shape of Ambition, of 'Honour': beyond money and money's worth, our only rational blessedness is Popularity. It were but a fool's trick to die for conscience. Only for 'character,' by duel, or in case of extremity, by suicide, is the wise man bound to die. By arguing on the 'force of circumstances,' we have argued away all force from ourselves; and stand leashed together, uniform in dress and movement, like the rowers of some boundless galley. This and that may be right and true; *but* we must not do it. Wonderful 'Force of Public Opinion'! We must act and walk in all points as it prescribes; follow the traffic it bids us, realise the sum of money, the degree of 'influence' it expects of us, *or* we shall be lightly esteemed; certain mouthfuls of articulate wind will be blown at us, and this what mortal courage can front? Thus, while civil liberty is more and more secured to us, our moral liberty is all but lost. Practically considered, our creed is Fatalism; and, free in hand and foot, we are shackled in heart and soul with far straiter than feudal chains. Truly may we say, with the Philosopher, 'the deep meaning of the Laws of Mechanism lies heavy on us'; and in the closet, in the marketplace, in the temple, by the social hearth, encumbers the whole movements of our mind, and over our noblest faculties is spreading a nightmare sleep.

These dark features, we are aware, belong more or less to other ages, as well as to ours. This faith in Mechanism, in the all-importance of physical things, is in every age the common refuge of Weakness and blind Discontent; of all who believe, as many will ever do, that man's true good lies without him, not within. We are aware also, that, as applied to ourselves in all their aggravation, they form but half a picture; that in the whole picture there are bright lights as well as gloomy shadows. If we here dwell chiefly on the latter, let us not be blamed: it is in general more profitable to reckon up our defects than to boast of our attainments.

Neither, with all these evils more or less clearly before us, have we at any time despaired of the fortunes of society. Despair, or even despondency, in that respect, appears to us, in all cases, a groundless feeling. We have a faith in the imperishable dignity of man; in the high vocation to which, throughout this his earthly history, he has been appointed. However it may be with individual nations, whatever melancholic speculators may assert, it seems a well-ascertained fact, that in all times, reckoning even from those of the Heraclides and Pelasgi, the happiness and greatness of mankind at large have been continually progressive. Doubtless this age also is advancing. Its very unrest, its ceaseless activity, its discontent contains matter of promise. Knowledge, education are opening the eyes of the humblest; are increasing the number of thinking minds without limit. This is as it should be; for not in turning back, not in resisting, but only in resolutely struggling forward, does our life consist.

Nay, after all, our spiritual maladies are but of Opinion; we are but fettered by chains of our own forging, and which ourselves also can rend asunder. This deep, paralysed subjection to physical objects comes not from Nature, but from our own unwise mode of *viewing* Nature. Neither can we understand that man wants, at this hour, any faculty of heart, soul or body, that ever belonged to him. 'He, who has been born, has been a First Man'; has had lying before his young eyes, and as yet unhardened into scientific shapes, a world as plastic, infinite, divine, as lay before the eyes of Adam himself. If Mechanism, like some glass bell, encircles and imprisons us; if the soul looks forth on a fair heavenly country which it cannot reach, and pines, and in its scanty atmosphere is ready to perish,—yet the bell is but of glass; 'one bold stroke to break the bell in pieces, and thou art delivered!' Not the invisible world is wanting, for it dwells in man's soul, and this last is still here. Are the solemn temples, in which the Divinity was once visibly revealed among us, crumbling away? We can repair them, we can rebuild them. The wisdom, the heroic worth of our forefathers, which we have lost, we can recover. That admiration of old nobleness, which now so often shows itself as a faint *dilettantism,* will one day become a generous emulation, and man may again be all that he has been, and more than he has been. Nor are these the mere daydreams of fancy; they are clear possibilities; nay, in this time they are even assuming the character of hopes. Indications we do see in other countries and in our own, signs infinitely cheering to us, that Mechanism is not always to be our hard taskmaster, but one day to be our pliant, all-ministering servant; that a new and brighter spiritual era is slowly evolving itself for all men. But on these things our present course forbids us to enter.

Meanwhile, that great outward changes are in progress can be doubtful to no one. The time is sick and out of joint. Many things have reached their height; and it is a wise adage that tells us, 'the darkest hour is nearest the dawn.' Wherever we can gather indication of the public thought, whether from printed books, as in France or Germany, or from Carbonari rebellions and other political tumults, as in Spain, Portugal, Italy and Greece, the voice it utters is the same. The thinking minds of all nations call for change. There is a deep-lying struggle in the whole fabric of society; a boundless grinding collision of the New with the Old. The French Revolution, as is now visible enough, was not the parent of this mighty movement, but its offspring. Those two hostile influences, which always exist in human things, and on the constant intercommunion of which depends their health and safety, had lain in separate masses, accumulating through generations, and France was the scene of their fiercest explosion; but the final issue was not unfolded in that country: nay, it is not yet anywhere unfolded. Political freedom is hitherto the object of these efforts; but they will not and cannot stop there. It is towards a higher freedom than mere freedom from oppression by his fellow-mortal, that man dimly aims. Of this higher, heavenly freedom, which is 'man's reasonable service,' all his noble institutions, his faithful endeavours and loftiest attainments, are but the body, and more and more approximated emblem.

On the whole, as this wondrous planet, Earth, is journeying with its fellows through infinite Space, so are the wondrous destinies embarked on it journeying through infinite Time, under a higher guidance than ours. For the present, as our astronomy informs us, its path lies towards *Hercules*, the constellation of *Physical Power*: but that is not our most pressing concern. Go where it will, the deep HEAVEN will be around it. Therein let us have hope and sure faith. To reform a world, to reform a nation, no wise man will undertake; and all but foolish men know, that the only solid, though a far slower reformation, is what each begins and perfects on *himself*.

On History

1 8 3 0

[This essay was first published in the November 1830 issue of *Fraser's Magazine*. It is a development of material Carlyle worked on in writing "A History of German Literature" in 1829-1830. The book was never finished and remained unpublished until 1951, but several essays, chiefly on German literary matters, were carved out of it. In this essay Carlyle enunciates his views on the meaning of history and the writing of history, views which determined his own approach in works like *The French Revolution* and *Past and Present*. Carlyle's theory of the commanding role of biography in history also anticipates the doctrine of the Hero.]

Clio was figured by the ancients as the eldest daughter of Memory, and chief of the Muses; which dignity, whether we regard the essential qualities of her art, or its practice and acceptance among men, we shall still find to have been fitly bestowed. History, as it lies at the root of all science, is also the first distinct product of man's spiritual nature; his earliest expression of what can be called Thought. It is a looking both before and after; as, indeed, the coming Time already waits, unseen, yet definitely shaped, predetermined and inevitable, in the Time come; and only by the combination of both is the meaning of either completed. The Sibylline Books, though old, are not the oldest. Some nations have prophecy, some have not: but of all mankind, there is no tribe so rude that it has not attempted History, though several have not arithmetic enough to count Five. History has been written with quipo-threads, with feather-pictures, with wampum-belts; still oftener with earth-mounds and monumental stone-heaps, whether as pyramid or cairn; for the Celt and the Copt, the Red man as well as the White, lives between two eternities, and warring against Oblivion, he would fain unite himself in clear conscious relation, as in dim unconscious relation he is already united, with the whole Future, and the whole Past.

A talent for History may be said to be born with us, as our chief inheritance. In a certain sense all men are historians. Is not every memory written quite full with Annals, wherein joy and mourning, conquest and loss manifoldly alternate; and, with or without philosophy, the whole fortunes of one little inward Kingdom, and all its politics, foreign and domestic, stand ineffaceably recorded? Our very speech is curiously historical. Most men, you may observe, speak only to narrate; not in imparting what they have thought, which indeed were often a very small matter, but in exhibiting what they have undergone or seen, which is a quite unlimited one, do talkers dilate. Cut us off from Narrative, how would the stream of conversation, even among the wisest, languish into detached handfuls, and among the foolish utterly evaporate! Thus, as we do nothing but enact History, we say little but recite it nay, rather, in that widest sense, our whole spiritual life is built thereon. For, strictly considered, what is all Knowledge too but recorded Experience, and a product of History; of which, therefore, Reasoning and Belief, no less than Action and Passion, are essential materials?

Under a limited, and the only practicable shape, History proper, that part of History which treats of remarkable action, has, in all modern as well as ancient times, ranked among the highest arts, and perhaps never stood higher than in these times of ours. For whereas, of old, the charm of History lay chiefly in gratifying our common appetite for the wonderful, for the unknown; and her office was but as that of a Minstrel and Story-teller, she has now farther become a School-mistress, and professes to instruct in gratifying. Whether, with the stateliness of that venerable character, she may not have taken up something of its austerity and frigidity; whether in the logical terseness of a Hume or Robertson, the graceful ease and gay pictorial heartiness of a Herodotus or Froissart may not be wanting, is not the question for us here. Enough that all learners, all inquiring minds of every order, are gathered round her footstool, and reverently pondering her lessons, as the true basis of Wisdom. Poetry, Divinity, Politics, Physics, have each their adherents and adversaries; each little guild supporting a defensive and offensive war for its own special domain; while the domain of History is as a Free Emporium, where all these belligerents peaceably meet and furnish themselves;

and Sentimentalist and Utilitarian, Sceptic and Theologian, with one voice advise us: Examine History, for it is 'Philosophy teaching by Experience.'

Far be it from us to disparage such teaching, the very attempt at which must be precious. Neither shall we too rigidly inquire: How much it has hitherto profited? Whether most of what little practical wisdom men have, has come from study of professed History, or from other less boasted sources, whereby, as matters now stand, a Marlborough may become great in the world's business, with no History save what he derives from Shakspeare's Plays? Nay, whether in that same teaching by Experience, historical Philosophy has yet properly deciphered the first element of all science in this kind: What the aim and significance of that wondrous changeful Life it investigates and paints may be? Whence the course of man's destinies in this Earth originated, and whither they are tending? Or, indeed, if they have any course and tendency, are really guided forward by an unseen mysterious Wisdom, or only circle in blind mazes without recognisable guidance? Which questions, altogether fundamental, one might think, in any Philosophy of History, have, since the era when Monkish Annalists were wont to answer them by the long-ago extinguished light of their Missal and Breviary, been by most philosophical Historians only glanced at dubiously and from afar; by many, not so much as glanced at.

The truth is, two difficulties, never wholly surmountable, lie in the way. Before Philosophy can teach by Experience, the Philosophy has to be in readiness, the Experience must be gathered and intelligibly recorded. Now, overlooking the former consideration, and with regard only to the latter, let any one who has examined the current of human affairs, and how intricate, perplexed, unfathomable, even when seen into with our own eyes, are their thousandfold blending movements, say whether the true representing of it is easy or impossible. Social Life is the aggregate of all the individual men's Lives who constitute society; History is the essence of innumerable Biographies. But if one Biography, nay, our own Biography, study and recapitulate it as we may, remains in so many points unintelligible to us; how much more must these million, the very facts of which, to say nothing of the purport of them, we know not, and cannot know!

Neither will it adequately avail us to assert that the general inward condition of Life is the same in all ages; and that only the remarkable deviations from the common endowment and common lot, and the more important variations which the outward figure of Life has from time to time undergone, deserve memory and record. The inward condition of Life, it may rather be affirmed, the conscious or half-conscious aim of mankind, so far as men are not mere digesting-machines, is the same in no two ages; neither are the more important outward variations easy to fix on, or always well capable of representation. Which was the greatest innovator, which was the more important personage in man's history, he who first led armies over the Alps, and gained the victories of Cannæ and Thrasymene; or the nameless boor who first hammered out for himself an iron spade? When the oak-tree is felled, the whole forest echoes with it; but a hundred acorns are planted silently by some unnoticed breeze. Battles and war-tumults, which for the time din every ear and with joy or terror intoxicate every heart, pass away, like tavern-brawls; and, except some few Marathons and Morgartens, are remembered by accident, not by desert. Laws themselves, political Constitutions, are not our Life, but only the house wherein our Life is led: nay, they are but the bare walls of the house: all whose essential furniture, the inventions and traditions, and daily habits that regulate and support our existence, are the work not of Dracos and Hampdens, but of Phœnician mariners, of Italian masons and Saxon metallurgists, of philosophers, alchymists, prophets, and all the long-forgotten train of artists and artisans; who from the first have been jointly teaching us how to think and how to act, how to rule over spiritual and over physical Nature. Well may we say that of our History the more important part is lost without recovery; and,—as thanksgivings were once wont to be offered 'for unrecognised mercies,'—look with reverence into the dark untenanted places of the Past, where, in formless oblivion, our chief benefactors, with all their sedulous endeavours, but not with the fruit of these, lie entombed.

So imperfect is that same Experience, by which Philosophy is to teach. Nay, even with regard to those occurrences which do stand recorded, which, at their origin have seemed worthy of record, and the summary of which constitutes what we now call History, is not our understanding of them altogether incomplete; is it even possible to represent them as they were? The old story of Sir Walter Raleigh's looking from his prison-window, on some street tumult, which afterwards three witnesses reported in three different ways, himself differing from them all, is still a true lesson for us. Consider how it is that historical documents and records originate; even honest records, where the reporters were unbiased by personal regard; a case which, were nothing more wanted, must ever be among the rarest. The real leading features of a historical Transaction, those movements that essentially characterise it, and alone deserve to be recorded, are nowise the foremost to be noted. At first, among the various witnesses, who are also parties interested, there is only vague wonder, and fear or hope, and the noise of Rumour's thousand tongues; till, after a season, the conflict of testimonies has subsided into some general issue; and then it is settled, by majority of votes, that such and such a 'Crossing of the Rubicon,' an 'Impeachment of Strafford,' a 'Convocation of the Notables,' are epochs in the world's history, cardinal points on which grand world-revolutions have hinged. Suppose, however, that the majority of votes was all wrong; that the real cardinal points lay far deeper: and had been passed over unnoticed, because no Seer, but only mere Onlookers, chanced to be there! Our clock strikes when there is a change from hour to hour; but no hammer in the Horologe of Time peals through the universe when there is a change from Era to Era. Men understand not what is among their hands: as calmness is the characteristic of strength, so the weightiest causes may be most silent. It is, in no case, the real historical Transaction, but only some more or less plausible scheme and theory of the Transaction, or the harmonised result of many such schemes, each varying from the other and all varying from truth, that we can ever hope to behold.

Nay, were our faculty of insight into passing things never so complete, there is still a fatal discrepancy between our manner of observing these, and their manner of occurring. The most gifted man can observe, still more can record, only the series of his own impressions: his observation, therefore, to say nothing of its other imperfections, must be *successive*, while the things done were often *simultaneous*; the things done were not a series, but a group. It is not in acted, as it is in written History: actual events are nowise so simply related to each other as parent and offspring are; every single event is the offspring not of one, but of all other events, prior or contemporaneous, and will in its turn combine with all others to give birth to new: it is an ever-living, ever-working Chaos of Being, wherein shape after shape bodies itself forth from innumerable elements. And this Chaos, boundless as the habitation and duration of man, unfathomable as the soul and destiny of man, is what the historian will depict, and scientifically gauge, we may say, by threading it with single lines of a few ells in length! For as all Action is, by its nature, to be figured as extended in breadth and in depth, as well as in length; that is to say, is based on Passion and Mystery, if we investigate its origin; and spreads abroad on all hands, modifying and modified; as well as advances towards completion,—so all Narrative is, by its nature, of only one dimension; only travels forward towards one, or towards successive points: Narrative is *linear,* Action is *solid.* Alas for our 'chains,' or chainlets, of 'causes and effects,' which we so assiduously track through certain handbreadths of years and square miles, when the whole is a broad, deep Immensity, and each atom is 'chained' and complected with all! Truly, if History is Philosophy teaching by Experience, the writer fitted to compose History is hitherto an unknown man. The Experience itself would require All-knowledge to record it,— were the All-wisdom needful for such Philosophy as would interpret it, to be had for asking. Better were it that mere earthly Historians should lower such pretensions, more suitable for Omniscience than for human science; and aiming only at some picture of the things acted, which picture itself will at best be a poor approximation, leave the inscrutable purport of them an acknowledged secret; or at most, in reverent Faith, far different from that teaching of Philosophy, pause over the mysterious vestiges of Him, whose path is in the great deep of Time, whom History indeed reveals, but only all History, and in Eternity, will clearly reveal.

Such considerations truly were of small profit, did they, instead of teaching us vigilance and reverent humility in our inquiries into History, abate our esteem for them, or discourage us from unweariedly prosecuting them. Let us search more and more into the Past; let all men explore it, as the true fountain of knowledge; by whose light alone, consciously or unconsciously employed, can the Present and the Future be interpreted or guessed at. For though the whole meaning lies far beyond our ken; yet in that complex Manuscript, covered over with formless inextricably-entangled unknown characters,—nay, which is a *Palimpsest,* and had once prophetic writing, still dimly legible there, —some letters, some words, may be deciphered; and if no complete Philosophy, here and there an intelligible precept, available in practice, be gathered: well understanding, in the mean while, that it is only a little portion we have deciphered; that much still remains to be interpreted; that History is a real Prophetic Manuscript, and can be fully interpreted by no man.

But the Artist in History may be distinguished from the Artisan in History; for here, as in all other provinces, there are Artists and Artisans; men who labour mechanically in a department, without eye for the Whole, not feeling that there is a Whole; and men who inform and ennoble the humblest department with an Idea of the Whole, and habitually know that only in the Whole is the Partial to be truly discerned. The proceedings and the duties of these two, in regard to History, must be altogether different. Not, indeed, that each has not a real worth, in his several degree. The simple husbandman can till his field, and by knowledge he has gained of its soil, sow it with the fit grain, though the deep rocks and central fires are unknown to him: his little crop hangs under and over the firmament of stars, and sails through whole untracked celestial spaces, between Aries and Libra; nevertheless it ripens for him in due season, and he gathers it safe into his barn. As a husbandman he is blameless in disregarding those higher wonders; but as a thinker, and faithful inquirer into Nature, he were wrong. So likewise is it with the Historian, who examines some special aspect of History; and from this or that combination of circumstances, political, moral, economical, and the issues it has led to, infers that such and such properties belong to human society, and that the like circumstances will produce the like issue; which inference, if other trials confirm it, must be held true and practically valuable. He is wrong only, and an artisan, when he fancies that these properties, discovered or discoverable, exhaust the matter: and sees not, at every step, that it is inexhaustible.

However, that class of cause-and-effect speculators, with

whom no wonder would remain wonderful, but all things in Heaven and Earth must be computed and 'accounted for'; and even the Unknown, the Infinite in man's Life, had under the words *enthusiasm, superstition, spirit of the age* and so forth, obtained, as it were, an algebraical symbol and given value,—have now wellnigh played their part in European culture; and may be considered, as in most countries, even in England itself where they linger the latest, verging towards extinction. He who reads the inscrutable Book of Nature as if it were a Merchant's Ledger, is justly suspected of having never seen that Book, but only some school Synopsis thereof; from which, if taken for the real Book, more error than insight is to be derived.

Doubtless also, it is with a growing feeling of the infinite nature of History, that in these times, the old principle, division of labour, has been so widely applied to it. The Political Historian, once almost the sole cultivator of History, has now found various associates, who strive to elucidate other phases of human Life; of which, as hinted above, the political conditions it is passed under are but one, and though the primary, perhaps not the most important, of the many outward arrangements. Of this Historian himself, moreover, in his own special department, new and higher things are beginning to be expected. From of old, it was too often to be reproachfully observed of him, that he dwelt with disproportionate fondness in Senate-houses, in Battlefields, nay, even in Kings' Antechambers; forgetting, that far away from such scenes, the mighty tide of Thought and Action was still rolling on its wondrous course, in gloom and brightness; and in its thousand remote valleys, a whole world of Existence, with or without an earthly sun of Happiness to warm it, with or without a heavenly sun of Holiness to purify and sanctify it, was blossoming and fading, whether the 'famous victory' were won or lost. The time seems coming when much of this must be amended; and he who sees no world but that of courts and camps; and writes only how soldiers were drilled and shot, and how this ministerial conjuror outconjured that other, and then guided, or at least held, something which he called the rudder of Government, but which was rather the spigot of Taxation, wherewith, in place of steering, he could tap, and the more cunningly the nearer the lees,—will pass for a more or less instructive Gazetteer, but will no longer be called a Historian.

However, the Political Historian, were his work performed with all conceivable perfection, can accomplish but a part, and still leaves room for numerous fellow-labourers. Foremost among these comes the Ecclesiastical Historian; endeavouring, with catholic or sectarian view, to trace the progress of the Church; of that portion of the social establishments, which respects our religious condition; as the other portion does our civil, or rather, in the long-run, our economical condition. Rightly conducted, this department were undoubtedly the more important of the two; inasmuch as it concerns us more to understand how man's moral well-being had been and might be promoted, than to understand in the like sort his physical well-being; which latter is ultimately the aim of all Political arrangements. For the physically happiest is simply the safest, the strongest; and, in all conditions of Government, Power (whether of wealth as in these days, or of arms and adherents as in old days) is the only outward emblem and purchase-money of Good. True Good, however, unless we reckon Pleasure synonymous with it, is said to be rarely, or rather never, offered for sale in the market where that coin passes current. So that, for man's true advantage, not the outward condition of his life, but the inward and spiritual, is of prime influence; not the form of Government he lives under, and the power he can accumulate there, but the Church he is a member of, and the degree of moral elevation he can acquire by means of its instruction. Church History, then, did it speak wisely, would have momentous secrets to teach us: nay, in its highest degree, it were a sort of continued Holy Writ; our Sacred Books being, indeed, only a History of the primeval Church, as it first arose in man's soul, and symbolically embodied itself in his external life. How far our actual Church Historians fall below such unattainable standards, nay, below quite attainable approximations thereto, we need not point out. Of the Ecclesiastical Historian we have to complain, as we did of his Political fellow-craftsman, that his inquiries turn rather on the outward mechanism, the mere hulls and superficial accidents of the object, than on the object itself: as if the Church lay in Bishops' Chapter-houses, and Ecumenic Council-halls, and

Cardinals' Conclaves, and not far more in the hearts of Believing Men; in whose walk and conversation, as influenced thereby, its chief manifestations were to be looked for, and its progress ᵒor decline ascertained. The History of the Church is a History of the Invisible as well as of the Visible Church; which latter, if disjoined from the former, is but a vacant edifice; gilded, it may be, and overhung with old votive gifts, yet useless, nay, pestilentially unclean; to write whose history is less important than to forward its down-fall.

Of a less ambitious character are the Histories that relate to special separate provinces of human Action; to Sciences, Practical Arts, Institutions and the like; matters which do not imply an epitome of man's whole interest and form of life; but wherein, though each is still connected with all, the spirit of each, at least its material results, may be in some degree evolved without so strict a reference to that of the others. Highest in dignity and difficulty, under this head, would be our histories of Philosophy, of man's opin-ions and theories respecting the nature of his Being, and re-lations to the Universe Visible and Invisible: which His-tory, indeed, were it fitly treated, or fit for right treatment, would be a province of Church History; the logical or dog-matical province thereof; for Philosophy, in its true sense, is or should be the soul, of which Religion, Worship is the body; in the healthy state of things the Philosopher and Priest were one and the same. But Philosophy itself is far enough from wearing this character; neither have its His-torians been men, generally speaking, that could in the smallest degree approximate it thereto. Scarcely since the rude era of the Magi and Druids has that same healthy iden-tification of Priest and Philosopher had place in any country: but rather the worship of divine things, and the scientific investigation of divine things, have been in quite different hands, their relations not friendly but hostile. Neither have the Brückers and Bühles, to say nothing of the many unhappy Enfields who have treated of that latter de-partment, been more than barren reporters, often unintel-ligent and unintelligible reporters, of the doctrine uttered; withou: force to discover how the doctrine originated, or what reference it bore to its time and country, to the spiritual position of mankind there and then. Nay, such a task did not perhaps lie before them, as a thing to be attempted.

Art also and Literature are intimately blended with Religion; as it were, outworks and abutments, by which that highest pinnacle in our inward world gradually connects itself with the general level, and becomes accessible therefrom. He who should write a proper History of Poetry, would depict for us the successive Revelations which man had obtained of the Spirit of Nature; under what aspects he had caught and endeavoured to body forth some glimpse of that unspeakable Beauty, which in its highest clearness is Religion, is the inspiration of a Prophet, yet in one or the other degree must inspire every true Singer, were his theme never so humble. We should see by what steps men had ascended to the Temple; how near they had approached; by what ill hap they had, for long periods, turned away from it, and grovelled on the plain with no music in the air, or blindly struggled towards other heights. That among all our Eichhorns and Wartons there is no such Historian, must be too clear to every one. Nevertheless let us not despair of far nearer approaches to that excellence. Above all, let us keep the Ideal of it ever in our eye; for thereby alone have we even a chance to reach it.

Our histories of Laws and Constitutions, wherein many a Montesquieu and Hallam has laboured with acceptance, are of a much simpler nature; yet deep enough if thoroughly investigated; and useful, when authentic, even with little depth. Then we have Histories of Medicine, of Mathematics, of Astronomy, Commerce, Chivalry, Monkery; and Goguets and Beckmanns have come forward with what might be the most bountiful contribution of all, a History of Inventions. Of all which sorts, and many more not here enumerated, not yet devised and put in practice, the merit and the proper scheme may, in our present limits, require no exposition.

In this manner, though, as above remarked, all Action is extended three ways, and the general sum of human Action is a whole Universe, with all limits of it unknown, does History strive by running path after path, through the Impassable, in manifold directions and intersections, to secure for us some oversight of the Whole; in which endeavour, if each Historian look well around him from his path, tracking it out with the *eye,* not, as is more common, with the *nose,* she may at last prove not altogether unsuccessful. Praying only that increased division of labour do not here, as elsewhere, aggravate our already strong Mechanical tendencies, so that in the manual dexterity for parts we lose all command over the whole, and the hope of any Philosophy of History be farther off than ever,—let us all wish her great and greater success.

Characteristics

1 8 3 1

[The *Charakteristik,* a characterization or sketch of a character, was a favorite literary type of the German romantics, the best known example being the *Charasteristiken und Kritken* of the brothers Schlegel (1801). Carlyle adopted the term to apply to his analysis of the condition of the age, which is the real point of this essay that purported to be a review of two books, Thomas Hope's *The Origin and Prospect of Man* (1830) and Friedrich Schlegel's *Philosophical Lectures* (1831). The essay was first published in the *Edinburgh Review* in December 1831. Along with "Signs of the Times," "Characteristics" proved to be a seminal essay for Carlyle's thought and for much of that of the Victorian age. Here he excoriates the utilitarian self-consciousness of the age and asserts the need for a religious belief to reanimate society.]

The healthy know not of their health, but only the sick: this is the Physician's Aphorism; and applicable in a far wider sense than he gives it. We may say, it holds no less in moral, intellectual, political, poetical, than in merely corporeal therapeutics; that wherever, or in what shape soever, powers of the sort which can be named *vital* are at work, herein lies the test of their working right or working wrong.

In the Body, for example, as all doctors are agreed, the first condition of complete health is, that each organ perform its function unconsciously, unheeded; let but any organ announce its separate existence, were it even boastfully, and for pleasure, not for pain, then already has one of those unfortunate 'false centres of sensibility' established itself, already is derangement there. The perfection of bodily well-being is, that the collective bodily activities seem one; and be manifested, moreover, not in themselves, but in the action they accomplish. If a Dr. Kitchiner boast that his system is in high order, Dietetic Philosophy may indeed take credit; but the true Peptician was that Countryman who answered that, "for his part, he had no system." In fact, unity, agreement is always silent, or soft-voiced; it is only discord that loudly proclaims itself. So long as the several elements of Life, all fitly adjusted, can pour forth their movement like harmonious tuned strings, it is a melody and unison; Life, from its mysterious fountains, flows out as in celestial music and diapason,—which also, like that other music of the spheres, even because it is perennial and complete, without interruption and without imperfection, might be fabled to escape the ear. Thus too, in some languages, is the state of health well denoted by a term expressing unity; when we feel ourselves as we wish to be, we say that we are *whole*.

Few mortals, it is to be feared, are permanently blessed with that felicity of 'having no system'; nevertheless, most of us, looking back on young years, may remember seasons of a light, aërial translucency and elasticity and perfect freedom; the body had not yet become the prison-house of the soul, but was its vehicle and implement, like a creature of the thought, and altogether pliant to its bidding. We knew not that we had limbs, we only lifted, hurled and leapt; through eye and ear, and all avenues of sense, came clear unimpeded tidings from without, and from within issued clear victorious force; we stood as in the centre of Nature, giving and receiving, in harmony with it all; unlike Virgil's Husbandmen, 'too happy *because* we did not know our blessedness.' In those days, health and sickness were foreign traditions that did not concern us; our whole being was as yet One, the whole man like an incorporated Will. Such, were Rest or ever-successful Labour the human lot, might our life continue to be: a pure, perpetual, unregarded music; a beam of perfect white light, rendering all things visible, but itself unseen, even because it was of that perfect whiteness, and no irregular obstruction had yet broken it into colours. The beginning of Inquiry is Disease: all Science, if we consider well, as it must have originated in the feeling of something being wrong, so it is and continues to be but Division, Dismemberment, and partial healing of the wrong. Thus, as was of old written, the Tree of Knowledge springs from a root of evil, and bears fruits of good and evil. Had Adam remained in Paradise, there had been no Anatomy and no Metaphysics.

But, alas, as the Philosopher declares, 'Life itself is a disease; a working incited by suffering'; action from passion! The memory of that first state of Freedom and paradisaic Unconsciousness has faded away into an ideal poetic dream. We stand here too conscious of many things: with Knowledge, the symptom of Derangement, we must even do our best to restore a little Order. Life is, in few instances, and at rare intervals, the diapason of a heavenly melody; oftenest the fierce jar of disruptions and convulsions, which, do what we will, there is no disregarding. Nevertheless, such is still the wish of Nature on our behalf; in all vital action, her manifest purpose and effort is, that we should be unconscious of it, and, like the peptic Countryman, never know that we 'have a system.' For, indeed, vital action everywhere is emphatically a means, not an end; Life is not given us for the mere sake of Living, but always with an ulterior external Aim: neither is it on the process, on the means, but rather on the result, that Nature, in any of her doings, is wont to intrust us with insight and volition. Boundless as is the domain of man, it is but a small fractional proportion of it that he rules with Consciousness and by Forethought: what he can contrive, nay, what he can altogether know and comprehend, is essentially the mechanical, small; the great is ever, in one sense or other, the vital; it is essentially the mysterious, and only the surface of it can be understood. But Nature, it might seem, strives, like a kind mother, to hide from us even this, that she is a mystery: she will have us rest on her beautiful and awful bosom as if it were our secure home; on the bottomless boundless Deep, whereon all human things fearfully and wonderfully swim, she will have us walk and build, as if the film which supported us there (which any scratch of a bare bodkin will rend asunder, any sputter of a pistol-shot instantaneously burn up) were no film, but a solid rock-foundation. Forever in the neighbourhood of an inevitable Death, man can forget that he is born to die; of his Life, which, strictly meditated, contains in it an Immensity and an Eternity, he can conceive lightly, as of a simple implement wherewith to do day-labour and earn wages. So cunningly does Nature, the mother of all highest Art, which only apes her from afar, 'body forth the Finite from the Infinite'; and guide man safe on his wondrous path, not more by endowing him with vision, than, at the right place, with blindness! Under all her works, chiefly under her noblest work, Life, lies a basis of Darkness, which she benignantly conceals; in Life too, the roots and inward circulations which stretch down fearfully to the regions of Death and

Night, shall not hint of their existence, and only the fair
stem with its leaves and flowers, shone on by the fair sun,
shall disclose itself, and joyfully grow.

However, without venturing into the abstruse, or too
eagerly asking Why and How, in things where our answer
must needs prove, in great part, an echo of the question,
let us be content to remark farther, in the merely historical
way, how that Aphorism of the bodily Physician holds good
in quite other departments. Of the Soul, with her activities,
we shall find it no less true than of the Body: nay, cry the
Spiritualists, is not that very division of the unity, Man, into
a dualism of Soul and Body, itself the symptom of disease;
as, perhaps, your frightful theory of Materialism, of his being but a Body, and therefore, at least, once more a unity,
may be the paroxysm which was critical, and the beginning of cure! But omitting this, we observe, with confidence
enough, that the truly strong mind, view it as Intellect, as
Morality, or under any other aspect, is nowise the mind
acquainted with its strength; that here as before the sign of
health is Unconsciousness. In our inward, as in our outward
world, what is mechanical lies open to us: not what is
dynamical and has vitality. Of our Thinking, we might say,
it is but the mere upper surface that we shape into articulate
Thoughts;—underneath the region of argument and conscious discourse, lies the region of meditation; here, in its
quiet mysterious depths, dwells what vital force is in us;
here, if aught is to be created, and not merely manufactured
and communicated, must the work go on. Manufacture is
intelligible, but trivial; Creation is great, and cannot be
understood. Thus if the Debater and Demonstrator, whom
we may rank as the lowest of true thinkers, knows what he
has done, and how he did it, the Artist, whom we rank as
the highest, knows not; must speak of Inspiration, and in
one or the other dialect, call his work the gift of a divinity.

But on the whole, 'genius is ever a secret to itself'; of this
old truth we háve, on all sides, daily evidence. The Shakspeare takes no airs for writing *Hamlet* and the *Tempest,*
understands not that it is anything surprising: Milton,
again, is more conscious of his faculty, which accordingly
is an inferior one. On the other hand, what cackling
and strutting must we not often hear and see, when, in some
shape of academical prolusion, maiden speech, review article, this or the other well-fledged goose has produced its

goose-egg, of quite measurable value, were it the pink of its whole kind; and wonders why all mortals do not wonder!

Foolish enough, too, was the College Tutor's surprise at Walter Shandy: how, though unread in Aristotle, he could nevertheless argue; and not knowing the name of any dialectic tool, handled them all to perfection. Is it the skilfulest anatomist that cuts the best figure at Sadler's Wells? or does the boxer hit better for knowing that he has a *flexor longus* and a *flexor brevis?* But indeed, as in the higher case of the Poet, so here in that of the Speaker and Inquirer, the true force is an unconscious one. The healthy Understanding, we should say, is not the Logical, argumentative, but the Intuitive; for the end of Understanding is not to prove and find reasons, but to know and believe. Of logic, and its limits, and uses and abuses, there were much to be said and examined; one fact, however, which chiefly concerns us here, has long been familiar: that the man of logic and the man of insight; the Reasoner and the Discoverer, or even Knower, are quite separable,—indeed, for most part, quite separate characters. In practical matters, for example, has it not become almost proverbial that the man of logic cannot prosper? This is he whom business-people call Systematic and Theoriser and Word-monger; his *vital* intellectual force lies dormant or extinct, his whole force is mechanical, conscious: of such a one it is foreseen that, when once confronted with the infinite complexities of the real world, his little compact theorem of the world will be found wanting; that unless he can throw it overboard and become a new creature, he will necessarily founder. Nay, in mere Speculation itself, the most ineffectual of all characters, generally speaking, is your dialectic man-at-arms; were he armed cap-à-pie in syllogistic mail of proof, and perfect master of logic-fence, how little does it avail him! Consider the old Schoolmen, and their pilgrimage towards Truth: the faithfulest endeavour, incessant unwearied motion, often great natural vigour; only no progress: nothing but antic feats of one limb poised against the other; there they balanced, somersetted, and made postures; at best gyrated swiftly, with some pleasure, like Spinning Dervishes, and ended where they began. So is it, so will it always be, with all System-makers and builders of logical card-castles; of which class a certain remnant must, in every age, as they do in our own, survive and build. Logic is good, but it is not

the best. The Irrefragable Doctor, with his chains of in-
duction, his corollaries, dilemmas and other cunning logical
diagrams and apparatus, will cast you a beautiful horoscope,
and speak reasonable things; nevertheless your stolen jewel,
which you wanted him to find you, is not forthcoming. Often
by some winged word, winged as the thunderbolt is, of a
Luther, a Napoleon, a Goethe, shall we see the difficulty split
asunder, and its secret laid bare; while the Irrefragable, with
all his logical tools, hews at it, and hovers around it, and
finds it on all hands too hard for him.

Again, in the difference between Oratory and Rhetoric,
as indeed everywhere in that superiority of what is called
the Natural over the Artificial, we find a similar illustration.
The Orator persuades and carries all with him, he knows not
how; the Rhetorician can prove that he ought to have persuaded and carried all with him: the one is in a state of
healthy unconsciousness, as if he 'had no system'; the other,
in virtue of regimen and dietetic punctuality, feels at best
that 'his system is in high order.' So stands it, in short, with
all the forms of Intellect, whether as directed to the finding
of truth, or to the fit imparting thereof; to Poetry, to Eloquence, to depth of Insight, which is the basis of both these;
always the characteristic of right performance is a certain
spontaneity, an unconsciousness; 'the healthy know not of
their health, but only the sick.' So that the old precept of
the critic, as crabbed as it looked to his ambitious disciple,
might contain in it a most fundamental truth, applicable to
us all, and in much else than Literature: "Whenever you
have written any sentence that looks particularly excellent,
be sure to blot it out." In like manner, under milder phraseology, and with a meaning purposely much wider, a living
Thinker has taught us: 'Of the Wrong we are always conscious, of the Right never.'

But if such is the law with regard to Speculation and the
Intellectual power of man, much more is it with regard to
Conduct, and the power, manifested chiefly therein, which
we name Moral. 'Let not thy left hand know what thy right
hand doeth': whisper not to thy own heart, How worthy is
this action!—for then it is already becoming worthless. The
good man is he who *works* continually in welldoing; to
whom welldoing is as his natural existence, awakening no
astonishment, requiring no commentary; but there, like a
thing of course, and as if it could not but be so. Self-con-

templation, on the other hand, is infallibly the symptom of disease, be it or be it not the sign of cure. An unhealthy Virtue is one that consumes itself to leanness in repenting and anxiety; or, still worse, that inflates itself into dropsical boastfulness and vain-glory: either way, there is a self-seeking; an unprofitable looking behind us to measure the way we have made: whereas the sole concern is to walk continually forward, and make more way. If in any sphere of man's life, then in the Moral sphere, as the inmost and most vital of all, it is good that there be wholeness; that there be unconsciousness, which is the evidence of this. Let the free, reasonable Will, which dwells in us, as in our Holy of Holies, be indeed free, and obeyed like a Divinity, as is its right and its effort: the perfect obedience will be the silent one. Such perhaps were the sense of that maxim, enunciating, as is usual, but the half of a truth: To say that we have a clear conscience, is to utter a solecism; had we never sinned, we should have had no conscience. Were defeat unknown, neither would victory be celebrated by songs of triumph.

This, true enough, is an ideal, impossible state of being; yet ever the goal towards which our actual state of being strives; which it is the more perfect the nearer it can approach. Nor, in our actual world, where Labour must often prove *in*effectual, and thus in all senses Light alternate with Darkness, and the nature of an ideal Morality be much modified, is the case, thus far, materially different. It is a fact which escapes no one, that, generally speaking, whoso is acquainted with his worth has but a little stock to cultivate acquaintance with. Above all, the public acknowledgment of such acquaintance, indicating that it has reached quite an intimate footing, bodes ill. Already, to the popular judgment, he who talks much about Virtue in the abstract, begins to be suspect; it is shrewdly guessed that where there is great preaching, there will be little almsgiving. Or again, on a wider scale, we can remark that ages of Heroism are not ages of Moral Philosophy; Virtue, when it can be philosophised of, has become aware of itself, is sickly and beginning to decline. A spontaneous habitual all-pervading spirit of Chivalrous Valour shrinks together, and perks itself up into shrivelled Points of Honour; humane Courtesy and Nobleness of mind dwindle into punctilious Politeness, 'avoiding meats'; 'paying tithe of mint and anise, neglecting the weightier matters of the law.' Goodness, which was a rule to itself, must now appeal to Precept, and seek strength from Sanctions; the Freewill no longer reigns unquestioned and by divine right, but like a mere earthly sovereign, by expediency, by Rewards and Punishments: or rather, let us say, the Freewill, so far as may be, has abdicated and withdrawn into the dark, and a spectral nightmare of a Necessity usurps its throne; for now that mysterious Self-impulse of the whole man, heaven-inspired, and in all senses partaking of the Infinite, being captiously questioned in a finite dialect, and answering, as it needs must, by silence,—is conceived as non-extant, and only the outward Mechanism of it remains acknowledged: of Volition, except as the synonym of Desire, we hear nothing; of 'Motives,' without any Mover, more than enough.

So too, when the generous Affections have become wellnigh paralytic, we have the reign of Sentimentality. The greatness, the profitableness, at any rate the extremely ornamental nature of high feeling, and the luxury of doing good; charity, love, self-forgetfulness, devotedness and all manner of godlike magnanimity,—are everywhere insisted on, and pressingly inculcated in speech and writing, in prose and verse; Socinian Preachers proclaim 'Benevolence' to all the four winds, and have TRUTH engraved on their watchseals: unhappily with little or no effect. Were the limbs in right walking order, why so much demonstrating of motion? The barrenest of all mortals is the Sentimentalist. Granting even that he were sincere, and did not wilfully deceive us, or without first deceiving himself, what good is in him? Does he not lie there as a perpetual lesson of despair, and type of bedrid valetudinarian impotence? His is emphatically a Virtue that has become, through every fibre, conscious of itself; it is all sick, and feels as if it were made of glass, and durst not touch or be touched; in the shape of work, it can do nothing; at the utmost, by incessant nursing and caudling, keep itself alive. As the last stage of all, when Virtue, properly so called, has ceased to be practised, and become extinct, and a mere remembrance, we have the era of Sophists, descanting of its existence, proving it, denying it, mechanically 'accounting' for it;—as dissectors and demonstrators cannot operate till once the body be dead.

Thus is true Moral genius, like true Intellectual, which indeed is but a lower phasis thereof, 'ever a secret to itself.'

The healthy moral nature loves Goodness, and without wonder wholly lives in it: the unhealthy makes love to it, and would fain get to live in it; or, finding such courtship fruitless, turns round, and not without contempt abandons it. These curious relations of the Voluntary and Conscious to the Involuntary and Unconscious, and the small proportion which, in all departments of our life, the former bears to the latter,—might lead us into deep questions of Psychology and Physiology: such, however, belong not to our present object. Enough, if the fact itself become apparent, that Nature so meant it with us; that in this wise we are made. We may now say, that view man's individual Existence under what aspect we will, under the highest spiritual, as under the merely animal aspect, everywhere the grand vital energy, while in its sound state, is an unseen unconscious one; or, in the words of our old Aphorism, 'the healthy know not of their health, but only the sick.'

To understand man, however, we must look beyond the individual man and his actions or interests, and view him in combination with his fellows. It is in Society that man first feels what he is; first becomes what he can be. In Society an altogether new set of spiritual activities are evolved in him, and the old immeasurably quickened and strengthened. Society is the genial element wherein his nature first lives and grows; the solitary man were but a small portion of himself, and must continue forever folded in, stunted and only half alive. 'Already,' says a deep Thinker, with more meaning than will disclose itself at once, 'my opinion, my conviction, gains *infinitely* in strength and sureness, the moment a second mind has adopted it.' Such, even in its simplest form, is association; so wondrous the communion of soul with soul as directed to the mere act of Knowing! In other higher acts, the wonder is still more manifest; as in that portion of our being which we name the Moral: for properly, indeed, all communion is of a moral sort, whereof such intellectual communion (in the act of knowing) is itself an example. But with regard to Morals strictly so called, it is in Society, we might almost say, that Morality begins; here at least it takes an altogether new form, and on every side, as in living growth, expands itself. The Duties of Man to himself, to what is Highest in himself, make but the First Table of the Law: to the First Table is now superadded a Second, with the Duties of Man to his Neighbour; whereby also the significance of the First now assumes its true importance. Man has joined himself with man; soul acts and reacts on soul; a mystic miraculous unfathomable Union establishes itself; Life, in all its elements, has become intensated, consecrated. The lightning-spark of Thought, generated, or say rather heaven-kindled, in the solitary mind, awakens its express likeness in another mind, in a thousand other minds, and all blaze-up together in combined fire; reverberated from mind to mind, fed also with fresh fuel in each, it acquires incalculable new light as Thought, incalculable new heat as converted into Action. By and by, a common store of Thought can accumulate, and be transmitted as an everlasting possession: Literature, whether as preserved in the memory of Bards, in Runes and Hieroglyphs engraved on stone, or in Books of written or printed paper, comes into existence, and begins to play its wondrous part. Polities are formed; the weak submitting to the strong; with a willing loyalty, giving obedience that he may receive guidance: or say rather, in honour of our nature, the ignorant submitting to the wise; for so it is in all even the rudest communities, man never yields himself wholly to brute Force, but always to moral Greatness; thus the universal title of respect, from the Oriental *Sheik,* from the *Sachem* of the Red Indians, down to our English *Sir,* implies only that he whom we mean to honour is our *senior.* Last, as the crown and all-supporting keystone of the fabric, Religion arises. The devout meditation of the isolated man, which flitted through his soul, like a transient tone of Love and Awe from unknown lands, acquires certainty, continuance, when it is shared-in by his brother men. 'Where two or three are gathered together' in the name of the Highest, then first does the Highest, as it is written, 'appear among them to bless them'; then first does an Altar and act of united Worship open a way from Earth to Heaven; whereon, were it but a simple Jacob's-ladder, the heavenly Messengers will travel, with glad tidings and unspeakable gifts for men. Such is SOCIETY, the vital articulation of many individuals into a new collective individual: greatly the most important of man's attainments on this earth; that in which, and by virtue of which, all his other attainments and attempts find their arena, and have their value. Considered well, Society is the standing wonder of our existence; a true region of the Supernatural; as it were, a second all-embracing Life, wherein our first individual Life becomes doubly and trebly alive, and whatever of Infinitude was in us bodies itself forth, and becomes visible and active.

To figure Society as endowed with life is scarcely a metaphor; but rather the statement of a fact by such imperfect methods as language affords. Look at it closely, that mystic Union, Nature's highest work with man, wherein man's volition plays an indispensable yet so subordinate a part, and the small Mechanical grows so mysteriously and indissolubly out of the infinite Dynamical, like Body out of Spirit,—is truly enough vital, what we can call vital, and bears the distinguishing character of life. In the same style also, we can say that Society has its periods of sickness and vigour, of youth, manhood, decrepitude, dissolution and new birth; in one or other of which stages we may, in all times, and all places where men inhabit, discern it; and do ourselves, in this time and place, whether as coöperating or as contending, as healthy members or as diseased ones, to our joy and sorrow, form part of it. The question, What is the actual condition of Society? has in these days unhappily become important enough. No one of us is unconcerned in that question; but for the majority of thinking men a true answer to it, such is the state of matters, appears almost as the one thing needful. Meanwhile, as the true answer, that is to say, the complete and fundamental answer and settlement, often as it has been demanded, is nowhere forthcoming, and indeed by its nature is impossible, any honest approximation towards such is not without value. The feeblest light, or even so much as a more precise recognition of the darkness, which is the first step to attainment of light, will be welcome.

This once understood, let it not seem idle if we remark that here too our old Aphorism holds; that again in the Body Politic, as in the animal body, the sign of right performance is Unconsciousness. Such indeed is virtually the meaning of that phrase, 'artificial state of society,' as contrasted with the natural state, and indicating something so inferior to it. For, in all vital things, men distinguish an Artificial and a Natural; founding on some dim perception or sentiment of the very truth we here insist on: the artificial is the conscious, mechanical; the natural is the unconscious, dynamical. Thus, as we have an artificial Poetry, and prize only the natural; so likewise we have an artificial Morality, an artificial Wisdom, an artificial Society. The artificial Society is precisely one that knows its own structure, its own internal functions; not in watching, not in knowing which, but in working outwardly to the fulfilment of its aim, does the wellbeing of a Society consist. Every Society, every Polity, has a spiritual principle; is the embodiment, tentative and more or less complete, of an Idea: all its tendencies of endeavour, specialties of custom, its laws, politics and whole procedure (as the glance of some Montesquieu, across innumerable superficial entanglements, can partly decipher), are prescribed by an Idea, and flow naturally from it, as movements from the living source of motion. This Idea, be it of devotion to a man or class of men, to a creed, to an institution, or even, as in more ancient times, to a piece of land, is ever a true Loyalty; has in it something of a religious, paramount, quite infinite character; it is properly the Soul of the State, its Life; mysterious as other forms of Life, and like these working secretly, and in a depth beyond that of consciousness.

Accordingly, it is not in the vigorous ages of a Roman Republic that Treatises of the Commonwealth are written: while the Decii are rushing with devoted bodies on the enemies of Rome, what need of preaching Patriotism? The virtue of Patriotism has already sunk from its pristine all-transcendent condition, before it has received a name. So long as the Commonwealth continues rightly athletic, it cares not to dabble in anatomy. Why teach obedience to the Sovereign; why so much as admire it, or separately recognise it, while a divine idea of Obedience perennially inspires all men? Loyalty, like Patriotism, of which it is a form, was not praised till it had begun to decline; the *Preux Chevaliers* first became rightly admirable, when 'dying for their king' had ceased to be a habit with chevaliers. For if the mystic significance of the State, let this be what it may, dwells vitally in every heart, encircles every life as with a second higher life, how should it stand self-questioning? It must rush outward, and express itself by works. Besides, if perfect, it is there as by necessity, and does not excite inquiry: it is also by nature infinite, has no limits; therefore can be circumscribed by no conditions and definitions; cannot be reasoned of; except *musically,* or in the language of Poetry, cannot yet so much as be spoken of.

In those days, Society was what we name healthy, sound at heart. Not indeed without suffering enough; not without perplexities, difficulty on every side: for such is the appointment of man; his highest and sole blessedness is, that he toil, and know what to toil at: not in ease, but in united victorious labour, which is at once evil and the victory over evil, does his Freedom lie. Nay, often, looking no deeper than such superficial perplexities of the early Time, historians have taught us that it was all one mass of contradiction and disease; and in the antique Republic or feudal Monarchy have seen only the confused chaotic quarry, not the robust labourer, or the stately edifice he was building of it.

If Society, in such ages, had its difficulty, it had also its strength; if sorrowful masses of rubbish so encumbered it, the tough sinews to hurl them aside, with indomitable heart, were not wanting. Society went along without complaint; did not stop to scrutinise itself, to say, How well I perform! or, Alas, how ill! Men did not yet feel themselves to be 'the envy of surrounding nations'; and were enviable on that very account. Society was what we can call *whole,* in both senses of the word. The individual man was in himself a whole, or complete union; and could combine with his fellows as the living member of a greater whole. For all men, through their life, were animated by one great Idea; thus all efforts pointed one way, everywhere there was *wholeness.* Opinion and Action had not yet become disunited; but the former could still produce the latter, or attempt to produce it; as the stamp does its impression while the wax is not hardened. Thought and the voice of thought were also a unison; thus, instead of Speculation, we had Poetry; Literature, in its rude utterance, was as yet a heroic Song, perhaps too a devotional Anthem.

Religion was everywhere; Philosophy lay hid under it, peaceably included in it. Herein, as in the life-centre of all, lay the true health and oneness. Only at a later era must Religion split itself into Philosophies; and thereby, the vital union of Thought being lost, disunion and mutual collision in all provinces of Speech and Action more and more prevail. For if the Poet, or Priest, or by whatever title the inspired thinker may be named, is the sign of vigour and well-being; so likewise is the Logician, or uninspired thinker, the sign of disease, probably of decrepitude and decay. Thus, not to mention other instances, one of them much nearer hand,—so soon as Prophecy among the Hebrews had ceased, then did the reign of Argumentation begin; and the ancient Theocracy, in its Sadduceeisms and Phariseeisms, and vain jangling of sects and doctors, give token that the *soul* of it had fled, and that the *body* itself, by natural dissolution, 'with the old forces still at work, but working in reverse order,' was on the road to final disappearance.

We might pursue this question into innumerable other ramifications; and everywhere, under new shapes, find the same truth, which we here so imperfectly enunciate, disclosed; that throughout the whole world of man, in all manifestations and performances of his nature, outward and inward, personal and social, the Perfect, the Great is a mystery to itself, knows not itself; whatsoever does know itself is already little, and more or less imperfect. Or otherwise, we may say, Unconsciousness belongs to pure unmixed life; Consciousness to a diseased mixture and conflict of life and death: Unconsciousness is the sign of creation; Consciousness, at best, that of manufacture. So deep, in this existence of ours, is the significance of Mystery. Well might the Ancients make Silence a god; for it is the element of all godhood, infinitude, or transcendental greatness; at once the source and the ocean wherein all such begins and ends. In the same sense, too, have Poets sung 'Hymns to the Night'; as if Night were nobler than Day; as if Day were but a small motley-coloured veil spread transiently over the infinite bosom of Night, and did but deform and hide from us its purely transparent eternal deeps. So likewise have they spoken and sung as if Silence were the grand epitome and complete sum-total of all Harmony; and Death, what mortals call Death, properly the beginning of Life. Under such figures, since except in figures there is no speaking of the Invisible, have men endeavoured to express a great Truth;—a Truth, in our Times, as nearly as is perhaps possible, forgotten by the most; which nevertheless continues forever true, forever all-important, and will one day, under new figures, be again brought home to the bosoms of all.

But indeed, in a far lower sense, the rudest mind has still some intimation of the greatness there is in Mystery. If Silence was made a god of by the Ancients, he still continues a government-clerk among us Moderns. To all quacks, moreover, of what sort soever, the effect of Mystery is well known: here and there some Cagliostro, even in latter days, turns it to notable account: the blockhead also, who is ambitious, and has no talent, finds sometimes in 'the talent of silence,' a kind of succedaneum. Or again, looking on the opposite side of the matter, do we not see, in the common understanding of mankind, a certain distrust, a certain contempt of what is altogether self-conscious and mechanical? As nothing that is wholly seen through has other than a trivial character; so anything professing to be great, and yet wholly to see through itself, is already known to be false, and a failure. The evil repute your 'theoretical men' stand in, the acknowledged inefficiency of 'paper constitutions,' and all that class of objects, are instances of this. Experience often repeated, and perhaps a certain instinct of something far deeper that lies under such experiences, has taught men so much. They know beforehand, that the loud is generally the insignificant, the empty. Whatsoever can proclaim itself from the house-tops may be fit for the hawker, and for those multitudes that must needs buy of him; but for any deeper use, might as well continue unproclaimed. Observe too, how the converse of the proposition holds; how the insignificant, the empty, is usually the loud; and, after the manner of a drum, is loud even because of its emptiness. The uses of some Patent Dinner Calefactor can be bruited abroad over the whole world in the course of the first winter; those of the Printing Press are not so well seen into for the first three centuries: the passing of the Select-Vestries Bill raises more noise and hopeful expectancy among mankind than did the promulgation of the Christian Religion. Again, and again, we say, the great, the creative and enduring is ever a secret to itself; only the small, the barren and transient is otherwise.

If we now, with a practical medical view, examine, by this same test of Unconsciousness, the Condition of our own Era, and of man's Life therein, the diagnosis we arrive at is nowise of a flattering sort. The state of Society in our days is, of all possible states, the least an unconscious one: this is specially the Era when all manner of Inquiries into what was once the unfelt, involuntary sphere of man's existence, find their place, and, as it were, occupy the whole domain of thought. What, for example, is all this that we hear, for the last generation or two, about the Improvement of the Age, the Spirit of the Age, Destruction of Prejudice, Progress of the Species, and the March of Intellect, but an unhealthy state of self-sentience, self-survey; the precursor and prognostic of still worse health? That Intellect do march, if possible at double-quick time, is very desirable; nevertheless, why should she turn round at every stride, and cry: See you what a stride I have taken! Such a marching of Intellect is distinctly of the spavined kind; what the Jockeys call 'all action and no go.' Or at best, if we examine well, it is the marching of that gouty Patient, whom his Doctors had clapt on a metal floor artificially heated to the searing point, so that he was obliged to march, and did march with a vengeance—nowhither. Intellect did not awaken for the first time yesterday; but has been under way from Noah's Flood downwards: greatly her best progress, moreover, was in the old times, when she said nothing about it. In those same 'dark ages,' Intellect (metaphorically as well as literally) could invent *glass*, which now she has enough ado to grind into *spectacles*. Intellect built not only Churches, but a Church, *the* Church, based on this firm Earth, yet reaching up, and leading up, as high as Heaven; and now it is all she can do to keep its doors bolted, that there be no tearing of the Surplices, no robbery of the Alms-box. She built a Senate-house likewise, glorious in its kind; and now it costs her a well-nigh mortal effort to sweep it clear of vermin, and get the roof made rain-tight.

But the truth is, with Intellect, as with most other things, we are now passing from that first or boastful stage of Self-sentience into the second or painful one: out of these often-asseverated declarations that 'our system is in high order,' we come now, by natural sequence, to the melancholy conviction that it is altogether the reverse. Thus, for instance, in the matter of Government, the period of the 'Invaluable Constitution' has to be followed by a Reform Bill; to laudatory De Lolmes succeed objurgatory Benthams. At any rate, what Treatises on the Social Contract, on the Elective Franchise, the Rights of Man, the Rights of Property, Codifications, Institutions, Constitutions, have we not, for long years, groaned under! Or again, with a wider survey, consider those Essays on Man, Thoughts on Man, Inquiries concerning Man; not to mention Evidences of the Christian Faith, Theories of Poetry, Considerations on the Origin of Evil, which during the last century have accumulated on us to a frightful extent. Never since the beginning of Time was there, that we hear or read of, so intensely self-conscious a Society. Our whole relations to the Universe and to our fellow-man have become an Inquiry, a Doubt; nothing will go on of its own accord, and do its function quietly; but all things must be probed into, the whole working of man's world be anatomically studied. Alas, anatomically studied, that it may be medically aided! Till at length indeed, we have come to such a pass, that except in this same *medicine,* with its artifices and appliances, few can so much as imagine any strength or hope to remain for us. The whole Life of Society must now be carried on by drugs: doctor after doctor appears with his nostrum, of Coöperative Societies, Universal Suffrage, Cottage-and-Cow systems, Repression of Population, Vote by Ballot. To such height has the dyspepsia of Society reached; as indeed the constant grinding internal pain, or from time to time the mad spasmodic throes, of all Society do otherwise too mournfully indicate.

Far be it from us to attribute, as some unwise persons do, the disease itself to this unhappy sensation that there is a disease! The Encyclopedists did not produce the troubles of France; but the troubles of France produced the Encyclopedists, and much else. The Self-consciousness is the symptom merely; nay, it is also the attempt towards cure. We record the fact, without special censure; not wondering that Society should feel itself, and in all ways complain of aches and twinges, for it has suffered enough. Napoleon was but a Job's-comforter, when he told his wounded staff-officer, twice unhorsed by cannon-balls, and with half his limbs blown to pieces: *"Vous vous écoutez trop!"*

On the outward, as it were Physical diseases of Society, it were beside our purpose to insist here. These are diseases which he who runs may read; and sorrow over, with or without hope. Wealth has accumulated itself into masses;

and Poverty, also in accumulation enough, lies impassably separated from it; opposed, uncommunicating, like forces in positive and negative poles. The gods of this lower world sit aloft on glittering thrones, less happy than Epicurus's gods, but as indolent, as impotent; while the boundless living chaos of Ignorance and Hunger welters terrific, in its dark fury, under their feet. How much among us might be likened to a whited sepulchre; outwardly all pomp and strength; but inwardly full of horror and despair and dead-men's bones! Iron highways, with their wains fire-winged, are uniting all ends of the firm Land; quays and moles, with their innumerable stately fleets, tame the Ocean into our pliant bearer of burdens; Labour's thousand arms, of sinew and of metal, all-conquering everywhere, from the tops of the mountain down to the depths of the mine and the caverns of the sea, ply unweariedly for the service of man: yet man remains unserved. He has subdued this Planet, his habitation and inheritance; yet reaps no profit from the victory.

Sad to look upon: in the highest stage of civilisation, nine tenths of mankind have to struggle in the lowest battle of savage or even animal man, the battle against Famine. Countries are rich, prosperous in all manner of increase, beyond example: but the Men of those countries are poor, needier than ever of all sustenance outward and inward; of Belief, of Knowledge, of Money, of Food. The rule, *Sic vos non vobis,* never altogether to be got rid of in men's Industry, now presses with such incubus weight, that Industry must shake it off, or utterly be strangled under it; and, alas, can as yet but gasp and rave, and aimlessly struggle, like one in the final deliration. Thus Change, or the inevitable approach of Change, is manifest everywhere. In one Country we have seen lava-torrents of fever-frenzy envelop all things; Government succeed Government, like the phantasms of a dying brain. In another Country, we can even now see, in maddest alternation, the Peasant governed by such guidance as this: To labour earnestly one month in raising wheat, and the next month labour earnestly in burning it. So that Society, were it not by nature immortal, and its death ever a new-birth, might appear, as it does in the eyes of some, to be sick to dissolution, and even now writhing in its last agony. Sick enough we must admit it to be, with disease enough, a whole nosology of diseases; wherein he perhaps is happiest that is not called to prescribe as physician;—wherein, however, one small piece of policy, that of summoning the Wisest in the Commonwealth, by the sole method yet known or thought of, to come together and with their whole soul consult for it, might, but for late tedious experiences, have seemed unquestionable enough.

But leaving this, let us rather look within, into the Spiritual condition of Society, and see what aspects and prospects offer themselves there. For after all, it is there properly that the secret and origin of the whole is to be sought: the Physical derangements of Society are but the image and impress of its Spiritual; while the heart continues sound, all other sickness is superficial, and temporary. False Action is the fruit of false Speculation; let the spirit of Society be free and strong, that is to say, let true Principles inspire the members of Society, then neither can disorders accumulate in its Practice; each disorder will be promptly, faithfully inquired into, and remedied as it arises. But alas, with us the Spiritual condition of Society is no less sickly than the Physical. Examine man's internal world, in any of its social relations and performances, here too all seems diseased self-consciousness, collision and mutually-destructive struggle. Nothing acts from within outwards in undivided healthy force; everything lies impotent, lamed, its force turned inwards, and painfully 'listens to itself.'

To begin with our highest Spiritual function, with Religion, we might ask, Whither has Religion now fled? Of Churches and their establishments we here say nothing; nor of the unhappy domains of Unbelief, and how innumerable men, blinded in their minds, have grown to 'live without God in the world'; but, taking the fairest side of the matter, we ask, What is the nature of that same Religion, which still lingers in the hearts of the few who are called, and call themselves, specially the Religious? Is it a healthy religion, vital, unconscious of itself; that shines forth spontaneously in doing of the Work, or even in preaching of the Word? Unhappily, no. Instead of heroic martyr Conduct, and inspired and soul-inspiring Eloquence, whereby Religion itself were brought home to our living bosoms, to live and reign there, we have 'Discourses on the Evidences,' endeavouring, with smallest result, to make it probable that such a thing as Religion exists. The most enthusiastic Evangelicals do not preach a Gospel, but keep describing how it should and might be preached: to awaken the sacred fire of faith, as by a sacred contagion, is not their endeavour; but, at most, to describe how Faith shows and acts, and scientifically distinguish true Faith from false. Religion, like all else, is conscious of itself, listens to itself; it becomes less and less creative, vital; more and more mechanical. Considered as a whole, the Christian Religion of late ages has been continually dissipating itself into Metaphysics; and threatens now to disappear, as some rivers do, in deserts of barren sand.

Of Literature, and its deep-seated, wide-spread maladies, why speak? Literature is but a branch of Religion, and always participates in its character: however, in our time, it is the only branch that still shows any greenness; and, as some think, must one day become the main stem. Now, apart from the subterranean and tartarean regions of Literature;—leaving out of view the frightful, scandalous statistics of Puffing, the mystery of Slander, Falsehood, Hatred and other convulsion-work of rabid Imbecility, and all that has rendered Literature on that side a perfect 'Babylon the mother of Abominations,' in very deed making the world 'drunk' with the wine of her iniquity;—forgetting all this, let us look only to the regions of the upper air; to such Literature as can be said to have some attempt towards truth in it, some tone of music, and if it be not poetical, to hold of the poetical. Among other characteristics, is not this manifest enough: that it knows itself? Spontaneous devotedness to the object, being wholly possessed by the object, what we can call Inspiration, has well-nigh ceased to appear in Literature. Which melodious Singer forgets that he is singing melodiously? We have not the love of greatness, but the love of the love of greatness. Hence infinite Affectations, Distractions; in every case inevitable Error. Consider, for one example, this peculiarity of Modern Literature, the sin that has been named View-hunting. In our elder writers, there are no paintings of scenery for its own sake; no euphuistic gallantries with Nature, but a constant heartlove for her, a constant dwelling in communion with her. View-hunting, with so much else that is of kin to it, first came decisively into action through the *Sorrows of Werter*; which wonderful Performance, indeed, may in many senses be regarded as the progenitor of all that has since become popular in Literature; whereof, in so far as concerns spirit and

tendency, it still offers the most instructive image; for nowhere, except in its own country, above all in the mind of
its illustrious Author, has it yet fallen wholly obsolete.
Scarcely ever, till that late epoch, did any worshipper of
Nature become entirely aware that he was worshipping,
much to his own credit; and think of saying to himself:
Come, let us make a description! Intolerable enough: when
every puny whipster plucks out his pencil, and insists on
painting you a scene; so that the instant you discern such a
thing as 'wavy outline,' 'mirror of the lake,' 'stern head-
land,' or the like, in any Book, you tremulously hasten on;
and scarcely the Author of Waverley himself can tempt
you not to skip.

Nay, is not the diseased self-conscious state of Literature
disclosed in this one fact, which lies so near us here, the
prevalence of Reviewing! Sterne's wish for a reader 'that
would give-up the reins of his imagination into his author's
hands, and be pleased he knew not why, and cared not
wherefore,' might lead him a long journey now. Indeed, for
our best class of readers, the chief pleasure, a very stinted
one, is this same knowing of the Why; which many a
Kames and Bossu has been, ineffectually enough, endeavouring to teach us: till at last these also have laid down their
trade; and now your Reviewer is a mere *taster;* who tastes,
and says, by the evidence of such palate, such tongue, as he
has got, It is good, It is bad. Was it thus that the French
carried out certain inferior creatures on their Algerine
Expedition, to taste the wells for them, and try whether
they were poisoned? Far be it from us to disparage our own
craft, whereby we have our living! Only we must note these
things: that Reviewing spreads with strange vigour; that
such a man as Byron reckons the Reviewer and the Poet
equal; that at the last Leipzig Fair, there was advertised a
Review of Reviews. By and by it will be found that all Literature has become one boundless self-devouring Review;
and, as in London routs, we have to *do* nothing, but only to
see others do nothing.—Thus does Literature also, like a
sick thing, superabundantly 'listen to itself.'

No less is this unhealthy symptom manifest, if we cast a
glance on our Philosophy, on the character of our speculative Thinking. Nay, already, as above hinted, the mere existence and necessity of a Philosophy is an evil. Man is sent
hither not to question, but to work: 'the end of man,' it was

long ago written, 'is an Action, not a Thought.' In the perfect state, all Thought were but the picture and inspiring symbol of Action; Philosophy, except as Poetry and Religion, would have no being. And yet how, in this imperfect state, can it be avoided, can it be dispensed with? Man stands as in the centre of Nature; his fraction of Time encircled by Eternity, his handbreadth of Space encircled by Infinitude: how shall he forbear asking himself, What am I; and Whence; and Whither? How too, except in slight partial hints, in kind asseverations and assurances, such as a mother quiets her fretfully inquisitive child with, shall he get answer to such inquiries?

The disease of Metaphysics, accordingly, is a perennial one. In all ages, those questions of Death and Immortality, Origin of Evil, Freedom and Necessity, must, under new forms, anew make their appearance; ever, from time to time, must the attempt to shape for ourselves some Theorem of the Universe be repeated. And ever unsuccessfully: for what Theorem of the Infinite can the Finite render complete? We, the whole species of Mankind, and our whole existence and history, are but a floating speck in the illimitable ocean of the All; yet *in* that ocean; indissoluble portion thereof; partaking of its infinite tendencies: borne this way and that by its deep-swelling tides, and grand ocean currents;—of which what faintest chance is there that we should ever exhaust the significance, ascertain the goings and comings? A region of Doubt, therefore, hovers forever in the background; in Action alone can we have certainty. Nay, properly Doubt is the indispensable inexhaustible material whereon Action works, which Action has to fashion into Certainty and Reality; only on a canvas of Darkness, such is man's way of being, could the many-coloured picture of our Life paint itself and shine.

Thus if our eldest system of Metaphysics is as old as the *Book of Genesis,* our latest is that of Mr. Thomas Hope, published only within the current year. It is a chronic malady that of Metaphysics, as we said, and perpetually recurs on us. At the utmost, there is a better and a worse in it; a stage of convalescence, and a stage of relapse with new sickness: these forever succeed each other, as is the nature of all Life-movement here below. The first, or convalescent stage, we might also name that of Dogmatical or Constructive Metaphysics; when the mind constructively endeavours to scheme out and assert for itself an actual The-orem of the Universe, and therewith for a time rests satis-fied. The second or sick stage might be called that of Scep-tical or Inquisitory Metaphysics; when the mind having widened its sphere of vision, the existing Theorem of the Universe no longer answers the phenomena, no longer yields contentment; but must be torn in pieces, and cer-tainty anew sought for in the endless realms of denial. All Theologies and sacred Cosmogonies belong, in some meas-ure, to the first class; in all Pyrrhonism, from Pyrrho down to Hume and the innumerable disciples of Hume, we have instances enough of the second. In the former, so far as it affords satisfaction, a temporary anodyne to doubt, an arena for wholesome action, there may be much good; in-deed in this case, it holds rather of Poetry than of Meta-physics, might be called Inspiration rather than Speculation. The latter is Metaphysics proper; a pure, unmixed, though from time to time a necessary evil.

For truly, if we look into it, there is no more fruitless en-deavour than this same, which the Metaphysician proper toils in: to educe Conviction out of Negation. How, by merely testing and rejecting what is not, shall we ever at-tain knowledge of what is? Metaphysical Speculation, as it begins in No or Nothingness, so it must needs end in Noth-ingness; circulates and must circulate in endless vortices; creating, swallowing—itself. Our being is made up of Light and Darkness, the Light resting on the Darkness, and bal-ancing it; everywhere there is Dualism, Equipoise; a per-petual Contradiction dwells in us: 'where shall I place my-self to escape from my own shadow?' Consider it well, Metaphysics is the attempt of the mind to rise above the mind; to environ and shut in, or as we say, *comprehend* the mind. Hopeless struggle, for the wisest, as for the fool-ishest! What strength of sinew, or athletic skill, will enable the stoutest athlete to fold his own body in his arms, and, by lifting, lift up *himself?* The Irish Saint swam the Chan-nel, 'carrying his head in his teeth'; but the feat has never been imitated.

That this is the age of Metaphysics, in the proper, or sceptical Inquisitory sense; that there was a necessity for its being such an age, we regard as our indubitable misfortune. From many causes, the arena of free Activity has long been narrowing, that of sceptical Inquiry becoming more and more universal, more and more perplexing. The Thought conducts not to the Deed; but in boundless chaos, self-devouring, engenders monstrosities, phantasms, fire-breathing chimeras. Profitable Speculation were this: What is to be done; and How is it to be done? But with us not so much as the What can be got sight of. For some generations, all Philosophy has been a painful, captious, hostile question towards everything in the Heaven above, and in the Earth beneath: Why art thou there? Till at length it has come to pass that the worth and authenticity of all things seems dubitable or deniable: our best effort must be unproductively spent not in working, but in ascertaining our mere Whereabout, and so much as whether we are to work at all. Doubt, which, as was said, ever hangs in the background of our world, has now become our middleground and foreground; whereon, for the time, no fair Life-picture can be painted, but only the dark air-canvas itself flow round us, bewildering and benighting.

Nevertheless, doubt as we will, man is actually Here; not to ask questions, but to do work: in this time, as in all times, it must be the heaviest evil for him, if his faculty of Action lie dormant, and only that of sceptical Inquiry exert itself. Accordingly, whoever looks abroad upon the world, comparing the Past with the Present, may find that the practical condition of man in these days is one of the saddest; burdened with miseries which are in a considerable degree peculiar. In no time was man's life what he calls a happy one; in no time can it be so. A perpetual dream there has been of Paradises, and some luxurious Lubberland, where the brooks should run wine, and the trees bend with ready-baked viands; but it was a dream merely; an impossible dream. Suffering, contradiction, error, have their quite perennial, and even indispensable abode in this Earth. Is not labour the inheritance of man? And what labour for the present is joyous, and not grievous? Labour, effort, is the very interruption of that ease, which man foolishly enough fancies to be his happiness; and yet without labour there were no ease, no rest, so much as conceivable. Thus Evil, what we call Evil, must ever exist while man exists: Evil, in the widest sense we can give it, is precisely the dark, disordered material out of which man's Freewill has to create an edifice of order and Good. Ever must Pain urge us to Labour; and only in free Effort can any blessedness be imagined for us.

But if man has, in all ages, had enough to encounter, there has, in most civilised ages, been an inward force vouchsafed him, whereby the pressure of things outward might be withstood. Obstruction abounded; but Faith also was not wanting. It is by Faith that man removes mountains: while he had Faith, his limbs might be wearied with toiling, his back galled with bearing; but the heart within him was peaceable and resolved. In the thickest gloom there burnt a lamp to guide him. If he struggled and suffered, he felt that it even should be so; knew for what he was suffering and struggling. Faith gave him an inward Willingness; a world of Strength wherewith to front a world of Difficulty. The true wretchedness lies here: that the Difficulty remain and the Strength be lost; that Pain cannot relieve itself in free Effort; that we have the Labour, and want the Willingness. Faith strengthens us, enlightens us, for all endeavours and endurances; with Faith we can do all, and dare all, and life itself has a thousand times been joyfully given away. But the sum of man's misery is even this, that he feel himself crushed under the Juggernaut wheels, and know that Juggernaut is no divinity, but a dead mechanical idol.

Now this is specially the misery which has fallen on man in our Era. Belief, Faith has well-nigh vanished from the world. The youth on awakening in this wondrous Universe no longer finds a competent theory of its wonders. Time was, when if he asked himself, What is man, What are the duties of man? the answer stood ready written for him. But now the ancient 'ground-plan of the All' belies itself when brought into contact with reality; Mother Church has, to the most, become a superannuated Step-mother, whose lessons go disregarded; or are spurned at, and scornfully gainsaid. For young Valour and thirst of Action no ideal Chivalry invites to heroism, prescribes what is heroic: the old ideal of Manhood has grown obsolete, and the new is still invisible to us, and we grope after it in darkness, one clutching this phantom, another that; Werterism, Byronism, even Brummelism, each has its day. For Contemplation and love of Wisdom, no Cloister now opens its religious shades; the Thinker must, in all senses, wander homeless, too often aimless, looking up to a Heaven which is dead for him, round to an Earth which is deaf. Action, in those old days, was easy, was voluntary, for the divine worth of human things lay acknowledged; Speculation was wholesome, for it ranged itself as the handmaid of Action; what could not so range itself died out by its natural death, by neglect. Loyalty still hallowed obedience, and made rule noble; there was still something to be loyal to: the Godlike stood embodied under many a symbol in men's interests and business; the Finite shadowed forth the Infinite; Eternity looked through Time. The Life of man was encompassed and overcanopied by a glory of Heaven, even as his dwelling-place by the azure vault.

How changed in these new days! Truly may it be said, the Divinity has withdrawn from the Earth; or veils himself in that wide-wasting Whirlwind of a departing Era, wherein the fewest can discern his goings. Not Godhead, but an iron, ignoble circle of Necessity embraces all things; binds the youth of these times into a sluggish thrall, or else exasperates him into a rebel. Heroic Action is paralysed; for what worth now remains unquestionable with him? At the fervid period when his whole nature cries aloud for Action, there is nothing sacred under whose banner he can act; the course and kind and conditions of free Action are all but undiscoverable. Doubt storms-in on him through every avenue; inquiries of the deepest, painfulest sort must be engaged with; and the invincible energy of young years waste itself in sceptical, suicidal cavillings; in passionate 'questionings of Destiny,' whereto no answer will be returned.

For men, in whom the old perennial principle of Hunger (be it Hunger of the poor Day-drudge who stills it with eighteenpence a-day, or of the ambitious Placehunter who can nowise still it with so little) suffices to fill-up existence, the case is bad; but not the worst. These men have an aim, such as it is; and can steer towards it, with chagrin enough truly; yet, as their hands are kept full, without desperation. Unhappier are they to whom a higher instinct has been given; who struggle to be persons, not machines; to whom the Universe is not a warehouse, or at best a fancy-bazaar, but a mystic temple and hall of doom. For such men there lie properly two courses open. The lower, yet still an estimable class, take up with worn-out Symbols of the

Godlike; keep trimming and trucking between these and Hypocrisy, purblindly enough, miserably enough. A numerous intermediate class end in Denial; and form a theory that there is no theory; that nothing is certain in the world, except this fact of Pleasure being pleasant; so they try to realise what trifling modicum of Pleasure they can come at, and to live contented therewith, winking hard. Of those we speak not here; but only of the second nobler class, who also have dared to say No, and cannot yet say Yea; but feel that in the No they dwell as in a Golgotha, where life enters not, where peace is not appointed them.

Hard, for most part, is the fate of such men; the harder the nobler they are. In dim forecastings, wrestles within them the 'Divine Idea of the World,' yet will nowhere visibly reveal itself. They have to realise a Worship for themselves, or live unworshipping. The Godlike has vanished from the world; and they, by the strong cry of their soul's agony, like true wonder-workers, must again evoke its presence. This miracle is their appointed task; which they must accomplish, or die wretchedly: this miracle has been accomplished by such; but not in our land; our land yet knows not of it. Behold a Byron, in melodious tones, 'cursing his day': he mistakes earthborn passionate Desire for heaven-inspired Freewill; without heavenly loadstar, rushes madly into the dance of meteoric lights that hover on the mad Mahlstrom; and goes down among its eddies. Hear a Shelley filling the earth with inarticulate wail; like the infinite, inarticulate grief and weeping of forsaken infants. A noble Friedrich Schlegel, stupefied in that fearful loneliness, as of a silenced battle-field, flies back to Catholicism; as a child might to its slain mother's bosom, and cling there. In lower regions, how many a poor Hazlitt must wander on God's verdant earth, like the Unblest on burning deserts; passionately dig wells, and draw up only the dry quicksand; believe that he is seeking Truth, yet only wrestle among endless Sophisms, doing desperate battle as with spectre-hosts; and die and make no sign!

To the better order of such minds any mad joy of Denial has long since ceased: the problem is not now to deny, but to ascertain and perform. Once in destroying the False, there was a certain inspiration; but now the genius of Destruction has done its work, there is now nothing more to destroy. The doom of the Old has long been pronounced, and irrevocable; the Old has passed away: but, alas, the New appears not in its stead; the Time is still in pangs of travail with the New. Man has walked by the light of conflagrations, and amid the sound of falling cities; and now there is darkness, and long watching till it be morning. The voice even of the faithful can but exclaim: 'As yet struggles the twelfth hour of the Night: birds of darkness are on the wing, spectres uproar, the dead walk, the living dream.— Thou, Eternal Providence, wilt cause the day to dawn!' [1]

Such being the condition, temporal and spiritual, of the world at our Epoch, can we wonder that the world 'listens to itself,' and struggles and writhes, everywhere externally and internally, like a thing in pain? Nay, is not even this unhealthy action of the world's Organisation, if the symptom of universal disease, yet also the symptom and sole means of restoration and cure? The effort of Nature, exerting her medicative force to cast-out foreign impediments, and once more become One, become whole? In Practice, still more in Opinion, which is the precursor and prototype of Practice, there must needs be collision, convulsion; much has to be ground away. Thought must needs be Doubt and Inquiry, before it can again be Affirmation and Sacred Precept. Innumerable 'Philosophies of Man,' contending in boundless hubbub, must annihilate each other, before an inspired Poesy and Faith for Man can fashion itself together.

From this stunning hubbub, a true Babel-like confusion of tongues, we have here selected two Voices; less as objects of praise or condemnation, than as signs how far the confusion has reached, what prospect there is of its abating. Friedrich Schlegel's *Lectures* delivered at Dresden, and Mr. Hope's *Essay* published in London, are the latest utterances of European Speculation: far asunder in external place, they stand at a still wider distance in inward purport; are, indeed, so opposite and yet so cognate that they may, in many senses, represent the two Extremes of our whole modern system of Thought; and be said to include between them all the Metaphysical Philosophies, so often alluded to here, which, of late times, from France, Germany, England, have agitated and almost overwhelmed us. Both in

[1] Jean Paul's *Hesperus* (Vorrede). [Carlyle's note.]

regard to matter and to form, the relation of these two Works is significant enough.

Speaking first of their cognate qualities, let us remark, not without emotion, one quite extraneous point of agreement; the fact that the Writers of both have departed from this world; they have now finished their search, and had all doubts resolved: while we listen to the voice, the tongue that uttered it has gone silent forever. But the fundamental, all-pervading similarity lies in this circumstance, well worthy of being noted, that both these Philosophies are of the Dogmatic or Constructive sort: each in its way is a kind of Genesis; an endeavour to bring the Phenomena of man's Universe once more under some theoretic Scheme: in both there is a decided principle of unity; they strive after a result which shall be positive; their aim is not to question, but to establish. This, especially if we consider with what comprehensive concentrated force it is here exhibited, forms a new feature in such works.

Under all other aspects, there is the most irreconcilable opposition; a staring contrariety, such as might provoke contrasts, were there far fewer points of comparison. If Schlegel's Work is the apotheosis of Spiritualism; Hope's again is the apotheosis of Materialism: in the one, all Matter is evaporated into a Phenomenon, and terrestrial Life itself, with its whole doings and showings, held out as a Disturbance (*Zerrüttung*) produced by the *Zeitgeist* (Spirit of Time); in the other, Matter is distilled and sublimated into some semblance of Divinity: the one regards Space and Time as mere forms of man's mind, and without external existence or reality; the other supposes Space and Time to be 'incessantly created,' and rayed-in upon us like a sort of 'gravitation.' Such is their difference in respect of purport: no less striking is it in respect of manner, talent, success and all outward characteristics. Thus, if in Schlegel we have to admire the power of Words, in Hope we stand astonished, it might almost be said, at the want of an articulate Language. To Schlegel his Philosophic Speech is obedient, dextrous, exact, like a promptly ministering genius; his names are so clear, so precise and vivid, that they almost (sometimes altogether) become things for him: with Hope there is no Philosophical Speech; but a painful, confused stammering, and struggling after such; or the tongue, as in doatish forgetfulness, maunders, low, long-winded, and speaks not the word intended, but another; so that here the scarcely intelligible, in these endless convolutions, becomes the wholly unreadable; and often we could ask, as that mad pupil did of his tutor in Philosophy, "But whether is Virtue a fluid, then, or a gas?" If the fact, that Schlegel, in the city of Dresden, could find audience for such high discourse, may excite our envy; this other fact, that a person of strong powers, skilled in English Thought and master of its Dialect, could write the *Origin and Prospects of Man,* may painfully remind us of the reproach, that England has now no language for Meditation; that England, the most calculative, is the least meditative, of all civilised countries.

It is not our purpose to offer any criticism of Schlegel's Book; in such limits as were possible here, we should despair of communicating even the faintest image of its significance. To the mass of readers, indeed, both among the Germans themselves, and still more elsewhere, it nowise addresses itself, and may lie forever sealed. We point it out as a remarkable document of the Time and of the Man; can recommend it, moreover, to all earnest Thinkers, as a work deserving their best regard; a work full of deep meditation, wherein the infinite mystery of Life, if not represented, is decisively recognised. Of Schlegel himself, and his character, and spiritual history, we can profess no thorough or final understanding; yet enough to make us view him with admiration and pity, nowise with harsh contemptuous censure; and must say, with clearest persuasion, that the outcry of his being 'a renegade,' and so forth, is but like other such outcries, a judgment where there was neither jury, nor evidence, nor judge. The candid reader, in this Book itself, to say nothing of all the rest, will find traces of a high, far-seeing, earnest spirit, to whom 'Austrian Pensions,' and the Kaiser's crown, and Austria altogether, were but a light matter to the finding and vitally appropriating of Truth. Let us respect the sacred mystery of a Person; rush not irreverently into man's Holy of Holies! Were the lost little one, as we said already, found 'sucking its dead mother, on the field of carnage,' could it be other than a spectacle for tears? A solemn mournful feeling comes over us when we see this last Work of Friedrich Schlegel, the unwearied seeker, end abruptly in the middle; and, as if he *had not* yet found, as if emblematically of much, end with an

'*Aber*—,' with a 'But—'! This was the last word that came from the Pen of Friedrich Schlegel: about eleven at night he wrote it down, and there paused sick; at one in the morning, Time for him had merged itself in Eternity; he was, as we say, no more.

Still less can we attempt any criticism of Mr. Hope's new Book of Genesis. Indeed, under any circumstances, criticism of it were now impossible. Such an utterance could only be responded to in peals of laughter; and laughter sounds hollow and hideous through the vaults of the dead. Of this monstrous Anomaly, where all sciences are heaped and huddled together, and the principles of all are, with a childlike innocence, plied hither and thither, or wholly abolished in case of need; where the First Cause is figured as a huge Circle, with nothing to do but radiate 'gravitation' towards its centre; and so construct a Universe, wherein all, from the lowest cucumber with its coolness, up to the highest seraph with his love, were but 'gravitation,' direct or reflex, 'in more or less central globes,'—what can we say, except, with sorrow and shame, that it could have originated nowhere save in England? It is a general agglomerate of all facts, notions, whims and observations, as they lie in the brain of an English gentleman; as an English gentleman, of unusual thinking power, is led to fashion them, in his schools and in his world: all these thrown into the crucible, and if not fused, yet soldered or conglutinated with boundless patience; and now tumbled out here, heterogeneous, amorphous, unspeakable, a world's wonder. Most melancholy must we name the whole business; full of long-continued thought, earnestness, loftiness of mind; not without glances into the Deepest, a constant fearless endeavour after truth; and with all this nothing accomplished, but the perhaps absurdest Book written in our century by a thinking man. A shameful Abortion; which, however, need not now be smothered or mangled, for it is already dead; only, in our love and sorrowing reverence for the writer of *Anastasius*, and the heroic seeker of Light, though not bringer thereof, let it be buried and forgotten.

For ourselves, the loud discord which jars in these two Works, in innumerable works of the like import, and generally in all the Thought and Action of this period, does not any longer utterly confuse us. Unhappy who, in such a time, felt not, at all conjunctures, ineradicably in his heart the knowledge that a God made this Universe, and a Demon not! And shall Evil always prosper, then? Out of all Evil comes Good? and no Good that is possible but shall one day be real. Deep and sad as is our feeling that we stand yet in the bodeful Night; equally deep, indestructible is our assurance that the Morning also will not fail. Nay, already, as we look round, streaks of a dayspring are in the east; it is dawning; when the time shall be fulfilled, it will be day. The progress of man towards higher and nobler developments of whatever is highest and noblest in him, lies not only prophesied to Faith, but now written to the eye of Observation, so that he who runs may read.

One great step of progress, for example, we should say, in actual circumstances, was this same; the clear ascertainment that we are in progress. About the grand Course of Providence, and his final Purposes with us, we can know nothing, or almost nothing: man begins in darkness, ends in darkness; mystery is everywhere around us and in us, under our feet, among our hands. Nevertheless so much has become evident to every one, that this wondrous Mankind is advancing somewhither; that at least all human things are, have been and forever will be, in Movement and Change;—as, indeed, for beings that exist in Time, by virtue of Time, and are made of Time, might have been long since understood. In some provinces, it is true, as in Experimental Science, this discovery is an old one; but in most others it belongs wholly to these latter days. How often, in former ages, by eternal Creeds, eternal Forms of Government and the like, has it been attempted, fiercely enough, and with destructive violence, to chain the Future under the Past; and say to the Providence, whose ways with man are mysterious, and through the great deep: Hitherto shalt thou come, but no farther! A wholly insane attempt; and for man himself, could it prosper, the frightfulest of all enchantments, a very Life-in-Death. Man's task here below, the destiny of every individual man, is to be in turns Apprentice and Workman; or say rather, Scholar, Teacher, Discoverer: by nature he has a strength for learning, for imitating; but also a strength for acting, for knowing on his own account. Are we not in a world seen to be Infinite; the relations lying closest together modified by those latest discovered and lying farthest asunder? Could you ever spell-bind man into a Scholar merely, so that he had nothing to discover, to correct; could you ever establish a Theory of the Universe that were entire, unimprovable, and which needed only to be got by heart; man then were spiritually defunct, the Species we now name Man had ceased to exist. But the gods, kinder to us than we are to ourselves, have forbidden such suicidal acts. As Phlogiston is displaced by Oxygen, and the Epicycles of Ptolemy by the Ellipses of Kepler; so does Paganism give place to Catholicism, Tyranny to Monarchy, and Feudalism to Representative Government,—where also the process does not stop. Perfection of Practice, like completeness of Opinion, is always approaching, never arrived; Truth, in the words of Schiller, *immer wird, nie ist;* never *is,* always *is a-being.*

Sad, truly, were our condition did we know but this, that Change is universal and inevitable. Launched into a dark shoreless sea of Pyrrhonism, what would remain for us but to sail aimless, hopeless; or make madly merry, while the devouring Death had not yet ingulfed us? As indeed, we have seen many, and still see many do. Nevertheless so stands it not. The venerator of the Past (and to what pure heart is the Past, in that 'moonlight of memory,' other than sad and holy?) sorrows not over its departure, as one utterly bereaved. The true Past departs not, nothing that was worthy in the Past departs; no Truth or Goodness realised by man ever dies, or can die; but is all still here, and, recognised or not, lives and works through endless changes. If all things, to speak in the German dialect, are discerned by us, and exist for us, in an element of Time, and therefore of Mortality and Mutability; yet Time itself reposes on Eternity: the truly Great and Transcendental has its basis and substance in Eternity; stands revealed to us as Eternity in a vesture of Time. Thus in all Poetry, Worship, Art, Society, as one form passes into another, nothing is lost: it is but the superficial, as it were the *body* only, that grows obsolete and dies; under the mortal body lies a *soul* which is immortal; which anew incarnates itself in fairer revelation; and the Present is the living sum-total of the whole Past.

In Change, therefore, there is nothing terrible, nothing supernatural: on the contrary, it lies in the very essence of our lot and life in this world. Today is not yesterday: we ourselves change; how can our Works and Thoughts, if they are always to be the fittest, continue always the same? Change, indeed, is painful; yet ever needful; and if Memory have its force and worth, so also has Hope. Nay, if we look well to it, what is all Derangement, and necessity of great Change, in itself such an evil, but the product simply of *increased resources* which the old *methods* can no longer administer; of new wealth which the old coffers will no longer contain? What is it, for example, that in our own day bursts asunder the bonds of ancient Political Systems, and perplexes all Europe with the fear of Change, but even this: the increase of social resources, which the old social methods will no longer sufficiently administer? The new omnipotence of the Steam-engine is hewing asunder quite other mountains than the physical. Have not our economical distresses, those barnyard Conflagrations themselves, the frightfulest madness of our mad epoch, their rise also in what is a real increase: increase of Men; of human Force; properly, in such a Planet as ours, the most precious of all increases? It is true again, the ancient methods of administration will no longer suffice. Must the indomitable millions, full of old Saxon energy and fire, lie cooped-up in this Western Nook, choking one another, as in a Blackhole of Calcutta, while a whole fertile untenanted Earth, desolate for want of the ploughshare, cries: Come and till me, come and reap me? If the ancient Captains can no longer yield guidance, new must be sought after: for the difficulty lies not in nature, but in artifice; the European Calcutta-Blackhole has no walls but air ones and paper ones.—So too, Scepticism itself, with its innumerable mischiefs, what is it but the sour fruit of a most blessed increase, that of Knowledge; a fruit too that will not always continue *sour?*

In fact, much as we have said and mourned about the unproductive prevalence of Metaphysics, it was not without some insight into the use that lies in them. Metaphysical Speculation, if a necessary evil, is the forerunner of much good. The fever of Scepticism must needs burn itself out, and burn out thereby the Impurities that caused it; then again will there be clearness, health. The principle of life, which now struggles painfully, in the outer, thin and barren domain of the Conscious or Mechanical, may then withdraw into its inner sanctuaries, its abysses of mystery and miracle; withdraw deeper than ever into that domain of the Unconscious, by nature infinite and inexhaustible; and creatively work there. From that mystic region, and from that alone, all wonders, all Poesies, and Religions, and Social Systems have proceeded: the like wonders, and greater and higher, lie slumbering there; and, brooded on by the spirit of the waters, will evolve themselves, and rise like exhalations from the Deep.

Of our Modern Metaphysics, accordingly, may not this already be said, that if they have produced no Affirmation, they have destroyed much Negation? It is a disease expelling a disease: the fire of Doubt, as above hinted, consuming away the Doubtful; that so the Certain come to light, and again lie visible on the surface. English or French Metaphysics, in reference to this last stage of the speculative process, are not what we allude to here; but only the Metaphysics of the Germans. In France or England, since the days of Diderot and Hume, though all thought has been of a sceptico-metaphysical texture, so far as there was any Thought, we have seen no Metaphysics; but only more or less ineffectual questionings whether such could be. In the Pyrrhonism of Hume and the Materialism of Diderot, Logic had, as it were, overshot itself, overset itself. Now, though the athlete, to use our old figure, cannot, by much lifting, lift up his own body, he may shift it out of a laming posture, and get to stand in a free one. Such a service have German Metaphysics done for man's mind. The second sickness of Speculation has abolished both itself and the first. Friedrich Schlegel complains much of the fruitlessness, the tumult and transiency of German as of all Metaphysics; and with reason. Yet in that wide-spreading, deep-whirling vortex of Kantism, so soon metamorphosed into Fichteism, Schellingism, and then as Hegelism, and Cousinism, perhaps finally evaporated, is not this issue visible enough, That Pyrrhonism and Materialism, themselves necessary phenomena in European culture, have disappeared; and a Faith in Religion has again become possible and inevitable for the scientific mind; and the word *Free*-thinker no longer means the Denier or Caviller, but the Believer, or the Ready to believe? Nay, in the higher Literature of Germany, there already lies, for him that can read it, the beginning of a new revelation of the Godlike; as yet unrecognised by the mass of the world; but waiting there for recognition, and sure to find it when the fit hour comes. This age also is not wholly without its Prophets.

Again, under another aspect, if Utilitarianism, or Radicalism, or the Mechanical Philosophy, or by whatever name it is called, has still its long task to do; nevertheless we can now see through it and beyond it: in the better heads, even among us English, it has become obsolete; as in other countries, it has been, in such heads, for some forty or even fifty years. What sound mind among the French, for example, now fancies that men can be governed by 'Constitutions'; by the never so cunning mechanising of Self-interests, and all conceivable adjustments of checking and balancing; in a word, by the best possible solution of this quite insoluble and impossible problem, *Given a world of Knaves, to produce an Honesty from their united action?* Were not experiments enough of this kind tried before all Europe, and found wanting, when, in that doomsday of France, the infinite gulf of human Passion shivered asunder the thin rinds of Habit; and burst forth all-devouring, as in seas of Nether Fire? Which cunningly-devised 'Constitution,' constitutional, republican, democratic, sansculottic, could bind that raging chasm together? Were they not all burnt up, like paper as they were, in its molten eddies; and still the fire-sea raged fiercer than before? It is not by Mechanism, but by Religion; not by Self-interest, but by Loyalty, that men are governed or governable.

Remarkable it is, truly, how everywhere the eternal fact begins again to be recognised, that there is a Godlike in human affairs; that God not only made us and beholds us, but is in us and around us; that the Age of Miracles, as it ever was, now is. Such recognition we discern on all hands and in all countries: in each country after its own ·fashion. In France, among the younger nobler minds, strangely enough; where, in their loud contention with the Actual and Conscious, the Ideal or Unconscious is, for the time, without exponent; where Religion means not the parent of Polity, as of all that is highest, but Polity itself; and this and the other earnest man has not been wanting, who could audibly whisper to himself: "Go to, I will make a religion." In England still more strangely; as in all things, worthy England will have its way: by the shrieking of hysterical women, casting out of devils, and other 'gifts of the Holy Ghost.' Well might Jean Paul say, in this his twelfth hour of the Night, 'the living dream'; well might he say, 'the dead walk.' Meanwhile let us rejoice rather that so much has been seen into, were it through never so diffracting media, and never so madly distorted; that in all dialects, though but half-articulately, this high Gospel begins to be preached: Man is still Man. The genius of Mechanism, as was once before predicted, will not always sit like a choking incubus on our soul; but at length, when by a new magic Word the old spell is broken, become our slave, and as familiar-spirit do all our bidding. 'We are near awakening when we dream that we dream.'

He that has an eye and a heart can even now say: Why should I falter? Light has come into the world; to such as love Light, so as Light must be loved, with a boundless all-doing, all-enduring love. For the rest, let that vain struggle to read the mystery of the Infinite cease to harass us. It is a mystery which, through all ages, we shall only read here a line of, there another line of. Do we not already know that the name of the Infinite is GOOD, is GOD? Here on Earth we are Soldiers, fighting in a foreign land; that understand not the plan of the campaign, and have no need to understand it; seeing well what is at our hand to be done. Let us do it like Soldiers; with submission, with courage, with a heroic joy. 'Whatsoever thy hand findeth to do, do it with all thy might.' Behind us, behind each one of us, lie Six Thousand Years of human effort, human conquest: before us is the boundless Time, with its as yet uncreated and unconquered Continents and Eldorados, which we, even we, have to conquer, to create; and from the bosom of Eternity there shine for us celestial guiding stars.

'My inheritance how wide and fair!
Time is my fair seed-field, of Time I'm heir.'

On History Again

1 8 3 3

[First published under the title *"Quae Cogitavit"* in the May 1833 *Fraser's,* this essay may have been an offshoot of Carlyle's work in the previous year on Diderot and therefore related to his study of the French Revolution, but the style, organization, and ideas reflect above all *Sartor Resartus,* which had been completed two years before but not yet published. The "D.T." of the prefatory note is, of course, Diogenes Teufelsdröckh, otherwise a name as yet unknown to the British public. "O.Y." are the initials of "Oliver Yorke," the pretended editor of *Fraser's Magazine.* The initials were freely used by the actual editor, William Maginn, and other contributors.]

The following singular Fragment on History *forms part, as may be recognised, of the Inaugural Discourse delivered by our assiduous 'D. T.' at the opening of the* Society for the Diffusion of Common Honesty. *The Discourse, if one may credit the Morning Papers, 'touched in the most wonderful manner, didactically, poetically, almost prophetically, on all things in this world and the next, in a strain of sustained or rather of suppressed passionate eloquence rarely witnessed in Parliament or out of it: the chief bursts were received with profound silence,'—interrupted, we fear, by snuff-taking. As will be seen, it is one of the didactic passages that we introduce here. The Editor of this Magazine is responsible for its accuracy, and publishes, if not with leave given, then with leave taken.—O. Y.*

* * * History recommends itself as the most profitable of all studies: and truly, for such a being as Man, who is born, and has to learn and work, and then after a measured term of years to depart, leaving descendants and performances, and so, in all ways, to vindicate himself as vital portion of a Mankind, no study could be fitter. History is the Letter of Instructions, which the old generations write and posthumously transmit to the new; nay, it may be called, more generally still, the Message, verbal or written, which all Mankind delivers to every man; it is the only *articulate* communication (when the inarticulate and mute, intelligible or not, lie round us and in us, so strangely through every fibre of our being, every step of our activity) which the Past can have with the Present, the Distant with what is Here. All Books, therefore, were they but Song-books or treatises on Mathematics, are in the long-run historical documents—as indeed all Speech itself is: thus might we say, History is not only the fittest study, but the only study, and includes all others whatsoever. The Perfect in History, he who understood, and saw and knew within himself, *all* that the whole Family of Adam had hitherto *been* and hitherto *done*, were perfect in all learning extant or possible; needed not thenceforth to *study* any more; had thenceforth nothing left but to *be* and to *do* something himself, that others might make History of it, and learn of *him*.

Perfection in any kind is well known not to be the lot of man: but of all supernatural perfect-characters this of the Perfect in History (so easily conceivable, too) were perhaps the most miraculous. Clearly a faultless monster which the world is not to see, not even on paper. Had the Wandering Jew, indeed, begun to wander at Eden, and with a Fortunatus's Hat on his head! Nanac Shah too, we remember, steeped himself three days in some sacred Well; and there learnt all things: Nanac's was a far easier method; but unhappily not practicable—in this climate. Consider, however, at what immeasurable distance from this perfect Nanac your highest imperfect Gibbons play their part! Were there no brave men, thinkest thou, before Agamemnon? Beyond the Thracian Bosphorus, was all dead and void; from Cape Horn to Nova Zembla, round the whole habitable Globe, not a mouse stirring? Or, again, in reference to Time:—the Creation of the World is indeed old, compare it to the Year One; yet young, of yesterday, compare it to Eternity! Alas, all Universal History is but a sort of Parish History; which the 'P. P. Clerk of this Parish,' member of 'our Ale-house Club' (instituted for what 'Psalmody' is in request there) puts together,—in such sort as his fellow-members will praise. Of the *thing* now gone silent, named Past, which was once Present, and loud enough, how much do we know? Our 'Letter of Instructions' comes to us in the saddest state; falsified, blotted out, torn, lost and but a shred of it in existence; this too so difficult to read or spell.

Unspeakably precious meanwhile is our shred of a Letter, is our written or spoken Message, such as we have it. Only he who understands what has been, can know what should be and will be. It is of the last importance that the individual have ascertained his relation to the whole; 'an individual helps not,' it has been written; 'only he who unites with many at the proper hour.' How easy, in a sense, for your all-instructed Nanac to work without waste or force (or what we call fault); and, in practice, act new History, as perfectly as, in theory, he knew the old! Comprehending what the given world was, what it had and what it wanted, how might his clear effort strike-in at the right time and the right point; wholly increasing the true current and tendency, nowhere cancelling itself in opposition thereto! Unhappily, such smooth-running, ever-accelerated course is nowise the one appointed us; cross-currents we have, perplexed back-floods; innumerable efforts (every new man is a new effort) consume themselves in aimless eddies: thus is the River of Existence so wild-flowing, wasteful; and whole multitudes, and whole generations, in painful unreason, spend and are spent on what can never profit. Of all which, does not one-half originate in this which we have named want of Perfection in History;—the other half, indeed, in another want still deeper, still more irremediable?

Here, however, let us grant that Nature, in regard to such historic want, is nowise blamable: taking up the other face of the matter, let us rather admire the pains she has been at, the truly magnificent provision she has made, that this same Message of Instructions might reach us in boundless plenitude. Endowments, faculties enough, we have: it is her wise will too that no faculty imparted to us shall rust from disuse; the miraculous faculty of Speech, once given, becomes not more a gift than a necessity; the Tongue, with or without much meaning, will keep in motion; and only in some La Trappe by unspeakable self-restraint forbear wagging. As little can the fingers that have learned the miracle of Writing lie idle; if there is a rage of speaking, we know also there is a rage of writing, perhaps the more furious of the two. It is said, 'so eager are men to speak, they will not let one another get to speech'; but, on the other hand, writing is usually transacted in private, and every man has his own desk and inkstand, and sits independent and unrestrainable there. Lastly, multiply this power of the Pen some ten-thousandfold: that is to say, invent the Printing-Press, with its Printer's Devils, with its Editors, Contributors, Booksellers, Billstickers, and see what it will do! Such are the means wherewith Nature, and Art the daughter of Nature, have equipped their favourite Man, for publishing himself to man.

Consider, now, two things: first, that one Tongue, of average velocity, will publish at the rate of a thick octavo volume per day; and then how many nimble-enough Tongues may be supposed to be at work on this Planet Earth, in this City London, at this hour! Secondly, that a Literary Contributor, if in good heart and urged by hunger, will many times, as we are credibly informed, accomplish his two Magazine sheets within the four-and-twenty hours; such Contributors being now numerable not by the thousand, but by the million. Nay, taking History, in its narrower, vulgar sense, as the mere chronicle of 'occurrences,' of things that can be, as we say, 'narrated,' our calculation is still but a little altered. Simple Narrative, it will be observed, is the grand staple of Speech; 'the common man,' says Jean Paul, 'is copious in Narrative, exiguous in Reflection; only with the cultivated man is it otherwise, reversewise.' Allow even the thousandth part of human publishing for the emission of Thought, though perhaps the millionth were enough, we have still the nine hundred and ninety-nine employed in History proper, in relating occurrences, or conjecturing probabilities of such; that is to say, either in History or Prophecy, which is a new form of History:—and so the reader can judge with what abundance this life-breath of the human intellect is furnished in our world; whether Nature has been stingy to him or munificent. Courage, reader! Never can the historical inquirer want pabulum, better or worse: are there not forty-eight longitudinal feet of small-printed History in thy Daily Newspaper?

The truth is, if Universal History is such a miserable defective 'shred' as we have named it, the fault lies not in our historic organs, but wholly in our misuse of these; say rather, in so many wants and obstructions, varying with the various age, that pervert our right use of them; especially two wants that press heavily in all ages: want of Honesty, want of Understanding. If the thing published is not true, is only a supposition, or even a wilful invention, what can be done with it, except abolish it and annihilate it? But again, Truth, says Horne Tooke, means simply the thing *trowed,* the thing believed; and now, from this to the thing *itself,* what a new fatal deduction have we to suffer! Without Understanding, Belief itself will profit little: and how can your publishing avail, when there was no vision in it, but mere blindness? For as in political appointments, the man you appoint is not he who was ablest to discharge the duty, but only he who was ablest to be appointed; so too, in all historic elections and selections, the maddest work goes on. The event worthiest to be known is perhaps of all others the least spoken of: nay, some say, it lies in the very nature of such events to be so. Thus, in those same forty-eight longitudinal feet of History, or even when they have stretched out into forty-eight longitudinal miles, of the like quality, there may not be the forty-eighth part of a hairsbreadth that will turn to anything. Truly, in these times, the quantity of printed Publication that will need to be consumed with fire, before the smallest permanent advantage can be drawn from it, might fill us with astonishment, almost with apprehension. Where, alas, is the intrepid Herculean Dr. Wagtail, that will reduce all these paper-mountains into tinder, and extract therefrom the three drops of Tinder-water Elixir?

For indeed, looking at the activity of the historic Pen and Press through this last half-century, and what bulk of History it yields for that period alone, and how it is henceforth like to increase in decimal or vigesimal geometric progression,—one might feel as if a day were not distant, when perceiving that the whole Earth would not now contain those writings of what was done in the Earth, the human memory must needs sink confounded, and cease remembering!—To some the reflection may be new and consolatory, that this state of ours is not so unexampled as it seems; that with memory and things memorable the case was always intrinsically similar. The Life of Nero occupies some diamond pages of our Tacitus: but in the parchment and papyrus archives of Nero's generation how many did it fill? The author of the *Vie de Sénèque,* at this distance, picking-up a few residuary snips, has with ease made two octavos of it. On the other hand, were the contents of the then extant Roman memories, or, going to the utmost length, were all that was then *spoken* on it, put in types, how many 'longitudinal feet' of small-pica had we,—in belts that would go round the Globe!

History, then, before it can become Universal History,

needs of all things to be compressed. Were there no epitomising of History, one could not remember beyond a week. Nay, go to that with it, and exclude compression altogether, we could not remember an hour, or at all: for Time, like Space, is *infinitely* divisible; and an hour with its events, with its sensations and emotions, might be diffused to such expansion as should cover the whole field of memory, and push all else over the limits. Habit, however, and the natural constitution of man, do themselves prescribe serviceable rules for remembering; and keep at a safe distance from us all such fantastic possibilities;—into which only some foolish Mahomedan Caliph, ducking his head in a bucket of enchanted water, and so beating-out one wet minute into seven long years of servitude and hardship, could fall. The rudest peasant has his complete set of Annual Registers legibly printed in his brain; and, without the smallest training in Mnemonics, the proper pauses, subdivisions and subordinations of the little to the great, all introduced there. Memory and Oblivion, like Day and Night, and indeed like all other Contradictions in this strange dualistic Life of ours, are necessary for each other's existence: Oblivion is the dark page, whereon Memory writes her light-beam characters, and makes them legible; were it all light, nothing could be read there, any more than if it were all darkness.

As with man and these autobiographic Annual-Registers of his, so goes it with Mankind and its Universal History, which also is *its* Autobiography: a like unconscious talent of remembering and of forgetting again does the work here. The transactions of the day, were they never so noisy, cannot remain loud forever; the morrow comes with its new noises, claiming also to be registered: in the immeasurable conflict and concert of this chaos of existence, figure after figure sinks, as *all* that has emerged must one day sink: what cannot be kept in mind will even go out of mind; History contracts itself into readable extent; and at last, in the hands of some Bossuet or Müller, the whole printed History of the World, from the Creation downwards, has grown shorter than that of the Ward of Portsoken for one solar day.

Whether such contraction and epitome is always wisely formed, might admit of question; or rather, as we say, admits of no question. Scandalous Cleopatras and Messalinas,

Caligulas and Commoduses, in unprofitable proportion, survive for memory; while a scientific Pancirollus has to write his Book of Arts Lost; and a moral Pancirollus, were the vision lent him, might write a still more mournful Book of Virtues Lost; of noble men, doing and daring and enduring, whose heroic life, as a new revelation and development of Life itself, were a possession for all, but is now lost and forgotten, History having otherwise filled her page. In fact, here as elsewhere, what we call Accident governs much; in any case, History must come together not as it should, but as it can and will.

Remark nevertheless how, by natural tendency alone, and as it were without man's forethought, a certain fitness of selection, and this even to a high degree, becomes inevitable. Wholly worthless the selection could not be, were there no better rule than this to guide it: that men permanently speak only of what is extant and actively alive beside them. Thus do the things that have produced fruit, nay, whose fruit still grows, turn out to be the things chosen for record and writing of; which things alone were great, and worth recording. The Battle of Châlons, where Hunland met Rome, and the Earth was played for, at swordfence, by two earth-bestriding giants, the sweep of whose swords cut kingdoms in pieces, hovers dim in the languid remembrance of a few; while the poor police-court Treachery of a wretched Iscariot, transacted in the wretched land of Palestine, centuries earlier, for 'thirty pieces of silver,' lives clear in the heads, in the hearts of all men. Nay, moreover, as only that which bore fruit was great; so of all things, that whose fruit is still here and growing must be the greatest, the best worth remembering; which again, as we see, by the very nature of the case, is mainly the thing remembered. Observe, too, how this 'mainly' tends always to become a 'solely,' and the approximate continually approaches nearer: for triviality after triviality, as it perishes from the living activity of men, drops away from their speech and memory, and the great and vital more and more exclusively survive there. Thus does Accident correct Accident; and in the wondrous boundless jostle of things (an aimful POWER presiding over it, say rather, dwelling *in* it), a result comes out that may be put-up with.

Curious, at all events, and worth looking at once in our life, is this same compressure of History, be the process thereof what it may. How the 'forty-eight longitudinal feet' have shrunk together after a century, after ten centuries! Look back from end to beginning, over any History; over our own *England:* how in rapidest law of perspective, it dwindles from the canvas! An unhappy Sybarite, if we stand within two centuries of him and name him Charles Second, shall have twelve times the space of a heroic Alfred; two or three thousand times, if we name him George the Fourth. The whole Saxon Heptarchy, though events, to which Magna Charta, and the world-famous Third Reading, are as dust in the balance, took place then,—for did not England, to mention nothing else, get itself, if not represented in Parliament, yet converted to Christianity?—the whole Saxon Heptarchy, I say, is summed-up practically in that one sentence of Milton's, the only one succeeding writers have copied, or readers remembered, of the 'fighting and flocking of kites and crows.' Neither was that an unimportant wassail-night, when the two black-browed Brothers, strongheaded, headstrong, Hengst and Horsa (*Stallion* and *Horse*), determined on a man-hunt in Britain, the boar-hunt at home having got over-crowded; and so, of a few hungry Angles made an English Nation, and planted it here, and—produced *thee,* O Reader! Of Hengst's whole campaignings scarcely half a page of good Narrative can now be written; the *Lord Mayor's Visit to Oxford* standing, meanwhile, revealed to mankind in a respectable volume. Nay, what of this? Does not the Destruction of a Brunswick Theatre take above a million times as much telling as the Creation of a World?

To use a ready-made similitude, we might liken Universal History to a magic web; and consider with astonishment how, by philosophic insight and indolent neglect, the ever-growing fabric wove itself forward, out of that ravelled immeasurable mass of threads and thrums, which we name *Memoirs;* nay, at each new lengthening, at each new *epoch,* changed its whole proportions, its hue and structure to the very origin. Thus, do not the records of a Tacitus acquire new meaning, after seventeen hundred years, in the hands of a Montesquieu? Niebuhr has to reinterpret for us, at a still greater distance, the writings of a Titus Livius: nay, the religious archaic chronicles of a Hebrew Prophet and Law-giver escape not the like fortune; and many a ponderous Eichhorn scans, with new-ground philosophic spectacles, the revelation of a Moses, and strives to reproduce for this century what, thirty centuries ago, was of plainly infinite significance to all. Consider History with the beginnings of it stretching dimly into the remote Time; emerging darkly out of the mysterious Eternity: the ends of it enveloping *us* at this hour, whereof we at this hour, both as actors and relators, form part! In shape we might mathematically name it *Hyperbolic-Asymptotic*; ever of *infinite* breadth around us; soon shrinking within narrow limits: ever narrowing more and more into the infinite depth behind us. In essence and significance it has been called 'the true Epic Poem, and universal Divine Scripture, *whose* "plenary inspiration" no man, out of Bedlam 'or in it, shall bring in question.'

*　　　　*　　　　*　　　　*　　　　*

Death of Edward Irving

1 8 3 5

[Edward Irving (1792-1834) had been Carlyle's closest friend since 1816, and no man's downfall could have offered a more melancholy spectacle for Carlyle. Irving's sensational rise and fall had all been accomplished before the Carlyles moved to London. When they saw him for the last time in 1834, he was already a broken man. He died in December of that year and was buried in the crypt of Glasgow Cathedral. Carlyle's tribute was first published in *Fraser's* in January 1835. The "one who knew him well" at the end of the essay is, of course, Carlyle himself.]

Edward Irving's warfare has closed; if not in victory, yet in invincibility, and faithful endurance to the end. The Spirit of the Time, which could not enlist him as its soldier, must needs, in all ways, fight against him as its enemy: it has done its part, and he has done his. One of the noblest natures; a man of antique heroic nature, in questionable modern garniture, which he could not wear! Around him a distracted society, vacant, prurient; heat and darkness, and what these two may breed: mad extremes of flattery, followed by madder contumely, by indifference and neglect! These were the conflicting elements; this is the result they have made out among them. The voice of our 'son of thunder,'—with its deep tone of wisdom that belonged to all articulate-speaking ages, never inaudible amid wildest dissonances that belong to this inarticulate age, which slumbers and somnambulates, which cannot *speak,* but only screech and gibber,—has gone silent so soon. Closed are those lips. The large heart, with its large bounty, where wretchedness found solacement, and they that were wandering in darkness the light as of a home, has paused. The strong man can no more: beaten-on from without, undermined from within, he has had to sink overwearied, as at nightfall, when it was yet but the mid-season of day. Irving was forty-two years and some months old: Scotland sent him forth a Herculean man; our mad Babylon wore him and wasted him, with all her engines; and it took her twelve years. He sleeps with his fathers, in that loved birth-land: Babylon with its deafening inanity rages on; but to him henceforth innocuous, unheeded—forever.

Reader, thou hast seen and heard the man, as who has not,—with wise or unwise wonder; thou shalt not see or hear him again. The work, be what it might, is *done;* dark curtains sink over it, enclose it ever deeper into the unchangeable Past. Think, for perhaps thou art one of a thousand, and worthy so to think, That here once more was a genuine man sent into this our *un*genuine phantasmagory of a world, which would go to ruin without such; that here once more, under thy own eyes, in this last decade, was enacted the old Tragedy, and has had its fifth-act now, of *The Messenger of Truth in the Age of Shams,*—and what relation thou thyself mayest have to that. Whether any? Beyond question, thou thyself art *here;* either a dreamer or awake; and one day shalt cease to dream.

This man was appointed a Christian Priest; and strove with the whole force that was in him to *be* it. To be it: in a time of Tithe Controversy, Encyclopedism, Catholic Rent, Philanthropism, and the Revolution of Three Days! He might have been so many things; not a speaker only, but a doer; the leader of hosts of men. For his head, when the Fog-Babylon had not yet obscured it, was of strong far-searching insight; his very enthusiasm was sanguine, not atrabiliar; he was so loving, full of hope, so simple-hearted, and made all that approached him his. A giant force of activity was in the man; speculation was accident, not nature. Chivalry, adventurous field-life of the old Border, and a far nobler sort than that, ran in his blood. There was in him a courage, dauntless not pugnacious, hardly fierce, by no possibility ferocious; as of the generous warhorse, gentle in its strength, yet that laughs at the shaking of the spear.— But, above all, be what he might, to be a *reality* was indispensable for him. In his simple Scottish circle, the highest form of manhood attainable or known was that of Christian; the highest Christian was the Teacher of such. Irving's lot was cast. For the foray-spears were all rusted into earth there; Annan Castle had become a Townhall; and Prophetic Knox had sent tidings thither: Prophetic Knox; and, alas, also Sceptic Hume: and, as the natural consequence,

Diplomatic Dundas! In such mixed incongruous element had the young soul to grow.

Grow, nevertheless, he did, with that strong vitality of his; grow and ripen. What the Scottish uncelebrated Irving was, they that have only seen the London celebrated and distorted one can never know. Bodily and spiritually, perhaps there was not, in that November 1822, when he first arrived here, a man more full of genial energetic life in all these Islands.

By a fatal chance, Fashion cast her eye on him, as on some impersonation of Novel-Cameronianism, some wild Product of Nature from the wild mountains; Fashion crowded round him, with her meteor lights and Bacchic dances; breathed her foul incense on him; intoxicating, poisoning. One may say, it was his own nobleness that forwarded such ruin; the excess of his sociability and sympathy, of his value for the suffrages and sympathies of men. Siren songs, as of a new Moral Reformation (sons of Mammon, and high sons of Belial and Beelzebub, to become sons of God, and the gumflowers of Almack's to be made living roses in a new Eden), sound in the inexperienced ear and heart. Most seductive, most delusive! Fashion went her idle way, to gaze on Egyptian Crocodiles, Iroquois Hunters, or what else there might be; forgot this man,—who unhappily could not in his turn forget. The intoxicating poison had been swallowed; no force of natural health could cast it out. Unconsciously, for most part in deep unconsciousness, there was now the impossibility to live neglected; to walk on the quiet paths, where alone it is well with us. Singularity must henceforth succeed Singularity. O foulest Circean draught, thou poison of Popular Applause! madness is in thee, and death; thy end is Bedlam and the Grave. For the last seven years, Irving, forsaken by the world, strove either to recall it, or to forsake it; shut himself up in a lesser world of ideas and persons, and lived isolated there. Neither in this was there health: for this man such isolation was not fit, such ideas, such persons.

One light still shone on him; alas, through a medium more and more turbid: the light from Heaven. His Bible was there, wherein must lie healing for all sorrows. To the Bible he more and more exclusively addressed himself. If it is the written Word of God, shall it not be the acted Word too?

Is it mere sound, then; black printer's-ink on white rag-paper? A half-man could have passed on without answering; a whole man must answer. Hence Prophecies of Millenniums, Gifts of Tongues,—whereat Orthodoxy prims herself into decent wonder, and waves her, Avaunt! Irving clave to his Belief, as to his soul's soul; followed it whithersoever, through earth or air, it might lead him; toiling as never man toiled to spread it, to gain the world's ear for it,—in vain. Ever wilder waxed the confusion without and within. The misguided noble-minded had now nothing left to do but die. He died the death of the true and brave. His last words, they say, were: "In life and in death I am the Lord's."—Amen! Amen!

One who knew him well, and may with good cause love him, has said: "But for Irving, I had never known what the communion of man with man means. His was the freest, brotherliest, bravest human soul mine ever came in contact with: I call him, on the whole, the best man I have ever, after trial enough, found in this world, or now hope to find.

"The first time I saw Irving was six-and-twenty years ago, in his native town, Annan. He was fresh from Edinburgh, with College prizes, high character and promise; he had come to see our Schoolmaster, who had also been his. We heard of famed Professors, of high matters classical, mathematical, a whole Wonderland of Knowledge: nothing but joy, health, hopefulness without end, looked out from the blooming young man. The last time I saw him was three months ago, in London. Friendliness still beamed in his eyes, but now from amid unquiet fire; his face was flaccid, wasted, unsound; hoary as with extreme age: he was trembling over the brink of the grave.—Adieu, thou first Friend; adieu, while this confused Twilight of Existence lasts! Might we meet where Twilight has become Day!"

LETTER TO J. W. VON GOETHE

[The Carlyle-Goethe correspondence arose as a result of Carlyle's intense interest in German literature and thought and his frequent essays on German matters. In the following letter Carlyle discusses some aspects of the state of German studies in England at the time and, toward the end, refers to his work on what was to become *Sartor Resartus* ("a Piece more immediately my own"), which he was soon to take to London in an unsuccessful attempt to find a publisher for it.]

LETTER TO GOETHE, *Weimar*
Craigenputtock, Dumfries, 10 June 1831

My dear and honoured Friend—If kind thoughts spontaneously transformed themselves into kind messages, you had many times heard from me since I last wrote. Here in our still solitudes, where the actual world is so little seen, and Memory and Fancy must be the busier, Weimar is not distant but near and friendly, a familiar city of the Mind. Daily must I send affectionate wishes thither; daily must I think, and oftenest speak also, of the Man to whom, more than to any other living, I stand indebted and united. For it can never be forgotten that to him I owe the all-precious knowledge and experience that Reverence is still possible, nay, Reverence for our fellow-man, as a true emblem of the Highest, even in these perturbed, chaotic times. That you have carried and will yet carry such life-giving Light into many a soul, wandering bewildered in the eclipse of Doubt; till at length whole generations have cause to bless you, that instead of Conjecturing and Denying they can again Believe and Know: herein truly is a Sovereignty of quite indisputable Legitimacy, and which it is our only Freedom to obey.

In anxious hours, when one is apt to figure misfortune for the absent and dear, I often look timorously into the Foreign Column of our Newspapers, lest it bring evil tidings of you, to me also so evil; again, I delight to figure you as still active and serene; busy at your high Task, in the high spirit of old Times.—*Wie das Gestirn, Ohne Hast, Aber Ohne Rast!*—May I beg for my own behoof, some few of those moments which belong to the world? It is chiefly in the hope of drawing a Letter from Weimar that I now write in the Scottish wilderness, where there can be so little to communicate. Our promised Packet has been detained longer than we looked for, and diminished in contents; by a circumstance, however, which, we hope, will render it the welcomer when it comes. We send it, this time, by London, where also it will have to linger, and be finally made up under the eye of a Proxy. For in that city, let me announce, there is a little poetic *Tugendbund* of Philo-Germans forming itself, whereof you are the Centre; the first public act of which should come to light at Weimar, on your approaching Birthday. That the Craigenputtock Packet might carry any little documents of *this* along with it, was the cause of our delay, and of the new route fixed on. In London, with which I can only communicate by writing, matters move slower than I could wish: nevertheless, it is confidently reckoned, the whole will be ready in time, and either through the hands of Messrs. Parish at Hamburg, or of the British Ambassador at Berlin, appear at Weimar before the 28 of August, where doubtless it will meet with the old friendly reception.

Of this little Philo-German Combination, and what it now specially proposes, and whether there is likelihood that it may grow into a more lasting union, for more complex purposes,—I hope to speak hereafter. The mere fact that such an attempt was possible among us, would have seemed strange some years ago; and gives one of many proofs that what you have named *World-Literature* is perhaps already not so distant. To the Berlin Friends from whom lately came a friendly Note, I purpose communicating some intelligence of this affair: it may be, we too in London shall have a little *Society for Foreign Literature*; which, in these days, I should regard as of good promise.

The chief item in our Packet for Weimar will be the Proof-sheets of my poor contributions as a Foreign Reviewer; the most of which I have had stitched up into a volume for your acceptance, till I can offer the whole in another form. If the last number of the *Edinburgh Review* has fallen into your hands, you have already seen the newest of these, the *Criticism of Taylor*; likewise in the same number, an Essay on the *Correspondence with Schiller*. This latter is by a Mr. Empson, a man of some rank and very considerable talent and learning; in whose spiritual progress, as manifested in his study of German, I see a curious triumph of Truth and

Belief over Falsehood and Dilettantism. He was the Reviewer of *Faust* in a former number; and on this occasion, still leaving somewhat to desire, he has greatly surpassed my expectations. Of young men that have an open sense for such Literature as the German, or of mature men that from youth upwards have been acquiring an open sense, there are now not a few in Britain: but the Critic here in question started at middle age, as I understand, and only a few years ago, from quite another point; is an *English Whig Politician,* which means generally a man of altogether mechanical intellect, looking to Elegance, Excitement, and a certain refined Utility, as the Highest; a man halting between two Opinions, and calling it Tolerance; to whom, on the whole, that Precept, *Im Ganzen, Guten, Wahren resolut zu leben,* were altogether a dead letter. How in this case the dry bones, blown upon by Heavenly Inspiration, have been made to live; and a naturally gifted spirit is freeing itself from that death-sleep,—is to me an interesting Phenomenon. It is on such grounds that the study of the best German writings is so incalculably important for us English at this Epoch. I am happy to report anew, that we make rapid progress in the matter; that the ultimate recognition and appropriation of what is worthy in German literature by all cultivated English minds, may be considered as not only indubitable, but even likely to be speedy.

For myself, though my labours in that province have of late been partially suspended, I hope they are yet nowise concluded. The *History,* when it sees the light, may be no worse for having waited; already, simply by the influence of Time, various matters have cleared up, and the form of the whole is much more decisively before me. As occasion serves, I can, either at once, or gradually as hitherto, speak out what further I have to say on it. But for these last months I have been busy with a Piece more immediately my own: of this, should it ever become a printed volume, and seem in the smallest worthy of such honour, a copy for Weimar will not be wanting. Alas! It is, after all, not a Picture that I am painting; it is but a half-reckless casting of the brush, with its many frustrated colours, against the canvas: whether it will make good Foam is still a venture.

In some six weeks I expect to be in London: I wish to look a little with my own eyes at the world; where much is getting enigmatic to me, so rapid have been its vicissitudes lately. The mountain-solitude, with its silent verdure and foliage, will be sweeter for the change; and my efforts there more precisely directed.

Here, however, are the limits of my paper, when there was scarcely a beginning of my utterance. How poor is all that a Letter, how poor were all that words, could say, when the heart is so full! Do you interpret for me, and of broken stammerings make speech.

Think now and then of your Scottish Friends; and know always that a Prophet is not without honour, that we love and reverence our Prophet. My wife unites with me in every friendliest wish. May all Good be with you and yours!— Ever your affectionate.

T. Carlyle.

LETTER ON *SARTOR RESARTUS*

[The following letter is Carlyle's offer of *Sartor Resartus* for serial publication in *Fraser's Magazine,* his second major attempt to market the manuscript and ultimately a successful one. The passage that follows is one of Carlyle's few sustained descriptions of the nature of *Sartor*.]

FROM A LETTER TO MR. FRASER, PUBLISHER, *London*

Craigenputtock, 27 May 1833

Most probably you recollect the Manuscript *Book* I had with me in London; and how during that Reform hurly-burly, which unluckily still continues and is like to continue, I failed to make any bargain about it. The Manuscript still lies in my drawer; and now after long deliberation I have determined to slit it up into strips, and send it forth in the Periodical way; for which in any case it was perhaps better adapted. The pains I took with the composition of it, truly, were greater than even I might have thought necessary, had this been foreseen: but what then? Care of that sort is never altogether thrown away; far better too much than too little. I reckon that it will be easy for the Magazine Printer to save me some thirty or forty complete copies, as he prints it; these can then be bound up and distributed among my Friends likely to profit thereby; and in the end of all we can *re*print it into a Book proper, if that seem good. Your Magazine is the first I think of for this object; and I must have got a distinct negative from you before I go any farther. Listen to me, then, and judge.

The Book is at present named "Thoughts on Clothes; or Life and Opinions of Herr D. Teufelsdröckh, D. U. J."; but perhaps we might see right to alter the title a little; for the rest, some brief Introduction could fit it handsomely enough into its new destination: it is already divided into three "Books," and farther into very short "Chapters," capable in all ways of subdivision. Nay some tell me, what perhaps is true, that taking a few chapters at a time is really the profitablest way of reading it. There may be in all some Eight sheets of *Fraser*. It is put together in the fashion of a kind of Didactic Novel; but indeed properly *like* nothing yet extant: I used to characterise it briefly as a kind of "Satirical Extravaganza on Things in General"; it contains more of my opinions on Art, Politics, Religion, Heaven, Earth and Air, than all the things I have yet written. The Creed promulgated on all these things, as you may judge, is *mine,* and firmly *believed:* for the rest, the main Actor in the business ("Editor of these Sheets," as he often calls himself) assumes a kind of Conservative (though Anti-quack) character; and would suit *Fraser* perhaps better than any other Magazine. The ultimate result, however, I need hardly premise, is a deep religious speculative-radicalism (so I call it for want of a better name), with which you are already well enough acquainted in me.

There are only five persons that have yet read this Manuscript: of whom two have expressed themselves (I mean convinced me that they *are*) considerably interested and gratified; two quite struck, "overwhelmed with astonishment and new hope" (this is the result I aimed at for souls worthy of hope); and one in secret discontented and displeased. William Fraser is a sixth reader, or rather half-reader; for I think he had only got half-way or so; and I never learned his opinion. With him, if you like, at this stage of the business you can consult freely about it. My own conjecture is that *Teufelsdröckh,* whenever published, will astonish most that read it, be wholly understood by very few; but to the astonishment of some will add touches of (almost the deepest) spiritual interest, with others quite the opposite feeling. I think I can practically prophesy that for some six or eight months (for it must be published without interruption), it would be apt at least to *keep the eyes* of the Public on you. . . .

Sartor Resartus

1 8 3 3 - 1 8 3 4

[Carlyle wrote *Sartor Resartus* in Craigenputtock in 1830-1831, beginning first with the germ of the "Clothes Philosophy," later expanding the work to include a biography of Teufelsdröckh and a third speculative section. He travelled to London in August 1831 with the completed work, then called "Thoughts on Clothes," in an effort to find a publisher for it. The heterodoxy of Carlyle's opinions and manner in *Sartor,* coupled with the extreme uncertainty of the times in the face of widespread agitation over the Reform Bill then being debated in Parliament, made publishers reluctant to undertake the venture of printing the work. Carlyle returned to Craigenputtock in the spring of 1832 without having found a publisher. In May 1833 he determined to offer *Sartor* for publication again, this time to *Fraser's* for serialization. It was accepted and published from November 1833 to August 1834, except for January and May.

Perhaps the publishers in 1831 had not been unwisely cautious. *Sartor* evoked intensely unfavorable response upon its appearance in *Fraser's.* But there were a few enthusiastic readers and Ralph Waldo Emerson was one. He arranged for the publication of the work in Boston in 1836, the first book publication of *Sartor.* The first English edition appeared in 1838; another followed in 1840. By that time *The French Revolution* had won a public for Carlyle and *Sartor* prospered. It eventually became one of the best-selling books of the Victorian Age.

Sartor Resartus is at once Carlyle's most perplexing and most characteristic work. It contains the ideas he was to elaborate for the rest of his career, and it exhibits the electrifying style that came to be known as Carlylese and that is as much Carlyle's trademark as his ideas. It is also a work of considerable artistic complexity and sophistication. Simultaneously essay and fiction, fantasy and social criticism, biography and autobiography, *Sartor Resartus* is a dazzling tour de force by one of the most inventive masters of English prose.

The central idea of the work lies in the title, which means the "tailor retailored," or the "patcher repatched," whereby Carlyle undertakes to refashion common ideas about life and society. All comes under the figure of clothing. When the eccentric German Professor of Things in General, Diogenes Teufelsdröckh (God-begotten Devil's-dung), writes his history of clothing, *Die*

Kleider, ihr Werden und Wirken (Clothes, their Origin and Influence), he finds that everything under the sun can be seen as one form or another of clothing: ideas, institutions, manners, aristocracies, religions—all are kinds of outward representations. All life is, in short, symbolic. What Teufelsdröckh's insight means is that all external reality is but the expression of a greater reality. That greater reality is the Divine Idea of the World, the momentous fact of God's existence and His maintenance of the universe. When, however, the outward forms no longer conform to any transcendent reality, the time is out of joint. Such is the condition of the contemporary world. Modern society is garbed in old clothes that increasingly fail to conceal inward emptiness. They must be retailored, indeed are even now being fashioned in mysterious ways ("organic filaments"), for the world cannot indefinitely ignore transcendent reality.

In order to present this thesis, Carlyle adopted an extremely complex structure, but one that comes clear on a little examination. The book is divided into three parts. The first part is the presentation of the Professor through the agency of a British editor who seeks to introduce *Die Kleider* to English readers. Part two is the biography of Teufelsdröckh as extracted by the Editor from autobiographical fragments in six paper bags. Part three is the presentation of the metaphysical and social applications of the Clothes Philosophy. The whole work is an unfolding and penetration of the life and thought of Teufelsdröckh and is designed to be grasped in its entirety rather than in parts. So it is presented here. But the passages that have become best known are those relating to Teufelsdröckh's despair and subsequent attainment of a positive belief (from the "Everlasting No" to the "Everlasting Yea" in Book II) and the heart of the Clothes Philosophy (from "Symbols" to "Natural Supernaturalism" in Book III).

No outline can do justice to the variety and range of *Sartor Resartus*. The foregoing is merely a starting point for a work that bubbles with an inexhaustible vitality and allusiveness, that encompasses rhapsodic joys and depths of sorrow.]

SARTOR RESARTUS

The Life and Opinions

of

Herr Teufelsdröckh

Mein Vermächtniss, wie herrlich weit und breit!
Die Zeit ist mein Vermächtniss, mein Acker ist die Zeit.

[My inheritance how wide and fair!
Time is my fair seed-field, of Time I'm heir.]

GOETHE

Die Welt ist ein Universaltropus des Geistes, ein sym-
bolisches Bild desselben . . .

[The world is a universal trope of the spirit, a symbolic picture of it.]

NOVALIS

Nicht blosses Wissen, sondern nach deinem Wissen
Thun *ist deine Bestimmung.*

[Not mere knowledge, but according to your knowledge
Doing is your commitment.]

FICHTE

BOOK FIRST / CHAPTER I

PRELIMINARY

No Philosophy of Clothes yet, notwithstanding all our Science. Strangely forgotten that Man is by nature a naked animal. The English mind all-too practically absorbed for any such inquiry. Not so, deep-thinking Germany. Advantage of Speculation having free course. Editor receives from Professor Teufelsdröckh his new Work on Clothes.

Considering our present advanced state of culture, and how the Torch of Science has now been brandished and borne about, with more or less effect, for five thousand years and upwards; how, in these times especially, not only the Torch still burns, and perhaps more fiercely than ever, but innumerable Rush-lights, and Sulphur-matches, kindled thereat, are also glancing in every direction, so that not the smallest cranny or doghole in Nature or Art can remain unilluminated,—it might strike the reflective mind with some surprise that hitherto little or nothing of a fundamental character, whether in the way of Philosophy or History, has been written on the subject of Clothes.

Our Theory of Gravitation is as good as perfect: Lagrange, it is well known, has proved that the Planetary System, on this scheme, will endure forever; Laplace, still more cunningly, even guesses that it could not have been made on any other scheme. Whereby, at least, our nautical Logbooks can be better kept; and water-transport of all kinds has grown more commodious. Of Geology and Geognosy we know enough: what with the labours of our Werners and Huttons, what with the ardent genius of their disciples, it has come about that now, to many a Royal Society, the Creation of a World is little more mysterious than the cooking of a dumpling; concerning which last, indeed, there have been minds to whom the question, *How the apples were got in,* presented difficulties. Why mention our disquisitions on the Social Contract, on the Standard of Taste, on the Migrations of the Herring? Then, have we not a Doctrine of Rent, a Theory of Value; Philosophies of Language, of History, of Pottery, of Apparitions, of Intoxicating Liquors? Man's whole life and environment have been laid open and elucidated; scarcely a fragment or fibre of his Soul, Body, and Possessions, but has been probed, dissected, distilled, desiccated, and scientifically decomposed: our spiritual Faculties, of which it appears there are not a few, have their Stewarts, Cousins, Royer Collards: every cellular, vascular, muscular Tissue glories in its Lawrences, Majendies, Bichâts.

How, then, comes it, may the reflective mind repeat, that the grand Tissue of all Tissues, the only real Tissue, should have been quite overlooked by Science,—the vestural Tissue, namely, of woollen or other cloth; which Man's Soul wears as its outmost wrappage and overall; wherein his whole other Tissues are included and screened, his whole Faculties work, his whole Self lives, moves, and has its being? For if, now and then, some straggling broken-winged thinker has cast an owl's-glance into this obscure region, the most have soared over it altogether heedless; regarding Clothes as a property, not an accident, as quite natural and spontaneous, like the leaves of trees, like the plumage of birds. In all speculations they have tacitly figured man as a *Clothed Animal*; whereas he is by nature a *Naked Animal*; and only in certain circumstances, by purpose and device, masks himself in Clothes. Shakespeare says, we are creatures that look before and after: the more surprising that we do not look round a little, and see what is passing under our very eyes.

But here, as in so many other cases, Germany, learned, indefatigable, deep-thinking Germany comes to our aid. It is, after all, a blessing that, in these revolutionary times, there should be one country where abstract Thought can still take shelter; that while the din and frenzy of Catholic Emancipations, and Rotten Boroughs, and Revolts of Paris, deafen every French and every English ear, the German can stand peaceful on his scientific watch-tower; and, to the raging, struggling multitude here and elsewhere, solemnly, from hour to hour, with preparatory blast of cowhorn, emit his *Höret ihr Herren und lasset's Euch sagen*; in other words, tell the Universe, which so often forgets that fact, what o'clock it really is. Not unfrequently the Germans have been blamed for an unprofitable diligence; as if they struck into devious courses, where nothing was to be had but the toil of a rough journey; as if, forsaking the gold-mines of finance and that political slaughter of fat oxen whereby a man himself grows fat, they were apt to run goose-hunting into regions of bilberries and crowberries, and be swallowed up at last in remote peat-bogs. Of that unwise science, which, as our Humorist expresses it,

'By geometric scale
Doth take the size of pots of ale;'

still more, of that altogether misdirected industry, which is seen vigorously thrashing mere straw, there can nothing defensive be said. In so far as the Germans are chargeable with such, let them take the consequence. Nevertheless be it remarked, that even a Russian steppe has tumuli and gold ornaments; also many a scene that looks desert and rock-bound from the distance, will unfold itself, when visited, into rare valleys. Nay, in any case, would Criticism erect not only finger-posts and turnpikes, but spiked gates and impassable barriers, for the mind of man? It is written, 'Many shall run to and fro, and knowledge shall be increased.' Surely the plain rule is, Let each considerate person have his way, and see what it will lead to. For not this man and that man, but all men make up mankind, and their united tasks the task of mankind. How often have we seen some such adventurous, and perhaps much-censured wanderer light on some out-lying, neglected, yet vitally momentous province; the hidden treasures of which he first discovered, and kept proclaiming till the general eye and effort were directed thither, and the conquest was completed;—thereby, in these his seemingly so aimless rambles, planting new standards, founding new habitable colonies, in the immeasurable circumambient realm of Nothingness and Night! Wise man was he who counselled that Speculation should have free course, and look fearlessly towards all the thirty-two points of the compass, whithersoever and howsoever it listed.

Perhaps it is proof of the stunted condition in which pure Science, especially pure moral Science, languishes among us English; and how our mercantile greatness, and invaluable Constitution, impressing a political or other immediately practical tendency on all English culture and endeavour, cramps the free flight of Thought,—that this, not Philosophy of Clothes, but recognition even that we have no such Philosophy, stands here for the first time published in our language. What English intellect could have chosen such a topic, or by chance stumbled on it? But for that same unshackled, and even sequestered condition of the German Learned, which permits and induces them to fish in all manner of waters, with all manner of nets, it seems probable enough, this abstruse Inquiry might, in spite of the results it leads to, have continued dormant for indefinite periods. The Editor of these sheets, though otherwise boasting himself a man of confirmed speculative habits, and perhaps discursive enough, is free to confess, that never, till these last months, did the above very plain considerations, on our total want of a Philosophy of Clothes, occur to him; and then, by quite foreign suggestion. By the arrival, namely, of a new Book from Professor Teufelsdröckh of Weissnichtwo; treating expressly of this subject, and in a style which, whether understood or not, could not even by the blindest be overlooked. In the present Editor's way of thought, this remarkable Treatise, with its Doctrines, whether as judicially acceded to, or judicially denied, has not remained without effect.

'*Die Kleider, ihr Werden und Wirken* (Clothes, their Origin and Influence): *von Diog. Teufelsdröckh, J.U.D. etc. Stillschweigen und Co* ^gnie^. *Weissnichtwo,* 1831.

'Here,' says the *Weissnichtwo'sche Anzeiger,* 'comes a Volume of that extensive, close-printed, close-meditated sort, which, be it spoken with pride, is seen only in Germany, perhaps only in Weissnichtwo. Issuing from the hitherto irreproachable Firm of Stillschweigen and Company, with every external furtherance, it is of such internal quality as to set Neglect at defiance.' * * * * 'A work,' concludes the well-nigh enthusiastic Reviewer, 'interesting alike to the antiquary, the historian, and the philosophic thinker; a masterpiece of boldness, lynx-eyed acuteness, and rugged independent Germanism and Philanthropy (*derber Kerndeutschheit und Menschenliebe*); which will not, assuredly, pass current without opposition in high places; but must and will exalt the almost new name of Teufelsdröckh to the first ranks of Philosophy, in our German Temple of Honour.'

Mindful of old friendship, the distinguished Professor, in this the first blaze of his fame, which however does not dazzle him, sends hither a Presentation-copy of his Book; with compliments and encomiums which modesty forbids the present Editor to rehearse; yet without indicated wish or hope of any kind, except what may be implied in the concluding phrase: *Möchte es* (this remarkable Treatise) *auch im Brittischen Boden gedeihen!*

CHAPTER II

EDITORIAL DIFFICULTIES

How to make known Teufelsdröckh and his Book to English readers; especially such a book? Editor receives from the Hofrath Heuschrecke a letter promising Biographic Documents. Negotiations with Oliver Yorke. Sartor Resartus *conceived. Editor's assurances and advice to his British reader.*

If for a speculative man, 'whose seedfield,' in the sublime words of the Poet, 'is Time,' no conquest is important but that of new ideas, then might the arrival of Professor Teufelsdröckh's Book be marked with chalk in the Editor's calendar. It is indeed an 'extensive Volume,' of boundless, almost formless contents, a very Sea of Thought; neither calm nor clear, if you will; yet wherein the toughest pearl-diver may dive to his utmost depth, and return not only with sea-wreck but with true orients.

Directly on the first perusal, almost on the first deliberate inspection, it became apparent that here a quite new Branch of Philosophy, leading to as yet undescried ulterior results, was disclosed; farther, what seemed scarcely less interesting, a quite new human Individuality, an almost unexampled personal character, that, namely, of Professor Teufelsdröckh the Discloser. Of both which novelties, as far as might be possible, we resolved to master the significance. But as man is emphatically a proselytising creature, no sooner was such mastery even fairly attempted, than the new question arose: How might this acquired good be imparted to others, perhaps in equal need thereof: how could the philosophy of Clothes, and the Author of such Philosophy, be brought home, in any measure, to the business and bosoms of our own English Nation? For if new-got gold is said to burn the pockets till it be cast forth into circulation, much more may new truth.

Here, however, difficulties occurred. The first thought naturally was to publish Article after Article on this remarkable Volume, in such widely-circulating Critical Journals as the Editor might stand connected with, or by money or love procure access to. But, on the other hand, was it not clear that such matter as must here be revealed, and treated of, might endanger the circulation of any Journal extant? If, indeed, all party-divisions in the State, could have been abolished, Whig, Tory, and Radical, embracing in discrepant union; and all the Journals of the Nation could have been jumbled into one Journal, and the Philosophy of Clothes poured forth in incessant torrents therefrom, the attempt had seemed possible. But, alas, what vehicle of that sort have we, except *Fraser's Magazine?* A vehicle all strewed (figuratively speaking) with the maddest Waterloo-Crackers, exploding distractively and destructively, wheresoever the mystified passenger stands or sits; nay, in any case, understood to be, of late years, a vehicle full to overflowing, and inexorably shut! Besides, to state the Philosophy of Clothes without the Philosopher, the ideas of Teufelsdröckh without something of his personality, was it not to insure both of entire misapprehension? Now for Biography, had it been otherwise admissible, there were no adequate documents, no hope of obtaining such, but rather, owing to circumstances, a special despair. Thus did the Editor see himself, for the while, shut out from all public utterance of these extraordinary Doctrines, and constrained to revolve them, not without disquietude, in the dark depths of his own mind.

So had it lasted for some months; and now the Volume on Clothes, read and again read, was in several points becoming lucid and lucent; the personality of its Author more and more surprising, but, in spite of all that memory and conjecture could do, more and more enigmatic; whereby the old disquietude seemed fast settling into fixed discontent, —when altogether unexpectedly arrives a Letter from Herr Hofrath Heuschrecke, our Professor's chief friend and associate in Weissnichtwo, with whom we had not previously corresponded. The Hofrath, after much quite extraneous matter, began dilating largely on the 'agitation and attention' which the Philosophy of Clothes was exciting in its own German Republic of Letters; on the deep significance and tendency of his Friend's Volume; and then, at length, with great circumlocution, hinted at the practicability of conveying 'some knowledge of it, and of him, to England, and through England to the distant West': a work on Professor Teufelsdröckh 'were undoubtedly welcome to the *Family,* the *National,* or any other of those patriotic *Li-*

braries, at present the glory of British Literature'; might work revolutions in Thought; and so forth;—in conclusion, intimating not obscurely, that should the present Editor feel disposed to undertake a Biography of Teufelsdröckh, he, Hofrath Heuschrecke, had it in his power to furnish the requisite Documents.

As in some chemical mixture, that has stood long evaporating, but would not crystallise, instantly when the wire or other fixed substance is introduced, crystallisation commences, and rapidly proceeds till the whole is finished, so was it with the Editor's mind and this offer of Heuschrecke's. Form rose out of void solution and discontinuity; like united itself with like in definite arrangement: and soon either in actual vision and possession, or in fixed reasonable hope, the image of the whole Enterprise had shaped itself, so to speak, into a solid mass. Cautiously yet courageously, through the twopenny post, application to the famed redoubtable OLIVER YORKE was now made: an interview, interviews with that singular man have taken place; with more of assurance on our side, with less of satire (at least of open satire) on his, than we anticipated;—for the rest, with such issue as is now visible. As to those same 'patriotic *Libraries,*' the Hofrath's counsel could only be viewed with silent amazement; but with his offer of Documents we joyfully and almost instantaneously closed. Thus, too, in the sure expectation of these, we already see our task begun; and this our *Sartor Resartus,* which is properly a 'Life and Opinions of Herr Teufelsdröckh,' hourly advancing.

Of our fitness for the Enterprise, to which we have such title and vocation, it were perhaps uninteresting to say more. Let the British reader study and enjoy, in simplicity of heart, what is here presented him, and with whatever metaphysical acumen and talent for meditation he is possessed of. Let him strive to keep a free, open sense; cleared from the mists of prejudice, above all from the paralysis of cant; and directed rather to the Book itself than to the Editor of the Book. Who or what such Editor may be, must remain conjectural, and even insignificant:[1] it is a voice publishing tidings of the Philosophy of Clothes; undoubtedly a Spirit addressing Spirits: whoso hath ears, let him hear.

---

[1] With us even he still communicates in some sort of mask, or muffler; and, we have reason to think, under a feigned name!—O.Y. [Carlyle's note.]

On one other point the Editor thinks it needful to give warning: namely, that he is animated with a true though perhaps a feeble attachment to the Institutions of our Ancestors; and minded to defend these, according to ability, at all hazards; nay, it was partly with a view to such defence that he engaged in this undertaking. To stem, or if that be impossible, profitably to divert the current of Innovation, such a Volume as Teufelsdröckh's, if cunningly planted down, were no despicable pile, or floodgate, in the logical wear.

For the rest, be it nowise apprehended, that any personal connexion of ours with Teufelsdröckh, Heuschrecke, or this Philosophy of Clothes, can pervert our judgment, or sway us to extenuate or exaggerate. Powerless, we venture to promise, are those private Compliments themselves. Grateful they may well be; as generous illusions of friendship; as fair mementos of bygone unions, of those nights and suppers of the gods, when, lapped in the symphonies and harmonies of Philosophic Eloquence, though with baser accompaniments, the present Editor revelled in that feast of reason, never since vouchsafed him in so full measure! But what then? *Amicus Plato, magis amica veritas*; Teufelsdröckh is our friend, Truth is our divinity. In our historical and critical capacity, we hope we are strangers to all the world; have feud or favour with no one,—save indeed the Devil, with whom, as with the Prince of Lies and Darkness, we do at all times wage internecine war. This assurance, at an epoch when puffery and quackery have reached a height unexampled in the annals of mankind, and even English Editors, like Chinese Shopkeepers, must write on their door-lintels *No cheating here*,—we thought it good to premise.

CHAPTER III

REMINISCENCES

Teufelsdröckh at Weissnichtwo. Professor of Things in General at the University there: Outward aspect and character; memorable coffee-house utterances; domicile and watch-tower: Sights thence of City-Life by day and by night; with reflections thereon. Old 'Liza and her ways. Character of Hofrath Heuschrecke, and his relation to Teufelsdröckh.

To the Author's private circle the appearance of this singular Work on Clothes must have occasioned little less surprise than it has to the rest of the world. For ourselves, at least, few things have been more unexpected. Professor Teufelsdröckh, at the period of our acquaintance with him, seemed to lead a quite still and self-contained life: a man devoted to the higher Philosophies, indeed; yet more likely, if he published at all, to publish a refutation of Hegel and Bardili, both of whom, strangely enough, he included under a common ban; than to descend, as he has here done, into the angry noisy Forum, with an Argument that cannot but exasperate and divide. Not, that we can remember, was the Philosophy of Clothes once touched upon between us. If through the high, silent, meditative Transcendentalism of our Friend we detected any practical tendency whatever, it was at most Political, and towards a certain prospective, and for the present quite speculative, Radicalism; as indeed some correspondence, on his part, with Herr Oken of Jena was now and then suspected; though his special contributions to the *Isis* could never be more than surmised at. But, at all events, nothing Moral, still less anything Didactico-Religious, was looked for from him.

Well do we recollect the last words he spoke in our hearing; which indeed, with the Night they were uttered in, are to be forever remembered. Lifting his huge tumbler of *Gukguk*,[1] and for a moment lowering his tobacco-pipe, he stood up in full coffeehouse (it was *Zur Grünen Gans,* the largest in Weissnichtwo, where all the Virtuosity, and nearly all the Intellect of the place assembled of an evening); and there, with low, soul-stirring tone, and the look truly of an angel, though whether of a white or of a black one might be dubious, proposed this toast: *Die Sache der Armen in Gottes und Teufels Namen* (The Cause of the Poor, in Heaven's name and ——'s)! One full shout, breaking the leaden silence; then a gurgle of innumerable emptying bumpers, again followed by universal cheering, returned him loud acclaim. It was the finale of the night: resuming their pipes; in the highest enthusiasm, amid volumes of tobacco-smoke; triumphant, cloud-capt without and within, the assembly broke up, each to his thoughtful pillow. *Bleibt doch ein echter Spass- und Galgen-vogel,* said several; meaning thereby that, one day, he would probably be hanged

[1] Gukguk is unhappily only an academical—beer. [Carlyle's note.]

for his democratic sentiments. *Wo steckt doch der Schalk?* added they, looking round: but Teufelsdröckh had retired by private alleys, and the Compiler of these pages beheld him no more.

In such scenes has it been our lot to live with this Philosopher, such estimate to form of his purposes and powers. And yet, thou brave Teufelsdröckh, who could tell what lurked in thee? Under those thick locks of thine, so long and lank, overlapping roof-wise the gravest face we ever in this world saw, there dwelt a most busy brain. In thy eyes too, deep under their shaggy brows, and looking out so still and dreamy, have we not noticed gleams of an ethereal or else a diabolic fire, and half-fancied that their stillness was but the rest of infinite motion, the *sleep* of a spinning-top? Thy little figure, there as, in loose ill-brushed threadbare habiliments, thou sattest, amid litter and lumber, whole days, to 'think and smoke tobacco,' held in it a mighty heart. The secrets of man's Life were laid open to thee; thou sawest into the mystery of the Universe, farther than another; thou hadst *in petto* thy remarkable Volume on Clothes. Nay, was there not in that clear logically-founded Transcendentalism of thine; still more, in thy meek, silent, deep-seated Sans-culottism, combined with a true princely Courtesy of inward nature, the visible rudiments of such speculation? But great men are too often unknown, or what is worse, mis-known. Already, when we dreamed not of it, the warp of thy remarkable Volume lay on the loom; and silently, mysterious shuttles were putting-in the woof!

How the Hofrath Heuschrecke is to furnish biographical data, in this case, may be a curious question; the answer of which, however, is happily not our concern, but his. To us it appeared, after repeated trial, that in Weissnichtwo, from the archives or memories of the best-informed classes, no Biography of Teufelsdröckh was to be gathered; not so much as a false one. He was a stranger there, wafted thither by what is called the course of circumstances; concerning whose parentage, birthplace, prospects, or pursuits, curiosity had indeed made inquiries, but satisfied herself with the most indistinct replies. For himself, he was a man so still and altogether unparticipating, that to question him even afar off on such particulars was a thing of more than usual delicacy: besides, in his sly way, he had ever some quaint turn, not without its satirical edge, wherewith to divert such intrusions, and deter you from the like. Wits spoke of him secretly as if he were a kind of Melchizedek, without father or mother of any kind; sometimes, with reference to his great historic and statistic knowledge, and the vivid way he had of expressing himself like an eye-witness of distant transactions and scenes, they called him the *Ewige Jude,* Everlasting, or as we say, Wandering Jew.

To the most, indeed, he had become not so much a Man as a Thing; which Thing doubtless they were accustomed to see, and with satisfaction; but no more thought of accounting for than for the fabrication of their daily *Allgemeine Zeitung,* or the domestic habits of the Sun. Both were there and welcome; the world enjoyed what good was in them, and thought no more of the matter. The man Teufelsdröckh passed and repassed, in his little circle, as one of those originals and nondescripts, more frequent in German Universities than elsewhere; of whom, though you see them alive, and feel certain enough that they must have a History, no History seems to be discoverable; or only such as men give of mountain rocks and antediluvian ruins: That they have been created by unknown agencies, are in a state of gradual decay, and for the present reflect light and resist pressure; that is, are visible and tangible objects in this phantasm world, where so much other mystery is.

It was to be remarked that though, by title and diploma, *Professor der Allerley-Wissenschaft,* or as we should say in English, 'Professor of Things in General,' he had never delivered any Course; perhaps never been incited thereto by any public furtherance or requisition. To all appearance, the enlightened Government of Weissnichtwo, in founding their New University, imagined they had done enough, if 'in times like ours,' as the half-official Program expressed it, 'when all things are, rapidly or slowly, resolving themselves into Chaos, a Professorship of this kind had been established; whereby, as occasion called, the task of bodying somewhat forth again from such Chaos might be, even slightly, facilitated.' That actual Lectures should be held, and Public Classes for the 'Science of Things in General,' they doubtless considered premature; on which ground too they had only established the Professorship, nowise endowed it; so that Teufelsdröckh, 'recommended by the highest Names,' had been promoted thereby to a Name merely.

Great, among the more enlightened classes, was the admiration of this new Professorship: how an enlightened Government had seen into the Want of the Age (*Zeit-bedürfniss*); how at length, instead of Denial and Destruction, we were to have a science of Affirmation and Reconstruction; and Germany and Weissnichtwo were where they should be, in the vanguard of the world. Considerable also was the wonder at the new Professor, dropt opportunely enough into the nascent University; so able to lecture, should occasion call; so ready to hold his peace for indefinite periods, should an enlightened Government consider that occasion did not call. But such admiration and such wonder, being followed by no act to keep them living, could last only nine days; and, long before our visit to that scene, had quite died away. The more cunning heads thought it was all an expiring clutch at popularity, on the part of a Minister, whom domestic embarrassments, court intrigues, old age, and dropsy soon afterwards finally drove from the helm.

As for Teufelsdröckh, except by his nightly appearances at the *Grüne Gans,* Weissnichtwo saw little of him, felt little of him. Here, over his tumbler of Gukguk, he sat reading Journals; sometimes contemplatively looking into the clouds of his tobacco-pipe, without other visible employment: always, from his mild ways, an agreeable phenomenon there; more especially when he opened his lips for speech; on which occasions the whole Coffee-house would hush itself into silence, as if sure to hear something noteworthy. Nay, perhaps to hear a whole series and river of the most memorable utterances; such as, when once thawed, he would for hours indulge in, with fit audience: and the more memorable, as issuing from a head apparently not more interested in them, not more conscious of them, than is the sculptured stone head of some public fountain, which through its brass mouth-tube emits water to the worthy and the unworthy; careless whether it be for cooking victuals or quenching conflagrations; indeed, maintains the same earnest assiduous look, whether any water be flowing or not.

To the Editor of these sheets, as to a young enthusiastic

Englishman, however unworthy, Teufelsdröckh opened himself perhaps more than to the most. Pity only that we could not then half guess his importance, and scrutinise him with due power of vision! We enjoyed, what not three men in Weissnichtwo could boast of, a certain degree of access to the Professor's private domicile. It was the attic floor of the highest house in the Wahngasse; and might truly be called the pinnacle of Weissnichtwo, for it rose sheer up above the contiguous roofs, themselves rising from elevated ground. Moreover, with its windows it looked towards all the four *Orte,* or as the Scotch say, and we ought to say, *Airts*: the sitting-room itself commanded three; another came to view in the *Schlafgemach* (bed-room) as the opposite end; to say nothing of the kitchen, which offered two, as it were, *duplicates,* and showing nothing new. So that it was in fact the speculum or watch-tower of Teufelsdröckh; wherefrom, sitting at ease, he might see the whole life-circulation of that considerable City; the streets and lanes of which, with all their doing and driving (*Thun und Treiben*), were for the most part visible there.

'I look down into all that wasp-nest or bee-hive,' have we heard him say, 'and witness their wax-laying and honey-making, and poison-brewing, and choking by sulphur. From the Palace esplanade, where music plays while Serene Highness is pleased to eat his victuals, down to the low lane, where in her door-sill the aged widow, knitting for a thin livelihood, sits to feel the afternoon sun, I see it all; for, except the Schlosskirche weathercock, no biped stands so high. Couriers arrive bestrapped and bebooted, bearing Joy and Sorrow bagged-up in pouches of leather; there, topladen, and with four swift horses, rolls-in the country Baron and his household; here, on timber-leg, the lamed Soldier hops painfully along, begging alms: a thousand carriages, and wains, and cars, come tumbling-in with Food, with young Rusticity, and other Raw Produce, inanimate or animate, and go tumbling out again with Produce manufactured. That living flood, pouring through these streets, of all qualities and ages, knowest thou whence it is coming, whither it is going? *Aus der Ewigkeit, zu der Ewigkeit hin*: From Eternity, onwards to Eternity! These are Apparitions: what else? Are they not Souls rendered visible: in Bodies, that took shape and will lose it, melting into air? Their solid Pavement is a Picture of the Sense; they walk on the bosom

of Nothing, blank Time is behind them and before them.
Or fanciest thou, the red and yellow Clothes-screen yonder, with spurs on its heels and feather in its crown, is but
of Today, without a Yesterday or a Tomorrow; and had
not rather its Ancestor alive when Hengst and Horsa over-
ran thy Island? Friend, thou seest here a living link in that
Tissue of History, which inweaves all Being: watch well, or
it will be past thee, and seen no more.

'Ach, mein Lieber!' said he once, at midnight, when we
had returned from the Coffee-house in rather earnest talk,
'it is a true sublimity to dwell here. These fringes of lamp-
light, struggling up through smoke and thousandfold exhala-
tion, some fathoms into the ancient reign of Night, what
thinks Boötes of them, as he leads his Hunting-dogs over
the Zenith in their leash of sidereal fire? That stifled hum
of Midnight, when Traffic has lain down to rest; and the
chariot-wheels of Vanity, still rolling here and there through
distant streets, are bearing her to Halls roofed-in, and lighted
to the due pitch for her; and only Vice and Misery, to prowl
or to moan like nightbirds, are abroad: that hum, I say,
like the stertorous, unquiet slumber of sick Life, is heard in
Heaven! Oh, under that hideous coverlet of vapours, and
putrefactions, and unimaginable gases, what a Fermenting-
vat lies simmering and hid! The joyful and the sorrowful
are there; men are dying there, men are being born; men
are praying,—on the other side of a brick partition, men are
cursing; and around them all is the vast, void Night. The
proud Grandee still lingers in his perfumed saloons, or reposes within damask curtains; Wretchedness cowers into
truckle-beds, or shivers hunger-stricken into its lair of straw:
in obscure cellars, *Rouge-et-Noir* languidly emits its voice-of-
destiny to haggard hungry Villains; while Councillors of
State sit plotting, and playing their high chess-game, whereof
the pawns are Men. The Lover whispers his mistress that
the coach is ready; and she, full of hope and fear, glides
down, to fly with him over the borders: the Thief, still
more silently, sets-to his picklocks and crowbars, or lurks in
wait till the watchmen first snore in their boxes. Gay man-
sions, with supper-rooms, and dancing-rooms, are full of
light and music and high-swelling hearts; but, in the Condemned Cells, the pulse of life beats tremulous and faint,
and bloodshot eyes look-out through the darkness, which is
around and within, for the light of a stern last morning.

Six men are to be hanged on the morrow: comes no hammering from the *Rabenstein?*—their gallows must even now be o'building. Upwards of five-hundred-thousand two-legged animals without feathers lie round us, in horizontal positions; their heads all in nightcaps, and full of the foolishest dreams. Riot cries aloud, and staggers and swaggers in his rank dens of shame; and the Mother, with streaming hair, kneels over her pallid dying infant, whose cracked lips only her tears now moisten.—All these heaped and huddled together, with nothing but a little carpentry and masonry between them;—crammed in, like salted fish in their barrel;—or weltering, shall I say, like an Egyptian pitcher of tamed vipers, each struggling to get its *head above* the others: *such* work goes on under that smoke-counterpane!—But I, *mein Werther,* sit above it all; I am alone with the Stars.'

We looked in his face to see whether, in the utterance of such extraordinary Night-thoughts, no feeling might be traced there; but with the light we had, which indeed was only a single tallow-light, and far enough from the window, nothing save that old calmness and fixedness was visible.

These were the Professor's talking seasons: most commonly he spoke in mere monosyllables, or sat altogether silent and smoked; while the visitor had liberty either to say what he listed, receiving for answer an occasional grunt; or to look round for a space, and then take himself away. It was a strange apartment; full of books and tattered papers, and miscellaneous shreds of all conceivable substances, 'united in a common element of dust.' Books lay on tables, and below tables; here fluttered a sheet of manuscript, there a torn handkerchief, or nightcap hastily thrown aside; ink-bottles alternated with bread-crusts, coffee-pots, tobacco-boxes, Periodical Literature, and Blücher Boots. Old Lieschen (Lisekin, 'Liza), who was his bed-maker and stove-lighter, his washer and wringer, cook, errand-maid, and general lion's-provider, and for the rest a very orderly creature, had no sovereign authority in this last citadel of Teufelsdröckh; only some once in the month she half-forcibly made her way thither, with broom and duster, and (Teufelsdröckh hastily saving his manuscripts) effected a partial clearance, a jail-delivery of such lumber as was not Literary. These were her *Erdbeben* (earthquakes), which Teufelsdröckh dreaded worse than the pestilence; nevertheless, to such length he had been forced to comply. Glad would he have been to sit here philosophising forever, or till the litter, by accumulation, drove him out of doors: but Lieschen was his right-arm, and spoon, and necessary of life, and would not be flatly gainsayed. We can still remember the ancient woman; so silent that some thought her dumb; deaf also you would often have supposed her; for Teufelsdröckh, and Teufelsdröckh only, would she serve or give heed to; and with him she seemed to communicate chiefly by signs; if it were not rather by some secret divination that she guessed all his wants, and supplied them. Assiduous old dame! she scoured, and sorted, and swept, in her kitchen, with the least possible violence to the ear; yet all was tight and right there: hot and black came the coffee ever at the due moment; and the speechless Lieschen herself looked out on you, from under her clean white coif with its lappets, through her clean withered face and wrinkles, with a look of helpful intelligence, almost of benevolence.

Few strangers, as above hinted, had admittance hither: the only one we ever saw there, ourselves excepted, was the Hofrath Heuschrecke, already known, by name and expectation, to the readers of these pages. To us, at that period, Herr Heuschrecke seemed one of those purse-mouthed, crane-necked, clean-brushed, pacific individuals, perhaps sufficiently distinguished in society by this fact, that, in dry weather or in wet, 'they never appear without their umbrella.' Had we not known with what 'little wisdom' the world is governed; and how, in Germany as elsewhere, the ninety-and-nine Public Men can for most part be but mute train-bearers to the hundredth, perhaps but stalking-horses and willing or unwilling dupes,—it might have seemed wonderful how Herr Heuschrecke should be named a *Rath*, or Councillor, and Counsellor, even in Weissnichtwo. What counsel to any man, or to any woman, could this particular Hofrath give; in whose loose, zigzag figure; in whose thin visage, as it went jerking to and fro, in minute incessant fluctuation,—you traced rather confusion worse confounded; at most, Timidity and physical Cold? Some indeed said withal, he was 'the very Spirit of Love embodied': blue earnest eyes, full of sadness and kindness; purse ever open, and so forth; the whole of which, we shall now hope, for many reasons, was not quite groundless. Nevertheless friend Teufelsdröckh's outline, who indeed handled the burin like few in these cases, was probably the best: *Er hat Gemüth und Geist, hat wenigstens gehabt, doch ohne Organ, ohne Schicksals-Gunst; ist gegenwärtig aber halb-zerrüttet, halb-erstarrt,* 'He has heart and talent, at least has had such, yet without fit mode of utterance, or favour of Fortune; and so is now half-cracked, half-congealed.'— What the Hofrath shall think of this when he sees it, readers may wonder: we, safe in the stronghold of Historical Fidelity, are careless.

The main point, doubtless, for us all, is his love of Teufelsdröckh, which indeed was also by far the most decisive feature of Heuschrecke himself. We are enabled to assert that he hung on the Professor with the fondness of a Boswell for his Johnson. And perhaps with the like return; for Teufelsdröckh treated his gaunt admirer with little outward regard, as some half-rational or altogether irrational friend, and at best loved him out of gratitude and by habit. On the other hand, it was curious to observe with what reverent kindness, and a sort of fatherly protection, our Hofrath, being the elder, richer, and as he fondly imagined far more practically influential of the two, looked and tended on his little Sage, whom he seemed to consider as a living oracle. Let but Teufelsdröckh open his mouth, Heuschrecke's also unpuckered itself into a free doorway, besides his being all eye and all ear, so that nothing might be lost: and then, at every pause in the harangue, he gurgled-out his pursy chuckle of a cough-laugh (for the machinery of laughter took some time to get in motion, and seemed crank and slack), or else his twanging nasal, *Bravo! Das glaub' ich;* in either case, by way of heartiest approval. In short, if Teufelsdröckh was Dalai-Lama, of which, except perhaps in his self-seclusion, and godlike indifference, there was no symptom, then might Heuschrecke pass for his chief Talapoin, to whom no dough-pill he could knead and publish was other than medicinal and sacred.

In such environment, social, domestic, physical, did Teufelsdröckh, at the time of our acquaintance, and most likely does he still, live and meditate. Here, perched-up in his high Wahngasse watch-tower, and often, in solitude, out-watching the Bear, it was that the indomitable Inquirer fought all his battles with Dulness and Darkness; here, in all probability, that he wrote this surprising Volume on

Clothes. Additional particulars: of his age, which was of that standing middle sort you could only guess at; of his wide surtout; the colour of his trousers, fashion of his broad-brimmed steeple-hat, and so forth, we might report, but do not. The Wisest truly is, in these times, the Greatest; so that an enlightened curiosity, leaving Kings and suchlike to rest very much on their own basis, turns more and more to the Philosophic Class: nevertheless, what reader expects that, with all our writing and reporting, Teufelsdröckh could be brought home to him, till once the Documents arrive? His Life, Fortunes, and Bodily Presence, are as yet hidden from us, or matter only of faint conjecture. But, on the other hand, does not his Soul lie enclosed in this remarkable Volume, much more truly than Pedro Garcia's did in the buried Bag of Doubloons? To the soul of Diogenes Teufelsdröckh, to his opinions, namely, on the 'Origin and Influence of Clothes,' we for the present gladly return.

CHAPTER IV

CHARACTERISTICS

Teufelsdröckh and his Work on Clothes: Strange freedom of speech; transcendentalism; force of insight and expression; multifarious learning: Style poetic, uncouth: Comprehensiveness of his humour and moral feeling. How the Editor once saw him laugh. Different kinds of Laughter and their significance.

It were a piece of vain flattery to pretend that this Work on Clothes entirely contents us; that it is not, like all works of genius, like the very Sun, which, though the highest published creation, or work of genius, has nevertheless black spots and troubled nebulosities amid its effulgence,—a mixture of insight, inspiration, with dulness, double-vision, and even utter blindness.

Without committing ourselves to those enthusiastic praises and prophesyings of the *Weissnichtwo'sche Anzeiger,* we admitted that the Book had in a high degree excited us to self-activity, which is the best effect of any book; that it had even operated changes in our way of thought; nay, that it promised to prove, as it were, the opening of a new mine-shaft, wherein the whole world of Speculation might henceforth dig to unknown depths. More especially it may now be declared that Professor Teufelsdröckh's acquirements, patience of research, philosophic and even poetic vigour, are here made indisputably manifest; and unhappily no less his prolixity and tortuosity and manifold ineptitude; that, on the whole, as in opening new mine-shafts is not unreasonable, there is much rubbish in his Book, though likewise specimens of almost invaluable ore. A paramount popularity in England we cannot promise him. Apart from the choice of such a topic as Clothes, too often the manner of treating it betokens in the Author a rusticity and academic seclusion, unblamable, indeed inevitable in a German, but fatal to his success with our public.

Of good society Teufelsdröckh appears to have seen little, or has mostly forgotten what he saw. He speaks-out with a strange plainness; calls many things by their mere dictionary names. To him the Upholsterer is no Pontiff, neither is any Drawing-room a Temple, were it never so begilt and overhung: 'a whole immensity of Brussels carpets, and pier-glasses, and or-molu,' as he himself expresses it, 'cannot hide from me that such Drawing-room is simply a section of Infinite Space, where so many God-created Souls do for the time meet together.' To Teufelsdröckh the highest Duchess is respectable, is venerable; but nowise for her pearl bracelets and Malines laces: in his eyes, the star of a Lord is little less and little more than the broad button of Birmingham spelter in a Clown's smock; 'each is an implement,' he says, 'in its kind; a tag for *hooking-together*; and, for the rest, was dug from the earth, and hammered on a stithy before smith's fingers.' Thus does the Professor look in men's faces with a strange impartiality, a strange scientific freedom; like a man unversed in the higher circles, like a man dropped thither from the Moon. Rightly considered, it is in this peculiarity, running through his whole system of thought, that all these shortcomings, over-shootings, and multiform perversities, take rise: if indeed they have not a second source, also natural enough, in his Transcendental Philosophies, and humour of looking at all Matter and Material things as Spirit; whereby truly his case were but the more hopeless, the more lamentable.

To the Thinkers of this nation, however, of which class it is firmly believed there are individuals yet extant, we can safely recommend the Work: nay, who knows but among the fashionable ranks too, if it be true, as Teufelsdröckh maintains, that 'within the most starched cravat there passes a windpipe and weasand, and under the thickliest embroidered waistcoat beats a heart,'—the force of that rapt earnestness may be felt, and here and there an arrow of the soul pierce through? In our wild Seer, shaggy, unkempt, like a Baptist living on locusts and wild honey, there is an untutored energy, a silent, as it were unconscious, strength, which except in the higher walks of Literature, must be rare. Many a deep glance, and often with unspeakable precision, has he cast into mysterious Nature, and the still more mysterious Life of Man. Wonderful it is with what cutting words, now and then, he severs asunder the confusion; shears down, were it furlongs deep, into the true centre of the matter; and there not only hits the nail on the head, but with crushing force smites it home, and buries it.—On the other hand, let us be free to admit, he is the most unequal writer breathing. Often after some such feat, he will play truant for long pages, and go dawdling and dreaming, and mumbling and maundering the merest commonplaces, as if he were asleep with eyes open, which indeed he is.

Of his boundless Learning, and how all reading and literature in most known tongues, from *Sanchoniathon* to *Dr. Lingard,* from your Oriental *Shasters,* and *Talmuds,* and *Korans,* with Cassini's *Siamese Tables,* and Laplace's *Mécanique Céleste,* down to *Robinson Crusoe* and the *Belfast Town and Country Almanack,* are familiar to him,—we shall say nothing: for unexampled as it is with us, to the Germans such universality of study passes without wonder, as a thing commendable, indeed, but natural, indispensable, and there of course. A man that devotes his life to learning, shall he not be learned?

In respect of style our Author manifests the same genial capability, marred too often by the same rudeness, inequality, and apparent want of intercourse with the higher classes. Occasionally, as above hinted, we find consummate vigour, a true inspiration; his burning thoughts step forth in fit burning words, like so many full-formed Minervas, issuing amid flame and splendour from Jove's head; a rich, idiomatic diction, picturesque allusions, fiery poetic emphasis, or quaint tricksy turns; all the graces and terrors of a wild Imagination, wedded to the clearest Intellect, alternate in beautiful vicissitude. Were it not that sheer sleeping and soporific passages; circumlocutions, repetitions, touches even of pure doting jargon, so often intervene! On the whole, Professor Teufelsdröckh is not a cultivated writer. Of his sentences perhaps not more than nine-tenths stand straight on their legs; the remainder are in quite angular attitudes, buttressed-up by props (of parentheses and dashes), and ever with this or the other tagrag hanging from them; a few even sprawl-out helplessly on all sides, quite broken-backed and dismembered. Nevertheless, in almost his very worst moods, there lies in him a singular attraction. A wild tone pervades the whole utterance of the man, like its keynote and regulator; now screwing itself aloft as into the Song of Spirits, or else the shrill mockery of Fiends; now sinking in cadences, not without melodious heartiness, though sometimes abrupt enough, into the common pitch, when we hear it only as a monotonous hum; of which hum the true character is extremely difficult to fix. Up to this hour we have never fully satisfied ourselves whether it is a tone and hum of real Humour, which we reckon among the very highest qualities of genius, or some echo of mere Insanity and Inanity, which doubtless ranks below the very lowest.

Under a like difficulty, in spite even of our personal intercourse, do we still lie with regard to the Professor's moral feeling. Gleams of an ethereal love burst forth from him, soft wailings of infinite pity; he could clasp the whole Universe into his bosom, and keep it warm; it seems as if under that rude exterior there dwelt a very seraph. Then again he is so sly and still, so imperturbably saturnine; shows such indifference, malign coolness towards all that men strive after; and ever with some half-visible wrinkle of a bitter sardonic humour, if indeed it be not mere stolid callousness,— that you look on him almost with a shudder, as on some incarnate Mephistopheles, to whom this great terrestrial and celestial Round, after all, were but some huge foolish Whirligig, where kings and beggars, and angels and demons, and stars and street-sweepings, were chaotically whirled, in which only children could take interest. His look, as we mentioned, is probably the gravest ever seen: yet it is not of that cast-iron gravity frequent enough among our own Chancery suitors; but rather the gravity as of some silent, high-encircled mountain-pool, perhaps the crater of an extinct volcano; into whose black deeps you fear to gaze:

those eyes, those lights that sparkle in it, may indeed be reflexes of the heavenly Stars, but perhaps also glances from the region of Nether Fire!

Certainly a most involved, self-secluded, altogether enigmatic nature, this of Teufelsdröckh! Here, however, we gladly recall to mind that once we saw him *laugh;* once only, perhaps it was the first and last time in his life; but then such a peal of laughter, enough to have awakened the Seven Sleepers! It was of Jean Paul's doing: some single billow in that vast World-Mahlstrom of Humour, with its heaven-kissing coruscations, which is now, alas, all congealed in the frost of death! The large-bodied Poet and the small, both large enough in soul, sat talking miscellaneously together, the present Editor being privileged to listen; and now Paul, in his serious way, was giving one of those inimitable 'Extra-harangues'; and, as it chanced, On the Proposal for a *Cast-metal King:* gradually a light kindled in our Professor's eyes and face, a beaming, mantling, loveliest light; through those murky features, a radiant, ever-young Apollo looked; and he burst forth like the neighing of all Tattersall's,—tears streaming down his cheeks, pipe held aloft, foot clutched into the air,—loud, long-continuing, uncontrollable; a laugh not of the face and diaphragm only, but of the whole man from head to heel. The present Editor, who laughed indeed, yet with measure, began to fear all was not right: however, Teufelsdröckh composed himself, and sank into his old stillness; on his inscrutable countenance there was, if anything, a slight look of shame; and Richter himself could not rouse him again. Readers who have any tincture of Psychology know how much is to be inferred from this; and that no man who has once heartily and wholly laughed can be altogether irreclaimably bad. How much lies in Laughter: the cipher-key, wherewith we decipher the whole man! Some men wear an everlasting barren simper; in the smile of others lies a cold glitter as of ice: the fewest are able to laugh, what can be called laughing, but only sniff and titter and snigger from the throat outwards; or at best, produce some whiffling husky cachinnation, as if they were laughing through wool: of none such comes good. The man who cannot laugh is not only fit for treasons, stratagems, and spoils; but his whole life is already a treason and a stratagem.

Considered as an Author, Herr Teufelsdröckh has one scarcely pardonable fault, doubtless his worst: an almost total want of arrangement. In this remarkable Volume, it is true, his adherence to the mere course of Time produces, through the Narrative portions, a certain show of outward method; but of true logical method and sequence there is too little. Apart from its multifarious sections and subdivisions, the Work naturally falls into two Parts; a Historical-Descriptive, and a Philosophical-Speculative: but falls, unhappily, by no firm line of demarcation; in that labyrinthic combination, each Part overlaps, and indents, and indeed runs quite through the other. Many sections are of a debatable rubric, or even quite nondescript and unnameable; whereby the Book not only loses in accessibility, but too often distresses us like some mad banquet, wherein all courses had been confounded, and fish and flesh, soup and solid, oyster-sauce, lettuces, Rhine-wine and French mustard, were hurled into one huge tureen or trough, and the hungry Public invited to help itself. To bring what order we can out of this Chaos shall be part of our endeavour.

CHAPTER V

THE WORLD IN CLOTHES

Futile cause-and-effect Philosophies. Teufelsdröckh's Orbis Vestitus. Clothes first invented for the sake of ornament. Picture of our progenitor, the Aborginal Savage. Wonders of growth and progress in mankind's history. Man defined as a Tool-using Animal.

'As Montesquieu wrote a *Spirit of Laws,*' observes our Professor, 'so could I write a *Spirit of Clothes*; thus, with an *Esprit des Lois,* properly an *Esprit de Coutumes,* we should have an *Esprit de Costumes.* For neither in tailoring nor in legislating does man proceed by mere Accident, but the hand is ever guided on by mysterious operations of the mind. In all his Modes, and habilatory endeavours, an Architectural Idea will be found lurking; his Body and the Cloth are the site and materials whereon and whereby his beautified edifice, of a Person, is to be built. Whether he flow gracefully out in folded mantles, based on light sandals; tower-up in high headgear, from amid peaks, spangles and bell-girdles; swell-out in starched ruffs, buckram stuffings, and monstrous tuberosities; or girth himself into separate sections, and front the world an Agglomeration of four limbs,—will depend on the nature of such Architectural Idea: whether Grecian, Gothic, Later-Gothic, or altogether Modern, and Parisian or Anglo-Dandiacal. Again, what meaning lies in Colour! From the soberest drab to the high-flaming scarlet, spiritual idiosyncrasies unfold themselves in choice of Colour: if the Cut betoken Intellect and Talent, so does the Colour betoken Temper and Heart. In all which, among nations as among individuals, there is an incessant, indubitable, though infinitely complex working of Cause and Effect: every snip of the Scissors has been regulated and prescribed by ever-active Influences, which doubtless to Intelligences of a superior order are neither invisible nor illegible.

'For such superior Intelligences a Cause-and-Effect Philosophy of Clothes, as of Laws, were probably a comfortable winter-evening entertainment: nevertheless, for inferior Intelligences, like men, such Philosophies have always seemed to me uninstructive enough. Nay, what is your Montesquieu himself but a clever infant spelling Letters from a hieroglyphical prophetic Book, the lexicon of which lies in Eternity, in Heaven?—Let any Cause-and-Effect Philosopher explain, not why I wear such and such a Garment, obey such and such a Law; but even why *I* am *here*, to wear and obey anything!—Much, therefore, if not the whole, of that same *Spirit of Clothes* I shall suppress, as hypothetical, ineffectual, and even impertinent: naked Facts, and Deductions drawn therefrom in quite another than that omniscient style, are my humbler and proper province.'

Acting on which prudent restriction, Teufelsdröckh has nevertheless contrived to take-in a well-nigh boundless extent of field; at least, the boundaries too often lie quite beyond our horizon. Selection being indispensable, we shall here glance-over his First Part only in the most cursory manner.

This First Part is, no doubt, distinguished by omnivorous

learning, and utmost patience and fairness: at the same time, in its results and delineations, it is much more likely to interest the Compilers of some *Library* of General, Entertaining, Useful, or even Useless Knowledge than the miscellaneous readers of these pages. Was it this Part of the Book which Heuschrecke had in view, when he recommended us to that joint-stock vehicle of publication, 'at present the glory of British Literature'? If so, the Library Editors are welcome to dig in it for their own behoof.

To the First Chapter, which turns on Paradise and Figleaves, and leads us into interminable disquisitions of a mythological, metaphorical, cabalistico-sartorial and quite antediluvian cast, we shall content ourselves with giving an unconcerned approval. Still less have we to do with 'Lilis, Adam's first wife, whom, according to the Talmudists, he had before Eve, and who bore him, in that wedlock, the whole progeny of aerial, aquatic, and terrestrial Devils,'— very needlessly, we think. On this portion of the Work, with its profound glances into the *Adam-Kadmon,* or Primeval Element, here strangely brought into relation with the *Nifl* and *Muspel* (Darkness and Light) of the antique North, it may be enough to say, that its correctness of deduction, and depth of Talmudic and Rabbinical lore have filled perhaps not the worst Hebraist in Britain with something like astonishment.

But, quitting this twilight region, Teufelsdröckh hastens from the Tower of Babel, to follow the dispersion of Mankind over the whole habitable and habilable globe. Walking by the light of Oriental, Pelasgic, Scandinavian, Egyptian, Otaheitean, Ancient and Modern researches of every conceivable kind, he strives to give us in compressed shape (as the Nürnbergers give an *Orbis Pictus*) an *Orbis Vestitus;* or view of the costumes of all mankind, in all countries, in all times. It is here that to the Antiquarian, to the Historian, we can triumphantly say: Fall to! Here is learning: an irregular Treasury, if you will; but inexhaustible as the Hoard of King Nibelung, which twelve wagons in twelve days, at the rate of three journeys a day, could not carry off. Sheepskin cloaks and wampum belts; phylacteries, stoles, albs; chlamydes, togas, Chinese silks, Afghaun shawls, trunk-hose, leather breeches, Celtic philibegs (though breeches, as the name *Gallia Braccata* indicates, are the

more ancient), Hussar cloaks, Vandyke tippets, ruffs, far-
dingales, are brought vividly before us,—even the Kilmar-
nock nightcap is not forgotten. For most part, too, we must
admit that the Learning, heterogeneous as it is, and tum-
bled-down quite pell-mell, is true concentrated and purified
Learning, the drossy parts smelted out and thrown aside.

Philosophical reflections intervene, and sometimes touching pictures of human life. Of this sort the following has
surprised us. The first purpose of Clothes, as our Professor
imagines, was not warmth or decency, but ornament. 'Miserable indeed,' says he, 'was the condition of the Aboriginal
Savage, glaring fiercely from under his fleece of hair, which
with the beard reached down to his loins, and hung round
him like a matted cloak; the rest of his body sheeted in its
thick natural fell. He loitered in the sunny glades of the
forest, living on wild-fruits; or, as the ancient Caledonian,
squatted himself in morasses, lurking for his bestial or human prey; without implements, without arms, save the ball
of heavy Flint, to which, that his sole possession and defence might not be lost, he had attached a long cord of
plaited thongs; thereby recovering as well as hurling it with
deadly unerring skill. Nevertheless, the pains of Hunger
and Revenge once satisfied, his next care was not Comfort
but Decoration (*Putz*). Warmth he found in the toils of the
chase; or amid dried leaves, in his hollow tree, in his bark
shed, or natural grotto: but for Decoration he must have
Clothes. Nay, among wild people, we find tattooing and
painting even prior to Clothes. The first spiritual want of a
barbarous man is Decoration, as indeed we still see among
the barbarous classes in civilised countries.

'Reader, the heaven-inspired melodious Singer; loftiest
Serene Highness; nay thy own amber-locked, snow-and-
rose-bloom Maiden, worthy to glide sylphlike almost on
air, whom thou lovest, worshippest as a divine Presence,
which, indeed, symbolically taken, she is,—has descended,
like thyself, from that same hair-mantled, flint-hurling Aboriginal Anthropophagus! Out of the eater cometh forth
meat; out of the strong cometh forth sweetness. What
changes are wrought, not by Time, yet in Time! For not
Mankind only, but all that Mankind does or beholds, is in
continual growth, regenesis and self-perfecting vitality. Cast
forth thy Act, thy Word, into the ever-living, ever-work-

ing Universe: it is a seed-grain that cannot die; unnoticed today (says one), it will be found flourishing as a Banyan-grove (perhaps, alas, as a Hemlock-forest!) after a thousand years.

'He who first shortened the labour of Copyists by device of *Movable Types* was disbanding hired Armies, and cashiering most Kings and Senates, and creating a whole new Democratic world: he had invented the Art of Printing. The first ground handful of Nitre, Sulphur, and Charcoal drove Monk Schwartz's pestle through the ceiling: what will the last do? Achieve the final undisputed prostration of Force under Thought, of Animal courage under Spiritual. A simple invention it was in the old-world Grazier,—sick of lugging his slow Ox about the country till he got it bartered for corn or oil,—to take a piece of Leather, and thereon scratch or stamp the mere Figure of an Ox (or *Pecus*); put it in his pocket, and call it *Pecunia,* Money. Yet hereby did Barter grow Sale, the Leather Money is now Golden and Paper, and all miracles have been out-miracled: for there are Rothschilds and English National Debts; and whoso has sixpence is sovereign (to the length of sixpence) over all men; commands cooks to feed him, philosophers to teach him, kings to mount guard over him,—to the length of sixpence.—Clothes too, which began in foolishest love of Ornament, what have they not become! Increased Security and pleasurable Heat soon followed: but what of these? Shame, divine Shame, (*Schaam,* Modesty), as yet a stranger to the Anthropophagous bosom, arose there mysteriously under Clothes; a mystic grove-encircled shrine for the Holy in man. Clothes gave us individuality, distinctions, social polity; Clothes have made Men of us; they are threatening to make Clothes-screens of us.

'But, on the whole,' continues our eloquent Professor, 'Man is a Tool-using Animal (*Handthierendes Thier*). Weak in himself, and of small stature, he stands on a basis, at most for the flattest-soled, of some half-square foot, insecurely enough; has to straddle out his legs, lest the very wind supplant him. Feeblest of bipeds! Three quintals are a crushing load for him; the steer of the meadow tosses him aloft, like a waste rag. Nevertheless he can use Tools, can devise Tools: with these the granite mountain melts into light dust before him; he kneads glowing iron, as if it were soft paste; seas are his smooth highway, winds and fire his unwearying steeds. Nowhere do you find him without Tools: without Tools he is nothing, with Tools he is all.'

Here may we not, for a moment, interrupt the stream of Oratory with a remark, that this Definition of the Tool-using Animal appears to us, of all that Animal-sort, considerably the precisest and best? Man is called a Laughing Animal: but do not the apes also laugh, or attempt to do it; and is the manliest man the greatest and oftenest laugher? Teufelsdröckh himself, as we said, laughed only once. Still less do we make of that other French Definition of the Cooking Animal; which, indeed, for rigorous scientific purposes, is as good as useless. Can a Tartar be said to cook, when he only readies his steak by riding on it? Again, what Cookery does the Greenlander use, beyond stowing-up his whale-blubber, as a marmot, in the like case, might do? Or how would Monsieur Ude prosper among those Orinocco Indians who, according to Humboldt, lodge in crow-nests, on the branches of trees; and, for half the year, have no victuals but pipe-clay, the whole country being under water? But, on the other hand, show us the human being, of any period or climate, without his Tools: those very Caledonians, as we saw, had their Flintball, and Thong to it, such as no brute has or can have.

'Man is a Tool-using Animal,' concludes Teufelsdröckh in his abrupt way; 'of which truth Clothes are but one example: and surely if we consider the interval between the first wooden Dibble fashioned by man, and those Liverpool Steam-carriages, or the British House of Commons, we shall note what progress he has made. He digs up certain black stones from the bosom of the earth, and says to them, *Transport me and this luggage at the rate of five-and-thirty miles an hour;* and they do it: he collects, apparently by lot, six-hundred and fifty-eight miscellaneous individuals, and says to them, *Make this nation toil for us, bleed for us, hunger and sorrow and sin for us;* and they do it.'

CHAPTER VI

APRONS

Divers Aprons in the world with divers uses. The Military and Police Establishment Society's working Apron. The Episcopal Apron with its corner tucked in. The Laystall. Journalists now our only Kings and Clergy.

One of the most unsatisfactory Sections in the whole Volume is that on *Aprons*. What though stout old Gao, the Persian Blacksmith, 'whose Apron, now indeed hidden under jewels, because raised in revolt which proved successful, is still the royal standard of that country'; what though John Knox's Daughter, 'who threatened Sovereign Majesty that she would catch her husband's head in her Apron, rather than he should lie and be a bishop'; what though the Landgravine Elizabeth, with many other Apron worthies,—figure here? An idle wire-drawing spirit, sometimes even a tone of levity, approaching to conventional satire, is too clearly discernible. What, for example, are we to make of such sentences as the following?

'Aprons are Defences; against injury to cleanliness, to safety, to modesty, sometimes to roguery. From the thin slip of notched silk (as it were, the emblem and beatified ghost of an Apron), which some highest-bred housewife, sitting at Nürnberg Workboxes and Toyboxes, has gracefully fastened on; to the thick-tanned hide, girt round him with thongs, wherein the Builder builds, and at evening sticks his trowel; or to those jingling sheet-iron Aprons, wherein your otherwise half-naked Vulcans hammer and smelt in their smelt-furnace,—is there not range enough in the fashion and uses of this Vestment? How much has been concealed, how much has been defended in Aprons! Nay, rightly considered, what is your whole Military and Police Establishment, charged at uncalculated millions, but a huge scarlet-coloured, iron-fastened Apron, wherein Society works (uneasily enough); guarding itself from some soil and stithy-sparks, in this Devil's-smithy (*Teufelsschmiede*) of a world? But of all Aprons the most puzzling to me hitherto has been the Episcopal or Cassock. Wherein consists the usefulness of this Apron? The Overseer (*Episcopus*) of Souls, I notice, has tucked in the corner of it, as if his day's work were done: what does he shadow forth thereby?' &c. &c.

Or again, has it often been the lot of our readers to read such stuff as we shall now quote?

'I consider those printed Paper Aprons, worn by the Parisian Cooks, as a new vent, though a slight one, for Typography; therefore as an encouragement to modern Literature, and deserving of approval; nor is it without satisfaction that I hear of a celebrated London Firm having in view to introduce the same fashion, with important extensions, in England.'—We who are on the spot hear of no such thing; and indeed have reason to be thankful that hitherto there are other vents for our Literature, exuberant as it is.—Teufelsdröckh continues: 'If such supply of printed Paper should rise so far as to choke-up the highways and public thoroughfares, new means must of necessity be had recourse to. In a world existing by Industry, we grudge to employ fire as a destroying element, and not as a creating one. However, Heaven is omnipotent, and will find us an outlet. In the mean while, is it not beautiful to see five-million quintals of Rags picked annually from the Laystall; and annually, after being macerated, hot-pressed, printed-on, and sold,—returned thither; filling so many hungry mouths by the way? Thus is the Laystall, especially with its Rags or Clothes-rubbish, the grand Electric Battery, and Fountain-of-motion, from which and to which the Social Activities (like vitreous and resinous Electricities) circulate, in larger or smaller circles, through the mighty, billowy, stormtost Chaos of Life, which they keep alive!'—Such passages fill us, who love the man, and partly esteem him, with a very mixed feeling.

Farther down we meet with this: 'The Journalists are now the true Kings and Clergy: henceforth Historians, unless they are fools, must write not of Bourbon Dynasties, and Tudors and Hapsburgs; but of Stamped Broad-sheet Dynasties, and quite new successive Names, according as this or the other Able Editor, or Combination of Able Editors, gains the world's ear. Of the British Newspaper Press, perhaps the most important of all, and wonderful enough in its secret constitution and procedure, a valuable descriptive History already exists, in that language, under the title of *Satan's Invisible World Displayed*; which, however, by search in all the Weissnichtwo Libraries, I have not yet succeeded in procuring (*vermöchte nicht aufzutreiben*).'

Thus does the good Homer not only nod, but snore. Thus does Teufelsdröckh, wandering in regions where he had little business, confound the old authentic Presbyterian Witchfinder with a new, spurious, imaginary Historian of the *Brittische Journalistik*; and so stumble on perhaps the most egregious blunder in Modern Literature!

CHAPTER VII

MISCELLANEOUS-HISTORICAL

How Men and Fashions come and go. German Costume in the fifteenth century. By what strange chances do we live in History! The costume of Bolivar's Cavalry.

Happier is our Professor, and more purely scientific and historic, when he reaches the Middle Ages in Europe, and down to the end of the Seventeenth Century; the true era of extravagance in Costume. It is here that the Antiquary and Student of Modes comes upon his richest harvest. Fantastic garbs, beggaring all fancy of a Teniers or a Callot, succeeded each other, like monster devouring monster in a Dream. The whole too in brief authentic strokes, and touched not seldom with that breath of genius which makes even old raiment live. Indeed, so learned, precise, graphical, and everyway interesting have we found these Chapters, that it may be thrown-out as a pertinent question for parties concerned, Whether or not a good English translation thereof might henceforth be profitably incorporated with Mr. Merrick's valuable Work *On Ancient Armour*? Take, by way of example, the following sketch; as authority for which Paulinus's *Zeitkürzende Lust* (ii. 678) is, with seeming confidence, referred to:

'Did we behold the German fashionable dress of the Fifteenth Century, we might smile; as perhaps those bygone Germans, were they to rise again, and see our haberdashery, would cross themselves, and invoke the Virgin. But happily no bygone German, or man, rises again; thus the

Present is not needlessly trammelled with the Past; and only grows out of it, like a Tree, whose roots are not intertangled with its branches, but lie peaceably underground. Nay it is very mournful, yet not useless, to see and know, how the Greatest and Dearest, in a short while, would find his place quite filled-up here, and no room for him; the very Napoleon, the very Byron, in some seven years, has become obsolete, and were now a foreigner to his Europe. This is the law of Progress secured; and in Clothes, as in all other external things whatsoever, no fashion will continue.

'Of the military classes in those old times, whose buff-belts, complicated chains and gorgets, huge churn-boots, and other riding and fighting gear have been bepainted in modern Romance, till the whole has acquired somewhat of a signpost character,—I shall here say nothing: the civil and pacific classes, less touched upon, are wonderful enough for us.

'Rich men, I find, have *Teusinke*' (a perhaps untranslateable article); 'also a silver girdle, whereat hang little bells; so that when a man walks, it is with continual jingling. Some few, of musical turn, have a whole chime of bells (*Glockenspiel*) fastened there; which, especially in sudden whirls, and the other accidents of walking, has a grateful effect. Observe too how fond they are of peaks, and Gothic-arch intersections. The male world wears peaked caps, an ell long, which hang bobbing over the side (*schief*): their shoes are peaked in front, also to the length of an ell, and laced on the side with tags; even the wooden shoes have their ell-long noses: some also clap bells on the peak. Further, according to my authority, the men have breeches without seat (*ohne Gesäss*): these they fasten peakwise to their shirts; and the long round doublet must overlap them.

'Rich maidens, again, flit abroad in gowns scolloped out behind and before, so that back and breast are almost bare. Wives of quality, on the other hand, have train-gowns four or five ells in length; which trains there are boys to carry. Brave Cleopatras, sailing in their silk-cloth Galley, with a Cupid for steersman! Consider their welts, a handbreadth thick, which waver round them by way of hem; the long flood of silver buttons, or rather silver shells, from throat to shoe, wherewith these same welt-gowns are buttoned. The maidens have bound silver snoods about their hair, with

gold spangles, and pendent flames (*Flammen*), that is, sparkling hair-drops: but of their mother's headgear who shall
speak? Neither in love of grace is comfort forgotten. In
winter weather you behold the whole fair creation (that can
afford it) in long mantles, with skirts wide below, and, for
hem, not one but two sufficient hand-broad welts; all ending atop in a thick well-starched Ruff, some twenty inches
broad: these are their Ruff-mantles (*Kragenmäntel*).

'As yet among the womankind hoop-petticoats are not;
but the men have doublets of fustian, under which lie mul-
tiple ruffs of cloth, pasted together with batter (*mit Teig
zusammengekleistert*), which create protuberance enough.
Thus do the two sexes vie with each other in the art of
Decoration; and as usual the stronger carries it.'

Our Professor, whether he have humour himself or not,
manifests a certain feeling of the Ludicrous, a sly observ-
ance of it, which, could emotion of any kind be confidently
predicated of so still a man, we might call a real love. None
of those bell-girdles, bushel-breeches, cornuted shoes, or
other the like phenomena, of which the History of Dress
offers so many, escape him: more especially the mischances,
or striking adventures, incident to the wearers of such, are
noticed with due fidelity. Sir Walter Raleigh's fine mantle,
which he spread in the mud under Queen Elizabeth's feet,
appears to provoke little enthusiasm in him; he merely
asks, Whether at that period the Maiden Queen 'was red-
painted on the nose, and white-painted on the cheeks, as
her tirewomen, when from spleen and wrinkles she would
no longer look in any glass, were wont to serve her?' We
can answer that Sir Walter knew well what he was doing,
and had the Maiden Queen been stuffed parchment dyed
in verdigris, would have done the same.

Thus too, treating of those enormous habiliments, that
were not only slashed and galooned, but artificially swollen-
out on the broader parts of the body, by introduction of
Bran,—our Professor fails not to comment on that luckless
Courtier, who having seated himself on a chair with some
projecting nail on it, and therefrom rising, to pay his *devoir*
on the entrance of Majesty, instantaneously emitted several
pecks of dry wheat-dust: and stood there diminished to a
spindle, his galoons and slashes dangling sorrowful and
flabby round him. Whereupon the Professor publishes this
reflection:

'By what strange chances do we live in History? Eros-
tratus by a torch; Milo by a bullock; Henry Darnley, an
unfledged booby and bustard, by his limbs; most Kings and
Queens by being born under such and such a bed-tester;
Boileau Despréaux (according to Helvetius) by the peck of
a turkey; and this ill-starred individual by a rent in his
breeches,—for no Memoirist of Kaiser Otto's Court omits
him. Vain was the prayer of Themistocles for a talent of
Forgetting: my Friends, yield cheerfully to Destiny, and
read since it is written.'—Has Teufelsdröckh to be put in
mind that, nearly related to the impossible talent of Forgetting, stands that talent of Silence, which even travelling
Englishmen manifest?

'The simplest costume,' observes our Professor, 'which I
anywhere find alluded to in History, is that used as regimental, by Bolivar's Cavalry, in the late Columbian wars. A
square Blanket, twelve feet in diagonal, is provided (some
were wont to cut-off the corners, and make it circular): in
the centre a slit is effected eighteen inches long; through
this the mother-naked Trooper introduces his head and
neck; and so rides shielded from all weather, and in battle
from many strokes (for he rolls it about his left arm); and
not only dressed, but harnessed and draperied.'

With which picture of a State of Nature, affecting by its
singularity, and Old-Roman contempt of the superfluous,
we shall quit this part of our subject.

CHAPTER VIII

THE WORLD OUT OF CLOTHES

*Teufelsdröckh's Theorem, 'Society founded upon Cloth'; his
Method, Intuition quickened by Experience.—The mysterious
question, Who am I? Philosophic systems all at fault: A deeper
meditation has always taught, here and there an individual, that
all visible things are appearances only; but also emblems and revelations of God. Teufelsdröckh first comes upon the question of
Clothes: Baseness to which Clothing may bring us.*

If in the Descriptive-Historical portion of this Volume,
Teufelsdröckh, discussing merely the *Werden* (Origin and
successive Improvement) of Clothes, has astonished many a

reader, much more will he in the Speculative-Philosophical portion, which treats of their *Wirken,* or Influences. It is here that the present Editor first feels the pressure of his task; for here properly the higher and new Philosophy of Clothes commences: an untried, almost inconceivable region, or chaos; in venturing upon which, how difficult, yet how unspeakably important is it to know what course, of survey and conquest, is the true one; where the footing is firm substance and will bear us, where it is hollow, or mere cloud, and may engulf us! Teufelsdröckh undertakes no less than to expound the moral, political, even religious Influences of Clothes; he undertakes to make manifest, in its thousandfold bearings, this grand Proposition, that Man's earthly interests, 'are all hooked and buttoned together, and held up, by Clothes.' He says in so many words, 'Society is founded upon Cloth'; and again, 'Society sails through the Infinitude on Cloth, as on a Faust's Mantle, or rather like the Sheet of clean and unclean beasts in the Apostle's Dream; and without such Sheet or Mantle, would sink to endless depths, or mount to inane limboes, and in either case be no more.'

By what chains, or indeed infinitely complected tissues, of meditation this grand Theorem is here unfolded, and innumerable practical Corollaries are drawn therefrom, it were perhaps a mad ambition to attempt exhibiting. Our Professor's method is not, in any case, that of common school Logic, where the truths all stand in a row, each holding by the skirts of the other; but at best that of practical Reason, proceeding by large Intuition over whole systematic groups and kingdoms; whereby, we might say, a noble complexity, almost like that of Nature, reigns in his Philosophy, or spiritual Picture of Nature: a mighty maze, yet, as faith whispers, not without a plan. Nay we complained above, that a certain ignoble complexity, what we must call mere confusion, was also discernible. Often, also, we have to exclaim: Would to Heaven those same Biographical Documents were come! For it seems as if the demonstration lay much in the Author's individuality; as if it were not Argument that had taught him, but Experience. At present it is only in local glimpses, and by significant fragments, picked often at wide-enough intervals from the original Volume, and carefully collated, that we can hope to impart some outline or foreshadow of this Doctrine. Readers of any intelligence are once more invited to favour us with their most concentrated attention: let these, after intense consideration, and not till then, pronounce, Whether on the utmost verge of our actual horizon there is not a looming as of Land; a promise of new Fortunate Islands, perhaps whole undiscovered Americas, for such as have canvas to sail thither?—As exordium to the whole, stand here the following long citation:

'With men of a speculative turn,' writes Teufelsdröckh, there come seasons, meditative, sweet, yet awful hours, when in wonder and fear you ask yourself that unanswerable question: Who am I; the thing that can say "I" (das Wesen das sich ICH nennt)? The world, with its loud trafficking, retires into the distance; and, through the paperhangings, and stone-walls, and thick-plied tissues of Commerce and Polity, and all the living and lifeless integuments (of Society and a Body), wherewith your Existence sits surrounded,—the sight reaches forth into the void Deep, and you are alone with the Universe, and silently commune with it, as one mysterious Presence with another.

'Who am I; what is this ME? A Voice, a Motion, an Appearance;—some embodied, visualised Idea in the Eternal Mind? Cogito, ergo sum. Alas, poor Cogitator, this takes us but a little way. Sure enough, I am; and lately was not: but Whence? How? Whereto? The answer lies around, written in all colours and motions, uttered in all tones of jubilee and wail, in thousand-figured, thousand-voiced, harmonious Nature: but where is the cunning eye and ear to whom that God-written Apocalypse will yield articulate meaning? We sit as in a boundless Phantasmagoria and Dream-grotto; boundless, for the faintest star, the remotest century, lies not even nearer the verge thereof: sounds and many-coloured visions flit round our sense; but Him, the Unslumbering, whose work both Dream and Dreamer are, we see not; except in rare half-waking moments, suspect not. Creation, says one, lies before us, like a glorious Rainbow; but the Sun that made it lies behind us, hidden from us. Then, in that strange Dream, how we clutch at shadows as if they were substances; and sleep deepest while fancying ourselves most awake! Which of your Philosophical Systems is other than a dream-theorem; a net quotient, confidently given out, where divisor and dividend are both unknown? What are all your national Wars, with their Moscow Retreats, and sanguinary hate-filled Revolutions, but the Somnambulism of uneasy Sleepers? This Dreaming, this Somnambulism is what we on Earth call Life; wherein the most indeed undoubtedly wander, as if they knew right hand from left; yet they only are wise who know that they know nothing.

'Pity that all Metaphysics had hitherto proved so inexpressibly unproductive! The secret of Man's Being is still like the Sphinx's secret: a riddle that he cannot rede; and for ignorance of which he suffers death, the worst death, a spiritual. What are your Axioms, and Categories, and Systems, and Aphorisms? Words, words. High Air-castles are cunningly built of Words, the Words well bedded also in good Logic-mortar; wherein, however, no Knowledge will come to lodge. *The whole is greater than the part:* how exceedingly true! *Nature abhors a vacuum:* how exceedingly false and calumnious! Again, *Nothing can act but where it is:* with all my heart; only, WHERE is it? Be not the slave of Words: is not the Distant, the Dead, while I love it, and long for it, and mourn for it, Here, in the genuine sense, as truly as the floor I stand on? But that same WHERE, with its brother WHEN, are from the first the master-colours of our Dream-grotto; say rather, the Canvas (the warp and woof thereof) whereon all our Dreams and Life-visions are painted. Nevertheless, has not a deeper meditation taught certain of every climate and age, that the WHERE and WHEN, so mysteriously inseparable from all our thoughts, are but superficial terrestrial adhesions to thought; that the Seer may discern them where they mount up out of the celestial EVERYWHERE and FOREVER: have not all nations conceived their God as Omnipresent and Eternal; as existing in a universal HERE, an everlasting Now? Think well, thou too wilt find that Space is but a mode of our human Sense, so likewise Time; there *is* no Space and no Time: WE are—we know not what;—light-sparkles floating in the æther of Deity!

'So that this so solid-seeming World, after all, were but an air-image, our ME the only reality: and Nature, with its thousandfold production and destruction, but the reflex of our own inward Force, the "phantasy of our Dream"; or what the Earth-Spirit in *Faust* names it, *the living visible Garment of God:*

' "In Being's floods, in Action's storm,
    I walk and work, above, beneath,

Work and weave in endless motion!
    Birth and Death,
    An infinite ocean;
    A seizing and giving
    The fire of Living:
'Tis thus at the roaring Loom of Time I ply,
And weave for God the Garment thou seest Him by."

Of twenty millions that have read and spouted this thunder-speech of the *Erdgeist,* are there yet twenty units of us that have learned the meaning thereof?

'It was in some such mood, when wearied and fordone with these high speculations, that I first came upon the question of Clothes. Strange enough, it strikes me, is this same fact of there being Tailors and Tailored. The Horse I ride has his own whole fell: strip him of the girths and flaps and extraneous tags I have fastened round him, and the noble creature is his own sempster and weaver and spinner; nay his own boot-maker, jeweller, and man-milliner; he bounds free through the valleys, with a perennial rain-proof court-suit on his body; wherein warmth and easiness of fit have reached perfection; nay, the graces also have been considered, and frills and fringes, with gay variety of colour, featly appended, and ever in the right place, are not wanting. While I—good Heaven!—have thatched myself over with the dead fleeces of sheep, the bark of vegetables, the entrails of worms, the hides of oxen or seals, the felt of furred beasts; and walk abroad a moving Rag-screen, over-heaped with shreds and tatters raked from the Charnel-house of Nature, where they would have rotted, to rot on me more slowly! Day after day, I must thatch myself anew; day after day, this despicable thatch must lose some film of its thickness; some film of it, frayed away by tear and wear, must be brushed-off into the Ashpit, into the Laystall; till by degrees the whole has been brushed thither, and I, the dust-making, patent Rag-grinder, get new material to grind down. O subter-brutish! vile! most vile! For have not I too a compact all-enclosing Skin, whiter or dingier? Am I a botched mass of tailors' and cobblers' shreds, then; or a tightly-articulated, homogeneous little Figure, automatic, nay alive?

'Strange enough how creatures of the human-kind shut their eyes to plainest facts; and by the mere inertia of Oblivion and Stupidity, live at ease in the midst of Wonders and Terrors. But indeed man is, and was always, a block-head and dullard; much readier to feel and digest, than to think and consider. Prejudice, which he pretends to hate, is his absolute lawgiver; mere use-and-wont everywhere leads him by the nose; thus let but a Rising of the Sun, let but a Creation of the World happen *twice,* and it ceases to be marvellous, to be noteworthy, or noticeable. Perhaps not once in a lifetime does it occur to your ordinary biped, of any country or generation, be he gold-mantled Prince, or russet-jerkined Peasant, that his Vestments and his Self are not one and indivisible; that *he* is naked, without vestments, till he buy or steal such, and by forethought sew and button them.

'For my own part, these considerations, of our Clothes-thatch, and how, reaching inwards even to our heart of hearts, it tailorises and demoralises us, fill me with a certain horror at myself and mankind; almost as one feels at those Dutch Cows, which, during the wet season, you see grazing deliberately with jackets and petticoats (of striped sacking), in the meadows of Gouda. Nevertheless there is something great in the moment when a man first strips himself of ad-ventitious wrappages; and sees indeed that he is naked, and, as Swift has it, "a forked straddling animal with bandy legs"; yet also a Spirit, and unutterable Mystery of Mys-teries.'

CHAPTER IX

ADAMITISM

The universal utility of Clothes, and their higher mystic virtue, illustrated. Conception of Mankind stripped naked; and immedi-ate consequent dissolution of civilised Society.

Let no courteous reader take offence at the opinions broached in the conclusion of the last Chapter. The Editor himself, on first glancing over that singular passage, was in-clined to exclaim: What, have we got not only a Sansculot-tist, but an enemy to Clothes in the abstract? A new

Adamite, in this century, which flatters itself that it is the Nineteenth, and destructive both to Superstition and Enthusiasm?

Consider, thou foolish Teufelsdröckh, what benefits unspeakable all ages and sexes derive from Clothes. For example, when thou thyself, a watery, pulpy, slobbery freshman and new-comer in this Planet, sattest muling and puking in thy nurse's arms; sucking thy coral, and looking forth into the world in the blankest manner, what hadst thou been without thy blankets, and bibs, and other nameless hulls? A terror to thyself and mankind! Or hast thou forgotten the day when thou first receivedst breeches, and thy long clothes became short? The village where thou livedst was all apprised of the fact; and neighbour after neighbour kissed thy pudding-cheek, and gave thee, as handsel, silver or copper coins, on that the first gala-day of thy existence. Again, wert not thou, at one period of life, a Buck, or Blood, or Macaroni, or Incroyable, or Dandy, or by whatever name, according to year and place, such phenomenon is distinguished? In that one word lie included mysterious volumes. Nay, now when the reign of folly is over, or altered, and thy clothes are not for triumph but for defence, hast thou always worn them perforce, and as a consequence of Man's Fall; never rejoiced in them as in a warm movable House, a Body round thy Body, wherein that strange THEE of thine sat snug, defying all variations of Climate? Girt with thick double-milled kerseys; half-buried under shawls and broadbrims, and over-alls and mud-boots, thy very fingers cased in doeskin and mittens, thou hast bestrode that 'Horse I ride'; and, though it were in wild winter, dashed through the world, glorying in it as if thou wert its lord. In vain did the sleet beat round thy temples; it lighted only on thy impenetrable, felted or woven, case of wool. In vain did the winds howl,—forests sounding and creaking, deep calling unto deep,—and the storms heap themselves together into one huge Arctic whirlpool: thou flewest through the middle thereof, striking fire from the highway; wild music hummed in thy ears, thou too wert as a 'sailor of the air'; the wreck of matter and the crash of worlds was thy element and propitiously wafting tide. Without Clothes, without bit or saddle, what hadst thou been; what had thy fleet quadruped been?—Nature is good, but she is not the best: here truly was the victory of Art over Nature. A thunderbolt indeed might have pierced thee; all short of this thou couldst defy.

Or, cries the courteous reader, has your Teufelsdröckh forgotten what he said lately about 'Aboriginal Savages,' and their 'condition miserable indeed'? Would he have all this unsaid; and us betake ourselves again to the 'matted cloak,' and go sheeted in a 'thick natural fell'?

Nowise, courteous reader! The Professor knows full well what he is saying; and both thou and we, in our haste, do him wrong. If Clothes, in these times, 'so tailorise and demoralise us,' have they no redeeming value; can they not be altered to serve better; must they of necessity be thrown to the dogs? The truth is, Teufelsdröckh, though a Sansculottist, is no Adamite; and much perhaps as he might wish to go forth before this degenerate age 'as a Sign,' would nowise wish to do it, as those old Adamites did, in a state of Nakedness. The utility of Clothes is altogether apparent to him: nay perhaps he has an insight into their more recondite, and almost mystic qualities, what we might call the omnipotent virtue of Clothes, such as was never before vouchsafed to any man. For example:

'You see two individuals,' he writes, 'one dressed in fine Red, the other in coarse threadbare Blue: Red says to Blue, "Be hanged and anatomised"; Blue hears with a shudder, and (O wonder of wonders!) marches sorrowfully to the gallows; is there noosed-up, vibrates his hour, and the surgeons dissect him, and fit his bones into a skeleton for medical purposes. How is this; or what make ye of your *Nothing can act but where it is?* Red has no physical hold of Blue, no *clutch* of him, is nowise in *contact* with him: neither are those ministering Sheriffs and Lord-Lieutenants and Hangmen and Tipstaves so related to commanding Red, that he can tug them hither and thither; but each stands distinct within his own skin. Nevertheless, as it is spoken, so is it done: the articulated Word sets all hands in Action; and Rope and Improved-drop perform their work.

'Thinking reader, the reason seems to me twofold: First, that *Man is a Spirit,* and bound by invisible bonds to *All Men;* secondly, that *he wears Clothes,* which are the visible emblems of that fact. Has not your Red hanging-individual a horsehair wig, squirrel-skins, and a plush-gown; whereby all mortals know that he is a JUDGE?—Society, which the more I think of it astonishes me the more, is founded upon Cloth.

'Often in my atrabiliar moods, when I read of pompous ceremonials, Frankfort Coronations, Royal Drawing-rooms, Levees, Couchees; and how the ushers and macers and pursuivants are all in waiting; how Duke this is presented by Archduke that, and Colonel A by General B, and innumerable Bishops, Admirals, and miscellaneous Functionaries, are advancing gallantly to the Anointed Presence; and I strive, in my remote privacy, to form a clear picture of that solemnity,—on a sudden, as by some enchanter's wand, the —shall I speak it?—the Clothes fly-off the whole dramatic corps; and Dukes, Grandees, Bishops, Generals, Anointed Presence itself, every mother's son of them, stand straddling there, not a shirt on them; and I know not whether to laugh or weep. This physical or psychical infirmity, in which perhaps I am not singular, I have, after hesitation, thought right to publish, for the solace of those afflicted with the like.'

Would to Heaven, say we, thou hadst thought right to keep it secret! Who is there now that can read the five columns of Presentations in his Morning Newspaper without a shudder? Hypochondriac men, and all men are to a certain extent hypochondriac, should be more gently treated. With what readiness our fancy, in this shattered state of the nerves, follows out the consequences which Teufelsdröckh, with a devilish coolness, goes on to draw:

'What would Majesty do, could such an accident befall in reality; should the buttons all simultaneously start, and the solid wool evaporate, in very Deed, as here in Dream? *Ach Gott!* How each skulks into the nearest hiding-place; their high State Tragedy (*Haupt- und Staats-Action*) becomes a Pickleherring-Farce to weep at, which is the worst kind of Farce; *the tables* (according to Horace), and with them, the whole fabric of Government, Legislation, Property, Police, and Civilised Society, *are dissolved,* in wails and howls.'

Lives the man that can figure a naked Duke of Windlestraw addressing a naked House of Lords? Imagination, choked as in mephitic air, recoils on itself, and will not forward with the picture. The Woolsack, the Ministerial, the Opposition Benches—*infandum! infandum!* And yet why is the thing impossible? Was not every soul, or rather every body, of these Guardians of our Liberties, naked, or nearly so, last night; 'a forked Radish with a head fantastically carved'? And why might he not, did our stern fate so order it, walk out to St. Stephen's, as well as into bed, in that no-fashion; and there, with other similar Radishes, hold a Bed of Justice? 'Solace of those afflicted with the like!' Unhappy Teufelsdröckh, had man ever such a 'physical or psychical infirmity' before? And now how many, perhaps, may thy unparalleled confession (which we, even to the sounder British world, and goaded-on by Critical and Biographical duty, grudge to reimpart) incurably infect therewith! Art thou the malignest of Sansculottists, or only the maddest?

'It will remain to be examined,' adds the inexorable Teu-felsdröckh, 'in how far the SCARECROW, as a Clothed Person, is not also entitled to benefit of clergy, and English trial by jury: nay perhaps, considering his high function (for is not he too a Defender of Property, and Sovereign armed with the *terrors* of the Law?), to a certain royal Immunity and Inviolability; which, however, misers and the meaner class of persons are not always voluntarily disposed to grant him.' * * * * 'O my friends, we are (in Yorick Sterne's words) but as "turkeys driven, with a stick and red clout, to the market": or if some drivers, as they do in Norfolk, take a dried bladder and put peas in it, the rattle thereof terrifies the boldest!'

CHAPTER X

PURE REASON

A Naked World possible, nay actually exists, under the clothed one. Man, in the eye of Pure Reason, a visible God's Presence. The beginning of all wisdom, to look fixedly on Clothes till they become transparent. Wonder, the basis of Worship: Perennial in man. Modern Sciolists who cannot wonder: Teufelsdröckh's contempt for, and advice to them.

It must now be apparent enough that our Professor, as above hinted, is a speculative Radical, and of the very darkest tinge; acknowledging, for most part, in the solemnities and paraphernalia of civilised Life, which we make so much of, nothing but so many Cloth-rags, turkey-poles, and 'bladders with dried peas.' To linger among such speculations, longer than mere Science requires, a discerning public can have no wish. For our purposes the simple fact that such a *Naked World* is possible, nay actually exists (under the Clothed one), will be sufficient. Much, therefore, we omit about 'Kings wrestling naked on the green with Carmen,' and the Kings being thrown: 'dissect them with scalpels,' says Teufelsdröckh; 'the same viscera, tissues, livers, lights, and other life-tackle, are there: examine their spiritual mechanism; the same great Need, great Greed, and little Faculty; nay ten to one but the Carman, who understands draught-cattle, the rimming of wheels, something of the laws of unstable and stable equilibrium, with other branches of wagon-science, and has actually put forth his hand and operated on Nature, is the more cunningly gifted of the two. Whence, then, their so unspeakable difference? From Clothes.' Much also we shall omit about confusion of Ranks, and Joan and My Lady, and how it would be everywhere 'Hail fellow well met,' and Chaos were come again: all which to any one that has once fairly pictured-out the grand mother-idea, *Society in a state of Nakedness,* will spontaneously suggest itself. Should some sceptical individual still entertain doubts whether in a world without Clothes, the smallest Politeness, Polity, or even Police, could exist, let him turn to the original Volume, and view there the boundless Serbonian Bog of Sansculottism, stretching sour and pestilential: over which we have lightly flown; where not only whole armies but whole nations might sink! If indeed the following argument, in its brief riveting emphasis, be not of itself incontrovertible and final:

'Are we Opossums; have we natural Pouches, like the Kangaroo? Or how, without Clothes, could we possess the master-organ, soul's seat, and true pineal gland of the Body Social: I mean, a PURSE?'

Nevertheless it is impossible to hate Professor Teufelsdröckh; at worst, one knows not whether to hate or to love him. For though, in looking at the fair tapestry of human Life, with its royal and even sacred figures, he dwells not on the obverse alone, but here chiefly on the reverse; and indeed turns out the rough seams, tatters, and manifold thrums of that unsightly wrong-side, with an almost diabolic patience and indifference, which must have sunk him in the estimation of most readers,—there is that within which unspeakably distinguishes him from all other past and present Sansculottists. The grand unparalleled peculiarity of Teufelsdröckh is, that with all this Descendentalism, he combines a Transcendentalism, no less superlative; whereby if on the one hand he degrade man below most animals, except those jacketed Gouda Cows, he, on the other, exalts him beyond the visible Heavens, almost to an equality with the Gods.

'To the eye of vulgar Logic,' says he, 'what is man? An omnivorous Biped that wears Breeches. To the eye of Pure Reason what is he? A Soul, a Spirit, and divine Apparition. Round his mysterious ME, there lies, under all those wool-rags, a Garment of Flesh (or of Senses), contextured in the Loom of Heaven; whereby he is revealed to his like, and dwells with them in UNION and DIVISION; and sees and fashions for himself a Universe, with azure Starry Spaces, and long Thousands of Years. Deep-hidden is he under that strange Garment; amid Sounds and Colours and Forms, as it were, swathed-in, and inextricably over-shrouded: yet it is sky-woven, and worthy of a God. Stands he not thereby in the centre of Immensities, in the conflux of Eternities? He feels; power has been given him to know, to believe; nay does not the spirit of Love, free in its celestial primeval brightness, even here, though but for moments, look through? Well said Saint Chrysostom, with his lips of gold, "the true SHEKINAH is Man": where else is the GOD's-PRESENCE manifested not to our eyes only, but to our hearts, as in our fellow-man?'

In such passages, unhappily too rare, the high Platonic Mysticism of our Author, which is perhaps the fundamental element of his nature, bursts forth, as it were, in full flood: and, through all the vapour and tarnish of what is often so perverse, so mean in his exterior and environment, we seem to look into a whole inward Sea of Light and Love;— though, alas, the grim coppery clouds soon roll together again, and hide it from view.

Such tendency to Mysticism is everywhere traceable in this man; and indeed, to attentive readers, must have been long ago apparent. Nothing that he sees but has more than a common meaning, but has two meanings: thus, if in the highest Imperial Sceptre and Charlemagne-Mantle, as well as in the poorest Ox-goad and Gipsy-Blanket, he finds Prose, Decay, Contemptibility; there is in each sort Poetry also, and a reverend Worth. For Matter, were it never so despicable, is Spirit, the manifestation of Spirit: were it never so honourable, can it be more? The thing Visible, nay the thing Imagined, the thing in any way conceived as Visible, what is it but a Garment, a Clothing of the higher, celestial Invisible, 'unimaginable, formless, dark with excess of bright'? Under which point of view the following passage, so strange in purport, so strange in phrase, seems characteristic enough:

'The beginning of all Wisdom is to look fixedly on Clothes, or even with armed eyesight, till they become *transparent*. "The Philosopher," says the wisest of this age, "must station himself in the middle": how true! The Philosopher is he to whom the Highest has descended, and the Lowest has mounted up; who is the equal and kindly brother of all.

'Shall we tremble before clothwebs and cobwebs, whether woven in Arkwright looms, or by the silent Arachnes that weave unrestingly in our imagination? Or, on the other hand, what is there that we cannot love; since all was created by God?

'Happy he who can look through the Clothes of a Man (the woollen, and fleshly, and official Bank-paper and State-paper Clothes) into the Man himself; and discern, it may be, in this or the other Dread Potentate, a more or less incompetent Digestive-apparatus; yet also an inscrutable venerable Mystery, in the meanest Tinker that sees with eyes!'

For the rest, as is natural to a man of this kind, he deals much in the feeling of Wonder; insists on the necessity and high worth of universal Wonder; which he holds to be the only reasonable temper for the denizen of so singular a Planet as ours. 'Wonder,' says he, 'is the basis of Worship: the reign of wonder is perennial, indestructible in Man; only at certain stages (as the present), it is, for some short season, a reign *in partibus infidelium.*' That progress of Science, which is to destroy Wonder, and in its stead substitute Mensuration and Numeration, finds small favour with Teufelsdröckh, much as he otherwise venerates these two latter processes.

'Shall your Science,' exclaims he, 'proceed in the small chink-lighted, or even oil-lighted, underground workshop of Logic alone; and man's mind become an Arithmetical Mill, whereof Memory is the Hopper, and mere Tables of Sines and Tangents, Codification, and Treatises of what you call Political Economy, are the Meal? And what is that Science, which the scientific head alone, were it screwed off, and (like the Doctor's in the Arabian Tale) set in a basin to keep it alive, could prosecute without shadow of a heart,— but one other of the mechanical and menial handicrafts, for which the Scientific Head (having a Soul in it) is too noble an organ? I mean that Thought without Reverence is barren, perhaps poisonous; at best, dies like cookery with the day that called it forth; does not live, like sowing, in successive tilths and wider-spreading harvests, bringing food and plenteous increase to all Time.'

In such wise does Teufelsdröckh deal hits, harder or softer, according to ability; yet ever, as we would fain persuade ourselves, with charitable intent. Above all, that class of 'Logic-choppers, and treble-pipe Scoffers, and professed Enemies to Wonder; who, in these days, so numerously patrol as night-constables about the Mechanics' Institute of Science, and cackle like true Old-Roman geese and goslings round their Capitol, on any alarm, or on none; nay who often, as illuminated Sceptics, walk abroad into peaceable society, in full daylight, with rattle and lantern, and insist on guiding you and guarding you therewith, though the Sun is shining, and the street populous with mere justice-loving men:' that whole class is inexpressibly wearisome to him. Hear with what uncommon animation he perorates:

'The man who cannot wonder, who does not habitually wonder (and worship), were he President of innumerable Royal Societies, and carried the whole *Mécanique Céleste* and *Hegel's Philosophy,* and the epitome of all Laboratories and Observatories with their results, in his single head,— is but a Pair of Spectacles behind which there is no Eye. Let those who have Eyes look through him, then he may be useful.

'Thou wilt have no Mystery and Mysticism; wilt walk through thy world by the sunshine of what thou callest Truth, or even by the hand-lamp of what I call Attorney-Logic; and "explain" all, "account" for all, or believe nothing of it? Nay, thou wilt attempt laughter; whoso recognises the unfathomable, all-pervading domain of Mystery, which is everywhere under our feet and among our hands; to whom the Universe is an Oracle and Temple, as well as a

Kitchen and Cattlestall,—he shall be a delirious Mystic; to him thou, with sniffing charity, wilt protrusively proffer thy hand-lamp, and shriek, as one injured, when he kicks his foot through it?—*Armer Teufel!* Doth not thy cow calve, doth not thy bull gender? Thou thyself, wert thou not born, wilt thou not die? "Explain" me all this, or do one of two things: Retire into private places with thy foolish cackle; or, what were better, give it up, and weep, not that the reign of wonder is done, and God's world all disembellished and prosaic, but that thou hitherto art a Dilettante and sandblind Pedant.'

CHAPTER XI

PROSPECTIVE

Nature not an Aggregate, but a Whole. All visible things are emblems, Clothes; and exist for a time only. The grand scope of the Philosophy of Clothes.—Biographic Documents arrive. Letter from Heuschrecke on the importance of Biography. Heterogeneous character of the documents: Editor sorely perplexed; but desperately grapples with his work.

The Philosophy of Clothes is now to all readers, as we predicted it would do, unfolding itself into new boundless expansions, of a cloudcapt, almost chimerical aspect, yet not without azure loomings in the far distance, and streaks as of an Elysian brightness; the highly questionable purport and promise of which it is becoming more and more important for us to ascertain. Is that a real Elysian brightness, cries many a timid wayfarer, or the reflex of Pandemonian lava? Is it of a truth leading us into beatific Asphodel meadows, or the yellow-burning marl of a Hell-on-Earth?

Our Professor, like other Mystics, whether delirious or inspired, gives an Editor enough to do. Ever higher and dizzier are the heights he leads us to; more piercing, all-comprehending, all-confounding are his views and glances. For example, this of Nature being not an Aggregate but a Whole:

'Well sang the Hebrew Psalmist: "If I take the wings of the morning and dwell in the uttermost parts of the universe, God is there." Thou thyself, O cultivated reader, who too probably art no Psalmist, but a Prosaist, knowing GOD only by tradition, knowest thou any corner of the world where at least FORCE is not? The drop which thou shakest from thy wet hand, rests not where it falls, but to-morrow thou findest it swept away; already on the wings of the Northwind, it is nearing the Tropic of Cancer. How came it to evaporate, and not lie motionless? Thinkest thou there is ought motionless; without Force, and utterly dead?

'As I rode through the Schwarzwald, I said to myself: That little fire which glows star-like across the dark-growing (*nachtende*) moor, where the sooty smith bends over his anvil, and thou hopest to replace thy lost horse-shoe,— is it a detached, separated speck, cut-off from the whole Universe; or indissolubly joined to the whole? Thou fool, that smithy-fire was (primarily) kindled at the Sun; is fed by air that circulates from before Noah's Deluge, from beyond the Dogstar; therein, with Iron Force, and Coal Force, and the far stranger Force of Man, are cunning affinities and battles and victories of Force brought about; it is a little ganglion, or nervous centre, in the great vital system of Immensity. Call it, if thou wilt, an unconscious Altar, kindled on the bosom of the All; whose iron sacrifice, whose iron smoke and influence reach quite through the All; whose dingy Priest, not by word, yet by brain and sinew, preaches forth the mystery of Force; nay preaches forth (exoterically enough) one little textlet from the Gospel of Freedom, the Gospel of Man's Force, commanding, and one day to be all-commanding.

'Detached, separated! I say there is no such separation: nothing hitherto was ever stranded, cast aside; but all, were it only a withered leaf, works together with all; is borne forward on the bottomless, shoreless flood of Action, and lives through perpetual metamorphoses. The withered leaf is not dead and lost, there are Forces in it and around it, though working in inverse order; else how could it *rot?* Despise not the rag from which man makes Paper, or the litter from which the earth makes Corn. Rightly viewed no meanest object is insignificant; all objects are as windows, through which the philosophic eye looks into Infinitude itself.'

Again, leaving that wondrous Schwarzwald Smithy-Altar, what vacant, high-sailing air-ships are these, and whither will they sail with us?

'All visible things are emblems; what thou seest is not there on its own account; strictly taken, is not there at all: Matter exists only spiritually, and to represent some Idea, and *body* it forth. Hence Clothes, as despicable as we think them, are so unspeakably significant. Clothes, from the King's mantle downwards, are emblematic, nor of want only, but of a manifold cunning Victory over Want. On the other hand, all Emblematic things are properly Clothes, thought-woven or hand-woven: must not the Imagination weave Garments, visible Bodies, wherein the else invisible creations and inspirations of our Reason are, like Spirits, revealed, and first become all-powerful;—the rather if, as we often see, the Hand too aid her, and (by wool Clothes or otherwise) reveal such even to the outward eye?

'Men are properly said to be clothed with Authority, clothed with Beauty, with Curses, and the like. Nay, if you consider it, what is Man himself, and his whole terrestrial Life, but an Emblem; a Clothing or visible Garment for that divine ME of his, cast hither, like a light-particle, down from Heaven? Thus is he said also to be clothed with a Body.

'Language is called the Garment of Thought: however, it should rather be, Language is the Flesh-Garment, the Body, of Thought. I said that Imagination wove this Flesh-Garment; and does not she? Metaphors are her stuff: examine Language; what, if you except some few primitive elements (of natural sound), what is it all but Metaphors, recognised as such, or no longer recognised; still fluid and florid, or now solid-grown and colourless? If those same primitive elements are the osseous fixtures in the Flesh-Garment, Language,—then are Metaphors its muscles and tissues and living integuments. An unmetaphorical style you shall in vain seek for: is not your very *Attention* a *Stretching-to?* The difference lies here: some styles are lean, adust, wiry, the muscle itself seems osseous; some are even quite pallid, hunger-bitten and dead-looking; while others again glow in the flush of health and vigorous self-growth, sometimes (as in my own case) not without an apoplectic tendency. More-over, there are sham Metaphors, which overhanging that same Thought's-Body (best naked), and deceptively bedizening, or bolstering it out, may be called its false stuffings, superfluous show-cloaks (*Putz-Mäntel*), and tawdry woollen rags: whereof he that runs and reads may gather whole hampers,—and burn them.'

Than which paragraph on Metaphors did the reader ever chance to see a more surprisingly metaphorical? However, that is not our chief grievance; the Professor continues:

'Why multiply instances? It is written, the Heavens and the Earth shall fade away like a Vesture; which indeed they are: the Time-vesture of the Eternal. Whatsoever sensibly exists, whatsoever represents Spirit to Spirit, is properly a Clothing, a suit of Raiment, put on for a season, and to be laid off. Thus in this one pregnant subject of CLOTHES, rightly understood, is included all that men have thought, dreamed, done, and been: the whole External Universe and what it holds is but Clothing; and the essence of all Science lies in the PHILOSOPHY OF CLOTHES.'

Towards these dim infinitely-expanded regions, close-bordering on the impalpable Inane, it is not without apprehension, and perpetual difficulties, that the Editor sees himself journeying and struggling. Till lately a cheerful daystar of hope hung before him, in the expected Aid of Hofrath Heuschrecke; which daystar, however, melts now, not into the red of morning, but into a vague, gray half-light, uncertain whether dawn of day or dusk of utter darkness. For the last week, these so-called Biographical Documents are in his hand. By the kindness of a Scottish Hamburg Merchant, whose name, known to the whole mercantile world, he must not mention; but whose honourable courtesy, now and often before spontaneously manifested to him, a mere literary stranger, he cannot soon forget,—the bulky Weissnichtwo Packet, with all its Customhouse seals, foreign hieroglyphs, and miscellaneous tokens of Travel, arrived here in perfect safety, and free of cost. The reader shall now fancy with what hot haste it was broken up, with what breathless expectation glanced over; and, alas, with what unquiet disappointment it has, since then, been often thrown down, and again taken up.

Hofrath Heuschrecke, in a too long-winded Letter, full of compliments, Weissnichtwo politics, dinners, dining repartees, and other ephemeral trivialities, proceeds to remind us of what we knew well already: that however it may be with Metaphysics, and other abstract Science originating in the Head (*Verstand*) alone, no Life-Philosophy (*Lebensphilo-*

sophie), such as this of Clothes pretends to be, which originates equally in the Character (*Gemüth*), and equally
speaks thereto, can attain its significance till the Character
itself is known and seen; 'till the Author's View of the World
(*Weltansicht*), and how he actively and passively came by
such view, are clear: in short till a Biography of him has
been philosophico-poetically written, and philosophico-poetically read.' 'Nay,' adds he, 'were the speculative scientific
Truth even known, you still, in this inquiring age, ask yourself, Whence came it, and Why, and How?—and rest not,
till, if no better may be, Fancy have shaped-out an answer;
and either in the authentic lineaments of Fact, or the
forged ones of Fiction, a complete picture and Genetical
History of the Man and his spiritual Endeavour lies before
you. But why,' says the Hofrath, and indeed say we, 'do I
dilate on the uses of our Teufelsdröckh's Biography? The
great Herr Minister von Goethe has penetratingly remarked that "Man is properly the *only* object that interests
man": thus I too have noted, that in Weissnichtwo our
whole conversation is little or nothing else but Biography
or Auto-Biography; ever humano-anecdotical (*menschlich-
anekdotisch*). Biography is by nature the most universally
profitable, universally pleasant of all things: especially Biography of distinguished individuals.

'By this time, *mein Verehrtester* (my Most Esteemed),'
continues he, with an eloquence which, unless the words
be purloined from Teufelsdröckh, or some trick of his, as
we suspect, is well-nigh unaccountable, 'by this time you are
fairly plunged (*vertieft*) in that mighty forest of Clothes-
Philosophy; and looking round, as all readers do, with astonishment enough. Such portions and passages as you
have already mastered, and brought to paper, could not
but awaken a strange curiosity touching the mind they issued from; the perhaps unparalleled psychical mechanism,
which manufactured such matter, and emitted it to the light
of day. Had Teufelsdröckh also a father and mother; did
he, at one time, wear drivel-bibs, and live on spoon-meat?
Did he ever, in rapture and tears, clasp a friend's bosom to
his; looks he also wistfully into the long burial-aisle of the
Past, where only winds, and their low harsh moan, give inarticulate answer? Has he fought duels;—good Heaven!
how did he comport himself when in Love? By what singular stair-steps, in short, and subterranean passages, and

sloughs of Despair, and steep Pisgah hills, has he reached this wonderful prophetic Hebron (a true Old-Clothes Jewry) where he now dwells?

'To all these natural questions the voice of public History is as yet silent. Certain only that he has been, and is, a Pilgrim, and a Traveller from a far Country; more or less footsore and travel-soiled; has parted with road-companions; fallen among thieves, been poisoned by bad cookery, blistered with bugbites; nevertheless, at every stage (for they have let him pass), has had the Bill to discharge. But the whole particulars of his Route, his Weather-observations, the picturesque Sketches he took, though all regularly jotted down (in indelible sympathetic-ink by an invisible interior Penman), are these nowhere forthcoming? Perhaps quite lost: one other leaf of that mighty Volume (of human Memory) left to fly abroad, unprinted, unpublished, unbound up, as waste paper; and to rot, the sport of rainy winds?

'No, *verehrtester Herr Herausgeber,* in no wise! I here, by the unexampled favour you stand in with our Sage, send not a Biography only, but an Autobiography: at least the materials for such; wherefrom, if I misreckon not, your perspicacity will draw fullest insight: and so the whole Philosophy and Philosopher of Clothes will stand clear to the wondering eyes of England, nay thence, through America, through Hindostan, and the antipodal New Holland, finally conquer (*einnehmen*) great part of this terrestrial Planet!'

And now let the sympathising reader judge of our feeling when, in place of this same Autobiography with 'fullest insight,' we find—Six considerable Paper-Bags, carefully sealed, and marked successively, in gilt China-ink, with the symbols of the Six southern Zodiacal Signs, beginning at Libra; in the inside of which sealed Bags lie miscellaneous masses of Sheets, and oftener Shreds and Snips, written in Professor Teufelsdröckh's scarce legible *cursiv-schrift;* and treating of all imaginable things under the Zodiac and above it, but of his own personal history only at rare intervals, and then in the most enigmatic manner.

Whole fascicles there are, wherein the Professor, or, as he here, speaking in the third person, calls himself, 'the Wanderer,' is not once named. Then again, amidst what seems to be a Metaphysico-theological Disquisition, 'Detached Thoughts on the Steam-engine,' or, 'The continued

Possibility of Prophecy,' we shall meet with some quite private, not unimportant Biographical fact. On certain sheets stand Dreams, authentic or not, while the circumjacent waking Actions are omitted. Anecdotes, oftenest without date of place or time, fly loosely on separate slips, like Sibylline leaves. Interspersed also are long purely Autobiographical delineations; yet without connexion, without recognisable coherence; so unimportant, so superfluously minute, they almost remind us of 'P.P. Clerk of this Parish.' Thus does famine of intelligence alternate with waste. Selection, order, appears to be unknown to the Professor. In all Bags the same imbroglio; only perhaps in the Bag *Capricorn,* and those near it, the confusion a little worse confounded. Close by a rather eloquent Oration, 'On receiving the Doctor's-Hat,' lie wash-bills, marked *bezahlt* (settled). His Travels are indicated by the Street-Advertisements of the various cities he has visited; of which Street-Advertisements, in most living tongues, here is perhaps the completest collection extant.

So that if the Clothes-Volume itself was too like a Chaos, we have now instead of the solar Luminary that should still it, the airy Limbo which by intermixture will farther volatilise and discompose it! As we shall perhaps see it our duty ultimately to deposit these Six Paper-Bags in the British Museum, farther description, and all vituperation of them, may be spared. Biography or Autobiography of Teufelsdröckh there is, clearly enough, none to be gleaned here: at most some sketchy, shadowy fugitive likeness of him may, by unheard-of efforts, partly of intellect, partly of imagination, on the side of Editor and of Reader, rise up between them. Only as a gaseous-chaotic Appendix to that aqueous-chaotic Volume can the contents of the Six Bags hover round us, and portions thereof be incorporated with our delineation of it.

Daily and nightly does the Editor sit (with green spectacles) deciphering these unimaginable Documents from their perplexed *cursiv-schrift;* collating them with the almost equally unimaginable Volume, which stands in legible print. Over such a universal medley of high and low, of hot, cold, moist and dry, is he here struggling (by union of like with like, which is Method) to build a firm Bridge for British travellers. Never perhaps since our first Bridge-builders, Sin and Death, built that stupendous Arch from Hell-gate to the Earth, did any Pontifex, or Pontiff, undertake such a task as the present Editor. For in this Arch too, leading, as we humbly presume, far otherwards than that grand primeval one, the materials are to be fished-up from the weltering deep, and down from the simmering air, here one mass, there another, and cunningly cemented, while the elements boil beneath: nor is there any supernatural force to do it with; but simply the Diligence and feeble thinking Faculty of an English Editor, endeavouring to evolve printed Creation out of a German printed and written Chaos, wherein, as he shoots to and fro in it, gathering, clutching, piecing the Why to the far-distant Wherefore, his whole Faculty and Self are like to be swallowed up.

Patiently, under these incessant toils and agitations, does the Editor, dismissing all anger, see his otherwise robust health declining; some fraction of his allotted natural sleep nightly leaving him, and little but an inflamed nervous-system to be looked for. What is the use of health, or of life, if not to do some work therewith? And what work nobler than transplanting foreign Thought into the barren domestic soil; except indeed planting Thought of your own, which the fewest are privileged to do? Wild as it looks, this Philosophy of Clothes, can we ever reach its real meaning, promises to reveal new-coming Eras, the first dim rudiments and already-budding germs of a nobler Era, in Universal History. Is not such a prize worth some striving? Forward with us, courageous reader; be it towards failure, or towards success! The latter thou sharest with us; the former also is not all our own.

BOOK SECOND / CHAPTER I

GENESIS

Old Andreas Futteral and Gretchen his wife: their quiet home. Advent of a mysterious stranger, who deposits with them a young infant, the future Herr Diogenes Teufelsdröckh. After-yearnings of the youth for his unknown Father. Sovereign power of Names and Naming. Diogenes a flourishing Infant.

In a psychological point of view, it is perhaps questionable whether from birth and genealogy, how closely scrutinised soever, much insight is to be gained. Nevertheless, as in every phenomenon the Beginning remains always the most notable moment; so, with regard to any great man, we rest not till, for our scientific profit or not, the whole circumstances of his first appearance in this Planet, and what manner of Public Entry he made, are with utmost completeness rendered manifest. To the Genesis of our Clothes-Philosopher, then, be this First Chapter consecrated. Unhappily, indeed, he seems to be of quite obscure extraction; uncertain, we might almost say, whether of any: so that this Genesis of his can properly be nothing but an Exodus (or transit out of Invisibility into Visibility); whereof the preliminary portion is nowhere forthcoming.

'In the village of Entepfuhl,' thus writes he, in the Bag *Libra,* on various Papers, which we arrange with difficulty, 'dwelt Andreas Futteral and his wife; childless, in still seclusion, and cheerful though now verging towards old age. Andreas had been grenadier Sergeant, and even regimental Schoolmaster under Frederick the Great; but now, quitting the halbert and ferule for the spade and pruning-hook, cultivated a little Orchard, on the produce of which he, Cincinnatus-like, lived not without dignity. Fruits, the peach, the apple, the grape, with other varieties came in their season; all which Andreas knew how to sell: on evenings he smoked largely, or read (as beseemed a regimental Schoolmaster), and talked to neighbours that would listen about the Victory of Rossbach; and how Fritz the Only (*der Einzige*) had once with his own royal lips spoken to him, had been pleased to say, when Andreas as camp-sentinel demanded the pass-word, *"Schweig Hund* (Peace, hound)!" before any of his staff-adjutants could answer. *"Das nenn' ich mir einen König.* There is what I call a King," would Andreas exclaim: "but the smoke of Kunersdorf was still smarting his eyes."

'Gretchen, the housewife, won like Desdemona by the deeds rather than the looks of her now veteran Othello, lived not in altogether military subordination; for, as Andreas said, "the womankind will not drill (*wer kann die Weiberchen dressiren*): nevertheless she at heart loved him both for valour and wisdom; to her a Prussian grenadier Sergeant and Regiment's Schoolmaster was little other than a Cicero and Cid: what you see, yet cannot see over, is as good as infinite. Nay, was not Andreas in very deed a man of order,

courage, downrightness (*Geradheit*); that understood Büsch-
ing's *Geography*, had been in the victory of Rossbach,
and left for dead in the camisade of Hochkirch? The good
Gretchen, for all her fretting, watched over him and hovered round him as only a true housemother can: assiduously
she cooked and sewed and scoured for him; so that not
only his old regimental sword and grenadier-cap, but the
whole habitation and environment, where on pegs of honour they hung, looked ever trim and gay: a roomy painted
Cottage, embowered in fruit-trees and forest-trees, ever-
greens and honeysuckles; rising many-coloured from amid
shaven grass-plots, flowers struggling-in through the very
windows; under its long projecting eaves nothing but gar-
den-tools in methodic piles (to screen them from rain), and
seats where, especially on summer nights, a King might have
wished to sit and smoke, and call it his. Such a *Bauergut*
(Copyhold) had Gretchen given her veteran; whose sinewy
arms, and long-disused gardening talent, had made it what
you saw.

'Into this umbrageous Man's-nest, one meek yellow evening or dusk, when the Sun, hidden indeed from terrestrial
Entepfuhl, did nevertheless journey visible and radiant along
the celestial Balance (*Libra*), it was that a Stranger of reverend aspect entered; and, with grave salutation, stood before the two rather astonished housemates. He was close-
muffled in a wide mantle; which without farther parley unfolding, he deposited therefrom what seemed some Basket,
overhung with green Persian silk; saying only: *Ihr lieben
Leute, hier bringe ein unschätzbares Verleihen; nehmt es
in aller Acht, sorgfältigst benützt es: mit hohem Lohn, oder
wohl mit schweren Zinsen, wird's einst zurückgefordert.*
"Good Christian people, here lies for you an invaluable
Loan; take all heed thereof, in all carefulness employ it:
with high recompense, or else with heavy penalty, will it one
day be required back." Uttering which singular words, in a
clear, bell-like, forever memorable tone, the Stranger gracefully withdrew; and before Andreas or his wife, gazing in
expectant wonder, had time to fashion either question or
answer, was clean gone. Neither out of doors could aught of
him be seen or heard; he had vanished in the thickets, in
the dusk; the Orchard-gate stood quietly closed: the Stranger
was gone once and always. So sudden had the whole transaction been, in the autumn stillness and twilight, so gentle,

noiseless, that the Futterals could have fancied it all a trick of Imagination, or some visit from an authentic Spirit. Only that the greensilk Basket, such as neither Imagination nor authentic Spirits are wont to carry, still stood visible and tangible on their little parlour-table. Towards this the astonished couple, now with lit candle, hastily turned their attention. Lifting the green veil, to see what invaluable it hid, they descried there, amid down and rich white wrappages, no Pitt Diamond or Hapsburg Regalia, but, in the softest sleep, a little red-coloured Infant! Beside it, lay a roll of gold Friedrichs, the exact amount of which was never publicly known; also a *Taufschein* (baptismal certificate), wherein unfortunately nothing but the Name was decipherable; other document or indication none whatever.

'To wonder and conjecture was unavailing, then and always thenceforth. Nowhere in Entepfuhl, on the morrow or next day, did tidings transpire of any such figure as the Stranger; nor could the Traveller, who had passed through the neighbouring Town in coach-and-four, be connected with this Apparition, except in the way of gratuitous surmise. Meanwhile, for Andreas and his wife, the grand practical problem was: What to do with this little sleeping red-coloured Infant? Amid amazements and curiosities, which had to die away without external satisfying, they resolved, as in such circumstances charitable prudent people needs must, on nursing it, though with spoon-meat, into whiteness, and if possible into manhood. The Heavens smiled on their endeavour: thus has that same mysterious Individual ever since had a status for himself in this visible Universe, some modicum of victual and lodging and parade-ground; and now expanded in bulk, faculty and knowledge of good and evil, he, as HERR DIOGENES TEUFELSDRÖCKH, professes or is ready to profess, perhaps not altogether without effect, in the New University of Weissnichtwo, the new Science of Things in General.'

Our Philosopher declares here, as indeed we should think he well might, that these facts, first communicated, by the good Gretchen Futteral, in his twelfth year, 'produced on the boyish heart and fancy a quite indelible impression. Who this reverend Personage,' he says, 'that glided into the Orchard Cottage when the Sun was in Libra, and then, as on spirit's wings, glided out again, might be? An inexpressible desire, full of love and of sadness, has often since struggled

within me to shape an answer. Ever, in my distresses and
my loneliness, has Fantasy turned, full of longing (*sehn-
suchtsvoll*), to that unknown Father, who perhaps far from
me, perhaps near, either way invisible, might have taken me
to his paternal bosom, there to lie screened from many a
woe. Thou beloved Father, dost thou still, shut out from me
only by thin penetrable curtains of earthly Space, wend to
and fro among the crowd of the living? Or art thou hidden by
those far thicker curtains of the Everlasting Night, or rather
of the Everlasting Day, through which my mortal eye and
outstretched arms need not strive to reach? Alas, I know not,
and in vain vex myself to know. More than once, heart-
deluded, have I taken for thee this and the other noble-
looking Stranger; and approached him wistfully, with infinite
regard; but he too had to repel me, he too was not thou.

'And yet, O Man born of Woman,' cries the Autobiographer, with one of his sudden whirls, 'wherein is my
case peculiar? Hadst thou, any more than I, a Father whom
thou knowest? The Andreas and Gretchen, or the Adam and
Eve, who led thee into Life, and for a time suckled and pap-
fed thee there, whom thou namest Father and Mother; these
were, like mine, but thy nursing-father and nursing-mother:
thy true Beginning and Father is in Heaven, whom with the
bodily eye thou shalt never behold, but only with the spiritual.'

'The little green veil,' adds he, among much similar moral-
ising, and embroiled discoursing, 'I yet keep; still more inseparably the Name, Diogenes Teufelsdröckh. From the veil
can nothing be inferred: a piece of now quite faded Persian
silk, like thousands of others. On the Name I have many times
meditated and conjectured; but neither in this lay there any
clue. That it was my unknown Father's name I must hesitate
to believe. To no purpose have I searched through all the
Herald's Books, in and without the German Empire, and
through all manner of Subscriber-Lists (*Pränumeranten*),
Militia-Rolls, and other Name-catalogues; extraordinary
names as we have in Germany, the name Teufelsdröckh, except as appended to my own person, nowhere occurs. Again,
what may the unchristian rather than Christian "Diogenes"
mean? Did that reverend Basket-bearer intend, by such
designation, to shadow-forth my future destiny, or his own
present malign humour? Perhaps the latter, perhaps both.
Thou ill-starred Parent, who like an Ostrich hadst to leave thy

ill-starred offspring to be hatched into self-support by the mere sky-influences of Chance, can thy pilgrimage have been a smooth one? Beset by Misfortune thou doubtless hast been; or indeed by the worst figure of Misfortune, by Misconduct. Often have I fanced how, in thy hard life-battle, thou wert shot at, and slung at, wounded, hand-fettered, hamstrung, browbeaten and bedevilled by the Time-Spirit (*Zeitgeist*) in thyself and others, till the good soul first given thee was seared into grim rage; and thou hadst nothing for it but to leave in me an indignant appeal to the Future, and living speaking Protest against the Devil, as that same Spirit not of the Time only, but of Time itself, is well named! Which Appeal and Protest, may I now modestly add, was not perhaps quite lost in air.

'For indeed, as Walter Shandy often insisted, there is much, nay almost all, in Names. The Name is the earliest Garment you wrap round the earth-visiting ME; to which it thenceforth cleaves, more tenaciously (for there are Names that have lasted nigh thirty centuries) than the very skin. And now from without, what mystic influences does it not send inwards, even to the centre; especially in those plastic first-times, when the whole soul is yet infantine, soft, and the invisible seedgrain will grow to be an all overshadowing tree! Names? Could I unfold the influence of Names, which are the most important of all Clothings, I were a second greater Trismegistus. Not only all common Speech, but Science, Poetry itself is no other, if thou consider it, than a right *Naming*. Adam's first task was giving names to natural Appearances: what is ours still but a continuation of the same; be the Appearances, exotic-vegetable, organic, mechanic, stars, or starry movements (as in Science); or (as in Poetry) passions, virtues, calamities, God-attributes, Gods?—In a very plain sense the Proverb says, *Call one a thief, and he will steal;* in an almost similar sense may we not perhaps say, *Call one Diogenes Teufelsdröckh, and he will open the Philosophy of Clothes?*'

'Meanwhile the incipient Diogenes, like others, all ignorant of his Why, his How or Whereabout, was opening his eyes to the kind Light; sprawling-out his ten fingers and toes; listening, tasting, feeling; in a word, by all his Five Senses, still more by his Sixth Sense of Hunger, and a whole infinitude of inward, spiritual, half-awakened Senses, endeavouring daily to acquire for himself some knowledge of this strange Universe where he had arrived, be his task therein what it might. Infinite was his progress; thus in some fifteen months, he could perform the miracle of—Speech! To breed a fresh Soul, is it not like brooding a fresh (celestial) Egg; wherein as yet all is formless, powerless; yet by degrees organic elements and fibres shoot through the watery albumen; and out of vague Sensation grows Thought, grows Fantasy and Force, and we have Philosophies, Dynasties, nay Poetries and Religions!

'Young Diogenes, or rather young Gneschen, for by such diminutive had they in their fondness named him, travelled forward to those high consummations, by quick yet easy stages. The Futterals, to avoid vain talk, and moreover keep the roll of gold Friedrichs safe, gave-out that he was a grand-nephew; the orphan of some sister's daughter, suddenly deceased, in Andreas's distant Prussian birthland; of whom, as of her indigent sorrowing widower, little enough was known at Entepfuhl. Heedless of all which, the Nurseling took to his spoon-meat, and throve. I have heard him noted as a still infant, that kept his mind much to himself; above all, that seldom or never cried. He already felt that time was precious; that he had other work cut-out for him than whimpering.'

Such, after utmost painful search and collation among these miscellaneous Paper-masses, is all the notice we can gather of Herr Teufelsdröckh's genealogy. More imperfect, more enigmatic it can seem to few readers than to us. The Professor, in whom truly we more and more discern a certain satirical turn, and deep under-currents of roguish whim, for the present stands pledged in honour, so we will not doubt him: but seems it not conceivable that, by the 'good Gretchen Futteral,' or some other perhaps interested party, he has himself been deceived? Should these sheets, translated or not, ever reach the Entepfuhl Circulating Library, some cultivated native of that district might feel called to afford explanation. Nay, since Books, like invisible scouts, permeate the whole habitable globe, and Timbuctoo itself is not safe from British Literature, may not some Copy find out even the mysterious basket-bearing Stranger, who in a state of extreme senility perhaps still exists; and gently force even him to disclose himself; to claim openly a son, in whom any father may feel pride?

CHAPTER II

IDYLLIC

Happy Childhood! Entepfuhl: Sights, hearings and experiences of the boy Teufelsdröckh; their manifold teaching. Education; what it can do, what cannot. Obedience our universal duty and destiny. Gneschen sees the good Gretchen pray.

'Happy season of Childhood!' exclaims Teufelsdröckh: 'Kind Nature, that art to all a bountiful mother; that visitest the poor man's hut with auroral radiance; and for thy Nurseling hast provided a soft swathing of Love and infinite Hope, wherein he waxes and slumbers, danced-round (*umgaukelt*) by sweetest Dreams! If the paternal Cottage still shuts us in, its roof still screens us; with a Father we have as yet a prophet, priest and king, and an Obedience that makes us free. The young spirit has awakened out of Eternity, and knows not what we mean by Time; as yet Time is no fast-hurrying stream, but a sportful sunlit ocean; years to the child are as ages: ah! the secret of Vicissitude, of that slower or quicker decay and ceaseless down-rushing of the universal World-fabric, from the granite mountain to the man or day-moth, is yet unknown; and in a motionless Universe, we taste, what afterwards in this quick-whirling Universe, is forever denied us, the balm of Rest. Sleep on, thou fair Child, for thy long rough journey is at hand! A little while, and thou too shalt sleep no more, but thy very dreams shall be mimic battles; thou too, with old Arnauld, wilt have to say in stern patience: "Rest? Rest? Shall I not have all Eternity to rest in?" Celestial Nepenthe! though a Pyrrhus conquer empires, and an Alexander sack the world, he finds thee not; and thou hast once fallen gently, of thy own accord, on the eyelids, on the heart of every mother's child. For as yet, sleep and waking are one: the fair Life-garden rustles infinite around, and everywhere is dewy fragrance, and the budding of Hope; which budding, if in youth, too frostnipt, it grow to flowers, will in manhood yield no fruit, but a prickly, bitter-rinded stone-fruit, of which the fewest can find the kernel.'

In such rose-coloured light does our Professor, as Poets

are wont, look back on his childhood; the historical details of which (to say nothing of much other vague oratorical matter) he accordingly dwells on with an almost wearisome minuteness. We hear of Entepfuhl standing 'in trustful derangement' among the woody slopes; the paternal Orchard flanking it as extreme outpost from below; the little Kuhbach gushing kindly by, among beech-rows, through river after river, into the Donau, into the Black Sea, into the Atmosphere and Universe; and how 'the brave old Linden,' stretching like a parasol of twenty ells in radius, overtopping all other rows and clumps, towered-up from the central *Agora* and *Campus Martius* of the Village, like its Sacred Tree; and how the old men sat talking under its shadow (Gneschen often greedily listening), and the wearied labourers reclined, and the unwearied children sported, and the young men and maidens often danced to flute-music. 'Glorious summer twilights,' cries Teufelsdröckh, 'when the Sun, like a proud Conqueror and Imperial Taskmaster, turned his back, with his gold-purple emblazonry, and all his fireclad body-guard (of Prismatic Colours); and the tired brickmakers of this clay Earth might steal a little frolic, and those few meek Stars would not tell of them!'

Then we have long details of the *Weinlesen* (Vintage), the Harvest-Home, Christmas, and so forth; with a whole cycle of the Entepfuhl Children's-games, differing apparently by mere superficial shades from those of other countries. Concerning all which, we shall here, for obvious reasons, say nothing. What cares the world for our as yet miniature Philosopher's achievements under that 'brave old Linden'? Or even where is the use of such practical reflections as the following? 'In all the sports of Children, were it only in their wanton breakages and defacements, you shall discern a creative instinct (*schaffenden Trieb*): the Mankin feels that he is a born Man, that his vocation is to work. The choicest present you can make him is a Tool; be it knife or pen-gun, for construction or for destruction; either way it is for Work, for Change. In gregarious sports of skill or strength, the Boy trains himself to Coöperation, for war or peace, as governor or governed: the little Maid again, provident of her domestic destiny, takes with preference to Dolls.'

Perhaps, however, we may give this anecdote, considering who it is that relates it: 'My first short-clothes were of yellow serge; or rather, I should say, my first short-cloth, for the vesture was one and indivisible, reaching from neck to ankle, a mere body with four limbs: of which fashion how little could I then divine the architectural, how much less the moral significance!'

More graceful is the following little picture: 'On fine evenings I was wont to carry-forth my supper (bread-crumb boiled in milk), and eat it out-of-doors. On the coping of the Orchard-wall, which I could reach by climbing, or still more easily if Father Andreas would set-up the pruning-ladder, my porringer was placed: there, many a sunset, have I, looking at the distant western Mountains, consumed, not without relish, my evening meal. Those hues of gold and azure, that hush of World's expectation as Day died, were still a Hebrew Speech for me; nevertheless I was looking at the fair illuminated Letters, and had an eye for their gilding.'

With 'the little one's friendship for cattle and poultry' we shall not much intermeddle. It may be that hereby he acquired a 'certain deeper sympathy with animated Nature': but when, we would ask, saw any man, in a collection of Biographical Documents, such a piece as this: 'Impressive enough (*bedeutungsvoll*) was it to hear, in early morning, the Swineherd's horn; and know that so many hungry happy quadrupeds were, on all sides, starting in hot haste to join him, for breakfast on the Heath. Or to see them at eventide, all marching-in again, with short squeak, almost in military order; and each, topographically correct, trotting-off in succession to the right or left, through its own lane, to its own dwelling; till old Kunz, at the Village-head, now left alone, blew his last blast, and retired for the night. We are wont to love the Hog chiefly in the form of Ham; yet did not these bristly thick-skinned beings here manifest intelligence, perhaps humour of character; at any rate, a touching, trustful submissiveness to Man,—who, were he but a Swineherd, in darned gabardine, and leather breeches more resembling slate or discoloured-tin breeches, is still the Hierarch of this lower world?'

It is maintained, by Helvetius and his set, that an infant of genius is quite the same as any other infant, only that certain surprisingly favourable influences accompany him through life, especially through childhood, and expand him, while others lie closefolded and continue dunces. Herein, say they, consists the whole difference between an inspired

Prophet and a double-barrelled Game-preserver: the inner man of the one has been fostered into generous development; that of the other, crushed-down perhaps by vigour of animal digestion, and the like, has exuded and evaporated, or at best sleeps now irresuscitably stagnant at the bottom of his stomach. 'With which opinion,' cries Teufelsdröckh, 'I should as soon agree as with this other, that an acorn might, by favourable or unfavourable influences of soil and climate, be nursed into a cabbage, or the cabbage-seed into an oak.

'Nevertheless,' continues he, 'I too acknowledge the all-but omnipotence of early culture and nurture: hereby we have either a doddered dwarf bush, or a high-towering, wide-shadowing tree; either a sick yellow cabbage, or an edible luxuriant green one. Of a truth, it is the duty of all men, especially of all philosophers, to note-down with accuracy the characteristic circumstances of their Education, what furthered, what hindered, what in any way modified it: to which duty, nowadays so pressing for many a German Autobiographer, I also zealously address myself.'—Thou rogue! Is it by short-clothes of yellow serge, and swineherd horns, that an infant of genius is educated? And yet, as usual, it ever remains doubtful whether he is laughing in his sleeve at these Autobiographical times of ours, or writing from the abundance of his own fond ineptitude. For he continues: 'If among the ever-streaming currents of Sights, Hearings, Feelings for Pain or Pleasure, whereby, as in a Magic Hall, young Gneschen went about environed, I might venture to select and specify, perhaps these following were also of the number:

'Doubtless, as childish sports call forth Intellect, Activity, so the young creature's Imagination was stirred up, and a Historical tendency given him by the narrative habits of Father Andreas; who, with his battle-reminiscences, and gray austere yet hearty patriarchal aspect, could not but appear another Ulysses and "much-enduring Man." Eagerly I hung upon his tales, when listening neighbours enlivened the hearth; from these perils and these travels, wild and far almost as Hades itself, a dim world of Adventure expanded itself within me. Incalculable also was the knowledge I acquired in standing by the Old Men under the Linden-tree: the whole of Immensity was yet new to me; and had not these reverend seniors, talkative enough, been employed in partial surveys thereof for nigh fourscore years? With amazement I began to discover that Entepfuhl stood in the middle of a Country, of a World; that there was such a thing as History, as Biography; to which I also, one day, by hand and tongue, might contribute.

'In a like sense worked the *Postwagen* (Stage-coach), which, slow-rolling under its mountains of men and luggage, wended through our Village: northwards, truly, in the dead of night; yet southwards visibly at eventide. Not till my eighth year did I reflect that this Postwagen could be other than some terrestrial Moon, rising and setting by mere Law of Nature, like the heavenly one; that it came on made highways, from far cities towards far cities; weaving them like a monstrous shuttle into closer and closer union. It was then that, independently of Schiller's *Wilhelm Tell,* I made this not quite insignificant reflection (so true also in spiritual things): *Any road, this simple Entepfuhl road, will lead you to the end of the World!*

'Why mention our Swallows, which, out of far Africa, as I learned, threading their way over seas and mountains, corporate cities and belligerent nations, yearly found themselves, with the month of May, snug-lodged in our Cottage Lobby? The hospitable Father (for cleanliness' sake) had fixed a little bracket plumb under their nest: there they built, and caught flies, and twittered, and bred; and all, I chiefly, from the heart loved them. Bright, nimble creatures, who taught *you* the mason-craft; nay, stranger still, gave you a masonic incorporation, almost social police? For if, by ill chance, and when time pressed, your House fell, have I not seen five neighbourly Helpers appear next day; and swashing to and fro with animated, loud, long-drawn chirpings, and activity almost super-hirundine, complete it again before nightfall?

'But undoubtedly the grand summary of Entepfuhl child's-culture, where as in a funnel its manifold influences were concentrated and simultaneously poured-down on us, was the annual Cattle-fair. Here, assembling from all the four winds, came the elements of an unspeakable hurly-burly. Nutbrown maids and nutbrown men, all clear-washed, loud-laughing, bedizened and beribanded; who came for dancing, for treating, and if possible, for happiness. Top-booted Graziers from the North; Swiss Brokers, Italian Drovers, also topbooted, from the South; these with their subalterns in leather jerkins, leather skull-caps, and long ox-goads; shouting in half-articulate speech, amid the inarticulate barking and bellowing. Apart stood Potters from far Saxony, with their crockery in fair rows; Nürnberg Pedlars, in booths that to me seemed richer than Ormuz bazaars; Showmen from the Lago Maggiore; detachments of the *Wiener Schub* (Offscourings of Vienna) vociferously superintending games of chance. Ballad-singers brayed, Auctioneers grew hoarse; cheap New Wine (*heuriger*) flowed like water, still worse confounding the confusion; and high over all, vaulted, in ground-and-lofty tumbling, a particoloured Merry-Andrew, like the genius of the place and of Life itself.

'Thus encircled by the mystery of Existence; under the deep heavenly Firmament; waited-on by the four golden Seasons, with their vicissitudes of contribution, for even grim Winter brought its skating-matches and shooting-matches, its snow-storms and Christmas-carols,—did the Child sit and learn. These things were the Alphabet, whereby in aftertime he was to syllable and partly read the grand Volume of the World: what matters it whether such Alphabet be in large gilt letters or in small ungilt ones, so you have an eye to read it? For Gneschen, eager to learn, the very act of looking thereon was a blessedness that gilded all: his existence was a bright, soft element of Joy; out of which, as in Prospero's Island, wonder after wonder bodied itself forth, to teach by charming.

'Nevertheless, I were but a vain dreamer to say, that even then my felicity was perfect. I had, once for all, come down from Heaven into the Earth. Among the rainbow colours that glowed on my horizon, lay even in childhood a dark ring of Care, as yet no thicker than a thread, and often quite overshone; yet always it reappeared, nay ever waxing broader and broader; till in after-years it almost over-shadowed my whole canopy, and threatened to engulf me in final night. It was the ring of Necessity whereby we are all begirt; happy he for whom a kind heavenly Sun brightens it into a ring of Duty, and plays round it with beautiful prismatic diffractions; yet ever, as basis and as bourne for our whole being, it is there.

'For the first few years of our terrestrial Apprenticeship, we have not much work to do; but, boarded and lodged gratis, are set down mostly to look about us over the work-shop, and see others work, till we have understood the tools a little, and can handle this and that. If good Passivity alone, and not good Passivity and good Activity together, were the thing wanted, then was my early position favourable be-yond the most. In all that respects openness of Sense, af-fectionate Temper, ingenuous Curiosity, and the fostering of these, what more could I have wished? On the other side, however, things went not so well. My Active Power (*Thatkraft*) was unfavourably hemmed-in; of which mis-fortune how many traces yet abide with me! In an orderly house, where the litter of children's sports is hateful enough, your training is too stoical; rather to bear and forbear than to make and do. I was forbid much: wishes in any measure bold I had to renounce; everywhere a strait bond of Obe-dience inflexibly held me down. Thus already Freewill often came in painful collision with Necessity; so that my tears flowed, and at seasons the Child itself might taste that root of bitterness, wherewith the whole fruitage of our life is mingled and tempered.

'In which habituation to Obedience, truly, it was beyond measure safer to err by excess than by defect. Obedience is our universal duty and destiny; wherein whoso will not bend must break: too early and too thoroughly we cannot be trained to know that Would, in this world of ours, is as mere zero to Should, and for most part as the smallest of fractions even to Shall. Hereby was laid for me the basis of worldly Discretion, nay of Morality itself. Let me not quarrel with my upbringing. It was rigorous, too frugal, compres-sively secluded, everyway unscientific: yet in that very strictness and domestic solitude might there not lie the root of deeper earnestness, of the stem from which all noble fruit must grow? Above all, how unskilful soever, it was lov-ing, it was well-meant, honest; whereby every deficiency was helped. My kind Mother, for as such I must ever love the good Gretchen, did me one altogether invaluable service: she taught me, less indeed by word than by act and daily rever-ent look and habitude, her own simple version of the Chris-tian Faith. Andreas too attended Church; yet more like a parade-duty, for which he in the other world expected pay with arrears,—as, I trust, he has received; but my Mother, with a true woman's heart, and fine though uncultivated sense, was in the strictest acceptation Religious. How indestructibly the Good grows, and propagates itself, even among the weedy entanglements of Evil! The highest whom I knew on Earth I here saw bowed down, with awe unspeakable, before a Higher in Heaven: such things, especially in infancy, reach inwards to the very core of your being; mysteriously does a Holy of Holies build itself into visibility in the mysterious deeps; and Reverence, the divinest in man, springs forth undying from its mean envelopment of Fear. Wouldst thou rather be a peasant's son that knew, were it never so rudely, there was a God in Heaven and in Man; or a duke's son that only knew there were two-and-thirty quarters on the family-coach?'

To which last question we must answer: Beware, O Teufelsdröckh, of spiritual pride!

CHAPTER III

PEDAGOGY

Teufelsdröckh's School. His Education. How the ever-flowing Kuhbach speaks of Time and Eternity. The Hinterschlag Gymnasium: rude Boys; and pedant Professors. The need of true Teachers, and their due recognition. Father Andreas dies; and Teufelsdröckh learns the secret of his birth: His reflections thereon. The Nameless University. Statistics of Imposture much wanted. Bitter fruits of Rationalism: Teufelsdröckh's religious difficulties. The young Englishman Herr Towgood. Modern Friendship.

Hitherto we see young Gneschen, in his indivisible case of yellow serge, borne forward mostly on the arms of kind Nature alone; seated, indeed, and much to his mind, in the terrestrial workshop, but (except his soft hazel eyes, which we doubt not already gleamed with a still intelligence) called upon for little voluntary movement there. Hitherto, accordingly, his aspect is rather generic, that of an incipient Philosopher and Poet in the abstract; perhaps it would puzzle Herr Heuschrecke himself to say wherein the special Doctrine of Clothes is as yet foreshadowed or betokened. For with Gneschen, as with others, the Man may indeed stand pictured in the Boy (at least all the pigments are there); yet only some half of the Man stands in the Child, or young Boy, namely, his Passive endowment, not his Active. The more impatient are we to discover what figure he cuts in this latter capacity; how, when, to use his own words, 'he understands the tools a little, and can handle this or that,' he will proceed to handle it.

Here, however, may be the place to state that, in much of our Philosopher's history, there is something of an almost Hindoo character: nay perhaps in that so well-fostered and every-way excellent 'Passivity' of his, which, with no free development of the antagonist Activity, distinguished his childhood, we may detect the rudiments of much that, in after days, and still in these present days, astonishes the world. For the shallow-sighted, Teufelsdröckh is oftenest a man without Activity of any kind, a No-man; for the deep-sighted, again, a man with Activity almost superabundant, yet so spiritual, close-hidden, enigmatic, that no mortal can foresee its explosions, or even when it has exploded, so much as ascertain its significance. A dangerous, difficult temper for the modern European; above all, disadvantageous in the hero of a Biography! Now as heretofore it will behoove the Editor of these pages, were it never so unsuccessfully, to do his endeavour.

Among the earliest tools of any complicacy which a man, especially a man of letters, gets to handle, are his Class-books. On this portion of his History, Teufelsdröckh looks down professedly as indifferent. Reading he 'cannot remember ever to have learned'; so perhaps had it by nature. He says generally: 'Of the insignificant portion of my Education, which depended on Schools, there need almost no notice be taken. I learned what others learn; and kept it stored-by in a corner of my head, seeing as yet no manner of use in it. My Schoolmaster, a downbent, brokenhearted, underfoot martyr, as others of that guild are, did little for me, except discover that he could do little: he, good soul, pronounced me a genius, fit for the learned professions; and that I must be sent to the Gymnasium, and one day to the University. Meanwhile, what printed thing soever I could meet with I read. My very copper pocket-money I laid-out on stall-literature; which, as it accumulated, I with my own hands sewed into volumes. By this means was the young head furnished with a considerable miscellany of things and shadows of things: History in authentic fragments lay mingled with Fabulous chimeras, wherein also was reality; and the whole not as dead stuff, but as living pabulum, tolerably nutritive for a mind as yet so peptic.'

That the Entepfuhl Schoolmaster judged well, we now know. Indeed, already in the youthful Gneschen, with all his outward stillness, there may have been manifest an inward vivacity that promised much; symptoms of a spirit singularly open, thoughtful, almost poetical. Thus, to say nothing of his Suppers on the Orchard-wall, and other phenomena of that earlier period, have many readers of these pages stumbled, in their twelfth year, on such reflections as the following? 'It struck me much, as I sat by the Kuhbach, one silent noontide, and watched it flowing, gurgling, to think how this same streamlet had flowed and gurgled, through all changes of weather and of fortune, from beyond the earliest date of History. Yes, probably on the morning when Joshua forded Jordan; even as at the mid-day when Cæsar, doubtless with difficulty, swam the Nile, yet kept his *Commentaries* dry,—this little Kuhbach, assiduous as Tiber, Eurotas or Siloa, was murmuring on across the wilderness, as yet unnamed, unseen: here, too, as in the Euphrates and the Ganges, is a vein or veinlet of the grand World-circulation of Waters, which, with its atmospheric arteries, has lasted and lasts simply with the World. Thou fool! Nature alone is antique, and the oldest art a mushroom; that idle crag thou sittest on is six-thousand years of age.' In which little thought, as in a little fountain, may there not lie the beginning of those well-nigh unutterable meditations on the grandeur and mystery of TIME, and its relation to ETERNITY, which play such a part in this Philosophy of Clothes?

Over his Gymnastic and Academic years the Professor by no means lingers so lyrical and joyful as over his childhood. Green sunny tracts there are still; but intersected by bitter rivulets of tears, here and there stagnating into sour marshes of discontent. 'With my first view of the Hinterschlag Gymnasium,' writes he, 'my evil days began. Well do I still remember the red sunny Whitsuntide morning, when, trotting full of hope by the side of Father Andreas, I entered the main street of the place, and saw its steeple-clock (then striking Eight) and *Schuldthurm* (Jail), and the aproned or disaproned Burghers moving-in to breakfast: a little dog, in mad terror, was rushing past; for some human imps had tied a tin-kettle to its tail; thus did the agonised creature,

loud-jingling, career through the whole length of the Borough, and become notable enough. Fit emblem of many a
Conquering Hero, to whom Fate (wedding Fantasy to Sense,
as it often elsewhere does) has malignantly appended a
tin-kettle of Ambition, to chase him on; which the faster he
runs, urges him the faster, the more loudly and more foolishly! Fit emblem also of much that awaited myself, in that
mischievous Den; as in the World, whereof it was a portion
and epitome!

'Alas, the kind beech-rows of Entepfuhl were hidden in
the distance: I was among strangers, harshly, at best in-
differently, disposed towards me; the young heart felt, for
the first time, quite orphaned and alone.' His schoolfellows,
as is usual, persecuted him: 'They were Boys,' he says,
'mostly rude Boys, and obeyed the impulse of rude Nature,
which bids the deerherd fall upon any stricken hart, the
duck-flock put to death any broken-winged brother or sister, and on all hands the strong tyrannise over the weak.' He
admits that though 'perhaps in an unusual degree morally
courageous,' he succeeded ill in battle, and would fain have
avoided it; a result, as would appear, owing less to his small
personal stature (for in passionate seasons he was 'incredi-
bly nimble'), than to his 'virtuous principles': 'if it was
disgraceful to be beaten,' says he, 'it was only a shade less
disgraceful to have so much as fought; thus was I drawn two
ways at once, and in this important element of school-his-
tory, the war-element, had little but sorrow.' On the whole,
that same excellent 'Passivity,' so notable in Teufelsdröckh's
childhood, is here visibly enough again getting nourishment.
'He wept often; indeed to such a degree that he was nicknamed *Der Weinende* (the Tearful), which epithet, till towards his thirteenth year, was indeed not quite unmerited.
Only at rare intervals did the young soul burst-forth into
fire-eyed rage, and, with a stormfulness (*Ungestüm*) under
which the boldest quailed, assert that he too had Rights of
Man, or at least of Mankin.' In all which, who does not discern a fine flower-tree and cinnamon-tree (of genius) nigh
choked among pumpkins, reed-grass and ignoble shrubs; and
forced if it would live, to struggle upwards only, and not outwards; into a *height* quite sickly, and disproportioned to its
breadth?

We find, moreover, that his Greek and Latin were 'mechanically' taught; Hebrew scarce even mechanically; much

else which they called History, Cosmography, Philosophy, and so forth, no better than not at all. So that, except inasmuch as Nature was still busy; and he himself 'went about, as was of old his wont, among the Craftsmen's workshops, there learning many things'; and farther lighted on some small store of curious reading, in Hans Wachtel the Cooper's house, where he lodged,—his time, it would appear, was utterly wasted. Which facts the Professor has not yet learned to look upon with any contentment. Indeed, throughout the whole of this Bag *Scorpio,* where we now are, and often in the following Bag, he shows himself unusually animated on the matter of Education, and not without some touch of what we might presume to be anger.

'My Teachers,' says he, 'were hide-bound Pedants, without knowledge of man's nature, or of boy's; or of aught save their lexicons and quarterly account-books. Innumerable dead Vocables (no dead Language, for they themselves knew no Language) they crammed into us, and called it fostering the growth of mind. How can an inanimate, mechanical Gerund grinder, the like of whom will, in a subsequent century, be manufactured at Nürnberg out of wood and leather, foster the growth of anything; much more of Mind, which grows, not like a vegetable (by having its roots littered with etymological compost), but like a spirit, by mysterious contact of Spirit; Thought kindling itself at the fire of living Thought? How shall *he* give kindling, in whose own inward man there is no live coal, but all is burnt-out to a dead grammatical cinder? The Hinterschlag Professors knew syntax enough; and of the human soul thus much: that it had a faculty called Memory, and could be acted-on through the muscular integument by appliance of birch-rods.

'Alas, so is it everywhere, so will it ever be; till the Hodman is discharged, or reduced to hodbearing; and an Architect is hired, and on all hands fitly encouraged: till communities and individuals discover, not without surprise, that fashioning the souls of a generation by Knowledge can rank on a level with blowing their bodies to pieces by Gunpowder; that with Generals and Fieldmarshals for killing, there should be world-honoured Dignitaries, and were it possible, true God-ordained Priests, for teaching. But as yet, though the Soldier wears openly, and even parades, his butchering-tool, nowhere, far as I have travelled, did the Schoolmaster make show of his instructing-tool: nay, were he to walk abroad with birch girt on thigh, as if he therefrom expected honour, would there not, among the idler class, perhaps a certain levity be excited?'

In the third year of this Gymnasic period, Father Andreas seems to have died: the young Scholar, otherwise so maltreated, saw himself for the first time clad outwardly in sables, and inwardly in quite inexpressible melancholy. 'The dark bottomless Abyss, that lies under our feet, had yawned open; the pale kingdoms of Death, with all their innumerable silent nations and generations, stood before him; the inexorable word, NEVER! now first showed its meaning. My Mother wept, and her sorrow got vent; but in my heart there lay a whole lake of tears, pent-up in silent desolation. Nevertheless the unworn Spirit is strong; Life is so healthful that it even finds nourishment in Death: these stern experiences, planted down by Memory in my Imagination, rose there to a whole cypress-forest, sad but beautiful; waving, with not unmelodious sighs, in dark luxuriance, in the hottest sunshine, through long years of youth:—as in manhood also it does, and will do; for I have now pitched my tent under a Cypress-tree; the Tomb is now my inexpugnable Fortress, ever close by the gate of which I look upon the hostile armaments, and pains and penalties of tyrannous Life placidly enough, and listen to its loudest threatenings with a still smile. O ye loved ones, that already sleep in the noiseless Bed of Rest, whom in life I could only weep for and never help; and ye, who wide-scattered still toil lonely in the monster-bearing Desert, dyeing the flinty ground with your blood,—yet a little while, and we shall all meet THERE, and our Mother's bosom will screen us all; and Oppression's harness, and Sorrow's fire-whip, and all the Gehenna Bailiffs that patrol and inhabit ever-vexed Time, cannot thenceforth harm us any more!'

Close by which rather beautiful apostrophe, lies a laboured Character of the deceased Andreas Futteral; of his natural ability, his deserts in life (as Prussian Sergeant); with long historical inquiries into the genealogy of the Futteral Family, here traced back as far as Henry the Fowler: the whole of which we pass over, not without astonishment. It only concerns us to add, that now was the time when Mother Gretchen revealed to her foster-son that he was not at all of this kindred; or indeed of any kindred, having come into historical existence in the way already known to us. 'Thus was I doubly orphaned,' says he; 'bereft not only of Possession, but even of Remembrance. Sorrow and Wonder, here suddenly united, could not but produce abundant fruit. Such a disclosure, in such a season, struck its roots through my whole nature: ever till the years of mature manhood, it mingled with my whole thoughts, was as the stem whereon all my day-dreams and night-dreams grew. A certain poetic elevation, yet also a corresponding civic depression, it naturally imparted: *I was like no other;* in which fixed-idea, leading sometimes to highest, and oftener to frightfullest results, may there not lie the first spring of tendencies, which in my Life have become remarkable enough? As in birth, so in action, speculation, and social position, my fellows are perhaps not numerous.'

In the Bag *Sagittarius,* as we at length discover, Teufelsdröckh has become a University man; though how, when, or of what quality, will nowhere disclose itself with the smallest certainty. Few things, in the way of confusion and capricious indistinctness, can now surprise our readers; not even the total want of dates, almost without parallel in a Biographical work. So enigmatic, so chaotic we have always found, and must always look to find, these scattered Leaves. In *Sagittarius,* however, Teufelsdröckh begins to show himself even more than usually Sibylline: fragments of all sorts; scraps of regular Memoir, College-Exercises, Programs, Professional Testimoniums, Milkscores, torn Billets, sometimes to appearance of an amatory cast; all blown together as if by merest chance, henceforth bewilder the sane Historian. To combine any picture of these University, and the subsequent, years; much more, to decipher therein any illustrative primordial elements of the Clothes-Philosophy, becomes such a problem as the reader may imagine.

So much we can see; darkly, as through the foliage of some wavering thicket: a youth of no common endowment, who has passed happily through Childhood, less happily yet still vigorously through Boyhood, now at length perfect in 'dead vocables,' and set down, as he hopes, by the living Fountain, there to superadd Ideas and Capabilities. From such Fountain he draws, diligently, thirstily, yet never or seldom with his whole heart, for the water nowise suits his palate; discouragements, entanglements, aberrations are discoverable or supposable. Nor perhaps are even pecuniary distresses wanting; for 'the good Gretchen, who in spite of advices from not disinterested relatives has sent him hither, must after a time withdraw her willing but too feeble hand.' Nevertheless in an atmosphere of Poverty and manifold Chagrin, the Humour of that young Soul, what character is in him, first decisively reveals itself; and, like strong sunshine in weeping skies, gives out variety of colours, some of which are prismatic. Thus, with the aid of Time and of what Time brings, has the stripling Diogenes Teufelsdröckh waxed into manly stature; and into so questionable an aspect, that we ask with new eagerness, How he specially came by it, and regret anew that there is no more explicit answer. Certain of the intelligible and partially significant fragments, which are few in number, shall be extracted from that Limbo of a Paper-bag, and presented with the usual preparation.

As if, in the Bag *Scorpio,* Teufelsdröckh had not already expectorated his antipedagogic spleen; as if, from the name *Sagittarius,* he had thought himself called upon to shoot arrows, we here again fall-in with such matter as this: 'The University where I was educated still stands vivid enough in my remembrance, and I know its name well; which name, however, I, from tenderness to existing interests and persons, shall in nowise divulge. It is my painful duty to say that, out of England and Spain, ours was the worst of all hitherto discovered Universities. This is indeed a time when right Education is, as nearly as may be, impossible: however, in degrees of wrongness there is no limit: nay, I can conceive a worse system than that of the Nameless itself; as poisoned victual may be worse than absolute hunger.

'It is written, When the blind lead the blind, both shall fall into the ditch: wherefore, in such circumstances, may it not sometimes be safer, if both leader and lead simply— sit still? Had you, anywhere in Crim Tartary, walled-in a square enclosure; furnished it with a small, ill-chosen Library; and then turned loose into it eleven-hundred Christian striplings, to tumble about as they listed, from three to seven years: certain persons, under the title of Professors, being stationed at the gates, to declare aloud that it was a University, and exact considerable admission-fees, —you had, not indeed in mechanical structure, yet in spirit and result, some imperfect resemblance of our High Seminary. I say, imperfect; for if our mechanical structure was quite other, so neither was our result altogether the same: unhappily, we were not in Crim Tartary, but in a corrupt European city, full of smoke and sin; moreover, in the middle of a Public, which, without far costlier apparatus than that of the Square Enclosure, and Declaration aloud, you could not be sure of gulling.

'Gullible, however, by fit apparatus, all Publics are; and gulled, with the most surprising profit. Towards anything like a *Statistics of Imposture,* indeed, little as yet has been done: with a strange indifference, our Economists, nigh buried under Tables for minor Branches of Industry, have altogether overlooked the grand all-overtopping Hypocrisy Branch; as if our whole arts of Puffery, of Quackery, Priestcraft, Kingcraft, and the innumerable other crafts and mysteries of that genus, had not ranked in Productive Industry at all! Can any one, for example, so much as say, What moneys, in Literature and Shoeblacking, are realised by actual instruction and actual jet Polish; what by fictitious-persuasive Proclamation of such; specifying, in distinct items, the distributions, circulations, disbursements, incomings of said moneys, with the smallest approach to accuracy? But to ask, How far, in all the several infinitely-complected departments of social business, in government, education, in manual, commercial, intellectual fabrication of every sort, man's Want is supplied by true Ware; how far by the mere Appearance of true Ware:—in other words, To what extent, by what methods, with what effects, in various times and countries, Deception takes the place of wages of Performance: here truly is an Inquiry big with results for the future time, but to which hitherto only the vaguest answer can be given. If for the present, in our Europe, we estimate the ratio of Ware to Appearance of Ware so high even as at One to a Hundred (which, considering the Wages of a Pope, Russian Autocrat, or English Game-Preserver, is probably not far from the mark),—what almost prodigious saving may there not be anticipated, as the *Statistics of Imposture* advances, and so the manufacturing of Shams (that of Realities rising into clearer and clearer distinction therefrom) gradually declines, and at length becomes all but wholly unnecessary!

'This for the coming golden ages. What I had to remark, for the present brazen one, is, that in several provinces, as in Education, Polity, Religion, where so much is wanted and indispensable, and so little can as yet be furnished, probably Imposture is of sanative, anodyne nature, and man's Gullibility not his worst blessing. Suppose your sinews of war quite broken; I mean your military chest insolvent, forage all but exhausted; and that the whole army is about to mutiny, disband, and cut your and each other's throat, —then were it not well could you, as if by miracle, pay them in any sort of fairy-money, feed them on coagulated water, or mere imagination of meat; whereby, till the real supply came up, they might be kept together and quiet? Such perhaps was the aim of Nature, who does nothing without aim, in furnishing her favourite, Man, with this his so omnipotent or rather omnipatient Talent of being Gulled.

'How beautifully it works, with a little mechanism; nay, almost makes mechanism for itself! These Professors in the Nameless lived with ease, with safety, by a mere Reputation, constructed in past times, and then too with no great effort, by quite another class of persons. Which Reputation, like a strong, brisk-going undershot wheel, sunk into the general current, bade fair, with only a little annual repainting on their part, to hold long together, and of its own accord assiduously grind for them. Happy that it was so, for the Millers! They themselves needed not to work; their attempts at working, at what they called Educating, now when I look back on it, fill me with a certain mute admiration.

'Besides all this, we boasted ourselves a Rational University; in the highest degree hostile to Mysticism; thus was the young vacant mind furnished with much talk about Progress of the Species, Dark Ages, Prejudice, and the like; so that all were quickly enough blown out into a state of windy argumentativeness; whereby the better sort had soon to end in sick, impotent Scepticism; the worser sort explode (*crepiren*) in finished Self-conceit, and to all spiritual intents become dead.—But this too is portion of mankind's lot. If our era is the Era of Unbelief, why murmur under it; is there not a better coming, nay come? As in long-drawn systole and long-drawn diastole, must the period of Faith alternate with the period of Denial; must the vernal growth, the summer luxuriance of all Opinions, Spiritual Representations and Creations, be followed by, and again follow, the autumnal decay, the winter dissolution. For man lives in Time, has his whole earthly being, endeavour and destiny shaped for him by Time: only in the transitory Time-Symbol is the ever-motionless Eternity we stand on made manifest. And yet, in such winter-seasons of Denial, it is for the nobler-minded perhaps a comparative misery to have been born, and to be awake and work; and for the duller a felicity, if, like hibernating animals, safe-lodged in some Salamanca University, or Sybaris City, or other superstitious or voluptuous Castle of Indolence, they can slumber-through in stupid dreams, and only awaken when the loud-roaring hailstorms have all done their work, and to our prayers and martyrdoms the new Spring has been vouchsafed.'

That in the environment, here mysteriously enough shadowed forth Teufelsdröckh must have felt ill at ease, cannot be doubtful. 'The hungry young,' he says, 'looked up to their spiritual Nurses; and, for food, were bidden eat the east-wind. What vain jargon of controversial Metaphysic, Etymology, and mechanical Manipulation falsely named Science, was current there, I indeed learned, better perhaps than the most. Among eleven-hundred Christian youths, there will not be wanting some eleven eager to learn. By collision with such, a certain warmth, a certain polish was communicated; by instinct and happy accident, I took less to rioting (*renommiren*), than to thinking and reading, which latter also I was free to do. Nay from the chaos of that Library, I succeeded in fishing-up more books perhaps than had been known to the very keepers thereof. The foundation of a Literary Life was hereby laid. I learned, on my own strength, to read fluently in almost all cultivated languages, on almost all subjects and sciences; farther, as man is ever the prime object to man, already it was my favourite employment to read character in speculation, and from the Writing to construe the Writer. A certain ground-plan of Human Nature and Life began to fashion itself in me; wondrous enough, now when I look back on it; for my whole Universe, physical and spiritual, was as yet a Machine! However, such a conscious, recognised groundplan, the truest I had, *was* beginning to be there, and by additional experiments might be corrected and indefinitely extended.'

Thus from poverty does the strong educe nobler wealth; thus in the destitution of the wild desert does our young Ishmael acquire for himself the highest of all possessions, that of Self-help. Nevertheless a desert this was, waste, and howling with savage monsters. Teufelsdröckh gives us long details of his 'fever-paroxysms of Doubt'; his Inquiries concerning Miracles, and the Evidences of religious Faith; and how 'in the silent night-watches, still darker in his heart than over sky and earth, he has cast himself before the All-seeing, and with audible prayers cried vehemently for Light, for deliverance from Death and the Grave. Not till after long years, and unspeakable agonies, did the believing heart surrender; sink into spell-bound sleep, under the nightmare, Unbelief; and, in this hag-ridden dream, mistake God's fair living world for a pallid, vacant Hades and extinct Pandemonium. But through such Purgatory pain,' continues he, 'it is appointed us to pass; first must the dead Letter of Religion own itself dead, and drop piecemeal into dust, if the living Spirit of Religion, freed from this its charnel-house, is to arise on us, newborn of Heaven, and with new healing under its wings.'

To which Purgatory pains, seemingly severe enough, if we add a liberal measure of Earthly distresses, want of practical guidance, want of sympathy, want of money, want of hope; and all this in the fervid season of youth, so exaggerated in imagining, so boundless in desires, yet here so poor in means,—do we not see a strong incipient spirit oppressed and overloaded from without and from within; the fire of genius struggling-up among fuel-wood of the greenest, and as yet with more of bitter vapour than of clear flame?

From various fragments of Letters and other documentary scraps, it is to be inferred that Teufelsdröckh, isolated, shy, retiring as he was, had not altogether escaped notice: certain established men are aware of his existence; and, if stretching-out no helpful hand, have at least their eyes on him. He appears, though in dreary enough humour, to be addressing himself to the Profession of Law;—whereof, indeed, the world has since seen him a public graduate. But omitting these broken, unsatisfactory thrums of Economical relation, let us present rather the following small thread of Moral relation; and therewith, the reader for himself weaving it in at the right place, conclude our dim arras-picture of these University years.

'Here also it was that I formed acquaintance with Herr Towgood, or, as it is perhaps better written, Herr Toughgut; a young person of quality (*von Adel*), from the interior parts of England. He stood connected, by blood and hospitality, with the Counts von Zähdarm, in this quarter of Germany; to which noble Family I likewise was, by his means, with all friendliness, brought near. Towgood had a fair talent, unspeakably ill-cultivated; with considerable humour of character: and, bating his total ignorance, for he knew nothing except Boxing and a little Grammar, showed less of that aristocratic impassivity, and silent fury, than for most part belongs to Travellers of his nation. To him I owe my first practical knowledge of the English and their ways; perhaps also something of the partiality with which I have ever since regarded that singular people. Towgood was not without an eye, could he have come at any light. Invited doubtless by the presence of the Zähdarm Family, he had travelled hither, in the almost frantic hope of perfecting his studies; he, whose studies had as yet been those of infancy, hither to a University where so much as the notion of perfection, not to say the effort after it, no longer existed! Often we would condole over the hard destiny of the Young in this era: how, after all our toil, we were to be turned-out into the world, with beards on our chins indeed, but with few other attributes of manhood; no existing thing that we were trained to Act on, nothing that we could so much as Believe. "How has our head on the outside a polished Hat," would Towgood exclaim, "and in the inside Vacancy, or a froth of Vocables and Attorney-Logic! At a small cost men are educated to make leather into shoes; but at a great cost, what am I educated to make? By Heaven, Brother! what I have already eaten and worn, as I came thus far, would endow a considerable Hospital of Incurables."—"Man, indeed," I would answer, "has a Digestive Faculty, which must be kept working, were it even partly by stealth. But as for our Miseducation, make not bad worse; waste not the time yet ours, in trampling on thistles because they have yielded us no figs. *Frisch zu, Bruder!* Here are Books, and we have brains to read them; here is a whole Earth and a whole Heaven, and we have eyes to look on them: *Frisch zu!*"

'Often also our talk was gay; not without brilliancy, and even fire. We looked-out on Life, with its strange scaffolding, where all at once harlequins dance, and men are beheaded and quartered: motley, not unterrific was the aspect; but we looked on it like brave youths. For myself, these were perhaps my most genial hours. Towards this young warmhearted, strongheaded and wrongheaded Herr Towgood I was even near experiencing the now obsolete sentiment of Friendship. Yes, foolish Heathen that I was, I felt that, under certain conditions, I could have loved this man, and taken him to my bosom, and been his brother once and always. By degrees, however, I understood the new time, and its wants. If man's *Soul* is indeed, as in the Finnish Language, and Utilitarian Philosophy, a kind of *Stomach,* what else is the true meaning of Spiritual Union but an Eating together? Thus we, instead of Friends, are Dinner-guests; and here as elsewhere have cast away chimeras.'

So ends, abruptly as is usual, and enigmatically, this little incipient romance. What henceforth becomes of the brave Herr Towgood, or Toughgut? He has dived-under, in the Autobiographical Chaos, and swims we see not where. Does any reader 'in the interior parts of England' know of such a man?

CHAPTER IV

GETTING UNDER WAY

The grand thaumaturgic Art of Thought. Difficulty in fitting Capability to Opportunity, or of getting under way. The advantage of Hunger and Bread-Studies. Teufelsdröckh has to enact the stern monodrama of No object and no rest. Sufferings as Auscultator. Given up as a man of genius. Zähdarm House. Intolerable presumption of young men. Irony and its consequences. Teufelsdröckh's Epitaph on Count Zähdarm.

'Thus nevertheless,' writes our Autobiographer, apparently as quitting College, 'was there realised Somewhat; namely, I, Diogenes Teufelsdröckh: a visible Temporary Figure (*Zeitbild*), occupying some cubic feet of Space, and containing within it Forces both physical and spiritual; hopes, passions, thoughts; the whole wondrous furniture, in more or less perfection, belonging to that mystery, a Man. Capabilities there were in me to give battle, in some small degree, against the great Empire of Darkness: does not the very Ditcher and Delver, with his spade, extinguish many a thistle and puddle; and so leave a little Order, where he found the opposite? Nay your very Daymoth has capabilities in this kind; and ever organises something (into its own Body, if no otherwise), which was before Inorganic; and of mute dead air makes living music, though only of the faintest, by humming.

'How much more, one whose capabilities are spiritual; who has learned, or begun learning, the grand thaumaturgic art of Thought! Thaumaturgic I name it; for hitherto all Miracles have been wrought thereby, and henceforth innumerable will be wrought; whereof we, even in these days, witness some. Of the Poet's and Prophet's inspired Message, and how it makes and unmakes whole worlds, I shall forbear mention: but cannot the dullest hear Steam-Engines clanking around him? Has he not seen the Scottish Brassmith's IDEA (and this but a mechanical one) travelling on fire-wings round the Cape, and across two Oceans; and stronger than any other Enchanter's Familiar, on all hands unweariedly fetching and carrying: at home, not only weaving Cloth; but rapidly enough overturning the whole old system of Society; and, for Feudalism and Preservation of the Game, preparing us, by indirect but sure methods, Industrialism and the Government of the Wisest? Truly a Thinking Man is the worst enemy the Prince of Darkness can have; every time such a one announces himself, I doubt not, there runs a shudder through the Nether Empire; and new Emissaries are trained, with new tactics, to, if possible, entrap him, and hoodwink and handcuff him.

'With such high vocation had I too, as denizen of the Universe, been called. Unhappy it is, however, that though born to the amplest Sovereignty, in this way, with no less than sovereign right of Peace and War against the Time-Prince (*Zeitfürst*), or Devil, and all his Dominions, your coronation-ceremony costs such trouble, your sceptre is so difficult to get at, or even to get eye on!'

By which last wiredrawn similitude does Teufelsdröckh mean no more than that young men find obstacles in what we call 'getting under way'? 'Not what I Have,' continues he, 'but what I Do is my Kingdom. To each is given a certain inward Talent, a certain outward Environment of Fortune; to each, by wisest combination of these two, a certain maximum of Capability. But the hardest problem were ever this first: To find by study of yourself, and of the ground you stand on, what your combined inward and outward Capability specially is. For, alas, our young soul is all budding with Capabilities, and we see not yet which is the main and true one. Always too the new man is in a new time, under new conditions; his course can be the *fac-simile* of no prior one, but is by its nature original. And then how seldom will the outward Capability fit the inward: though talented wonderfully enough, we are poor, unfriended, dyspeptical, bashful; nay what is worse than all, we are foolish. Thus, in a whole imbroglio of Capabilities, we go stupidly groping about, to grope which is ours, and often clutch the wrong one: in this mad work must several years of our small term be spent, till the purblind Youth, by practice, acquire notions of distance, and become a seeing Man. Nay, many so spend their whole term, and in ever-new expectation, ever-new disappointment, shift from enterprise to enterprise, and from side to side: till at length, as exasperated striplings of threescore-and-ten, they shift into their last enterprise, that of getting buried.

'Such, since the most of us are too ophthalmic, would be the general fate; were it not that one thing saves us: our Hunger. For on this ground, as the prompt nature of Hunger is well known, must a prompt choice be made: hence have we, with wise foresight, Indentures and Apprenticeships for our irrational young; whereby, in due season, the vague universality of a Man shall find himself ready-moulded into a specific Craftsman; and so thenceforth work, with much or with little waste of Capability as it may be; yet not with the worst waste, that of time. Nay even in matters spiritual, since the spiritual artist too is born blind, and does not, like certain other creatures, receive sight in nine days, but far later, sometimes never,—is it not well that there should be what we call Professions, or Bread-studies (*Brodzwecke*), pre-appointed us? Here, circling like the gin-horse, for whom partial or total blindness is no evil, the Bread-artist can travel contentedly round and round, still fancying that it is forward and forward; and realise much: for himself victual; for the world an additional horse's power in the grand corn-mill or hemp-mill of Economic Society. For me too had such a leading-string been provided; only that it proved a neck-halter, and had nigh throttled me, till I broke it off. Then, in the words of Ancient Pistol, did the world generally become mine oyster, which I, by strength or cunning, was to open, as I would and could. Almost had I deceased (*fast wär ich umgekommen*), so obstinately did it continue shut.'

We see here, significantly foreshadowed, the spirit of much that was to befall our Autobiographer; the historical embodiment of which, as it painfully takes shape in his Life, lies scattered, in dim disastrous details, through this Bag *Pisces,* and those that follow. A young man of high talent, and high though still temper, like a young mettled colt, 'breaks-off his neck-halter,' and bounds forth, from his peculiar manger, into the wide world; which, alas, he finds all rigorously fenced-in. Richest clover-fields tempt his eye; but to him they are forbidden pasture: either pining in progressive starvation, he must stand; or, in mad exasperation, must rush to and fro, leaping against sheer stone-walls, which he cannot leap over, which only lacerate and lame him; till at last, after thousand attempts and endurances, he, as if by miracle, clears his way; not indeed into luxuriant and luxurious clover, yet into a certain bosky wilderness where existence is still possible, and Freedom, though waited on by Scarcity, is not without sweetness. In a word, Teufelsdröckh having thrown-up his legal Profession, finds himself without landmark of outward guidance; whereby his previous want of decided Belief, or inward guidance, is frightfully aggravated. Necessity urges him on; Time will not stop, neither can he, a Son of Time; wild passions without solacement, wild faculties without employment, ever vex and agitate him. He too must enact that stern Monodrama, *No Object and No Rest;* must front its successive destinies, work through to its catastrophe, and deduce therefrom what moral he can.

Yet let us be just to him, let us admit that his 'neckhalter' sat nowise easy on him; that he was in some degree forced to break it off. If we look at the young man's civic position, in this Nameless capital, as he emerges from its Nameless University, we can discern well that it was far from enviable. His first Law-Examination he has come through triumphantly; and can even boast that the *Examen Rigorosum* need not have frightened him: but though he is hereby 'an *Auscultator* of respectability,' what avails it? There is next to no employment to be had. Neither, for a youth without connexions, is the process of Expectation very hopeful in itself; nor for one of his disposition much cheered from without. 'My fellow Auscultators,' he says, 'were Auscultators: they dressed, and digested, and talked articulate words; other vitality showed they almost none. Small speculation in those eyes, that they did glare withal! Sense neither for the high nor for the deep, nor for aught human or divine, save only for the faintest scent of coming Preferment.' In which words, indicating a total estrangement on the part of Teufelsdröckh, may there not also lurk traces of a bitterness as from wounded vanity? Doubtless these prosaic Auscultators may have sniffed at him, with his strange ways; and tried to hate, and what was much more impossible, to despise him. Friendly communion, in any case, there could not be: already has the young Teufelsdröckh left the other young geese; and swims apart, though as yet uncertain whether he himself is cygnet or gosling.

Perhaps, too, what little employment he had was performed ill, at best unpleasantly. 'Great practical method and expertness' he may brag of; but is there not also great practical pride, though deep-hidden, only the deeper-seated? So shy a man can never have been popular. We figure to ourselves, how in those days he may have played strange freaks with his independence, and so forth: do not his own words betoken as much? 'Like a very young person, I imagined it was with Work alone, and not also with Folly and Sin, in myself and others, that I had been appointed to struggle.' Be this as it may, his progress from the passive Auscultatorship, towards any active Assessorship, is evidently of the slowest. By degrees, those same established men, once partially inclined to patronise him, seem to withdraw their countenance, and give him up as 'a man of genius': against which procedure he, in these Papers, loudly protests. 'As if,' says he, 'the higher did not presuppose the lower; as if he who can fly into heaven, could not also walk post if he resolved on it! But the world is an old woman, and mistakes any gilt farthing for a gold coin; whereby being often cheated, she will thenceforth trust nothing but the common copper.'

How our winged sky-messenger, unaccepted as a terrestrial runner, contrived, in the mean while, to keep himself from flying skyward without return, is not too clear from these Documents. Good old Gretchen seems to have vanished from the scene, perhaps from the Earth; other Horn of Plenty, or even of Parsimony, nowhere flows for him; so that 'the prompt nature of Hunger being well known,' we are not without our anxiety. From private Tuition, in never so many languages and sciences, the aid derivable is small; neither, to use his own words, 'does the young Adventurer hitherto suspect in himself any literary gift; but at best earns bread-and-water wages, by his wide faculty of Translation. Nevertheless,' continues he, 'that I subsisted is clear, for you find me even now alive.' Which fact, however, except upon the principle of our true-hearted, kind old Proverb, that 'there is always life for a living one,' we must profess ourselves unable to explain.

Certain Landlords' Bills, and other economic Documents, bearing the mark of Settlement, indicate that he was not without money; but, like an independent Hearth-holder, if not House-holder, paid his way. Here also occur, among many others, two little mutilated Notes, which perhaps throw light on his condition. The first has now no date, or writer's name, but a huge Blot; and runs to this effect: 'The (*Inkblot*), tied-down by previous promise, cannot, except by best wishes, forward the Herr Teufelsdröckh's views on the Assessorship in question; and sees himself under the cruel necessity of forbearing, for the present, what were otherwise his duty and joy, to assist in opening the career for a man of genius, on whom far higher triumphs are yet waiting.' The other is on gilt paper; and interests us like a sort of epistolary mummy now dead, yet which once lived and beneficently worked. We give it in the original: '*Herr Teufelsdröckh wird von der Frau Gräfinn, auf Donnerstag, zum ÆSTHETISCHEN THEE schönstens eingeladen.*'

Thus, in answer to a cry for solid pudding, whereof there is the most urgent need, comes, epigrammatically enough, the invitation to a wash of quite fluid *Æsthetic Tea!* How Teufelsdröckh, now at actual handgrips with Destiny herself, may have comported himself among these Musical and Literary Dilettanti of both sexes, like a hungry lion invited to a feast of chickenweed, we can only conjecture. Perhaps in expressive silence, and abstinence: otherwise if the lion, in such case, is to feast at all, it cannot be on the chickenweed, but only on the chickens. For the rest, as this Frau Gräfinn dates from the *Zähdarm House,* she can be no other than the Countess and mistress of the same; whose intellectual tendencies, and good-will to Teufelsdröckh, whether on the footing of Herr Towgood, or on his own footing, are hereby manifest. That some sort of relation, indeed, continued, for a time, to connect our Autobiographer, though perhaps feebly enough, with this noble House, we have elsewhere express evidence. Doubtless, if he expected patronage, it was in vain; enough for him if he here obtained occasional glimpses of the great world, from which we at one time fancied him to have been always excluded. 'The Zähdarms,' says he, 'lived in the soft, sumptuous garniture of Aristocracy; whereto Literature and Art, attracted and attached from without, were to serve as the handsomest fringing. It was to the *Gnädigen Frau* (her Ladyship) that this latter improvement was due: assiduously she gathered, dextrously she fitted-on, what fringing was to be had; lace or cobweb, as the place yielded.' Was Teufelsdröckh also a fringe, of lace or cobweb; or promising to be such? 'With his *Excellenz* (the Count),' continues he, 'I have more than once had the honour to converse; chiefly on general affairs, and the aspect of the world, which he, though now past middle life, viewed in no unfavourable light; finding indeed, except the Outrooting of Journalism (*die auszurottende Journalistik*), little to desiderate therein. On some points, as his *Excellenz* was not uncholeric, I found it more pleasant to keep silence. Besides, his occupation being that of Owning Land, there might be faculties enough, which, as superfluous for such use, were little developed in him.'

That to Teufelsdröckh the aspect of the world was nowise so faultless, and many things besides 'the Outrooting of Journalism' might have seemed improvements, we can readily conjecture. With nothing but a barren Auscultatorship from without, and so many mutinous thoughts and wishes from within, his position was no easy one. 'The Universe,' he says, 'was a mighty Sphinx-riddle, which I knew so little of, yet must rede, or be devoured. In red streaks of unspeakable grandeur, yet also in the blackness of darkness, was Life, to my too-unfurnished Thought, unfolding itself. A strange contradiction lay in me; and I as yet knew not the solution of it; knew not that spiritual music can spring only from discords set in harmony; that but for Evil there were no Good, as victory is only possible by battle.'

'I have heard affirmed (surely in jest),' observes he elsewhere, 'by not unphilanthropic persons, that it were a real increase of human happiness, could all young men from the age of nineteen be covered under barrels, or rendered otherwise invisible; and there left to follow their lawful studies and callings, till they emerged, sadder and wiser, at the age of twenty-five. With which suggestion, at least as considered in the light of a practical scheme, I need scarcely say that I nowise coincide. Nevertheless it is plausibly urged that, as young ladies (*Mädchen*) are, to mankind, precisely the most delightful in those years; so young gentlemen (*Bübchen*) do then attain their maximum of detestability. Such gawks (*Gecken*) are they, and foolish peacocks, and yet with such a vulturous hunger for self-indulgence; so obstinate, obstreperous, vain-glorious; in all senses, so froward and so forward. No mortal's endeavour or attainment will, in the smallest, content the as yet unendeavouring, unattaining young gentleman; but he could make it all infinitely better, were it worthy of him. Life everywhere is the most manageable matter, simple as a question in the Rule-of-Three: multiply your second and third term together, divide the product by the first, and your quotient will be the answer,—which you are but an ass if you cannot come at. The booby has not yet found-out, by any trial, that, do what one will, there is ever a cursed fraction, oftenest a decimal repeater, and no net integer quotient so much as to be thought of.'

In which passage does not there lie an implied confession that Teufelsdröckh himself, besides his outward obstructions, had an inward, still greater, to contend with; namely, a certain temporary, youthful, yet still afflictive derangement of head? Alas, on the former side alone, his case was hard enough. 'It continues ever true,' says he, 'that Saturn, or Chronos, or what we call TIME, devours all his Children: only by incessant Running, by incessant Working, may you (for some threescore-and-ten years) escape him; and you too he devours at last. Can any Sovereign, or Holy Alliance of Sovereigns, bid Time stand still; even in thought, shake themselves free of Time? Our whole terrestrial being is based on Time, and built of Time; it is wholly a Movement, a Time-impulse; Time is the author of it, the material of it. Hence also our Whole Duty, which is to move, to work, —in the right direction. Are not our Bodies and our Souls in continual movement, whether we will or not; in a continual Waste, requiring a continual Repair? Utmost satisfaction of our whole outward and inward Wants were but satisfaction for a space of Time; thus, whatso we have done, is done, and for us annihilated, and ever must we go and do anew. O Time-Spirit, how hast thou environed and imprisoned us, and sunk us so deep in thy troublous dim Time-Element, that only in lucid moments can so much as glimpses of our upper Azure Home be revealed to us! Me, however, as a Son of Time, unhappier than some others, was Time threatening to eat quite prematurely; for, strive as I might, there was no good Running, so obstructed was the path, so gyved were the feet.' That is to say, we presume, speaking in the dialect of this lower world, that Teufelsdröckh's whole duty and necessity was, like other men's, 'to work,—in the right direction,' and that no work was to be had; whereby he became wretched enough. As was natural: with haggard Scarcity threatening him in the distance; and so vehement a soul languishing in restless inaction, and forced thereby, like Sir Hudibras's sword by rust,

> To eat into itself, for lack
> Of something else to hew and hack!

But on the whole, that same 'excellent Passivity,' as it has all along done, is here again vigorously flourishing; in which circumstance may we not trace the beginnings of much that now characterises our Professor; and perhaps, in faint rudiments, the origin of the Clothes-Philosophy itself? Already the attitude he has assumed towards the World is too defensive; not, as would have been desirable, a bold attitude of attack. 'So far hitherto,' he says, 'as I had mingled with mankind, I was notable, if for anything, for a certain stillness of manner, which, as my friends often rebukingly declared, did but ill express the keen ardour of my feelings. I, in truth, regarded men with an excess both of love and of fear. The mystery of a Person, indeed, is ever divine to him that has a sense for the Godlike. Often, notwithstanding, was I blamed, and by half-strangers hated, for my so-called Hardness (*Härte*), my Indifferentism towards men; and the seemingly ironic tone I had adopted, as my favourite dialect in conversation. Alas, the panoply of Sarcasm was but as a buckram case, wherein I had striven to envelope myself; that so my own poor Person might live safe there, and in all friendliness, being no longer exasperated by wounds. Sarcasm I now see to be, in general, the language of the Devil; for which reason I have long since as good as renounced it. But how many individuals did I, in those days, provoke into some degree of hostility thereby! An ironic man, with his sly stillness, and ambuscading ways, more especially an ironic young man, from whom it is least expected, may be viewed as a pest to society. Have we not seen persons of weight and name coming forward, with gentlest indifference, to tread such a one out of sight, as an insignificancy and worm, start ceiling-high (*balkenhoch*), and thence fall shattered and supine, to be borne home on shutters, not without indignation, when he proved electric and a torpedo!'

Alas, how can a man with this devilishness of temper make way for himself in Life; where the first problem, as Teufelsdröckh too admits, is 'to unite yourself with some one and with somewhat (*sich anzuschliessen*)'? Division, not union, is written on most part of his procedure. Let us add too that, in no great length of time, the only important connexion he had ever succeeded in forming, his connexion with the Zähdarm Family, seems to have been paralysed, for all practical uses, by the death of the 'not uncholeric' old Count. This fact stands recorded, quite incidentally, in a certain *Discourse on Epitaphs,* huddled into the present Bag, among so much else; of which Essay the learning and curious penetration are more to be approved of than the spirit. His grand principle is, that lapidary inscriptions, of what sort soever, should be Historical rather than Lyrical. 'By request of that worthy Nobleman's survivors,' says he, 'I undertook to compose his Epitaph; and not unmindful of my own rules, produced the following; which however, for an alleged defect of Latinity, a defect never yet fully visible to myself, still remains unengraven;'—wherein, we may predict, there is more than the Latinity that will surprise an English reader:

HIC JACET

PHILIPPUS ZAEHDARM,
COGNOMINE MAGNUS,
ZAEHDARMI COMES,
EX IMPERII CONCILIO,

VELLERIS AUREI, PERISCELIDIS, NECNON
VULTURIS NIGRI EQUES.
QUI DUM SUB LUNA AGEBAT,

QUINQUIES MILLE PERDICES
PLUMBO CONFECIT:

VARII CIBI
CENTUMPONDIA MILLIES CENTENA MILLIA,
PER SE, PERQUE SERVOS QUADRUPEDES BIPEDESVE,
HAUD SINE TUMULTU DEVOLVENS,

IN STERCUS
PALAM CONVERTIT.
NUNC A LABORE REQUIESCENTEM
OPERA SEQUUNTUR.
SI MONUMENTUM QUÆRIS,
FIMETUM ADSPICE.

PRIMUM IN ORBE DEJECIT [*sub dato*];
POSTREMUM [*sub dato*].[1]

CHAPTER V

ROMANCE

*Teufelsdröckh gives up his Profession. The heavenly mystery of
Love. Teufelsdröckh's feeling of worship towards women. First
and only love. Blumine. Happy hearts and free tongues. The infinite nature of Fantasy. Love's joyful progress; sudden dissolution; and final catastrophe.*

'For long years,' writes Teufelsdröckh, 'had the poor Hebrew, in this Egypt of an Auscultatorship, painfully toiled,
baking bricks without stubble, before ever the question

---

[1] "Here lies Philip Zaehdarm [literally, tough-gut], called the Great,
Count of Zaehdarm, Member of the Imperial Council, Knight of the
Golden Fleece, of the Garter, and of the Black Vulture. Who, while
he lived on earth, shot five thousand partridges: a hundred million
hundred-weights of various kinds of food he openly, by himself and
by his servants, quadrupeds and bipeds, not without tumult in the
course of it, converted into manure. Now resting from his labor, his
works follow him. If you seek his monument, look at this pile. Commenced [on the date]; finished [on the date]."

once struck him with entire force: For what?—*Beym Himmel!* For Food and Warmth! And are Food and Warmth nowhere else, in the whole wide Universe, discoverable?— Come of it what might, I resolved to try.'

Thus then are we to see him in a new independent capacity, though perhaps far from an improved one. Teufelsdröckh is now a man without Profession. Quitting the common Fleet of herring-busses and whalers, where indeed his leeward, laggard condition was painful enough, he desperately steers off, on a course of his own, by sextant and compass of his own. Unhappy Teufelsdröckh! Though neither Fleet, nor Traffic, nor Commodores pleased thee, still was it not *a Fleet,* sailing in prescribed track, for fixed objects; above all, in combination, wherein, by mutual guidance, by all manner of loans and borrowings, each could manifoldly aid the other? How wilt thou sail in unknown seas; and for thyself find that shorter North-west Passage to thy fair Spice-country of a Nowhere?—A solitary rover, on such a voyage, with such nautical tactics, will meet with adventures. Nay, as we forthwith discover, a certain Calypso-Island detains him at the very outset; and as it were falsifies and oversets his whole reckoning.

'If in youth,' writes he once, 'the Universe is majestically unveiling, and everywhere Heaven revealing itself on Earth, nowhere to the Young Man does this Heaven on Earth so immediately reveal itself as in the Young Maiden. Strangely enough, in this strange life of ours, it has been so appointed. On the whole, as I have often said, a Person (*Persönlichkeit*) is ever holy to us; a certain orthodox Anthropomorphism connects my *Me* with all *Thees* in bonds of Love: but it is in this approximation of the Like and Unlike, that such heavenly attraction, as between Negative and Positive, first burns-out into a flame. Is the pitifullest mortal Person, think you, indifferent to us? Is it not rather our heartfelt wish to be made one with him; to unite him to us, by gratitude, by admiration, even by fear; or failing all these, unite ourselves to him? But how much more, in this case of the Like-Unlike! Here is conceded us the higher mystic possibility of such a union, the highest in our Earth; thus, in the conducting medium of Fantasy, flames-forth that *fire*-development of the universal Spiritual Electricity, which, as unfolded between man and woman, we first emphatically denominate LOVE.

'In every well-conditioned stripling, as I conjecture, there already blooms a certain prospective Paradise, cheered by some fairest Eve; nor, in the stately vistas, and flowerage and foliage of that Garden, is a Tree of Knowledge, beautiful and awful in the midst thereof, wanting. Perhaps too the whole is but the lovelier, if Cherubim and a Flaming Sword divide it from all footsteps of men; and grant him, the imaginative stripling, only the view, not the entrance. Happy season of virtuous youth, when shame is still an impassable celestial barrier; and the sacred air-cities of Hope have not shrunk into the mean clay-hamlets of Reality; and man, by his nature, is yet infinite and free!

'As for our young Forlorn,' continues Teufelsdröckh, evidently meaning himself, 'in his secluded way of life, and with his glowing Fantasy, the more fiery that it burnt under cover, as in a reverberating furnace, his feeling towards the Queens of this Earth was, and indeed is, altogether unspeakable. A visible Divinity dwelt in them; to our young Friend all women were holy, were heavenly. As yet he but saw them flitting past, in their many-coloured angel-plumage; or hovering mute and inaccessible on the outskirts of *Æsthetic Tea:* all of air they were, all Soul and Form; so lovely, like mysterious priestesses, in whose hand was the invisible Jacob's-ladder, whereby man might mount into very Heaven. That he, our poor Friend, should ever win for himself one of these Gracefuls (*Holden*)—*Ach Gott!* how could he hope it; should he not have died under it? There was a certain delirious vertigo in the thought.

'Thus was the young man, if all-sceptical of Demons and Angels such as the vulgar had once believed in, nevertheless not unvisited by hosts of true Sky-born, who visibly and audibly hovered round him wheresoever he went; and they had that religious worship in his thought, though as yet it was by their mere earthly and trivial name that he named them. But now, if on a soul so circumstanced, some actual Air-maiden, incorporated into tangibility and reality, should cast any electric glance of kind eyes, saying thereby, "Thou too mayst love and be loved"; and so kindle him,—good Heaven, what a volcanic, earthquake-bringing, all-consuming fire were probably kindled!'

Such a fire, it afterwards appears, did actually burst-forth, with explosions more or less Vesuvian, in the inner man of Herr Diogenes; as indeed how could it fail? A nature, which, in his own figurative style, we might say, had now not a little carbonised tinder, of Irritability; with so much nitre of latent Passion, and sulphurous Humour enough; the whole lying in such hot neighbourhood, close by 'a reverberating furnace of Fantasy': have we not here the components of driest Gunpowder, ready, on occasion of the smallest spark, to blaze-up? Neither, in this our Life-element, are sparks anywhere wanting. Without doubt, some Angel, whereof so many hovered round, would one day, leaving 'the outskirts of *Æsthetic Tea*,' flit nigher; and, by electric Promethean glance, kindle no despicable firework. Happy, if it indeed proved a Firework, and flamed-off rocket-wise, in successive beautiful bursts of splendour, each growing naturally from the other, through the several stages of a happy Youthful Love; till the whole were safely burnt-out; and the young soul relieved with little damage! Happy, if it did not rather prove a Conflagration and mad Explosion; painfully lacerating the heart itself; nay perhaps bursting the heart in pieces (which were Death); or at best, bursting the thin walls of your 'reverberating furnace,' so that it rage thenceforth all unchecked among the contiguous combustibles (which were Madness): till of the so fair and manifold internal world of our Diogenes, there remained Nothing, or only the 'crater of an extinct volcano'!

From multifarious Documents in this Bag *Capricornus,* and in the adjacent ones on both sides thereof, it becomes manifest that our philosopher, as stoical and cynical as he now looks, was heartily and even frantically in Love: here therefore may our old doubts whether his heart were of stone or of flesh give way. He loved once; not wisely but too well. And once only: for as your Congreve needs a new case or wrappage for every new rocket, so each human heart can properly exhibit but one Love, if even one; the 'First Love which is infinite' can be followed by no second like unto it. In more recent years, accordingly, the Editor of these Sheets was led to regard Teufelsdröckh as a man not only who would never wed, but who would never even flirt; whom the grand-climacteric itself, and *St. Martin's Summer* of incipient Dotage, would crown with no new myrtle-garland. To the Professor, women are henceforth Pieces of Art; of Celestial Art, indeed; which celestial pieces he glories to survey in galleries, but has lost thought of purchasing.

Psychological readers are not without curiosity to see how

Teufelsdröckh, in this for him unexampled predicament, demeans himself; with what specialties of successive configuration, splendour and colour, his Firework blazes-off. Small, as usual, is the satisfaction that such can meet with here. From amid these confused masses of Eulogy and Elegy, with their mad Petrarchan and Werterean ware lying madly scattered among all sorts of quite extraneous matter, not so much as the fair one's name can be deciphered. For, without doubt, the title *Blumine,* whereby she is here designated, and which means simply Goddess of Flowers, must be fictitious. Was her real name Flora, then? But what was her surname, or had she none? Of what station in Life was she; of what parentage, fortune, aspect? Specially, by what Preëstablished Harmony of occurrences did the Lover and the Loved meet one another in so wide a world; how did they behave in such a meeting? To all which questions, not unessential in a Biographic work, mere Conjecture must for most part return answer. 'It was appointed,' says our Philosopher, 'that the high celestial orbit of Blumine should intersect the low sublunary one of our Forlorn; that he, looking in her empyrean eyes, should fancy the upper Sphere of Light was come down into this nether sphere of Shadows; and finding himself mistaken, make noise enough.'

We seem to gather that she was young, hazel-eyed, beautiful, and some one's Cousin; highborn, and of high spirit; but unhappily dependent and insolvent; living, perhaps, on the not too gracious bounty of moneyed relatives. But how came 'the Wanderer' into her circle? Was it by the humid vehicle of *Æsthetic Tea,* or by the arid one of mere Business? Was it on the hand of Herr Towgood; or of the Gnädige Frau, who, as an ornamental Artist, might sometimes like to promote flirtation, especially for young cynical Nondescripts? To all appearance, it was chiefly by Accident, and the grace of Nature.

'Thou fair Waldschloss,' writes our Autobiographer, 'what stranger ever saw thee, were it even an absolved Auscultator, officially bearing in his pocket the last *Relatio ex Actis* he would ever write, but must have paused to wonder! Noble Mansion! There stoodest thou, in deep Mountain Amphitheatre, on umbrageous lawns, in thy serene solitude; stately, massive, all of granite; glittering in the western sunbeams, like a palace of El Dorado, overlaid with precious metal. Beautiful rose up, in wavy curvature, the slope of thy guardian Hills; of the greenest was their sward, embossed with its dark-brown frets of crag, or spotted by some spreading solitary Tree and its shadow. To the unconscious Wayfarer thou wert also as an Ammon's Temple, in the Libyan Waste; where, for joy and woe, the tablet of his Destiny lay written. Well might he pause and gaze; in that glance of his were prophecy and nameless forebodings.'

But now let us conjecture that the so presentient Ausculator has handed-in his *Relatio ex Actis;* been invited to a glass of Rhine-wine; and so, instead of returning dispirited and athirst to his dusty Town-home, is ushered into the Gardenhouse, where sit the choicest party of dames and cavaliers: if not engaged in Æsthetic Tea, yet in trustful evening conversation, and perhaps Musical Coffee, for we hear of 'harps and pure voices making the stillness live.' Scarcely, it would seem, is the Gardenhouse inferior in respectability to the noble mansion itself. 'Embowered amid rich foliage, rose-clusters, and the hues and odours of thousand flowers, here sat that brave company; in front, from the wide-opened doors, fair outlook over blossom and bush, over grove and velvet green, stretching, undulating onwards to the remote Mountain peaks: so bright, so mild, and everywhere the melody of birds and happy creatures: it was all as if man had stolen a shelter from the Sun in the bosom-vesture of Summer herself. How came it that the Wanderer advanced thither with such forecasting heart (*ahndungs-voll*), by the side of his gay host? Did he feel that to these soft influences his hard bosom ought to be shut; that here, once more, Fate had it in view to try him; to mock him, and see whether there were Humour in him?

'Next moment he finds himself presented to the party; and especially by name to—Blumine! Peculiar among all dames and damosels glanced Blumine, there in her modesty, like a star among earthly lights. Noblest maiden! whom he bent to, in body and in soul; yet scarcely dared look at, for the presence filled him with painful yet sweetest embarrassment.

'Blumine's was a name well known to him; far and wide was the fair one heard of, for her gifts, her graces, her caprices: from all which vague colourings of Rumour, from the censures no less than from the praises, had our friend painted for himself a certain imperious Queen of Hearts, and blooming warm Earth-angel, much more enchanting than your mere white Heaven-angels of women, in whose placid veins circulates too little naphtha-fire. Herself also he had seen in public places; that light yet so stately form; those dark tresses, shading a face where smiles and sunlight played over earnest deeps: but all this he had seen only as a magic vision, for him inaccessible, almost without reality. Her sphere was too far from his; how should she ever think of him; O Heaven! how should they so much as once meet together? And now that Rose-goddess sits in the same circle with him; the light of *her* eyes has smiled on him; if he speak, she will hear it! Nay, who knows, since the heavenly Sun looks into lowest valleys, but Blumine herself might have aforetime noted the so unnotable; perhaps, from his very gainsayers, as he had from hers, gathered wonder, gathered favour for him? Was the attraction, the agitation mutual, then; pole and pole trembling towards contact, when once brought into neighbourhood? Say rather, heart swelling in presence of the Queen of Hearts; like the Sea swelling when once near its Moon! With the Wanderer it was even so: as in heavenward gravitation, suddenly as at the touch of a Seraph's wand, his whole soul is roused from its deepest recesses; and all that was painful and that was blissful there, dim images, vague feelings of a whole Past and a whole Future, are heaving in unquiet eddies within him.

'Often, in far less agitating scenes, had our still Friend shrunk forcibly together; and shrouded-up his tremors and flutterings, of what sort soever, in a safe cover of Silence, and perhaps of seeming Stolidity. How was it, then, that here, when trembling to the core of his heart, he did not sink into swoons, but rose into strength, into fearlessness and clearness? It was his guiding Genius (*Dämon*) that inspired him; he must go forth and meet his Destiny. Show thyself now, whispered it, or be forever hid. Thus sometimes it is even when your anxiety becomes transcendental, that the soul first feels herself able to transcend it; that she rises above it, in fiery victory; and borne on new-found wings of victory, moves so calmly, even because so rapidly, so irresistibly. Always must the Wanderer remember, with a certain satisfaction and surprise, how in this case he sat not silent, but struck adroitly into the stream of conversation; which thenceforth, to speak with an apparent not a real vanity, he may say that he continued to lead. Surely, in those hours, a certain inspiration was imparted him, such inspiration as is still possible in our late era. The self-secluded unfolds himself in noble thoughts, in free, glowing words; his soul is as one sea of light, the peculiar home of Truth and Intellect; wherein also Fantasy bodies-forth form after form, radiant with all prismatic hues.'

It appears, in this otherwise so happy meeting, there talked one 'Philistine'; who even now, to the general weariness, was dominantly pouring-forth Philistinism (*Philistriositäten*); little witting what hero was here entering to demolish him! We omit the series of Socratic, or rather Diogenic utterances, not unhappy in their way, whereby the monster, 'persuaded into silence,' seems soon after to have withdrawn for the night. 'Of which dialectic marauder,' writes our hero, 'the discomfiture was visibly felt as a benefit by most: but what were all applauses to the glad smile, threatening every moment to become a laugh, wherewith Blumine herself repaid the victor? He ventured to address her, she answered with attention: nay what if there were a slight tremor in that silver voice; what if the red glow of evening were hiding a transient blush!

'The conversation took a higher tone, one fine thought called forth another: it was one of those rare seasons, when the soul expands with full freedom, and man feels himself brought near to man. Gaily in light, graceful abandonment, the friendly talk played round that circle; for the burden was rolled from every heart; the barriers of Ceremony, which are indeed the laws of polite living, had melted as into vapour; and the poor claims of *Me* and *Thee,* no longer parted by rigid fences, now flowed softly into one another; and Life lay all harmonious, many-tinted, like some fair royal champaign, the sovereign and owner of which were Love only. Such music springs from kind hearts, in a kind environment of place and time. And yet as the light grew more aërial on the mountaintops, and the shadows fell longer over the valley, some faint tone of sadness may have breathed through the heart; and, in whispers more or less audible, reminded every one that as this bright day was drawing towards its close, so likewise must the Day of Man's Existence decline into dust and darkness; and with all its sick toilings, and joyful and mournful noises, sink in the still Eternity.

'To our Friend the hours seemed moments; holy was he

and happy: the words from those sweetest lips came over him like dew on thirsty grass; all better feelings in his soul seemed to whisper, It is good for us to be here. At parting, the Blumine's hand was in his: in the balmy twilight, with the kind stars above them, he spoke something of meeting again, which was not contradicted; he pressed gently those small soft fingers, and it seemed as if they were not hastily, not angrily withdrawn.'

Poor Teufelsdröckh! it is clear to demonstration thou art smit: the Queen of Hearts would see a 'man of genius' also sigh for her; and there, by art-magic, in that preternatural hour, has she bound and spell-bound thee. 'Love is not altogether a Delirium,' says he elsewhere; 'yet has it many points in common therewith. I call it rather a discerning of the Infinite in the Finite, of the Idea made Real; which discerning again may be either true or false, either seraphic or demoniac, Inspiration or Insanity. But in the former case too, as in common Madness, it is Fantasy that superadds itself to sight; on the so petty domain of the Actual plants its Archimedes-lever, whereby to move at will the infinite Spiritual. Fantasy I might call the true Heaven-gate and Hell-gate of man: his sensuous life is but the small temporary stage (Zeitbühne), whereon thick-streaming influences from both these far yet near regions meet visibly, and act tragedy and melodrama. Sense can support herself handsomely, in most countries, for some eighteen-pence a day; but for Fantasy planets and solar-systems will not suffice. Witness your Pyrrhus conquering the world, yet drinking no better red wine than he had before.' Alas! witness also your Diogenes, flame-clad, scaling the upper Heaven, and verging towards Insanity, for prize of a 'high-souled Brunette,' as if the earth held but one and not several of these!

He says that, in Town, they met again: 'day after day, like his heart's sun, the blooming Blumine shone on him. Ah! a little while ago, and he was yet in all darkness: him what Graceful (Holde) would ever love? Disbelieving all things, the poor youth had never learned to believe in himself. Withdrawn, in proud timidity, within his own fastnesses; solitary from men, yet baited by night-spectres enough, he saw himself, with a sad indignation, constrained to renounce the fairest hopes of existence. And now, O now! "She looks on thee," cried he: "she the fairest, noblest; do not her dark eyes tell thee, thou art not despised?

The Heaven's-Messenger! All Heaven's blessings be hers!"
Thus did soft melodies flow through his heart; tones of an
infinite gratitude; sweetest intimations that he also was a
man, that for him also unutterable joys had been provided.

'In free speech, earnest or gay, amid lambent glances,
laughter, tears, and often with the inarticulate mystic speech
of Music: such was the element they now lived in; in such a
many-tinted, radiant Aurora, and by this fairest of Orient
Light-bringers must our Friend be blandished, and the new
Apocalypse of Nature unrolled to him. Fairest Blumine!
And, even as a Star, all Fire and humid Softness, a very
Light-ray incarnate! Was there so much as a fault, a
"caprice," he could have dispensed with? Was she not to
him in very deed a Morning-Star; did not her presence
bring with it airs from Heaven? As from Æolian Harps in
the breath of dawn, as from the Memnon's Statue struck by
the rosy finger of Aurora, unearthly music was around him,
and lapped him into untried balmy Rest. Pale Doubt fled
away to the distance; Life bloomed-up with happiness and
hope. The past, then, was all a haggard dream; he had been
in the Garden of Eden, then, and could not discern it! But
lo now! the black walls of his prison melt away; the captive is
alive, is free. If he loved his Disenchantress? *Ach Gott!* His
whole heart and soul and life were hers, but never had he
named it Love: existence was all a Feeling, not yet shaped
into a Thought.'

Nevertheless, into a Thought, nay into an Action, it must
be shaped; for neither Disenchanter nor Disenchantress,
mere 'Children of Time,' can abide by Feeling alone. The
Professor knows not, to this day, 'how in her soft, fervid
bosom the Lovely found determination, even on hest of
Necessity, to cut asunder these so blissful bonds.' He even
appears surprised at the 'Duenna Cousin,' whoever she may
have been, 'in whose meagre, hunger-bitten philosophy, the
religion of young hearts was, from the first, faintly approved
of.' We, even at such distance, can explain it without necro-
mancy. Let the Philosopher answer this one question. What
figure, at that period, was a Mrs. Teufelsdröckh likely to make
in polished society? Could she have driven so much as a
brass-bound Gig, or even a simple iron-spring one? Thou
foolish 'absolved Auscultator,' before whom lies no prospect
of capital, will any yet known 'religion of young hearts'
keep the human kitchen warm? Pshaw! thy divine Blumine,

when she 'resigned herself to wed some richer,' shows more philosophy, though but 'a woman of genius,' than thou, a pretended man.

Our readers have witnessed the origin of this Love-mania, and with what royal splendour it waxes, and rises. Let no one ask us to unfold the glories of its dominant state; much less the horrors of its almost instantaneous dissolution. How from such inorganic masses, henceforth madder than ever, as lie in these Bags, can even fragments of a living delineation be organised? Besides, of what profit were it? We view, with a lively pleasure, the gay silk Montgolfier start from the ground, and shoot upwards, cleaving the liquid deeps, till it dwindle to a luminous star: but what is there to look longer on, when once, by natural elasticity, or accident of fire, it has exploded? A hapless air-navigator, plunging, amid torn parachutes, sand-bags, and confused wreck, fast enough into the jaws of the Devil! Suffice it to know that Teufelsdröckh rose into the highest regions of the Empyrean, by a natural parabolic track, and returned thence in a quick perpendicular one. For the rest, let any feeling reader, who has been unhappy enough to do the like, paint it out for himself: considering only that if he, for his perhaps comparatively insignificant mistress, underwent such agonies and frenzies, what must Teufelsdröckh's have been, with a fire-heart, and for a nonpareil Blumine! We glance merely at the final scene:

'One morning, he found his Morning-star all dimmed and dusky-red; the fair creature was silent, absent, she seemed to have been weeping. Alas, no longer a Morning-star, but a troublous skyey Portent, announcing that the Doomsday had dawned! She said, in a tremulous voice, They were to meet no more.' The thunderstruck Air-sailor is not wanting to himself in this dread hour: but what avails it? We omit the passionate expostulations, entreaties, indignations, since all was vain, and not even an explanation was conceded him; and hasten to the catastrophe. ' "Farewell, then, Madam!" said he, not without sternness, for his stung pride helped him. She put her hand in his, she looked in his face, tears started to her eyes; in wild audacity he clasped her to his bosom; their lips were joined, their two souls, like two dew-drops, rushed into one,—for the first time, and for the last!' Thus was Teufelsdröckh made immortal by a kiss. And then? Why, then—'thick curtains of Night rushed over his soul, as rose the immeasurable Crash of Doom; and through the ruins as of a shivered Universe was he falling, falling, towards the Abyss.'

CHAPTER VI

SORROWS OF TEUFELSDRÖCKH

Teufelsdröckh's demeanour thereupon. Turns pilgrim. A last wistful look on native Entepfuhl: Sunset amongst primitive Mountains. Basilisk glance of the Barouche-and-four. Thoughts on View-hunting. Wanderings and Sorrowings.

We have long felt that, with a man like our Professor, matters must often be expected to take a course of their own; that in so multiplex, intricate a nature, there might be channels, both for admitting and emitting, such as the Psychologist had seldom noted; in short, that on no grand occasion and convulsion, neither in the joy-storm nor in the woe-storm, could you predict his demeanour.

To our less philosophical readers, for example, it is now clear that the so passionate Teufelsdröckh, precipitated through 'a shivered Universe' in this extraordinary way has only one of three things which he can next do: Establish himself in Bedlam; begin writing Satanic Poetry; or blow-out his brains. In the progress towards any of which consummations, do not such readers anticipate extravagance enough; breast-beating, brow-beating (against walls), lion-bellowings of blasphemy and the like, stampings, smitings, breakages of furniture, if not arson itself?

Nowise so does Teufelsdröckh deport him. He quietly lifts his *Pilgerstab* (Pilgrim-staff), 'old business being soon wound-up'; and begins a perambulation and circumambulation of the terraqueous Globe! Curious it is, indeed, how with such vivacity of conception, such intensity of feeling, above all, with these unconscionable habits of Exaggeration in speech, he combines that wonderful stillness of his, that stoicism in external procedure. Thus, if his sudden bereavement, in this matter of the Flower-goddess, is talked of as a real Doomsday and Dissolution of Nature, in which light doubtless it partly appeared to himself, his own nature is nowise dissolved thereby; but rather is compressed closer. For once, as we might say, a Blumine by magic appliances has unlocked that shut heart of his, and its hidden things rush-out tumultuous, boundless, like genii enfranchised from their glass phial: but no sooner are your magic appliances withdrawn, than the strange casket of a heart springs-to again; and perhaps there is now no key extant that will open it; for a Teufelsdröckh, as we remarked, will not love a second time. Singular Diogenes! No sooner has that heart-rending occurrence fairly taken place, than he affects to regard it as a thing natural, of which there is nothing more to be said. 'One highest hope, seemingly legible in the eyes of an Angel, had recalled him as out of Death-shadows into celestial Life: but a gleam of Tophet passed over the face of his Angel; he was rapt away in whirlwinds, and heard the laughter of Demons. It was a Calenture,' adds he, 'whereby the Youth saw green Paradise-groves in the waste Ocean-waters: a lying vision, yet not wholly a lie, for *he* saw it.' But what things soever passed in him, when he ceased to see it; what ragings and despairings soever Teufelsdröckh's soul was the scene of, he has the goodness to conceal under a quite opaque cover of Silence. We know it well; the first mad paroxysm past, our brave Gneschen collected his dismembered philosophies, and buttoned himself together; he was meek, silent, or spoke of the weather and the Journals: only by a transient knitting of those shaggy brows, by some deep flash of those eyes, glancing one knew not whether with tear-dew or with fierce fire,—might you have guessed what a Gehenna was within; that a whole Satanic School were spouting, though inaudibly, there. To consume your own choler, as some chimneys consume their own smoke; to keep a whole Satanic School spouting, if it must spout, inaudibly, is a negative yet no slight virtue, nor one of the commonest in these times.

Nevertheless, we will not take upon us to say, that in the strange measure he fell upon, there was not a touch of latent Insanity; whereof indeed the actual condition of these Documents in *Capricornus* and *Aquarius* is no bad emblem. His so unlimited Wanderings, toilsome enough, are without assigned or perhaps assignable aim; internal Unrest seems his sole guidance; he wanders, wanders, as if that curse of the Prophet had fallen on him, and he were 'made like unto a wheel.' Doubtless, too, the chaotic nature of these Paper-bags aggravates our obscurity. Quite without note of preparation, for example, we come upon the following slip: 'A peculiar feeling it is that will rise in the Travelier, when turning some hill-range in his desert road, he descries lying far below, embosomed among its groves and green natural bulwarks, and all diminished to a toybox, the fair Town, where so many souls, as it were seen and yet unseen, are driving their multifarious traffic. Its white steeple is then truly a starward-pointing finger; the canopy of blue smoke seems like a sort of Life-breath: for always, of its own unity, the soul gives unity to whatsoever it looks on with love; thus does the little Dwellingplace of men, in itself a congeries of houses and huts, become for us an individual, almost a person. But what thousand other thoughts unite thereto, if the place has to ourselves been the arena of joyous or mournful experiences; if perhaps the cradle we were rocked in still stands there, if our Loving ones still dwell there, if our Buried ones there slumber!' Does Teufelsdröckh, as the wounded eagle is said to make for its own eyrie, and indeed military deserters, and all hunted outcast creatures, turn as if by instinct in the direction of their birthland,—fly first, in this extremity, towards his native Entepfuhl; but reflecting that there no help awaits him, take only one wistful look from the distance, and then wend elsewhither?

Little happier seems to be his next flight: into the wilds of Nature; as if in her mother-bosom he would seek healing. So at least we incline to interpret the following Notice, separated from the former by some considerable space, wherein, however, is nothing noteworthy:

'Mountains were not new to him; but rarely are Mountains seen in such combined majesty and grace as here. The rocks are of that sort called Primitive by the mineralogists, which always arrange themselves in masses of a rugged, gigantic character; which ruggedness, however, is here tempered by a singular airiness of form, and softness of environment: in a climate favourable to vegetation, the gray cliff, itself covered with lichens, shoots-up through a garment of foliage or verdure; and white, bright cottages, tree-shaded, cluster round the everlasting granite. In fine vicissitude, Beauty alternates with Grandeur: you ride through stony hollows, along strait passes, traversed by torrents, overhung by high walls of rock; now winding amid broken shaggy chasms, and huge fragments; now suddenly

emerging into some emerald valley, where the streamlet collects itself into a Lake, and man has again found a fair
dwelling, and it seems as if Peace had established herself in
the bosom of Strength.

'To Peace, however, in this vortex of existence, can the
Son of Time not pretend: still less if some Spectre haunt
him from the Past; and the Future is wholly a Stygian Darkness, spectre-bearing. Reasonably might the Wanderer exclaim to himself: Are not the gates of this world's Happiness inexorably shut against thee; hast thou a hope that is
not mad? Nevertheless, one may still murmur audibly, or in
the original Greek if that suit thee better: "Whoso can look
on Death will start at no shadows."

'From such meditations is the Wanderer's attention called
outwards; for now the Valley closes-in abruptly, intersected
by a huge mountain mass, the stony water-worn ascent of
which is not to be accomplished on horseback. Arrived
aloft, he finds himself again lifted into the evening sunset
light; and cannot but pause, and gaze round him, some moments there. An upland irregular expanse of wold, where
valleys in complex branchings are suddenly or slowly arranging their descent towards every quarter of the sky. The
mountain-ranges are beneath your feet, and folded together:
only the loftier summits look down here and there as on a
second plain; lakes also lie clear and earnest in their solitude. No trace of man now visible; unless indeed it were he
who fashioned that little visible link of Highway, here, as
would seem, scaling the inaccessible, to unite Province with
Province. But sun-wards, lo you! how it towers sheer up, a
world of Mountains, the diadem and centre of the mountain region! A hundred and a hundred savage peaks, in the
last light of Day; all glowing, of gold and amethyst, like giant spirits of the wilderness; there in their silence, in their
solitude, even as on the night when Noah's Deluge first dried!
Beautiful, nay solemn, was the sudden aspect to our Wanderer. He gazed over those stupendous masses with wonder, almost with longing desire; never till this hour had he
known Nature, that she was One, that she was his Mother
and divine. And as the ruddy glow was fading into clearness
in the sky, and the Sun had now departed, a murmur of
Eternity and Immensity, of Death and of Life, stole through
his soul; and he felt as if Death and Life were one, as if the
Earth were not dead, as if the Spirit of the Earth had its

throne in that splendour, and his own spirit were therewith holding communion.

'The spell was broken by a sound of carriage-wheels. Emerging from the hidden Northward, to sink soon into the hidden Southward, came a gay Barouche-and-four: it was open; servants and postillions wore wedding-favours: that happy pair, then, had found each other, it was their marriage evening! Few moments brought them near: *Du Himmel!* It was Herr Towgood and——Blumine! With slight unrecognising salutation they passed me; plunged down amid the neighbouring thickets, onwards, to Heaven, and to England; and I, in my friend Richter's words, *I re-mained alone, behind them, with the Night.'*

Were it not cruel in these circumstances, here might be the place to insert an observation, gleaned long ago from the great *Clothes-Volume,* where it stands with quite other intent: 'Some time before Small-pox was extirpated,' says the Professor, there came a new malady of the spiritual sort on Europe: I mean the epidemic, now endemical, of View-hunting. Poets of old date, being privileged with Senses, had also enjoyed external Nature; but chiefly as we enjoy the crystal cup which holds good or bad liquor for us; that is to say, in silence, or with slight incidental com-mentary: never, as I compute, till after the *Sorrows of Werter,* was there man found who would say: Come let us make a Description! Having drunk the liquor, come let us eat the glass! Of which endemic the Jenner is unhappily still to seek.' Too true!

We reckon it more important to remark that the Pro-fessor's Wanderings, so far as his stoical and cynical en-velopment admits us to clear insight, here first take their permanent character, fatuous or not. That Basilisk-glance of the Barouche-and-four seems to have withered-up what little remnant of a purpose may have still lurked in him: Life has become wholly a dark labyrinth; wherein, through long years, our Friend, flying from spectres, has to stumble about at random, and naturally with more haste than prog-ress.

Foolish were it in us to attempt following him, even from afar, in this extraordinary world-pilgrimage of his; the simplest record of which, were clear record possible, would fill volumes. Hopeless is the obscurity, unspeakable the con-fusion. He glides from country to country, from condition

to condition; vanishing and re-appearing, no man can calculate how or where. Through all quarters of the world he
wanders, and apparently through all circles of society. If in
any scene, perhaps difficult to fix geographically, he settles
for a time, and forms connexions, be sure he will snap
them abruptly asunder. Let him sink out of sight as Private
Scholar (*Privatisirender*), living by the grace of God in
some European capital, you may next find him as Hadjee in
the neighbourhood of Mecca. It is an inexplicable Phantasmagoria, capricious, quick-changing; as if our Traveller,
instead of limbs and highways, had transported himself by
some wishing-carpet, or Fortunatus' Hat. The whole, too,
imparted emblematically, in dim multifarious tokens (as that
collection of Street-Advertisements); with only some touch
of direct historical notice sparingly interspersed: little light-
islets in the world of haze! So that, from this point, the Professor is more of an enigma than ever. In figurative language, we might say he becomes, not indeed a spirit, yet
spiritualised, vaporised. Fact unparalleled in Biography: The
river of his History, which we have traced from its tiniest
fountains, and hoped to see flow onward, with increasing
current, into the ocean, here dashes itself over that terrific
Lover's Leap; and, as a mad-foaming cataract, flies wholly
into tumultuous clouds of spray! Low down it indeed collects again into pools and plashes; yet only at a great distance, and with difficulty, if at all, into a general stream. To
cast a glance into certain of those pools and plashes, and
trace whither they run, must, for a chapter or two, form the
limit of our endeavour.

For which end doubtless those direct historical Notices,
where they can be met with, are the best. Nevertheless, of
this sort too there occurs much, which, with our present light,
it were questionable to emit. Teufelsdröckh, vibrating everywhere between the highest and the lowest levels, comes
into contact with public History itself. For example, those
conversations and relations with illustrious Persons, as Sultan Mahmoud, the Emperor Napoleon, and others, are they
not as yet rather of a diplomatic character than of a biographic? The Editor, appreciating the sacredness of crowned
heads, nay perhaps suspecting the possible trickeries of a
Clothes-Philosopher, will eschew this province for the present; a new time may bring new insight and a different duty.

If we ask now, not indeed with what ulterior Purpose, for

there was none, yet with what immediate outlooks; at all events, in what mood of mind, the Professor undertook and prosecuted this world-pilgrimage,—the answer is more distinct than favourable. 'A nameless Unrest,' says he, 'urged me forward; to which the outward motion was some momentary lying solace. Whither should I go? My Loadstars were blotted out; in that canopy of grim fire shone no star. Yet forward must I; the ground burnt under me; there was no rest for the sole of my foot. I was alone, alone! Ever too the strong inward longing shaped Fantasms for itself: towards these, one after the other, must I fruitlessly wander. A feeling I had, that for my fever-thirst there was and must be somewhere a healing Fountain. To many fondly imagined Fountains, the Saints' Wells of these days, did I pilgrim; to great Men, to great Cities, to great Events: but found there no healing. In strange countries, as in the well-known; in savage deserts, as in the press of corrupt civilisation, it was ever the same: how could your Wanderer escape from—*his own Shadow?* Nevertheless still Forward! I felt as if in great haste; to do I saw not what. From the depths of my own heart, it called to me, Forwards! The winds and the streams, and all Nature sounded to me, Forwards! *Ach Gott,* I was even, once for all, a Son of Time.'

From which is it not clear that the internal Satanic School was still active enough? He says elsewhere: 'The *Enchiridion of Epictetus* I had ever with me, often as my sole rational companion; and regret to mention that the nourishment it yielded was trifling.' Thou foolish Teufelsdröckh! How could it else? Hadst thou not Greek enough to understand thus much: *The End of Man is an Action, and not a Thought,* though it were the noblest?

'How I lived?' writes he once: 'Friend, hast thou considered the "rugged all-nourishing Earth," as Sophocles well names her; how she feeds the sparrow on the housetop much more her darling, man? While thou stirrest and livest, thou hast a probability of victual. My breakfast of tea has been cooked by a Tartar woman, with water of the Amur, who wiped her earthen kettle with a horse-tail. I have roasted wild-eggs in the sand of Sahara; I have awakened in Paris *Estrapades* and Vienna *Malzleins,* with no prospect of breakfast beyond elemental liquid. That I had my Living to seek saved me from Dying,—by suicide. In our busy Europe, is there not an everlasting demand for

Intellect, in the chemical, mechanical, political, religious, educational, commercial departments? In Pagan countries, cannot one write Fetishes? Living! Little knowest thou what alchemy is in an inventive Soul; how, as with its little finger, it can create provision enough for the body (of a Philosopher); and then, as with both hands, create quite other than provision; namely, spectres to torment itself withal.'

Poor Teufelsdröckh! Flying with Hunger always parallel to him; and a whole Infernal Chase in his rear; so that the countenance of Hunger is comparatively a friend's! Thus must he, in the temper of ancient Cain, or of the modern Wandering Jew,—save only that he feels himself not guilty and but suffering the pains of guilt,—wend to and fro with aimless speed. Thus must he, over the whole surface of the Earth (by footprints), write his *Sorrows of Teufelsdröckh*; even as the great Goethe, in passionate words, had to write his *Sorrows of Werter,* before the spirit freed herself, and he could become a Man. Vain truly is the hope of your swiftest Runner to escape 'from his own Shadow'! Nevertheless, in these sick days, when the Born of Heaven first descries himself (about the age of twenty) in a world such as ours, richer than usual in two things, in Truths grown obsolete, and Trades grown obsolete,—what can the fool think but that it is all a Den of Lies, wherein whoso will not speak Lies and act Lies, must stand idle and despair? Whereby it happens that, for your nobler minds, the publishing of some such Work of Art, in one or the other dialect, becomes almost a necessity. For what is it properly but an Altercation with the Devil, before you begin honestly Fighting him? Your Byron publishes his *Sorrows of Lord George,* in verse and in prose, and copiously otherwise: your Bonaparte represents his *Sorrows of Napoleon* Opera, in an all-too stupendous style; with music of cannon-volleys, and murder-shrieks of a world; his stagelights are the fires of Conflagration; his rhyme and recitative are the tramp of embattled Hosts and the sound of falling Cities.—Happier is he who, like our Clothes-Philosopher, can write such matter, since it must be written, on the insensible Earth, with his shoe-soles only; and also survive the writing thereof!

CHAPTER VII

THE EVERLASTING NO

Loss of Hope, and of Belief. Profit-and-Loss Philosophy. Teufels-dröckh in his darkness and despair still clings to Truth and follows Duty. Inexpressible pains and fears of Unbelief. Fever-crisis: Protest against the Everlasting No: Baphometic Fire-Baptism.

Under the strange nebulous envelopment, wherein our Professor has now shrouded himself, no doubt but his spiritual nature is nevertheless progressive, and growing: for how can the 'Son of Time,' in any case, stand still? We behold him, through those dim years, in a state of crisis, of transition: his mad Pilgrimings, and general solution into aimless Discontinuity, what is all this but a mad Fermentation; wherefrom, the fiercer it is, the clearer product will one day evolve itself?

Such transitions are ever full of pain: thus the Eagle when he moults is sickly; and, to attain his new beak, must harshly dash-off the old one upon rocks. What Stoicism soever our Wanderer, in his individual acts and motions, may affect, it is clear that there is a hot fever of anarchy and misery raging within; coruscations of which flash out: as, indeed, how could there be other? Have we not seen him disappointed, bemocked of Destiny, through long years? All that the young heart might desire and pray for has been denied; nay, as in the last worst instance, offered and then snatched away. Ever an 'excellent Passivity'; but of useful, reasonable Activity, essential to the former as Food to Hunger, nothing granted: till at length, in this wild Pilgrimage, he must forcibly seize for himself an Activity, though useless, unreasonable. Alas, his cup of bitterness, which had been filling drop by drop, ever since that first 'ruddy morning' in the Hinterschlag Gymnasium, was at the very lip; and then with that poison-drop, of the Towgood-and-Blumine business, it runs over, and even hisses over in a deluge of foam.

He himself says once, with more justice than originality: 'Man is, properly speaking, based upon Hope, he has no other possession but Hope; this world of his is emphatically the 'Place of Hope.' What, then, was our Professor's possession? We see him, for the present, quite shut-out from Hope; looking not into the golden orient, but vaguely all round into a dim copper firmament, pregnant with earthquake and tornado.

Alas, shut-out from Hope, in a deeper sense than we yet dream of! For, as he wanders wearisomely through this world, he has now lost all tidings of another and higher. Full of religion, or at least of religiosity, as our Friend has since exhibited himself, he hides not that, in those days, he was wholly irreligious: 'Doubt had darkened into Unbelief,' says he; 'shade after shade goes grimly over your soul, till you have the fixed, starless, Tartarean black.' To such readers as have reflected, what can be called reflecting, on man's life, and happily discovered, in contradiction to much Profit-and-Loss Philosophy, speculative and practical, that Soul is *not* synonymous with Stomach; who understand, therefore, in our Friend's words, 'that, for man's well-being, Faith is properly the one thing needful; how, with it, Martyrs, otherwise weak, can cheerfully endure the shame and the cross; and without it, Worldlings puke-up their sick existence, by suicide, in the midst of luxury': to such it will be clear that, for a pure moral nature, the loss of his religious Belief was the loss of everything. Unhappy young man! All wounds, the crush of long-continued Destitution, the stab of false Friendship and of false Love, all wounds in thy so genial heart, would have healed again, had not its life-warmth been withdrawn. Well might he exclaim, in his wild way: 'Is there no God, then; but at best an absentee God, sitting idle, ever since the first Sabbath, at the outside of his Universe, and *see*ing it go? Has the word Duty no meaning; is what we call Duty no divine Messenger and Guide, but a false earthly Fantasm, made-up of Desire and Fear, of emanations from the Gallows and from Doctor Graham's Celestial-Bed? Happiness of an approving Conscience! Did not Paul of Tarsus, whom admiring men have since named Saint, feel that *he* was "the chief of sinners"; and Nero of Rome, jocund in spirit (*wohlgemuth*), spend much of his time in fiddling? Foolish Wordmonger and Motive-grinder, who in thy Logic-mill hast an earthly mechanism for the Godlike itself, and wouldst fain grind me out Virtue from the husks of Pleasure,—I tell thee, Nay! To the unregenerate Prometheus Vinctus of a man, it is ever the bitterest aggravation of his wretchedness that he is conscious of Virtue, that he feels himself the victim not of suffering only, but of injustice. What then? Is the heroic inspiration we name Virtue but some Passion; some bubble of the blood, bubbling in the direction others *profit* by? I know not: only this I know, If what thou namest Happiness be our true aim, then are we all astray. With Stupidity and sound Digestion man may front much. But what, in these dull unimaginative days, are the terrors of Conscience to the diseases of the Liver! Not on Morality, but on Cookery, let us build our stronghold: there brandishing our frying-pan, as censer, let us offer sweet incense to the Devil, and live at ease on the fat things *he* has provided for his Elect!'

Thus has the bewildered Wanderer to stand, as so many have done, shouting question after question into the Sibyl-cave of Destiny, and receive no Answer but an Echo. It is all a grim Desert, this once-fair world of his; wherein is heard only the howling of wild-beasts, or the shrieks of despairing, hate-filled·men; and no Pillar of Cloud by day, and no Pillar of Fire by night, any longer guides the Pilgrim. To such length has the spirit of Inquiry carried him. 'But what boots it (*was thut's*)?' cries he: 'it is but the common lot in this era. Not having come to spiritual majority prior to the *Siècle de Louis Quinze,* and not being born purely a Loghead (*Dummkopf*), thou hadst no other outlook. The whole world is, like thee, sold to Unbelief; their old Temples of the Godhead, which for long have not been rain-proof, crumble down; and men ask now: Where is the God-head; our eyes never saw him?'

Pitiful enough were it, for all these wild utterances, to call our Diogenes wicked. Unprofitable servants as we all are, perhaps at no era of his life was he more decisively the Servant of Goodness, the Servant of God, than even now when doubting God's existence. 'One circumstance I note,' says he: 'after all the nameless woe that Inquiry, which for me, what it is not always, was genuine Love of Truth, had wrought me, I nevertheless still loved Truth, and would bate no jot of my allegiance to her. "Truth!" I cried, "though the Heavens crush me for following her: no Falsehood! though a whole celestial Lubberland were the price of Apostasy." In conduct it was the same. Had a divine Messenger from the clouds, or miraculous Handwriting on the wall, convincingly proclaimed to me *This thou shalt do,* with what passionate readiness, as I often thought, would I have done it, had it been leaping into the infernal Fire. Thus, in spite of all Motive-grinders, and Mechanical Profit-and-Loss Philosophies, with the sick ophthalmia and hallucination they had brought on, was the Infinite nature of Duty still dimly present to me: living without God in the world, of God's light I was not utterly bereft; if my as yet sealed eyes, with their unspeakable longing, could nowhere see Him, nevertheless in my heart He was present, and His heaven-written Law still stood legible and sacred there.'

Meanwhile, under all these tribulations, and temporal and spiritual destitutions, what must the Wanderer, in his silent soul, have endured! 'The painfullest feeling,' writes he, 'is that of your own Feebleness (*Unkraft*); ever, as the English Milton says, to be weak is the true misery. And yet of your Strength there is and can be no clear feeling, save by what you have prospered in, by what you have done. Between vague wavering Capability and fixed indubitable Performance, what a difference! A certain inarticulate Self-consciousness dwells dimly in us; which only our Works can render articulate and decisively discernible. Our Works are the mirror wherein the spirit first sees its natural lineaments. Hence, too, the folly of that impossible Precept, *Know thyself;* till it be translated into this partially possible one, *Know what thou canst work at.*

'But for me, so strangely unprosperous had I been, the net-result of my Workings amounted as yet simply to— Nothing. How then could I believe in my Strength, when there was as yet no mirror to see it in? Ever did this agitating, yet, as I now perceive, quite frivolous question, remain to me insoluble: Hast thou a certain Faculty, a certain Worth, such even as the most have not; or art thou the completest Dullard of these modern times? Alas, the fearful Unbelief is unbelief in yourself; and how could I believe? Had not my first, last Faith in myself, when even to me the Heavens seemed laid open, and I dared to love, been all-too cruelly belied? The speculative Mystery of Life grew ever more mysterious to me: neither in the practical Mystery had I made the slightest progress, but been everywhere buffeted, foiled, and contemptuously cast out. A feeble unit in the middle of a threatening Infinitude, I seemed to have nothing given me but eyes, whereby to discern my own wretchedness. Invisible yet impenetrable walls, as of Enchantment, divided me from all living: was there, in the wide world, any true bosom I could press trustfully to mine? O Heaven, No, there was none! I kept a lock upon my lips: why should I speak much with that shifting variety of so-called Friends, in whose withered, vain and too-hungry souls Friendship was but an incredible tradition? In such cases, your resource is to talk little, and that little mostly from the Newspapers. Now when I look back, it was a strange isolation I then lived in. The men and women around me, even speaking with me, were but Figures; I had, practically, forgotten that they were alive that they were not merely automatic. In the midst of their crowded streets and assemblages, I walked solitary; and (except as it was my own heart, not another's, that I kept devouring) savage also, as the tiger in his jungle. Some comfort it would have been, could I, like a Faust, have fancied myself tempted and tormented of the Devil; for a Hell, as I imagine, without Life, though only diabolic Life, were more frightful: but in our age of Down-pulling and Disbelief, the very Devil has been pulled down, you cannot so much as believe in a Devil. To me the Universe was all void of Life, of Purpose, of Volition, even of Hostility: it was one huge, dead, immeasurable Steam-engine, rolling on, in its dead indifference, to grind me limb from limb. O, the vast, gloomy, solitary Golgotha, and Mill of Death! Why was the Living banished thither companionless, conscious? Why, if there is no Devil; nay, unless the Devil is your God?'

A prey incessantly to such corrosions, might not, moreover, as the worst aggravation to them, the iron constitution even of a Teufelsdröckh threaten to fail? We conjecture that he has known sickness; and, in spite of his locomotive habits, perhaps sickness of the chronic sort. Hear this, for example: 'How beautiful to die of broken-heart, on Paper! Quite another thing in practice; every window of your Feeling, even of your Intellect, as it were, begrimed and mud-bespattered, so that no pure ray can enter; a whole Drugshop in your inwards; the fordone soul drowning slowly in quagmires of Disgust!'

Putting all which external and internal miseries together, may we not find in the following sentences, quite in our Professor's still vein, significance enough? 'From Suicide a certain aftershine (*Nachschein*) of Christianity withheld me: perhaps also a certain indolence of character; for, was not that a remedy I had at any time within reach? Often, however, was there a question present to me: Should some one now, at the turning of that corner, blow thee suddenly out of Space, into the other World, or other No-world, by pistol-shot,—how were it? On which ground, too, I often, in sea-storms and sieged cities and other death-scenes, exhibited an imperturbability, which passed, falsely enough, for courage.

'So had it lasted,' concludes the Wanderer, 'so had it lasted, as in bitter protracted Death-agony, through long years. The heart within me, unvisited by any heavenly dew-drop was smouldering in sulphurous, slow-consuming fire. Almost since earliest memory I had shed no tear; or once only when I, murmuring half-audibly, recited Faust's Death-song, that wild *Selig der den er im Siegesglanze findet* (Happy whom *he* finds in Battle's splendour), and thought that of this last Friend even I was not forsaken, that Destiny itself could not doom me not to die. Having no hope, neither had I any definite fear, were it of Man or of Devil: nay, I often felt as if it might be solacing, could the Arch-Devil himself, though in Tartarean terrors, but rise to me, that I might tell him a little of my mind. And yet, strangely enough, I lived in a continual, indefinite, pining fear; tremulous, pusillanimous, apprehensive of I knew not what; it seemed as if all things in the Heavens above and the Earth beneath would hurt me; as if the Heavens and the Earth were but boundless jaws of a devouring monster, wherein I, palpitating, waited to be devoured.

'Full of such humour, and perhaps the miserablest man in the whole French Capital or Suburbs, was I, one sultry Dog-day, after much perambulation, toiling along the dirty little *Rue Saint-Thomas de l'Enfer,* among civic rubbish enough, in a close atmosphere, and over pavements hot as Nebuchadnezzar's Furnace; whereby doubtless my spirits were little cheered; when, all at once, there rose a Thought in me, and I asked myself: "What *art* thou afraid of? Wherefore, like a coward, dost thou forever pip and whimper, and go cowering and trembling? Despicable biped! what is the sum-total of the worst that lies before thee? Death? Well, Death; and say the pangs of Tophet too, and all that the Devil and Man may, will or can do against thee! Hast thou not a heart; canst thou not suffer whatsoever it be; and, as a Child of Freedom, though outcast, trample Tophet itself under thy feet, while it consumes thee? Let it come, then; I will meet it and defy it!" And as I so thought, there rushed like a stream of fire over my whole soul; and I shook base Fear away from me forever. I was strong, of unknown strength; a spirit, almost a god. Ever from that time, the temper of my misery was changed: not Fear or whining Sorrow was it, but Indignation and grim fire-eyed Defiance.

'Thus had the EVERLASTING NO (*das ewige Nein*) pealed authoritatively through all the recesses of my Being, of my ME; and then was it that my whole ME stood up, in native God-created majesty, and with emphasis recorded its Protest. Such a Protest, the most important transaction in Life, may that same Indignation and Defiance, in a psychological point of view, be fitly called. The Everlasting No had said: "Behold, thou art fatherless, outcast, and the Universe is mine (the Devil's)"; to which my whole ME now made answer: "*I* am not thine, but Free, and forever hate thee!"

'It is from this hour that I incline to date my Spiritual New-birth, or Baphometic Fire-baptism; perhaps I directly thereupon began to be a Man.'

CHAPTER VIII

CENTRE OF INDIFFERENCE

Teufelsdröckh turns now outwardly to the Not-me; *and finds wholesomer food. Ancient Cities: Mystery of their origin and growth: Invisible inheritances and possessions. Power and virtue of a true Book. Wagram Battlefield: War. Great Scenes beheld by the Pilgrim: Great Events, and Great Men. Napoleon, a divine missionary, preaching* La carrière ouverte aux talens. *Teufelsdröckh at the North Cape: Modern means of self-defence. Gunpowder and duelling. The Pilgrim, despising his miseries, reaches the Centre of Indifference.*

Though, after this 'Baphometic Fire-baptism' of his, our Wanderer signifies that his Unrest was but increased; as, indeed, 'Indignation and Defiance,' especially against things in general, are not the most peaceable inmates; yet can the Psychologist surmise that it was no longer a quite hopeless Unrest; that henceforth it had at least a fixed centre to revolve round. For the fire-baptised soul, long so scathed and thunder-riven, here feels its own Freedom, which feeling is its Baphometic Baptism: the citadel of its whole kingdom it has thus gained by assault, and will keep inexpugnable; outwards from which the remaining dominions, not indeed without hard battling, will doubtless by degrees be conquered and pacificated. Under another figure, we might say, if in that great moment, in the *Rue Saint-Thomas de l'Enfer,* the old inward Satanic School was not yet thrown out of doors, it received peremptory judicial notice to quit; —whereby, for the rest, its howl-chantings, Ernulphus-cursings, and rebellious gnashings of teeth, might, in the meanwhile, become only the more tumultuous, and difficult to keep secret.

Accordingly, if we scrutinise these Pilgrimings well, there is perhaps discernible henceforth a certain incipient method in their madness. Not wholly as a Spectre does Teufelsdröckh now storm through the world; at worst as a spectre-fighting Man, nay who will one day be a Spectre-queller. If pilgriming restlessly to so many 'Saints' Wells,' and ever without quenching of his thirst, he nevertheless finds little secular wells, whereby from time to time some alleviation is ministered. In a word, he is now, if not ceasing, yet intermitting to 'eat his own heart'; and clutches round him outwardly on the NOT-ME for wholesomer food. Does not the following glimpse exhibit him in a much more natural state?

'Towns also and Cities, especially the ancient, I failed not to look upon with interest. How beautiful to see thereby, as through a long vista, into the remote Time; to have as it were, an actual section of almost the earliest Past brought safe into the Present, and set before your eyes! There, in that old City, was a live ember of Culinary Fire put down, say only two-thousand years ago; and there, burning more or less triumphantly, with such fuel as the region yielded, it has burnt, and still burns, and thou thyself seest the very smoke thereof. Ah! and the far more mysterious live ember of Vital Fire was then also put down there; and still miraculously burns and spreads; and the smoke and ashes thereof (in these Judgment-Halls and Churchyards), and its bellows-engines (in these Churches), thou still seest; and its flame, looking out from every kind countenance, and every hateful one, still warms thee or scorches thee.

'Of Man's Activity and Attainment the chief results are

aeriform, mystic, and preserved in Tradition only: such are his Forms of Government, with the Authority they rest on; his Customs, or Fashions both of Cloth-habits and of Soul-habits; much more his collective stock of Handicrafts, the whole Faculty he has acquired of manipulating Nature: all these things, as indispensable and priceless as they are, cannot in any way be fixed under lock and key, but must flit, spirit-like, on impalpable vehicles, from Father to Son; if you demand sight of them, they are nowhere to be met with. Visible Ploughmen and Hammermen there have been, ever from Cain and Tubalcain downwards: but where does your accumulated Agricultural, Metallurgic, and other Manufacturing SKILL lie warehoused? It transmits itself on the atmospheric air, on the sun's rays (by Hearing and by Vision); it is a thing aeriform, impalpable, of quite spiritual sort. In like manner, ask me not, Where are the LAWS; where is the GOVERNMENT? In vain wilt thou go to Schönbrunn, to Downing Street, to the Palais Bourbon: thou findest nothing there but brick or stone houses, and some bundles of Papers tied with tape. Where, then, is that same cunningly-devised almighty GOVERNMENT of theirs to be laid hands on? Everywhere, yet nowhere: seen only in its works, this too is a thing aeriform, invisible; or if you will, mystic and miraculous. So spiritual (*geistig*) is our whole daily Life: all that we do springs out of Mystery, Spirit, invisible Force; only like a little Cloud-image, or Armida's Palace, air-built, does the Actual body itself forth from the great mystic Deep.

'Visible and tangible products of the Past, again, I reckon-up to the extent of three: Cities, with their Cabinets and Arsenals; then tilled Fields, to either or to both of which divisions Roads with their Bridges, may belong; and thirdly —————— Books. In which third truly, the last invented, lies a worth far surpassing that of the two others. Wondrous indeed is the virtue of a true Book. Not like a dead city of stones, yearly crumbling, yearly needing repair; more like a tilled field, but then a spiritual field: like a spiritual tree, let me rather say, it stands from year to year, and from age to age (we have Books that already number some hundred-and-fifty human ages); and yearly comes its new produce of leaves (Commentaries, Deductions, Philosophical, Political Systems; or were it only Sermons, Pamphlets, Journalistic Essays), every one of which is talismanic and thau-

244 / A CARLYLE READER

maturgic, for it can persuade men. O thou who art able to write a Book, which once in the two centuries or oftener there is a man gifted to do, envy not him whom they name City-builder, and inexpressibly pity him whom they name Conqueror or City-burner! Thou too art a Conqueror and Victor; but of the true sort, namely over the Devil: thou too hast built what will outlast all marble and metal, and be a wonder-bringing City of the Mind, a Temple and Seminary and Prophetic Mount, whereto all kindreds of the Earth will pilgrim.—Fool! why journeyest thou wearisomely, in thy antiquarian fervour, to gaze on the stone pyramids of Geeza, or the clay ones of Sacchara? These stand there, as I can tell thee, idle and inert, looking over the Desert, foolishly enough, for the last three-thousand years: but canst thou not open thy Hebrew BIBLE, then, or even Luther's Version thereof?'

No less satisfactory is his sudden appearance not in Battle, yet on some Battle-field; which, we soon gather, must be that of Wagram; so that here, for once, is a certain approximation to distinctiveness of date. Omitting much, let us impart what follows:

'Horrible enough! A whole Marchfeld strewed with shell-splinters, cannon-shot, ruined tumbrils, and dead men and horses; stragglers still remaining not so much as buried. And those red mould heaps: ay, there lie the Shells of Men, out of which all the Life and Virtue has been blown; and now are they swept together, and crammed-down out of sight, like blown Egg-shells!—Did Nature, when she bade the Donau bring down his mould-cargoes from the Carinthian and Carpathian Heights, and spread them out here into the softest, richest level,—intend thee, O Marchfeld, for a corn-bearing Nursery, whereon her children might be nursed; or for a Cockpit, wherein they might the more commodiously be throttled and tattered? Were thy three broad Highways, meeting here from the ends of Europe, made for Ammunition-wagons, then? Were thy Wagrams and Stillfrieds but so many ready-built Casemates, wherein the house of Hapsburg might batter with artillery, and with artillery be battered? König Ottokar, amid yonder hillocks, dies under Rodolf's truncheon; here Kaiser Franz falls a-swoon under Napoleon's: within which five centuries, to omit the others, how has thy breast, fair Plain, been defaced and defiled! The greensward is torn-up and trampled-down; man's fond care of it, his fruit-trees, hedge-rows, and pleasant dwellings, blown away with gunpowder; and the kind seedfield lies a desolate, hideous Place of Sculls.—Nevertheless, Nature is at work; neither shall these Powder-Devilkins with their utmost devilry gainsay her: but all that gore and carnage will be shrouded-in, absorbed into manure; and next year the Marchfeld will be green, nay greener. Thrifty unwearied Nature, ever out of our great waste educing some little profit of thy own,—how dost thou, from the very carcass of the Killer, bring Life for the Living!

'What, speaking in quite unofficial language, is the net-purport and upshot of war? To my own knowledge, for example, there dwell and toil, in the British village of Dumdrudge, usually some five-hundred souls. From these, by certain "Natural Enemies" of the French, there are successively selected, during the French war, say thirty able-bodied men: Dumdrudge, at her own expense, has suckled and nursed them: she has, not without difficulty and sorrow, fed them up to manhood, and even trained them to crafts, so that one can weave, another build, another hammer, and the weakest can stand under thirty stone avoirdupois. Nevertheless, amid much weeping and swearing, they are selected; all dressed in red; and shipped away, at the public charges, some two-thousand miles, or say only to the south of Spain; and fed there till wanted. And now to that same spot, in the south of Spain, are thirty similar French artisans, from a French Dumdrudge, in like manner wending: till at length, after infinite effort, the two parties come into actual juxtaposition; and Thirty stands fronting Thirty, each with a gun in his hand. Straightway the word "Fire!" is given: and they blow the souls out of one another; and in place of sixty brisk useful craftsmen, the world has sixty dead carcasses, which it must bury, and anew shed tears for. Had these men any quarrel? Busy as the Devil is, not the smallest! They lived far enough apart; were the entirest strangers; nay, in so wide a Universe, there was even, unconsciously, by Commerce, some mutual helpfulness between them. How then? Simpleton! their Governors had fallen-out; and, instead of shooting one another, had the cunning to make these poor blockheads shoot.—Alas, so is it in Deutschland, and hitherto in all other lands; still as of old, "what devilry soever Kings do, the Greeks must pay the piper!"—In that fiction of the English Smollet, it is true, the final Cessation of War is perhaps prophetically shadowed forth; where the two Natural Enemies, in person, take each a Tobacco-pipe, filled with Brimstone; light the same, and smoke in one another's faces, till the weaker gives in: but from such predicted Peace-Era, what blood-filled trenches, and contentious centuries, may still divide us!'

Thus can the Professor, at least in lucid intervals, look away from his own sorrows, over the many-coloured world, and pertinently enough note what is passing there. We may remark, indeed, that for the matter of spiritual culture, if for nothing else, perhaps few periods of his life were richer than this. Internally, there is the most momentous instructive Course of Practical Philosophy, with Experiments, going on; towards the right comprehension of which his Peripatetic habits, favourable to Meditation, might help him rather than hinder. Externally, again, as he wanders to and fro, there are, if for the longing heart little substance, yet for the seeing eye sights enough: in these so boundless Travels of his, granting that the Satanic School was even partially kept down, what an incredible knowledge of our Planet, and its Inhabitants and their Works, that is to say, of all knowable things, might not Teufelsdröckh acquire!

'I have read in most Public Libraries,' says he, 'including those of Constantinople and Samarcand: in most Colleges, except the Chinese Mandarin ones, I have studied, or seen that there was no studying. Unknown Languages have I oftenest gathered from their natural repertory, the Air, by my organ of Hearing; Statistics, Geographics, Topographics came, through the Eye, almost of their own accord. The ways of Man, how he seeks food, and warmth, and protection for himself, in most regions, are ocularly known to me. Like the great Hadrian, I meted-out much of the terraqueous Globe with a pair of Compasses that belonged to myself only.

'Of great Scenes why speak? Three summer days, I lingered reflecting, and even composing (*dichtete*), by the Pinechasms of Vaucluse; and in that clear Lakelet moistened my bread. I have sat under the Palm-trees of Tadmor; smoked a pipe among the ruins of Babylon. The great Wall of China I have seen; and can testify that it is of gray brick, coped and covered with granite, and shows only second-rate masonry.—Great Events, also, have not I witnessed? Kings sweated-down (*ausgemergelt*) into Berlin-and-Milan

Customhouse-Officers; the World well won, and the World well lost; oftener than once a hundred-thousand individuals shot (by each other) in one day. All kindreds and peoples and nations dashed together, and shifted and shovelled into heaps, that they might ferment there, and in time unite. The birth-pangs of Democracy, wherewith convulsed Europe was groaning in cries that reached Heaven, could not escape me.

'For great Men I have ever had the warmest predilection; and can perhaps boast that few such in this era have wholly escaped me. Great Men are the inspired (speaking and acting) Texts of that divine BOOK OF REVELATIONS, whereof a Chapter is completed from epoch to epoch, and by some named HISTORY; to which inspired Texts your numerous talented men, and your innumerable untalented men, are the better or worse exegetic Commentaries, and wagonload of too-stupid, heretical or orthodox, weekly Sermons. For my study, the inspired Texts themselves! Thus did not I, in very early days, having disguised me as tavern-waiter, stand behind the field-chairs, under that shady Tree at Treisnitz by the Jena Highway; waiting upon the great Schiller and greater Goethe; and hearing what I have not forgotten. For————'

————But at this point the Editor recalls his principle of caution, some time ago laid down, and must suppress much. Let not the sacredness of Laurelled, still more, of Crowned Heads, be tampered with. Should we, at a future day, find circumstances altered, and the time come for Publication, then may these glimpses into the privacy of the Illustrious be conceded; which for the present were little better than treacherous, perhaps traitorous Eavesdroppings. Of Lord Byron, therefore, of Pope Pius, Emperor Tarakwang, and the 'White Water-roses' (Chinese Carbonari) with their mysteries, no notice here! Of Napoleon himself we shall only, glancing from afar, remark that Teufelsdröckh's relation to him seems to have been of very varied character. At first we find our poor Professor on the point of being shot as a spy; then taken into private conversation, even pinched on the ear, yet presented with no money; at last indignantly dismissed, almost thrown out of doors, as an 'Ideologist.' 'He himself,' says the Professor, 'was among the completest Ideologists, at least Ideopraxists: in the Idea (*in der Idee*) he lived, moved and fought. The man was a Divine Missionary, though unconscious of it; and preached, through the cannon's throat, that great doctrine, *La carrière ouverte aux talens* (The Tools to him that can handle them), which is our ultimate Political Evangel, wherein alone can liberty lie. Madly enough he preached, it is true, as Enthusiasts and first Missionaries are wont, with imperfect utterance, amid much frothy rant; yet as articulately perhaps as the case admitted. Or call him, if you will, an American Backwoodsman, who had to fell unpenetrated forests, and battle with innumerable wolves, and did not entirely forbear strong liquor, rioting, and even theft; whom, notwithstanding, the peaceful Sower will follow, and, as he cuts the boundless harvest, bless.'

More legitimate and decisively authentic is Teufelsdröckh's appearance and emergence (we know not well whence) in the solitude of the North Cape, on that June Midnight. He has a 'light-blue Spanish cloak' hanging round him, as his 'most commodious, principal, indeed sole upper-garment'; and stands there, on the World-promontory, looking over the infinite Brine, like a little blue Belfry (as we figure), now motionless indeed, yet ready, if stirred, to ring quaintest changes.

'Silence as of death,' writes he; 'for Midnight, even in the Arctic latitudes, has its character: nothing but the granite cliffs ruddy-tinged, the peaceable gurgle of that slow-heaving Polar Ocean, over which in the utmost North the great Sun hangs low and lazy, as if he too were slumbering. Yet is his cloud-couch wrought of crimson and cloth-of-gold; yet does his light stream over the mirror of waters, like a tremulous fire-pillar, shooting downwards to the abyss, and hide itself under my feet. In such moments, Solitude also is invaluable; for who would speak, or be looked on, when behind him lies all Europe and Africa, fast asleep, except the watchmen; and before him the silent Immensity, and Palace of the Eternal, whereof our Sun is but a porch-lamp?

'Nevertheless, in this solemn moment comes a man, or monster, scrambling from among the rock-hollows; and, shaggy, huge as the Hyperborean Bear, hails me in Russian speech: most probably, therefore, a Russian Smuggler. With courteous brevity, I signify my indifference to contraband trade, my humane intentions, yet strong wish to be private. In vain: the monster, counting doubtless on his superior stature, and minded to make sport for himself, or perhaps profit, were it with murder, continues to advance; ever assailing me with his importunate train-oil breath; and now has advanced, till we stand both on the verge of the rock, the deep Sea rippling greedily down below. What argument will avail? On the thick Hyperborean, cherubic reasoning, seraphic eloquence were lost. Prepared for such extremity, I, deftly enough, whisk aside one step; draw out, from my interior reservoirs, a sufficient Birmingham Horse-pistol, and say, "Be so obliging as to retire, Friend (*Er ziehe sich zurück, Freund*), and with promptitude!" This logic even the Hyperborean understands: fast enough, with apologetic, petitionary growl, he sidles off; and, except for suicidal as well as homicidal purposes, need not return.

'Such I hold to be the genuine use of Gunpowder: that it makes all men alike tall. Nay, if thou be cooler, cleverer than I, if thou have more *Mind,* though all but no *Body* whatever, then canst thou kill me first, and art the taller. Hereby, at last, is the Goliath powerless, and the David resistless; savage Animalism is nothing, inventive Spiritualism is all.

'With respect to Duels, indeed, I have my own ideas. Few things, in this so surprising world, strike me with more surprise. Two little visual Spectra of men, hovering with insecure enough cohesion in the midst of the UNFATHOMABLE, and to dissolve therein, at any rate, very soon,—make pause at the distance of twelve paces asunder; whirl round; and, simultaneously by the cunningest mechanism, explode one another into Dissolution; and off-hand become Air, and Non-extant! Deuce on it (*verdammt*), the little spitfires!—Nay, I think with old Hugo von Trimberg: "God must needs laugh outright, could such a thing be, to see his wondrous Manikins here below." '

But amid these specialties, let us not forget the great generality, which is our chief quest here: How prospered the inner man of Teufelsdröckh under so much outward shifting? Does Legion still lurk in him, though repressed; or has he exorcised that Devil's Brood? We can answer that the symptoms continue promising. Experience is the grand spiritual Doctor; and with him Teufelsdröckh has been long a patient, swallowing many a bitter bolus. Unless our poor Friend belong to the numerous class of Incurables, which seems not likely, some cure will doubtless be effected. We should rather say that Legion, or the Satanic School, was now pretty well extirpated and cast out, but next to nothing introduced in its room; whereby the heart remains, for the while, in a quiet but no comfortable state.

'At length, after so much roasting,' thus writes our Autobiographer, 'I was what you might name calcined. Pray only that it be not rather, as is the more frequent issue, reduced to a *caput-mortuum!* But in any case, by mere dint of practice, I had grown familiar with many things. Wretchedness was still wretched; but I could now partly see through it, and despise it. Which highest mortal, in this inane Existence, had I not found a Shadow-hunter, or Shadow-hunted; and, when I looked through his brave garnitures, miserable enough? Thy wishes have all been sniffed aside, thought I: but what, had they even been all granted! Did not the Boy Alexander weep because he had not two Planets to conquer; or a whole Solar System; or after that, a whole Universe? *Ach Gott,* when I gazed into these Stars, have they not looked-down on me as if with pity, from their serene spaces; like Eyes glistening with heavenly tears over the little lot of man! Thousands of human generations, all as noisy as our own, have been swallowed-up of Time, and there remains no wreck of them any more; and Arcturus and Orion and Sirius and the Pleiades are still shining in their courses, clear and young, as when the Shepherd first noted them in the plain of Shinar. Pshaw! what is this paltry little Dog-cage of an Earth; what art thou that sittest whining there? Thou art still Nothing, Nobody: true; but who, then, is Something, Somebody? For thee the Family of Man has no use; it rejects thee; thou art wholly as a dissevered limb; so be it; perhaps it is better so!'

Too-heavy-laden Teufelsdröckh! Yet surely his bands are loosening; one day he will hurl the burden far from him, and bound forth free and with a second youth.

'This,' says our Professor, 'was the CENTRE OF INDIFFERENCE I had now reached; through which whoso travels from the Negative Pole to the Positive must necessarily pass.'

CHAPTER IX

THE EVERLASTING YEA

Temptations in the Wilderness: Victory over the Tempter. An-
nihilation of Self. Belief in God, and love to Man. The Origin
of Evil, a problem ever requiring to be solved anew: Teufels-
dröckh's solution. Love of Happiness a vain whim: A Higher
in man than Love of Happiness. The Everlasting Yea. Worship
of Sorrow. Voltaire: his task now finished. Conviction worthless,
impossible, without Conduct. The true Ideal, the Actual: Up and
work!

'Temptations in the Wilderness!' exclaims Teufelsdröckh:
'Have we not all to be tried with such? Not so easily can the
old Adam, lodged in us by birth, be dispossessed. Our Life is
compassed round with Necessity; yet is the meaning of Life
itself no other than Freedom, than Voluntary Force: thus
have we a warfare; in the beginning, especially, a hard-
fought battle. For the God-given mandate, *Work thou in*
Welldoing, lies mysteriously written, in Promethean Prophetic Characters, in our hearts; and leaves us no rest,
night or day, till it be deciphered and obeyed; till it burn
forth, in our conduct, a visible, acted Gospel of Freedom.
And as the clay-given mandate, *Eat thou and be filled,* at
the same time persuasively proclaims itself through every
nerve,—must not there be a confusion, a contest, before
the better Influence can become the upper?
　'To me nothing seems more natural than that the Son
of Man, when such God-given mandate first prophetically
stirs within him, and the Clay must now be vanquished or
vanquish,—should be carried of the spirit into grim Solitudes, and there fronting the Tempter do grimmest battle
with him; defiantly setting him at naught, till he yield and
fly. Name it as we choose: with or without visible Devil,
whether in the natural Desert of rocks and sands, or in
the populous moral Desert of selfishness and baseness,—to
such Temptation are we all called. Unhappy if we are not!
Unhappy if we are but Half-men, in whom that divine
handwriting has never blazed forth, all-subduing, in true
sun-splendour; but quivers dubiously amid meaner

lights: or smoulders, in dull pain, in darkness, under earthly vapours!—Our Wilderness is the wide World in an Atheistic Century; our Forty Days are long years of suffering and fasting: nevertheless, to these also comes an end. Yes, to me also was given, if not Victory, yet the consciousness of Battle, and the resolve to persevere therein while life or faculty is left. To me also, entangled in the enchanted forests, demon-peopled, doleful of sight and of sound, it was given, after weariest wanderings, to work out my way into the higher sunlight slopes—of that Mountain which has no summit, or whose summit is in Heaven only!'

He says elsewhere, under a less ambitious figure; as figures are, once for all, natural to him: 'Has not thy Life been that of most sufficient men (*tüchtigen Männer*) thou hast known in this generation? An outflush of foolish young Enthusiasm, like the first fallow-crop, wherein are as many weeds as valuable herbs: this all parched away, under the Droughts of practical and spiritual Unbelief, as Disappointment, in thought and act, often-repeated gave rise to Doubt, and Doubt gradually settled into Denial! If I have had a second-crop, and now see the perennial greensward, and sit under umbrageous cedars, which defy all Drought (and Doubt); herein too, be the Heavens praised, I am not without examples, and even exemplars.'

So that, for Teufelsdröckh also, there has been a 'glorious revolution': these mad shadow-hunting and shadow-hunted Pilgrimings of his were but some purifying 'Temptation in the Wilderness,' before his apostolic work (such as it was) could begin; which Temptation is now happily over, and the Devil once more worsted! Was 'that high moment in the *Rue de l'Enfer*,' then, properly the turning-point of the battle; when the Fiend said, *Worship me, or be torn in shreds;* and was answered valiantly with an *Apage Satana?*—Singular Teufelsdröckh, would thou hadst told thy singular story in plain words! But it is fruitless to look there, in those Paper-bags, for such. Nothing but innuendoes, figurative crotchets: a typical Shadow, fitfully wavering, prophetico-satiric; no clear logical Picture. 'How paint to the sensual eye,' asks he once, 'what passes in the Holy-of-Holies of Man's Soul; in what words, known to these profane times, speak even afar-off of the unspeakable?' We ask in turn: Why perplex these times, profane as they are, with needless obscurity, by omission and by commission? Not mystical only is our Professor, but whimsical; and involves himself, now more than ever, in eye-bewildering *chiaroscuro*. Successive glimpses, here faithfully imparted, our more gifted readers must endeavour to combine for their own behoof.

He says: 'The hot Harmattan wind had raged itself out; its howl went silent within me; and the long-deafened soul could now hear. I paused in my wild wanderings; and sat me down to wait, and consider; for it was as if the hour of change drew nigh. I seemed to surrender, to renounce utterly, and say: Fly, then, false shadows of Hope; I will chase you no more, I will believe you no more. And ye too, haggard spectres of Fear, I care not for you; ye too are all shadows and a lie. Let me rest here: for I am way-weary and life-weary; I will rest here, were it but to die: to die or to live is alike to me; alike insignificant.'—And again: 'Here, then, as I lay in that CENTRE OF INDIFFERENCE; cast, doubtless by benignant upper Influence, into a healing sleep, the heavy dreams rolled gradually away, and I awoke to a new Heaven and a new Earth. The first preliminary moral Act, Annihilation of Self (*Selbst-tödtung*), had been happily accomplished; and my mind's eyes were now unsealed, and its hands ungyved.'

Might we not also conjecture that the following passage refers to his Locality, during this same 'healing sleep'; that his Pilgrim-staff lies cast aside here, on 'the high table-land'; and indeed that the repose is already taking wholesome effect on him? If it were not that the tone, in some parts, has more of riancy, even of levity, than we could have expected! However, in Teufelsdröckh, there is always the strangest Dualism: light dancing, with guitar-music, will be going on in the fore-court, while by fits from within comes the faint whimpering of woe and wail. We transcribe the piece entire.

'Beautiful it was to sit there, as in my skyey Tent, musing and meditating; on the high table-land, in front of the Mountains; over me, as roof, the azure Dome, and around me, for walls, four azure-flowing curtains,—namely, of the Four azure Winds, on whose bottom-fringes also I have seen gilding. And then to fancy the fair Castles that stood sheltered in these Mountain hollows; with their green flower-lawns, and white dames and damosels, lovely enough: or better still, the straw-roofed Cottages, wherein stood many a Mother baking bread, with her children round her:—all hidden and protectingly folded-up in the valley-folds; yet there and alive, as sure as if I beheld them. Or to see, as well as fancy, the nine Towns and Villages, that lay round my mountain-seat, which, in still weather, were wont to speak to me (by their steeple-bells) with metal tongue; and, in almost all weather, proclaimed their vitality by repeated Smoke-clouds; whereon, as on a culinary horologe, I might read the hour of the day. For it was the smoke of cookery, as kind housewives at morning, midday, eventide, were boiling their husbands' kettles; and ever a blue pillar rose up into the air, successively or simultaneously, from each of the nine, saying, as plainly as smoke could say: Such and such a meal is getting ready here. Not uninteresting! For you have the whole Borough, with all its love-makings and scandal-mongeries, contentions and contentments, as in miniature, and could cover it all with your hat.—If, in my wide Wayfarings, I had learned to look into the business of the World in its details, here perhaps was the place for combining it into general propositions, and deducing inferences therefrom.

'Often also could I see the black Tempest marching in anger through the Distance: round some Schreckhorn, as yet grim-blue, would the eddying vapour gather, and there tumultuously eddy, and flow down like a mad witch's hair; till, after a space, it vanished, and, in the clear sunbeam, your Schreckhorn stood smiling grim-white, for the vapour had held snow. How thou fermentest and elaboratest, in thy great fermenting-vat and laboratory of an Atmosphere, of a World, O Nature!—Or what is Nature? Ha! why do I not name thee God? Art not thou the "Living Garment of God"? O Heavens, is it, in very deed, HE, then, that ever speaks through thee; that lives and loves in thee, that lives and loves in me?

'Fore-shadows, call them rather fore-splendours, of that Truth, and Beginning of Truths, fell mysteriously over my soul. Sweeter than Dayspring to the Shipwrecked in Nova Zembla; ah, like the mother's voice to her little child that strays bewildered, weeping, in unknown tumults; like soft streamings of celestial music to my too-exasperated heart, came that Evangel. The Universe is not dead and demoniacal, a charnel-house with spectres; but godlike, and my Father's!

'With other eyes, too, could I now look upon my fellow man: with an infinite Love, an infinite Pity. Poor, wandering, wayward man! Art thou not tried, and beaten with stripes, even as I am? Ever, whether thou bear the royal mantle or the beggar's gabardine, art thou not so weary, so heavy-laden; and thy Bed of Rest is but a Grave. O my Brother, my Brother, why cannot I shelter thee in my bosom, and wipe away all tears from thy eyes!—Truly, the din of many-voiced Life, which, in this solitude, with the mind's organ, I could hear, was no longer a maddening discord, but a melting one; like inarticulate cries, and sobbings of a dumb creature, which in the ear of Heaven are prayers. The poor Earth, with her poor joys, was now my needy Mother, not my cruel Stepdame; Man, with his so mad Wants and so mean Endeavours, had become the dearer to me; and even for his sufferings and his sins, I now first named him Brother. Thus was I standing in the porch of that *"Sanctuary of Sorrow"*; by strange, steep ways had I too been guided thither; and ere long its sacred gates would open, and the *"Divine Depth of Sorrow"* lie disclosed to me.'

The Professor says, he here first got eye on the Knot that had been strangling him, and straightway could unfasten it, and was free. 'A vain interminable controversy,' writes he, 'touching what is at present called Origin of Evil, or some such thing, arises in every soul, since the beginning of the world; and in every soul, that would pass from idle Suffering into actual Endeavouring, must first be put an end to. The most, in our time, have to go content with a simple, incomplete enough Suppression of this controversy; to a few some Solution of it is indispensable. In every new era, too, such Solution comes-out in different terms; and ever the Solution of the last era has become obsolete, and is found unserviceable. For it is man's nature to change his Dialect from century to century; he cannot help it though he would. The authentic *Church-Catechism* of our present century has not yet fallen into my hands: meanwhile, for my own private behoof, I attempt to elucidate the matter so. Man's Unhappiness as I construe, comes of his Greatness; it is because there is an

Infinite in him, which with all his cunning he cannot quite bury under the Finite. Will the whole Finance Ministers and Upholsterers and Confectioners of modern Europe undertake, in joint-stock company, to make one Shoeblack HAPPY? They cannot accomplish it, above an hour or two: for the Shoeblack also has a Soul quite other than his Stomach; and would require, if you consider it, for his permanent satisfaction and saturation, simply this allotment, no more, and no less: *God's infinite Universe altogether to himself,* therein to enjoy infinitely, and fill every wish as fast as it rose. Oceans of Hochheimer, a Throat like that of Ophiuchus: speak not of them; to the infinite Shoeblack they are as nothing. No sooner is your ocean filled, then he grumbles that it might have been of better vintage. Try him with half of a Universe, of an Omnipotence, he sets to quarrelling with the proprietor of the other half, and declares himself the most maltreated of men.—Always there is a black spot in our sunshine: it is even, as I said, the *Shadow of Ourselves.*

'But the whim we have of Happiness is somewhat thus. By certain valuations, and averages, of our own striking, we come upon some sort of average terrestrial lot; this we fancy belongs to us by nature, and of indefeasible right. It is simple payment of our wages, of our deserts; requires neither thanks nor complaint; only such *overplus* as there may be do we account Happiness; any *deficit* again is Misery. Now consider that we have the valuation of our own deserts ourselves, and what a fund of Self-conceit there is in each of us,—do you wonder that the balance should so often dip the wrong way, and many a Blockhead cry: See there, what a payment; was ever worthy gentleman so used!—I tell thee, Blockhead, it all comes of thy Vanity; of what thou *fanciest* those same deserts of thine to be. Fancy that thou deservest to be hanged (as is most likely), thou wilt feel it happiness to be only shot: fancy that thou deservest to be hanged in a hair-halter, it will be a luxury to die in hemp.

'So true is it, what I then said, that *the Fraction of Life can be increased in value not so much by increasing your Numerator as by lessening your Denominator.* Nay, unless my Algebra deceive me, *Unity* itself divided by *Zero* will give *Infinity.* Make thy claim of wages a zero, then; thou hast the world under thy feet. Well did the Wisest of our time write: "It is only with Renunciation (*Entsagen*) that Life, properly speaking, can be said to begin."

'I asked myself: What is this that, ever since earliest years, thou hast been fretting and fuming, and lamenting and self-tormenting, on account of? Say it in a word: is it not because thou art not HAPPY? Because the THOU (sweet gentleman) is not sufficiently honoured, nourished, soft-bedded, and lovingly cared-for? Foolish soul! What Act of Legislature was there that *thou* shouldst be Happy? A little while ago thou hadst no right to *be* at all. What if thou wert born and predestined not to be Happy, but to be Unhappy! Art thou nothing other than a Vulture, then, that fliest through the Universe seeking after somewhat to *eat;* and shrieking dolefully because carrion enough is not given thee? Close thy *Byron;* open thy *Goethe.*'

'*Es leuchtet mir ein,* I see a glimpse of it!' cries he elsewhere: 'there is in man a HIGHER than Love of Happiness: he can do without Happiness, and instead thereof find Blessedness! Was it not to preach-forth this same HIGHER that sages and martyrs, the Poet and the Priest, in all times, have spoken and suffered; bearing testimony, through life and through death, of the Godlike that is in Man, and how in the Godlike only has he Strength and Freedom? Which God-inspired Doctrine art thou also honoured to be taught; O Heavens! and broken with manifold merciful Afflictions, even till thou become contrite, and learn it! O, thank thy Destiny for these; thankfully bear what yet remain: thou hadst need of them; the Self in thee needed to be annihilated. By benignant fever-paroxysms is Life rooting out the deep-seated chronic Disease, and triumphs over Death. On the roaring billows of Time, thou art not engulfed, but borne aloft into the azure of Eternity. Love not Pleasure; love God. This is the EVERLASTING YEA, wherein all contradiction is solved: wherein whoso walks and works, it is well with him.'

And again: 'Small is it that thou canst trample the Earth with its injuries under thy feet, as old Greek Zeno trained thee: thou canst love the Earth while it injures thee, and even because it injures thee; for this a Greater than Zeno was needed, and he too was sent. Knowest thou that "*Worship of Sorrow*"? The Temple thereof, founded some eighteen centuries ago, now lies in ruins, overgrown with jungle, the habitation of doleful creatures: nevertheless, venture forward; in a low crypt, arched out of falling fragments, thou findest the Altar still there, and its sacred Lamp perennially burning.'

Without pretending to comment on which strange utterances, the Editor will only remark, that there lies beside them much of a still more questionable character; unsuited to the general apprehension; nay wherein he himself does not see his way. Nebulous disquisitions on Religion, yet not without bursts of splendour; on the 'perennial continuance of Inspiration'; on Prophecy; that there are 'true Priests, as well as Baal-Priests, in our own day': with more of the like sort. We select some fractions, by way of finish to this farrago.

'Cease, my much-respected Herr von Voltaire,' thus apostrophises the Professor: 'shut thy sweet voice; for the task appointed thee seems finished. Sufficiently hast thou demonstrated this proposition, considerable or otherwise: That the Mythus of the Christian Religion looks not in the eighteenth century as it did in the eighth. Alas, were thy six-and-thirty quartos, and the six-and-thirty thousand other quartos and folios, and flying sheets or reams, printed before and since on the same subject, all needed to convince us of so little! But what next? Wilt thou help us to embody the divine Spirit of that Religion in a new Mythus, in a new vehicle and vesture, that our Souls, otherwise too like perishing, may live? What! thou hast no faculty in that kind? Only a torch for burning, no hammer for building? Take our thanks, then, and——thyself away.

'Meanwhile what are antiquated Mythuses to me? Or is the God present, felt in my own heart, a thing which Herr von Voltaire will dispute out of me; or dispute into me? To the "Worship of Sorrow" ascribe what origin and genesis thou pleasest, has not that Worship originated, and been generated; is it not here? Feel it in thy heart, and then say whether it is of God! This is Belief; all else is Opinion, —for which latter whoso will, let him worry and be worried.'

'Neither,' observes he elsewhere, 'shall ye tear-out one another's eyes, struggling over "Plenary Inspiration," and such-like: try rather to get a little even Partial Inspiration, each of you for himself. One BIBLE I know, of whose Plenary Inspiration doubt is not so much as possible; nay with my own eyes I saw the God's-Hand writing it: thereof all other Bibles are but Leaves,—say, in Picture-Writing to assist the weaker faculty.'

Or, to give the wearied reader relief, and bring it to an end, let him take the following perhaps more intelligible passage:

'To me, in this our life,' says the Professor, 'which is an internecine warfare with the Time-spirit, other warfare seems questionable. Hast thou in any way a Contention with thy brother, I advise thee, think well what the meaning thereof is. If thou gauge it to the bottom, it is simply this: "Fellow, see! thou art taking more than thy share of Happiness in the world, something from *my* share: which, by the Heavens, thou shalt not; nay I will fight thee rather." —Alas, and the whole lot to be divided is such a beggarly matter, truly a "feast of shells," for the substance has been spilled out: not enough to quench one Appetite; and the collective human species clutching at them!—Can we not, in all such cases, rather say: "Take it, thou too-ravenous individual; take that pitiful additional fraction of a share, which I reckoned mine, but which thou so wantest; take it with a blessing: would to Heaven I had enough for thee!"— If Fichte's *Wissenschaftslehre* be, "to a certain extent, Applied Christianity," surely to a still greater extent, so is this. We have here not a Whole Duty of Man, yet a Half Duty, namely the Passive half: could we but do it, as we can demonstrate it!

'But indeed Conviction, were it never so excellent, is worthless till it convert itself into Conduct. Nay properly Conviction is not possible till then; inasmuch as all Speculation is by nature endless, formless, a vortex amid vortices: only by a felt indubitable certainty of Experience does it find any centre to revolve round, and so fashion itself into a system. Most true is it, as a wise man teaches us, that "Doubt of any sort cannot be removed except by Action." On which ground, too, let him who gropes painfully in darkness or uncertain light, and prays vehemently that the dawn may ripen into day, lay this other precept well to heart, which to me was of invaluable service: *"Do the Duty which lies nearest thee,"* which thou knowest to be a Duty! Thy second Duty will already have become clearer.

'May we not say, however, that the hour of Spiritual

Enfranchisement is even this: When your Ideal World, wherein the whole man has been dimly struggling and inexpressibly languishing to work, becomes revealed, and thrown open; and you discover, with amazement enough, like the Lothario in *Wilhelm Meister,* that your "America is here or nowhere"? The Situation that has not its Duty, its Ideal, was never yet occupied by man. Yes here, in this poor, miserable, hampered, despicable Actual, wherein thou even now standest, here or nowhere is thy Ideal: work it out therefrom; and working, believe, live, be free. Fool! the Ideal is in thyself, the impediment too is in thyself: thy Condition is but the stuff thou art to shape that same Ideal out of: what matters whether such stuff be of this sort or that, so the Form thou give it be heroic, be poetic? O thou that pinest in the imprisonment of the Actual, and criest bitterly to the gods for a kingdom wherein to rule and create, know this of a truth: the thing thou seekest is already with thee, "here or nowhere," couldst thou only see!

'But it is with man's Soul as it was with Nature: the beginning of Creation is—Light. Till the eye have vision, the whole members are in bonds. Divine moment, when over the tempest-tost Soul, as once over the wild-weltering Chaos, it is spoken: Let there be Light! Ever to the greatest that has felt such moment, is it not miraculous and God-announcing; even as, under simpler figures, to the simplest and least. The mad primeval Discord is hushed; the rudely-jumbled conflicting elements bind themselves into separate Firmaments: deep silent rock-foundations are built beneath; and the skyey vault with its everlasting Luminaries above: instead of a dark wasteful Chaos, we have a blooming, fertile, heaven-encompassed World.

'I too could now say to myself: Be no longer a Chaos, but a World, or even Worldkin. Produce! Produce! Were it but the pitifullest infinitesimal fraction of a Product, produce it, in God's name! 'Tis the utmost thou hast in thee: out with it, then. Up, up! Whatsoever thy hand findeth to do, do it with thy whole might. Work while it is called Today; for · the Night cometh, wherein no man can work.'

CHAPTER X

PAUSE

Conversion; a spiritual attainment peculiar to the modern Era. Teufelsdröckh accepts Authorship as his divine calling. The scope of the command Thou shalt not steal.—*Editor begins to suspect the authenticity of the Biographical documents; and abandons them for the great Clothes volume. Result of the preceding ten Chapters: Insight into the character of Teufelsdröckh: His fundamental beliefs, and how he was forced to seek and find them.*

Thus have we, as closely and perhaps satisfactorily as, in such circumstances, might be, followed Teufelsdröckh through the various successive states and stages of Growth, Entanglement, Unbelief, and almost Reprobation, into a certain clearer state of what he himself seems to consider as Conversion. 'Blame not the word,' says he; 'rejoice rather that such a word, signifying such a thing, has come to light in our modern Era, though hidden from the wisest Ancients. The Old World knew nothing of Conversion; instead of an *Ecce Homo,* they had only some *Choice of Hercules.* It was a new-attained progress in the Moral Development of man: hereby has the Highest come home to the bosoms of the most Limited; what to Plato was but a hallucination, and to Socrates a chimera, is now clear and certain to your Zinzendorfs, your Wesleys, and the poorest of their Pietists and Methodists.'

It is here, then, that the spiritual majority of Teufelsdröckh commences: we are henceforth to see him 'work in well-doing,' with the spirit and clear aims of a Man. He has discovered that the Ideal Workshop he so panted for is even this same Actual ill-furnished Workshop he has so long been stumbling in. He can say to himself: 'Tools? Thou hast no Tools? Why, there is not a Man, or a Thing, now alive but has tools. The basest of created animalcules, the Spider itself, has a spinning-jenny, and warping-mill, and power-loom within its head: the stupidest of Oysters has a Papin's-Digester, with stone-and-lime house to hold it in: every being that can live can do something: this let him *do.*—Tools? Hast thou not a Brain, furnished, furnishable with some glimmerings of Light; and three fingers to hold a Pen withal? Never since Aaron's rod went out of practice, or even before it, was there such a wonder-working Tool: greater than all recorded miracles have been performed by Pens. For strangely in this so solid-seeming World, which nevertheless is in continual restless flux, it is appointed that *Sound,* to appearance the most fleeting, should be the most continuing of all things. The WORD is well said to be omnipotent in this world; man, thereby divine, can create as by a *Fiat.* Awake, arise! Speak forth what is in thee; what God has given thee, what the Devil shall not take away. Higher task than that of Priesthood was allotted to no man: wert thou but the meanest in that sacred Hierarchy, is it not honour enough therein to spend and be spent?

'By this Art, which whoso will may sacrilegiously degrade into a handicraft,' adds Teufelsdröckh, 'have I thenceforth abidden. Writings of mine, not indeed known as mine (for what am *I?*), have fallen, perhaps not altogether void, into the mighty seed-field of Opinion; fruits of my unseen sowing gratifyingly meet me here and there. I thank the Heavens that I have now found my Calling; wherein, with or without perceptible result, I am minded diligently to persevere.

'Nay how knowest thou,' cries he, 'but this and the other pregnant Device, now grown to be a world-renowned far-working Institution; like a grain of right mustard-seed once cast into the right soil, and now stretching-out strong boughs to the four winds, for the birds of the air to lodge in,—may have been properly my doing? Some one's doing, it without doubt was; from some Idea, in some single Head, it did first of all take beginning: why not from some Idea in mine?' Does Teufelsdröckh here glance at that 'SOCIETY FOR THE CONSERVATION OF PROPERTY (*Eigenthums-conservirende Gesellschaft*),' of which so many ambiguous notices glide spectre-like through these inexpressible Paper-bags? 'An Institution,' hints he, 'not unsuitable to the wants of the time; as indeed such sudden extension proves: for already can the Society number, among its office-bearers or corresponding members, the highest Names, if not the highest Persons, in Germany, England, France; and contributions, both of money and of meditation, pour in from all quarters; to, if possible, enlist the remaining Integrity of the world, and, defensively and with forethought, marshal it round this Palladium.' Does Teufelsdröckh mean, then, to give himself out as the originator of that so notable *Eigenthums-conservirende* ('Owndom-conserving') *Gesellschaft;* and if so, what, in the Devil's name, is it? He again hints: 'At a time when the divine Commandment, *Thou shalt not steal,* wherein truly, if well understood, is comprised the whole Hebrew Decalogue, with Solon's and Lycurgus's Constitutions, Justinian's Pandects, the Code Napoléon, and all Codes, Catechisms, Divinities, Moralities whatsoever, that man has hitherto devised (and enforced with Altar-fire and Gallows-ropes) for his social guidance: at a time, I say, when this divine Commandment has all-but faded away from the general remembrance; and, with little disguise, a new opposite Commandment, *Thou shalt steal,* is everywhere promulgated,—it perhaps behooved, in this universal dotage and deliration, the sound portion of mankind to bestir themselves and rally. When the widest and wildest violations of that divine right of Property, the only divine right now extant or conceivable, are sanctioned and recommended by a vicious Press, and the world has lived to hear it asserted that *we have no Property in our very Bodies, but only an accidental Possession and Life-rent,* what is the issue to be looked for? Hangmen and Catchpoles may, by their noose-gins and baited fall-traps, keep down the smaller sort of vermin; but what, except perhaps some such Universal Association, can protect us against whole meat-devouring and man-devouring hosts of Boa-constrictors? If, therefore, the more sequestered Thinker have wondered, in his privacy, from what hand that perhaps not ill-written *Program* in the Public Journals, with its high *Prize-Questions* and so liberal *Prizes,* could have proceeded, —let him now cease such wonder; and, with undivided faculty, betake himself to the *Concurrenz* (Competition).'

We ask: Has this same 'perhaps not ill-written *Program,*' or any other authentic Transaction of that Property-conserving Society, fallen under the eye of the British Reader, in any Journal foreign or domestic? If so, what are those *Prize-Questions;* what are the terms of Competition, and when and where? No printed Newspaper-leaf, no farther light of any sort, to be met with in these Paper-bags! Or is the whole business one other of those whimsicalities and perverse inexplicabilities, whereby Herr Teufelsdröckh, meaning much or nothing, is pleased so often to play fast-and-loose with us?

Here, indeed, at length, must the Editor give utterance to a painful suspicion, which, through late Chapters, has begun to haunt him; paralysing any little enthusiasm that might still have rendered his thorny Biographical task a labour of love. It is a suspicion grounded perhaps on trifles, yet confirmed almost into certainty by the more and more discernible humoristico-satirical tendency of Teufelsdröckh, in whom underground humours and intricate sardonic rogueries, wheel within wheel, defy all reckoning: a suspicion, in one word, that these Autobiographical Documents are partly a mystification! What if many a so-called Fact were little better than a Fiction; if here we had no direct Camera-obscura Picture of the Professor's History; but only some more or less fantastic Adumbration, symbolically, perhaps significantly enough, shadowing-forth the same! Our theory begins to be that, in receiving as literally authentic what was but hieroglyphically so, Hofrath Heuschrecke, whom in that case we scruple not to name Hofrath Nose-of-Wax, was made a fool of, and set adrift to make fools of others. Could it be expected, indeed, that a man so known for impenetrable reticence as Teufelsdröckh, would all at once frankly unlock his private citadel to an English Editor and a German Hofrath; and not rather deceptively *in*lock both Editor and Hofrath in the labyrinthic tortuosities and covered-ways of said citadel (having enticed them thither), to see, in his half-devilish way, how the fools would look?

Of one fool, however, the Herr Professor will perhaps find himself short. On a small slip, formerly thrown aside as blank, the ink being all-but invisible, we lately notice, and with effort decipher, the following: 'What are your historical Facts; still more your biographical? Wilt thou know a Man, above all a Mankind, by stringing-together bead-rolls of what thou namest Facts? The Man is the spirit he worked in; not what he did, but what he became. Facts are engraved Hierograms, for which the fewest have the key. And then how your Block-head (*Dummkopf*) studies not their Meaning; but simply whether they are well or ill cut, what he calls Moral or Immoral! Still worse is it with your Bungler (*Pfuscher*): such I have seen reading some Rousseau, with pretences of interpretation; and mistaking the ill-cut Serpent-of-Eternity for a common poisonous reptile.' Was the Professor apprehensive lest an Editor, selected as the present boasts himself, might mistake the Teufelsdröckh Serpent-of-Eternity in like manner? For which reason it was to be altered, not without underhand satire, into a plainer Symbol? Or is this merely one of his half-sophisms, half-truisms, which if he can but set on the back of a Figure, he cares not whither it gallop? We say not with certainty; and indeed, so strange is the Professor, can never say. If our suspicion be wholly unfounded, let his own questionable ways, not our necessary circumspectness, bear the blame.

But be this as it will, the somewhat exasperated and indeed exhausted Editor determines here to shut these Paper-bags for the present. Let it suffice that we know of Teufelsdröckh, so far, if 'not what he did, yet what he became': the rather, as his character has now taken its ultimate bent, and no new revolution, of importance, is to be looked for. The imprisoned Chrysalis is now a winged Psyche: and such, wheresoever be its flight, it will continue. To trace by what complex gyrations (flights or involuntary waftings) through the mere external Life-element, Teufelsdröckh reaches his University Professorship, and the Psyche clothes herself in civic Titles, without altering her now fixed nature,—would be comparatively an unproductive task, were we even unsuspicious of its being, for us at least, a false and impossible one. His outward Biography, therefore, which, at the Blumine Lover's-Leap, we saw churned utterly into spray-vapour, may hover in that condition, for aught that concerns us here. Enough that by survey of certain 'pools and plashes,' we have ascertained its general direction; do we not already know that, by one way and other, it *has* long since rained-down again into a stream; and even now, at Weissnichtwo, flows deep and still, fraught with the *Philosophy of Clothes,* and visible to whoso will cast eye thereon? Over much invaluable matter, that lies scattered, like jewels among quarry-rubbish, in those Paper-catacombs, we may have occasion to glance back, and somewhat will demand insertion at the right place: meanwhile be our tiresome diggings therein suspended.

If now, before reopening the great *Clothes-Volume,* we

ask what our degree of progress, during these Ten Chapters, has been, towards right understanding of the *Clothes-Philosophy*, let not our discouragement become total. To speak in that old figure of the Hell-gate Bridge over Chaos, a few flying pontoons have perhaps been added, though as yet they drift straggling on the Flood; how far they will reach, when once the chains are straightened and fastened, can, at present, only be matter of conjecture.

So much we already calculate: Through many a little loophole, we have had glimpses into the internal world of Teufelsdröckh; his strange mystic, almost magic Diagram of the Universe, and how it was gradually drawn, is not henceforth altogether dark to us. Those mysterious ideas on TIME, which merit consideration, and are not wholly unintelligible with such, may by and by prove significant. Still more may his somewhat peculiar view of Nature, the decisive Oneness he ascribes to Nature. How all Nature and Life are but one *Garment,* a 'Living Garment,' woven and ever aweaving in the 'Loom of Time'; is not here, indeed, the outline of a whole *Clothes-Philosophy;* at least the arena it is to work in? Remark, too, that the Character of the Man, nowise without meaning in such a matter, becomes less enigmatic: amid so much tumultuous obscurity, almost like diluted madness, do not a certain indomitable Defiance and yet a boundless Reverence seem to loom forth, as the two mountain-summits, on whose rock-strata all the rest were based and built?

Nay further, may we not say that Teufelsdröckh's Biography, allowing it even, as suspected, only a hieroglyphical truth, exhibits a man, as it were preappointed for Clothes-Philosophy? To look through the Shows of things into Things themselves he is led and compelled. The 'Passivity' given him by birth is fostered by all turns of his fortune. Everywhere cast out, like oil out of water, from mingling in any Employment, in any public Communion, he has no portion but Solitude, and a life of Meditation. The whole energy of his existence is directed, through long years, on one task: that of enduring pain, if he cannot cure it. Thus everywhere do the Shows of things oppress him, withstand him, threaten him with fearfullest destruction: only by victoriously penetrating into Things themselves can he find peace and a stronghold. But is not this same looking-through the Shows, or Vestures, into the

Things, even the first preliminary to a *Philosophy of Clothes?* Do we not, in all this, discern some beckonings towards the true higher purport of such a Philosophy; and what shape it must assume with such a man, in such an era?

Perhaps in entering on Book Third, the courteous Reader is not utterly without guess whither he is bound: nor, let us hope, for all the fantastic Dream-Grottoes through which, as is our lot with Teufelsdröckh, he must wander, will there be wanting between whiles some twinkling of a steady Polar Star.

BOOK THIRD   CHAPTER I

INCIDENT IN MODERN HISTORY

Story of George Fox the Quaker; and his perennial suit of Leather. A man God-possessed, witnessing for spiritual freedom and manhood.

As a wonder-loving and wonder-seeking man, Teufelsdröckh, from an early part of this Clothes-Volume, has more and more exhibited himself. Striking it was, amid all his perverse cloudiness, with what force of vision and of heart he pierced into the mystery of the World; recognising in the highest sensible phenomena, so far as Sense went, only fresh or faded Raiment; yet ever, under this, a celestial Essence thereby rendered visible: and while, on the one hand, he trod the old rags of Matter, with their tinsels, into the mire, he on the other everywhere exalted Spirit above all earthly principalities and powers, and worshipped it, though under the meanest shapes, with a true Platonic mysticism. What the man ultimately purposed by thus casting his Greek-fire into the general Wardrobe of the Universe; what such, more or less complete, rending and burning of Garments throughout the whole compass of Civilised Life and Speculation, should lead to; the rather as he was no Adamite, in any sense, and could not, like Rousseau, recommend either bodily or intellectual Nudity, and a return to the savage state: all this our readers are now bent to discover; this is, in fact, properly the gist and purport of Professor Teufelsdröckh's Philosophy of Clothes.

Be it remembered, however, that such purport is here not so much evolved, as detected to lie ready for evolving. We are to guide our British Friends into the new Gold-country, and show them the mines; nowise to dig-out and exhaust its wealth, which indeed remains for all time inexhaustible. Once there, let each dig for his own behoof, and enrich himself.

Neither, in so capricious inexpressible a Work as this of the Professor's, can our course now more than formerly be straightforward, step by step, but at best leap by leap. Significant Indications stand-out here and there; which for the critical eye, that looks both widely and narrowly, shape themselves into some ground-scheme of a Whole: to select these with judgment, so that a leap from one to the other be possible, and (in our old figure) by chaining them together, a passable Bridge be effected: this, as heretofore, continues our only method. Among such light-spots, the following, floating in much wild matter about *Perfectibility,* has seemed worth clutching at:

'Perhaps the most remarkable incident in Modern History,' says Teufelsdröckh, 'is not the Diet of Worms, still less the Battle of Austerlitz, Waterloo, Peterloo, or any other Battle; but an incident passed carelessly over by most Historians, and treated with some degree of ridicule by others: namely, George Fox's making to himself a suit of Leather. This man, the first of the Quakers, and by trade a Shoemaker, was one of those, to whom, under ruder or purer form, the Divine Idea of the Universe is pleased to manifest itself; and, across all the hulls of Ignorance and earthly Degradation, shine through, in unspeakable Awfulness, unspeakable Beauty, on their souls: who therefore are rightly accounted Prophets, God-possessed; or even Gods, as in some periods it has chanced. Sitting in his stall; working on tanned hides, amid pincers, paste-horns, rosin, swine-bristles, and a nameless flood of rubbish, this youth had, nevertheless, a Living Spirit belonging to him; also an antique Inspired Volume, through which, as through a window, it could look upwards, and discern its celestial Home. The task of a daily pair of shoes, coupled even with some prospect of victuals, and an honourable Mastership in Cordwainery, and perhaps the post of Thirdborough in his hundred, as the crown of long faithful sewing,—was nowise satisfaction enough to such a mind: but ever amid the boring and hammering came tones from that far country, came Splendours and Terrors; for this poor Cordwainer, as we said, was a Man; and the Temple of Immensity, wherein as Man he had been sent to minister, was full of holy mystery to him.

'The Clergy of the neighbourhood, the ordained Watchers and Interpreters of that same holy mystery, listened with unaffected tedium to his consultations, and advised him, as the solution of such doubts, to "drink beer and dance with the girls." Blind leaders of the blind! For what end were their tithes levied and eaten; for what were their shovel-hats scooped-out, and their surplices and cassock-aprons girt-on; and such a church-repairing, and chaffering, and organing, and other racketing, held over that spot of God's Earth,—if Man were but a Patent Digester, and the Belly with its adjuncts the grand Reality? Fox turned from them, with tears and a sacred scorn, back to his Leather-parings and his Bible. Mountains of encumbrance, higher than Ætna, had been heaped over that Spirit: but it was a Spirit, and would not lie buried there. Through long days and nights of silent agony, it struggled and wrestled, with a man's force, to be free: how its prison-mountains heaved and swayed tumultuously, as the giant spirit shook them to this hand and that, and emerged into the light of Heaven! That Leicester shoe-shop, had men known it, was a holier place than any Vatican or Loretto-shrine. —"So bandaged, and hampered, and hemmed in," groaned he, "with thousand requisitions, obligations, straps, tatters, and tagrags, I can neither see nor move: not my own am I, but the World's; and Time flies fast, and Heaven is high, and Hell is deep: Man! bethink thee, if thou hast power of Thought! Why not; what binds me here? Want, want!—Ha, of what? Will all the shoe-wages under the Moon ferry me across into that far Land of Light? Only Meditation can, and devout Prayer to God. I will to the woods: the hollow of a tree will lodge me, wildberries feed me; and for Clothes, cannot I stitch myself one perennial suit of Leather!"

'Historical Oil-painting,' continues Teufelsdröckh, 'is one of the Arts I never practised; therefore shall I not decide whether this subject were easy of execution on the canvas. Yet often has it seemed to me as if such first out-flashing of man's Freewill, to lighten, more and more into Day, the Chaotic Night that threatened to engulf him in its hindrances and its horrors, were properly the only grandeur there is in History. Let some living Angelo or Rosa, with seeing eye and understanding heart, picture George Fox on that morning, when he spreads-out his cutting-board for the last time, and cuts cowhides by unwonted patterns, and stitches them together into one continuous all-including Case, the farewell service of his awl! Stitch away, thou noble Fox: every prick of that little instrument is pricking into the heart of Slavery, and World-worship, and the Mammon-god. Thy elbows jerk, as in strong swimmer-strokes, and every stroke is bearing thee across the Prison-ditch, within which Vanity holds her Workhouse and Ragfair, into lands of true Liberty; were the work done, there is in broad Europe one Free Man, and thou art he!

'Thus from the lowest depth there is a path to the loftiest height; and for the Poor also a Gospel has been published. Surely if, as D'Alembert asserts, my illustrious namesake, Diogenes, was the greatest man of Antiquity, only that he wanted Decency, then by stronger reason is George Fox the greatest of the Moderns, and greater than Diogenes himself: for he too stands on the adamantine basis of his Manhood, casting aside all props and shoars; yet not, in half-savage Pride, undervaluing the Earth; valuing it rather, as a place to yield him warmth and food, he looks Heavenward from his Earth, and dwells in an element of Mercy and Worship, with a still Strength, such as the Cynic's Tub did nowise witness. Great, truly, was that Tub; a temple from which man's dignity and divinity was scornfully preached abroad: but greater is the Leather Hull, for the same sermon was preached there, and not in Scorn but in Love.'

George Fox's 'perennial suit,' with all that it held, has been worn quite into ashes for nigh two centuries: why, in a discussion on the *Perfectibility of Society,* reproduce it now? Not out of blind sectarian partisanship: Teufelsdröckh himself is no Quaker; with all his pacific tendencies, did not we see him, in that scene at the North Cape, with the Archangel Smuggler, exhibit fire-arms?

For us, aware of his deep Sansculottism, there is more meant in this passage than meets the ear. At the same time,

who can avoid smiling at the earnestness and Bœotian simplicity (if indeed there be not an underhand satire in it),
with which that 'Incident' is here brought forward; and,
in the Professor's ambiguous way, as clearly perhaps as
he durst in Weissnichtwo, recommended to imitation!
Does Teufelsdröckh anticipate that, in this age of refinement, any considerable class of the community, by way of
testifying against the 'Mammon-god,' and escaping from
what he calls 'Vanity's Workhouse and Ragfair,' where
doubtless some of them are toiled and whipped and hoodwinked sufficiently,—will sheathe themselves in close-fit-
ting cases of Leather? The idea is ridiculous in the extreme.
Will Majesty lay aside its robes of state, and Beauty its frills
and train-gowns, for a second-skin of tanned hide? By
which change Huddersfield and Manchester, and Coven-
try and Paisley, and the Fancy-Bazaar, were reduced to
hungry solitudes; and only Day and Martin could profit.
For neither would Teufelsdröckh's mad daydream, here as
we presume covertly intended, of levelling Society (*levelling*
it indeed with a vengeance, into one huge drowned
marsh!), and so attaining the political effects of Nudity
without its frigorific or other consequences,—be thereby
realised. Would not the rich man purchase a water-proof
suit of Russia Leather; and the high-born Belle step-forth in
red or azure morocco, lined with shamoy: the black cow-
hide being left to the Drudges and Gibeonites of the world;
and so all the old Distinctions be reëstablished?

Or has the Professor his own deeper intention; and
laughs in his sleeve at our strictures and glosses, which indeed are but a part thereof?

CHAPTER II

CHURCH-CLOTHES

*Church-Clothes defined; the Forms under which the Religious
Principle is temporarily embodied. Outward Religion originates
by Society: Society becomes possible by Religion. The condition
of Church-Clothes in our time.*

Not less questionable is his Chapter on *Church-Clothes*,
which has the farther distinction of being the shortest in
the Volume. We here translate it entire:

'By Church-Clothes, it need not be premised that I mean infinitely more than Cassocks and Surplices; and do not at all mean the mere haberdasher Sunday Clothes that men go to Church in. Far from it! Church-Clothes, are, in our vocabulary, the Forms, the *Vestures,* under which men have at various periods embodied and represented for themselves the Religious Principle; that is to say, invested the Divine Idea of the World with a sensible and practically active Body, so that it might dwell among them as a living and life-giving WORD.

'These are unspeakably the most important of all the vestures and garnitures of Human Existence. They are first spun and woven, I may say, by that wonder of wonders, SOCIETY; for it is still only when "two or three are gathered together," that Religion, spiritually existent, and indeed indestructible, however latent, in each, first outwardly manifests itself (as with "cloven tongues of fire"), and seeks to be embodied in a visible Communion and Church Militant. Mystical, more than magical, is that Communing of Soul with Soul, both looking heavenward: here properly Soul first speaks with Soul; for only in looking heavenward, take it in what sense you may, not in looking earthward, does what we can call Union, mutual Love, Society, begin to be possible. How true is that of Novalis: "It is certain, my Belief gains quite *infinitely* the moment I can convince another mind thereof"! Gaze thou in the face of thy Brother, in those eyes where plays the lambent fire of Kindness, or in those where rages the lurid conflagration of Anger; feel how thy own so quiet Soul is straightway involuntarily kindled with the like, and ye blaze and reverberate on each other, till it is all one limitless confluent flame (of embracing Love, or of deadly-grappling Hate); and then say what miraculous virtue goes out of man into man. But if so, through all the thick-plied hulls of our Earthly Life; how much more when it is of the Divine Life we speak, and inmost ME is, as it were, brought into contact with inmost ME!

'Thus was it that I said, the Church-Clothes are first spun and woven by Society; outward Religion originates by Society, Society becomes possible by Religion. Nay, perhaps, every conceivable Society, past and present, may well be figured as properly and wholly a Church, in one or other of these three predicaments: an audibly preaching and prophesying Church, which is the best; second, a Church that struggles to preach and prophesy, but cannot as yet, till its Pentecost come; and third and worst, a Church gone dumb with old age, or which only mumbles delirium prior to dissolution. Whoso fancies that by Church is here meant Chapterhouses and Cathedrals, or by preaching and prophesying, mere speech and chanting, let him,' says the oracular Professor, 'read on, light of heart (*getrosten Muthes*).

'But with regard to your Church proper, and the Church-Clothes specially recognised as Church-Clothes, I remark, fearlessly enough, that without such Vestures and sacred Tissues Society has not existed, and will not exist. For if Government is, so to speak, the outward Skin of the Body Politic, holding the whole together and protecting it; and all your Craft-Guilds, and Associations for Industry, of hand or of head, are the Fleshly Clothes, the muscular and osseous Tissues (lying *under* such Skin), whereby Society stands and works;—then is Religion the inmost Pericardial and Nervous Tissue, which ministers Life and warm Circulation to the whole. Without which Pericardial Tissue the Bones and Muscles (of Industry) were inert, or animated only by a Galvanic vitality; the Skin would become a shrivelled pelt, or fast-rotting rawhide; and Society itself a dead carcass,—deserving to be buried. Men were no longer Social, but Gregarious; which latter state also could not continue, but must gradually issue in universal selfish discord, hatred, savage isolation, and dispersion;—whereby, as we might continue to say, the very dust and dead body of Society would have evaporated and become abolished. Such, and so all-important, all-sustaining, are the Church-Clothes to civilised or even to rational men.

'Meanwhile, in our era of the World, those same Church-Clothes have gone sorrowfully out-at-elbows: nay, far worse, many of them have become mere hollow Shapes, or Masks, under which no living Figure or Spirit any longer dwells; but only spiders and unclean beetles, in horrid accumulation, drive their trade; and the mask still glares on you with its glass-eyes, in ghastly affectation of Life,—some generation-and-half after Religion has quite withdrawn from it, and in unnoticed nooks is weaving for herself new Vestures, wherewith to reappear, and bless us, or our sons or grandsons. As a Priest, or Interpreter of the Holy, is the noblest and highest of all men, so is a Sham-priest (*Schein-priester*) the falsest and basest; neither is it doubtful that his Canonicals, were they Popes' Tiaras, will one day be torn from him, to make bandages for the wounds of mankind; or even to burn into tinder, for general scientific or culinary purposes.

'All which, as out of place here, falls to be handled in my Second Volume, *On the Palingenesia, or Newbirth of Society*; which volume, as treating pràctically of the Wear, Destruction, and Retexture of Spiritual Tissues, or Garments, forms, properly speaking, the Transcendental or ultimate Portion of this my work *on Clothes*, and is already in a state of forwardness.'

And herewith, no farther exposition, note, or commentary being added, does Teufelsdröckh, and must his Editor now, terminate the singular chapter on Church-Clothes!

CHAPTER III

SYMBOLS

The benignant efficacies of Silence and Secrecy. Symbols; revelations of the Infinite in the Finite: Man everywhere encompassed by them; lives and works by them. Theory of Motive-millwrights, a false account of human nature. Symbols of an extrinsic value; as Banners, Standards: Of intrinsic value; as Works of Art, Lives and Deaths of Heroic men. Religious Symbols; Christianity. Symbols hallowed by Time; but finally defaced and desecrated. Many superannuated Symbols in our time, needing removal.

Probably it will elucidate the drift of these foregoing obscure utterances, if we here insert somewhat of our Professor's speculations on *Symbols*. To state his whole doctrine, indeed, were beyond our compass: nowhere is he more mysterious, impalpable, than in this of 'Fantasy being the organ of the Godlike'; and how 'Man thereby, though based, to all seeming, on the small Visible, does nevertheless extend down into the infinite deeps of the

Invisible, of which Invisible, indeed, his Life is properly the bodying forth.' Let us, omitting these high transcendental aspects of the matter, study to glean (whether from the Paper-bags or the Printed Volume) what little seems logical and practical, and cunningly arrange it into such degree of coherence as it will assume. By way of proem, take the following not injudicious remarks:

'The benignant efficacies of Concealment,' cries our Professor, 'who shall speak or sing? SILENCE and SECRECY! Altars might still be raised to them (were this an altar-building time) for universal worship. Silence is the element in which great things fashion themselves together; that at length they may emerge, full-formed and majestic, into the daylight of Life, which they are thenceforth to rule. Not William the Silent only, but all the considerable men I have known, and the most undiplomatic and unstrategic of these, forbore to babble of what they were creating and projecting. Nay, in thy own mean perplexities, do thou thyself but *hold thy tongue for one day:* on the morrow, how much clearer are thy purposes and duties; what wreck and rubbish have those mute workmen within thee swept away, when intrusive noises were shut out! Speech is too often not, as the Frenchman defined it, the art of concealing Thought; but of quite stifling and suspending Thought, so that there is none to conceal. Speech too is great, but not the greatest. As the Swiss Inscription says: *Sprechen ist silbern, Schweigen ist golden* (Speech is silvern, Silence is golden); or as I might rather express it: Speech is of Time, Silence is of Eternity.

'Bees will not work except in darkness; Thought will not work except in Silence: neither will Virtue work except in Secrecy. Let not thy left hand know what thy right hand doeth! Neither shalt thou prate even to thy own heart of "those secrets known to all." Is not Shame (*Schaam*) the soil of all Virtue, of all good manners and good morals? Like other plants, Virtue will not grow unless its root be hidden, buried from the eye of the sun. Let the sun shine on it, nay do but look at it privily thyself, the root withers, and no flowers will glad thee. O my Friends, when we view the fair clustering flowers that overwreathe, for example, the Marriage-bower, and encircle man's life with the fragrance and hues of Heaven, what hand will not smite the foul plunderer that grubs them up by the roots, and with grinning, grunting satisfaction, shows us the dung they flourish in! Men speak much of the Printing-Press with its Newspapers: *du Himmel!* what are these to Clothes and the Tailor's Goose?'

'Of kin to the so incalculable influences of Conceal-ment, and connected with still greater things, is the won-drous agency of *Symbols*. In a Symbol there is concealment and yet revelation: here therefore, by Silence and by Speech acting together, comes a double significance. And if both the Speech be itself high, and the Silence fit and noble, how expressive will their union be! Thus in many a painted Device, or simple Seal-emblem, the commonest Truth stands out to us proclaimed with quite new emphasis.

'For it is here that Fantasy with her mystic won-derland plays into the small prose domain of Sense, and becomes incorporated therewith. In the Symbol proper, what we can call a Symbol, there is ever, more or less dis-tinctly and directly, some embodiment and revelation of the Infinite; the Infinite is made to blend itself with the Finite, to stand visible, and as it were, attainable there. By Symbols, accordingly, is man guided and commanded, made happy, made wretched. He everywhere finds him-self encompassed with Symbols, recognised as such or not recognised: the Universe is but one vast Symbol of God; nay if thou wilt have it, what is man himself but a Sym-bol of God; is not all that he does symbolical; a revelation to Sense of the mystic god-given force that is in him; a "Gospel of Freedom," which he, the "Messias of Nature," preaches, as he can, by act and word? Not a Hut he builds but is the visible embodiment of a Thought; but bears visi-ble record of invisible things; but is, in the transcendental sense, symbolical as well as real.'

'Man,' says the Professor elsewhere, in quite antipodal contrast with these high-soaring delineations, which we have here cut-short on the verge of the inane, 'Man is by birth somewhat of an owl. Perhaps, too, of all the owl-eries that ever possessed him, the most owlish, if we con-sider it, is that of your actually existing Motive-Millwrights. Fantastic tricks enough man has played, in his time; has fancied himself to be most things, down even to an ani-mated heap of Glass: but to fancy himself a dead Iron-Balance for weighing Pains and Pleasures on, was re-served for this his latter era. There stands he, his Universe one huge Manger, filled with hay and thistles to be weighed against each other; and looks long-eared enough. Alas, poor devil! spectres are appointed to haunt him: one age he is hagridden, bewitched; the next, priestridden, befooled; in all ages, bedevilled. And now the Genius of Mechanism smothers him worse than any Nightmare did; till the Soul is nigh choked out of him, and only a kind of Digestive, Mechanic life remains. In Earth and in Heaven he can see nothing but Mechanism; has fear for nothing else, hope in nothing else: the world would indeed grind him to pieces; but cannot he fathom the Doctrine of Motives, and cunningly compute these, and mechanise them to grind the other way?

'Were he not, as has been said, purblinded by enchantment, you had but to bid him open his eyes and look. In which country, in which time, was it hitherto that man's history, or the history of any man, went-on by calculated or calculable "Motives"? What make ye of your Christianities, and Chivalries, and Reformations, and Marseillese Hymns, and Reigns of Terror? Nay, has not perhaps the Motive-grinder himself been *in Love?* Did he never stand so much as a contested Election? Leave him to Time, and the medicating virtue of Nature.'

'Yes, Friends,' elsewhere observes the Professor, 'not our Logical, Mensurative faculty, but our Imaginative one is King over us; I might say, Priest and Prophet to lead us heavenward; or Magician and Wizard to lead us hellward. Nay, even for the basest Sensualist, what is Sense but the implement of Fantasy; the vessel it drinks out of? Ever in the dullest existence there is a sheen either of Inspiration or of Madness (thou partly hast it in thy choice, which of the two), that gleams-in from the circumambient Eternity, and colours with its own hues our little islet of Time. The Understanding is indeed thy window, too clear thou canst not make it; but Fantasy is thy eye, with its colour-giving retina, healthy or diseased. Have not I myself known five-hundred living soldiers sabred into crows'-meat for a piece of glazed cotton, which they called their Flag; which, had you sold it at any market-cross, would not have brought above three groschen? Did not the whole Hungarian Nation rise, like some tumultuous moon-stirred Atlantic, when Kaiser Joseph pocketed their Iron Crown; an implement, as was sagaciously observed, in size and commercial value little differing from a horse-shoe? It is in and through *Symbols* that man, consciously or unconsciously, lives, works, and has his being: those ages, moreover, are accounted the noblest which can the best recognise symbolical worth, and prize it the highest. For is not a Symbol ever, to him who has eyes for it, some dimmer or clearer revelation of the Godlike?

'Of Symbols, however, I remark farther, that they have both an extrinsic and intrinsic value; oftenest the former only. What, for instance, was in that clouted Shoe, which the Peasants bore aloft with them as ensign in their *Bauern-krieg* (Peasants' War)? Or in the Wallet-and-staff round which the Netherland *Gueux,* glorying in that nickname of Beggars, heroically rallied and prevailed, though against King Philip himself? Intrinsic significance these had none; only extrinsic; as the accidental Standards of multitudes more or less sacredly uniting together; in which union itself, as above noted, there is ever something mystical and borrowing of the Godlike. Under a like category, too, stand, or stood, the stupidest heraldic Coats-of-arms; military Banners everywhere; and generally all national or other sectarian Costumes and Customs: they have no intrinsic, necessary divineness, or even worth; but have acquired an extrinsic one. Nevertheless through all these there glimmers something of a Divine Idea; as through military Banners themselves, the Divine Idea of Duty, of heroic Daring; in some instances of Freedom, of Right. Nay the highest ensign that men ever met and embraced under, the Cross itself, had no meaning save an accidental extrinsic one.

'Another matter it is, however, when your Symbol has intrinsic meaning, and is of itself *fit* that men should unite round it. Let but the Godlike manifest itself to Sense; let but Eternity look, more or less visibly, through the Time-Figure (*Zeitbild*)! Then is it fit that men unite there; and worship together before such Symbol; and so from day to day, and from age to age, superadd to it new divineness.

'Of this latter sort are all true Works of Art: in them (if thou know a Work of Art from a Daub of Artifice) wilt thou discern Eternity looking through Time; the Godlike rendered visible. Here too may an extrinsic value gradually superadd itself: thus certain *Iliads,* and the like, have, in three-thousand years, attained quite new significance. But nobler than all in this kind are the Lives of heroic god-inspired Men; for what other Work of Art is so divine? In Death too, in the Death of the Just, as the last perfection of a Work of Art, may we not discern symbolic meaning? In that divinely transfigured Sleep, as of Victory, resting over the beloved face which now knows thee no more, read (if thou canst for tears) the confluence of Time with Eternity, and some gleam of the latter peering through.

'Highest of all Symbols are those wherein the Artist or Poet has risen into Prophet, and all men can recognise a present God, and worship the same: I mean religious Symbols. Various enough have been such religious Symbols, what we call *Religions*; as men stood in this stage of culture or the other, and could worse or better body-forth the Godlike: some Symbols with a transient intrinsic worth; many with only an extrinsic. If thou ask to what height man has carried it in this manner, look on our divinest Symbol: on Jesus of Nazareth, and his Life, and his Biography, and what followed therefrom. Higher has the human Thought not yet reached: this is Christianity and Christendom; a Symbol of quite perennial, infinite character; whose significance will ever demand to be anew inquired into, and anew made manifest.

'But, on the whole, as Time adds much to the sacredness of Symbols, so likewise in his progress he at length defaces, or even desecrates them; and Symbols, like all terrestrial Garments, wax old. Homer's Epos has not ceased to be true; yet it is no longer *our* Epos, but shines in the distance, if clearer and clearer, yet also smaller and smaller, like a receding Star. It needs a scientific telescope, it needs to be reinterpreted and artificially brought near us, before we can so much as know that it *was* a Sun. So likewise a day comes when the Runic Thor, with his Eddas, must withdraw into dimness; and many an African Mumbo-Jumbo and Indian Pawaw be utterly abolished. For all things, even Celestial Luminaries, much more atmospheric meteors, have their rise, their culmination, their decline.'

'Small is this which thou tellest me, that the Royal Sceptre is but a piece of gilt-wood; that the Pyx has become a most foolish box, and truly, as Ancient Pistol thought, "of little price." A right Conjuror might I name thee, couldst thou conjure back into these wooden tools the divine virtue they once held.'

'Of this thing, however, be certain: wouldst thou plant for Eternity, then plant into the deep infinite faculties of man, his Fantasy and Heart; wouldst thou plant for Year and Day, then plant into his shallow superficial faculties, his Self-love and Arithmetical Understanding, what will grow there. A Hierarch, therefore, and Pontiff of the World will we call him, the Poet and inspired Maker; who, Prometheus-like, can shape new Symbols, and bring new Fire from Heaven to fix it there. Such too will not always be wanting; neither perhaps now are. Meanwhile, as the average of matters goes, we account him Legislator and wise who can so much as tell when a Symbol has grown old, and gently remove it.

'When, as the last English Coronation was preparing,' concludes this wonderful Professor, 'I read in their Newspapers that the "Champion of England," he who has to offer battle to the Universe for his new King, had brought it so far that he could now "mount his horse with little assistance," I said to myself: Here also we have a Symbol well-nigh superannuated. Alas, move whithersoever you may, are not the tatters and rags of superannuated worn-out Symbols (in this Ragfair of a World) dropping off everwhere, to hoodwink, to halter, to tether you; nay, if you shake them not aside, threatening to accumulate, and perhaps produce suffocation?'

CHAPTER IV

HELOTAGE

Heuschrecke's Malthusian Tract, and Teufelsdröckh's marginal notes thereon. The true workman, for daily bread, or spiritual bread, to be honoured; and no other. The real privation of the Poor not poverty or toil, but ignorance. Over-population: With a world like ours and wide as ours, can there be too many men? Emigration.

At this point we determine on adverting shortly, or rather reverting, to a certain Tract of Hofrath Heuschrecke's, entitled *Institute for the Repression of Population*; which lies, dishonourably enough (with torn leaves, and a perceptible smell of aloetic drugs), stuffed into the Bag *Pisces.* Not indeed for the sake of the Tract itself, which we admire little; but of the marginal Notes, evidently in Teufelsdröckh's hand, which rather copiously fringe it. A few of these may be in their right place here.

Into the Hofrath's *Institute,* with its extraordinary schemes, and machinery of Corresponding Boards and the like, we shall not so much as glance. Enough for us to understand that Heuschrecke is a disciple of Malthus; and so zealous for the doctrine, that his zeal almost literally eats him up. A deadly fear of Population possesses the Hofrath; something like a fixed-idea; undoubtedly akin to the more diluted forms of Madness. Nowhere, in that quarter of his intellectual world, is there light; nothing but a grim shadow of Hunger; open mouths opening wider and wider; a world to terminate by the frightfullest consummation: by its too dense inhabitants, famished into delirium, universally eating one another. To make air for himself in which strangulation, choking enough to a benevolent heart, the Hofrath founds, or proposes to found, this *Institute* of his, as the best he can do. It is only with our Professor's comments thereon that we concern ourselves.

First, then, remark that Teufelsdröckh, as a speculative Radical, has his own notions about human dignity; that the Zähdarm palaces and courtesies have not made him forgetful of the Futteral cottages. On the blank cover of Heuschrecke's Tract we find the following indistinctly engrossed:

'Two men I honour, and no third. First, the toilworn Craftsman that with earth-made Implement laboriously conquers the Earth, and makes her man's. Venerable to me is the hard Hand; crooked, coarse; wherein notwithstanding lies a cunning virtue, indefeasibly royal, as of the Sceptre of this Planet. Venerable too is the rugged face, all weather-tanned, besoiled, with its rude intelligence; for it is the face of a Man living manlike. O, but the more venerable for thy rudeness, and even because we must pity as well as love thee! Hardly-entreated Brother! For us was thy back so bent, for us were thy straight limbs and fingers so deformed: thou wert our Conscript, on whom the lot fell, and fighting our battles wert so marred. For in thee too lay a god-created Form, but it was not to be unfolded;

encrusted must it stand with the thick adhesions and defacements of Labour: and thy body, like thy soul, was not to know freedom. Yet toil on, toil on: *thou* art in thy duty, be out of it who may; thou toilest for the altogether indispensable, for daily bread.

'A second man I honour, and still more highly: Him who is seen toiling for the spiritually indispensable; not daily bread, but the bread of Life. Is not he too in his duty; endeavouring towards inward Harmony; revealing this, by act or by word, through all his outward endeavours, be they high or low? Highest of all, when his outward and his inward endeavour are one: when we can name him Artist; not earthly Craftsman only, but inspired Thinker, who with heaven-made Implement conquers Heaven for us! If the poor and humble toil that we have Food, must not the high and glorious toil for him in return, that he have Light, have Guidance, Freedom, Immortality?— These two, in all their degrees, I honour: all else is chaff and dust, which let the wind blow whither it listeth.

'Unspeakably touching is it, however, when I find both dignities united; and he that must toil outwardly for the lowest of man's wants, is also toiling inwardly for the highest. Sublimer in this world know I nothing than a Peasant Saint, could such now anywhere be met with. Such a one will take thee back to Nazareth itself; thou wilt see the splendour of Heaven spring forth from the humblest depths of Earth, like a light shining in great darkness.'

And again: 'It is not because of his toils that I lament for the poor: we must all toil, or steal (howsoever we name our stealing), which is worse; no faithful workman finds his task a pastime. The poor is hungry and athirst; but for him also there is food and drink: he is heavy-laden and weary; but for him also the Heavens send Sleep, and of the deepest; in his smoky cribs, a clear dewy heaven of Rest envelops him, and fitful glitterings of cloud-skirted Dreams. But what I do mourn over is, that the lamp of his soul should go out; that no ray of heavenly, or even of earthly knowledge, should visit him; but only, in the haggard darkness, like two spectres, Fear and Indignation bear him company. Alas, while the body stands so broad and brawny, must the Soul lie blinded, dwarfed, stupefied, almost annihilated! Alas, was this too a Breath of God; bestowed in Heaven, but on earth never to be unfolded!—

That there should one Man die ignorant who had capacity for Knowledge, this I call a tragedy, were it to happen more than twenty times in the minute, as by some computations it does. The miserable fraction of Science which our united Mankind, in a wide Universe of Nescience, has acquired, why is not this, with all diligence, imparted to all?'

Quite in an opposite strain is the following: 'The old Spartans had a wiser method; and went out and hunted-down their Helots, and speared and spitted them, when they grew too numerous. With our improved fashions of hunting, Herr Hofrath, now after the invention of fire-arms, and standing-armies, how much easier were such a hunt! Perhaps in the most thickly-peopled country, some three days annually might suffice to shoot all the able-bodied Paupers that had accumulated within the year. Let Governments think of this. The expense were trifling: nay the very carcasses would pay it. Have them salted and barrelled; could not you victual therewith, if not Army and Navy, yet richly such infirm Paupers, in workhouses and elsewhere, as enlightened Charity, dreading no evil of them, might see good to keep alive?'

'And yet,' writes he farther on, 'there must be something wrong. A full-formed Horse will. in any market, bring from twenty to as high as two-hundred Friedrichs d'or: such is his worth to the world. A full-formed Man is not only worth nothing to the world, but the world could afford him a round sum would he simply engage to go and hang himself. Nevertheless, which of the two was the more cunningly-devised article, even as an Engine? Good Heavens! A white European Man, standing on his two Legs, with his two five-fingered Hands at his shackle-bones, and miraculous Head on his shoulders, is worth, I should say, from fifty to a hundred Horses'!

'True, thou Gold-Hofrath,' cries the Professor elsewhere: 'too crowded indeed! Meanwhile, what portion of this inconsiderable terraqueous Globe have ye actually tilled and delved, till it will grow no more? How thick stands your Population in the Pampas and Savannas of America; round ancient Carthage, and in the interior of Africa; on both slopes of the Altaic chain, in the central Platform of Asia; in Spain, Greece, Turkey, Crim Tartary, the Curragh of Kildare? One man, in one year, as I have understood it, if you lend him Earth, will feed himself and nine others. Alas, where now are the Hengsts and Alarics of our still-glowing, still-expanding Europe; who, when their home is grown too narrow, will enlist, and, like Fire-pillars, guide onwards those superfluous masses of indomitable living Valour; equipped, not now with the battle-axe and war-chariot, but with the steam-engine and ploughshare? Where are they?—Preserving their Game!'

CHAPTER V

THE PHŒNIX

Teufelsdröckh considers Society as dead; its soul (Religion) gone, its body (existing Institutions) going. Utilitarianism, needing little farther preaching, is now in full activity of destruction. —Teufelsdröckh would yield to the Inevitable, accounting that the best: Assurance of a fairer Living Society, arising, Phœnix-like, out of the ruins of the old dead one. Before that Phœnix death-birth is accomplished, long time, struggle, and suffering must intervene.

Putting which four singular Chapters together, and alongside of them numerous hints, and even direct utterances, scattered over these Writings of his, we come upon the startling yet not quite unlooked-for conclusion, that Teufelsdröckh is one of those who consider Society, properly so called, to be as good as extinct; and that only the gregarious feelings, and old inherited habitudes, at this juncture, hold us from Dispersion, and universal national, civil, domestic and personal war! He says expressly: 'For the last three centuries, above all for the last three quarters of a century, that same Pericardial Nervous Tissue (as we named it) of Religion, where lies the Life-essence of Society, has been smote-at and perforated, needfully and needlessly; till now it is quite rent into shreds; and Society, long pining, diabetic, consumptive, can be regarded as defunct; for those spasmodic, galvanic sprawlings are not life; neither indeed will they endure, galvanise as you may, beyond two days.'

'Call ye that a Society,' cries he again, 'where there is no longer any Social Idea extant; not so much as the Idea of a common Home, but only of a common over-crowded

Lodging-house? Where each, isolated, regardless of his neighbour, turned against his neighbour, clutches what he can get, and cries "Mine!" and calls it Peace, because, in the cut-purse and cut-throat Scramble, no steel knives, but only a far cunninger sort, can be employed? Where Friendship, Communion, has become an incredible tradition; and your holiest Sacramental Supper is a smoking Tavern Dinner, with Cook for Evangelist? Where your Priest has no tongue but for plate-licking: and your high Guides and Governors cannot guide; but on all hands hear it passionately proclaimed: *Laissez faire;* Leave us alone of *your* guidance, such light is darker than darkness; eat you your wages, and sleep!

'Thus, too,' continues he, 'does an observant eye discern everywhere that saddest spectacle: The Poor perishing, like neglected, foundered Draught-Cattle, of Hunger and Over-work; the Rich, still more wretchedly, of Idleness, Satiety, and Over-growth. The Highest in rank, at length, without honour from the Lowest; scarcely, with a little mouth-honour, as from tavern-waiters who expect to put it in the bill. Once-sacred Symbols fluttering as empty Pageants, whereof men grudge even the expense; a World becoming dismantled: in one word, the CHURCH fallen speechless, from obesity and apoplexy; the STATE shrunken into a Police-Office, straitened to get its pay!'

We might ask, are there many 'observant eyes,' belonging to practical men in England or elsewhere, which have descried these phenomena; or is it only from the mystic elevation of a German *Wahngasse* that such wonders are visible? Teufelsdröckh contends that the aspect of a 'deceased or expiring Society' fronts us everywhere, so that whoso runs may read. 'What, for example,' says he, 'is the universally-arrogated Virtue, almost the sole remaining Catholic Virtue, of these days? For some half century, it has been the thing you name "Independence." Suspicion of "Servility," of reverence for Superiors, the very dogleech is anxious to disavow. Fools! Were your Superiors worthy to govern, and you worthy to obey, reverence for them were even your only possible freedom. Independence, in all kinds, is rebellion; if unjust rebellion, why parade it, and everywhere prescribe it?'

But what then? Are we returning, as Rousseau prayed, to the state of Nature? 'The Soul Politic having departed,' says Teufelsdröckh, 'what can follow but that the Body Politic be decently interred, to avoid putrescence? Liberals, Economists, Utilitarians enough I see marching with its bier, and chanting loud pæans, towards the funeral-pile, where, amid wailings from some, and saturnalian revelries from the most, the venerable Corpse is to be burnt. Or, in plain words, that these men, Liberals, Utilitarians, or whatsoever they are called, will ultimately carry their point, and dissever and destroy most existing Institutions of Society, seems a thing which has some time ago ceased to be doubtful.

'Do we not see a little subdivision of the grand Utilitarian Armament come to light even in insulated England? A living nucleus, that will attract and grow, does at length appear there also; and under curious phasis; properly as the inconsiderable fag-end, and so far in the rear of the others as to fancy itself the van. Our European Mechanisers are a sect of boundless diffusion, activity, and coöperative spirit: has not Utilitarianism flourished in high places of Thought, here among ourselves, and in every European country, at some time or other, within the last fifty years? If now in all countries, except perhaps England, it has ceased to flourish, or indeed to exist, among Thinkers, and sunk to Journalists and the popular mass,—who sees not that, as hereby it no longer preaches, so the reason is, it now needs no Preaching, but is in full universal Action, the doctrine everywhere known, and enthusiastically laid to heart? The fit pabulum, in these times, for a certain rugged workshop intellect and heart, nowise without their corresponding workshop strength and ferocity, it requires but to be stated in such scenes to make proselytes enough.—Admirably calculated for destroying, only not for rebuilding! It spreads like a sort of Dog-madness; till the whole World-kennel will be rabid: then woe to the Huntsmen, with or without their whips! They should have given the quadrupeds water,' adds he; 'the water, namely, of Knowledge and of Life, while it was yet time.'

Thus, if Professor Teufelsdröckh can be relied on, we are at this hour in a most critical condition; beleaguered by that boundless 'Armament of Mechanisers' and Unbelievers, threatening to strip us bare! 'The World,' says he, 'as it needs must, is under a process of devastation and waste, which, whether by silent assiduous corrosion, or open quicker combustion, as the case chances, will effectually enough annihilate the past Forms of Society; replace them with what it may. For the present, it is contemplated that when man's whole Spiritual Interests are once *divested*, these innumerable stript-off Garments shall mostly be burnt; but the sounder Rags among them be quilted together into one huge Irish watch-coat for the defence of the Body only!'—This, we think, is but Job's-news to the humane reader.

'Nevertheless,' cries Teufelsdröckh, 'who can hinder it; who is there that can clutch into the wheelspokes of Destiny, and say to the Spirit of the Time: Turn back, I command thee?—Wiser were it that we yielded to the Inevitable and Inexorable, and accounted even this the best.'

Nay, might not an attentive Editor, drawing his own inferences from what stands written, conjecture that Teufelsdröckh individually had yielded to this same 'Inevitable and Inexorable' heartily enough; and now sat waiting the issue, with his natural diabolico-angelical Indifference, if not even Placidity? Did we not hear him complain that the World was a 'huge Ragfair,' and the 'rags and tatters of old Symbols' were raining-down everywhere, like to drift him in, and suffocate him? What with those 'unhunted Helots' of his; and the uneven *sic vos non vobis* pressure and hard-crashing collision he is pleased to discern in existing things; what with the so hateful 'empty Masks,' full of beetles and spiders, yet glaring out on him, from their glass eyes, 'with a ghastly affectation of life,'—we feel entitled to conclude him even willing that much should be thrown to the Devil, so it were but done gently! Safe himself in that 'Pinnacle of Weissnichtwo,' he would consent, with a tragic solemnity, that the monster UTILITARIA, held back, indeed, and moderated by nose-rings, halters, foot-shackles, and every conceivable modification of rope, should go forth to do her work;—to tread down old ruinous Palaces and Temples with her broad hoof, till the whole were trodden down, that new and better might be built! Remarkable in this point of view are the following sentences.

'Society,' says he, 'is not dead: that Carcass, which you call dead Society, is but her mortal coil which she has shuffled-off, to assume a nobler; she herself, through perpetual metamorphoses, in fairer and fairer development, has to live till Time also merge in Eternity. Wheresoever two or three Living Men are gathered together, there is Society; or there it will be, with its cunning mechanisms and stupendous structures, overspreading this little Globe, and reaching upwards to Heaven and downwards to Gehenna: for always, under one or the other figure, it has two authentic Revelations, of a God and of a Devil; the Pulpit, namely, and the Gallows.'

Indeed, we already heard him speak of 'Religion, in unnoticed nooks, weaving for herself new Vestures';—Teufelsdröckh himself being one of the loom-treadles? Elsewhere he quotes without censure that strange aphorism of Saint-Simon's, concerning which and whom so much were to be said: '*L'âge d'or, qu'une aveugle tradition a placé jusqu'ici dans le passé, est devant nous;* The golden age, which a blind tradition has hitherto placed in the Past, is Before us.' —But listen again:

'When the Phœnix is fanning her funeral pyre, will there not be sparks flying! Alas, some millions of men, and among them such as a Napoleon, have already been licked into that high-eddying Flame, and like moths consumed there. Still also have we to fear that incautious beards will get singed.

'For the rest, in what year of grace such Phœnix-cremation will be completed, you need not ask. The law of Perseverance is among the deepest in man: by nature he hates change; seldom will he quit his old house till it has actually fallen about his ears. Thus have I seen Solemnities linger as Ceremonies, sacred Symbols as idle Pageants, to the extent of three-hundred years and more after all life and sacredness had evaporated out of them. And then, finally, what time the Phœnix Death-Birth itself will require, depends on unseen contingencies.—Meanwhile, would Destiny offer Mankind, that after, say two centuries of convulsion and conflagration, more or less vivid, the fire-creation should be accomplished, and we to find ourselves again in a Living Society, and no longer fighting but working,—were it not perhaps prudent in Mankind to strike the bargain?'

Thus is Teufelsdröckh content that old sick Society should be deliberately burnt (alas, with quite other fuel than spice-wood); in the faith that she is a Phœnix; and that a new heavenborn young one will rise out of her ashes! We ourselves, restricted to the duty of Indicator, shall forbear commentary. Meanwhile, will not the judicious reader shake his head, and reproachfully, yet more in sorrow than in anger, say or think: From a *Doctor utriusque Juris,* titular Professor in a University, and man to whom hitherto, for his services, Society, bad as she is, has given not only food and raiment (of a kind), but books, tobacco and guk-guk, we expected more gratitude to his benefactress; and less of a blind trust in the future, which resembles that rather of a philosophical Fatalist and Enthusiast, than of a solid householder paying scot-and-lot in a Christian country.

CHAPTER VI

OLD CLOTHES

Courtesy due from all men to all men: The Body of Man a Revelation in the Flesh. Teufelsdröckh's respect for Old Clothes, as the 'Ghosts of life.' Walk in Monmouth Street, and meditations there.

As mentioned above, Teufelsdröckh, though a sansculot-tist, is in practice probably the politest man extant: his whole heart and life are penetrated and informed with the spirit of politeness; a noble natural Courtesy shines through him, beautifying his vagaries; like sun-light, making a rosy-fingered, rainbow-dyed Aurora out of mere aqueous clouds; nay brightening London-smoke itself into gold vapour, as from the crucible of an alchemist. Hear in what earnest though fantastic wise he expresses himself on this head:

'Shall Courtesy be done only to the rich, and only by the rich? In Good-breeding, which differs, if at all, from High-breeding, only as it gracefully remembers the rights of others, rather than gracefully insists on its own rights, I discern no special connexion with wealth or birth: but rather that it lies in human nature itself, and is due from all men towards all men. Of a truth, were your Schoolmaster at his post, and worth anything when there, this, with so much else, would be reformed. Nay, each man were then also his neighbour's schoolmaster; till at length a rude-visaged, unmannered Peasant could no more be met with, than a Peasant unacquainted with botanical Physiology, or who felt not that the clod he broke was created in Heaven.

'For whether thou bear a sceptre or a sledge-hammer,

art not thou ALIVE; is not this thy brother ALIVE? "There is but one temple in the world," says Novalis, "and that temple is the Body of Man. Nothing is holier than this high Form. Bending before men is a reverence done to this Revelation in the Flesh. We touch Heaven, when we lay our hands on a human Body."

'On which ground, I would fain carry it farther than most do; and whereas the English Johnson only bowed to every Clergyman, or man with a shovel-hat, I would bow to every Man with any sort of hat, or with no hat whatever. Is not he a Temple, then; the visible Manifestation and Impersonation of the Divinity? And yet, alas, such indiscriminate bowing serves not. For there is a Devil dwells in man, as well as a Divinity; and too often the bow is but pocketed by the *former*. It would go to the pocket of Vanity (which is your clearest phasis of the Devil, in these times); therefore must we withhold it.

'The gladder am I, on the other hand, to do reverence to those Shells and outer Husks of the Body, wherein no devilish passion any longer lodges, but only the pure emblem and effigies of Man: I mean, to Empty, or even to Cast Clothes. Nay, is it not to Clothes that most men do reverence: to the fine frogged broadcloth, nowise to the "straddling animal with bandy legs" which it holds, and makes a Dignitary of? Who ever saw any Lord my-lorded in tattered blanket fastened with wooden skewer? Nevertheless, I say, there is in such worship a shade of hypocrisy, a practical deception: for how often does the Body appropriate what was meant for the Cloth only! Whoso would avoid falsehood, which is the essence of all Sin, will perhaps see good to take a different course. That reverence which cannot act without obstruction and perversion when the Clothes are full, may have free course when they are empty. Even as, for Hindoo Worshippers, the Pagoda is not less sacred than the God; so do I too worship the hollow cloth Garment with equal fervour, as when it contained the Man: nay, with more, for I now fear no deception, of myself or of others.

'Did not King *Toomtabard,* or, in other words, John Baliol, reign long over Scotland; the man John Baliol being quite gone, and only the "Toom Tabard" (Empty Gown) remaining? What still dignity dwells in a suit of Cast Clothes! How meekly it bears its honours! No haughty looks, no scornful gesture: silent and serene, it fronts the world; neither demanding worship, nor afraid to miss it. The Hat still carries the physiognomy of its Head: but the vanity and the stupidity, and goose-speech which was the sign of these two, are gone. The Coat-arm is stretched out, but not to strike; the Breeches, in modest simplicity, depend at ease, and now at last have a graceful flow; the Waistcoat hides no evil passion, no riotous desire; hunger or thirst now dwells not in it. Thus all is purged from the grossness of sense, from the carking cares and foul vices of the World; and rides there, on its Clothes-horse; as, on a Pegasus, might some skyey Messenger, or purified Apparition, visiting our low Earth.

'Often, while I sojourned in that monstrous tuberosity of Civilised Life, the Capital of England; and meditated, and questioned Destiny, under that ink-sea of vapour, black, thick, and multifarious as Spartan broth; and was one lone soul amid those grinding millions;—often have I turned into their Old-Clothes Market to worship. With awe-struck heart I walk through that Monmouth Street, with its empty Suits, as through a Sanhedrim of stainless Ghosts. Silent are they, but expressive in their silence: the past witnesses and instruments of Woe and Joy, of Passions, Virtues, Crimes, and all the fathomless tumult of Good and Evil in "the Prison men call Life." Friends! trust not the heart of that man for whom Old Clothes are not venerable. Watch, too, with reverence, that bearded Jewish High-priest, who with hoarse voice, like some Angel of Doom, summons them from the four winds! On his head, like the Pope, he has three Hats,—a real triple tiara; on either hand are the similitude of wings, whereon the summoned Garments come to alight; and ever, as he slowly cleaves the air, sounds forth his deep fateful note, as if through a trumpet he were proclaiming: "Ghosts of Life, come to Judgment!" Reck not, ye fluttering Ghosts: he will purify you in his Purgatory, with fire and with water; and, one day, new-created ye shall reappear. O, let him in whom the flame of Devotion is ready to go out, who has never worshipped, and knows not what to worship, pace and repace, with austerest thought, the pavement of Monmouth Street, and say whether his heart and his eyes still continue dry. If Field Lane, with its long fluttering rows of yellow handkerchiefs, be a Dionysius' Ear, where, in stifled jarring hubbub, we

292 / A CARLYLE READER

hear the Indictment which Poverty and Vice bring against lazy Wealth, that it has left them there cast-out and trodden under foot of Want, Darkness and the Devil,—then is Monmouth Street a Mirza's Hill, where, in motley vision, the whole Pageant of Existence passes awfully before us; with its wail and jubilee, mad loves and mad hatreds, church-bells and gallows-ropes, farce-tragedy, beast-godhood,—the Bedlam of Creation!'

To most men, as it does to ourselves, all this will seem overcharged. We too have walked through Monmouth Street; but with little feeling of 'Devotion': probably in part because the contemplative process is so fatally broken in upon by the brood of money-changers who nestle in that Church, and importune the worshipper with merely secular proposals. Whereas Teufelsdröckh might be in that happy middle state, which leaves to the Clothes-broker no hope either of sale or of purchase, and so be allowed to linger there without molestation.—Something we would have given to see the little philosophical figure, with its steeple-hat and loose flowing skirts, and eyes in a fine frenzy, 'pacing and repacing in austerest thought' that foolish Street; which to him was a true Delphic avenue, and supernatural Whispering-gallery, where the 'Ghosts of Life' rounded strange secrets in his ear. O thou philosophic Teufelsdröckh, that listenest while others only gabble, and with thy quick tympanum hearest the grass grow!

At the same time, is it not strange that, in Paper-bag Documents destined for an English work, there exists nothing like an authentic diary of this his sojourn in London; and of his Meditations among the Clothes-shops only the obscurest emblematic shadows? Neither, in conversation (for, indeed, he was not a man to pester you with his Travels), have we heard him more than allude to the subject.

For the rest, however, it cannot be uninteresting that we here find how early the significance of Clothes had dawned on the now so distinguished Clothes-Professor. Might we but fancy it to have been even in Monmouth Street, at the bottom of our own English 'ink-sea,' that this remarkable Volume first took being, and shot forth its salient point in his soul,—as in Chaos did the Egg of Eros, one day to be hatched into a Universe!

CHAPTER VII

ORGANIC FILAMENTS

Destruction and Creation ever proceed together; and organic filaments of the Future are even now spinning. Wonderful connection of each man with all men; and of each generation with all generations, before and after: Mankind is One. Sequence and progress of all human work, whether of creation or destruction, from age to age.—Titles, hitherto derived from Fighting, must give way to others. Kings will remain and their title. Political Freedom, not to be attained by any mechanical contrivance. Hero-worship, perennial amongst men; the cornerstone of polities in the Future. Organic filaments of the New Religion: Newspapers and Literature. Let the faithful soul take courage!

For us, who happen to live while the World-Phœnix is burning herself, and burning so slowly that, as Teufelsdröckh calculates, it were a handsome bargain would she engage to have done 'within two centuries,' there seems to lie but an ashy prospect. Not altogether so, however, does the Professor figure it. 'In the living subject,' says he, 'change is wont to be gradual: thus, while the serpent sheds its old skin, the new is already formed beneath. Little knowest thou of the burning of a World-Phœnix, who fanciest that she must first burn-out, and lie as a dead cinereous heap; and therefrom the young one start-up by miracle, and fly heavenward. Far otherwise! In that Fire-whirlwind, Creation and Destruction proceed together; ever as the ashes of the Old are blown about, do organic filaments of the New mysteriously spin themselves: and amid the rushing and the waving of the Whirlwind-element come tones of a melodious Deathsong, which end not but in tones of a more melodious Birthsong. Nay, look into the Fire-whirlwind with thy own eyes, and thou wilt see.' Let us actually look, then: to poor individuals, who cannot expect to live two centuries, those same organic filaments, mysteriously spinning themselves, will be the best part of the spectacle. First, therefore, this of Mankind in general:

'In vain thou deniest it,' says the Professor; 'thou *art* my Brother. Thy very Hatred, thy very Envy, those foolish Lies thou tellest of me in thy splenetic humour: what is all this but an inverted Sympathy? Were I a Steam-engine, wouldst thou take the trouble to tell lies of me? Not thou! I should grind all unheeded, whether badly or well.

'Wondrous truly are the bonds that unite us one and all; whether by the soft binding of Love, or the iron chaining of Necessity, as we like to choose it. More than once have I said to myself, of some perhaps whimsically strutting Figure, such as provokes whimsical thoughts: "Wert thou, my little Brotherkin, suddenly covered-up within the largest imaginable Glass-bell,—what a thing it were, not for thyself only, but for the world! Post Letters, more or fewer, from all the four winds, impinge against thy Glass walls, but have to drop unread: neither from within comes there question or response into any Postbag; thy Thoughts fall into no friendly ear or heart, thy Manufacture into no purchasing hand: thou art no longer a circulating venous-arterial Heart, that, taking and giving, circulatest through all Space and all Time: there has a Hole fallen-out in the immeasurable, universal World-tissue, which must be darned-up again!"

'Such venous-arterial circulation, of Letters, verbal Messages, paper and other Packages, going out from him and coming in, are a blood-circulation, visible to the eye: but the finer nervous circulation, by which all things, the minutest that he does, minutely influence all men, and the very look of his face blesses or curses whomso it lights on, and so generates ever new blessing or new cursing: all this you cannot see, but only imagine. I say, there is not a red Indian, hunting by Lake Winnipic, can quarrel with his squaw, but the whole world must smart for it: will not the price of beaver rise? It is a mathematical fact that the casting of this pebble from my hand alters the centre of gravity of the Universe.

'If now an existing generation of men stand so woven together, not less indissolubly does generation with generation. Hast thou ever meditated on that word, Tradition: how we inherit not Life only, but all the garniture and form of Life; and work, and speak, and even think and feel, as our Fathers, and primeval grandfathers, from the beginning, have given it us?—Who printed thee, for example, this unpretending Volume on the Philosophy of Clothes? Not the Herren Stillschweigen and Company; but

Cadmus of Thebes, Faust of Mentz, and innumerable others whom thou knowest not. Had there been no Mœsogothic Ulfila, there had been no English Shakspeare, or a different one. Simpleton! it was Tubalcain that made thy very Tailor's needle, and sewed that court-suit of thine.

'Yes, truly, if Nature is one, and a living indivisible whole, much more is Mankind, the Image that reflects and creates Nature, without which Nature were not. As palpable life-streams in that wondrous Individual Mankind, among so many life-streams that are not palpable, flow on those main-currents of what we call Opinion; as preserved in Institutions, Polities, Churches, above all in Books. Beautiful it is to understand and know that a Thought did never yet die; that as thou, the originator thereof, hast gathered it and created it from the whole Past, so thou wilt transmit it to the whole Future. It is thus that the heroic heart, the seeing eye of the first times, still feels and sees in us of the latest; that the Wise Man stands ever encompassed, and spiritually embraced, by a cloud of witnesses and brothers; and there is a living, literal *Communion of Saints,* wide as the World itself, and as the History of the World.

'Noteworthy also, and serviceable for the progress of this same Individual, wilt thou find his subdivision into Generations. Generations are as the Days of toilsome Mankind: Death and Birth are the vesper and the matin bells, that summon Mankind to sleep, and to rise refreshed for new advancement. What the Father has made, the Son can make and enjoy; but has also work of his own appointed him. Thus all things wax, and roll onwards; Arts, Establishments, Opinions, nothing is completed, but ever completing. Newton has learned to see what Kepler saw; but there is also a fresh heaven-derived force in Newton; he must mount to still higher points of vision. So too the Hebrew Lawgiver is, in due time, followed by an Apostle of the Gentiles. In the business of Destruction, as this also is from time to time a necessary work, thou findest a like sequence and perseverance: for Luther it was as yet hot enough to stand by that burning of the Pope's Bull; Voltaire could not warm himself at the glimmering ashes, but required quite other fuel. Thus likewise, I note, the English Whig has, in the second generation, become an English Radical; who, in the third again, it is to be hoped, will become an English Rebuilder. Find Mankind where thou wilt, thou findest it in living movement, in progress faster or slower: the Phœnix soars aloft, hovers with outstretched wings, filling Earth with her music; or, as now, she sinks, and with spheral swan-song immolates herself in flame, that she may soar the higher and sing the clearer.'

Let the friends of social order, in such a disastrous period, lay this to heart, and derive from it any little comfort they can. We subjoin another passage, concerning Titles:

'Remark, not without surprise,' says Teufelsdröckh, 'how all high Titles of Honour come hitherto from Fighting. Your *Herzog* (Duke, *Dux*) is Leader of Armies; your Earl (*Jarl*) is Strong Man; your Marshal cavalry Horse-shoer. A Millennium, or reign of Peace and Wisdom, having from of old been prophesied, and becoming now daily more and more indubitable, may it not be apprehended that such Fighting-titles will cease to be palatable, and new and higher need to be devised?

'The only Title wherein I, with confidence, trace eternity, is that of King. *König* (King), anciently *Könning,* means Ken-ning (Cunning), or which is the same thing, Can-ning. Ever must the Sovereign of Mankind be fitly entitled King.'

'Well, also,' says he elsewhere, 'was it written by Theologians: a King rules by divine right. He carries in him an authority from God, or man will never give it him. Can I choose my own King? I can choose my own King Popinjay, and play what farce or tragedy I may with him: but he who is to be my Ruler, whose will is to be higher than my will, was chosen for me in Heaven. Neither except in such Obedience to the Heaven-chosen is Freedom so much as conceivable.'

The Editor will here admit that, among all the wondrous provinces of Teufelsdröckh's spiritual world, there is none he walks in with such astonishment, hesitation, and even pain, as in the Political. How, with our English love of Ministry and Opposition, and that generous conflict of Parties, mind warming itself against mind in their mutual wrestle for the Public Good, by which wrestle, indeed, is our invaluable Constitution kept warm and alive; how shall we domesticate ourselves in this spectral Necropolis, or rather City both of the Dead and of the Unborn, where the Present seems little other than an inconsiderable Film dividing the Past and the Future? In those dim long-drawn expanses, all is so immeasurable; much so disastrous, ghastly; your very radiances and straggling light-beams have a supernatural character. And then with such an indifference, such a prophetic peacefulness (accounting the inevitably coming as already here, to him all one whether it be distant by centuries or only by days), does he sit;— and live, you would say, rather in any other age than in his own! It is our painful duty to announce, or repeat, that, looking into this man, we discern a deep, silent, slow-burning, inextinguishable Radicalism, such as fills us with shuddering admiration.

Thus, for example, he appears to make little even of the Elective Franchise; at least so we interpret the following: 'Satisfy yourselves,' he says, 'by universal, indubitable experiment, even as ye are now doing or will do, whether FREEDOM, heavenborn and leading heavenward, and so vitally essential for us all, cannot peradventure be mechanically hatched and brought to light in that same Ballot-Box of yours; or at worst, in some other discoverable or devisable Box, Edifice, or Steam-mechanism. It were a mighty convenience; and beyond all feats of manufacture witnessed hitherto.' Is Teufelsdröckh acquainted with the British Constitution, even slightly?—He says, under another figure: 'But after all, were the problem, as indeed it now everywhere is, To rebuild your old House from the top downwards (since you must live in it the while), what better, what other, than the Representative Machine will serve your turn? Meanwhile, however, mock me not with the name of Free, "when you have but knit-up my chains into ornamental festoons." '—Or what will any member of the Peace Society make of such an assertion as this: 'The lower people everywhere desire War. Not so unwisely; there is then a demand for lower people—to be shot!'

Gladly, therefore, do we emerge from those soul-confusing labyrinths of speculative Radicalism, into somewhat clearer regions. Here, looking round, as was our hest, for 'organic filaments,' we ask, May not this, touching 'Hero-worship,' be of the number? It seems of a cheerful character; yet so quaint, so mystical, one knows not what, or how little, may lie under it. Our readers shall look with their own eyes:

'True is it that, in these days, man can do almost all things, only not obey. True likewise that whoso cannot obey cannot be free, still less bear rule; he that is the inferior of nothing, can be the superior of nothing, the equal of nothing. Nevertheless, believe not that man has lost his faculty of Reverence; that if it slumber in him, it has gone dead. Painful for man is that same rebellious Independence, when it has become inevitable; only in loving companionship with his fellows does he feel safe; only in reverently bowing down before the Higher does he feel himself exalted.

'Or what if the character of our so troublous Era lay even in this: that man had forever cast away Fear, which is the lower; but not yet risen into perennial Reverence, which is the higher and highest?

'Meanwhile, observe with joy, so cunningly has Nature ordered it, that whatsoever man ought to obey, he cannot but obey. Before no faintest revelation of the Godlike did he ever stand irreverent; least of all, when the Godlike showed itself revealed in his fellow-man. Thus is there a true religious Loyalty forever rooted in his heart; nay in all ages, even in ours, it manifests itself as a more or less orthodox *Hero-worship*. In which fact, that Hero-worship exists, has existed, and will forever exist, universally among Mankind, mayest thou discern the corner-stone of living-rock, whereon all Polities for the remotest time may stand secure.'

Do our readers discern any such corner-stone, or even so much as what Teufelsdröckh is looking at? He exclaims, 'Or hast thou forgotten Paris and Voltaire? How the aged, withered man, though but a Sceptic, Mocker, and millinery Court-poet, yet because even he seemed the Wisest, Best, could drag mankind at his chariot-wheels, so that princes coveted a smile from him, and the loveliest of France would have laid their hair beneath his feet! All Paris was one vast Temple of Hero-worship; though their Divinity, moreover, was of feature too apish.

'But if such things,' continues he, 'were done in the dry tree, what will be done in the green? If, in the most parched season of Man's History, in the most parched spot of Europe, when Parisian life was at best but a scientific *Hortus Siccus,* bedizened with some Italian Gumflowers, such virtue could come out of it; what is to be looked for when Life again waves leafy and bloomy, and your Hero-Divinity shall have nothing apelike, but be wholly human? Know that there is in man a quite indestructible Reverence for whatsoever holds of Heaven, or even plausibly counterfeits such holding. Show the dullest clodpole, show the haughtiest featherhead, that a soul higher than himself is actually here; were his knees stiffened into brass, he must down and worship.'

Organic filaments, of a more authentic sort, mysteriously spinning themselves, some will perhaps discover in the following passage:

'There is no Church, sayest thou? The voice of Prophecy has gone dumb? This is even what I dispute: but in any case, hast thou not still Preaching enough? A Preaching Friar settles himself in every village; and builds a pulpit, which he calls Newspaper. Therefrom he preaches what most momentous doctrine is in him, for man's salvation; and dost not thou listen, and believe? Look well, thou seest everywhere a new Clergy of the Mendicant Orders, some bare-footed, some almost bare-backed, fashion itself into shape, and teach and preach, zealously enough, for copper alms and the love of God. These break in pieces the ancient idols; and, though themselves too often reprobate, as idol-breakers are wont to be, mark out the sites of new Churches, where the true God-ordained, that are to follow, may find audience, and minister. Said I not, Before the old skin was shed, the new had formed itself beneath it?'

Perhaps also in the following; wherewith we now hasten to knit-up this ravelled sleeve:

'But there is no Religion?' reiterates the Professor. 'Fool! I tell thee, there is. Hast thou well considered all that lies in this immeasurable froth-ocean we name LITERATURE? Fragments of a genuine Church-*Homiletic* lie scattered there, which Time will assort: nay fractions even of a *Liturgy* could I point out. And knowest thou no Prophet, even in the vesture, environment, and dialect of this age? None to whom the Godlike had revealed itself, through all meanest and highest forms of the Common; and by him been again prophetically revealed: in whose inspired melody, even in these rag-gathering and rag-burning days, Man's Life again begins, were it but afar off, to be divine? Knowest thou none such? I know him, and name him—Goethe.

'But thou as yet standest in no Temple; joinest in no Psalm-worship; feelest well that, where there is no ministering Priest, the people perish? Be of comfort! Thou art not alone, if thou have Faith. Spake we not of a Communion of Saints, unseen, yet not unreal, accompanying and brother-like embracing thee, so thou be worthy? Their heroic Sufferings rise up melodiously together to Heaven, out of all lands, and out of all times, as a sacred *Miserere;* their heroic Actions also, as a boundless everlasting Psalm of Triumph. Neither say that thou hast now no Symbol of the Godlike. Is not God's Universe a Symbol of the Godlike; is not Immensity a Temple; is not Man's History, and Men's History, a perpetual Evangel? Listen, and for organ-music thou wilt ever, as of old, hear the Morning Stars sing together.'

CHAPTER VIII

NATURAL SUPERNATURALISM

Deep significance of Miracles. Littleness of human Science: Divine incomprehensibility of Nature. Custom blinds us to the miraculousness of daily-recurring miracles; so do Names. Space and Time, appearances only; forms of human Thought: A glimpse of Immortality. How Space hides from us the wondrousness of our commonest powers; and Time, the divinely miraculous course of human history.

It is in his stupendous Section, headed *Natural Supernaturalism,* that the Professor first becomes a Seer; and, after long effort, such as we have witnessed, finally subdues under his feet this refractory Clothes-Philosophy, and takes victorious possession thereof. Phantasms enough he has had to struggle with; 'Cloth-webs and Cob-webs,' of Imperial Mantles, Superannuated Symbols, and what not: yet still did he courageously pierce through. Nay, worst of all, two quite mysterious, world-embracing Phantasms, TIME and SPACE, have ever hovered round him, perplexing and bewildering: but with these also he now resolutely grapples, these also he victoriously rends asunder. In a word, he has looked fixedly on Existence, till, one after the other, its earthly hulls and garnitures have all melted away;

and now, to his rapt vision, the interior celestial Holy of Holies lies disclosed.

Here, therefore, properly it is that the Philosophy of Clothes attains to Transcendentalism; this last leap, can we but clear it, takes us safe into the promised land, where *Palingenesia,* in all senses, may be considered as beginning. 'Courage, then!' may our Diogenes exclaim, with better right than Diogenes the First once did. This stupendous Section we, after long painful meditation, have found not to be unintelligible; but, on the contrary, to grow clear, nay radiant, and all-illuminating. Let the reader, turning on it what utmost force of speculative intellect is in him, do his part; as we, by judicious selection and adjustment, shall study to do ours:

'Deep has been, and is, the significance of Miracles,' thus quietly begins the Professor; 'far deeper perhaps than we imagine. Meanwhile, the question of questions were: What specially is a Miracle? To that Dutch King of Siam, an icicle had been a miracle; whoso had carried with him an air-pump, and vial of vitriolic ether, might have worked a miracle. To my Horse, again, who unhappily is still more unscientific, do not I work a miracle, and magical *"Open sesame!"* every time I please to pay twopence, and open for him an impassable *Schlagbaum,* or shut Turnpike?

' "But is not a real Miracle simply a violation of the Laws of Nature?" ask several. Whom I answer by this new question: Where are the Laws of Nature? To me perhaps the rising of one from the dead were no violation of these Laws, but a confirmation; were some far deeper Law, now first penetrated into, and by Spiritual Force, even as the rest have all been, brought to bear on us with its Material Force.

'Here too may some inquire, not without astonishment: On what ground shall one, that can make Iron swim, come and declare that therefore he can teach Religion? To us, truly, of the Nineteenth Century, such declaration were inept enough; which nevertheless to our fathers, of the First Century, was full of meaning.

' "But is it not the deepest Law of Nature that she be constant?" cries an illuminated class: "Is not the Machine of the Universe fixed to move by unalterable rules?" Probable enough, good friends: nay I, too, must believe that the God, whom ancient inspired men assert to be "without variableness or shadow of turning," does indeed never change; that

Nature, that the Universe, which no one whom it so pleases can be prevented from calling a Machine, does move by the most unalterable rules. And now of you, too, I make the old inquiry: What those same unalterable rules, forming the complete Statute-Book of Nature, may possibly be?

'They stand written in our Works of Science, say you; in the accumulated records of Man's Experience?—Was Man with his Experience present at the Creation, then, to see how it all went on? Have any deepest scientific individuals yet dived down to the foundations of the Universe, and gauged everything there? Did the Maker take them into His counsel; that they read His groundplan of the incomprehensible All; and can say, This stands marked therein, and no more than this? Alas, not in anywise! These scientific individuals have been nowhere but where we also are; have seen some handbreadths deeper than we see into the Deep that is infinite, without bottom as without shore.

'Laplace's Book on the Stars, wherein he exhibits that certain Planets, with their Satellites, gyrate round our worthy Sun, at a rate and in a course, which, by greatest good fortune, he and the like of him have succeeded in detecting,—is to me as precious as to another. But is this what thou namest "Mechanism of the Heavens," and "System of the World"; this, wherein Sirius and the Pleiades, and all Herschel's Fifteen-thousand Suns per minute, being left out, some paltry handful of Moons, and inert Balls, had been—looked at, nicknamed, and marked in the Zodiacal Way-bill; so that we can now prate of their Whereabout; their How, their Why, their What, being hid from us, as in the signless Inane?

'System of Nature! To the wisest man, wide as is his vision, Nature remains of quite *infinite* depth, of quite infinite expansion; and all Experience thereof limits itself to some few computed centuries and measured square-miles. The course of Nature's phases, on this our little fraction of a Planet, is partially known to us: but who knows what deeper courses these depend on; what infinitely larger Cycle (of causes) our little Epicycle revolves on? To the Minnow every cranny and pebble, and quality and accident, of its little native Creek may have become familiar: but does the Minnow understand the Ocean Tides and periodic Currents, the Trade-winds, and Monsoons, and Moon's Eclipses; by all which the condition of its little Creek is regulated, and may, from time to time (*un*miraculously enough), be quite overset and reversed? Such a minnow is Man; his Creek this Planet Earth; his Ocean the immeasurable All; his Monsoons and periodic Currents the mysterious Course of Providence through Æons of Æons.

'We speak of the Volume of Nature: and truly a Volume it is,—whose Author and Writer is God. To read it! Dost thou, does man, so much as well know the Alphabet thereof? With its Words, Sentences, and grand descriptive Pages, poetical and philosophical, spread out through Solar Systems, and Thousands of Years, we shall not try thee. It is a Volume written in celestial hieroglyphs, in the true Sacred-writing; of which even Prophets are happy that they can read here a line and there a line. As for your Institutes, and Academies of Science, they strive bravely; and, from amid the thick-crowded, inextricably intertwisted hieroglyphic writing, pick out, by dextrous combination, some Letters in the vulgar Character, and therefrom put together this and the other economic Recipe, of high avail in Practice. That Nature is more than some boundless Volume of such Recipes, or huge, well-nigh inexhaustible Domestic-Cookery Book, of which the whole secret will in this manner one day evolve itself, the fewest dream.

'Custom,' continues the Professor, 'doth make dotards of us all. Consider well, thou wilt find that Custom is the greatest of Weavers; and weaves air-raiment for all the Spirits of the Universe; whereby indeed these dwell with us visibly, as ministering servants, in our houses and workshops; but their spiritual nature becomes, to the most, forever hidden. Philosophy complains that Custom has hoodwinked us, from the first; that we do everything by Custom, even Believe by it; that our very Axioms, let us boast of Free-thinking as we may, are oftenest simply such Beliefs as we have never heard questioned. Nay, what is Philosophy throughout but a continual battle against Custom; an ever-renewed effort to *transcend* the sphere of blind Custom, and so become Transcendental?

'Innumerable are the illusions and legerdemain-tricks of Custom: but of all these, perhaps the cleverest is her knack of persuading us that the Miraculous, by simple repetition, ceases to be Miraculous. True, it is by this means we live; for man must work as well as wonder: and herein is Custom so far a kind nurse, guiding him to his true benefit. But she is a fond foolish nurse, or rather we are false foolish nurselings, when, in our resting and reflecting hours, we prolong the same deception. Am I to view the Stupendous with stupid indifference, because I have seen it twice, or two-hundred, or two-million times? There is no reason in Nature or in Art why I should: unless, indeed, I am a mere Work-Machine, for whom the divine gift of Thought were no other than the terrestrial gift of Steam is to the Steam-engine; a power whereby cotton might be spun, and money and money's worth realised.

'Notable enough too, here as elsewhere, wilt thou find the potency of Names; which indeed are but one kind of such custom-woven, wonder-hiding Garments. Witchcraft, and all manner of Spectre-work, and Demonology, we have now named Madness and Diseases of the Nerves. Seldom reflecting that still the new question comes upon us: What is Madness, what are Nerves? Ever, as before, does Madness remain a mysterious-terrific, altogether *infernal* boiling-up of the Nether Chaotic Deep, through this fair-painted Vision of Creation, which swims thereon, which we name the Real. Was Luther's Picture of the Devil less a Reality, whether it were formed within the bodily eye, or without it? In every the wisest Soul lies a whole world of internal Madness, an authentic Demon-Empire; out of which, indeed, his world of Wisdom has been creatively built together, and now rests there, as on its dark foundations does a habitable flowery Earth-rind.

'But deepest of all illusory Appearances, for hiding Wonder, as for many other ends, are your two grand fundamental world-enveloping Appearances, SPACE and TIME. These, as spun and woven for us from before Birth itself, to clothe our celestial ME, for dwelling here, and yet to blind it,—lie all-embracing, as the universal canvas, or warp and woof, whereby all minor Illusions, in this Phantasm Existence, weave and paint themselves. In vain, while here on Earth, shall you endeavour to strip them off; you can, at best, but rend them asunder for moments, and look through.

'Fortunatus had a wishing Hat, which when he put on, and wished himself Anywhere, behold he was There. By this means had Fortunatus triumphed over Space, he had annihilated Space; for him there was no Where, but all was

Here. Were a Hatter to establish himself, in the Wahngasse of Weissnichtwo, and make felts of this sort for all mankind, what a world we should have of it! Still stranger, should, on the opposite side of the street, another Hatter establish himself; and, as his fellow-craftsman made Space-annihilating Hats, make Time-annihilating! Of both would I purchase, were it with my last groschen; but chiefly of this latter. To clap-on your felt, and, simply by wishing that you were Any*where,* straightway to be *There!* Next to clap-on your other felt, and, simply by wishing that you were Any*when,* straightway to be *Then!* This were indeed the grander: shooting at will from the Fire-Creation of the World to its Fire-Consummation; here historically present in the First Century, conversing face to face with Paul and Seneca; there prophetically in the Thirty-first, conversing also face to face with other Pauls and Senecas, who as yet stand hidden in the depth of that late Time!

'Or thinkest thou it were impossible, unimaginable? Is the Past annihilated, then, or only past; is the Future non-extant, or only future? Those mystic faculties of thine, Memory and Hope, already answer: already through those mystic avenues, thou the Earth-blinded summonest both Past and Future, and communest with them, though as yet darkly, and with mute beckonings. The curtains of Yesterday drop down, the curtains of Tomorrow roll up; but Yesterday and Tomorrow both *are.* Pierce through the Time-element, glance into the Eternal. Believe what thou findest written in the sanctuaries of Man's Soul, even as all Thinkers, in all ages, have devoutly read it there: that Time and Space are not God, but creations of God; that with God as it is a universal HERE, so is it an everlasting NOW.

'And seest thou therein any glimpse of IMMORTALITY? —O Heaven! Is the white Tomb of our Loved One, who died from our arms, and had to be left behind us there, which rises in the distance, like a pale, mournfully receding Milestone, to tell how many toilsome uncheered miles we have journeyed on alone,—but a pale spectral Illusion! Is the lost Friend still mysteriously Here, even as we are Here mysteriously, with God!—Know of a truth that only the Time-shadows have perished, or are perishable; that the real Being of whatever was, and whatever is, and whatever will be, *is* even now and forever. This, should it unhappily seem new, thou mayest ponder at thy leisure; for the next twenty years, or the next twenty centuries: believe it thou must; understand it thou canst not.

'That the Thought-forms, Space and Time, wherein, once for all, we are sent into this Earth to live, should condition and determine our whole Practical reasonings, conceptions, and imagings or imaginings, seems altogether fit, just, and unavoidable. But that they should, furthermore, usurp such sway over pure spiritual Meditation, and blind us to the wonder everywhere lying close on us, seems nowise so. Admit Space and Time to their due rank as Forms of Thought; nay even, if thou wilt, to their quite undue rank of Realities: and consider, then, with thyself how their thin disguises hide from us the brightest God-effulgences! Thus, were it not miraculous, could I stretch forth my hand and clutch the Sun? Yet thou seest me daily stretch forth my hand and therewith clutch many a thing, and swing it hither and thither. Art thou a grown baby, then, to fancy that the Miracle lies in miles of distance, or in pounds avoirdupois of weight; and not to see that the true inexplicable God-revealing Miracle lies in this, that I can stretch forth my hand at all; that I have free Force to clutch aught therewith? Innumerable other of this sort are the deceptions, and wonder-hiding stupefactions, which Space practises on us.

'Still worse is it with regard to Time. Your grand antimagician, and universal wonder-hider, is this same lying Time. Had we but the Time-annihilating Hat, to put on for once only, we should see ourselves in a World of Miracles, wherein all fabled or authentic Thaumaturgy, and feats of Magic, were outdone. But unhappily we have not such a Hat; and man, poor fool that he is, can seldom and scantily help himself without one.

'Were it not wonderful, for instance, had Orpheus, or Amphion, built the walls of Thebes by the mere sound of his Lyre? Yet tell me, Who built these walls of Weissnichtwo; summoning out all the sandstone rocks, to dance along from the *Steinbruch* (now a huge Troglodyte Chasm, with frightful green-mantled pools); and shape themselves into Doric and Ionic pillars, squared ashlar houses and noble streets? Was it not the still higher Orpheus, or Orpheuses, who, in past centuries, by the divine Music of Wisdom, succeeded in civilising Man? Our highest Orpheus walked in Judea, eighteen-hundred years ago: his sphere-

melody, flowing in wild native tones, took captive the rav-
ished souls of men; and, being of a true sphere-melody still
flows and sounds, though now with thousandfold accompaniments, and rich symphonies, through all our hearts;
and modulates, and divinely leads them. Is that a wonder,
which happens in two hours; and does it cease to be wonderful if happening in two million? Not only was Thebes
built by the music of an Orpheus; but without the music of
some inspired Orpheus was no city ever built, no work that
man glories in ever done.

'Sweep away the Illusion of Time; glance, if thou have
eyes, from the near moving-cause to its far-distant Mover:
The stroke that came transmitted through a whole galaxy of
elastic balls, was it less a stroke than if the last ball only
had been struck, and sent flying? O, could I (with the
Time-annihilating Hat) transport thee direct from the Beginnings to the Endings, how were thy eyesight unsealed,
and thy heart set flaming in the Light-sea of celestial wonder! Then sawest thou that this fair Universe, were it in the
meanest province thereof, is in very deed the star-doomed
City of God; that through every star, through every grass-
blade, and most through every Living Soul, the glory of a
present God still beams. But Nature, which is the Time-
vesture of God, and reveals Him to the wise, hides Him from
the foolish.

'Again, could anything be more miraculous than an
actual authentic Ghost? The English Johnson longed, all
his life, to see one; but could not, though he went to Cock
Lane, and thence to the church-vaults, and tapped on cof-
fins. Foolish Doctor! Did he never, with the mind's eye as
well as with the body's, look round him into that full tide
of human Life he so loved; did he never so much as look
into Himself? The good Doctor was a Ghost, as actual and
authentic as heart could wish; well-nigh a million of Ghosts
were travelling the streets by his side. Once more I
say, sweep away the illusion of Time; compress the threescore years into three minutes: what else was he, what else
are we? Are we not Spirits, that are shaped into a body,
into an Appearance; and that fade away again into air and
Invisibility? This is no metaphor, it is a simple scientific *fact;*
we start out of Nothingness, take figure, and are Apparitions; round us, as round the veriest spectre, is Eternity;
and to Eternity minutes are as years and æons. Come

there not tones of Love and Faith, as from celestial harp-
strings, like the Song of beatified Souls? And again, do not
we squeak and jibber (in our discordant, screech-owlish
debatings and recriminatings); and glide bodeful, and
feeble, and fearful; or uproar (*poltern*), and revel in our
mad Dance of the Dead,—till the scent of the morning air
summons us to our still Home; and dreamy Night becomes
awake and Day? Where now is Alexander of Macedon: does
the steel Host, that yelled in fierce battle-shouts at Issus
and Arbela, remain behind him; or have they all vanished
utterly, even as perturbed Goblins must? Napoleon too, and
his Moscow Retreats and Austerlitz Campaigns! Was it all
other than the veriest Spectre-hunt; which has now, with
its howling tumult that made Night hideous, flitted away?
—Ghosts! There are nigh a thousand-million walking the
Earth openly at noontide; some half-hundred have vanished
from it, some half-hundred have arisen in it, ere thy watch
ticks once.

'O Heaven, it is mysterious, it is awful to consider that we
not only carry each a future Ghost within Him; but are, in
very deed, Ghosts! These Limbs, whence had we them; this
stormy Force; this life-blood with its burning Passion? They
are dust and shadow; a Shadow-system gathered round our
ME; wherein, through some moments or years, the Divine
Essence is to be revealed in the Flesh. That warrior on his
strong war-horse, fire flashes through his eyes; force dwells
in his arm and heart: but warrior and war-horse are a vision; a revealed Force, nothing more. Stately they tread the
Earth, as if it were a firm substance: fool! the Earth is but a
film; it cracks in twain, and warrior and war-horse sink beyond plummet's sounding. Plummet's? Fantasy herself will
not follow them. A little while ago, they were not; a little
while, and they are not, their very ashes are not.

'So has it been from the beginning, so will it be to the
end. Generation after generation takes to itself the Form
of a Body; and forth-issuing from Cimmerian Night, on
Heaven's mission APPEARS. What Force and Fire is in each
he expends: one grinding in the mill of Industry; one
hunter-like climbing the giddy Alpine heights of Science;
one madly dashed in pieces on the rocks of Strife, in war
with his fellow:—and then the Heaven-sent is recalled; his
earthly Vesture falls away, and soon even to sense be-

comes a vanished Shadow. Thus, like some wild-flaming, wild-thundering train of Heaven's Artillery, does this mysterious MANKIND thunder and flame, in long-drawn, quick-succeeding grandeur, through the unknown Deep. Thus, like a God-created, fire-breathing Spirit-host, we emerge from the Inane; haste stormfully across the astonished Earth; then plunge again into the Inane. Earth's mountains are levelled, and her seas filled up, in our passage: can the Earth, which is but dead and a vision, resist Spirits which have reality and are alive? On the hardest adamant some footprint of us is stamped-in; the last Rear of the host will read traces of the earliest Van. But whence?—O Heaven, whither? Sense knows not; Faith knows not; only that it is through Mystery to Mystery, from God and to God.

> "We *are such stuff*
> As dreams are made of, and our little Life
> Is rounded with a sleep!" '

CHAPTER IX

CIRCUMSPECTIVE

Recapitulation. Editor congratulates the few British readers who have accompanied Teufelsdröckh through all his speculations. The true use of the Sartor Resartus, *to exhibit the Wonder of daily life and common things; and to show that all Forms are but Clothes, and temporary. Practical inferences enough will follow.*

Here, then, arises the so momentous question: Have many British Readers actually arrived with us at the new promised country; is the Philosophy of Clothes now at last opening around them? Long and adventurous has the journey been: from those outmost vulgar, palpable Woollen Hulls of Man; through his wondrous Flesh-Garment, and his wondrous Social Garnitures; inwards to the Garments of his very Soul's Soul, to Time and Space themselves! And now does the spiritual, eternal Essence of Man, and of Mankind, bared of such wrappages, begin in any measure to reveal itself? Can many readers discern, as through a glass darkly, in huge wavering outlines, some primeval rudiments of Man's Being, what is changeable divided from what is unchangeable? Does that Earth-Spirit's speech in *Faust*,—

> 'Tis thus at the roaring Loom of Time I ply,
> And weave for God the Garment thou see'st Him by';

or that other thousand-times repeated speech of the Magician, Shakspeare,—

> 'And like the baseless fabric of this vision,
> The cloudcapt Towers, the gorgeous Palaces,
> The solemn Temples, the great Globe itself,
> And all which it inherit, shall dissolve;
> And like this unsubstantial pageant faded,
> Leave not a wrack behind';

begin to have some meaning for us? In a word, do we at length stand safe in the far region of Poetic Creation and Palingenesia, where that Phœnix Death-Birth of Human Society, and of all Human Things, appears possible, is seen to be inevitable?

Along this most insufficient, unheard-of Bridge, which the Editor, by Heaven's blessing, has now seen himself enabled to conclude if not complete, it cannot be his sober calculation, but only his fond hope, that many have travelled without accident. No firm arch, overspanning the Impassable with paved highway, could the Editor construct; only, as was said, some zigzag series of rafts floating tumultuously thereon. Alas, and the leaps from raft to raft, were too often of a breakneck character; the darkness, the nature of the element, all was against us!

Nevertheless, may not here and there one of a thousand, provided with a discursiveness of intellect rare in our day, have cleared the passage, in spite of all? Happy few! little band of Friends! be welcome, be of courage. By degrees, the eye grows accustomed to its new Whereabout; the hand can stretch itself forth to work there: it is in this grand and indeed highest work of Palingenesia that ye shall labour, each according to ability. New labourers will arrive; new Bridges will be built; nay, may not our own poor rope-and-raft Bridge, in your passings and repassings, be mended in many a point, till it grows quite firm, passable even for the halt?

Meanwhile, of the innumerable multitude that started with us, joyous and full of hope, where now is the innumerable remainder, whom we see no longer by our side? The most have recoiled, and stand gazing afar off, in unsympathetic astonishment, at our career: not a few, pressing forward with more courage, have missed footing, or leaped short; and now swim weltering in the Chaos-flood, some towards this shore, some towards that. To these also a helping hand should be held out; at least some word of encouragement be said.

Or, to speak without metaphor, with which mode of utterance Teufelsdröckh unhappily has somewhat infected us,—can it be hidden from the Editor that many a British reader sits reading quite bewildered in head, and afflicted rather than instructed by the present Work? Yes, long ago has many a British Reader been, as now, demanding with something like a snarl: Whereto does all this lead; or what use is in it?

In the way of replenishing thy purse, or otherwise aiding thy digestive faculty, O British Reader, it leads to nothing, and there is no use in it; but rather the reverse, for it costs thee somewhat. Nevertheless, if through this unpromising Horn-gate, Teufelsdröckh, and we by means of him, have led thee into the true Land of Dreams; and through the Clothes-Screen, as through a magical *Pierre-Pertuis,* thou lookest, even for moments, into the region of the Wonderful, and seest and feelest that thy daily life is girt with Wonder, and based on Wonder, and thy very blankets and breeches are Miracles,—then art thou profited beyond money's worth; and hast a thankfulness towards our Professor; nay, perhaps in many a literary Tea-circle wilt open they kind lips, and audibly express that same.

Nay further, art not thou too perhaps by this time made aware that all Symbols are properly Clothes; that all Forms whereby Spirit manifests itself to sense, whether outwardly or in the imagination, are Clothes; and thus not only the parchment Magna Charta, which a Tailor was nigh cutting into measures, but the Pomp and Authority of Law, the sacredness of Majesty, and all inferior Worships (Worthships) are properly a Vesture and Raiment; and the Thirty-nine Articles themselves are articles of wearing-apparel (for the Religious Idea)? In which case, must it not also be admitted that this Science of Clothes is a high one, and may with infinitely deeper study on thy part yield richer fruit: that it takes scientific rank beside Codification, and Political Economy, and the Theory of the British Constitution; nay rather, from its prophetic height looks down on all these, as on so many weaving-shops and spinning-mills, where the Vestures which *it* has to fashion, and consecrate and distribute, are, too often by haggard hungry operatives who see no farther than their nose, mechanically woven and spun?

But omitting all this, much more all that concerns Natural Supernaturalism, and indeed whatever has reference to the Ulterior or Transcendental portion of the Science, or bears never so remotely on that promised Volume of the *Palingenesie der menschlichen Gesellschaft* (Newbirth of Society),—we humbly suggest that no province of Clothes-Philosophy, even the lowest, is without its direct value, but that innumerable inferences of a practical nature may be drawn therefrom. To say nothing of those pregnant considerations, ethical, political, symbolical, which crowd on the Clothes-Philosopher from the very threshold of his Science; nothing even of those 'architectural ideas,' which, as we have seen, lurk at the bottom of all Modes, and will one day, better unfolding themselves, lead to important revolutions,—let us glance for a moment, and with the faintest light of Clothes-Philosophy, on what may be called the Habilatory Class of our fellow-men. Here too overlooking, where so much were to be looked on, the million spinners, weavers, fullers, dyers, washers, and wringers, that puddle and muddle in their dark recesses, to make us Clothes, and die that we may live,—let us but turn the reader's attention upon two small divisions of mankind, who, like moths, may be regarded as Cloth-animals, creatures that live, move, and have their being in Cloth: we mean, Dandies and Tailors.

In regard to both which small divisions it may be asserted without scruple, that the public feeling, unenlightened by Philosophy, is at fault; and even that the dictates of humanity are violated. As will perhaps abundantly appear to readers of the two following Chapters.

CHAPTER X

THE DANDIACAL BODY

The Dandy defined. The Dandiacal Sect a new modification of the primeval superstition Self-worship: How to be distinguished. Their Sacred Books (Fashionable Novels) unreadable. Dandyism's Articles of Faith.—Brotherhood of Poor-Slaves; vowed to perpetual Poverty; worshippers of Earth; distinguished by peculiar costume and diet. Picture of a Poor-Slave Household; and of a Dandiacal. Teufelsdröckh fears these two Sects may spread, till they part all England between them, and then frightfully collide.

First, touching Dandies, let us consider, with some scientific strictness, what a Dandy specially is. A Dandy is a Clothes-wearing Man, a Man whose trade, office, and existence consists in the wearing of Clothes. Every faculty of his soul, spirit, purse, and person is heroically consecrated to this one object, the wearing of Clothes wisely and well: so that as others dress to live, he lives to dress. The all-importance of Clothes, which a German Professor, of un-equalled learning and acumen, writes his enormous Volume to demonstrate, has sprung up in the intellect of the Dandy without effort, like an instinct of genius; he is inspired with Cloth, a Poet of Cloth. What Teufelsdröckh would call a 'Divine Idea of Cloth' is born with him; and this, like other such Ideas, will express itself outwardly, or wring his heart asunder with unutterable throes.

But, like a generous, creative enthusiast, he fearlessly makes his Idea an Action; shows himself in peculiar guise to mankind; walks forth, a witness and living Martyr to the eternal world of Clothes. We called him a Poet: is not his body the (stuffed) parchment-skin whereon he writes, with cunning Huddersfield dyes, a Sonnet to his mistress' eye-brow? Say, rather, an Epos, and *Clotha Virumque cano,* to the whole world, in Macaronic verses, which he that runs may read. Nay, if you grant, what seems to be admissible, that the Dandy has a Thinking-principle in him, and some notions of Time and Space, is there not in this Life-devoted-ness to Cloth, in this so willing sacrifice of the Immortal to the Perishable, something (though in reverse order) of that blending and identification of Eternity with Time, which, as we have seen, constitutes the Prophetic character?

And now, for all this perennial Martyrdom, and Poesy, and even Prophecy, what is it that the Dandy asks in return? Solely, we may say, that you would recognise his existence; would admit him to be a living object; or even failing this, a visual object, or thing that will reflect rays of light. Your silver or your gold (beyond what the niggardly Law has already secured him) he solicits not; simply the glance of your eyes. Understand his mystic significance, or altogether miss and misinterpret it; do but look at him, and he is contented. May we not well cry shame on an ungrateful world, which refuses even this poor boon; which will waste its optic faculty on dried Crocodiles, and Siamese Twins; and over the domestic wonderful wonder of wonders, a live Dandy, glance with hasty indifference, and a scarcely concealed contempt! Him no Zoologist classes among the Mammalia, no Anatomist dissects with care: when did we see any injected Preparation of the Dandy in our Museums; any specimen of him preserved in spirits? Lord Herringbone may dress himself in a snuff-brown suit, with snuff-brown shirt and shoes: it skills not; the undiscerning public, occupied with grosser wants, passes by regardless on the other side.

The age of Curiosity, like that of Chivalry, is indeed, properly speaking, gone. Yet perhaps only gone to sleep: for here arises the Clothes-Philosophy to resuscitate, strangely enough, both the one and the other! Should sound views of this Science come to prevail, the essential nature of the British Dandy, and the mystic significance that lies in him, cannot always remain hidden under laughable and lamentable hallucination. The following long Extract from Professor Teufelsdröckh may set the matter, if not in its true light, yet in the way towards such. It is to be regretted, however, that here, as so often elsewhere, the Professor's keen philosophic perspicacity is somewhat marred by a certain mixture of almost owlish purblindness, or else of some perverse, ineffectual, ironic tendency; our readers shall judge which:

'In these distracted times,' writes he, 'when the Religious

Principle, driven out of most Churches, either lies unseen in the hearts of good men, looking and longing and silently working there towards some new Revelation; or else wanders homeless over the world, like a disembodied soul seeking its terrestrial organisation,—into how many strange shapes, of Superstition and Fanaticism, does it not tentatively and errantly cast itself! The higher Enthusiasm of man's nature is for the while without Exponent; yet does it continue indestructible, unweariedly active, and work blindly in the great chaotic deep: thus Sect after Sect, and Church after Church, bodies itself forth, and melts again into new metamorphosis.

'Chiefly is this observable in England, which, as the wealthiest and worst-instructed of European nations, offers precisely the elements (of Heat, namely, and of Darkness), in which such moon-calves and monstrosities are best generated. Among the newer Sects of that country, one of the most notable, and closely connected with our present subject, is that of the *Dandies*; concerning which, what little information I have been able to procure may fitly stand here.

'It is true, certain of the English Journalists, men generally without sense for the Religious Principle, or judgment for its manifestations, speak, in their brief enigmatic notices, as if this were perhaps rather a Secular Sect, and not a Religious one; nevertheless, to the psychologic eye its devotional and even sacrificial character plainly enough reveals itself. Whether it belongs to the class of Fetich-worships, or of Hero-worships or Polytheisms, or to what other class, may in the present state of our intelligence remain undecided (*schweben*). A certain touch of Manicheism, not indeed in the Gnostic shape, is discernible enough: also (for human Error walks in a cycle, and reappears at intervals) a not-inconsiderable resemblance to that Superstition of the Athos Monks, who by fasting from all nourishment, and looking intensely for a length of time into their own navels, came to discern therein the true Apocalypse of Nature, and Heaven Unveiled. To my own surmise, it appears as if this Dandiacal Sect were but a new modification, adapted to the new time, of that primeval Superstition, *Self-worship*; which Zerdusht, Quangfoutchee, Mohamed, and others, strove rather to subordinate and restrain than to eradicate, and which only in the purer forms of Religion has been altogether rejected. Wherefore, if any one chooses to name it revived Ahrimanism, or a new figure of Demon-worship, I have, so far as is yet visible, no objection.

'For the rest, these people, animated with the zeal of a new Sect, display courage and perseverance, and what force there is in man's nature, though never so enslaved. They affect great purity and separatism; distinguish themselves by a particular costume (whereof some notices were given in the earlier part of this Volume); likewise, so far as possible, by a particular speech (apparently some broken *Lingua-franca,* or English-French); and, on the whole, strive to maintain a true Nazarene deportment, and keep themselves unspotted from the world.

'They have their Temples, whereof the chief, as the Jewish Temple did, stands in their metropolis; and is named *Almack's,* a word of uncertain etymology. They worship principally by night; and have their Highpriests and Highpriestesses, who, however, do not continue for life. The rites, by some supposed to be of the Menadic sort, or perhaps with an Eleusinian or Cabiric character, are held strictly secret. Nor are Sacred Books wanting to the Sect; these they call *Fashionable Novels*: however, the Canon is not completed, and some are canonical and others not.

'Of such Sacred Books I, not without expense, procured myself some samples; and in hope of true insight, and with the zeal which beseems an Inquirer into Clothes, set to interpret and study them. But wholly to no purpose: that tough faculty of reading, for which the world will not refuse me credit, was here for the first time foiled and set at naught. In vain that I summoned my whole energies (*mich weidlich anstrengte*), and did my very utmost; at the end of some short space, I was uniformly seized with not so much what I can call a drumming in my ears, as a kind of infinite, unsufferable, Jew's harping and scrannel-piping there; to which the frightfullest species of Magnetic Sleep soon supervened. And if I strove to shake this away, and absolutely would not yield, there came a hitherto unfelt sensation, as of *Delirium Tremens,* and a melting into total deliquium: till at last, by order of the Doctor, dreading ruin to my whole intellectual and bodily faculties, and a general breaking-up of the constitution, I reluctantly but determinedly forbore. Was there some miracle at work here; like those Fire-balls, and supernal and infernal prodigies, which, in the case of the Jewish Mysteries, have also more than once scared-back the Alien? Be this as it may, such failure on my part, after best efforts, must excuse the imperfection of this sketch; altogether incomplete, yet the completest I could give of a Sect too singular to be omitted.

'Loving my own life and senses as I do, no power shall induce me, as a private individual, to open another *Fashionable Novel*. But luckily, in this dilemma, comes a hand from the clouds; whereby if not victory, deliverance is held out to me. Round one of those Book-packages, which the *Stillschweigen'sche Buchandlung* is in the habit of importing from England, come, as is usual, various waste printed-sheets (*Maculatur-blätter*), by way of interior wrappage: into these the Clothes-Philosopher, with a certain Mohamedan reverence even for waste-paper, where curious knowledge will sometimes hover, disdains not to cast his eye. Readers may judge of his astonishment when on such a defaced stray-sheet, probably the outcast fraction of some English Periodical, such as they name *Magazine*, appears something like a Dissertation on this very subject of *Fashionable Novels*! It sets out, indeed, chiefly from a Secular point of view; directing itself, not without asperity, against some to me unknown individual named *Pelham*, who seems to be a Mystagogue, and leading Teacher and Preacher of the Sect; so that, what indeed otherwise was not to be expected in such a fugitive fragmentary sheet, the true secret, the Religious physiognomy and physiology of the Dandiacal Body, is nowise laid fully open there. Nevertheless, scattered lights do from time to time sparkle out, whereby I have endeavoured to profit. Nay, in one passage selected from the Prophecies, or Mythic Theogonies, or whatever they are (for the style seems very mixed) of this Mystagogue, I find what appears to be a Confession of Faith, or Whole Duty of Man, according to the tenets of that Sect. Which Confession or Whole Duty, therefore, as proceeding from a source so authentic, I shall here arrange under Seven distinct Articles, and in very abridged shape lay before the German world; therewith taking leave of this

318 / A CARLYLE READER

matter. Observe also, that to avoid possibility of error, I, as far as may be, quote literally from the Original:

'ARTICLES OF FAITH.

"1. Coats should have nothing of the triangle about them; at the same time, wrinkles behind should be carefully avoided.

"2. The collar is a very important point: it should be low behind, and slightly rolled.

"3. No licence of fashion can allow a man of delicate taste to adopt the posterial luxuriance of a Hottentot.

"4. There is safety in a swallow-tail.

"5. The good sense of a gentleman is nowhere more finally developed than in his rings.

"6. It is permitted to mankind, under certain restrictions, to wear white waistcoats.

"7. The trousers must be exceedingly tight across the hips."

'All which Propositions I, for the present, content myself with modestly but peremptorily and irrevocably denying.

'In strange contrast with this Dandiacal Body stands another British Sect, originally, as I understand, of Ireland, where its chief seat still is; but known also in the main Island, and indeed everywhere rapidly spreading. As this Sect has hitherto emitted no Canonical Books, it remains to me in the same state of obscurity as the Dandiacal, which has published Books that the unassisted human faculties are inadequate to read. The members appear to be designated by a considerable diversity of names, according to their various places of establishment: in England they are generally called the *Drudge* Sect; also, unphilosophically enough, the *White Negroes*; and, chiefly in scorn by those of other communions, the *Ragged-Beggar* Sect. In Scotland, again, I find them entitled *Hallanshakers*, or the *Stook of Duds* Sect; any individual communicant is named *Stook of Duds* (that is, Shock of Rags), in allusion, doubtless, to their professional Costume. While in Ireland, which, as mentioned, is their grand parent hive, they go by a perplexing multiplicity of designations, such as *Bogtrotters, Redshanks, Ribbonmen, Cottiers, Peep-of-Day Boys, Babes of the Wood, Rockites, Poor-Slaves:* which last, however, seems to be the primary and generic name; whereto, probably enough, the others are only subsidiary species, or slight varieties; or, at most, propagated offsets from the parent stem, whose minute subdivisions, and shades of difference, it were here loss of time to dwell on. Enough for us to understand, what seems indubitable, that the original Sect is that of the *Poor-Slaves*; whose doctrines, practices, and fundamental characteristics pervade and animate the whole Body, howsoever denominated or outwardly diversified.

'The precise speculative tenets of this Brotherhood: how the Universe, and Man, and Man's Life, picture themselves to the mind of an Irish Poor-Slave; with what feelings and opinions he looks forward on the Future, round on the Present, back on the Past, it were extremely difficult to specify. Something Monastic there appears to be in their Constitution: we find them bound by the two Monastic Vows, of Poverty and Obedience; which Vows, especially the former, it is said, they observe with great strictness; nay, as I have understood it, they are pledged, and be it by any solemn Nazarene ordination or not, irrevocably consecrated thereto, even *before* birth. That the third Monastic Vow, of Chastity, is rigidly enforced among them, I find no ground to conjecture.

'Furthermore, they appear to imitate the Dandiacal Sect in their grand principle of wearing a peculiar Costume. Of which Irish Poor-Slave Costume no description will indeed be found in the present Volume; for this reason, that by the imperfect organ of Language it did not seem describable. Their raiment consists of innumerable skirts, lappets and iregular wings, of all cloths and of all colours; through the labyrinthic intricacies of which their bodies are introduced by some unknown process. It is fastened together by a multiplex combination of buttons, thrums, and skewers; to which frequently is added a girdle of leather, of hempen or even of straw rope, round the loins. To straw rope, indeed, they seem partial, and often wear it by way of sandals. In headdress they affect a certain freedom: hats with partial brim, without crown, or with only a loose, hinged, or valved crown; in the former case, they sometimes invert the hat, and wear it brim uppermost, like a University-cap, with what view is unknown.

'The name Poor-Slaves seems to indicate a Slavonic, Polish, or Russian origin: not so, however, the interior essence and spirit of their Superstition, which rather displays a Teutonic or Druidical character. One might fancy them worshippers of Hertha, or the Earth: for they dig and affectionately work continually in her bosom; or else, shut-up in private Oratories, meditate and manipulate the substances derived from her; seldom looking-up towards the Heavenly Luminaries, and then with comparative indifference. Like the Druids, on the other hand, they live in dark dwellings; often even breaking their glass-windows, where they find such, and stuffing them up with pieces of raiment, or other opaque substances, till the fit obscurity is restored. Again, like all followers of Nature-Worship, they are liable to outbreakings of an enthusiasm rising to ferocity; and burn men, if not in wicker idols, yet in sod cottages.

'In respect of diet, they have also their observances. All Poor-Slaves are Rhizophagous (or Root-eaters); a few are Ichthyophagous, and use Salted Herrings: other animal food they abstain from; except indeed, with perhaps some strange inverted fragment of a Brahminical feeling, such animals as die a natural death. Their universal sustenance is the root named Potato, cooked by fire alone; and generally without condiment or relish of any kind, save an unknown condiment named *Point*, into the meaning of which I have vainly inquired; the victual *Potatoes-and-Point* not appearing, at least not with specific accuracy of description, in any European Cookery-Book whatever. For drink, they use, with an almost epigrammatic counterpoise of taste, Milk, which is the mildest of liquors, and *Potheen*, which is the fiercest. This latter I have tasted, as well as the English *Blue-Ruin*, and the Scotch *Whisky*, analogous fluids used by the Sect in those countries: it evidently contains some form of alcohol, in the highest state of concentration, though disguised with acrid oils; and is, on the whole, the most pungent substance known to me,—indeed, a perfect liquid fire. In all their Religious Solemnities, Potheen is said to be an indispensable requisite, and largely consumed.

'An Irish Traveller, of perhaps common veracity, who presents himself under the to me unmeaning title of *The late John Bernard*, offers the following sketch of a domestic establishment; the inmates whereof, though such is not stated expressly, appear to have been of that Faith. Thereby shall my German readers now behold an Irish Poor-Slave, as it were with their own eyes; and even see him at meat.

Moreover, in the so precious waste-paper sheet above mentioned, I have found some corresponding picture of a Dandiacal Household, painted by that same Dandiacal Mystagogue, or Theogonist: this also, by way of counterpart and contrast, the world shall look into.

'First, therefore, of the Poor-Slave, who appears likewise to have been a species of Innkeeper. I quote from the original:

Poor-Slave Household

' "The furniture of this Caravansera consisted of a large iron Pot, two oaken Tables, two Benches, two Chairs, and a Potheen Noggin. There was a Loft above (attainable by a ladder), upon which the inmates slept; and the space below was divided by a hurdle into two Apartments; the one for their cow and pig, the other for themselves and guests. On entering the house we discovered the family, eleven in number, at dinner: the father sitting at the top, the mother at the bottom, the children on each side, of a large oaken Board, which was scooped-out in the middle, like a trough, to receive the contents of their Pot of Potatoes. Little holes were cut at equal distances to contain Salt; and a bowl of Milk stood on the table: all the luxuries of meat and beer, bread, knives and dishes were dispensed with." The Poor-Slave himself our Traveller found, as he says, broad-backed, black-browed, of great personal strength, and mouth from ear to ear. His Wife was a sun-browned but well-featured woman; and his young ones, bare and chubby, had the appetite of ravens. Of their Philosophical or Religious tenets or observances, no notice or hint.

'But now, secondly, of the Dandiacal Household; in which, truly, that often-mentioned Mystagogue and inspired Penman himself has his abode:

Dandiacal Household

' "A Dressing-room splendidly furnished; violet-coloured curtains, chairs and ottomans of the same hue. Two full-length Mirrors are placed, one on each side of a table, which supports the luxuries of the Toilet. Several Bottles of Perfumes, arranged in a peculiar fashion, stand upon a smaller table of mother-of-pearl: opposite to these are placed the appurtenances of Lavation richly wrought in frosted silver. A Wardrobe of Buhl is on the left; the doors of which, being partly open, discover a profusion of Clothes: Shoes of a singularly small size monopolise the lower shelves. Fronting the wardrobe a door ajar gives some slight glimpse of a Bathroom. Folding-doors in the background.—Enter the Author," our Theogonist in person, "obsequiously preceded by a French Valet, in white silk Jacket and cambric Apron."

'Such are the two Sects which, at this moment, divide the more unsettled portion of the British People; and agitate that ever-vexed country. To the eye of the political Seer, their mutual relation, pregnant with the elements of discord and hostility, is far from consoling. These two principles of Dandiacal Self-worship or Demon-worship, and Poor-Slavish or Drudgical Earth-worship, or whatever that same Drudgism may be, do as yet indeed manifest themselves under distant and nowise considerable shapes: nevertheless, in their roots and subterranean ramifications, they extend through the entire structure of Society, and work unweariedly in the secret depths of English national Existence; striving to separate and isolate it into two contradictory, uncommunicating masses.

'In numbers, and even individual strength, the Poor-Slaves or Drudges, it would seem, are hourly increasing. The Dandiacal, again, is by nature no proselytising Sect; but it boasts of great hereditary resources, and is strong by union; whereas the Drudges, split into parties, have as yet no rallying-point; or at best only coöperate by means of partial secret affiliations. If, indeed, there were to arise a *Communion of Drudges*, as there is already a Communion of Saints, what strangest effects would follow therefrom! Dandyism as yet affects to look-down on Drudgism: but perhaps the hour of trial, when it will be practically seen which ought to look down, and which up, is not so distant.

'To me it seems probable that the two Sects will one day part England between them; each recruiting itself from the intermediate ranks, till there be none left to enlist on either side. Those Dandiacal Manicheans, with the host of Dandyising Christians, will form one body: the Drudges, gathering round them whosoever is Drudgical, be he Christian or Infidel Pagan; sweeping-up likewise all manner of Utilitarians, Radicals, refractory Potwallopers, and so forth, into their general mass, will form another. I could liken Dandyism and Drudgism to two bottomless boiling Whirlpools that had broken-out on opposite quarters of the firm land: as yet they appear only disquieted, foolishly bubbling wells, which man's art might cover-in; yet mark them, their diameter is daily widening: they are hollow Cones that boil-up from the infinite Deep, over which your firm land is but a thin crust or rind! Thus daily is the intermediate land crumbling-in, daily the empire of the two Buchan-Bullers extending; till now there is but a foot-plank, a mere film of Land between them; this too is washed away: and then—we have the true Hell of Waters, and Noah's Deluge is outdeluged!

'Or better, I might call them two boundless, and indeed unexampled Electric Machines (turned by the "Machinery of Society"), with batteries of opposite quality; Drudgism the Negative, Dandyism the Positive: one attracts hourly towards it and appropriates all the Positive Electricity of the nation (namely, the Money thereof); the other is equally busy with the Negative (that is to say the Hunger), which is equally potent. Hitherto you see only partial transient sparkles and sputters: but wait a little, till the entire nation is in an electric state; till your whole vital Electricity, no longer healthfully Neutral, is cut into two isolated portions of Positive and Negative (of Money and of Hunger); and stands there bottled-up in two World-Batteries! The stirring of a child's finger brings the two together; and then —What then? The Earth is but shivered into impalpable smoke by that Doom's-thunderpeal; the Sun misses one of his Planets in Space, and thenceforth there are no eclipses of the Moon.—Or better still, I might liken——'

O, enough, enough of likenings and similitudes; in excess of which, truly, it is hard to say whether Teufelsdröckh or ourselves sin the more.

We have often blamed him for a habit of wire-drawing and over-refining; from of old we have been familiar with his tendency to Mysticism and Religiosity, whereby in everything he was still scenting-out Religion: but never perhaps did these amaurosis-suffusions so cloud and distort his otherwise most piercing vision, as in this of the *Dandiacal Body!* Or was there something of intended satire; is the Professor and Seer not quite the blinkard he affects to be? Of an ordinary mortal we should have decisively answered in the affirmative; but with a Teufelsdröckh there ever hovers some shade of doubt. In the meanwhile, if satire were actually intended the case is little better. There are not wanting men who will answer: Does your Professor take us for simpletons? His irony has overshot itself; we see through it, and perhaps through him.

CHAPTER XI

TAILORS

Injustice done to Tailors, actual and metaphorical. Their rights and great services will one day be duly recognised.

Thus, however, has our first Practical Inference from the Clothes-Philosophy, that which respects Dandies, been sufficiently drawn; and we come now to the second, concerning Tailors. On this latter our opinion happily quite coincides with that of Teufelsdröckh himself, as expressed in the concluding page of his Volume, to whom, therefore, we willingly give place. Let him speak his own last words, in his own way:

'Upwards of a century,' says he, 'must elapse, and still the bleeding fight of Freedom be fought, whoso is noblest perishing in the van, and thrones be hurled on altars like Pelion on Ossa, and the Moloch of Iniquity have his victims, and the Michael of Justice his martyrs, before Tailors can be admitted to their true prerogatives of manhood, and this last wound of suffering Humanity be closed.

'If aught in the history of the world's blindness could surprise us, here might we indeed pause and wonder. An idea has gone abroad, and fixed itself down into a wide-spreading rooted error, that Tailors are a distinct species in Physiology, not Men, but fractional Parts of a Man. Call any one a *Schneider* (Cutter, Tailor), is it not, in our dislocated, hoodwinked, and indeed delirious condition of Society, equivalent to defying his perpetual fellest enmity? The epithet *schneidermässig* (tailor-like) betokens an otherwise unapproachable degree of pusillanimity: we introduce a *Tailor's-Melancholy*, more opprobrious than any Leprosy, into our Books of Medicine; and fable I know not what of his generating it by living on Cabbage. Why should I speak of Hans Sachs (himself a Shoemaker, or kind of Leather-Tailor), with his *Schneider mit dem Panier*? Why of Shakspeare, in his *Taming of the Shrew*, and elsewhere? Does it not stand on record that the English Queen Elizabeth, receiving a deputation of Eighteen Tailors, addressed them with a "Good-morning, gentlemen both!" Did not the same virago boast that she had a Cavalry Regiment, whereof neither horse nor man could be injured; her Regiment, namely, of Tailors on Mares? Thus everywhere is the falsehood taken for granted, and acted on as an indisputable fact.

'Nevertheless, need I put the question to any Physiologist, whether it is disputable or not? Seems it not at least presumable, that, under his Clothes, the Tailor has bones and viscera, and other muscles than the sartorious? Which function of manhood is the Tailor not conjectured to perform? Can he not arrest for debt? Is he not in most countries a tax-paying animal?

'To no reader of this Volume can it be doubtful which conviction is mine. Nay if the fruit of these long vigils, and almost preternatural Inquiries, is not to perish utterly, the world will have approximated towards a higher Truth; and the doctrine, which Swift, with the keen forecast of genius, dimly anticipated, will stand revealed in clear light: that the Tailor is not only a Man, but something of a Creator or Divinity. Of Franklin it was said, that "he snatched the Thunder from Heaven and the Sceptre from Kings": but which is greater, I would ask, he that lends, or he that snatches? For, looking away from individual cases, and how a Man is by the Tailor new-created into a Nobleman, and clothed not only with Wool but with Dignity and a Mystic Dominion,—is not the fair fabric of Society itself, with all its royal mantles and pontifical stoles, whereby, from nakedness and dismemberment, we are organised into Polities, into nations, and a whole coöperating Mankind, the creation, as has here been often irrefragably evinced, of the Tailor alone?—What too are all Poets and moral Teachers, but a species of Metaphorical Tailors? Touching which high Guild the greatest living Guild-brother has triumphantly asked us: "Nay if thou wilt have it, who but the Poet first made Gods for men; brought them down to us; and raised us up to them?"

'And this is he, whom sitting downcast, on the hard basis of his Shopboard, the world treats with contumely, as the ninth part of a man! Look up, thou much-injured one, look up with the kindling eye of hope, and prophetic bodings of a noble better time. Too long hast thou sat there, on crossed legs, wearing thy ankle-joints to horn; like some sacred Anchorite, or Catholic Fakir, doing penance, drawing down Heaven's richest blessings, for a world that scoffed at thee. Be of hope! Already streaks of blue peer through our clouds; the thick gloom of Ignorance is rolling asunder, and it will be Day. Mankind will repay with interest their long-accumulated debt: the Anchorite that was scoffed at will be worshipped; the Fraction will become not an Integer only, but a Square and Cube. With astonishment the world will recognise that the Tailor is its Hierophant and Hierarch, or even its God.

'As I stood in the Mosque of St. Sophia, and looked upon these Four-and-Twenty Tailors, sewing and embroidering that rich Cloth, which the Sultan sends yearly for the Caaba of Mecca, I thought within myself: How many other Unholies has your covering Art made holy, besides this Arabian Whin-stone!

'Still more touching was it when, turning the corner of a lane, in the Scottish Town of Edinburgh, I came upon a Signpost, whereon stood written that such and such a one was "Breeches-Maker to his Majesty"; and stood painted the Effigies of a Pair of Leather Breeches, and between the knees these memorable words, SIC ITUR AD ASTRA. Was not this the martyr prison-speech of a Tailor sighing indeed in bonds, yet sighing towards deliverance, and prophetically appealing to a better day? A day of justice, when the worth of Breeches would be revealed to man, and the Scissors become forever venerable.

'Neither, perhaps, may I now say, has his appeal been altogether in vain. It was in this high moment, when the soul, rent, as it were, and shed asunder, is open to inspiring influence, that I first conceived this Work on Clothes: the greatest I can ever hope to do; which has already, after long retardations, occupied, and will yet occupy, so large a section of my Life; and of which the Primary and simpler Portion may here find its conclusion.'

CHAPTER XII

FAREWELL

Teufelsdröckh's strange manner of speech, but resolute, truthful character. His purpose seemingly to proselytise, to unite the wakeful earnest in these dark times. Letter from Hofrath Heuschrecke announcing that Teufelsdröckh has disappeared from Weissnichtwo. Editor guesses he will appear again. Friendly Farewell.

So have we endeavoured, from the enormous, amorphous Plum-pudding, more like a Scottish Haggis, which Herr Teufelsdröckh had kneaded for his fellow-mortals, to pick out the choicest Plums, and present them separately on a cover of our own. A laborious, perhaps a thankless enterprise; in which, however, something of hope has occasionally cheered us, and of which we can now wash our hands not altogether without satisfaction. If hereby, though in barbaric wise, some morsel of spiritual nourishment have been added to the scanty ration of our beloved British world, what nobler recompense could the Editor desire? If it prove otherwise, why should he murmur? Was not this a Task which Destiny, in any case, had appointed him; which having now done with, he sees his general Day's-work so much the lighter, so much the shorter?

Of Professor Teufelsdröckh it seems impossible to take leave without a mingled feeling of astonishment, gratitude, and disapproval. Who will not regret that talents, which might have profited in the higher walks of Philosophy, or in Art itself, have been so much devoted to a rummaging among lumber-rooms; nay too often to a scraping in kennels, where lost rings and diamond-necklaces are nowise the sole conquests? Regret is unavoidable; yet censure were loss of time. To cure him of his mad humours British Criticism would essay in vain: enough for her if she can, by vigilance, prevent the spreading of such among ourselves. What a result, should this piebald, entangled, hyper-metaphorical style of writing, not to say of thinking, become general among our Literary men! As it might so easily do. Thus has not the Editor himself, working over Teufelsdröckh's German, lost much of his own English purity? Even as the smaller whirlpool is sucked into the larger, and made to whirl along with it, so has the lesser mind, in this instance, been forced to become portion of the greater, and, like it, see all things figuratively: which habit time and assiduous effort will be needed to eradicate.

Nevertheless, wayward as our Professor shows himself, is there any reader that can part with him in declared enmity? Let us confess, there is that in the wild, much-suffering, much-inflicting man, which almost attaches us. His attitude, we will hope and believe, is that of a man who had said to Cant, Begone; and to Dilettantism, Here thou canst not be; and to Truth, Be thou in place of all to me: a man who had manfully defied the 'Time-prince,' or Devil, to his face; nay perhaps, Hannibal-like, was mysteriously consecrated from birth to that warfare, and now stood minded to wage the same, by all weapons, in all places, at all times. In such a cause, any soldier, were he but a Polack Scythe-man, shall be welcome.

Still the question returns on us: How could a man occasionally of keen insight, not without keen sense of propriety, who had real Thoughts to communicate, resolve to emit them in a shape bordering so closely on the absurd? Which question he were wiser than the present Editor who should satisfactorily answer. Our conjecture has sometimes been, that perhaps Necessity as well as Choice was concerned in it. Seems it not conceivable that, in a Life like our Professor's, where so much bountifully given by Nature had in Practice failed and misgone, Literature also would never rightly prosper: that striving with his characteristic vehemence to paint this and the other Picture, and ever without success, he at last desperately dashes his sponge, full of all colours, against the canvas, to try whether it will paint Foam? With all his stillness, there were perhaps in Teufelsdröckh desperation enough for this.

A second conjecture we hazard with even less warranty. It is, that Teufelsdröckh is not without some touch of the universal feeling, a wish to proselytise. How often already have we paused, uncertain whether the basis of this so enigmatic nature were really Stoicism and Despair, or Love and Hope only seared into the figure of these! Remarkable, moreover, is this saying of his: 'How were Friendship possible? In mutual devotedness to the Good and True: otherwise impossible; except as Armed Neutrality, or hollow Commercial League. A man, be the Heavens ever praised, is sufficient for himself; yet were ten men, united in Love, capable of being and of doing what ten thousand singly would fail in. Infinite is the help man can yield to man.' And now in conjunction therewith consider this other: 'It is the Night of the World, and still long till it be Day: we wander amid the glimmer of smoking ruins, and the Sun and the Stars of Heaven are as if blotted out for a season; and two immeasurable Phantoms, HYPOCRISY and ATHEÏSM, with the Gowl, SENSUALITY, stalk abroad over the Earth, and call it theirs: well at ease are the Sleepers for whom Existence is a shallow Dream.'

But what of the awestruck Wakeful who find it a Reality? Should not these unite; since even an authentic Spectre is not visible to Two?—In which case were this enormous Clothes-Volume properly an enormous Pitchpan, which our Teufelsdröckh in his lone watchtower had kindled, that it might flame far and wide through the Night, and many a disconsolately wandering spirit be guided thither to a Brother's bosom!—We say as before, with all his malign Indifference, who knows what mad Hopes this man may harbour?

Meanwhile there is one fact to be stated here, which harmonises ill with such conjecture; and, indeed, were Teufelsdröckh made like other men, might as good as altogether subvert it. Namely, that while the Beacon-fire blazed its brightest, the Watchman had quitted it; that no pilgrim could now ask him: Watchman, what of the Night? Professor Teufelsdröckh, be it known, is no longer visibly present at Weissnichtwo, but again to all appearance lost in space! Sometime ago, the Hofrath Heuschrecke was pleased to favour us with another copious Epistle; wherein much is said about the 'Population-Institute'; much repeated in praise of the Paper-bag Documents, the hieroglyphic nature of which our Hofrath still seems not to have surmised; and, lastly, the strangest occurrence communicated, to us for the first time, in the following paragraph:

'*Ew. Wohlgeboren* will have seen from the public Prints, with what affectionate and hitherto fruitless solicitude Weissnichtwo regards the disappearance of her Sage. Might but the united voice of Germany prevail on him to return; nay could we but so much as elucidate for ourselves by what mystery he went away! But, alas, old Lieschen experiences or affects the profoundest deafness, the profoundest ignorance: in the Wahngasse all lies swept, silent, sealed up; the Privy Council itself can hitherto elicit no answer.

'It had been remarked that while the agitating news of those Parisian Three Days flew from mouth to mouth, and dinned every ear in Weissnichtwo, Herr Teufelsdröckh was not known, at the *Gans* or elsewhere, to have spoken, for a whole week, any syllable except once these three: *Es geht an* (It is beginning). Shortly after, as *Ew. Wohlgeboren* knows, was the public tranquillity here, as in Berlin, threatened by a Sedition of the Tailors. Nor did there want Evil-wishers, or perhaps mere desperate Alarmists, who asserted that the closing Chapter of the Clothes-Volume was to blame. In this appalling crisis, the serenity of our Philosopher was indescribable: nay, perhaps through one humble individual, something thereof might pass into the *Rath* (Council) itself, and so contribute to the country's deliverance. The Tailors are now entirely pacificated.—

'To neither of these two incidents can I attribute our loss; yet still comes there the shadow of a suspicion out of Paris and its Politics. For example, when the *Saint-Simonian Society* transmitted its Propositions hither, and the whole *Gans* was one vast cackle of laughter, lamentation, and astonishment, our Sage sat mute; and at the end of the third evening said merely: "Here also are men who have discovered, not without amazement, that Man is still Man; of which high, long-forgotten Truth you already see them make a false application." Since then, as has been ascertained by examination of the Post-Director, there passed at least one Letter with its Answer between the Messieurs Bazard-Enfantin and our Professor himself; of what tenor can now only be conjectured. On the fifth night following, he was seen for the last time!

'Has this invaluable man, so obnoxious to most of the hostile Sects that convulse our Era, been spirited away by certain of their emissaries; or did he go forth voluntarily to their head-quarters to confer with them and confront them? Reason we have, at least of a negative sort, to believe the Lost still living; our widowed heart also whispers that ere long he will himself give a sign. Otherwise, indeed, his archives must, one day, be opened by Authority; where much, perhaps the *Palingenesie* itself, is thought to be reposited.'

Thus far the Hofrath; who vanishes, as is his wont, too like an Ignis Fatuus, leaving the dark still darker.

So that Teufelsdröckh's public History were not done, then, or reduced to an even, unromantic tenor: nay, perhaps the better part thereof were only beginning? We stand in a region of conjectures, where substance has melted into shadow, and one cannot be distinguished from the other. May Time, which solves or suppresses all problems, throw glad light on this also! Our own private conjecture, now amounting almost to certainty, is that, safe-moored in some stillest obscurity, not to lie always still, Teufelsdröckh is actually in London!

Here, however, can the present Editor, with an ambrosial joy as of over-weariness falling into sleep, lay down his pen. Well does he know, if human testimony be worth aught, that to innumerable British readers likewise, this is a satisfying consummation; that innumerable British readers consider him, during these current months, but as an uneasy interruption to their ways of thought and digestion; and indicate so much, not without a certain irritancy and even spoken invective. For which, as for other mercies, ought not he to thank the Upper Powers? To one and all of you, O irritated readers, he, with outstretched arms and open heart, will wave a kind farewell. Thou too, miraculous Entity, who namest thyself YORKE and OLIVER, and with thy vivacities and genialities, with thy all-too Irish mirth and madness, and odour of palled punch, makest such strange work, farewell; long as thou canst, fare-*well!* Have we not, in the course of Eternity, travelled some months of our Life-journey in partial sight of one another; have we not existed together, though in a state of quarrel?

APPENDIX

TESTIMONIES OF AUTHORS

[Carlyle first added this appendix to the first English edition, 1838. No. I is the opinion, possibly by John Gibson Lockhart, that caused the rejection of *Sartor* for publication in 1831; No. IV is from Emerson's preface to the first American edition.]

This questionable little Book was undoubtedly written among the mountain solitudes, in 1831; but, owing to impediments natural and accidental, could not, for seven years more, appear as a Volume in England;—and had at last to clip itself in pieces, and be content to struggle out, bit by bit, in some courageous *Magazine* that offered. Whereby now, to certain idly curious readers, and even to myself till I make study, the insignificant but at last irritating question, What its real history and chronology are, is, if not insoluble, considerably involved in haze.

To the first English Edition, 1838, which an American, or two Americans had now opened the way for, there was slightingly prefixed, under the title *'Testimonies of Authors,'* some straggle of real documents, which, now that I find it again, sets the matter into clear light and sequence;—and shall here, for removal of idle stumbling-blocks and nugatory guessings from the path of every reader, be reprinted as it stood. (*Author's Note of* 1868.)

I. Highest Class, Bookseller's Taster

Taster to Bookseller.—'The Author of *Teufelsdröckh* is a person of talent; his work displays here and there some felicity of thought and expression, considerable fancy and knowledge: but whether or not it would take with the public seems doubtful. For a *jeu d'esprit* of that kind it is too long; it would have suited better as an essay or article than as a volume. The Author has no great tact; his wit is frequently heavy; and reminds one of the German Baron who took to leaping on tables, and answered that he was learning to be lively. *Is* the work a translation?'

Bookseller to Editor.—'Allow me to say that such a writer requires only a little more tact to produce a popular as well as an able work. Directly on receiving your permission, I sent your *Ms.* to a gentleman in the highest class of men of letters, and an accomplished German scholar: I now enclose you his opinion, which, you may rely upon it, is a just one; and I have too high an opinion of your good sense to' &c. &c.—*Ms.* (*penes nos*), *London,* 17*th September* 1831.

II. Critic of the Sun

'Fraser's Magazine' exhibits the usual brilliancy, and also the' &c. 'Sartor Resartus is what old Dennis used to call "a heap of clotted nonsense," mixed however, here and there, with passages marked by thought and striking poetic vigour. But what does the writer mean by "Baphometic fire-baptism"? Why cannot he lay aside his pedantry, and write so as to make himself generally intelligible? We quote by way of curiosity a sentence from the *Sartor Resartus*; which may be read either backwards or forwards, for it is equally intelligible either way: indeed, by beginning at the tail, and so working up to the head, we think the reader will stand the fairest chance of getting at its meaning: "The fire-baptized soul, long so scathed and thunder-riven, here feels its own freedom; which feeling is its Baphometic baptism: the citadel of its whole kingdom it has thus gained by assault, and will keep inexpugnable; outwards from which the remaining dominions, not indeed without hard battering, will doubtless by degrees be conquered and pacificated." Here is a'— . . . . . —*Sun Newspaper,* 1*st April* 1834.

III. North-American Reviewer

. . . . . . 'After a careful survey of the whole ground, our belief is that no such persons as Professor Teufelsdröckh or Counsellor Heuschrecke ever existed; that the six Paperbags, with their China-ink inscriptions and multifarious contents, are a mere figment of the brain; that the "present Editor" is the only person who has ever written upon the Philosophy of Clothes; and that the *Sartor Resartus* is the only treatise that has yet appeared upon that subject;— in short, that the whole account of the origin of the work before us, which the supposed Editor relates with so much gravity, and of which we have given a brief abstract, is, in plain English, a *hum.*

'Without troubling our readers at any great length with our reasons for entertaining these suspicions, we may remark, that the absence of all other information on the subject, except what is contained in the work, is itself a fact of a most significant character. The whole German press, as well as the particular one where the work purports to have been printed, seems to be under the control of *Stillsch-weigen and Co.*—Silence and Company. If the Clothes-Philosophy and its author are making so great a sensation throughout Germany as is pretended, how happens it that the only notice we have of the fact is contained in a few numbers of a monthly Magazine published at London? How happens it that no intelligence about the matter has come out directly to this country? We pique ourselves here in New England upon knowing at least as much of what is going on in the literary way in the old Dutch Mother-land as our brethren of the fast-anchored Isle; but thus far we have no tidings whatever of the "extensive close-printed close-meditated volume," which forms the subject of this pre-tended commentary. Again, we would respectfully inquire of the "present Editor" upon what part of the map of Ger-many we are to look for the city of *Weissnichtwo*—"Know-not-where"—at which place the work is supposed to have been printed, and the Author to have resided. It has been our fortune to visit several portions of the German territory, and to examine pretty carefully, at different times and for various purposes, maps of the whole; but we have no recol-lection of any such place. We suspect that the city of *Know-not-where* might be called, with at least as much pro-priety, *Nobody-knows-where,* and is to be found in the kingdom of *Nowhere.* Again, the village of *Entepfuhl* —"Duck-pond"—where the supposed Author of the work is said to have passed his youth, and that of *Hinterschlag,* where he had his education, are equally foreign to our geography. Duck-ponds enough there undoubtedly are in almost every village in Germany, as the traveller in that country knows too well to his cost, but any particular village denominated Duck-pond is to us altogether *terra incognita.* The names of the personages are not less singular than those of the places. Who can refrain from a smile at the yoking together of such a pair of appellatives as Diogenes Teufelsdröckh? The supposed bearer of this strange title is represented as admitting, in his pretended autobiography, that "he had searched to no purpose through all the Heralds' books in and without the German empire, and through all manner of Subscribers'-lists, Militia-rolls, and other Name-catalogues," but had nowhere been able to find "the name Teufelsdröckh, except as appended to his own person." We can readily believe this, and we doubt very much whether any Christian parent would think of condemning a son to carry through life the burden of so unpleasant a title. That of Counsellor Heuschrecke—"Grasshopper"—though not offensive, looks much more like a piece of fancy work than a "fair business transaction." The same may be said of *Blumine*—"Flower-Goddess"—the heroine of the fable; and so of the rest.

'In short, our private opinion is, as we have remarked, that the whole story of a correspondence with Germany, a university of Nobody-knows-where, a Professor of Things in General, a Counsellor Grasshopper, a Flower-Goddess Blumine, and so forth, has about as much foundation in truth as the late entertaining account of Sir John Herschel's discoveries in the moon. Fictions of this kind are, however, not uncommon, and ought not, perhaps, to be condemned with too much severity; but we are not sure that we can exercise the same indulgence in regard to the attempt, which seems to be made to mislead the public as to the substance of the work before us, and its pretended German original. Both purport, as we have seen, to be upon the subject of Clothes, or dress. *Clothes, their Origin and Influence,* is the title of the supposed German treatise of Professor Teufelsdröckh, and the rather odd name of *Sartor Resartus*—the Tailor Patched—which the present Editor has affixed to his pretended commentary, seems to look the same way. But though there is a good deal of remark throughout the work in a half-serious, half-comic style upon dress, it seems to be in reality a treatise upon the great science of Things in General, which Teufelsdröckh is supposed to have professed at the university of Nobody-knows-where. Now, without intending to adopt a too rigid standard of morals, we own that we doubt a little the propriety of offering to the public a treatise on Things in General, under the name and in the form of an Essay on Dress. For ourselves, advanced as we unfortunately are in all the journey of life, far beyond the period when dress is practically a matter of interest, we have no hesitation in saying, that the real subject of the work is to us more attractive than the ostensible one. But this is probably not the case with the mass of readers. To the younger portion of the community, which constitutes everywhere the very great majority, the subject of dress is one of intense and paramount importance. An author who treats it appeals, like the poet, to the young men and maidens—*virginibus puerisque*—and calls upon them, by all the motives which habitually operate most strongly upon their feelings, to buy his book. When, after opening their purses for this purpose, they have carried home the work in triumph, expecting to find in it some particular instruction in regard to the tying of their neckcloths, or the cut of their corsets, and meet with nothing better than a dissertation on Things in General, they will—to use the mildest term—not be in very good humour. If the last improvements in legislation, which we have made in this country, should have found their way to England, the author, we think, would stand some chance of being *Lynched*. Whether his object in this piece of *supercherie* be merely pecuniary profit, or whether he takes a malicious pleasure in quizzing the Dandies, we shall not undertake to say. In the latter part of the work, he devotes a separate chapter to this class of persons, from the tenor of which we should be disposed to conclude, that he would consider any mode of divesting them of their property very much in the nature of a spoiling of the Egyptians.

'The only thing about the work, tending to prove that it is what it purports to be, a commentary on a real German treatise, is the style, which is a sort of Babylonish dialect, not destitute, it is true, of richness, vigour, and at times a sort of singular felicity of expression, but very strongly tinged throughout with the peculiar idiom of the German language. This quality in the style, however, may be a mere result of a great familiarity with German literature; and we cannot, therefore, look upon it as in itself decisive, still less as outweighing so much evidence of an opposite character.'—*North-American Review, No. 89, October* 1835.

IV. New-England Editors

'The Editors have been induced, by the express desire of many persons, to collect the following sheets out of the ephemeral pamphlets in which they first appeared, under the conviction that they contain in themselves the assurance of a longer date.

'The Editors have no expectation that this little Work will have a sudden and general popularity. They will not undertake, as there is no need, to justify the gay costume in which the Author delights to dress his thoughts, or the

German idioms with which he has sportively sprinkled his pages. It is his humour to advance the gravest speculations upon the gravest topics in a quaint and burlesque style. If his masquerade offend any of his audience, to that degree that they will not hear what he has to say, it may chance to draw others to listen to his wisdom; and what work of imagination can hope to please all? But we will venture to remark that the distaste excited by these peculiarities in some readers is greatest at first, and is soon forgotten; and that the foreign dress and aspect of the Work are quite superficial, and cover a genuine Saxon heart. We believe, no book has been published for many years, written in a more sincere style of idiomatic English, or which discovers an equal mastery over all the riches of the language. The Author makes ample amends for the occasional eccentricity of his genius, not only by frequent bursts of pure splendour, but by the wit and sense which never fail him.

'But what will chiefly commend the Book to the discerning reader is the manifest design of the work, which is, a Criticism upon the Spirit of the Age—we had almost said, of the hour—in which we live; exhibiting in the most just and novel light the present aspects of Religion, Politics, Literature, Arts, and Social Life. Under all his gaiety the Writer has an earnest meaning, and discovers an insight into the manifold wants and tendencies of human nature, which is very rare among our popular authors. The philanthropy and the purity of moral sentiment, which inspire the work, will find their way to the heart of every lover of virtue.'—*Preface to Sartor Resartus: Boston*, 1835, 1837.

SUNT, FUERUNT VEL FUERE.

London, 30th June 1838.

LETTERS ON *SARTOR RESARTUS*

[Emerson was one of the very few readers who responded favorably to *Sartor*. He had earlier recognized Carlyle's genius and in 1828 had made a special trip to remote Craigenputtock to meet him. In 1836 Emerson arranged for the first book publication of *Sartor* in Boston. The first English edition did not appear until 1838, but from the 1840s on, *Sartor* enjoyed steady popularity. The selection that follows offers an interesting insight into Carlyle's attitudes toward *Sartor* just after it was published when the general critical reaction was unfavorable.]

FROM A LETTER TO
RALPH WALDO EMERSON, *Boston*

5 Great Cheyne Row, Chelsea, London, 12 August 1834
. . . You thank me for Teufelsdröckh: how much more ought I to thank you for your hearty, genuine tho' extravagant acknowledgement of it! Blessed is the voice that amid dispiritment stupidity and contradiction proclaims to us: *Euge!* Nothing ever was more ungenial than the soil this poor Teufelsdröckhish seedcorn has been thrown on here; none cries, God speed to it; the sorriest nettle or hemlock seed, one would think, had been more welcome. For indeed our British periodical critics, and especially the public of Fraser's Magazine (which I believe I have now done with) exceed all speech; require not even contempt, only oblivion. Poor Teufelsdröckh! Creature of mischance, miscalculation, and thousandfold obstruction! Here nevertheless he is as you see; has struggled across the Stygian marshes, and now, as a stitched Pamphlet "for Friends," cannot be *burnt,* or lost—before his time. I send you one copy for your own behoof; three others you yourself can perhaps find fit readers for: as you spoke in the plural number, I thought there might be three; more would rather surprise me. From the British side of the water, I have met simply *one* intelligent response; clear, true, tho' almost enthusiastic as your own: my British Friend too is utterly a stranger, whose very name I know not, who did not print, but only write and to an *unknown* third party. Shall I say then: "In the mouth of *two* witnesses"? In any case, God be thanked, I am done with it, can wash my hands of it, and send it forth; sure that the Devil will get his full share of it, and not a whit *more,* clutch as he may. But as for you, my Transoceanic Brothers, read this earnestly, for it *was* earnestly meant and written, and contains no *voluntary* falsehood of mine. For the rest if you dislike it, say that I wrote it four years ago, and could not now so write it, and on the whole (as Fritz the Only said) "will do better another time."— With regard to style and so forth, what you call your "saucy" objections are not only most intelligible to me, but welcome

and instructive. You say well that I take up that attitude because I have no known public, am *alone* under the Heavens, speaking into friendly or unfriendly space; add only that I will not defend such attitude, that I call it questionable, tentative, and only the best that I in these mad times could conveniently hit upon. For you are to know, my view is that now at last we have lived to see all manner of Poetics and Rhetorics and Sermonics, and one may say generally all manner of *Pulpits* for addressing mankind from, as good as broken and abolished: alas, yes; if you have any earnest meaning, which demands to be not only listened to but *believed* and *done,* you cannot (at least I cannot) utter it *there,* but the sound sticks in my throat, as when a Solemnity were *felt* to have become a Mummery; and so one leaves the pasteboard coulisses, and three unities, and Blair's lectures, quite behind; and feels only that there is *nothing sacred,* then, but the *Speech of Man* to believing Men! *This,* come what will, was, is, and forever must be *sacred;* and will one day doubtless anew environ itself with fit modes, with Solemnities that are *not* Mummeries. Meanwhile, however, is it not pitiable? For tho' Teufelsdröckh exclaims: "Pulpit! canst thou not *make* a pulpit, by simply *inverting the nearest tub*"; yet alas he does not sufficiently reflect that it is still only a *tub,* that the most inspired utterance will come from *it,* inconceivable, misconceivable to the million; questionable (not of *ascertained* significance) even to the few. Pity us therefore; and with your just shake of the head join a sympathetic even a hopeful smile. Since I saw you, I have been trying and still trying, other methods, and shall surely get nearer the truth, as I honestly strive for it. Meanwhile I know no method of much consequence, except that of *believing,* of being sincere: from *Homer* and the *Bible* down to the poorest Burns's *Song* I find no other *Art* that promises to be perennial. . . .

[The following letter is Carlyle's reply to criticisms of *Sartor Resartus* from John Sterling, Carlyle's friend and a leading intellectual figure of the day. After Sterling's death Carlyle wrote a biography of him. See the references to Sterling below in Carlyle's letter of 1844 and in the selection from the *Reminiscences.*]

LETTER TO JOHN STERLING,

Herstmonceux, Sussex

5 Cheyne Row, Chelsea, 4 June 1835

My dear Sterling,

I said to Mill the other day that your Name was Hopeful; of which truth surely this copious refreshing shower of really kind and genial criticism you have bestowed on the hardened, kiln-burnt, altogether contradictory Professor Teufelsdröckh, is new proof. Greater faith I have not found in Israel! Neither here shall faith and hope wholly fail: know, my Friend, that your shower does not fall as on mere barren bricks, like water spilt on the ground; that I take it hopefully in, with great desire (knowing what spirit it is of) to *assimilate* such portion of it as the nature of things will allow. So much, on this sheet, I must announce to you, were it at full gallop, and in the most imperfect words.

Your objections as to phraseology and style have good grounds to stand on; many of them indeed are considerations to which I myself was not blind; which there (unluckily) were no means of doing more than nodding to as one passed. A man has but a certain strength; imperfections cling to him, which if he wait till he have brushed off entirely, he will spin forever on his axis, advancing nowhither. Know thy thought, *believe* it; front Heaven and Earth with it,—in whatsoever *words,* Nature and Art have made readiest for thee! If one has thoughts not hitherto uttered in English Books, I see nothing for it but that you must use words not found there, must *make* words,—with moderation and discretion, of course. That I have not always done it *so,* proves only that I was not strong enough; an accusation to which I for one will never plead not guilty. For the rest, pray that I may have more and more strength! Surely too, as I said, all these *coal-marks* of yours shall be duly considered, for the first and even for the second time, and help me on my way. With unspeakable cheerfulness I give up *"Talented"*: indeed, but for the plain statement you make, I could have sworn such word had never, except for parodistic, ironical purposes, risen from my inkhorn, or passed my lips. Too much evil can hardly be said of it: while speech of it at all is necessary.—But finally, do you reckon this really a time for Purism of Style; or that Style (mere dictionary Style) has much to do with the worth or un-worth of a Book? I do not: with whole ragged battalions of Scott's-Novel Scotch, with Irish, German, French, and even Newspaper Cockney (when "Literature" is little other than a Newspaper) storming in on us, and the whole structure of our Johnsonian English breaking up from its foundations, —revolution *there* as visible as anywhere else!

You ask, How it comes that none of the "leading minds" of this country (if one knew where to find them) have given the "Clothes-Philosophy" any response? Why, my good friend, not one of them has had the happiness of seeing it! It issued thro' one of the main *cloacas* of Periodi-cal Literature, where no leading mind, I fancy, looks, if he can help it: the poor Book cannot be destroyed by fire or other violence now, but solely by the *general* law of Destiny; and I have nothing more to do with it henceforth. How it chanced that no Bookseller would print it (in an epoch when Satan Montgomery runs, or seems to run, thro' thirteen editions), and the morning Papers (on its issuing thro' the *cloaca*) sang together in mere discord over such a creation: this truly is a question, but a different one. Mean-while, do not suppose the poor Book has *not* been responded to; for the historical fact is, I could show very curious re-sponse to it here; not ungratifying, and fully three times as much as I counted on, as the wretched farrago itself de-served.

You say finally, as the key to the whole mystery, that Teufelsdröckh does not believe in a "personal God." It is frankly said, with a friendly honesty for which I love you. A grave charge nevertheless, an *awful* charge: to which, if I mistake not, the Professor, laying his hand on his heart, will reply with some gesture expressing the solemnest *denial*. In gesture, rather than in speech; for "the Highest *cannot* be spoken of in words." *"Personal,"* "impersonal," One, Three, *what* meaning can any mortal (after all) attach to them in reference to such an object? *Wer darf ihn* NENNEN? I dare not, and do not. That you dare and do (to some greater extent) is a matter I am far from taking offence at: nay, with all sincerity, I can rejoice that you have a creed of that kind, which gives you happy thoughts, nerves you for good actions, brings you into readier communion with many good men; my true wish is that such creed may long hold compactly together in you, and be "a covert from the

342 / A CARLYLE READER

heat, a shelter from the storm, as the shadow of a great rock in a weary land." Well is it if we have a printed Litany to pray from; and yet not ill if we *can* pray even in *silence,* for silence too is audible *there.* Finally, assure yourself, I am neither Pagan nor Turk, not circumcised Jew, but an unfortunate Christian individual resident at Chelsea in *this* year of Grace; neither Pantheist nor Pottheist, nor any Theist or *ist* whatsoever, having the most decided contempt for all manner of Systembuilders and Sectfounders—so far as contempt may be compatible with so mild a nature; feeling well beforehand (taught by experience) that all such are and even must be *wrong.* By God's blessing, one has got two eyes to look with; and also a mind capable of knowing, of believing: that is all the creed I will at this time insist on. And now may I beg one thing: that whenever in my thoughts or your own you fall on any dogma that tends to estrange you from me, pray believe *that* to be *false;*—false as Beelzebub till you get clearer evidence.

However, descending from the Empyrean to London pavements, let me tell you that I am actually bestirring myself to try whether the people will give me any employment in this matter of National Education. Mill and some others undertake to help me, but have not reported yet. It is a confused business; out of which darkness is rayed forth on me hitherto. If we fail in it, there is some likelihood I may cross the Atlantic soon. The Book-trade seems to me *done* here: a man must go where his work lies, where they will keep him in existence for his work.

Your good Mother shocked us a little by the news that your return hither was uncertain. We will still hope to see you ere long. May you come for the better, not for the worse, when you do come! That is very sincerely my prayer; for I do believe you to be a very honest fellow; and, alas, I have never known Destiny too kind to such. God bless you and guide you!

I remain always,

Yours with great sincerity,

T. Carlyle.

LETTERS ON
THE FRENCH REVOLUTION

[Carlyle's oft-quoted statement that *The French Revolution* was a book that came "flamingly from the heart" probably has something to do with the fact that it was largely a twice-written book, the second time under very painful circumstances. The completed manuscript of half of the three-volume work was given to John Stuart Mill to read. What happened is told in the following selections from Carlyle's letters. Other versions of the story say the manuscript was burnt. See the selection from *Reminiscences* below.]

FROM A LETTER TO HIS MOTHER
Scotsbrig

Chelsea, 25 March 1835

. . . I had some occasion lately for a portion of your faith; in a most unexpected *accident* (what we call *accident*) that befell me; of which I delayed writing till I could not only say that I *would* get over it, but that I had got over it. Be of good cheer, therefore, as to that: it is all right (and for the best, I am persuaded); and you shall now hear about it fully. To sum up all in a word: the *First Volume* of my poor Book is utterly destroyed! Mill, to whom I had lent it to read, and write Notes on (for he is skilled in that subject), and who was full of admiration for the bit of work, had left it carelessly out in his house: some of the people saw it lying; tore it up as waste paper; and when he noticed it, there were only some three or four fractions of leaves remaining. He came hither to me, in a state looking not unlike insanity; and gasped out (for he could hardly speak) his Job's news. I am very glad that I got it borne so well; for it was a hard thing. It never got the better of me; and by next morning the bitterness of it was all over; and I had determined that there must be a finger of Providence in it; that it meant simply I was to write the thing over again *truer* than it was. My little Dame stood faithfully by me too, and was very good and brave. Having finished out the new Chapter I was upon therefore, I resolutely turned back to the beginning again; and have this day finished the First Chapter of all a second time, certainly no *worse* than it

343

was; a thing that gives me great comfort, for I now find that I *can* do it; of which, before trial (so *irksome* was the business), I had no certainty, except in the determination to "*gar* myself do it." . . . I do really believe the Book will be the better.—I must not forget to say that poor Mill next day sent a passionate entreaty to be allowed to pay me, what money could pay; to which I, as to a reasonable thing, acceded; and so he sent me soon after a Draught for £200, —which however I returned the same day saying it was just *twice* the sum due. I have seen Mill since, and we talked of it; he this day sends me another Letter still wishing I would stand by the original sum, or some intermediate one: but I had explained to him that £100 was fully my expenses during the time of writing the thing; and so I fancy we will still adhere to that computation; for if any one had asked me to throw the writing into the fire, and said, What would I take? I could have given him no definite answer—except that I would be *ill, ill indeed* to deal with. In this rather handsome way, has the matter been brought to a bearing. One other thing I proposed that it should never *be spoken of* (except to you and Jack and the kindred) till it was all made good again. . . .

[Following is the letter Carlyle wrote to Mill the day after Mill told him of the catastrophe with the manuscript.]

LETTER TO JOHN STUART MILL
India House

Chelsea, [7 March 1835]

My dear Mill,

How are you? You left me last night with a look which I shall not soon forget. Is there anything that I could do or suffer or say to alleviate you? For I feel that your sorrow must be far sharper than *mine;* yours bound to be a *passive* one. How true is this of Richter: "*All* Evil is like a nightmare; the instant you begin to *stir* under it, it is *gone.*"

I have ordered a *Biographie Universelle,* this morning; —and a better sort of paper. Thus, far from giving up the game, you see, I am risking another £10 on it. Courage, my Friend!

That I can never write *that* Volume again is indubitable: singular enough, the whole Earth could not get *it* back; but only a better or a worse one. There is the strangest dimness over it. A figure thrown into the melting-pot; but the metal (all that was golden or gold-like of that,—and *copper,* can be gathered) is there; the model also *is,* in my head. O my Friend, how easily might the bursting of some puny ligament or filament have abolished all light *there* too!

That I *can* write a Book on the French Revolution is (God be thanked for it) as clear to me as ever; also that if life be given me so long, I will. To it again, therefore! *Andar con Dios!*

I think you once said you could borrow me a *Campan?* Have you any more of *Lacretelle's* things; his 18me *Siècle?* (that is of almost no moment) The first vol. of *Genlis's Mém.?* Etc. But I find *Campan* (if I get the *Biographie*) is the only one I shall really want much. Had I been a *trained* Compiler, I should not have wanted that. To make some search for it, I know, will be a kind of solace to you.

Thanks to Mrs. Taylor for her kind sympathies. May God guide, and bless you both! That is my true prayer.

Ever your affectionate Friend,
T. Carlyle.

FROM *The French Revolution*

1837

[The French Revolution is a great watershed of modern times and its meaning a standing challenge to the historian. The Revolution had initially sparked the enthusiasm of such men as the English romantics, then soured them by its excesses. Since Burke's *Reflections on the Revolution in France* (1795), which painted in somber hues the consequences of Jacobinism, no major English author had attempted to assess the Revolution. But its shadow was cast athwart the entire nineteenth century. Carlyle took up the challenge and wrote a history and assessment of the cataclysm. His history—remarkably accurate as history, given the materials available to him—has more often been likened to poetry, especially epic poetry. Following his own theory of history, Carlyle sought to place the Revolution in its world-historical context, to show it as a kind of divine judgment upon a society gone astray. He was severe in condemning the selfish, game-preserving aristocracy of eighteenth-century France and equally severe in depicting the horrors of anarchy and mob rule. Here, as everywhere, Carlyle sought to fathom the role of the divine in history, to show men of all social stations that judgment may be delayed but can never be averted. In so doing he found the perfect correlative for his thunderous and portentous style. The work strikes the reader not only as history, but as poetry, as prophecy, and as inspiration.

The French Revolution was published in 1837 in three volumes, each containing six to seven "books" of from four to twelve chapters each, for a total of more than 300,000 words. It was the first work to appear with Carlyle's name on the title page. The work proceeds chronologically, from the death of Louis XV (1774) to Vendémiaire (October) of 1795. The selections printed here constitute whole chapters from each of the volumes, showing the range of Carlyle's coverage of the revolution, from his treatment of the theories of the age to portraits of principal participants, to the picture of the revolution devouring its own children. Carlyle's commentary footnotes on the text have been retained, but his documentary references to texts consulted have been omitted. Dates given at the beginning of each chapter are expansions of Carlyle's abbreviated running dates for each chapter; they include dates on the Christian calendar and, after 1792, dates by the revolutionary calendar (beginning year one of the Revolution September 22, 1792).]

FROM VOLUME I, BOOK II—THE PAPER
AGE / CHAPTER I

ASTRÆA REDUX

[1 7 7 4-1 7 8 4]

A paradoxical philosopher, carrying to the uttermost length
that aphorism of Montesquieu's, 'Happy the people whose
annals are tiresome,' has said, 'Happy the people whose
annals are vacant.' In which saying, mad as it looks, may
there not still be found some grain of reason? For truly,
as it has been written, 'Silence is divine,' and of Heaven; so
in all earthly things too there is a silence which is better
than any speech. Consider it well, the Event, the thing
which can be spoken of and recorded, is it not, in all cases,
some disruption, some solution of continuity? Were it even
a glad Event, it involves change, involves loss (of active
Force); and so far, either in the past or in the present, is
an irregularity, a disease. Stillest perseverance were our
blessedness; not dislocation and alternation,—could they
be avoided.

The oak grows silently, in the forest, a thousand years;
only in the thousandth year, when the woodman arrives
with his axe, is there heard an echoing through the solitudes; and the oak announces itself when, with far-sound-
ing crash, it *falls.* How silent too was the planting of the
acorn; scattered from the lap of some wandering wind!
Nay, when our oak flowered, or put on its leaves (its glad
Events), what shout of proclamation could there be? Hardly
from the most observant a word of recognition. These
things *befell* not, they were slowly *done*; not in an hour,
but through the flight of days: what was to be said of it?
This hour seemed altogether as the last was, as the next
would be.

It is thus everywhere that foolish Rumour babbles not
of what was done, but of what was misdone or undone;
and foolish History (ever, more or less, the written epito-
mised synopsis of Rumour) knows so little that were not
as well unknown. Attila Invasions, Walter-the-Penniless
Crusades, Sicilian Vespers, Thirty-Years Wars: mere sin

and misery; not work, but hindrance of work! For the Earth, all this while, was yearly green and yellow with her kind harvests; the hand of the craftsman, the mind of the thinker rested not: and so, after all, and in spite of all, we have this so glorious high-domed blossoming World; concerning which, poor History may well ask, with wonder, Whence *it* came? She knows so little of it, knows so much of what obstructed it, what would have rendered it impossible. Such, nevertheless, by necessity or foolish choice, is her rule and practice; whereby that paradox, 'Happy the people whose annals are vacant,' is not without its true side.

And yet, what seems more pertinent to note here, there is a stillness, not of unobstructed growth, but of passive inertness, the symptom of imminent downfall. As victory is silent, so is defeat. Of the opposing forces the weaker has resigned itself; the stronger marches on, noiseless now, but rapid, inevitable: the fall and overturn will not be noiseless. How all grows, and has its period, even as the herbs of the fields, be it annual, centennial, millennial! All grows and dies, each by its own wondrous laws, in wondrous fashion of its own; spiritual things most wondrously of all. Inscrutable, to the wisest, are these latter; not to be prophesied of, or understood. If when the oak stands proudliest flourishing to the eye, you know that its heart is sound, it is not so with the man; how much less with the Society, with the Nation of men! Of such it may be affirmed even that the superficial aspect, that the inward feeling of full health, is generally ominous. For indeed it is of apoplexy, so to speak, and a plethoric lazy habit of body, that Churches, Kingships, Social Institutions, oftenest die. Sad, when such Institution plethorically says to itself, Take thy ease, thou hast goods laid up;—like the fool of the Gospel, to whom it was answered, Fool, *this night* thy life shall be required of thee!

Is it the healthy peace, or the ominous unhealthy, that rests on France, for these next Ten Years? Over which the Historian can· pass lightly, without call to linger: for as yet events are not, much less performances. Time of sunniest stillness;—shall we call it, what all men thought it, the new Age of Gold? Call it at least, of Paper; which in many ways is the succedaneum of Gold. Bank-paper, wherewith you can still buy when there is no gold left; Book-paper, splen-

dent with Theories, Philosophies, Sensibilities,—beautiful
art, not only of revealing Thought, but also of so beautifully hiding from us the want of Thought! Paper is made
from the *rags* of things that did once exist; there are endless excellences in Paper.—What wisest Philosophe, in this
halcyon uneventful period, could prophesy that there was
approaching, big with darkness and confusion, the event of
events? Hope ushers in a Revolution,—as earthquakes are
preceded by bright weather. On the Fifth of May, fifteen
years hence, old Louis will not be sending for the Sacra-
ments; but a new Louis, his grandson, with the whole pomp
of astonished intoxicated France, will be opening the States-
General.

Dubarrydom and its D'Aiguillons are gone for ever.
There is a young, still docile, well-intentioned King; a
young, beautiful and bountiful, well-intentioned Queen;
and with them all France, as it were, become young.
Maupeou and his Parlement have to vanish into thick
night; respectable Magistrates, not indifferent to the Nation, were it only for having been opponents of the Court,
descend now unchained from their 'steep rocks at Croe in
Combrailles' and elsewhere, and return singing praises: the
old Parlement of Paris resumes its functions. Instead of
a profligate bankrupt Abbé Terray, we have now, for Con-
troller-General, a virtuous philosophic Turgot, with a
whole Reformed France in his head. By whom whatsoever
is wrong, in Finance or otherwise, will be righted,—as far
as possible. Is it not as if Wisdom herself were henceforth
to have seat and voice in the Council of Kings? Turgot has
taken office with the noblest plainness of speech to that
effect; been listened to with the noblest royal trustfulness.[1]
It is true, as King Louis objects, 'They say he never goes
to mass'; but liberal France likes him little worse for that;
liberal France answers, 'The Abbé Terray always went.'
Philosophism sees, for the first time, a Philosophe (or even
a Philosopher) in office: she in all things will applausively
second him; neither will light old Maurepas obstruct, if
he can easily help it.
    Then how 'sweet' are the manners; vice 'losing all its
deformity'; becoming *decent* (as established things, making

[1] The date is 24th August 1774. [Carlyle's note.]

regulations for themselves, do); becoming almost a kind of 'sweet' virtue! Intelligence so abounds; irradiated by wit and the art of conversation. Philosophism sits joyful in her glittering saloons, the dinner-guest of Opulence grown ingenuous, the very nobles proud to sit by her; and preaches, lifted up over all Bastilles, a coming millennium. From far Ferney, Patriarch Voltaire gives sign: veterans Diderot, D'Alembert have lived to see this day; these with their younger Marmontels, Morellets, Chamforts, Raynals, make glad the spicy board of rich ministering Dowager, of philosophic Farmer-General. O nights and suppers of the gods! Of a truth, the long-demonstrated will now be done: 'the Age of Revolutions approaches' (as Jean Jacques wrote), but then of happy blessed ones. Man awakens from his long somnambulism; chases the Phantasms that beleaguered and bewitched him. Behold the new morning glittering down the eastern steeps; fly, false Phantasms, from its shafts of light; let the Absurd fly utterly, forsaking this lower Earth for ever. It is Truth and *Astræa Redux* that (in the shape of Philosophism) henceforth reign. For what imaginable purpose was man made, if not to be 'happy'? By victorious Analysis, and Progress of the Species, happiness enough now awaits him. Kings can become philosophers; or else philosophers Kings. Let but Society be once rightly constituted,—by victorious Analysis. The stomach that is empty shall be filled; the throat that is dry shall be wetted with wine. Labour itself shall be all one as rest; not grievous, but joyous. Wheat-fields, one would think, cannot come to grow untilled; no man made clayey, or made weary thereby;—unless indeed machinery will do it? Gratuitous Tailors and Restaurateurs may start up, at fit intervals, one as yet sees not how. But if each will, according to rule of Benevolence, have a care for all, then surely—no one will be uncared for. Nay, who knows but, by sufficiently victorious Analysis, 'human life may be indefinitely lengthened,' and men get rid of Death, as they have already done of the Devil? We shall then be happy in spite of Death and the Devil.—So preaches magniloquent Philosophism her *Redeunt Saturnia regna*.

The prophetic song of Paris and its Philosophes is audible enough in the Versailles Œil-de-Bœuf; and the Œil-de-Bœuf, intent chiefly on nearer blessedness, can answer, at worst, with a polite 'Why not?' Good old cheery Maurepas is too joyful a Prime Minister to dash the world's joy. Sufficient for the day be its own evil. Cheery old man, he cuts his jokes, and hovers careless along; his cloak well adjusted to the wind, if so be he may please all persons. The simple young King, whom a Maurepas cannot think of troubling with business, has retired into the interior apartments; taciturn, irresolute; though with a sharpness of temper at times: he, at length, determines on a little smith-work; and so, in apprenticeship with a Sieur Gamain (whom one day he shall have little cause to bless), is learning to make locks. It appears further, he understood Geography; and could read English. Unhappy young King, his childlike trust in that foolish old Maurepas deserved another return. But friend and foe, destiny and himself have combined to do him hurt.

Meanwhile the fair young Queen, in her halls of state, walks like a goddess of Beauty, the cynosure of all eyes; as yet mingles not with affairs; heeds not the future; least of all, dreads it. Weber and Campan have pictured her, there within the royal tapestries, in bright boudoirs, baths, peignoirs, and the Grand and Little Toilette; with a whole brilliant world waiting obsequious on her glance: fair young daughter of Time, what things has Time in store for thee! Like Earth's brightest Appearance, she moves gracefully, environed with grandeur of Earth: a reality, and yet a magic vision; for, behold, shall not utter Darkness swallow it! The soft young heart adopts orphans, portions meritorious maids, delights to succour the poor,—such poor as come picturesquely in her way; and sets the fashion of doing it; for, as was said, Benevolence has now begun reigning. In her Duchess de Polignac, in her Princess de Lamballe, she enjoys something almost like friendship: now too, after seven long years, she has a child, and soon even a Dauphin, of her own; can reckon herself, as Queens go, happy in a husband.

Events? The grand events are but charitable Feasts of Morals (*Fêtes des mœurs*), with their Prizes and Speeches; Poissarde Processions to the Dauphin's cradle; above all, Flirtations, their rise, progress, decline and fall. There are Snow-statues raised by the poor in hard winter to a Queen who has given them fuel. There are masquerades, theatricals; beautifyings of little Trianon, purchase and repair of St. Cloud; journeyings from the summer Court-Elysium to the winter one. There are poutings and grudgings from the Sardinian Sisters-in-law (for the Princes too are wedded); little jealousies, which Court-Etiquette can moderate. Wholly the lightest-hearted frivolous foam of Existence; yet an artfully refined foam; pleasant were it not so costly, like that which mantles on the wine of Champagne!

Monsieur, the King's elder Brother, has set up for a kind of wit; and leans towards the Philosophe side. Monseigneur d'Artois pulls the mask from a fair impertinent; fights a duel in consequence,—almost drawing blood. He has breeches of a kind new in this world;—a fabulous kind; 'four tall lackeys,' says Mercier, as if he had seen it, 'hold him up in the air, that he may fall into the garment without vestige of wrinkle; from which rigorous encasement the same four, in the same way, and with more effort, have to deliver him at night.' This last is he who now, as a grey timeworn man, sits desolate at Grätz; having winded up his destiny with the Three Days. In such sort are poor mortals swept and shovelled to and fro.

CHAPTER VII

CONTRAT SOCIAL

[1 7 8 1-1 7 8 8]

In such succession of singular prismatic tints, flush after flush suffusing our horizon, does the Era of Hope dawn on towards fulfilment. Questionable! As indeed, with an Era of Hope that rests on mere universal Benevolence, victorious Analysis, Vice cured of its deformity; and, in the long-run, on Twenty-five dark savage Millions, looking up, in hunger and weariness, to that *Ecce-signum* of theirs 'forty feet high,'—how could it but be questionable?

Through all time, if we read aright, sin was, is, will be, the parent of misery. This land calls itself most Christian, and has crosses and cathedrals; but its High-priest is some Roche-Aymon, some Necklace-Cardinal Louis de Rohan. The voice of the poor, through long years, ascends inarticulate, in *Jacqueries*, meal-mobs; low-whimpering of infinite moan: unheeded of the Earth; not unheeded of Heaven. Always moreover where the Millions are wretched, there are the Thousands straitened, unhappy; only the Units can flourish; or say rather, be ruined the last. Industry, all noosed and haltered, as if it too were some beast of chase for the mighty hunters of this world to bait, and cut slices from,—cries passionately to these its well-paid guides and watchers, not, *Guide me*; but, *Laissez faire,* Leave me alone of *your* guidance! What market has Industry in this France? For two things there may be market and demand: for the coarser kind of field-fruits, since the Millions will live: for the finer kinds of luxury and spicery,—of multiform taste, from opera-melodies down to racers and courtesans; since the Units will be amused. It is at bottom but a mad state of things.

To mend and remake all which we have, indeed, victorious Analysis. Honour to victorious Analysis; nevertheless, out of the Workshop and Laboratory, what thing was victorious Analysis yet known to make? Detection of incoherences, mainly; destruction of the incoherent. From of old, Doubt was but half a magician; she evokes the spectres which she cannot quell. We shall have 'endless vortices of froth-logic'; whereon first words, and then things, are whirled and swallowed. Remark, accordingly, as acknowledged grounds of Hope, at bottom mere precursors of Despair, this perpetual theorising about Man, the Mind of Man, Philosophy of Government, Progress of the Species and such-like; the main thinking furniture of every head. Time, and so many Montesquieus, Mablys, spokesmen of Time, have discovered innumerable things: and now has not Jean Jacques promulgated his new Evangel of a *Contrat Social*; explaining the whole mystery of Government, and how it is *contracted* and bargained for,—to universal satisfaction? Theories of Government! Such have been, and will be; in ages of decadence. Acknowledge them in their degree; as processes of Nature, who does nothing in vain; as steps in her great process. Meanwhile, what theory is so certain as this, That all theories, were they never so earnest, painfully elaborated, are, and, by the very conditions of them, must be incomplete, questionable, and even false? Thou shalt know that this Universe is, what it professes to be, an *infinite* one. Attempt not to swallow *it,* for thy logical digestion; be thankful, if skilfully planting down this and the other fixed pillar in the chaos, thou prevent its swallowing *thee*. That a new young generation has exchanged the Sceptic Creed, *What shall I believe?* for pas-

sionate Faith in this Gospel according to Jean Jacques is a
further step in the business; and betokens much.

Blessed also is Hope; and always from the beginning
there was some Millennium prophesied; Millennium of Holiness; but (what is notable) never till this new Era, any
Millennium of mere Ease and plentiful Supply. In such
prophesied Lubberland, of Happiness, Benevolence, and Vice
cured of its deformity, trust not, my friends! Man is not
what one calls a happy animal; his appetite for sweet victual is so enormous. How, in this wild Universe, which
storms in on him, infinite, vague-menacing, shall poor
man find, say not happiness, but existence, and footing to
stand on, if it be not by girding himself together for continual endeavour and endurance? Wo, if in his heart there
dwelt no devout Faith; if the word Duty had lost its meaning for him! For as to this of Sentimentalism, so useful for
weeping with over romances and on pathetic occasions, it
otherwise verily will avail nothing; nay less. The healthy
heart that said to itself, 'How healthy am I!' was already
fallen into the fatalest sort of disease. Is not Sentimentalism
twin-sister to Cant, if not one and the same with it? Is not
Cant the *materia prima* of the Devil; from which all false-
hoods, imbecilities, abominations body themselves; from
which no true thing *can* come? For Cant is itself properly
a double-distilled Lie; the second-power of a Lie.

And now if a whole Nation fall into that? In such case, I
answer, infallibly they will return out of it! For life is no
cunningly-devised deception or self-deception: it is a great
truth that thou art alive, that thou hast desires, necessities;
neither can these subsist and satisfy themselves on delusions, but on fact. To fact, depend on it, we shall come
back: to such fact, blessed or cursed, as we have wisdom
for. The lowest, least blessed fact one knows of, on which
necessitous mortals have ever based themselves, seems to
be the primitive one of Cannibalism: That *I* can devour
Thee. What if such Primitive Fact were precisely the one
we had (with our improved methods) to revert to, and begin anew from!

FROM VOLUME I, BOOK VII—THE IN-
SURRECTION OF WOMEN / CHAPTER IV

THE MENADS

[October 5, 1789]

If Voltaire once, in splenetic humour, asked his countrymen: 'But you, *Gualches,* what have you invented?' they
can now answer: The Art of Insurrection. It was an art
needed in these last singular times: an art for which
the French nature, so full of vehemence, so free from
depth, was perhaps of all others the fittest.

Accordingly, to what a height, one may well say of perfection, has this branch of human industry been carried by
France, within the last half-century! Insurrection, which
Lafayette thought might be 'the most sacred of duties,'
ranks now, for the French people, among the duties which
they can perform. Other mobs are dull masses; which roll
onwards with a dull fierce heat, but emit no light-flashes
of genius as they go. The French mob, again, is among the
liveliest phenomena of our world. So rapid, audacious; so
clear-sighted, inventive, prompt to seize the moment; instinct with life to its finger-ends! That talent, were there
no other, of spontaneously standing in queue, distinguishes,
as we said, the French People from all Peoples, ancient
and modern.

Let the Reader confess too that, taking one thing with
another, perhaps few terrestrial Appearances are better
worth considering than mobs. Your mob is a genuine outburst of Nature; issuing from, or communicating with, the
deepest deep of Nature. When so much goes grinning and
grimacing as a lifeless Formality, and under the stiff buckram no heart can be felt beating, here once more, if nowhere else, is a Sincerity and Reality. Shudder at it; or
even shriek over it, if thou must; nevertheless consider it.
Such a Complex of human Forces and Individualities
hurled forth, in their transcendental mood, to act and re-
act, on circumstances and on one another; to work out
what it is in them to work. The thing they will do is known
to no man; least of all to themselves. It is the inflamma-

blest immeasurable Firework, generating, consuming itself. With what phases, to what extent, with what results it
will burn off, Philosophy and Perspicacity conjecture in
vain.

'Man,' as has been written, 'is for ever interesting to
man; nay properly there is nothing else interesting.' In
which light also may we not discern why most Battles have
become so wearisome? Battles, in these ages, are transacted
by mechanism; with the slightest possible development of
human individuality or spontaneity: men now even die,
and kill one another, in an artificial manner. Battles ever
since Homer's time, when they were Fighting Mobs, have
mostly ceased to be worth looking at, worth reading of or
remembering. How many wearisome bloody Battles does
History strive to represent; or even, in a husky way, to
sing:—and she would omit or carelessly slur-over this one
Insurrection of Women?

A thought, or dim raw-material of a thought, was fer-
menting all night, universally in the female head, and might
explode. In squalid garret, on Monday morning, Maternity
awakes, to hear children weeping for bread. Maternity
must forth to the streets, to the herb-markets and Bakers'-
queues; meets there with hunger-stricken Maternity, sympathetic, exasperative. O we unhappy women! But, instead
of Bakers'-queues, why not to Aristocrats' palaces, the root
of the matter? *Allons!* Let us assemble. To the Hôtel-de-
Ville; to Versailles; to the Lanterne!

In one of the Guardhouses of the Quartier Saint-Eustache,
'a young woman' seizes a drum—for how shall National
Guards give fire on women, on a young woman? The young
woman seizes the drum; sets forth, beating it, 'uttering cries
relative to the dearth of grains.' Descend, O mothers; descend, ye Judiths, to food and revenge!—All women gather
and go; crowds storm all stairs, force out all women: the
female Insurrectionary Force, according to Camille, resembles the English Naval one; there is a universal 'Press
of women.' Robust Dames of the Halle, slim Mantuamak-
ers, assiduous, risen with the dawn; ancient Virginity trip-
ping to matins; the Housemaid, with early broom; all
must go. Rouse ye, O women; the laggard men will not
act; they say, we ourselves may act!

And so, like snowbreak from the mountains, for every

staircase is a melted brook, it storms; tumultuous, wild-shrilling, towards the Hôtel-de-Ville. Tumultuous; with or without drum-music: for the Faubourg Saint-Antoine also has tucked-up its gown; and with besom-staves, fire-irons, and even rusty pistols (void of ammunition), is flowing on. Sound of it flies, with a velocity of sound, to the utmost Barriers. By seven o'clock, on this raw October morning, fifth of the month, the Townhall will see wonders. Nay, as chance would have it, a male party are already there; clustering tumultuously round some National Patrol, and a Baker who has been seized with short weights. They are there; and have even lowered the rope of the Lanterne. So that the official persons have to smuggle forth the short-weighing Baker by back-doors, and even send 'to all the Districts' for more force.

Grand it was, says Camille, to see so many Judiths, from eight to ten thousand of them in all, rushing out to search into the root of the matter! Not unfrightful it must have been; ludicro-terrific, and most unmanageable. At such hour the overwatched Three Hundred are not yet stirring: none but some Clerks, a company of National Guards; and M. de Gouvion, the Major-general. Gouvion has fought in America for the cause of civil Liberty; a man of no inconsiderable heart, but deficient in head. He is, for the moment, in his back apartment; assuaging Usher Maillard, the Bastille-sergeant, who has come, as too many do, with 'representations.' The assuagement is still incomplete when our Judiths arrive.

The National Guards form on the outer stairs with levelled bayonets; the ten thousand Judiths press up, resistless; with obtestations, with outspread hands,—merely to speak to the Mayor. The rear forces them; nay from male hands in the rear, stones already fly: the National Guard must do one of two things; sweep the Place de Grève with cannon, or else open to right and left. They open; the living deluge rushes in. Through all rooms and cabinets, upwards to the topmost belfry: ravenous; seeking arms, seeking Mayors, seeking justice;—while, again, the better-dressed speak kindly to the Clerks; point out the misery of these poor women; also their ailments, some even of an interesting sort.

Poor M. de Gouvion is shiftless in this extremity;—a man shiftless, perturbed: who will one day commit suicide. How happy for him that Usher Maillard the shifty was there, at the moment, though making representations! Fly back, thou shifty Maillard: seek the Bastille Company; and O return fast with it; above all, with thy own shifty head. For, behold, the Judiths can find no Mayor or Municipal; scarcely, in the topmost belfry, can they find poor Abbé Lefèvre the Powder-distributor. Him, for want of a better, they suspend there: in the pale morning light; over the top of all Paris, which swims in one's failing eyes:—a horrible end? Nay the rope broke, as French ropes often did; or else an Amazon cut it. Abbé Lefèvre falls, some twenty feet, rattling among the leads; and lives long years after, though always with 'a *tremblement* in the limbs.'

And now doors fly under hatchets; the Judiths have broken the Armory; have seized guns and cannons, three money-bags, paper-heaps; torches flare: in few minutes, our brave Hôtel-de-Ville, which dates from the Fourth Henry, will, with all that it holds, be in flames!

FROM VOLUME II, BOOK III—THE TUILERIES / CHAPTER VII

DEATH OF MIRABEAU

[March-April 1791]

But Mirabeau could not live another year, any more than he could live another thousand years. Men's years are numbered, and the tale of Mirabeau's was now complete. Important or unimportant; to be mentioned in World-History for some centuries, or not to be mentioned there beyond a day or two,—it matters not to peremptory Fate. From amid the press of ruddy busy Life, the Pale Messenger beckons silently: wide-spreading interests, projects, salvation of French Monarchies, what thing soever man has on hand, he must suddenly quit it all, and go. Wert thou saving French Monarchies; wert thou blacking shoes on the Pont Neuf! The most important of men cannot stay; did the World's History depend on an hour, that hour is not to be given. Whereby, indeed, it comes that these same *would-have-beens* are mostly a vanity; and the World's History could never in the least be what it would, or might, or should, by any manner of potentiality, but simply and altogether what it *is*.

The fierce wear and tear of such an existence has wasted out the giant oaken strength of Mirabeau. A fret and fever that keeps heart and brain on fire: excess of effort, of excitement; excess of all kinds: labour incessant, almost beyond credibility! 'If I had not lived with him,' says Dumont, 'I never should have known what a man can make of one day; what things may be placed within the interval of twelve hours. A day for this man was more than a week or a month is for others: the mass of things he guided on together was prodigious; from the scheming to the executing not a moment lost.'—'Monsieur le Comte,' said his Secretary to him once, 'what you require is impossible.' —'Impossible!'—answered he, starting from his chair, *'Ne me dites jamais ce bête de mot,* Never name to me that blockhead of a word.' And then the social repasts; the dinner which he gives as Commandant of National Guards, which 'cost five hundred pounds'; alas, and 'the Syrens of the Opera'; and all the ginger that is hot in the mouth:— down what a course is this man hurled! Cannot Mirabeau stop; cannot he fly, and save himself alive? No! there is a Nessus-Shirt on this Hercules; he must storm and burn there, without rest, till he be consumed. Human strength, never so Herculean, has its measure. Herald shadows flit pale across the fire-brain of Mirabeau; heralds of the pale repose. While he tosses and storms, straining every nerve, in that sea of ambition and confusion, there comes, sombre and still, a monition that for him the issue of it will be swift death.

In January last, you might see him as President of the Assembly; 'his neck wrapt in linen cloths, at the evening session': there was sick heat of the blood, alternate darkening and flashing in the eyesight; he had to apply leeches, after the morning labour, and preside bandaged. 'At parting he embraced me,' says Dumont, 'with an emotion I had never seen in him: "I am dying, my friend; dying as by slow fire; we shall perhaps not meet again. When I am gone, they will know what the value of me was. The miseries I have held back will burst from all sides on France." ' Sickness gives louder warning; but cannot be listened to. On the 27th day of March, proceeding towards the Assembly, he had to seek rest and help in Friend de Lamarck's, by the road; and lay there, for an hour, half-fainted, stretched on a sofa. To the Assembly nevertheless he went, as if in spite of Destiny itself; spoke, loud and eager, five several times; then quitted the Tribune—for ever. He steps out, utterly exhausted, into the Tuileries Gardens; many people press round him, as usual, with applications, memorials; he says to the Friend who was with him: 'Take me out of this!'

And so, on the last day of March 1791, endless anxious multitudes beset the Rue de la Chaussée d'Antin; incessantly inquiring: within doors there, in that House numbered, in our time, 42, the overwearied giant has fallen down, to die. Crowds of all parties and kinds; of all ranks from the King to the meanest man! The King sends publicly twice a-day to inquire; privately besides: from the world at large there is no end of inquiring. 'A written bulletin is handed out every three hours,' is copied and circulated; in the end, it is printed. The People spontaneously keep silence; no carriage shall enter with its noise: there is crowding pressure; but the Sister of Mirabeau is reverently recognised, and has free way made for her. The People stand mute, heart-stricken; to all it seems as if a great calamity were nigh: as if the last man of France, who could have swayed these coming troubles, lay there at hand-grips with the unearthly Power.

The silence of a whole People, the wakeful toil of Cabanis, Friend and Physician, skills not: on Saturday the second day of April, Mirabeau feels that the last of the Days has risen for him; that on this day he has to depart and be no more. His death is Titanic, as his life has been! Lit up, for the last time, in the glare of coming dissolution, the mind of the man is all glowing and burning; utters itself in sayings, such as men long remember. He longs to live, yet acquiesces in death, argues not with the inexorable. His speech is wild and wondrous: unearthly Phantasms dancing now their torch-dance round his soul; the soul itself looking out, fire-radiant, motionless, girt together for that great hour! At times comes a beam of light from him on the world he is quitting. 'I carry in my heart the death-dirge of the French Monarchy; the dead remains of it will now be the spoil of the factious.' Or again, when he heard the cannon fire, what is characteristic too: 'Have we the

Achilles' Funeral already?' So likewise, while some friend is supporting him: 'Yes, support that head; would I could bequeath it thee!' For the man dies as he has lived; self-conscious, conscious of a world looking on. He gazes forth on the young Spring, which for him will never be Summer. The Sun has risen; he says, *'Si ce n'est pas là Dieu, c'est du moins son cousin germain.'*—Death has mastered the outworks; power of speech is gone; the citadel of the heart still holding out: the moribund giant, passionately, by sign, demands paper and pen; writes his passionate demand for opium, to end these agonies. The sorrowful Doctor shakes his head: *Dormir,* 'To sleep,' writes the other, passionately pointing at it! So dies a gigantic Heathen and Titan; stumbling blindly, undismayed, down to his rest. At half-past eight in the morning, Doctor Petit, standing at the foot of the bed, says, *'Il ne souffre plus.'* His suffering and his working are now ended.

Even so, ye silent Patriot multitudes, all ye men of France; this man is rapt away from you. He has fallen suddenly, without bending till he broke; as a tower falls, smitten by sudden lightning. His word ye shall hear no more, his guidance follow no more.—The multitudes depart, heart-struck; spread the sad tidings. How touching is the loyalty of men to their Sovereign Man! All theatres, public amusements close; no joyful meeting can be held in these nights, joy is not for them: the People break in upon private dancing-parties, and sullenly command that they cease. Of such dancing-parties apparently but two came to light, and these also have gone out. The gloom is universal; never in this City was such sorrow for one death; never since that old night when Louis XII. departed, 'and the *Crieurs des Corps* went sounding their bells, and crying along the streets: *Le bon roi Louis, père du peuple, est mort,* The good King Louis, Father of the People, is dead!' King Mirabeau is now the lost King; and one may say with little exaggeration, all the People mourns for him.

For three days there is low wide moan; weeping in the National Assembly itself. The streets are all mournful; orators mounted on the *bornes,* with large silent audience, preaching the funeral sermon of the dead. Let no coachman whip fast, distractively with his rolling wheels, or almost at all, through these groups! His traces may be cut; himself and his fare, as incurable Aristocrats, hurled sulkily into the kennels. The bourne-stone orators speak as it is given them; the Sansculottic People, with its rude soul, listens eager,—as men will to any Sermon, or *Sermo,* when it *is* a spoken Word meaning a Thing, and not a Babblement meaning No-thing. In the Restaurateur's of the Palais-Royal, the waiter remarks, 'Fine weather, Monsieur': —'Yes, my friend,' answers the ancient Man of Letters, 'very fine; but Mirabeau is dead.' Hoarse rhythmic threnodies come also from the throats of ballad-singers; are sold on grey-white paper at a *sou* each. But of Portraits, engraved, painted, hewn and written; of Eulogies, Reminiscences, Biographies, nay *Vaudevilles,* Dramas and Melodramas, in all Provinces of France, there will, through these coming months, be the due immeasurable crop; thick as the leaves of Spring. Nor, that a tincture of burlesque might be in it, is Gobel's Episcopal *Mandement* wanting; goose Gobel, who has just been made Constitutional Bishop of Paris. A Mandement wherein *Ça ira* alternates very strangely with *Nomine Domini*; and you are, with a grave countenance, invited to 'rejoice at possessing in the midst of you a body of Prelates created by Mirabeau, zealous followers of his doctrine, faithful imitators of his virtues.' So speaks, and cackles manifold, the Sorrow of France; wailing articulately, inarticulately, as it can, that a Sovereign Man is snatched away. In the National Assembly, when difficult questions are astir, all eyes will 'turn mechanically to the place where Mirabeau sat,'—and Mirabeau is absent now.

On the third evening of the lamentation, the fourth of April, there is solemn Public Funeral; such as deceased mortal seldom had. Procession of a league in length; of mourners reckoned loosely at a hundred thousand. All roofs are thronged with on-lookers, all windows, lamp-irons, branches of trees. 'Sadness is painted on every countenance; many persons weep.' There is double hedge of National Guards; there is National Assembly in a body; Jacobin Society, and Societies; King's Ministers, Municipals, and all Notabilities, Patriot or Aristocrat. Bouillé is noticeable there, 'with his hat on'; say, hat drawn over his brow, hiding many thoughts! Slow-wending, in religious silence, the Procession of a league in length, under the level sun-rays, for it is five o'clock, moves and marches: with its sable plumes; itself in a religious silence; but, by

fits with the muffled roll of drums, by fits with some
drawn wail of music, and strange new clangour of
bones, and metallic dirge-voice; amid the infinite hu
men. In the Church of Saint-Eustache, there is f
oration by Cerutti; and discharge of fire-arms, which
'brings down pieces of the plaster.' Thence, forward again
to the Church of Sainte-Geneviève; which has been consecrated, by supreme decree, on the spur of this time, into
a Pantheon for the Great Men of the Fatherland, *Aux
Grands Hommes la Patrie réconnaissante*. Hardly at midnight is the business done; and Mirabeau left in his dark
dwelling: first tenant of that Fatherland's Pantheon.

Tenant, alas, who inhabits but at will, and shall be cast
out. For, in these days of convulsion and disjection, not
even the dust of the dead is permitted to rest. Voltaire's
bones are, by and by, to be carried from their stolen grave
in the Abbey of Scellières, to an eager *stealing* grave, in
Paris his birth-city: all mortals processioning and perorating
there; cars drawn by eight white horses, goadsters in classical costume, with fillets and wheat-ears enough;—though
the weather is of the wettest. Evangelist Jean Jacques too, as
is most proper, must be dug up from Ermenonville, and
processioned, with pomp, with sensibility, to the Pantheon
of the Fatherland. He and others: while again Mirabeau, we
say, is cast forth from it, happily incapable of being *re-*
placed; and rests now, irrecognisable, reburied hastily at
dead of night 'in the central part of the Churchyard Sainte-
Catherine, in the Suburb Saint-Marceau,' to be disturbed
no further.

So blazes out, far-seen, a Man's Life, and becomes ashes
and a *caput mortuum,* in this World-Pyre, which we name
French Revolution: not the first that consumed itself
there; nor, by thousands and many millions, the last! A man
who 'had swallowed all formulas'; who, in these strange
times and circumstances, felt called to live Titanically,
and also to die so. As he, for his part, had swallowed all
formulas, what Formula is there, never so comprehensive,
that will express truly the *plus* and the *minus* of him, give
us the accurate net-result of him? There is hitherto none
such. Moralities not a few must shriek condemnatory over
this Mirabeau; the Morality by which he could be judged
has not yet got uttered in the speech of men. We will say
this of him again: That he is a Reality and no Simulacrum;

a living Son of Nature our general Mother; not a hollow Artifice, and mechanism of Conventionalities, son of nothing, *brother* to nothing. In which little word, let the earnest man, walking sorrowful in a world mostly of 'Stuffed Clothes-suits,' that chatter and grin meaningless on him, quite *ghastly* to the earnest soul,—think what significance there is!

Of men who, in such sense, are alive, and see with eyes, the number is now not great: it may be well, if in this huge French Revolution itself, with its all-developing fury, we find some Three. Mortals driven rabid we find; sputtering the acridest logic; baring their breast to the battle-hail, their neck to the guillotine:—of whom it is so painful to say that they too are still, in good part, manufactured Formalities, not Facts but Hearsays!

Honour to the strong man, in these ages, who has shaken himself loose of shams, and *is* something. For in the way of being *worthy,* the first condition surely is that one *be.* Let Cant cease, at all risks and at all costs: till Cant cease, nothing else can begin. Of human Criminals, in these centuries, writes the Moralist, I find but one unforgivable: the Quack. 'Hateful to God,' as divine Dante sings, 'and to the Enemies of God,

'A Dio spiacente ed a' nemici sui!'

But whoever will, with sympathy, which is the first essential towards insight, look at this questionable Mirabeau, may find that there lay verily in him, as the basis of all, a Sincerity, a great free Earnestness; nay call it Honesty, for the man did before all things see, with that clear flashing vision, into what *was,* into what existed as fact; and did, with his wild heart, follow that and no other. Whereby on what ways soever he travels and struggles, often enough falling, he is still a brother man. Hate him not; thou canst not hate him! Shining through such soil and tarnish, and now victorious effulgent, and oftenest struggling eclipsed, the light of genius itself is in this man; which was never yet base and hateful; but at worst was lamentable, lovable with pity. They say that he was ambitious, that he wanted to be Minister. It is most true. And was he not simply the one man in France who could have done any good as Minister? Not vanity alone, not pride alone; far from that! Wild burstings of affection were in this great heart; of fierce lightning, and soft dew of pity. So sunk bemired in wretchedest defacements, it may be said of him, like the Magdalen of old, that he loved much: his Father, the harshest of old crabbed men, he loved with warmth, with veneration.

Be it that his falls and follies are manifold,—as himself often lamented even with tears. Alas, is not the Life of every such man already a poetic Tragedy; made up 'of Fate and of one's own Deservings,' of *Schicksal und eigene Schuld*; full of the elements of Pity and Fear? This brother man, if not Epic for us, is Tragic; if not great, is large, large in his qualities, world-large in his destinies. Whom other men, recognising him as such, may, through long times, remember, and draw nigh to examine and consider: these, in their several dialects, will say of him and sing of him,—till the right thing be said; and so the Formula that *can* judge him be no longer an undiscovered one.

Here then the wild Gabriel Honoré drops from the tissue of our History; not without a tragic farewell. He is gone: the flower of the wild Riquetti or Arrighetti kindred; which seems as if in him, with one last effort, it had done its best, and then expired, or sunk down to the undistinguished level. Crabbed old Marquis Mirabeau, the Friend of Men, sleeps sound. The Bailli Mirabeau, worthy Uncle, will soon die forlorn, alone. Barrel-Mirabeau, already gone across the Rhine, his Regiment of Emigrants will drive nigh desperate. 'Barrel-Mirabeau,' says a biographer of his, 'went indignantly across the Rhine, and drilled Emigrant Regiments. But as he sat one morning in his tent, sour of stomach doubtless and of heart, meditating in Tartarean humour on the turn things took, a certain Captain or Subaltern demanded admittance on business. Such Captain is refused; he again demands, with refusal; and then again; till Colonel Viscount Barrel-Mirabeau, blazing up into a mere burning brandy-barrel, clutches his sword, and tumbles out on this *canaille* of an intruder,—alas, on the *canaille* of an intruder's sword-point, who had drawn with swift dexterity; and dies, and the Newspapers name it *apoplexy* and *alarming accident*.' So die the Mirabeaus.

New Mirabeaus one hears not of: the wild kindred, as we said, is gone out with this its greatest. As families and kindreds sometimes do; producing, after long ages of unnoted notability, some living quintessence of all the qualities they had, to flame forth as a man world-noted; after whom they rest as if exhausted; the sceptre passing to others. The chosen Last of the Mirabeaus is gone; the chosen man of France is gone. It was he who shook old France from its basis; and, as if with his single hand, has held it toppling there, still unfallen. What things depended on that one man! He is as a ship suddenly shivered on sunk rocks: much swims on the waste waters, far from help.

FROM VOLUME III, BOOK IV—
TERROR / CHAPTER VII

MARIE-ANTOINETTE

[October 14-30, 1793;
Year 2, Vendémiaire 23]

On Monday the Fourteenth of October 1793, a Cause is pending in the Palais de Justice, in the new Revolutionary Court, such as those old stone-walls never witnessed: the Trial of Marie-Antoinette. The once brightest of Queens, now tarnished, defaced, forsaken, stands here at Fouquier-Tinville's Judgment-bar; answering for her life. The Indictment was delivered her last night. To such changes of human fortune what words are adequate? Silence alone is adequate.

There are few Printed things one meets with of such tragic, almost ghastly, significance as those bald Pages of the *Bulletin du Tribunal Révolutionnaire,* which beàr title, *Trial of the Widow Capet.* Dim, dim, as if in disastrous eclipse; like the pale kingdoms of Dis! Plutonic Judges, Plutonic Tinville; encircled, nine times, with Styx and Lethe, with Fire-Phlegethon and Cocytus named of Lamentation! The very witnesses summoned are like Ghosts: exculpatory, inculpatory, they themselves are all hovering over death and doom; they are known, in our imagination, as the prey of the Guillotine. Tall *ci-devant* Count d'Estaing, anxious to show himself Patriot, cannot escape; nor Bailly, who, when asked If he knows the Accused, answers with a reverent inclination towards her, 'Ah, yes, I know Madame.' Ex-Patriots are here, sharply dealt with, as Procureur Manuel; Ex-Ministers, shorn of their splendour. We have cold Aristocratic impassivity, faithful to itself even in Tartarus; rabid stupidity, of Patriot Corporals, Patriot Washerwomen, who have much to say of Plots, Treasons, August Tenth, old Insurrection of Women. For all now has become a crime in her who has *lost*.

Marie-Antoinette, in this her utter abandonment, and hour of extreme need, is not wanting to herself, the imperial woman. Her look, they say, as that hideous Indictment was reading, continued calm; 'she was sometimes observed moving her fingers, as when one plays on the piano.' You discern, not without interest, across that dim Revolutionary Bulletin itself, how she bears herself queenlike. Her answers are prompt, clear, often of Laconic brevity; resolution, which has grown contemptuous without ceasing to be dignified, veils itself in calm words. 'You persist, then, in denial?'—'My plan is not denial: it is the truth I have said, and I persist in that.' Scandalous Hébert has borne his testimony as to many things: as to one thing, concerning Marie-Antoinette and her little Son,—wherewith Human Speech had better not further be soiled. She has answered Hébert; a Juryman begs to observe that she has not answered as to *this*. 'I have not answered,' she exclaims with noble emotion, 'because Nature refuses to answer such a charge brought against a Mother. I appeal to all the Mothers that are here.' Robespierre, when he heard of it, broke out into something almost like swearing at the brutish blockheadism of this Hébert; on whose foul head his foul lie has recoiled. At four o'clock on Wednesday morning, after two days and two nights of interrogating, jurycharging, and other darkening of counsel, the result comes out: sentence of Death. 'Have you anything to say?' The Accused shook her head, without speech. Night's candles are burning out; and with her too Time is finishing, and it will be Eternity and Day. This Hall of Tinville's is dark, illlighted except where she stands. Silently she withdraws from it, to die.

Two Processions, or Royal Progresses, three-and-twenty years apart, have often struck us with a strange feeling of contrast. The first is of a beautiful Archduchess and Dauphiness, quitting her Mother's City, at the age of Fifteen; towards hopes such as no other Daughter of Eve then had: 'On the morrow,' says Weber an eye-witness, 'the Dauphiness left Vienna. The whole city crowded out; at first with a sorrow which was silent. She appeared: you saw her sunk back into her carriage; her face bathed in tears; hiding her eyes now with her handkerchief, now with her hands; several times putting out her head to see yet again this Palace of her Fathers, whither she was to return no more. She motioned her regret, her gratitude to the good Nation, which was crowding here to bid her farewell. Then arose not only tears; but piercing cries, on all sides. Men and women alike abandoned themselves to such expression of their sorrow. It was an audible sound of wail, in the streets and avenues of Vienna. The last Courier that followed her disappeared, and the crowd melted away.'

The young imperial Maiden of Fifteen has now become a worn discrowned Widow of Thirty-eight; grey before her time: this is the last Procession: 'Few minutes after the Trial ended, the drums were beating to arms in all Sections; at sunrise the armed force was on foot, cannons getting placed at the extremities of the Bridges, in the Squares, Crossways, all along from the Palais de Justice to the Place de la Révolution. By ten o'clock, numerous patrols were circulating in the Streets; thirty thousand foot and horse drawn up under arms. At eleven, Marie-Antoinette was brought out. She had on an undress of *piqué blanc*: she was led to the place of execution, in the same manner as an ordinary criminal; bound, on a Cart; accompanied by a Constitutional Priest in Lay dress; escorted by numerous detachments of infantry and cavalry. These, and the double row of troops all along her road, she appeared to regard with indifference. On her countenance there was visible neither abashment nor pride. To the cries of *Vive la République* and *Down with Tyranny*, which attended her all the way, she seemed to pay no heed. She spoke little to her Confessor. The tricolor Streamers on the housetops occupied her attention, in the Streets du Roule and Saint-Honoré; she also noticed the Inscriptions on the house-fronts. On reaching the Place de la Révolution, her looks turned towards the *Jardin National,* whilom Tuileries; her face at that moment gave signs of lively emotion. She mounted the Scaffold with courage enough; at a quarter past Twelve, her head fell; the Executioner showed it to the people, amid universal long-continued cries of *Vive la République*.'

FROM VOLUME III, BOOK VI—
THERMIDOR / CHAPTER I

THE GODS ARE ATHIRST

[March 1794; Year 2,
Ventose and Germinal]

What, then, is this Thing called *La Révolution,* which, like
an Angel of Death, hangs over France, noyading, fusillad-
ing, fighting, gun-boring, tanning human skins? *La Révolution* is but so many Alphabetic Letters; a thing nowhere to
be laid hands on, to be clapt under lock and key: where is
it? what is it? It is the Madness that dwells in the hearts of
men. In this man it is, and in that man; as a rage or as a
terror, it is in all men. Invisible, impalpable; and yet no
black Azrael, with wings spread over half a continent, with
sword sweeping from sea to sea, could be a truer Reality.

To explain, what is called explaining, the march of this
Revolutionary Government, be no task of ours. Man cannot
explain it. A paralytic Couthon, asking in the Jacobins,
'What hast thou done to be hanged if Counter-Revolution
should arrive?' a sombre Saint-Just, not yet six-and-twenty,
declaring that 'for Revolutionists there is no rest but in the
tomb'; a seagreen Robespierre converted into vinegar and
gall; much more an Amar and Vadier, a Collot and Billaud:
to inquire what thoughts, predetermination or prevision,
might be in the head of these men! Record of their
thought remains not; Death and Darkness have swept it
out utterly. Nay, if we even had their thought, all that they
could have articulately spoken to us, how insignificant a
fraction were that of the Thing which realised itself, which
decreed itself, on signal given by them! As has been said
more than once, this Revolutionary Government is not a
self-conscious but a blind fatal one. Each man, enveloped
in his ambient-atmosphere of revolutionary fanatic Madness, rushes on, impelled and impelling; and has become
a blind brute Force; no rest for him but in the grave!
Darkness and the mystery of horrid cruelty cover it for us,
in History; as they did in Nature. The chaotic Thunder-
cloud, with its pitchy black, and its tumult of dazzling jag-

ged fire, in a world all electric: thou wilt not undertake to show how that comported itself,—what the secrets of its dark womb were; from what sources, with what specialties, the lightning it held did, in confused brightness of terror, strike forth, destructive and self-destructive, till it ended? Like a Blackness naturally of Erebus, which by will of Providence had for once mounted itself into dominion and the Azure: is not this properly the nature of Sansculottism consummating itself? Of which Erebus Blackness be it enough to discern that this and the other dazzling fire-bolt, dazzling fire-torrent, does by small Volition and great Necessity, verily issue,—in such and such succession; destructive so and so, self-destructive so and so: till it end.

Royalism is extinct; 'sunk,' as they say, 'in the mud of the Loire'; Republicanism dominates without and within: what, therefore, on the 15th day of March 1794, is this? Arrestment, sudden really as a bolt out of the Blue, has hit strange victims: Hébert *Père Duchesne,* Bibliopolist Momoro, Clerk Vincent, General Ronsin; high Cordelier Patriots, red-capped Magistrates of Paris, Worshippers of Reason, Commanders of Revolutionary Army! Eight short days ago, their Cordelier Club was loud, and louder than ever, with Patriot denunciations. Hébert *Père Duchesne* had 'held his tongue and his heart these two months, at sight of Moderates. Crypto-Aristocrats, Camilles, *Scélérats* in the Convention itself: but could not do it any longer; would, if other remedy were not, invoke the sacred right of Insurrection.' So spake Hébert in Cordelier Session; with vivats, till the roofs rang again. Eight short days ago; and now already! They rub their eyes: it is no dream; they find themselves in the Luxembourg. Goose Gobel too; and they that burnt Churches! Chaumette himself, potent Procurer, *Agent National* as they now call it, who could 'recognise the Suspect by the very face of them,' he lingers but three days; on the third day he too is hurled in. Most chopfallen, blue, enters the National Agent this Limbo whither he has sent so many. Prisoners crowd round, gibing and jeering; 'Sublime National Agent,' says one, 'in virtue of thy immortal Proclamation, lo there! I am suspect, thou art suspect, he is suspect, we are suspect, ye are suspect, they are suspect'!

The meaning of these things? Meaning! It is a Plot;

Plot of the most extensive ramifications; which, however,
Barrère holds the threads of. Such Church-burning and
scandalous masquerades of Atheism, fit to make the Revolution odious: where indeed could they originate but in the
gold of Pitt? Pitt indubitably, as Preternatural Insight will
teach one, did hire this Faction of *Enragés,* to play their
fantastic tricks; to roar in their Cordeliers Club about Mod-
eratism; to print their *Père Duchesne;* worship skyblue
Reason in red nightcap; rob Altars,—and bring the spoil
to *us!*

Still more indubitable, visible to the mere bodily sight, is
this: that the Cordeliers Club sits pale, with anger and terror; and has 'veiled the Rights of Man,'—without effect.
Likewise that the Jacobins are in considerable confusion;
busy 'purging themselves, *s'épurant,'* as in times of Plot and
public Calamity they have repeatedly had to do. Not even
Camille Desmoulins but has given offence: nay there have
risen murmurs against Danton himself; though he bellowed
them down, and Robespierre finished the matter by 'embracing him in the Tribune.'

Whom shall the Republic and a jealous Mother Society
trust? In these times of temptation, of Preternatural Insight!
For there are Factions of the Stranger, *'de l'étranger,'*
Factions of Moderates, of Enraged; all manner of Factions:
we walk in a world of Plots; strings universally spread, of
deadly gins and falltraps, baited by the gold of Pitt! Clootz,
Speaker of Mankind so-called, with his *Evidences of
Mahometan Religion,* and babble of Universal Republic,
him an incorruptible Robespierre has purged away. Baron
Clootz, and Paine rebellious Needleman lie, these two
months, in the Luxembourg; limbs of the Faction *de l'étranger.* Representative Phélippeaux is purged out: he came
back from La Vendée with an ill report in his mouth
against rogue Rossignol, and our method of warfare there.
Recant it, O Phélippeaux, we entreat thee! Phélippeaux will
not recant; and is purged out. Representative Fabre d'Eglan-
tine, famed Nomenclator of Romme's Calendar, is purged
out; nay, is cast into the Luxembourg: accused of Legisla-
tive Swindling 'in regard to moneys of the India Company.'
There with his Chabots, Bazires, guilty of the like, let Fabre
wait his destiny. And Westermann friend of Danton, he
who led the Marseillese on the Tenth of August, and fought
well in La Vendée, but spoke not well of rogue Rossignol, is

372 / A CARLYLE READER

purged out. Lucky, if he too go not to the Luxembourg. And your Prolys, Guzmans, of the Faction of the Stranger, they have gone; Pereyra, though he fled, is gone, 'taken in the disguise of a Tavern Cook.' I am suspect, thou art suspect, he is suspect!—

The great heart of Danton is weary of it. Danton is gone to native Arcis, for a little breathing-time of peace: Away, black Arachne-webs, thou world of Fury, Terror, and Suspicion; welcome, thou everlasting Mother, with thy spring greenness, thy kind household loves and memories; true art thou, were all else untrue! The great Titan walks silent, by the banks of the murmuring Aube, in young native haunts that knew him when a boy; wonders what the end of these things may be.

But strangest of all, Camille Desmoulins is purged out. Couthon gave as a test in regard to Jacobin purgation the question, 'What hast thou done to be hanged if Counter-Revolution should arrive?' Yet Camille, who could so well answer this question, is purged out! The truth is, Camille, early in December last, began publishing a new Journal, or Series of Pamphlets, entitled the *Vieux Cordelier,* Old Cordelier. Camille, not afraid at one time to 'embrace Liberty on a heap of dead bodies,' begins to ask now, Whether among so many arresting and punishing Committees, there ought not to be a 'Committee of Mercy'? Saint-Just, he observes, is an extremely solemn young Republican, who 'carries his head as if it were a *Saint-Sacrement,*' adorable Hostie, or divine Real-Presence! Sharply enough, this *old* Cordelier,—Danton and he were of the earliest primary Cordeliers,—shoots his glittering war-shafts into your *new* Cordeliers, your Héberts, Momoros, with their brawling brutalities and despicabilities; say, as the Sun-god (for poor Camille is a Poet) shot into that Python Serpent sprung of mud.

Whereat, as was natural, the Hébertist Python did hiss and writhe amazingly; and threaten 'sacred right of Insurrection';—and, as we saw, get cast into Prison. Nay, with all the old wit, dexterity and light graceful poignancy, Camille, translating 'out of *Tacitus,* from the Reign of Tiberius,' pricks into the *Law of the Suspect* itself; making it odious! Twice, in the Decade, his wild Leaves issue; full of wit, nay of humour, of harmonious ingenuity and insight,—one of the strangest phenomena of that dark time;

and smite, in their wild-sparkling way, at various monstrosities, Saint-Sacrament heads, and Juggernaut idols, in a rather reckless manner. To the great joy of Josephine Beauharnais, and the other Five-thousand and odd Suspect, who fill the Twelve Houses of Arrest; on whom a ray of hope dawns! Robespierre, at first approbatory, knew not at last what to think; then thought, with his Jacobins, that Camille must be expelled. A man of true Revolutionary spirit, this Camille; but with the unwisest sallies; whom Aristocrats and Moderates have the art to corrupt! Jacobinism is in uttermost crisis and struggle; enmeshed wholly in plots, corruptibilities, neck-gins and baited falltraps of Pitt *ennemi du genre humain.* Camille's First Number begins with *'O Pitt!'*—his last is dated 15 Pluviose, Year 2, 3d February 1794; and ends with these words of Montezuma's, *'Les dieux ont soif,* The gods are athirst.'

Be this as it may, the Hébertists lie in Prison only some nine days. On the 24th of March, therefore, the Revolution Tumbrils carry through that Life-tumult a new cargo: Hébert, Vincent, Momoro, Ronsin, Nineteen of them in all; with whom, curious enough, sits Clootz Speaker of Mankind. They have been massed swiftly into a lump, this miscellany of Nondescripts; and travel now their last road. No help. They too must 'look through the little window'; they too 'must sneeze into the sack,' *éternuer dans le sac*; as they have done to others, so is it done to them. *Sainte-Guillotine,* meseems, is worse than the old Saints of Superstition; a man-devouring Saint? Clootz, still with an air of polished sarcasm, endeavours to jest, to offer cheering 'arguments of Materialism'; he requested to be executed last, 'in order to establish certain principles,'—which hitherto, I think, Philosophy has got no good of. General Ronsin too, he still looks forth with some air of defiance, eye of command: the rest are sunk in a stony paleness of despair. Momoro, poor Bibliopolist, no Agrarian Law yet realised,—they might as well have hanged thee at Evreux, twenty months ago, when Girondin Buzot hindered them. Hébert *Père Duchesne* shall never in this world rise in sacred right of insurrection; he sits there low enough, head sunk on breast; Red Nightcaps shouting round him, in frightful parody of his Newspaper Articles, 'Grand choler of the Père Duchesne!' Thus perish they; the sack receives all their heads. Through some section of History, Nineteen spectre-chimeras shall flit, squeaking and gibbering; till Oblivion swallow them.

In the course of a week, the Revolutionary Army itself is disbanded; the General having become spectral. This Faction of Rabids, therefore, is also purged from the Republican soil; here also the baited falltraps of that Pitt have been wrenched up harmless; and anew there is joy over a Plot Discovered. The Revolution, then, is verily devouring its own children? All Anarchy, by the nature of it, is not only destructive but self-destructive.

CHAPTER III

THE TUMBRILS

[April-May 1794; Year 2, Floréal]

Next week, it is still but the 10th of April, there comes a new Nineteen; Chaumette, Gobel, Hébert's Widow, the Widow of Camille: these also roll their fated journey; black Death devours them. Mean Hébert's Widow was weeping, Camille's Widow tried to speak comfort to her. O ye kind Heavens, azure, beautiful, eternal behind your tempests and Time-clouds, is there not pity in store for all! Gobel, it seems, was repentant; he begged absolution of a Priest; died as a Gobel best could. For Anaxagoras Chaumette, the sleek head now stripped of its *bonnet rouge,* what hope is there? Unless Death *were* 'an eternal sleep'? Wretched Anaxagoras, God shall judge thee, not I.

Hébert, therefore, is gone, and the Hebertists; they that robbed Churches, and adored blue Reason in red nightcap. Great Danton, and the Dantonists; they also are gone. Down to the catacombs; they are become silent men! Let no Paris Municipality, no Sect or Party of this hue or that, resist the will of Robespierre and *Salut.* Mayor Pache, not prompt enough in denouncing these Pitt Plots, may congratulate about them now. Never so heartily; it skills not! His course likewise is to the Luxembourg. We appoint one Fleuriot-Lescot Interim-Mayor in his stead: an 'architect from Belgium,' they say, this Fleuriot; he is a man one can depend on. Our new Agent-National is Payan, lately Juryman; whose cynosure also is Robespierre.

Thus then, we perceive, this confusedly electric Erebus-cloud of Revolutionary Government has altered its shape somewhat. Two masses, or wings, belonging to it; an over-electric mass of Cordelier Rabids, and an under-electric of Dantonist Moderates and Clemency-men,—these two masses, shooting bolts at one another, so to speak, have annihilated one another. For the Erebus-cloud, as we often remark, is of suicidal nature; and, in jagged irregularity, darts its lightning withal into itself. But now these two discrepant masses being mutually annihilated, it is as if the Erebus-cloud had got to internal composure; and did only pour its hellfire lightning on the World that lay under it. In plain words, Terror of the Guillotine was never terrible till now. Systole, diastole, swift and ever swifter goes the Axe of Samson. Indictments cease by degrees to have so much as plausibility: Fouquier chooses from the Twelve Houses of Arrest what he calls Batches, '*Fournées*,' a score or more at a time; his Jurymen are charged to make *feu de file*, file-firing till the ground be *clear*. Citizen Laflotte's report of Plot in the Luxembourg is verily bearing fruit! If no speakable charge exist against a man, or Batch of men, Fouquier has always this: a Plot in the Prison. Swift and ever swifter goes Samson; up, finally to threescore and more at a Batch. It is the highday of Death: none but the Dead return not.

O dusky D'Espréménil, what a day is this the 22d of April, thy last day! The Palais Hall here is the same stone Hall, where thou, five years ago, stoodest perorating, amid endless pathos of rebellious Parlement, in the grey of the morning; bound to march with D'Agoust to the Isles of Hières. The stones are the same stones: but the rest, Men, Rebellion, Pathos, Peroration, see, it has all fled, like a gibbering troop of ghosts, like the phantasms of a dying brain. With D'Espréménil, in the same line of Tumbrils, goes the mournfulest medley. Chapelier goes, *ci-devant* popular President of the Constituent; whom the Menads and Maillard met in his carriage, on the Versailles Road. Thouret likewise, *ci-devant* President, father of Constitutional Law-acts; he whom we heard saying, long since, with a loud voice, 'The Constituent Assembly has fulfilled its mission!' And the noble old Malesherbes, who defended Louis and could not speak, like a grey old rock dissolving into sudden water: he journeys here now, with his kindred, daughters, sons, and grandsons, his Lamoignons, Châteaubriands; silent, towards Death.—One young Châteaubriand alone is wandering amid the Natchez, by the roar of Niagara Falls, the moan of endless forests: Welcome thou great Nature, savage, but not false, not unkind, unmotherly; no Formula thou, or rabid jangle of Hypothesis, Parliamentary Eloquence, Constitution-building and the Guillotine; speak thou to me, O Mother, and sing my sick heart thy mystic everlasting lullaby-song, and let all the rest be far!—

Another row of Tumbrils we must notice: that which holds Elizabeth, the Sister of Louis. Her Trial was like the rest; for Plots, for Plots. She was among the kindliest, most innocent of women. There sat with her, amid four-and-twenty others, a once timorous Marchioness de Crussol; courageous now; expressing towards her the liveliest loyalty. At the foot of the Scaffold, Elizabeth with tears in her eyes thanked this Marchioness; said she was grieved she could not reward her. 'Ah, Madame, would your Royal Highness deign to embrace me, my wishes were complete!' —'Right willingly, Marquise de Crussol, and with my whole heart.' Thus they: at the foot of the Scaffold. The Royal Family is now reduced to two: a girl and a little boy. The boy, once named Dauphin, was taken from his Mother while she yet lived; and given to one Simon, by trade a Cordwainer, on service then about the Temple-Prison, to bring him up in principles of Sansculottism. Simon taught him to drink, to swear, to sing the *carmagnole*. Simon is now gone to the Municipality: and the poor boy, hidden in a tower of the Temple, from which in his fright and bewilderment and early decrepitude he wishes not to stir out, lies perishing, 'his shirt not changed for six months'; amid squalor and darkness, lamentably,—so as none but poor Factory Children and the like are wont to perish, and *not* be lamented!

The Spring sends its green leaves and bright weather, bright May, brighter than ever: Death pauses not. Lavoisier, famed Chemist, shall die and not live: Chemist Lavoisier was Farmer-General Lavoisier too, and now 'all the Farmers-General are arrested'; all, and shall give an account of their moneys and incomings; and die for 'putting water in the tobacco' they sold. Lavoisier begged a fortnight more of life, to finish some experiments: but 'the Republic does not need such'; the axe must do its work. Cynic Chamfort, reading these inscriptions of *Brotherhood or Death,* says, 'it is a Brotherhood of Cain': arrested, then liberated; then about to be arrested again, this Chamfort cuts and slashes himself with frantic uncertain hand; gains, not without difficulty, the refuge of death. Condorcet has lurked deep, these many months; Argus-eyes watching and searching for him. His concealment is become dangerous to others and himself; he has to fly again, to skulk, round Paris, in thickets and stone-quarries. And so at the Village of Clamars, one bleared May morning, there enters a Figure ragged, rough-bearded, hunger-stricken; asks breakfast in the tavern there. Suspect, by the look of him! 'Servant out of place, sayest thou?' Committee-President of Forty-Sous finds a Latin Horace on him: 'Art not thou one of those *Ci-devants* that were wont to keep servants? *Suspect!*' He is haled forthwith, breakfast unfinished, towards Bourg-la-Reine, on foot: he faints with exhaustion; is set on a peasant's horse; is flung into his damp prison-cell: on the morrow, recollecting him, you enter; Condorcet lies dead on the floor. They die fast, and disappear: the Notabilities of France disappear, one after one, like lights in a Theatre, which you are snuffing out.

Under which circumstances, is it not singular, and almost touching, to see Paris City drawn out, in the meek May nights, in civic ceremony, which they call *'Souper Fraternel,'* Brotherly Supper? Spontaneous, or partially spontaneous, in the twelfth, thirteenth, fourteenth nights of this May month, it is seen. Along the Rue Saint-Honoré, and main Streets and Spaces, each Citoyen brings forth what of supper the stingy *Maximum* has yielded him, to the open air; joins it to his neighbour's supper; and with common table, cheerful light burning frequent, and what due modicum of cut-glass and other garnish and relish is convenient, they eat frugally together, under the kind stars. See it, O Night! With cheerfully pledged wine-cup, hobnobbing to the Reign of Liberty, Equality, Brotherhood, with their wives in best ribands with their little ones romping round, the Citoyens, in frugal Love-feast, sit there. Night in her wide empire sees nothing similar. O my brothers, why is the reign of Brotherhood *not* come! It is come, it shall have come, say the Citoyens frugally hobnobbing.—Ah me! these everlasting stars, do they not look down 'like glistening eyes, bright with immortal pity, over the lot of man'!—

One lamentable thing, however, is, that individuals will attempt assassination—of Representatives of the People. Representative Collot, Member even of *Salut,* returning home, 'about one in the morning,' probably touched with liquor, as he is apt to be, meets on the stairs the cry '*Scélérat!*' and also the snap of a pistol: which latter flashes in the pan; disclosing to him, momentarily, a pair of truculent saucer-eyes, swart grim-clenched countenance; recognisable as that of our little fellow-lodger, Citoyen Amiral, formerly 'a clerk in the Lotteries.' Collot shouts *Murder,* with lungs fit to awaken all the *Rue Favart*; Amiral snaps a second time; a second time flashes in the pan; then darts up into his apartment; and, after there firing, still with inadequate effect, one musket at himself and another at his captor, is clutched and locked in Prison. An indignant little man this Amiral, of Southern temper and complexion, of 'considerable muscular force.' He denies not that he meant to 'purge France of a Tyrant'; nay avows that he had an eye to the Incorruptible himself, but took Collot as more convenient!

Rumour enough hereupon; heaven-high congratulation of Collot, fraternal embracing, at the Jacobins and elsewhere. And yet, it would seem, the assassin mood proves catching. Two days more, it is still but the 23d of May, and towards nine in the evening, Cécile Rénault, Paper-dealer's daughter, a young woman of soft blooming look, presents herself at the Cabinet-maker's in the Rue Saint-Honoré; desires to see Robespierre. Robespierre cannot be seen; she grumbles irreverently. They lay hold of her. She has left a basket in a shop hard by: in the basket are female change of raiment and two knives! Poor Cécile, examined by Committee, declares she 'wanted to see what a tyrant was like'; the change of raiment was 'for my own use in the place I am surely going to.'—'What place?'— 'Prison; and then the Guillotine,' answered she.—Such things come of Charlotte Corday; in a people prone to imitation, and monomania! Swart choleric men try Charlotte's feat, and their pistols miss fire; soft blooming young women try it, and, only half-resolute, leave their knives in a shop.

O Pitt, and ye Faction of the Stranger, shall the Republic

never have rest; but be torn continually by baited springes, by wires of explosive spring-guns? Swart Amiral, fair young Cécile, and all that knew them, and many that did not know them, lie locked, waiting the scrutiny of Tinville.

FROM VOLUME III, BOOK VII—
VENDÉMIAIRE / CHAPTER VII

THE WHIFF OF GRAPESHOT

[October 4-5, 1795; Year 4,
Vendémiaire 12-13]

In fact, what can be more natural, one may say inevitable, as a Post-Sansculottic transitionary state, than even this? Confused wreck of a Republic of the Poverties, which ended in Reign of Terror, is arranging itself into such composure as it can. Evangel of Jean-Jacques, and most other Evangels, becoming incredible, what is there for it but return to the old Evangel of Mammon? *Contrat-Social* is true or untrue, Brotherhood is Brotherhood or Death; but money always will buy money's worth: in the wreck of human dubitations, this remains indubitable, that Pleasure is pleasant. Aristocracy of Feudal Parchment has passed away with a mighty rushing; and now, by a natural course, we arrive at Aristocracy of the Moneybag. It is the course through which all European Societies are, at this hour, travelling. Apparently a still baser sort of Aristocracy? An infinitely baser; the basest yet known.

In which, however, there is this advantage, that, like Anarchy itself, it cannot continue. Hast thou considered how Thought is stronger than Artillery-parks, and (were it fifty years after death and martyrdom, or were it two thousand years) writes and unwrites Acts of Parliament, removes mountains; models the World like soft clay? Also how the beginning of all Thought, worth the name, is Love; and the wise head never yet was, without first the generous heart? The Heavens cease not their bounty; they send us generous hearts into every generation. And now what generous heart can pretend to itself, or be hoodwinked into believing, that Loyalty to the Moneybag is a noble Loyalty? Mammon, cries the generous heart out of all ages and countries, is the basest of known Gods, even of known Devils. In him what glory is there, that ye should worship him? No glory discernible; not even terror: at best, detestability, ill-matched with despicability!—Generous hearts, discerning, on this hand, wide-spread Wretchedness, dark without and within, moistening its ounce-and-half of bread with tears; and, on that hand, mere Balls in flesh-coloured drawers, and inane or foul glitter of such sort, —cannot but ejaculate, cannot but announce: Too much, O divine Mammon; somewhat too much!—The voice of these, once announcing itself, carries *fiat* and *pereat* in it, for all things here below.

Meanwhile we will hate Anarchy as Death, which it is; and the things worse than Anarchy shall be hated *more*. Surely Peace alone is fruitful. Anarchy is destruction; a burning up, say, of Shams and Insupportabilities; but which leaves Vacancy behind. Know this also, that out of a world of Unwise nothing but an Unwisdom can be made. Arrange it, constitution-build it, sift it through ballot-boxes as thou wilt, it is and remains an Unwisdom,—the new prey of new quacks and unclean things, the latter end of it slightly better than the beginning. Who can bring a wise thing out of men unwise? Not one. And so Vacancy and general Abolition having come for this France, what can Anarchy do more? Let there be Order, were it under the Soldier's Sword; let there be Peace, that the bounty of the Heavens be not spilt; that what of Wisdom they do send us bring fruit in its season!—It remains to be seen how the quellers of Sansculottism were themselves quelled, and sacred right of Insurrection was blown away by gunpowder; wherewith this singular eventful History called *French Revolution* ends.

The Convention, driven such a course by wild wind, wild tide, and steerage and non-steerage, these three years, has become weary of its own existence, sees all men weary of it; and wishes heartily to finish. To the last it has to strive with contradictions: it is now getting fast ready with a Constitution, yet knows no peace. Sieyes, we say, is making the Constitution once more; has as good as made it. Warned by experience, the great Architect alters much, admits much. Distinction of Active and Passive Citizen, that is, Money-qualification for Electors: nay Two Chambers,

'Council of Ancients,' as well as 'Council of Five-hundred'; to that conclusion have we come! In a like spirit, eschewing that fatal self-denying ordinance of your Old Constituents, we enact not only that actual Convention Members are reëligible, but that Two-thirds of them must be reëlected. The Active Citizen Electors shall for this time have free choice of only One-third of their National Assembly. Such enactment, of Two-thirds to be reëlected, we append to our Constitution; we submit our Constitution to the Townships of France, and say, Accept *both,* or reject both. Unsavoury as this appendix may be, the Townships, by overwhelming majority, accept and ratify. With Directory of Five; with Two good Chambers, double-majority of them nominated by ourselves, one hopes this Constitution may prove final. *March* it will; for the legs of it, the reëlected Two-thirds, are already here, able to march. Sieyes looks at his paper-fabric with just pride.

But now see how the contumacious Sections, Lepelletier foremost, kick against the pricks. Is it not manifest infraction of one's Elective Franchise, Rights of Man, and Sovereignty of the People, this appendix of reëlecting *your* Two-thirds? Greedy tyrants, who would perpetuate yourselves!— For the truth is, victory over Saint-Antoine, and long right of Insurrection, has spoiled these men. Nay spoiled all men. Consider, too, how each man was free to hope what he liked; and now there is to be no hope, there is to be fruition, fruition of *this.*

In men spoiled by long right of Insurrection, what confused ferments will rise, tongues once begun wagging! Journalists declaim, your Lacretelles, Laharpes; Orators spout. There is Royalism traceable in it, and Jacobinism. On the West Frontier, in deep secrecy, Pichegru, durst he trust his Army, is treating with Condé: in these Sections, there spout wolves in sheep's clothing, masked Emigrants and Royalists. All men, as we say, had hoped, each that the Election would do something for his own side: and now there is no Election, or only the third of one. Black is united with white against this clause of the Two-thirds; all the Unruly of France, who see their trade thereby near ending.

Section Lepelletier, after Addresses enough, finds that such clause is a manifest infraction; that it, Lepelletier for one, will simply not conform thereto; and invites all other free Sections to join it, 'in central Committee,' in resistance to oppression. The Sections join it, nearly all; strong with their Forty-thousand fighting men. The Convention therefore may look to itself! Lepelletier, on this 12th day of Vendémiaire, 4th of October 1795, is sitting in open contravention, in its Convent of Filles Saint-Thomas, Rue Vivienne, with guns primed. The Convention has some Five-thousand regular troops at hand; Generals in abundance; and a Fifteen-hundred of miscellaneous persecuted Ultra-Jacobins, whom in this crisis it has hastily got together and armed, under the title of *Patriots of Eighty-nine*. Strong in Law, it sends its General Menou to disarm Lepelletier.

General Menou marches accordingly, with due summons and demonstration; with no result. General Menou, about eight in the evening, finds that he is standing ranked in the Rue Vivienne, emitting vain summonses; with primed guns pointed out of every window at him; and that he cannot disarm Lepelletier. He has to return, with whole skin, but without success; and be thrown into arrest, as 'a traitor.' Whereupon the whole Forty-thousand join this Lepelletier which cannot be vanquished: to what hand shall a quaking Convention now turn? Or poor Convention, after such voyaging, just entering harbour, so to speak, has *struck on the bar*;—and labours there frightfully, with breakers roaring round it, Forty-thousand of them, like to wash it, and its Sieyes Cargo and the whole future of France, into the deep! Yet one last time, it struggles, ready to perish.

Some call for Barras to be made Commandant; he conquered in Thermidor. Some, what is more to the purpose, bethink them of the Citizen Buonaparte, unemployed Artillery-Officer, who took Toulon. A man of head, a man of action: Barras is named Commandant's-Cloak; this young Artillery-Officer is named Commandant. He was in the Gallery at the moment, and heard it; he withdrew, some half-hour, to consider with himself: after a half-hour of grim compressed considering, to be or not to be, he answers *Yea*.

And now, a man of head being at the centre of it, the whole matter gets vital. Swift, to Camp of Sablons; to secure the Artillery, there are not twenty men guarding it! A swift Adjutant, Murat is the name of him, gallops; gets thither some minutes within time, for Lepelletier was also on march that way: the Cannon are ours. And now beset this post, and beset that; rapid and firm: at Wicket of the

Louvre, in Cul-de-sac Dauphin, in Rue Saint-Honoré, from Pont-Neuf all along the north Quays, southward to Pont *ci-devant* Royal,—rank round the Sanctuary of the Tuileries, a ring of steel discipline; let every gunner have his match burning, and all men stand to their arms!

Thus there is Permanent-session through the night; and thus at sunrise of the morrow, there is seen sacred Insurrection once again: vessel of State labouring on the bar; and tumultuous sea all round her, beating *générale,* arming and sounding,—not ringing tocsin, for we have left no tocsin, but our own in the Pavilion of Unity. It is an imminence of shipwreck, for the whole world to gaze at. Frightfully she labours, that poor ship, within cable-length of port; huge peril for her. However, she has a man at the helm. Insurgent messages, received and not received; messenger admitted blindfolded; counsel and counter-counsel: the poor ship labours!—Vendémiaire 13th, year 4: curious enough, of all days, it is the 5th day of October, anniversary of that Menadmarch, six years ago; by sacred right of Insurrection we are got thus far.

Lepelletier has seized the Church of Saint-Roch; has seized the Pont-Neuf, our piquet there retreating without fire. Stray shots fall from Lepelletier; rattle down on the very Tuileries Staircase. On the other hand, women advance dishevelled, shrieking, Peace; Lepelletier behind them waving his hat in sign that we shall fraternise. Steady! The Artillery-Officer is steady as bronze; can, if need were, be quick as lightning. He sends eight-hundred muskets with ball-cartridges to the Convention itself; honourable Members shall act with these in case of extremity: whereat they look grave enough. Four of the afternoon is struck. Lepelletier, making nothing by messengers, by fraternity or hat-waving, bursts out, along the Southern Quai Voltaire, along streets and passages, treble-quick, in huge veritable onslaught! Whereupon, thou bronze Artillery-Officer—? 'Fire'! say the bronze lips. And roar and thunder, roar and again roar, continual, volcano-like, goes his great gun, in the Cul-de-sac Dauphin against the Church of Saint-Roch; go his great guns on the Pont-Royal; go all his great guns; —blow to air some two-hundred men, mainly about the Church of Saint-Roch! Lepelletier cannot stand such horseplay; no Sectioner can stand it; the Forty-thousand yield on all sides, scour towards covert. 'Some hundred or so of them gathered about the Théâtre de la République; but,' says he, 'a few shells dislodged them. It was all finished at six.'

The Ship is *over* the bar, then; free she bounds shore-ward—amid shouting and vivats! Citoyen Buonaparte is 'named General of the Interior, by acclamation'; quelled Sections have to disarm in such humour as they may; sacred right of Insurrection is gone for ever! The Sieyes Constitution can disembark itself, and begin marching. The miraculous Convention Ship has got to land;—and is there, shall we figuratively say, changed, as Epic Ships are wont, into a kind of *Sea Nymph,* never to sail more; to roam the waste Azure, a Miracle in History!

'It is false,' says Napoleon, 'that we fired first with blank charge; it had been a waste of life to do that.' Most false: the firing was with sharp and sharpest shot: to all men it was plain that here was no sport; the rabbets and plinths of Saint-Roch Church show splintered by it to this hour.— Singular: in old Broglie's time, six years ago, this Whiff of Grapeshot was promised; but it could not be given then; could not have profited then. Now, however, the time is come for it, and the man; and behold, you have it; and the thing we specifically call *French Revolution* is blown into space by it, and become a thing that was!—

CHAPTER VIII

FINIS

Homer's Epos, it is remarked, is like a Bas-Relief sculpture: it does not conclude, but merely ceases. Such, indeed, is the Epos of Universal History itself. Directorates, Consulates, Emperorships, Restorations, Citizen-Kingships succeed this Business in due series, in due genesis one out of the other. Nevertheless the First-parent of all these may be said to have gone to air in the way we see. A Babœuf Insurrection, next year, will die in the birth; stifled by the Soldiery. A Senate, if tinged with Royalism, can be purged by the Soldiery; and an Eighteenth of Fructidor transacted by the mere show of bayonets. Nay Soldiers' bayonets can be used *à posteriori* on a Senate, and make it leap out of window,—still bloodless; and produce an Eighteenth of Brumaire.[1] Such changes must happen: but they are managed by intriguings, caballings, and then by orderly word of command; almost like mere changes of Ministry. Not in general by sacred right of Insurrection, but by milder methods growing ever milder, shall the events of French History be henceforth brought to pass.

It is admitted that this Directorate, which owned, at its starting, these three things, an 'old table, a sheet of paper, and an inkbottle,' and no visible money or arrangement whatever, did wonders: that France, since the Reign of Terror hushed itself, has been a new France, awakened like a giant out of torpor; and has gone on, in the Internal Life of it, with continual progress. As for the External form and forms of Life, what can we say, except that out of the Eater there comes Strength; out of the Unwise there comes *not* Wisdom!—Shams are burnt up; nay, what as yet is the peculiarity of France, the very Cant of them is burnt up. The new Realities are not yet come: ah no, only Phantasms, Paper models, tentative Prefigurements of such! In France there are now Four Million Landed Properties; that black portent of an Agrarian Law is, as it were, *realised*. What is still stranger, we understand all Frenchmen have 'the right of duel'; the Hackney-coachman with the Peer, if insult be given: such is the law of Public Opinion. Equality at least in death! The Form of Government is by Citizen King, frequently shot at, not yet shot.

On the whole, therefore, has it not been fulfilled what was prophesied, *ex postfacto* indeed, by the Arch-quack Cagliostro, or another? He, as he looked in rapt vision and amazement into these things, thus spake: 'Ha! What is *this*? Angels, Uriel, Anachiel, and ye other Five; Pentagon of Rejuvenescence; Power that destroyedst Original Sin; Earth, Heaven, and thou Outer Limbo, which men name Hell! Does the Empire of Imposture waver? Burst there, in starry sheen, updarting, Light-rays from out of *its* dark foundations; as it rocks and heaves, not in travail-throes but in death-throes? Yea, Light-rays, piercing, clear, that salute the Heavens,—lo, they *kindle* it; their starry clearness becomes as red Hellfire!

'Imposture is in flames, Imposture is burnt up: one

[1] 9th November 1799. [Carlyle's note.]

red sea of Fire, wild-billowing, enwraps the World; with its fire-tongue licks at the very Stars. Thrones are hurled into it, and Dubois Mitres, and Prebendal Stalls that drop fatness, and—ha! what see I?—all the *Gigs* of Creation: all, all! Wo is me! Never since Pharaoh's Chariots, in the Red Sea of water, was there wreck of Wheel-vehicles like this in the Sea of Fire. Desolate, as ashes, as gases, shall they wander in the wind.

'Higher, higher yet flames the Fire-Sea; crackling with new dislocated timber; hissing with leather and prunella. The metal Images are molten; the marble Images become mortar-lime; the stone Mountains sulkily explode. RESPECT-ABILITY, with all her collected Gigs inflamed for funeral pyre, wailing, leaves the Earth: not to return save under new Avatar. Imposture how it burns, through generations: how it is burnt up; for a time. The World is black ashes;—which, ah, when will they grow green? The Images all run into amorphous Corinthian brass; all Dwellings of men destroyed; the very mountains peeled and riven, the valleys black and dead: it is an empty World! Wo to them that shall be born then!——A King, a Queen (ah me!) were hurled in; did rustle once; flew aloft, crackling, like paper-scroll. Iscariot Egalité was hurled in; thou grim De Launay, with thy grim Bastille; whole kindreds and peoples; five millions of mutually destroying Men. For it is the End of the dominion of IMPOSTURE (which is Darkness and opaque Fire-damp); and the burning up, with unquenchable fire, of all the Gigs that are in the Earth.' This Prophecy, we say, has it not been fulfilled, is it not fulfilling?

And so here, O Reader, has the time come for us two to part. Toilsome was our journeying together; not without offence; but it is done. To me thou wert as a beloved shade, the disembodied or not yet embodied spirit of a Brother. To thee I was but as a Voice. Yet was our relation a kind of sacred one; doubt not that! For whatsoever once sacred things become hollow jargons, yet while the Voice of Man speaks with Man, hast thou not there the living fountain out of which all sacrednesses sprang, and will yet spring? Man, by the nature of him, is definable as 'an incarnated Word.' Ill stands it with me if I have spoken falsely: thine also it was to hear truly. Farewell.

FROM *On Heroes and Hero-Worship and the Heroic in History*

1 8 4 1

[In May 1840 Carlyle delivered a series of six public lectures which appeared in print the following year and are generally referred to as *On Heroes and Hero-Worship*. The lectures on heroes were Carlyle's fourth lecture series, the first being on German literature in 1837, the second on the history of literature and culture in 1838, and the third on modern revolutions in 1839. Only the series on heroes was published by Carlyle. Fashionable London attended the lectures and marvelled at the obvious sincerity and the equally obvious difficulty with which Carlyle expressed his thought, for Carlyle, who was a vivid and fluent conversationalist, was terrified of the lecture platform. He insisted upon lecturing without notes, and this only aggravated his uneasiness. But the result was a series of lectures remarkable for their intensity and originality.

Carlyle's view of the hero as presented in these lectures is at once a call for a strong (not a despotic or lawless) leader and an attempt to delineate the terms and conditions under which leadership had flourished in the past. Beginning with Odin and the heroes of mythology, Carlyle takes his subject through six stages, the hero as divinity (Odin), as prophet (Mohammed), as poet (Dante, Shakespeare), as priest (Luther, Knox), as man of letters (Johnson, Rousseau, Burns), and finally as king (Cromwell, Napoleon). The selection printed here contains the introduction and the second part of the lecture on the Hero as Poet, originally delivered May 12, 1840, omitting the section on Dante. In this lecture Carlyle presents his favorite idea of the poet, or man of letters, as seer and prophet. The hero, in whatever form he appears, must be such a seer, must be in contact with and subordinate to the overarching moral law.]

FROM LECTURE III

THE HERO AS POET. DANTE; SHAKSPEARE

The Hero as Divinity, the Hero as Prophet, are productions of old ages; not to be repeated in the new. They presuppose a certain rudeness of conception, which the progress of mere scientific knowledge puts an end to. There needs to be, as it were, a world vacant, or almost vacant of scientific forms, if men in their loving wonder are to fancy their fellow-man either a god or one speaking with the voice of a god. Divinity and Prophet are past. We are now to see our Hero in the less ambitious, but also less questionable, character of Poet; a character which does not pass. The Poet is a heroic figure belonging to all ages; whom all ages possess, when once he is produced, whom the newest age as the oldest may produce;—and will produce, always when Nature pleases. Let Nature send a Hero-soul; in no age is it other than possible that he may be shaped into a Poet.

Hero, Prophet, Poet,—many different names, in different times and places, do we give to Great Men; according to varieties we note in them, according to the sphere in which they have displayed themselves! We might give many more names, on this same principle. I will remark again, how-ever, as a fact not unimportant to be understood, that the different *sphere* constitutes the grand origin of such distinc-tion; that the Hero can be Poet, Prophet, King, Priest or what you will, according to the kind of world he finds him-self born into. I confess, I have no notion of a truly great man that could not be *all* sorts of men. The Poet who could merely sit on a chair, and compose stanzas, would never make a stanza worth much. He could not sing the Heroic warrior, unless he himself were at least a Heroic warrior too. I fancy there is in him the Politician, the Thinker, Legislator, Philosopher;—in one or the other degree, he could have been, he is all these. So too I cannot understand how a Mirabeau, with that great glowing heart, with the fire that was in it, with the bursting tears that were in it, could not have written verses, tragedies, poems, and touched all hearts in that way, had his course of life and education led him thitherward. The grand fundamental character is that of Great Man; that the man be great. Napoleon has words in him which are like Austerlitz Battles. Louis Fourteenth's Marshals are a kind of poetical men withal; the things Turenne says are full of sagacity and geniality, like sayings of Samuel Johnson. The great heart, the clear deep-seeing eye: there it lies; no man whatever, in what province soever, can prosper at all without these. Petrarch and Boccaccio did diplomatic messages, it seems, quite well: one can easily believe it; they had done things a little harder than these! Burns, a gifted song-writer, might have made a still better Mirabeau. Shakspeare,—one knows not what *he* could not have made, in the supreme degree.

True, there are aptitudes of Nature too. Nature does not make all great men, more than all other men, in the self-same mould. Varieties of aptitude doubtless; but infinitely more of circumstance; and far oftenest it is the *latter* only that are looked to. But it is as with common men in the learning of trades. You take any man, as yet a vague capability of a man, who could be any kind of craftsman; and make him into a smith, a carpenter, a mason: he is then and thenceforth that and nothing else. And if, as Addison complains, you sometimes see a street-porter staggering under his load on spindle-shanks, and near at hand a tailor with the frame of a Samson handling a bit of cloth and small Whitechapel needle,—it cannot be considered that aptitude of Nature alone has been consulted here either!— The Great Man also, to what shall he be bound apprentice? Given your Hero, is he to become Conqueror, King, Philosopher, Poet? It is an inexplicably complex controversial-calculation between the world and him! He will read the world and its laws; the world with its laws will be there to be read. What the world, on *this* matter, shall permit and bid is, as we said, the most important fact about the world.—

Poet and Prophet differ greatly in our loose modern notions of them. In some old languages, again, the titles are synonymous; *Vates* means both Prophet and Poet: and indeed at all times, Prophet and Poet, well understood, have much kindred of meaning. Fundamentally indeed they are still the same; in this most important respect especially,

That they have penetrated both of them into the sacred mystery of the Universe; what Goethe calls 'the open secret.' 'Which is the great secret?' asks one.—'The *open* secret,'—open to all, seen by almost none! That divine mystery, which lies everywhere in all Beings, 'the Divine Idea of the World,' that which lies at 'the bottom of Appearance,' as Fichte styles it; of which all Appearance, from the starry sky to the grass of the field, but especially the Appearance of Man and his work, is but the *vesture,* the embodiment that renders it visible. This divine mystery *is* in all times and in all places; veritably is. In most times and places it is greatly overlooked; and the Universe, definable always in one or the other dialect, as the realised Thought of God, is considered a trivial, inert, commonplace matter,—as if, says the Satirist, it were a dead thing, which some upholsterer had put together! It could do no good, at present, to *speak* much about this; but it is a pity for every one of us if we do not know it, live ever in the knowledge of it. Really a most mournful pity;—a failure to live at all, if we live otherwise!

But now, I say, whoever may forget this divine mystery, the *Vates,* whether Prophet or Poet, has penetrated into it; is a man sent hither to make it more impressively known to us. That always is his message; he is to reveal that to us, —that sacred mystery which he more than others lives ever present with. While others forget it, he knows it;—I might say, he has been driven to know it; without consent asked of *him,* he finds himself living in it, bound to live in it. Once more, here is no Hearsay, but a direct Insight and Belief; this man too could not help being a sincere man! Whosoever may live in the shows of things, it is for him a necessity of nature to live in the very fact of things. A man once more, in earnest with the Universe, though all others were but toying with it. He is a *Vates,* first of all, in virtue of being sincere. So far Poet and Prophet, participators in the 'open secret,' are one.

With respect to their distinction again: The *Vates* Prophet, we might say, has seized that sacred mystery rather on the moral side, as Good and Evil, Duty and Prohibition; the *Vates* Poet on what the Germans call the æsthetic side, as Beautiful, and the like. The one we may call a revealer of what we are to do, the other of what we are to love. But indeed these two provinces run into one another, and cannot be disjoined. The Prophet too has his eye on what we are to love: how else shall he know what it is we are to do? The highest Voice ever heard on this earth said withal, 'Consider the lilies of the field; they toil not, neither do they spin: yet Solomon in all his glory was not arrayed like one of these.' A glance, that, into the deepest deep of Beauty. 'The lilies of the field,'—dressed finer than earthly princes, springing-up there in the humble furrow-field; a beautiful *eye* looking-out on you, from the great inner Sea of Beauty! How could the rude Earth make these, if her Essence, rugged as she looks and is, were not inwardly Beauty? In this point of view, too, a saying of Goethe's, which has staggered several, may have meaning: 'The Beautiful,' he intimates, 'is higher than the Good; the Beautiful includes in it the Good.' The *true* Beautiful; which however, I have said somewhere, 'differs from the *false* as Heaven does from Vauxhall!' So much for the distinction and identity of Poet and Prophet.—

In ancient and also in modern periods we find a few Poets who are accounted perfect; whom it were a kind of treason to find fault with. This is noteworthy; this is right: yet in strictness it is only an illusion. At bottom, clearly enough, there is no perfect Poet! A vein of Poetry exists in the hearts of all men; no man is made altogether of Poetry. We are all poets when we *read* a poem well. The 'imagination that shudders at the Hell of Dante,' is not that the same faculty, weaker in degree, as Dante's own? No one but Shakspeare can embody, out of *Saxo Grammaticus,* the story of *Hamlet* as Shakspeare did: but every one models some kind of story out of it; every one embodies it better or worse. We need not spend time in defining. Where there is no specific difference, as between round and square, all definition must be more or less arbitrary. A man that has *so* much more of the poetic element developed in him as to have become noticeable, will be called Poet by his neighbours. World-Poets too, those whom we are to take for perfect Poets, are settled by critics in the same way. One who rises *so* far above the general level of Poets will, to such and such critics, seem a Universal Poet; as he ought to do. And yet it is, and must be, an arbitrary distinction. All Poets, all men, have some touches of the Universal; no man is wholly made of that. Most Poets are very soon forgotten: but not the noblest Shakspeare or Homer of them can be remembered *for ever*;—a day comes when he too is not!

Nevertheless, you will say, there must be a difference between true Poetry and true Speech not poetical: what is the difference? On this point many things have been written, especially by late German Critics, some of which are not very intelligible at first. They say, for example, that the Poet has an *infinitude* in him; communicates an *Unendlich-keit*, a certain character of 'infinitude,' to whatsoever he delineates. This, though not very precise, yet on so vague a matter is worth remembering: if well meditated, some meaning will gradually be found in it. For my own part, I find considerable meaning in the old vulgar distinction of Poetry being *metrical*, having music in it, being a Song. Truly, if pressed to give a definition, one might say this as soon as anything else: If your delineation be authentically *musical*, musical not in word only, but in heart and sub-stance, in all the thoughts and utterances of it, in the whole conception of it, then it will be poetical; if not, not.—Musi-cal: how much lies in that? A *musical* thought is one spoken by a mind that has penetrated into the inmost heart of the thing; detected the inmost mystery of it, namely the *melody* that lies hidden in it; the inward harmony of coherence which is its soul, whereby it exists, and has a right to be, here in this world. All inmost things, we may say, are me-lodious; naturally utter themselves in Song. The meaning of Song goes deep. Who is there that, in logical words, can express the effect music has on us? A kind of inarticulate unfathomable speech, which leads us to the edge of the In-finite, and lets us for moments gaze into that!

Nay all speech, even the commonest speech, has some-thing of song in it: not a parish in the world but has its parish-accent;—the rhythm or *tune* to which the people there *sing* what they have to say! Accent is a kind of chant-ing; all men have accent of their own,—though they only *notice* that of others. Observe too how all passionate lan-guage does of itself become musical,—with a finer music than the mere accent; the speech of a man even in zealous anger becomes a chant, a song. All deep things are Song. It seems somehow the very central essence of us, Song; as if all the rest were but wrappages and hulls! The primal ele-ment of us; of us, and of all things. The Greeks fabled of

Sphere-Harmonies: it was the feeling they had of the inner structure of Nature; that the soul of all her voices and utterances was perfect music. Poetry, therefore, we will call *musical Thought*. The Poet is he who *thinks* in that manner. At bottom, it turns still on power of intellect; it is a man's sincerity and depth of vision that makes him a Poet. See deep enough, and you see musically; the heart of Nature *being* everywhere music, if you can only reach it.

The *Vates* Poet, with his melodious Apocalypse of Nature, seems to hold a poor rank among us, in comparison with the *Vates* Prophet; his function, and our esteem of him for his function, alike slight. The Hero taken as Divinity; the Hero taken as Prophet; then next the Hero taken only as Poet: does it not look as if our estimate of the Great Man, epoch after epoch, were continually diminishing? We take him first for a god, then for one god-inspired; and now in the next stage of it, his most miraculous word gains from us only the recognition that he is a Poet, beautiful verse-maker, man of genius, or suchlike!—It looks so; but I persuade myself that intrinsically it is not so. If we consider well, it will perhaps appear that in man still there is the *same* altogether peculiar admiration for the Heroic Gift, by what name soever called, that there at any time was.

I should say, if we do not now reckon a Great Man literally divine, it is that our notions of God, of the supreme unattainable Fountain of Splendour, Wisdom, and Heroism, are ever rising *higher*; not altogether that our reverence for these qualities, as manifested in our like, is getting lower. This is worth taking thought of. Sceptical Dilettantism, the curse of these ages, a curse which will not last for ever, does indeed in this the highest province of human things, as in all provinces, make sad work; and our reverence for great men, all crippled, blinded, paralytic as it is, comes out in poor plight, hardly recognisable. Men worship the shows of great men; the most disbelieve that there is any reality of great men to worship. The dreariest, fatalest faith; believing which, one would literally despair of human things. Nevertheless look, for example, at Napoleon! A Corsican lieutenant of artillery; that is the show of *him*: yet is he not obeyed, *worshipped* after his sort, as all the Tiaraed and Diademed of the world put together could not be? High Duchesses, and ostlers of inns, gather round the Scottish rustic, Burns;—a strange feeling dwelling in each that they

never heard a man like this; that, on the whole, this is the
man! In the secret heart of these people it still dimly reveals
itself, though there is no accredited way of uttering it at
present, that this rustic, with his black brows and flashing
sun-eyes, and strange words moving laughter and tears, is
of a dignity far beyond all others, incommensurable with
all others. Do not we feel it so? But now, were Dilettantism,
Scepticism, Triviality, and all that sorrowful brood, cast-
out of us,—as, by God's blessing, they shall one day be;
were faith in the shows of things entirely swept-out, replaced by clear faith in the *things,* so that a man acted on
the impulse of that only, and counted the other non-extant;
what a new livelier feeling towards this Burns were it!

Nay here in these ages, such as they are, have we not
two mere Poets, if not deified, yet we may say beatified?
Shakspeare and Dante are Saints of Poetry; really, if we
will think of it, *canonised,* so that it is impiety to meddle
with them. The unguided instinct of the world, working
across all these perverse impediments, has arrived at such
result. Dante and Shakspeare are a peculiar Two. They
dwell apart, in a kind of royal solitude; none equal, none
second to them: in the general feeling of the world, a certain transcendentalism, a glory as of complete perfection,
invests these two. They *are* canonised, though no Pope or
Cardinals took hand in doing it! Such, in spite of every per-
verting influence, in the most unheroic times, is still our
indestructible reverence for heroism.—We will look a little
at these Two, the Poet Dante and the Poet Shakspeare:
what little it is permitted us to say here of the Hero as Poet
will most fitly arrange itself in that fashion.

* * *

As Dante, the Italian man, was sent into our world to
embody musically the Religion of the Middle Ages, the
Religion of our Modern Europe, its Inner Life; so Shakspeare, we may say, embodies for us the Outer Life of our
Europe as developed then, its chivalries, courtesies, humours, ambitions, what practical way of thinking, acting,
looking at the world, men then had. As in Homer we may
still construe Old Greece; so in Shakspeare and Dante,
after thousands of years, what our modern Europe was, in
Faith and in Practice, will still be legible. Dante has given
us the Faith or soul; Shakspeare, in a not less noble way,

has given us the Practice or body. This latter also we were to have; a man was sent for it, the man Shakspeare. Just when that chivalry way of life had reached its last finish, and was on the point of breaking down into slow or swift dissolution, as we now see it everywhere, this other sovereign Poet, with his seeing eye, with his perennial singing voice, was sent to take note of it, to give long-enduring record of it. Two fit men: Dante, deep, fierce as the central fire of the world; Shakspeare, wide, placid, far-seeing, as the Sun, the upper light of the world. Italy produced the one world-voice; we English had the honour of producing the other.

Curious enough how, as it were by mere accident, this man came to us. I think always, so great, quiet, complete and self-sufficing is this Shakspeare, had the Warwickshire Squire not prosecuted him for deer-stealing, we had perhaps never heard of him as a Poet! The woods and skies, the rustic Life of Man in Stratford there, had been enough for this man! But indeed that strange outbudding of our whole English Existence, which we call the Elizabethan Era, did not it too come as of its own accord? The 'Tree Igdrasil' buds and withers by its own laws,—too deep for our scanning. Yet it does bud and wither, and every bough and leaf of it is there, by fixed eternal laws; not a Sir Thomas Lucy but comes at the hour fit for him. Curious, I say, and not sufficiently considered: how everything does coöperate with all; not a leaf rotting on the highway but is indissoluble portion of solar and stellar systems; no thought, word or act of man but has sprung withal out of all men, and works sooner or later, recognisably or irrecognisably, on all men! It is all a Tree: circulation of sap and influences, mutual communication of every minutest leaf with the lowest talon of a root, with every other greatest and minutest portion of the whole. The Tree Igdrasil, that has its roots down in the Kingdoms of Hela and Death, and whose boughs overspread the highest Heaven!—

In some sense it may be said that this glorious Elizabethan Era with its Shakspeare, as the outcome and flowerage of all which had preceded it, is itself attributable to the Catholicism of the Middle Ages. The Christian Faith, which was the theme of Dante's Song, had produced this Practical Life which Shakspeare was to sing. For Religion then, as it now and always is, was the soul of Practice; the primary vital fact in men's life. And remark here, as rather curious, that Middle-Age Catholicism was abolished, so far as Acts of Parliament could abolish it, before Shakspeare, the noblest product of it, made his appearance. He did make his appearance nevertheless. Nature at her own time, with Catholicism or what else might be necessary, sent him forth; taking small thought of Acts of Parliament. King-Henrys, Queen-Elizabeths go their way; and Nature too goes hers. Acts of Parliament, on the whole, are small, notwithstanding the noise they make. What Act of Parliament, debate at St. Stephen's, on the hustings or elsewhere, was it that brought this Shakspeare into being? No dining at Freemasons' Tavern, opening subscription-lists, selling of shares, and infinite other jangling and true or false endeavouring! This Elizabethan Era, and all its nobleness and blessedness, came without proclamation, preparation of ours. Priceless Shakspeare was the free gift of Nature; given altogether silently;—received altogether silently, as if it had been a thing of little account. And yet, very literally, it is a priceless thing. One should look at that side of matters too.

Of this Shakspeare of ours, perhaps the opinion one sometimes hears a little idolatrously expressed is, in fact, the right one; I think the best judgment not of this country only, but of Europe at large, is slowly pointing to the conclusion, That Shakspeare is the chief of all Poets hitherto; the greatest intellect who, in our recorded world, has left record of himself in the way of Literature. On the whole, I know not such a power of vision, such a faculty of thought, if we take all the characters of it, in any other man. Such a calmness of depth; placid joyous strength; all things imaged in that great soul of his so true and clear, as in a tranquil unfathomable sea! It has been said, that in the constructing of Shakspeare's Dramas there is, apart from all other 'faculties' as they are called, an understanding manifested, equal to that in Bacon's *Novum Organum*. That is true; and it is not a truth that strikes every one. It would become more apparent if we tried, any of us for himself, how, out of Shakspeare's dramatic materials, *we* could fashion such a result! The built house seems all so fit,—everyway as it should be, as if it came there by its own law and the nature of things,—we forget the rude disorderly quarry it was shaped from. The very perfection of the house,

as if Nature herself had made it, hides the builder's merit.
Perfect, more perfect than any other man, we may call
Shakspeare in this: he discerns, knows as by instinct,
what condition he works under, what his materials are,
what his own force and its relation to them is. It is not
a transitory glance of insight that will suffice; it is deliberate
illumination of the whole matter; it is a calmly *seeing* eye;
a great intellect, in short. How a man, of some wide thing
that he has witnessed, will construct a narrative, what kind
of picture and delineation he will give of it,—is the best
measure you could get of what intellect is in the man. Which
circumstance is vital and shall stand prominent; which unessential, fit to be suppressed; where is the true *beginning,*
the true sequence and ending? To find out this, you task
the whole force of insight that is in the man. He must
understand the thing; according to the depth of his understanding, will the fitness of his answer be. You will try him
so. Does like join itself to like; does the spirit of method
stir in that confusion, so that its embroilment becomes
order? Can the man say, *Fiat lux,* Let there be light; and
out of chaos make a world? Precisely as there is *light* in himself, will he accomplish this.

Or indeed we may say again, it is in what I called Por-
trait-painting, delineating of men and things, especially of
men, that Shakspeare is great. All the greatness of the
man comes out decisively here. It is unexampled, I think,
that calm creative perspicacity of Shakspeare. The thing
he looks at reveals not this or that face of it, but its inmost
heart, and generic secret: it dissolves itself as in light before him, so that he discerns the perfect structure of it.
Creative, we said: poetic creation, what is this too but *seeing* the thing sufficiently? The *word* that will describe the
thing, follows of itself from such clear intense sight of the
thing. And is not Shakspeare's *morality,* his valour, candour, tolerance, truthfulness; his whole victorious strength
and greatness, which can triumph over such obstructions,
visible there too? Great as the world! No *twisted,* poor
convex-concave mirror, reflecting all objects with its own
convexities and concavities; a perfectly *level* mirror;—that
is to say withal, if we will understand it, a man justly related to all things and men, a good man. It is truly a lordly
spectacle how this great soul takes-in all kinds of men and
objects, a Falstaff, an Othello, a Juliet, a Coriolanus; sets

them all forth to us in their round completeness; loving, just, the equal brother of all. *Novum Organum,* and all the intellect you will find in Bacon, is of a quite secondary order; earthly, material, poor in comparison with this. Among modern men, one finds, in strictness, almost nothing of the same rank. Goethe alone, since the days of Shakspeare, reminds me of it. Of him too you say that he *saw* the object; you may say what he himself says of Shakspeare: 'His characters are like watches with dial-plates of transparent crystal; they show you the hour like others, and the inward mechanism also is all visible.'

The seeing eye! It is this that discloses the inner harmony of things; what Nature meant, what musical idea Nature has wrapped-up in these often rough embodiments. Something she did mean. To the seeing eye that something were discernible. Are they base, miserable things? You can laugh over them, you can weep over them; you can in some way or other genially relate yourself to them;—you can, at lowest, hold your peace about them, turn away your own and others' face from them, till the hour come for practically exterminating and extinguishing them! At bottom, it is the Poet's first gift, as it is all men's, that he have intellect enough. He will be a Poet if he have: a Poet in word; or failing that, perhaps still better, a Poet in act. Whether he write at all; and if so, whether in prose or in verse, will depend on accidents: who knows on what extremely trivial accidents,—perhaps on his having had a singing-master, on his being taught to sing in his boyhood! But the faculty which enables him to discern the inner heart of things, and the harmony that dwells there (for whatsoever exists has a harmony in the heart of it, or it would not hold together and exist), is not the result of habits or accidents, but the gift of Nature herself; the primary outfit for a Heroic Man in what sort soever. To the Poet, as to every other, we say first of all, *See.* If you cannot do that, it is of no use to keep stringing rhymes together, jingling sensibilities against each other, and *name* yourself a Poet; there is no hope for you. If you can, there is, in prose or verse, in action or speculation, all manner of hope. The crabbed old Schoolmaster used to ask, when they brought him a new pupil, 'But are ye sure he's *not a dunce?*' Why, really one might ask the same thing, in regard to every man proposed for whatsoever function; and consider it as the one inquiry needful: Are ye sure he's not a dunce? There is, in this world, no other entirely fatal person.

For, in fact, I say the degree of vision that dwells in a man is a correct measure of the man. If called to define Shakspeare's faculty, I should say superiority of Intellect, and think I had included all under that. What indeed are faculties? We talk of faculties as if they were distinct, things separable; as if a man had intellect, imagination, fancy, etc., as he has hands, feet, and arms. That is a capital error. Then again, we hear of a man's 'intellectual nature,' and of his 'moral nature,' as if these again were divisible, and existed apart. Necessities of language do perhaps prescribe such forms of utterance; we must speak, I am aware, in that way, if we are to speak at all. But words ought not to harden into things for us. It seems to me, our apprehension of this matter is, for most part, radically falsified thereby. We ought to know withal, and to keep for ever in mind, that these divisions are at bottom but *names*; that man's spiritual nature, the vital Force which dwells in him, is essentially one and indivisible; that what we call imagination, fancy, understanding, and so forth, are but different figures of the same Power of Insight, all indissolubly connected with each other, physiognomically related; that if we knew one of them, we might know all of them. Morality itself, what we call the moral quality of a man, what is this but another *side* of the one vital Force whereby he is and works? All that a man does is physiognomical of him. You may see how a man would fight, by the way in which he sings; his courage, or want of courage, is visible in the word he utters, in the opinion he has formed, no less than in the stroke he strikes. He is *one*; and preaches the same Self abroad in all these ways.

Without hands a man might have feet, and could still walk: but, consider it,—without morality, intellect were impossible for him; a thoroughly immoral *man* could not know anything at all! To know a thing, what we can call knowing, a man must first *love* the thing, sympathise with it: that is, be *virtuously* related to it. If he have not the justice to put down his own selfishness at every turn, the courage to stand by the dangerous-true at every turn, how shall he know? His virtues, all of them, will lie recorded in his knowledge. Nature, with her truth, remains to the bad, to the selfish and the pusillanimous for ever a sealed book: what such can know of Nature is mean, superficial, small; for the uses of the day merely.—But does not the very Fox know something of Nature? Exactly so: it knows where the geese lodge! The human Reynard, very frequent everywhere in the world, what more does he know but this and the like of this? Nay, it should be considered too, that if the Fox had not a certain vulpine *morality*, he could not even know where the geese were, or get at the geese! If he spent his time in splenetic atrabiliar reflections on his own misery, his ill usage by Nature, Fortune and other Foxes, and so forth; and had not courage, promptitude, practicality, and other suitable vulpine gifts and graces, he would catch no geese. We may say of the Fox too, that his morality and insight are of the same dimensions; different faces of the same internal unity of vulpine life!—These things are worth stating; for the contrary of them acts with manifold very baleful perversion, in this time: what limitations, modifications they require, your own candour will supply.

If I say therefore, that Shakspeare is the greatest of Intellects, I have said all concerning him. But there is more in Shakspeare's intellect than we have yet seen. It is what I call an unconscious intellect; there is more virtue in it than he himself is aware of. Novalis beautifully remarks of him, that those Dramas of his are Products of Nature too, deep as Nature herself. I find a great truth in this saying. Shakspeare's Art is not Artifice; the noblest worth of it is not there by plan or precontrivance. It grows-up from the deeps of Nature, through this noble sincere soul, who is a voice of Nature. The latest generations of men will find new meanings in Shakspeare, new elucidations of their own human being; 'new harmonies with the infinite structure of the Universe; concurrences with later ideas, affinities with the higher powers and senses of man.' This well deserves meditating. It is Nature's highest reward to a true simple great soul, that he get thus to be *a part of herself*. Such a man's works, whatsoever he with utmost conscious exertion and forethought shall accomplish, grow up withal *un*consciously, from the unknown deeps in him;—as the oak-tree grows from the Earth's bosom, as the mountains and waters shape themselves; with a symmetry grounded on

Nature's own laws, conformable to all Truth whatsoever. How much in Shakspeare lies hid; his sorrows, his silent struggles known to himself; much that was not known at all, not speakable at all: like *roots,* like sap and forces working underground! Speech is great; but Silence is greater.

Withal the joyful tranquillity of this man is notable. I will not blame Dante for his misery: it is as battle without victory; but true battle,—the first, indispensable thing. Yet I call Shakspeare greater than Dante, in that he fought truly, and did conquer. Doubt it not, he had his own sorrows: those *Sonnets* of his will even testify expressly in what deep waters he had waded, and swum struggling for his life;—as what man like him ever failed to have to do? It seems to me a heedless notion, our common one, that he sat like a bird on the bough; and sang forth, free and off-hand, never knowing the troubles of other men. Not so; with no man is it so. How could a man travel forward from rustic deer-poaching to such tragedy-writing, and not fall-in with sorrows by the way? Or, still better, how could a man delineate a Hamlet, a Coriolanus, a Macbeth, so many suffering heroic hearts, if his own heroic heart had never suffered?—And now, in contrast with all this, observe his mirthfulness, his genuine overflowing love of laughter! You would say, in no point does he *exaggerate* but only in laughter. Fiery objurgations, words that pierce and burn, are to be found in Shakspeare; yet he is always in measure here; never what Johnson would remark as a specially 'good hater.' But his laughter seems to pour from him in floods; he heaps all manner of ridiculous nicknames on the butt he is bantering, tumbles and tosses him in all sorts of horse-play; you would say, with his whole heart laughs. And then, if not always the finest, it is always a genial laughter. Not at mere weakness, at misery or poverty; never. No man who *can* laugh, what we call laughing, will laugh at these things. It is some poor character only *desiring* to laugh, and have the credit of wit, that does so. Laughter means sympathy; good laughter is not 'the crackling of thorns under the pot.' Even at stupidity and pretension this Shakespeare does not laugh otherwise than genially. Dogberry and Verges tickle our very hearts; and we dismiss them covered with explosions of laughter: but we like the poor fellows only the better for our laughing; and hope they will get on well there, and continue Presidents of the City-watch. Such laughter, like sunshine on the deep sea, is very beautiful to me.

We have no room to speak of Shakspeare's individual works; though perhaps there is much still waiting to be said on that head. Had we, for instance, all his plays reviewed as *Hamlet,* in *Wilhelm Meister,* is! A thing which might, one day, be done. August Wilhelm Schlegel has a remark on his Historical Plays, *Henry Fifth* and the others, which is worth remembering. He calls them a kind of National Epic. Marlborough, you recollect, said, he knew no English History but what he had learned from Shakspeare. There are really, if we look to it, few as memorable Histories. The great salient points are admirably seized; all rounds itself off, into a kind of rhythmic coherence; it is, as Schlegel says, *epic;*—as indeed all delineation by a great thinker will be. There are right beautiful things in those Pieces, which indeed together form one beautiful thing. That battle of Agincourt strikes me as one of the most perfect things, in its sort, we anywhere have of Shakspeare's. The description of the two hosts: the worn-out, jaded English; the dread hour, big with destiny, when the battle shall begin; and then that deathless valour: 'Ye good yeomen, whose limbs were made in England!' There is a noble Patriotism in it,— far other than the 'indifference' you sometimes hear ascribed to Shakspeare. A true English heart breathes, calm and strong, through the whole business; not boisterous, protrusive; all the better for that. There is a sound in it like the ring of steel. This man too had a right stroke in him, had it come to that!

But I will say, of Shakspeare's works generally, that we have no full impress of him there; even as full as we have of many men. His works are so many windows, through which we see a glimpse of the world that was in him. All his works seem, comparatively speaking, cursory, imperfect, written under cramping circumstances; giving only here and there a note of the full utterance of the man. Passages there are that come upon you like splendour out of Heaven; bursts of radiance, illuminating the very heart of the thing: you say, 'That is *true,* spoken once and for ever; wheresoever and whensoever there is an open human soul, that will be recognised as true!' Such bursts, however, make us feel that the surrounding matter is not radiant; that it is, in part, temporary, conventional. Alas, Shakspeare had to write for the Globe Playhouse: his great soul had to crush itself, as it could, into that and no other mould. It was with him, then, as it is with us all. No man works save under conditions. The sculptor cannot set his own free Thought before us; but his Thought as he could translate it into the stone that was given, with the tools that were given. *Disjecta membra* are all that we find of any Poet, or of any man.

Whoever looks intelligently at this Shakspeare may recognise that he too was a *Prophet,* in his way; of an insight analogous to the Prophetic, though he took it up in another strain. Nature seemed to this man also divine; *un*speakable, deep as Tophet, high as Heaven: 'We are such stuff as Dreams are made of!' That scroll in Westminster Abbey, which few read with understanding, is of the depth of any seer. But the man sang; did not preach, except musically. We called Dante the melodious Priest of Middle-Age Catholicism. May we not call Shakspeare the still more melodious Priest of a *true* Catholicism, the 'Universal Church' of the Future and of all times? No narrow superstition, harsh asceticism, intolerance, fanatical fierceness or perversion: a Revelation, so far as it goes, that such a thousand-fold hidden beauty and divineness dwells in all Nature; which let all men worship as they can! We may say without offence, that there rises a kind of universal Psalm out of this Shakspeare too; not unfit to make itself heard among the still more sacred Psalms. Not in disharmony with these, if we understood them, but in harmony!—I cannot call this Shakspeare a 'Sceptic,' as some do; his indifference to the creeds and theological quarrels of his time misleading them. No: neither unpatriotic, though he says little about his Patriotism; nor sceptic, though he says little about his Faith. Such 'indifference' was the fruit of his greatness withal: his whole heart was in his own grand sphere of worship (we may call it such); these other controversies, vitally important to other men, were not vital to him.

But call it worship, call it what you will, is it not a right glorious thing, and set of things, this that Shakspeare has brought us? For myself, I feel that there is actually a kind of sacredness in the fact of such a man being sent into this Earth. Is he not an eye to us all; a blessed heaven-sent Bringer of Light?—And, at bottom, was it not perhaps far better that this Shakspeare, everyway an unconscious man, was *conscious* of no Heavenly message? He did not feel, like Mahomet, because he saw into those internal Splendours, that he specially was the 'Prophet of God': and was he not greater than Mahomet in that? Greater; and also, if we compute strictly, as we did in Dante's case, more successful. It was intrinsically an error that notion of Mahomet's, of his supreme Prophethood; and has come down to us inextricably involved in error to this day; dragging along with it such a coil of fables, impurities, intolerances, as makes it a questionable step for me here and now to say, as I have done, that Mahomet was a true Speaker at all, and not rather an ambitious charlatan, perversity and simulacrum; no Speaker, but a Babbler! Even in Arabia, as I compute, Mahomet will have exhausted himself and become obsolete, while this Shakspeare, this Dante may still be young;—while this Shakspeare may still pretend to be a Priest of Mankind, of Arabia as of other places, for unlimited periods to come!

Compared with any speaker or singer one knows, even with Æschylus or Homer, why should he not, for veracity and universality, last like them? He is *sincere* as they; reaches deep down like them, to the universal and perennial. But as for Mahomet, I think it had been better for him *not* to be so conscious! Alas, poor Mahomet; all that he was *conscious* of was a mere error; a futility and triviality,—as indeed such ever is. The truly great in him too was the unconscious that he was a wild Arab lion of the desert, and did speak-out with that great thunder-voice of his, not by words which he *thought* to be great, but by actions, by feelings, by a history which *were* great! His Koran has become a stupid piece of prolix absurdity; we do not believe, like him, that God wrote that! The Great Man here too, as always, is a Force of Nature: whatsoever is truly great in him springs-up from the *in*articulate deeps.

Well: this is our poor Warwickshire Peasant, who rose to be Manager of a Playhouse, so that he could live without begging; whom the Earl of Southampton cast some kind glances on; whom Sir Thomas Lucy, many thanks to him, was for sending to the Treadmill! We did not account him a god, like Odin, while he dwelt with us;—on which point there were much to be said. But I will say rather, or repeat: In spite of the sad state Hero-worship now lies in, consider

what this Shakspeare has actually become among us.
Which Englishman we ever made, in this land of ours,
which million of Englishmen, would we not give-up rather
than the Stratford Peasant? There is no regiment of highest
Dignitaries that we would sell him for. He is the grandest
thing we have yet done. For our honour among foreign
nations, as an ornament to our English Household, what
item is there that we would not surrender rather than him?
Consider now, if they asked us, Will you give-up your Indian Empire or your Shakspeare, you English; never have
had any Indian Empire, or never have had any Shakspeare?
Really it were a grave question. Official persons would answer doubtless in official language; but we, for our part too,
should not we be forced to answer: Indian Empire, or no
Indian Empire; we cannot do without Shakspeare! Indian
Empire will go, at any rate, some day; but this Shakspeare
does not go, he lasts for ever with us; we cannot give-up
our Shakspeare!

Nay, apart from spiritualities; and considering him
merely as a real, marketable, tangibly-useful possession. England, before long, this Island of ours, will hold but a small
fraction of the English: in America, in New Holland, east
and west to the very Antipodes, there will be a Saxondom
covering great spaces of the Globe. And now, what is it
that can keep all these together into virtually one Nation, so
that they do not fall-out and fight, but live at peace, in
brotherlike intercourse, helping one another? This is justly
regarded as the greatest practical problem, the thing all
manner of sovereignties and governments are here to accomplish: what is it that will accomplish this? Acts of Parliament, administrative prime-ministers cannot. America is
parted from us, so far as Parliament could part it. Call it not
fantastic, for there is much reality in it: Here, I say, is an
English King, whom no time or chance, Parliament or combination of Parliaments, can dethrone! This King Shakspeare, does not he shine, in crowned sovereignty, over us
all, as the noblest, gentlest, yet strongest of rallying-signs;
*in*destructible; really more valuable in that point of view
than any other means or appliance whatsoever? We can
fancy him as radiant aloft over all the Nations of Englishmen, a thousand years hence. From Paramatta, from New
York, wheresoever, under what sort of Parish-Constable
soever, English men and women are, they will say to one

another: 'Yes, this Shakspeare is ours; we produced him, we speak and think by him; we are of one blood and kind with him.' The most common-sense politician, too, if he pleases, may think of that.

Yes, truly, it is a great thing for a Nation that it get an articulate voice; that it produce a man who will speak-forth melodiously what the heart of it means! Italy, for example, poor Italy lies dismembered, scattered asunder, not appearing in any protocol or treaty as a unity at all; yet the noble Italy is actually *one*: Italy produced its Dante; Italy can speak! The Czar of all the Russias, he is strong, with so many bayonets, Cossacks, and cannons; and does a great feat in keeping such a tract of Earth politically together; but he cannot yet speak. Something great in him, but it is a dumb greatness. He has had no voice of genius, to be heard of all men and times. He must learn to speak. He is a great dumb monster hitherto. His cannons and Cossacks will all have rusted into nonentity, while that Dante's voice is still audible. The Nation that has Dante is bound together as no dumb Russia can be.—We must here end what we had to say of the *Hero-Poet*.

FROM *Past and Present*

1 8 4 3

[*Chartism* (1839) had expressed Carlyle's dismay over the "Con-
dition-of-England question," the matter of the estrangement between social classes that many believed threatened revolution.
The abortive Chartist movement of the late eighteen-thirties and
eighteen-forties was the occasion for Carlyle to lash out against
the deficiencies of the English ruling class. Then, following his
last lecture series in 1840, he began gathering materials for a
life of Oliver Cromwell (1599-1658). He visited the workhouse
of St. Ives, Huntingdonshire, and saw the disastrous effects of
the Poor Laws which compelled many able-bodied men to sit
idle. In Suffolk he visited the ruins of Bury St. Edmunds monastery, which was of particular interest because of the publication
in 1840 by the Camden Society of the chronicle of Jocelin of
Brakelond, a monk of Bury St. Edmunds in the twelfth century.
Carlyle interrupted his work on Cromwell and fused these other
two matters. In a brilliant counterpointing of the old and the
new he wrote *Past and Present,* contrasting the ordered, hierarchical life of an English abbey of the twelfth century with the
squalid, disoriented life of contemporary industrial England.
He showed that, for all its faults, medieval monastic life was
capable of just government because it was governed by an aristocracy of talent, whereas modern English life was governed by
the likes of Sir Jabesh Windbag and was fast hurtling toward
the chaos of democracy, which Carlyle had come to detest. The
great power of *Past and Present* lies in the abuse Carlyle heaped
on ideas and institutions he disliked and the vibrant and luminous
evocation of monastic and medieval life, far more compelling
than the airy confections of much gothic revival poetry.

The brief selections that follow are taken from Book II, "The
Ancient Monk," and depict, first the chronicler Jocelin, and then
life in the Abbey of Bury St. Edmunds itself.]

FROM BOOK II—THE ANCIENT
MONK / CHAPTER I

JOCELIN OF BRAKELOND

We will, in this Second Portion of our Work, strive to penetrate a little, by means of certain confused Papers, printed
and other, into a somewhat remote Century; and to look
face to face on it, in hope of perhaps illustrating our own
poor Century thereby. It seems a circuitous way; but it may
prove a way nevertheless. For man has ever been a striving,
struggling, and, in spite of wide-spread calumnies to the
contrary, a veracious creature: the Centuries too are all
lineal children of one another; and often, in the portrait
of early grandfathers, this and the other enigmatic feature
of the newest grandson shall disclose itself, to mutual elucidation. This Editor will venture on such a thing.

Besides, in Editors' Books, and indeed everywhere else
in the world of Today, a certain latitude of movement grows
more and more becoming for the practical man. Salvation
lies not in tight lacing, in these times;—how far from
that, in any province whatsoever! Readers and men generally are getting into strange habits of asking all persons
and things, from poor Editors' Books up to Church Bishops
and State Potentates, not, By what designation art thou
called; in what wig and black triangle dost thou walk
abroad? Heavens, I know thy designation and black triangle
well enough! But in God's name, what *art* thou? Not Nothing, sayest thou! Then, How much and what? This is the
thing I would know; and even *must* soon know, such a pass
am I come to!——What weather-symptoms,—not for the
poor Editor of Books alone! The Editor of Books may
understand withal that if, as is said, 'many kinds are permissible,' there is one kind not permissible, 'the kind that has
nothing in it, *le genre ennuyeux*'; and go on his way accordingly.

A certain Jocelinus de Brakelonda, a natural-born Englishman, has left us an extremely foreign Book,[1] which the

---

[1] *Chronica* JOCELINI DE BRAKELONDA, *de rebus gestis Samsonis Abbatis
Monasterii Sancti Edmundi: nunc primum typis mandata, curante
Johanne Gage Rokewood.* (Camden Society, London, 1840.) [Carlyle's
note.]

labours of the Camden Society have brought to light in these days. Jocelin's Book, the 'Chronicle,' or private Boswellean Notebook, of Jocelin, a certain old St. Edmundsbury Monk and Boswell, now seven centuries old, how remote is it from us; exotic, extraneous; in all ways, coming from far abroad! The language of it is not foreign only but dead: Monk-Latin lies across not the British Channel, but the ninefold Stygian Marshes, Stream of Lethe, and one knows not where! Roman Latin itself, still alive for us in the Elysian Fields of Memory, is domestic in comparison. And then the ideas, life-furniture, whole workings and ways of this worthy Jocelin; covered deeper than Pompeii with the lava-ashes and inarticulate wreck of seven hundred years!

Jocelin of Brakelond cannot be called a conspicuous literary character; indeed few mortals that have left so visible a work, or footmark, behind them can be more obscure. One other of those vanished Existences, whose work has not yet vanished;—almost a pathetic phenomenon, were not the whole world full of such! The builders of Stonehenge, for example:—or, alas, what say we, Stonehenge and builders? The writers of the *Universal Review* and *Homer's Iliad*; the paviors of London streets;—sooner or later, the entire Posterity of Adam! It is a pathetic phenomenon; but an irremediable, nay, if well meditated, a consoling one.

By his dialect of Monk-Latin, and indeed by his name, this Jocelin seems to have been a Norman Englishman; the surname *de Brakelonda* indicates a native of St. Edmundsbury itself, *Brakelond* being the known old name of a street or quarter in that venerable Town. Then farther, sure enough, our Jocelin was a Monk of St. Edmundsbury Convent; held some '*obedientia*,' subaltern officiality there, or rather, in succession several; was, for one thing, 'chaplain to my Lord Abbot, living beside him night and day for the space of six years';—which last, indeed, is the grand fact of Jocelin's existence, and properly the origin of this present Book, and of the chief meaning it has for us now. He was, as we have hinted, a kind of born *Boswell*, though an infinitesimally small one; neither did he altogether want his *Johnson* even there and then. Johnsons are rare; yet, as has been asserted, Boswells perhaps still rarer,—the more is the pity on both sides! This Jocelin, as we can discern well, was an ingenious and ingenuous, a cheery-hearted, innocent, yet withal shrewd, noticing, quick-witted man; and from under his monk's cowl has looked out on that narrow section of the world in a really *human* manner; not in any *simial,* canine, ovine, or otherwise *in*human manner,—afflictive to all that have humanity! The man is of patient, peaceable, loving, clear-smiling nature; open for this and that. A wise simplicity is in him; much natural sense; a *veracity* that goes deeper than words. Veracity: it is the basis of all; and, some say, means genius itself; the prime essence of all genius whatsoever. Our Jocelin, for the rest, has read his classical manuscripts, his Virgilius, his Flaccus, Ovidius Naso; of course still more, his Homilies and Breviaries, and if not the Bible, considerable extracts of the Bible. Then also he has a pleasant wit; and loves a timely joke, though in mild subdued manner: very amiable to see. A learned grown man, yet with the heart as of a good child; whose whole life indeed has been that of a child,—St. Edmundsbury Monastery a larger kind of cradle for him, in which his whole prescribed duty was to *sleep* kindly, and love his mother well! This is the Biography of Jocelin; 'a man of excellent religion,' says one of his contemporary Brother Monks, *'eximiæ religionis, potens sermone et opere.'*

For one thing, he had learned to write a kind of Monk or Dog-Latin, still readable to mankind; and, by good luck for us, had bethought him of noting down thereby what things seemed notablest to him. Hence gradually resulted a *Chronica Jocelini;* new Manuscript in the *Liber Albus* of St. Edmundsbury. Which Chronicle, once written in its child-like transparency, in its innocent good-humour, not without touches of ready pleasant wit and many kinds of worth, other men liked naturally to read: whereby it failed not to be copied, to be multiplied, to be inserted in the *Liber Albus*; and so surviving Henry the Eighth, Putney Cromwell, the Dissolution of Monasteries, and all accidents of malice and neglect for six centuries or so, it got into the *Harleian Collection,*—and has now therefrom, by Mr. Rokewood of the Camden Society, been deciphered into clear print; and lies before us, a dainty thin quarto, to interest for a few minutes whomsoever it can.

Here too it will behove a just Historian gratefully to say that Mr. Rokewood, Jocelin's Editor, has done his editorial function well. Not only has he deciphered his crabbed Manuscript into clear print; but he has attended, what his fellow editors are not always in the habit of doing, to the important truth that the Manuscript so deciphered ought to have a meaning for the reader. Standing faithfully by his text, and printing its very errors in spelling, in grammar or otherwise, he has taken care by some note to indicate that they are errors, and what the correction of them ought to be. Jocelin's Monk-Latin is generally transparent, as shallow limpid water. But at any stop that may occur, of which there a few, and only a very few, we have the comfortable assurance that a meaning does lie in the passage, and may by industry be got at; that a faithful editor's industry had already got at it before passing on. A compendious useful Glossary is given; nearly adequate to help the uninitiated through: sometimes one wishes it had been a trifle larger; but, with a Spelman and Ducange at your elbow, how easy to have made it far too large! Notes are added, generally brief; sufficiently explanatory of most points. Lastly, a copious correct Index; which no such Book should want, and which unluckily very few possess. And so, in a word, the *Chronicle of Jocelin* is, as it professes to be, unwrapped from its thick cerements, and fairly brought forth into the common daylight, so that he who runs, and has a smattering of grammar, may read.

We have heard so much of Monks; everywhere, in real and fictitious History, from Muratori Annals to Radcliffe Romances, these singular two-legged animals, with their rosaries and breviaries, with their shaven crowns, hair-cilices, and vows of poverty, masquerade so strangely through our fancy; and they are in fact so very strange an extinct species of the human family,—a veritable Monk of Bury St. Edmunds is worth attending to, if by chance made visible and audible. Here he is; and in his hand a magical speculum, much gone to rust indeed, yet in fragments still clear; wherein the marvellous image of his existence does still shadow itself, though fitfully, and as with an intermittent light! Will not the reader peep with us into this singular *camera lucida,* where an extinct species, though fitfully, can still be seen alive? Extinct species, we say; for the live specimens which still go about under that character are too evidently to be classed as spurious in Natural History: the Gospel of Richard Arkwright once promulgated, no Monk of the old sort is any longer possible in this world. But fancy a deep-buried Mastodon, some fossil Megatherion, Ichthyosaurus, were to begin to *speak* from amid its rock-swath-ings, never so indistinctly! The most extinct fossil species of Men or Monks can do, and does this miracle,—thanks to the Letters of the Alphabet, good for so many things.

Jocelin, we said, was somewhat of a Boswell; but un-fortunately, by Nature, he is none of the largest, and dis-tance has now dwarfed him to an extreme degree. His light is most feeble, intermittent, and requires the intensest, kind-est inspection; otherwise it will disclose mere vacant haze. It must be owned, the good Jocelin, spite of his beautiful child-like character, is but an altogether imperfect 'mirror' of these old-world things! The good man, he looks on us so clear and cheery, and in his neighbourly soft-smiling eyes we see so well our *own* shadow—we have a longing always to cross-question him, to force from him an explanation of much. But no; Jocelin, though he talks with such clear familiarity, like a next-door neighbour, will not answer any questions; that is the peculiarity of him, dead these six hun-dred and fifty years, and quite deaf to us, though still so audible! The good man, he cannot help it, nor can we.

But truly it is a strange consideration this simple one, as we go on with him, or indeed with any lucid simple-hearted soul like him: Behold therefore, this England of the Year 1200 was no chimerical vacuity or dreamland, peopled with mere vapourous Fantasms, Rymer's Fœdera, and Doc-trines of the Constitution; but a green solid place, that grew corn and several other things. The Sun shone on it; the vicissitude of seasons and human fortunes. Cloth was woven and worn; ditches were dug, furrow-fields ploughed, and houses built. Day by day all men and cattle rose to labour, and night by night returned home weary to their several lairs. In wondrous Dualism, then as now, lived na-tions of breathing men; alternating, in all ways, between Light and Dark; between joy and sorrow, between rest and toil,—between hope, hope reaching high as heaven, and fear deep as very Hell. Not vapour Fantasms, Rymer's Fœdera at all! Cœur-de-Lion was not a theatrical popinjay with greaves and steel-cap on it, but a man living upon vic-tuals,—*not* imported by Peel's Tariff. Cœur-de-Lion came palpably athwart this Jocelin at St. Edmundsbury; and had almost peeled the sacred gold 'Feretrum,' or St. Edmund Shrine itself, to ransom him out of the Danube Jail.

These clear eyes of neighbour Jocelin looked on the

bodily presence of King John; the very John *Sansterre,* or
Lackland, who signed *Magna Charta* afterwards in Runny-
mede. Lackland, with a great retinue, boarded once, for
the matter of a fortnight, in St. Edmundsbury Convent;
daily in the very eye-sight, palpable to the very fingers of
our Jocelin: O Jocelin, what did he say, what did he do;
how looked he, lived he;—at the very lowest, what coat or
breeches had he on? Jocelin is obstinately silent. Jocelin
marks down what interests *him*; entirely deaf to *us*. With
Jocelin's eyes we discern nothing of John Lackland. As
through a glass darkly, we with our own eyes and appliances, intensely looking, discern at most: A blustering,
dissipated human figure, with a kind of blackguard quality
air, in cramoisy velvet, or other uncertain texture, uncertain cut, with much plumage and fringing; amid numerous
other human figures of the like; riding abroad with hawks;
talking noisy nonsense;—tearing out the bowels of St.
Edmundsbury Convent (its larders namely and cellars) in
the most ruinous way, by living at rack and manger there.
Jocelin notes only, with a slight subacidity of manner, that
the King's Majesty, *Dominus Rex,* did leave, as gift for our
St. Edmund Shrine, a handsome enough silk-cloak—or
rather pretended to leave, for one of his retinue borrowed
it of us, and *we* never got sight of it again; and, on the
whole, that the *Dominus Rex,* at departing, gave us 'thirteen
sterlingii,' one shilling and one penny, to say a mass for
him; and so departed,—like a shabby Lackland as he was!
'Thirteen pence sterling,' this was what the Convent got
from Lackland, for all the victuals he and his had made
away with. We of course said our mass for him, having
covenanted to do it,—but let impartial posterity judge
with what degree of fervour!

And in this manner vanishes King Lackland; traverses
swiftly our strange intermittent magic-mirror, jingling the
shabby thirteen pence merely; and rides with his hawks into
Egyptian night again. It is Jocelin's manner with all things;
and it is men's manner and men's necessity. How intermittent is our good Jocelin; marking down, without eye to *us*,
what *he* finds interesting! How much in Jocelin, as in all
History, and indeed in all Nature, is at once inscrutable and
certain; so dim, yet so indubitable; exciting us to endless
considerations. For King Lackland *was* there, verily he; and
did leave these *tredecim sterlingii,* if nothing more, and did

live and look in one way or the other, and a whole world was living and looking along with him! There, we say, is the grand peculiarity; the immeasurable one; distinguishng, to a really infinite degree, the poorest historical Fact from all Fiction whatsoever. Fiction, 'Imagination,' 'Imaginative Poetry,' etc. etc., except as the vehicle for truth, or *fact* of some sort,—which surely a man should first try various other ways of vehiculating, and conveying safe,—what is it? Let the Minerva and other Presses respond!—

But it is time we were in St. Edmundsbury Monastery and Seven good Centuries off. If indeed it be possible, by any aid of Jocelin, by any human art, to get thither, with a reader or two still following us?

CHAPTER II

ST. EDMUNDSBURY

The *Burg,* Bury, or 'Berry' as they call it, of St. Edmund is still a prosperous brisk Town; beautifully diversifying, with its clear brick houses, ancient clean streets, and twenty or fifteen thousand busy souls, the general grassy face of Suffolk; looking out right pleasantly, from its hill-slope, towards the rising Sun: and on the eastern edge of it, still runs, long, black and massive, a range of monastic ruins; into the wide internal spaces of which the stranger is admitted on payment of one shilling. Internal spaces laid out, at present, as a botanic garden. Here stranger or towns-man sauntering at his leisure amid these vast grim venerable ruins, may persuade himself that an Abbey of St. Edmunds-bury did once exist; nay there is no doubt of it: see here the ancient massive Gateway, of architecture interesting to the eye of Dilettantism; and farther on, that other ancient Gateway, now about to tumble, unless Dilettantism, in these very months, can subscribe money to cramp it and prop it!

Here, sure enough, is an Abbey; beautiful in the eye of Dilettantism, Giant Pedantry also will step in, with its huge *Dugdale* and other enormous *Monasticons* under its arm, and cheerfully apprise you, That this was a very great Ab-bey, owner and indeed creator of St. Edmund's Town itself, owner of wide lands and revenues; nay that its lands were once a county of themselves; that indeed King Canute or Knut was very kind to it, and gave St. Edmund his own gold crown off his head, on one occasion: for the rest, that the Monks were of such and such a genus, such and such a number; that they had so many carucates of land in this hundred, and so many in that; and then farther that the large Tower or Belfry was built by such a one, and the smaller Belfry was built by etc. etc.—Till human nature can stand no more of it; till human nature desperately take refuge in forgetfulness, almost in flat disbelief of the whole business, Monks, Monastery, Belfries, Carucates and all! Alas, what mountains of dead ashes, wreck and burnt bones, does assiduous Pedantry dig up from the Past Time, and name it History, and Philosophy of History; till, as we say, the human soul sinks wearied and bewildered; till the Past Time seems all one infinite incredible gray void, without sun, stars, hearth-fires, or candle-light; dim offensive dust-whirlwinds filling universal Nature; and over your Historical Library, it is as if all the Titans had written for themselves: DRY RUBBISH SHOT HERE!

And yet these grim old walls are not a dilettantism and dubiety; they are an earnest fact. It was a most real and serious purpose they were built for! Yes, another world it was, when these black ruins, white in their new mortar and fresh chiselling, first saw the sun as walls, long ago. Gauge not, with thy dilettante compasses, with that placid dilet-tante simper, the Heaven's-Watchtower of our Fathers, the fallen God's-Houses, the Golgotha of true Souls departed!

Their architecture, belfries, land-carucates? Yes,—and that is but a small item of the matter. Does it never give thee pause, this other strange item of it, that men then had a *soul*,—not by hearsay alone, and as a figure of speech; but as a truth that they *knew*, and practically went upon! Verily it was another world then. Their Missals have be-come incredible, a sheer platitude, sayest thou? Yes, a most poor platitude; and even, if thou wilt, an idolatry and blas-phemy, should any one persuade *thee* to believe them, to pretend praying by them. But yet it is pity we had lost tid-ings of our souls:—actually we shall have to go in quest of them again, or worse in all ways will befall! A certain de-gree of soul, as Ben Jonson reminds us, is indispensable to keep the very body from destruction of the frightfulest sort; to 'save us,' says he, 'the expense of *salt*.' Ben has known men who had soul enough to keep their body and five senses from becoming carrion, and save salt:—men, and also Nations. You may look in Manchester Hunger-mobs and Corn-law Commons Houses, and various other quarters, and say whether either soul or else salt is not somewhat wanted at present!—

Another world, truly: and this present poor distressed world might get some profit by looking wisely into it, instead of foolishly. But at lowest, O dilettante friend, let us know always that it *was* a world, and not a void infinite of gray haze with fantasms swimming in it. These old St. Edmundsbury walls, I say, were not peopled with fantasms; but with men of flesh and blood, made altogether as we are. Had thou and I then been, who knows but we ourselves had taken refuge from an evil Time, and fled to dwell here, and meditate on an Eternity, in such fashion as we could? Alas, how like an old osseous fragment, a broken blackened shinbone of the old dead Ages, this black ruin looks out, not yet covered by the soil; still indicating what a once gigantic Life lies buried there! It is dead now, and dumb; but was alive once, and spake. For twenty generations, here was the earthly arena where painful living men worked out their life-wrestle,—looked at by Earth, by Heaven and Hell. Bells tolled to prayers; and men, of many humours, various thoughts, chanted vespers, matins;—and round the little islet of their life rolled forever (as round ours still rolls, though we are blind and deaf) the illimitable Ocean, tinting all things with *its* eternal hues and reflexes; making strange prophetic music! How silent now; all departed, clean gone. The World-Dramaturgist has written: *Exeunt.* The devouring Time-Demons have made away with it all: and in its stead, there is either nothing; or what is worse, offensive universal dust-clouds, and gray eclipse of Earth and Heaven, from 'dry rubbish shot here'!—

Truly it is no easy matter to get across the chasm of Seven Centuries, filled with such material. But here, of all helps, is not a Boswell the welcomest; even a small Boswell? Veracity, true simplicity of heart, how valuable are these always! He that speaks what *is* really in him, will find men to listen, though under never such impediments. Even gossip, springing free and cheery from a human heart, this too is a kind of veracity and *speech*;—much preferable to pedantry and inane gray haze; Jocelin is weak and garrulous, but he is human. Through the thin watery gossip of our Jocelin, we do get some glimpses of that deep-buried Time; discern veritably, though in a fitful intermittent manner, these antique figures and their life-method, face to face! Beautifully, in our earnest loving glance, the old centuries melt from opaque to partially translucent, transparent here and there; and the void black Night, one finds, is but the summing-up of innumerable peopled luminous *Days*. Not parchment Chartularies, Doctrines of the Constitution, O Dryasdust; not altogether, my erudite friend!—

Readers who please to go along with us into this poor *Jocelini Chronica* shall wander inconveniently enough, as in wintry twilight, through some poor stript hazel-grove, rustling with foolish noises, and perpetually hindering the eyesight; but across which, here and there, some real human figure is seen moving: very strange; whom we could hail if he would answer;—and we look into a pair of eyes deep as our own, *imagining* our own, but all unconscious of us; to whom we, for the time, are become as spirits and invisible!

LETTER TO JOHN STERLING

[This is Carlyle's farewell letter to John Sterling, written shortly before Sterling's death.]

Letter to John Sterling, *Ventnor*

Chelsea, 27 August 1844

My Friend,

Today another little Note from you makes the hearts start within us. On Sunday morning gone a fortnight there came another; which will dwell in my memory, I think, while I have any memory left. Ever since, it mingles with every thought, or is itself my thought; neither do I wish to exclude it, if I could. To me there is a tone in it as of Sphere-music, of the Eternal Melodies which we know well to be sacred,—sadder than any tears, and yet withal more beautiful than any joy. My Friend, my brave Sterling! A right valiant man; very beautiful, very dear to me; whose like I shall not see again in this world!

We are journeying towards the Grand Silence; what lies beyond it earthly man has never known, nor will know: but all brave men have known that it was Godlike, that it was right Good,—that the name of it was God. *Wir heissen euch hoffen.* What is right and best for us will full surely be. Tho' He slay me, yet will I trust in Him. "Eterno Amore"; that is the ultimate significance of this wild clashing whirlwind which is named Life, where the Sons of Adam flicker painfully for an hour.

My Wife is all in tears: no tear of mine, dear Sterling, shall, if I can help it, deface a scene so sacred. The memory of the Brother that is gone, like a brave one, shall be divine to us; and, if it please the Supreme Wisdom, we shall—O my friend, my friend!

In some moods it strikes me, with a reproachful emphasis, that there would be a kind of satisfaction for me could I see you with these eyes yet again. But you are in great suffering; perhaps I should be but a disturbance? There is a natural longing that way; but perhaps it is a false pusillanimous one: I have, at bottom, no speech for you which

418

could be so eloquent as my silence is. And yet I could be silent there too; silent and quiet. I shall let Anthony decide it between us, to whom I write today.

Adieu, my brave and dear one.

Yours evermore,
T. Carlyle.

FROM *Latter-Day Pamphlets*

1850

[The years following the publication of *Past and Present* in 1843 saw the completion of Carlyle's work on Cromwell, *Oliver Cromwell's Letters and Speeches, with Elucidations,* in two volumes, a groundbreaking study that initiated a general historical revaluation of the life and character of the seventeenth-century ruler. Carlyle's next work, *Latter-Day Pamphlets,* marked a deepening of his pessimism and his contempt for contemporary government. Planned originally to run to twelve pamphlets, the series stopped at eight. These were issued separately between February and August 1850 and subsequently issued in book form. They aroused almost universal disapprobation, for Carlyle was unsparing in his assaults on cherished Victorian ideas. The selection that follows reprints the whole of the first pamphlet, originally issued February 1, 1850. Here again Carlyle is assessing the character and the spirit of the age.]

NUMBER I. THE PRESENT TIME

The Present Time, youngest-born of Eternity, child and heir of all the Past Times with their good and evil, and parent of all the Future, is ever a 'New Era' to the thinking man; and comes with new questions and significance, however commonplace it look: to know *it,* and what it bids us do, is ever the sum of knowledge for all of us. This new Day, sent us out of Heaven, this also has its heavenly omens;—amid the bustling trivialities and loud empty noises, its silent monitions, which, if we cannot read and obey, it will not be well with us! No;—nor is there any sin more fearfully avenged on men and Nations than that same, which indeed includes and presupposes all manner of sins: the sin which our old pious fathers called 'judicial blindness';— which we, with our light habits, may still call misinterpretation of the Time that now is; disloyalty to its real meanings and monitions, stupid disregard of these, stupid adherence active or passive to the counterfeits and mere current semblances of these. This is true of all times and days.

But in the days that are now passing-over us, even fools

are arrested to ask the meaning of them; few of the generations of men have seen more impressive days. Days of endless calamity, disruption, dislocation, confusion worse confounded: if they are not days of endless hope too, then they are days of utter despair. For it is not a small hope that will suffice, the ruin being clearly, either in action or in prospect, universal. There must be a new world, if there is to be any world at all! That human things in our Europe can ever return to the old sorry routine, and proceed with any steadiness or continuance there; this small hope is not now a tenable one. These days of universal death must be days of universal newbirth, if the ruin is not to be total and final! It is a Time to make the dullest man consider; and ask himself, Whence *he* came? Whither he is bound?—A veritable 'New Era,' to the foolish as well as to the wise.

Not long ago, the world saw, with thoughtless joy which might have been very thoughtful joy, a real miracle not heretofore considered possible or conceivable in the world, —a Reforming Pope. A simple pious creature, a good country-priest, invested unexpectedly with the tiara, takes up the New Testament, declares that this henceforth shall be his rule of governing. No more finesse, chicanery, hypocrisy, or false or foul dealing of any kind: God's truth shall be spoken, God's justice shall be done, on the throne called of St. Peter: an honest Pope, Papa, or Father of Christendom, shall preside there. And such a throne of St. Peter; and such a Christendom, for an honest Papa to preside in! The European populations everywhere hailed the omen; with shouting and rejoicing, leading-articles and tar-barrels; thinking people listened with astonishment,—not with sorrow if they were faithful or wise; with awe rather as at the heralding of death, and with a joy as of victory beyond death! Something pious, grand and as if awful in that joy, revealing once more the Presence of a Divine Justice in this world. For, to such men it was very clear how this poor devoted Pope would prosper, with his New Testament in his hand. An alarming business, that of governing in the throne of St. Peter by the rule of veracity! By the rule of veracity, the so-called throne of St. Peter was openly declared, above three-hundred years ago, to be a falsity, a huge mistake, a pestilent dead carcass, which this Sun was

weary of. More than three hundred years ago, the throne of
St. Peter received peremptory judicial notice to quit;
authentic order, registered in Heaven's chancery and since
legible in the hearts of all brave men, to take itself away,—
to begone, and let us have no more to do with *it* and its
delusions and impious deliriums;—and it has been sitting
every day since, it may depend upon it, at its own peril
withal, and will have to pay exact damages yet for every
day it has so sat. Law of veracity? What this Popedom had
to do by the law of veracity, was to give-up its own foul
galvanic life, an offence to gods and men; honestly to die,
and get itself buried!

Far from this was the thing the poor Pope undertook in
regard to it;—and yet, on the whole, it was essentially this
too. "Reforming Pope?" said one of our acquaintance, often
in those weeks, "Was there ever such a miracle? About
to break-up that huge imposthume too, by 'curing' it? Turgot and Necker were nothing to this. God is great; and when
a scandal is to end, brings some devoted man to take charge
of it in hope, not in despair!"—But cannot he reform?
asked many simple persons;—to whom our friend in grim
banter would reply: "Reform a Popedom,—hardly. A
wretched old kettle, ruined from top to bottom, and con-
sisting mainly now of foul *grime* and *rust*: stop the holes
of it, as your antecessors have been doing, with temporary putty, it may hang-together yet a while; begin to hammer at it, solder at it, to what you call mend and rectify
it,—it will fall to sherds, as sure as rust is rust; go all into
nameless dissolution,—and the fat in the fire will be a
thing worth looking at, poor Pope!"— —So accordingly
it has proved. The poor Pope, amid felicitations and tar-
barrels of various kinds, went on joyfully for a season: but
he had awakened, he as no other man could do, the sleeping elements; mothers of the whirlwinds, conflagrations,
earthquakes. Questions not very soluble at present, were
even sages and heroes set to solve them, began everywhere
with new emphasis to be asked. Questions which all official
men wished, and almost hoped, to postpone till Doomsday. Doomsday itself *had* come; that was the terrible
truth!—

For, sure enough, if once the law of veracity be acknowledged as the rule for human things, there will not anywhere be want of work for the reformer; in very few places

do human things adhere quite closely to that law! Here was
the Papa of Christendom proclaiming that such was actually the case;—whereupon all over Christendom such results as we have seen. The Sicilians, I think, were the first
notable body that set-about applying this new strange rule
sanctioned by the general Father; they said to themselves,
We do not by the law of veracity belong to Naples and these
Neapolitan Officials; we will, by favour of Heaven and
the Pope, be free of these. Fighting ensued; insurrection,
fiercely maintained in the Sicilian Cities; with much blood-
shed, much tumult and loud noise, vociferation extending
through all newspapers and countries. The effect of this,
carried abroad by newspapers and rumour, was great in all
places; greatest perhaps in Paris, which for sixty years past
has been the City of Insurrections. The French People had
plumed themselves on being, whatever else they were not,
at least the chosen 'soldiers of liberty,' who took the lead of
all creatures in that pursuit, at least; and had become,
as their orators, editors and litterateurs diligently taught
them, a People whose bayonets were sacred, a kind of
Messiah People, saving a blind world in its own despite,
and earning for themselves a terrestrial and even celestial
glory very considerable indeed. And here were the wretched
downtrodden populations of Sicily risen to rival them, and
threatening to take the trade out of their hand.

No doubt of it, this hearing continually of the very
Pope's glory as a Reformer, of the very Sicilians fighting
divinely for liberty behind barricades,—must have bitterly
aggravated the feeling of every Frenchman, as he looked
around him, at home, on a Louis-Philippism which had become the scorn of all the world. "*Ichabod*; is the glory departing from us? Under the sun is nothing baser, by all ac-
counts and evidences, than the system of repression and
corruption, of shameless dishonesty and unbelief in anything but human baseness, that we now live under. The
Italians, the very Pope, have become apostles of liberty,
and France is— —what is France!"—We know what
France suddenly became in the end of February next; and
by a clear enough genealogy, we can trace a considerable
share in that event to the good simple Pope with the New
Testament in his hand. An outbreak, or at least a radical
change and even inversion of affairs hardly to be achieved
without an outbreak, everybody felt was inevitable in

France: but it had been universally expected that France would as usual take the initiative in that matter; and had there been no reforming Pope, no insurrectionary Sicily, France had certainly not broken-out then and so, but only afterwards and otherwise. The French explosion, not anticipated by the cunningest men there on the spot scrutinising it, burst-up unlimited, complete, defying computation or control.

Close following which, as if by sympathetic subterranean electricities, all Europe exploded, boundless, uncontrollable; and we had the year 1848, one of the most singular, disastrous, amazing, and, on the whole, humiliating years the European world ever saw. Not since the irruption of the Northern Barbarians has there been the like. Everywhere immeasurable Democracy rose monstrous, loud, blatant, inarticulate as the voice of Chaos. Everywhere the Official holy-of-holies was scandalously laid bare to dogs and the profane:—Enter, all the world, see what kind of Official holy it is. Kings everywhere, and reigning persons, stared in sudden horror, the voice of the whole world bellowing in their ear, "Begone, ye imbecile hypocrites, histrios not heroes! Off with you, off!"—and, what was peculiar and notable in this year for the first time, the Kings all made haste to go, as if exclaiming, "We *are* poor histrios, we sure enough;—did you want heroes? Don't kill us; we couldn't help it!" Not one of them turned round, and stood upon his Kingship, as upon a right he could afford to die for, or to risk his skin upon; by no manner of means. That, I say, is the alarming peculiarity at present. Democracy, on this new occasion, finds all Kings *conscious* that they are but Playactors. The miserable mortals, enacting their High Life Below Stairs, with faith only that this Universe may perhaps be all a phantasm and hypocrisis,—the truculent Constable of the Destinies suddenly enters: "Scandalous Phantasms, what do *you* here? Are 'solemnly constituted Impostors' the proper Kings of men? Did you think the Life of Man was a grimacing dance of apes? To be led always by the squeak of your paltry fiddle? Ye miserable, this Universe is not an upholstery Puppet-play, but a terrible God's Fact; and you, I think,—had not you better begone!" They fled precipitately, some of them with what we may call an exquisite ignominy,—in terror of the treadmill or worse. And everywhere the people, or the populace, take their own government upon themselves; and open 'kinglessness,' what we call *anarchy*,—how happy if it be anarchy *plus* a street-constable!—is everywhere the order of the day. Such was the history, from Baltic to Mediterranean, in Italy, France, Prussia, Austria, from end to end of Europe, in those March days of 1848. Since the destruction of the old Roman Empire by inroad of the Northern Barbarians, I have known nothing similar.

And so, then, there remained no King in Europe; no King except the Public Haranguer, haranguing on barrel-head, in leading-article; or getting himself aggregated into a National Parliament to harangue. And for about four months all France, and to a great degree all Europe, rough-ridden by every species of delirium, except happily the murderous for most part, was a weltering mob, presided over by M. de Lamartine at the Hôtel-de-Ville; a most eloquent fair-spoken literary gentleman, whom thoughtless persons took for a prophet, priest and heaven-sent evangelist, and whom a wise Yankee-friend of mine discerned to be properly 'the first stump-orator in the world, standing too on the highest stump,—for the time.' A sorrowful spectacle to men of reflection, during the time he lasted, that poor M. de Lamartine; with nothing in him but melodious wind and *soft sowder,* which he and others took for something divine and not diabolic! Sad enough: the eloquent latest impersonation of Chaos-come-again; able to talk for itself, and declare persuasively that *it* is Cosmos! However, you have but to wait a little, in such cases; all balloons do and must give-up their gas in the pressure of things, and are collapsed in a sufficiently wretched manner before long.

And so in City after City, street-barricades are piled, and truculent, more or less murderous insurrection begins; populace after populace rises, King after King capitulates or absconds; and from end to end of Europe Democracy has blazed-up explosive, much higher, more irresistible and less resisted than ever before; testifying too sadly on what a bottomless volcano, or universal powder-mine of most inflammable mutinous chaotic elements, separated from us by a thin earth-rind, Society with all its arrangements and acquirements everywhere, in the present epoch, rests! The kind of persons who excite or give signal to such revolutions, —students, young men of letters, advocates, editors, hot inexperienced enthusiasts, or fierce and justly bankrupt desperadoes, acting everywhere on the discontent of the millions and blowing it into flame,—might give rise to reflections as to the character of our epoch. Never till now did young men, and almost children, take such a command in human affairs. A changed time since the word *Senior* (Seigneur, or *Elder*) was first devised to signify 'lord,' or superior;—as in all languages of men we find it to have been! Not an honourable document this either, as to the spiritual condition of our epoch. In times when men love wisdom, the old man will ever be venerable, and be venerated, and reckoned noble: in times that love something else than wisdom, and indeed have little or no wisdom, and see little or none to love, the old man will cease to be venerated;—and looking more closely, also, you will find that in fact he has ceased to be venerable, and has begun to be contemptible; a foolish *boy* still, a boy without the graces, generosities, and opulent strength of young boys. In these days, what of *lordship* or leadership is still to be done, the youth must do it, not the mature or aged man; the mature man, hardened into sceptical egoism, knows no monition but that of his own frigid cautions, avarices, mean timidities; and can lead nowhither towards an object that even seems noble. But to return.

This mad state of matters will of course before long allay itself, as it has everywhere begun to do; the ordinary necessities of men's daily existence cannot comport with it, and these, whatever else is cast aside, will have their way. Some remounting,—very temporary remounting,—of the old machine, under new colours and altered forms, will probably ensue soon in most countries: the old histrionic Kings will be admitted back under conditions, under 'Constitutions,' with national Parliaments, or the like fashionable adjuncts; and everywhere the old daily life will try to begin again. But there is now no hope that such arrangements can be permanent; that they can be other than poor temporary makeshifts, which, if they try to fancy and make themselves permanent, will be displaced by new explosions, recurring more speedily than last time. In such baleful oscillation, afloat as amid raging bottomless eddies and conflicting sea-currents, not steadfast as on fixed foundations, must European Society continue swaying, now disastrously tumbling, then painfully readjusting itself, at ever shorter intervals,—till once the *new* rock-basis does come to light, and the weltering deluges of mutiny, and of need to mutiny, abate again!

For universal *Democracy,* whatever we may think of it, has declared itself as an inevitable fact of the days in which we live; and he who has any chance to instruct, or lead, in his days, must begin by admitting that: new street-barricades, and new anarchies, still more scandalous if still less sanguinary, must return and again return, till governing persons everywhere know and admit that. Democracy, it may be said everywhere, is here:—for sixty years now, ever since the grand or *First* French Revolution, that fact has been terribly announced to all the world; in message after message, some of them very terrible indeed; and now at last all the world ought really to believe it. That the world does believe it; that even Kings now as good as believe it, and know, or with just terror surmise, that they are but temporary phantasm Playactors, and that Democracy is the grand, alarming, imminent and indisputable Reality: this, among the scandalous phases we witnessed in the last two years, is a phasis full of hope: a sign that we are advancing closer and closer to the very Problem itself, which it will behove us to solve or die;—that all fighting and campaigning and coalitioning in regard to the *existence* of the Problem, is hopeless and superfluous henceforth. The gods have appointed it *so*; no Pitt, nor body of Pitts or mortal creatures can appoint it otherwise. Democracy, sure enough, is here: one knows not how long it will keep hidden underground even in Russia;—and here in England, though we object to it resolutely in the form of street-barricades and insurrectionary pikes, and decidedly will not open doors to it on those terms, the tramp of its million feet is on all streets and thoroughfares, the sound of its bewildered thousandfold voice is in all writings and speakings, in all thinkings and modes and activities of men: the soul that does not now, with hope or terror, discern *it,* is not the one we address on this occasion.

What *is* Democracy; this huge inevitable Product of the Destinies, which is everywhere the portion of our Europe in these latter days? There lies the question for us. Whence comes it, this universal big black Democracy; whither tends it; what is the meaning of it? A meaning it must have, or it would not be here. If we can find the right meaning of it, we may, wisely submitting or wisely resisting and controlling, still hope to live in the midst of it; if we cannot find the right meaning, if we find only the wrong or no meaning in it, to live will not be possible!—The whole social wisdom of the Present Time is summoned, in the name of the Giver of Wisdom, to make clear to itself, and lay deeply to heart with an eye to strenuous valiant practice and effort, what the meaning of this universal revolt of the European Populations, which calls itself Democracy, and decides to continue permanent, may be.

Certainly it is a drama full of action, event fast following event; in which curiosity finds endless scope, and there are interests at stake, enough to rivet the attention of all men, simple and wise. Whereat the idle multitude lift-up their voices, gratulating, celebrating sky-high; in rhyme and prose announcement, more than plentiful, that *now* the New Era, and long-expected Year One of Perfect Human Felicity has come. Glorious and immortal people, sublime French citizens, heroic barricades; triumph of civil and religious liberty—O Heaven! one of the inevitablest private miseries, to an earnest man in such circumstances, is this multitudinous efflux of oratory and psalmody, from the universal foolish human throat; drowning for the moment all reflection whatsoever, except the sorrowful one that you are fallen in an evil, heavy-laden, long-eared age, and must resignedly bear your part in the same. The front wall of your wretched old crazy dwelling, long denounced by you to no purpose, having at last fairly folded itself over, and fallen prostrate into the street, the floors, as may happen, will still hang-on by the mere beam-ends, and coherency of old carpentry, though in a sloping direction, and depend there till certain poor rusty nails and wormeaten dovetailings give way:—but is it cheering, in such circumstances, that the whole household burst-forth into celebrating the new joys of light and ventilation, liberty and picturesqueness of position, and thank God that now they have got a house to their mind? My dear household, cease singing and psalmodying; lay aside your fiddles, take out your work-implements, if you have any; for I can say with confidence the laws of gravitation are still active, and rusty nails, wormeaten dovetailings, and secret coherency of old carpentry, are not the best basis for a household!—In the lanes of Irish cities, I have heard say, the wretched people are sometimes found living, and perilously boiling their potatoes, on such swing-floors and inclined planes hanging-on by the joist-ends; but I did not hear that they sang very much in celebration of such lodging. No, they slid gently about, sat near the back wall, and perilously boiled their potatoes, in silence for most part!—

High shouts of exultation, in every dialect, by every vehicle of speech and writing, rise from far and near over this last avatar of Democracy in 1848: and yet, to wise minds, the first aspect it presents seems rather to be one of boundless misery and sorrow. What can be more miserable than this universal hunting-out of the high dignitaries, solemn functionaries, and potent, grave and reverend signiors of the world; this stormful rising-up of the inarticulate dumb masses everywhere, against those who pretended to be speaking for them and guiding them? These guides, then, were mere blind men only pretending to see? These rulers were not ruling at all; they had merely got-on the attributes and clothes of rulers, and were surreptitiously drawing the wages, while the work remained undone? The Kings were Sham-Kings, playacting as at Drury Lane;—and what were the people withal that took them for real?

It is probably the hugest disclosure of *falsity* in human things that was ever at one time made. These reverend Dignitaries that sat amid their far-shining symbols and long-sounding long-admitted professions, were mere Impostors, then? Not a true thing they were doing, but a false thing. The story they told men was a cunningly-devised fable; the gospels they preached to them were *not* an account of man's real position in this world, but an incoherent fabrication, of dead ghosts and unborn shadows, of traditions, cants, indolences, cowardices,—a falsity of falsities, which at last *ceases* to stick together. Wilfully and against their will, these high units of mankind were cheats, then; and the low millions who believed in them were dupes,—a kind of *inverse* cheats, too, or they would not have believed in them so long. A universal *Bankruptcy of Imposture;* that may be the brief definition of it. Imposture everywhere declared once more to be contrary to Nature; nobody will change its word into an act any farther:—fallen insolvent; unable to keep its head up by these false pretences, or make its pot boil any more for the present! A more scandalous phenomenon, wide as Europe, never afflicted the face of the sun.

Bankruptcy everywhere; foul ignominy, and the abomination of desolation, in all high places: odious to look upon, as the carnage of a battle-field on the morrow morning;—a massacre not of the innocents; we cannot call it a massacre of the innocents; but a universal tumbling of Impostors and of Impostures into the street!—

Such a spectacle, can we call it joyful? There is a joy in it, to the wise man too; yes, but a joy full of awe, and as it were sadder than any sorrow,—like the vision of immortality, unattainable except through death and the grave! And yet who would not, in his heart of hearts, feel piously thankful that Imposture has fallen bankrupt? By all means let it fall bankrupt; in the name of God let it do so, with whatever misery to itself and to all of us. Imposture, be it known then, —known it must and shall be,—is hateful, unendurable to God and man. Let it understand this everywhere; and swiftly make ready for departure, wherever it yet lingers; and let it learn never to return, if possible! The eternal voices, very audibly again, are speaking to proclaim this message, from side to side of the world. Not a very cheering message, but a very indispensable one.

Alas, it is sad enough that Anarchy is here; that we are not permitted to regret its being here,—for who that had, for this divine Universe, an eye which was human at all, could wish that Shams of any kind, especially that Sham-Kings should continue? No: at all costs, it is to be prayed by all men that Shams may *cease*. Good Heavens, to what depths have we got, when this to many a man seems strange! Yet strange to many a man it does seem; and to many a solid Englishman, wholesomely digesting his pudding among what are called the cultivated classes, it seems strange exceedingly; a mad ignorant notion, quite heterodox, and big with mere ruin. He has been used to decent forms long since fallen empty of meaning, to plausible modes, solemnities grown ceremonial,—what you in your iconoclast humour call shams,—all his life long; never heard that there was any harm in them, that there was any getting-on without them. Did not cotton spin itself, beef grow, and groceries and spiceries come in from the East and the West, quite comfortably by the side of shams? Kings reigned, what they were pleased to call reigning; lawyers pleaded, bishops preached, and honourable members perorated; and to crown the whole, as if it were all real and no sham there, did not scrip continue saleable, and the banker pay in bullion, or paper with a metallic basis? "The greatest sham, I have always thought, is he that would destroy shams."

Even so. To such depth have *I,* the poor knowing person of this epoch, got;—almost below the level of lowest humanity, and down towards the state of apehood and oxhood! For never till in quite recent generations was such a scandalous blasphemy quietly set forth among the sons of Adam; never before did the creature called man believe generally in his heart that lies were the rule in this Earth; that in deliberate long-established lying could there be help or salvation for him, could there be at length other than hindrance and destruction for him. O Heavyside, my solid friend, this is the sorrow of sorrows: what on earth can become of us till this accursed enchantment, the general summary and consecration of delusions, be cast forth from the heart and life of one and all! Cast forth it will be; it must, or we are tending at all moments,—whitherward I do not like to name. Alas, and the casting of it out, to what heights and what depths will it lead us, in the sad universe mostly of lies and shams and hollow phantasms (grown very ghastly now), in which, as in a safe home, we have lived this century or two! To heights and depths of social and individual *divorce* from delusions,—of 'reform' in right sacred earnest, of indispensable amendment, and stern sorrowful abrogation and order to depart,—such as cannot well be spoken at present; as dare scarcely be thought at present; which nevertheless are very inevitable, and perhaps rather imminent several of them! Truly we have a heavy task of work before us; and there is a pressing call that we should seriously begin upon it, before it tumble into an inextricable mass, in which there will be no working, but only suffering and hopelessly perishing!—

Or perhaps Democracy, which we announce as now come, will itself manage it? Democracy, once modelled into suffrages, furnished with ballot-boxes and suchlike, will itself accomplish the salutary universal change from Delusive to Real, and make a new blessed world of us by and by?—To the great mass of men, I am aware, the matter presents itself quite on this hopeful side. Democracy they consider to *be* a kind of 'Government.' The old model, formed long since, and brought to perfection in England now two hundred years ago, has proclaimed itself to all Nations as the new healing for every woe: "Set-up a Parliament," the Nations everywhere say, when the old King is detected to be a Sham-King, and hunted out or not; "set-up a Parliament; let us have suffrages, universal suffrages; and all either at once or by due degrees will be right, and a real Millennium come!" Such is their way of construing the matter.

Such, alas, is by no means my way of construing the matter; if it were, I should have had the happiness of remaining silent, and been without call to speak here. It is because the contrary of all this is deeply manifest to me, and appears to be forgotten by multitudes of my contemporaries, that I have had to undertake addressing a word to them. The contrary of all this;—and the farther I look into the roots of all this, the more hateful, ruinous and dismal does the state of mind all this could have originated in appear to me. To examine this recipe of a Parliament, how fit it is for governing Nations, nay, how fit it may now be, in these new times, for governing England itself where we are used to it so long: this, too, is an alarming inquiry, to which all thinking men, and good citizens of their country, who have an ear for the small still voices and eternal intimations, across the temporary clamours and loud blaring proclamations, are now solemnly invited. Invited by the rigorous fact itself; which will one day, and that perhaps soon, demand practical decision or redecision of it from us,—with enormous penalty if we decide it wrong! I think we shall all have to consider this question, one day; better perhaps now than later, when the leisure may be less. If a Parliament, with suffrages and universal or any conceivable kind of suffrages, *is* the method, then certainly let us set about discovering the kind of suffrages, and rest no moment till we have got them. But it is possible a Parliament may not be the method! Possible the inveterate notions of the English People may have settled it as the method, and the Everlasting Laws of Nature may have settled it as not the method! Not the whole method; nor the method at all, if taken as the whole? If a Parliament with never such suffrages is *not* the method settled by this latter authority, then it will urgently behove us to become aware of that fact, and to quit such method;—we may de-

pend upon it, however unanimous *we* be, every step taken
in that direction will, by the Eternal Law of things, be a
step *from* improvement, not towards it.

Not towards it, I say, if so! Unanimity of voting,—that
will do nothing for us if *so*. Your ship cannot double Cape
Horn by its excellent plans of voting. The ship may vote
this and that, above decks and below, in the most harmonious exquisitely constitutional manner: the ship, to get round
Cape Horn, will find a set of conditions already voted for,
and fixed with adamantine rigour by the ancient Elemental
Powers, who are entirely careless how you vote. If you
can, by voting or without voting, ascertain these conditions,
and valiantly conform to them, you will get round the
Cape: if you cannot,—the ruffian Winds will blow you ever
back again; the inexorable Icebergs, dumb privy-council-
lors from Chaos, will nudge you with most chaotic 'admoni-
tion'; you will be flung half-frozen on the Patagonian
cliffs, or admonished into shivers by your iceberg councillors, and sent sheer down to Davy Jones, and will never
get round Cape Horn at all! Unanimity on board ship;—
yes, indeed, the ship's crew may be very unanimous,
which doubtless, for the time being, will be very comfortable to the ship's crew, and to their Phantasm Captain if
they have one: but if the tack they unanimously steer upon
is guiding them into the belly of the Abyss, it will not profit
them much!—Ships accordingly do not use the ballot-box
at all; and they reject the Phantasm species of Captains:
one wishes much some other Entities,—since all entities
lie under the same rigorous set of laws,—could be brought
to show as much wisdom, and sense at least of self-preser-
vation, the *first* command of Nature. Phantasm Captains
with unanimous votings: this is considered to be all the law
and all the prophets, at present.

If a man could shake-out of his mind the universal noise
of political doctors in this generation and in the last generation or two, and consider the matter face to face, with
his own sincere intelligence looking at it, I venture to say
he would find this a very extraordinary method of navi-
gating, whether in the Straits of Magellan or the undiscovered Sea of Time. To prosper in this world, to gain felicity,
victory and improvement, either for a man or a nation,
there is but one thing requisite, That the man or nation
can discern what the true regulations of the Universe are in

regard to him and his pursuit, and can faithfully and steadfastly follow these. These will lead him to victory; whoever it may be that sets him in the way of these,—were it Russian Autocrat, Chartist Parliament, Grand Lama, Force of Public Opinion, Archbishop of Canterbury, M'Croudy the Seraphic Doctor with his Last-evangel of Political Economy, —sets him in the sure way to please the Author of this Universe, and is his friend of friends. And again, whoever does the contrary is, for a like reason, his enemy of enemies. This may be taken as fixed.

And now by what method ascertain the monition of the gods in regard to our affairs? How decipher, with best fidelity, the eternal regulation of the Universe; and read, from amid such confused embroilments of human clamour and folly, what the real Divine Message to us is? A divine message, or eternal regulation of the Universe, there verily is, in regard to every conceivable procedure and affair of man: faithfully following this, said procedure or affair will prosper, and have the whole Universe to second it, and carry it, across the fluctuating contradictions, towards a victorious goal; not following this, mistaking this, disregarding this, destruction and wreck are certain for every affair. How find it? All the world answers me, "Count heads; ask Universal Suffrage, by the ballot-boxes, and that will tell." Universal Suffrage, ballot-boxes, count of heads? Well,—I perceive we have got into strange spiritual latitudes indeed. Within the last half century or so, either the Universe or else the heads of men must have altered very much. Half a century ago, and down from Father Adam's time till then, the Universe, wherever I could hear tell of it, was wont to be of somewhat abstruse nature; by no means carrying its secret written on its face, legible to every passer-by; on the contrary, obstinately hiding its secret from all foolish, slavish, wicked, insincere persons, and partially disclosing it to the wise and noble-minded alone, whose number was not the majority in my time!

Or perhaps the chief end of man being now, in these improved epochs, to make money and spend it, his interests in the Universe have become amazingly simplified of late; capable of being voted-on with effect by almost anybody? 'To buy in the cheapest market, and sell in the dearest': truly if that is the summary of his social duties, and the final divine-message he has to follow, we may trust him extensively to vote upon that. But if it is *not,* and never was, or can be? If the Universe will not carry on its divine bosom any commonwealth of mortals that have no higher aim,—being still 'a Temple and Hall of Doom,' not a mere Weaving-shop and Cattle-pen? If the unfathomable Universe has decided to *reject* Human Beavers pretending to be Men; and will abolish, pretty rapidly perhaps, in hideous mud-deluges, their 'markets' and them, unless they think of it?—In that case it were better to think of it: and the Democracies and Universal Suffrages, I can observe, will require to modify themselves a good deal!

Historically speaking, I believe there was no Nation that could subsist upon Democracy. Of ancient Republics, and *Demoi* and *Populi,* we have heard much; but it is now pretty well admitted to be nothing to our purpose;—a universal-suffrage republic, or a general-suffrage one, or any but a most-limited-suffrage one, never came to light, or dreamed of doing so, in ancient times. When the mass of the population were slaves, and the voters intrinsically a kind of *kings,* or men born to rule others; when the voters were *real* 'aristocrats' and manageable dependents of such, —then doubtless voting, and confused jumbling of talk and intrigue, might, without immediate destruction, or the need of a Cavaignac to intervene with cannon and sweep the streets clear of it, go on; and beautiful developments of manhood might be possible beside it, for a season. Beside it; or even, if you will, by means of it, and in virtue of it, though that is by no means so certain as is often supposed. Alas, no: the reflective constitutional mind has misgivings as to the origin of old Greek and Roman nobleness; and indeed knows not how this or any other human nobleness could well be 'originated,' or brought to pass, by voting or without voting, in this world, except by the grace of God very mainly;—and remembers, with a sigh, that of the Seven Sages themselves no fewer than three were bits of Despotic Kings, Τύραννοι, 'Tyrants' so-called (such being greatly wanted there); and that the other four were very far from Red Republicans, if of any political faith whatever! We may quit the Ancient Classical concern, and leave it to College-clubs and speculative debating-societies, in these late days.

Of the various French Republics that have been tried, or that are still on trial,—of these also it is not needful to say any word. But there is one modern instance of Democracy nearly perfect, the Republic of the United States, which has actually subsisted for threescore years or more, with immense success as is affirmed; to which many still appeal, as to a sign of hope for all nations, and a 'Model Republic.' Is not America an instance in point? Why should not all Nations subsist and flourish on Democracy, as America does?

Of America it would ill beseem any Englishman, and me perhaps as little as another, to speak unkindly, to speak *unpatriotically,* if any of us even felt so. Sure enough, America is a great, and in many respects a blessed and hopeful phenomenon. Sure enough, these hardy millions of Anglo-saxon men prove themselves worthy of their genealogy; and, with the axe and plough and hammer, if not yet with any much finer kind of implements, are triumphantly clearing-out wide spaces, seedfields for the sustenance and refuge of mankind, arenas for the future history of the world; doing, in their day and generation, a creditable and cheering feat under the sun. But as to a Model Republic, or a model anything, the wise among themselves know too well that there is nothing to be said. Nay, the title hitherto to be a Commonwealth or Nation at all, among the ἔθνη of the world, is, strictly considered, still a thing they are but striving for, and indeed have not yet done much towards attaining. Their Constitution, such as it may be, was made here, not there; went over with them from the Old-Puritan English workshop ready-made. Deduct what they carried with them from England ready-made,—their common English Language, and that same Constitution, or rather elixir of constitutions, their inveterate and now, as it were, inborn reverence for the Constable's Staff; two quite immense attainments, which England had to spend much blood, and valiant sweat of brow and brain, for centuries long, in achieving;—and what new elements of polity or nationhood, what noble new phasis of human arrangement, or social device worthy of Prometheus or of Epimetheus, yet comes to light in America? Cotton-crops and Indian-corn and dollars come to light; and half a world of untilled land, where populations that respect the constable can live, for the present *without* Government: this comes to light; and the profound sorrow of all nobler hearts, here uttering itself as silent patient unspeakable

ennui, there coming out as vague elegiac wailings, that there
is still next to nothing more. 'Anarchy *plus* a street-constable': that also is anarchic to me, and other than quite
lovely!

I foresee, too, that, long before the waste lands are full,
the very street-constable, on these poor terms, will have
become impossible: without the waste lands, as here in our
Europe, I do not see how he could continue possible many
weeks. Cease to brag to me of America, and its model institutions and constitutions. To men in their sleep there is
nothing granted in this world: nothing, or as good as nothing, to men that sit idly *caucusing* and ballot-boxing on the
graves of their heroic ancestors, saying, 'It is well, it is
well!' Corn and bacon are granted: not a very sublime boon,
on such conditions; a boon moreover which, on such conditions, cannot last! No: America too will have to strain its
energies, in quite other fashion than this; to crack its sinews,
and all-but break its heart, as the rest of us have had to
do, in thousandfold wrestle with the Pythons and mud-
demons, before it can become a habitation for the gods.
America's battle is yet to fight; and we, sorrowful though
nothing doubting, will wish her strength for it. New
Spiritual Pythons, plenty of them; enormous Megatherions,
as ugly as were ever born of mud, loom huge and hideous
out of the twilight Future on America; and she will have
her own agony, and her own victory, but on other terms
than she is yet quite aware of. Hitherto she but ploughs and
hammers, in a very successful manner; hitherto, in spite of
her 'roast-goose with apple-sauce,' she is not much. 'Roast-
goose with apple-sauce for the poorest working-man': well,
surely that is something,—thanks to your respect for the
street-constable, and to your continents of fertile waste
land;—but that, even if it could continue, is by no means
enough; that is not even an instalment towards what will
be required of you. My friend, brag not yet of our American cousins! Their quantity of cotton, dollars, industry and
resources, I believe to be almost unspeakable; but I can by
no means worship the like of these. What great human soul,
what great thought, what great noble thing that one could
worship, or loyally admire, has yet been produced there?
None: the American cousins have yet done none of these
things. "What they have done?" growls Smelfungus, tired
of the subject: "They have doubled their population

every twenty years. They have begotten, with a rapidity beyond recorded example, Eighteen Millions of the greatest *bores* ever seen in this world before,—that hitherto is their feat in History!"—And so we leave them, for the present; and cannot predict the success of Democracy, on this side of the Atlantic, from their example.

Alas, on this side of the Atlantic and on that, Democracy, we apprehend, is forever impossible! So much, with certainty of loud astonished contradiction from all manner of men at present, but with sure appeal to the Law of Nature and the ever-abiding Fact, may be suggested and asserted once more. The Universe itself is a Monarchy and Hierarchy; large liberty of 'voting' there, all manner of choice, utmost freewill, but with conditions inexorable and immeasurable annexed to every exercise of the same. A most free commonwealth of 'voters'; but with Eternal Justice to preside over it, Eternal Justice enforced by Almighty Power! This is the model of 'constitutions'; this: nor in any Nation where there has not yet (in some supportable and withal some constantly-increasing degree) been confided to the *Noblest,* with his select series of *Nobler,* the divine everlasting duty of directing and controlling the Ignoble, has the 'Kingdom of God,' which we all pray for, 'come,' nor can 'His will' even *tend* to be 'done on Earth as it is in Heaven' till then. My Christian friends, and indeed my Sham-Christian and Anti-Christian, and all manner of men, are invited to reflect on this. They will find it to be the truth of the case. The Noble in the high place, the Ignoble in the low; that is, in all times and in all countries, the Almighty Maker's Law.

To raise the Sham-Noblest, and solemnly consecrate *him* by whatever method, new-devised, or slavishly adhered to from old wont, this, little as we may regard it, is, in all times and countries, a practical blasphemy, and Nature will in no wise forget it. Alas, there lies the origin, the fatal necessity, of modern Democracy everywhere. It is the Noblest, not the Sham-Noblest; it is God-Almighty's Noble, not the Court-Tailor's Noble, nor the Able-Editor's Noble, that must in some approximate degree, be raised to the supreme place; he and not a counterfeit,—under penalties! Penalties deep as death, and at length terrible as hell-on-earth, my constitutional friend!—Will the ballot-box raise the Noblest to the chief place; does any sane man deliberately believe such a thing? That nevertheless is the indispensable result, attain it how we may: if that is attained, all is attained; if not that, nothing. He that cannot believe the ballot-box to be attaining it, will be comparatively indifferent to the ballot-box. Excellent for keeping the ship's crew at peace under their Phantasm Captain; but unserviceable, under such, for getting round Cape Horn. Alas, that there should be human beings requiring to have these things argued of, at this late time of day!

I say, it is the everlasting privilege of the foolish to be governed by the wise; to be guided in the right path by those who know it better than they. This is the first 'right of man'; compared with which all other rights are as nothing,—mere superfluities, corollaries which will follow of their own accord out of this; if they be not contradictions to this, and less than nothing! To the wise it is not a privilege; far other indeed. Doubtless, as bringing preservation to their country, it implies preservation of themselves withal; but intrinsically it is the harshest duty a wise man, if he be indeed wise, has laid to his hand. A duty which he would fain enough shirk; which accordingly, in these sad times of doubt and cowardly sloth, he has long everywhere been endeavouring to reduce to its minimum, and has in fact in most cases nearly escaped altogether. It is an ungoverned world; a world which we flatter ourselves will henceforth need no governing. On the dust of our heroic ancestors we too sit ballot-boxing, saying to one another, It is well, it is well! By inheritance of their noble struggles, we have been permitted to sit slothful so long. By noble toil, not by shallow laughter and vain talk, they made this English Existence from a savage forest into an arable inhabitable field for us; and we, idly dreaming it would grow spontaneous crops forever,—find it now in a too questionable state; peremptorily requiring real labour and agriculture again. Real 'agriculture' is not pleasant; much pleasanter to reap and winnow (with ballot-box or otherwise) than to plough!

Who would govern that can get along without governing? He that is fittest for it, is of all men the unwillingest unless constrained. By multifarious devices we have been endeavouring to dispense with governing; and by very superficial speculations, of *laissez-faire,* supply-and-demand, etc. etc. to persuade ourselves that it is best so.

The Real Captain, unless it be some Captain of mechanical Industry hired by Mammon, where is he in these days? Most likely, in silence, in sad isolation somewhere, in remote obscurity; trying if, in an evil ungoverned time, he cannot at least govern himself. The Real Captain undiscoverable; the Phantasm Captain everywhere very conspicuous:—it is thought Phantasm Captains, aided by ballot-boxes, are the true method, after all. They are much the pleasantest for the time being! And so no *Dux* or Duke of any sort, in any province of our affairs, now *leads*: the Duke's Bailiff *leads,* what little leading is required for getting-in the rents; and the Duke merely rides in the state-coach. It is everywhere so: and now at last we see a world all rushing towards strange consummations, because it is and has long been so!

I do not suppose any reader of mine, or many persons in England at all, have much faith in Fraternity, Equality and the Revolutionary Millenniums preached by the French Prophets in this age: but there are many movements here too which tend inevitably in the like direction; and good men, who would stand aghast at Red Republic and its adjuncts, seem to me travelling at full speed towards that or a similar goal! Certainly the notion everywhere prevails among us too, and preaches itself abroad in every dialect, uncontradicted anywhere so far as I can hear, That the grand panacea for social woes is what we call 'enfranchisement,' 'emancipation'; or, translated into practical language, the cutting asunder of human relations, wherever they are found grievous, as is like to be pretty universally the case at the rate we have been going for some generations past. Let us all be 'free' of one another; we shall then be happy. Free, without bond or connection except that of cash payment; fair day's wages for the fair day's work; bargained for by voluntary contract, and law of supply-and-demand: this is thought to be the true solution of all difficulties and injustices that have occurred between man and man.

To rectify the relation that exists between two men, is there no method, then, but that of ending it? The old relation has become unsuitable, obsolete, perhaps unjust; it imperatively requires to be amended; and the remedy is,

Abolish it, let there henceforth be no relation at all. From the 'Sacrament of Marriage' downwards, human beings used to be manifoldly related, one to another, and each to all; and there was no relation among human beings, just or unjust, that had not its grievances and difficulties, its necessities on both sides to bear and forbear. But henceforth, be it known, we have changed all that, by favour of Heaven: 'the voluntary principle' has come-up, which will itself do the business for us; and now let a new Sacrament, that of *Divorce,* which we call emancipation, and spout-of on our platforms, be universally the order of the day!—Have men considered whither all this is tending, and what it certainly enough betokens? Cut every human relation which has anywhere grown uneasy sheer asunder; reduce whatsoever was compulsory to voluntary, whatsoever was permanent among us to the condition of nomadic:—in other words, loosen by assiduous wedges in every joint, the whole fabric of social existence, stone from stone; till at last, all now being loose enough, it can, as we already see in most countries, be overset by sudden outburst of revolutionary rage; and, lying as mere mountains of anarchic rubbish, solicit you to sing Fraternity etc. over it, and to rejoice in the new remarkable era of human progress we have arrived at.

Certainly Emancipation proceeds with rapid strides among us, this good while; and has got to such a length as might give rise to reflections in men of a serious turn. West-Indian Blacks are emancipated, and it appears refuse to work: Irish Whites have long been entirely emancipated; and nobody asks them to work, or on condition of finding them potatoes (which, of course, is indispensable), permits them to work.—Among speculative persons, a question has sometimes risen: In the progress of Emancipation, are we to look for a time when all the Horses also are to be emancipated, and brought to the supply-and-demand principle? Horses too have 'motives'; are acted-on by hunger, fear, hope, love of oats, terror of platted leather; nay, they have vanity, ambition, emulation, thankfulness, vindictiveness; some rude outline of all our human spiritualities,—a rude resemblance to us in mind and intelligence, even as they have in bodily frame. The Horse, poor dumb four-footed fellow, he too has his private feelings, his affections, gratitudes; and deserves good usage; no human master, without crime, shall treat him unjustly either, or recklessly lay-on the whip where it is not needed:—I am sure if I could make him 'happy,' I should be willing to grant a small vote (in addition to the late twenty millions) for that object!

Him too you occasionally tyrannise over; and with bad result to yourselves, among others; using the leather in a tyrannous unnecessary manner; withholding, or scantily furnishing, the oats and ventilated stabling that are due. Rugged horse-subduers, one fears they are a little tyrannous at times. 'Am I not a horse, and *half*-brother?'—To remedy which, so far as remediable, fancy—the horses all 'emancipated'; restored to their primeval right of property in the grass of this Globe: turned-out to graze in an independent supply-and-demand manner! So long as grass lasts, I dare say they are very happy, or think themselves so. And Farmer Hodge sallying forth, on a dry spring morning, with a sieve of oats in his hand, and agony of eager expectation in his heart, is he happy? Help me to plough this day, Black Dobbin: oats in full measure if thou wilt. 'Hlunh, No—thank!' snorts Black Dobbin; he prefers glorious liberty and the grass. Bay Darby, wilt not thou perhaps? 'Hlunh!' Gray Joan, then, my beautiful broad-bottomed mare,—O Heaven, she too answers Hlunh! Not a quadruped of them will plough a stroke for me. Corn-crops are *ended* in this world!—For the sake, if not of Hodge, then of Hodge's horses, one prays this benevolent practice might now cease, and a new and better one try to begin. Small kindness to Hodge's horses to emancipate them! The fate of all emancipated horses is, sooner or later, inevitable. To have in this habitable Earth no grass to eat,—in Black Jamaica gradually none, as in White Connemara already none;—to roam aimless, wasting the seed-fields of the world; and be hunted home to Chaos, by the due watch-dogs and due hell-dogs, with such horrors of forsaken wretchedness as were never seen before! These things are not sport; they are terribly true, in this country at this hour.

Between our Black West Indies and our White Ireland, between these two extremes of lazy refusal to work, and of famishing inability to find any work, what a world have we made of it, with our fierce Mammon-worships, and our benevolent philanderings, and idle godless nonsenses of one kind and another! Supply-and-demand, Leave-it-alone, Voluntary Principle, Time will mend it:—till British industrial existence seems fast becoming one huge poison-swamp of reeking pestilence physical and moral; a hideous *living* Golgotha of souls and bodies buried alive; such a Curtius' gulf, communicating with the Nether Deeps, as the Sun never saw till now. These scenes, which the *Morning Chronicle* is bringing home to all minds of men,—thanks to it for a service such as Newspapers have seldom done,—ought to excite unspeakable reflections in every mind. Thirty-thousand outcast Needlewomen working themselves swiftly to death; three-million Paupers rotting in forced idleness, *helping* said Needlewomen to die: these are but items in the sad ledger of despair.

Thirty-thousand wretched women, sunk in that putrefy-ing well of abominations; they have oozed-in upon London, from the universal Stygian quagmire of British industrial life; are accumulated in the *well* of the concern, to that ex-tent. British charity is smitten to the heart, at the laying-bare of such a scene; passionately undertakes, by enormous subscription of money, or by other enormous effort, to re-dress that individual horror; as I and all men hope it may. But, alas, what next? This general well and cesspool once baled clean out today, will begin before night to fill itself anew. The universal Stygian quagmire is still there; opulent in women ready to be ruined, and in men ready. Towards the same sad cesspool will these waste currents of human ruin ooze and gravitate as heretofore; except in draining the universal quagmire itself there is no remedy. "And for that, what is the method?" cry many in an angry manner. To whom, for the present, I answer only, "Not 'emanci-pation,' it would seem, my friends; not the cutting-loose of human ties, something far the reverse of that!"

Many things have been written about shirtmaking; but here perhaps is the saddest thing of all, not written any-where till now, that I know of. Shirts by the thirty-thou-sand are made at twopence-halfpenny each;—and in the mean while no needlewoman, distressed or other, can be procured in London by any housewife to give, for fair wages, fair help in sewing. Ask any thrifty house-mother, high or low, and she will answer. In high houses and in low, there is the same answer: no *real* needlewoman, 'distressed' or other, has been found attainable in any of the houses I frequent. Imaginary needlewomen, who demand consid-erable wages, and have a deepish appetite for beer and

444 / A CARLYLE READER

viands, I hear of everywhere; but their sewing proves too often a distracted puckering and botching; not sewing, only the fallacious hope of it, a fond imagination of the mind. Good sempstresses are to be hired in every village; and in London, with its famishing thirty-thousand, not at all, or hardly.—Is not No-government beautiful in human business? To such length has the Leave-alone principle carried it, by way of organising labour, in this affair of shirtmaking. Let us hope the Leave-alone principle has now got its apotheosis; and taken wing towards higher regions than ours, to deal henceforth with a class of affairs more appropriate for it!

Reader, did you ever hear of 'Constituted Anarchy'? Anarchy; the choking, sweltering, deadly and killing rule of No-rule; the consecration of cupidity, and braying folly, and dim stupidity and baseness, in most of the affairs of men? Slopshirts attainable three-halfpence cheaper, by the ruin of living bodies and immortal souls? Solemn Bishops and high Dignitaries, *our* divine 'Pillars of Fire by night,' debating meanwhile, with their largest wigs and gravest look, upon something they call 'prevenient grace'? Alas, our noble men of genius, Heaven's *real* messengers to us, they also rendered nearly futile by the wasteful time;—preappointed they everywhere, and assiduously trained by all their pedagogues and monitors, to 'rise in Parliament,' to compose orations, write books, or in short speak *words,* for the approval of reviewers; instead of doing real kingly *work* to be approved of by the gods! Our 'Government,' a highly 'responsible' one; responsible to no God that I can hear of, but to the twenty-seven million *gods* of the shilling gallery. A Government tumbling and drifting on the whirlpools and mud-deluges, floating atop in a conspicuous manner, nowhither,—like the carcass of a drowned ass. Authentic *Chaos* come up into this sunny Cosmos again; and all men singing *Gloria in excelsis* to it. In spirituals and temporals, in field and workshop, from Manchester to Dorsetshire, from Lambeth Palace to the Lanes of Whitechapel, wherever men meet and toil and traffic together,—Anarchy, Anarchy; and only the street-constable (though with ever-increasing difficulty) still maintaining himself in the middle of it; that so, for one thing, this blessed exchange of slop-shirts for the souls of women may transact itself in a peaceable manner!—I, for my part, do profess myself in eternal opposition to this, and discern well that universal Ruin has us in the wind, unless we can get out of this. My friend Crabbe, in a late number of his *Intermittent Radiator,* pertinently enough exclaims:

'When shall we have done with all this of British Liberty, Voluntary Principle, Dangers of Centralisation, and the like? It is really getting too bad. For British Liberty, it seems, the people cannot be taught to read. British Liberty, shuddering to interfere with the rights of capital, takes six or eight millions of money annually to feed the idle labourer whom it dare not employ. For British Liberty we live over poisonous cesspools, gully-drains, and detestable abominations; and omnipotent London cannot sweep the dirt out of itself. British Liberty produces—what? Floods of Hansard Debates every year, and apparently little else at present. If these are the results of British Liberty, I, for one, move we should lay it on the shelf a little, and look-out for something other and farther. We have achieved British Liberty hundreds of years ago; and are fast growing, on the strength of it, one of the most absurd populations the Sun, among his great Museum of Absurdities, looks down upon at present.'

Curious enough: the model of the world just now is England and her Constitution; all Nations striving towards it: poor France swimming these last sixty years in seas of horrid dissolution and confusion, resolute to attain this blessedness of free voting, or to die in chase of it. Prussia too, solid Germany itself, has all broken out into crackling of musketry, loud pamphleteering and Frankfort parliamenting and palavering; Germany too will scale the sacred mountains, how steep soever, and, by talisman of ballot-box, inhabit a political Elysium henceforth. All the Nations have that one hope. Very notable, and rather sad to the humane onlooker. For it is sadly conjectured, all the Nations labour somewhat under a mistake as to England, and the causes of her freedom and her prosperous cotton-spinning; and have much misread the nature of her Parliament, and the effect of ballot-boxes and universal-suffrages there.

What if it were because the English Parliament was from the first, and is only just now ceasing to be, a Council of actual Rulers, real Governing Persons (called Peers, Mitred Abbots, Lords, Knights of the Shire, or howsoever called), actually *ruling* each his section of the country,—and possessing (it must be said) in the lump, or when assembled as a Council, uncommon patience, devoutness, probity, discretion and good fortune,—that the said Parliament ever came to be good for much? In that case it will not be easy to 'imitate' the English Parliament; and the ballot-box and suffrage will be the mere bow of Robin Hood, which it is given to very few to bend, or shoot with to any perfection. And if the Peers become mere big Capitalists, Railway Directors, gigantic Hucksters, Kings of Scrip, *without* lordly quality, or other virtue except cash; and the Mitred Abbots change to mere Able-Editors, masters of Parliamentary Eloquence, Doctors of Political Economy, and suchlike; and all *have* to be elected by a universal-suffrage ballot-box,—I do not see how the English Parliament itself will long continue sea-worthy! Nay, I find England in her own big dumb heart, wherever you come upon her in a silent meditative hour, begins to have dreadful misgivings about it.

The model of the world, then, is at once unattainable by the world, and not much worth attaining? England, as I read the omens, is now called a second time to 'show the Nations how to live'; for by her Parliament, as chief governing entity, I fear she is not long for this world! Poor England must herself again, in these new strange times, the old methods being quite worn out, 'learn how to live.' That now is the terrible problem for England, as for all the Nations; and she alone of all, not *yet* sunk into open Anarchy, but left with time for repentance and amendment; she, wealthiest of all in material resource, in spiritual energy, in ancient loyalty to law, and in the qualities that yield such loyalty,—she perhaps alone of all may be able, with huge travail, and the strain of all her faculties, to accomplish some solution. She will have to try it, she has now to try it; she must accomplish it, or perish from her place in the world!

England, as I persuade myself, still contains in it many *kings*; possesses, as Old Rome did, many men not needing 'election' to command, but eternally elected for it by the Maker Himself. England's one hope is in these, just now. They are among the silent, I believe; mostly far away from platforms and public palaverings; not speaking forth the image of their nobleness in transitory words, but imprinting it, each on his own little section of the world, in silent facts, in modest valiant actions, that will endure forevermore. They must sit silent no longer. They are summoned to assert themselves; to act forth, and articulately vindicate, in the teeth of howling multitudes, of a world too justly *maddened* into all manner of delirious clamours, what of wisdom they derive from God. England, and the Eternal Voices, summon them; poor England never so needed them as now. Up, be doing everywhere: the hour of crisis has verily come! In all sections of English life, the god-made *king* is needed; is pressingly demanded in most; in some, cannot longer, without peril as of conflagration, be dispensed with. He, wheresoever he finds himself, can say, "Here too am I wanted; here is the kingdom I have to subjugate, and introduce God's Laws into,—God's Laws, instead of Mammon's and M'Croudy's and the Old Anarch's! Here is my work, here or nowhere."——Are there many such, who will answer to the call, in England? It turns on that, whether England, rapidly crumbling in these very years and months, shall go down to the Abyss as her neighbours have all done, or survive to new grander destinies *without* solution of continuity! Probably the chief question of the world at present.

The true 'commander' and king; he who knows for himself the divine Appointments of this Universe, the Eternal Laws ordained by God the Maker, in conforming to which lies victory and felicity, in departing from which lies, and forever must lie, sorrow and defeat, for each and all of the Posterity of Adam in every time and every place; he who has sworn fealty to these, and dare alone against the world assert these, and dare not with the whole world at his back deflect from these;—he, I know too well, is a rare man. Difficult to discover; not quite discoverable, I apprehend, by manœuvring of ballot-boxes, and riddling of the popular clamour according to the most approved methods. He is not sold at any shop I know of,—though sometimes, as at the sign of the Ballot-box, he is advertised for sale. Difficult indeed to discover: and not very much assisted, or encouraged in late times, to discover *himself*;—which, I think, might be a kind of help? Encouraged rather, and commanded in all ways, if he be wise, to *hide* himself, and give place to the windy Counterfeit of himself; such as the universal-suffrages can recognise, such as loves the most sweet voices of the universal-suffrages!—O Peter, what becomes of such a People; what can become?

Did you never hear, with the mind's ear as well, that fateful Hebrew Prophecy, I think the fatefulest of all, which sounds daily through the streets, "Ou' clo'! Ou' clo'!"—A certain People, once upon a time, clamorously voted by overwhelming majority, "Not *he*; Barabbas, not he! *Him,* and what he is, and what he deserves, we know well enough: a reviler of the Chief Priests and sacred Chancery wigs; a seditious Heretic, physical-force Chartist, and enemy of his country and mankind: To the gallows and the cross with him! Barabbas is our man; Barabbas, we are for Barabbas!" They got Barabbas:—have you well considered what a fund of purblind obduracy, of opaque *flunkyism* grown truculent and transcendent; what an eye for the phylacteries, and want of eye for the eternal noblenesses; sordid loyalty to the prosperous Semblances, and high-treason against the Supreme Fact, such a vote betokens in these natures? For it was the consummation of a long series of such; they and their fathers had long kept voting so. A singular People; who could both produce such divine men, and then could so stone and crucify them; a People terrible from the beginning!—Well, they got Barabbas; and they got, of course, such guidance as Barabbas and the like of him could give them; and, of course, they stumbled ever downwards and devilwards, in their truculent stiffnecked way; and—and, at this hour, after eighteen centuries of sad fortune, they prophetically sing "Ou' clo'!" in all the cities of the world. Might the world, at this late hour, but take note of them, and understand their song a little!

Yes, there are some things the universal-suffrage can decide,—and about these it will be exceedingly useful to consult the universal-suffrage: but in regard to most things of importance, and in regard to the choice of men especially, there is (astonishing as it may seem) next to no capability on the part of universal-suffrage.—I request all candid persons, who have never so little originality of mind, and every man has a little, to consider this. If true, it involves such a change in our now-fashionable modes of procedure as fills me with astonishment and alarm. *If* popular suffrage is not the way of ascertaining what the Laws of the Universe are, and who it is that will best guide us in the way of these,—then woe is to us if we do not take another method. Delolme on the British Constitution will not save us; deaf will the Parcæ be to votes of the House, to leading-articles, constitutional philosophies. The other method—alas, it involves a stopping short, or vital change of direction, in the glorious career which all Europe, with shouts heaven-high, is now galloping along: and that, happen when it may, will, to many of us, be probably a rather surprising business!

One thing I do know, and can again assert with great confidence, supported by the whole Universe, and by some Two-hundred generations of men, who have left us some record of themselves there, That the few Wise will have, by one method or another, to take command of the innumerable Foolish; that they must be got to take it;—and that, in fact, since Wisdom, which means also Valour and heroic Nobleness, is alone strong in this world, and one wise man is stronger than all men unwise, they can be got. That they must take it; and having taken, must keep it, and do their God's-Message in it, and defend the same, at their life's peril, against all men and devils. This I do clearly believe to be the backbone of all Future Society, as it has been of all Past; and that without it, there is no Society possible in the world. And what a business *this* will be, before it end in some degree of victory again, and whether the time for shouts of triumph and tremendous cheers upon it is yet come, or not yet by a great way, I perceive too well! A business to make us all very serious indeed. A business not to be accomplished but by noble manhood, and devout all-daring, all-enduring loyalty to Heaven, such as fatally *sleeps* at present,—such as is not *dead* at present either, unless the gods have doomed this world of theirs to die! A business which long centuries of faithful travail and heroic agony, on the part of all the noble that are born to us, will not end; and which to us, of this 'tremendous cheering' century, it were blessedness very great to see successfully begun. Begun, tried by all manner of methods, if there is one wise Statesman or man left among us, it verily must be;—begun, successfully or unsuccessfully, we do hope to see it!

In all European countries, especially in England, one class of Captains and commanders of men, recognisable as

the beginning of a new real and not imaginary 'Aristocracy,' has already in some measure developed itself: the
Captains of Industry;—happily the class who above all, or
at least first of all, are wanted in this time. In the doing of
material work, we have already men among us that can
command bodies of men. And surely, on the other hand,
there is no lack of men needing to be commanded: the
sad class of brother-men whom we had to describe as
'Hodge's emancipated horses,' reduced to roving famine,—
this too has in all countries developed itself; and, in fatal
geometrical progression, is ever more developing itself,
with a rapidity which alarms every one. On this ground, if
not on all manner of other grounds, it may be truly said,
the 'Organisation of Labour' (*not* organisable by the mad
methods tried hitherto) is the universal vital Problem of
the world.

To bring these hordes of outcast captainless soldiers
under due captaincy? This is really the question of questions; on the answer to which turns, among other things,
the fate of all Governments, constitutional and other,—the
possibility of their continuing to exist, or the impossibility.
Captainless, uncommanded, these wretched outcast 'soldiers,' since they cannot starve, must needs become
banditti, street-barricaders—destroyers of every Government that *cannot* put them under captains, and send them
upon enterprises, and in short render life human to them.
Our English plan of Poor Laws, which we once piqued ourselves upon as sovereign, is evidently fast breaking down.
Ireland, now admitted into the Idle Workhouse, is rapidly
bursting it in pieces. That never was a 'human' destiny
for any honest son of Adam; nowhere but in England
could it have lasted at all; and now, with Ireland sharer
in it, and the fulness of time come, it is as good as ended.
Alas, yes. Here in Connemara, your crazy Ship of the
State, otherwise dreadfully rotten in many of its timbers I
believe, has sprung a leak: spite of all hands at the pump,
the water is rising; the Ship, I perceive, will founder, if
you cannot stop this leak!

To bring these Captainless under due captaincy? The
anxious thoughts of all men that do think are turned upon
that question; and their efforts, though as yet blindly and
to no purpose, under the multifarious impediments and
obscurations, all point thitherward. Isolated men, and their

vague efforts, cannot do it. Government everywhere is called upon,—in England as loudly as elsewhere,—to give the initiative. A new strange task of these new epochs; which no Government, never so 'constitutional,' can escape from undertaking. For it is vitally necessary to the existence of Society itself; it must be undertaken, and succeeded in too, or worse will follow,—and, as we already see in Irish Connaught and some other places, will follow soon. To whatever thing still calls itself by the name of Government, were it never so constitutional and impeded by official impossibilities, all men will naturally look for help, and direction what to do, in this extremity. If help or direction is not given; if the thing called Government merely drift and tumble to and fro, nowhither, on the popular vortexes, like some carcass of a drowned ass, constitutionally put 'at the top of affairs'—popular indignation will infallibly accumulate upon it; one day, the popular lightning, descending forked and horrible from the black air, will annihilate said supreme carcass, and smite *it* home to its native ooze again!—Your Lordship, this is too true, though irreverently spoken: indeed one knows not how to speak of it; and to me it is infinitely sad and miserable, spoken or not! —Unless perhaps the Voluntary Principle will still help us through? Perhaps this Irish leak, in such a rotten distressed condition of the Ship, with all the crew so anxious about it, will be kind enough to stop of itself?—

Dismiss that hope, your Lordship! Let all real and imaginary Governors of England, at the pass we have arrived at, dismiss forever that fallacious fatal solace to their donothingism: of itself, too clearly, the leak will never stop; by human skill and energy it must be stopped, or there is nothing but the sea-bottom for us all! A Chief Governor of England really ought to recognise his situation; to discern that, doing nothing, and merely drifting to and fro, in however constitutional a manner, he is a squanderer of precious moments, moments that perhaps are priceless; a truly alarming Chief Governor. Surely, to a Chief Governor of England, worthy of that high name,—surely to him, as to every living man, in every conceivable situation short of the Kingdom of the Dead,—there is *something* possible; some plan of action other than that of standing mildly, with crossed arms, till he and we—sink? Complex as his situation is, he, of all Governors now extant among these distracted Nations, has, as I compute, by far the greatest possibilities. The Captains, actual or potential, are there, and the million Captainless: and such resources for bringing them together as no other has. To these outcast soldiers of his, unregimented roving banditti for the present, or unworking workhouse prisoners who are almost uglier than banditti; to these floods of Irish Beggars, Able-bodied Paupers, and nomadic Lackalls, now stagnating or roaming everywhere, drowning the face of the world (too truly) into an untenantable swamp and Stygian quagmire, has the Chief Governor of this country no word whatever to say? Nothing but "Rate in aid," "Time will mend it," "Necessary business of the Session"; and "After me the Deluge"? A Chief Governor that can front his Irish difficulty, and steadily contemplate the horoscope of Irish and British Pauperism, and whitherward it is leading him and us, in this humour, must be a—What shall we call such a Chief Governor? Alas, in spite of old use and wont,—little other than a tolerated Solecism, growing daily more intolerable! He decidedly ought to have some word to say on this matter,—to be incessantly occupied in getting something which he could practically say!—Perhaps to the following, or a much finer effect?

––––––––––––––––

Speech of the British Prime-Minister to the floods of Irish and other Beggars, the able-bodied Lackalls, nomadic or stationary, and the general assembly, outdoor and indoor, of the Pauper Populations of these Realms

"Vagrant Lackalls, foolish most of you, criminal many of you, miserable all; the sight of you fills me with astonishment and despair. What to do with you I know not; long have I been meditating, and it is hard to tell. Here are some three millions of you, as I count: so many of you fallen sheer over into the abysses of open Beggary; and, fearful to think, every new unit that falls is *loading* so much more the chain that drags the others over. On the edge of the precipice hang uncounted millions; increasing, I am told, at the rate of 1200 a-day. They hang there on the giddy edge, poor souls, cramping themselves down, holding-on with all their strength; but falling, falling one after another; and the chain is getting *heavy*, so that ever

more fall; and who at last will stand? What to do with you?
The question, What to do with you? especially since the
potato died, is like to break my heart!

"One thing, after much meditating, I have at last discovered, and now know for some time back: That you
cannot be left to roam abroad in this unguided manner,
stumbling over the precipices, and loading ever heavier
the fatal *chain* upon those who might be able to stand;
that this of locking you up in temporary Idle Workhouses,
when you stumble, and subsisting you on Indian meal, till
you can sally forth again on fresh roamings, and fresh
stumblings, and ultimate descent to the devil;—that this is
not the plan; and that it never was, or could out of England have been supposed to be, much as I have prided myself upon it!

"Vagrant Lackalls, I at last perceive, all this that has been
sung and spoken, for a long while, about enfranchisement,
emancipation, freedom, suffrage, civil and religious liberty
over the world, is little other than sad temporary jargon,
brought upon us by a stern necessity,—but now ordered
by a sterner to take itself away again a little. Sad temporary
jargon, I say: made-up of sense and nonsense,—sense in
small quantities, and nonsense in very large;—and, if taken
for the whole or permanent truth of human things, it is no
better than fatal infinite nonsense eternally *untrue*. All
men, I think, will soon have to quit this, to consider this as
a thing pretty well achieved; and to look-out towards another thing much more needing achievement at the time
that now is.

"All men will have to quit it, I believe. But to you, my
indigent friends, the time for quitting it has palpably arrived! To talk of glorious self-government, of suffrages and
hustings, and the fight of freedom and suchlike, is a vain
thing in your case. By all human definitions and conceptions of the said fight of freedom, you for your part have
lost it, and can fight no more. Glorious self-government is
a glory not for you,—not for Hodge's emancipated horses,
nor you. No; I say, No. You, for your part, have tried it,
and *failed*. Left to walk your own road, the will-o'-wisps
beguiled you, your short sight could not descry the pitfalls;
the deadly tumult and press has whirled you hither and
thither, regardless of your struggles and your shrieks;
and here at last you lie; fallen flat into the ditch, drown-

ing there and dying, unless the others that are still standing please to pick you up. The others that still stand have their own difficulties, I can tell you!—But you, by imperfect energy and redundant appetite, by doing too little work and drinking too much beer, you (I bid you observe) have proved that you cannot do it! You lie there plainly in the ditch. And I am to pick you up again, on these mad terms; help you ever again, as with our best heart's-blood, to do what, once for all, the gods have made impossible? To load the fatal *chain* with your perpetual staggerings and sprawlings; and ever again load it, till we all lie sprawling? My indigent, incompetent friends, I will not! Know that, whoever may be 'sons of freedom,' you for your part are not and cannot be such. Not 'free' you, I think, whoever may be free. You palpably are fallen captive,— *caitiff,* as they once named it:—you do, silently, but eloquently, demand, in the name of mercy itself, that some genuine command be taken of you.

"Yes, my indigent incompetent friends; some genuine practical command. Such,—if I rightly interpret those mad Chartisms, Repeal Agitations, Red Republics, and other delirious inarticulate howlings and bellowings which all the populations of the world now utter, evidently cries of pain on their and your part,—is the demand which you, Captives, make of all men that are not Captive, but are still Free. Free men,—alas, had you ever any notion who the free men were, who the not-free, the incapable of freedom! The free men, if you could have understood it, they are the wise men; the patient, self-denying, valiant; the Nobles of the World; who can discern the Law of this Universe, what it is, and piously *obey* it; these, in late sad times, having cast you loose, you are fallen captive to greedy sons of profit-and-loss; to bad and ever to worse; and at length to Beer and the Devil. Algiers, Brazil or Dahomey hold nothing in them so authentically *slave* as you are, my indigent incompetent friends!

"Good Heavens, and I have to raise some eight or nine millions annually, six for England itself, and to wreck the morals of my working population beyond all money's worth, to keep the life from going out of *you*: a small service to you, as I many times bitterly repeat! Alas, yes; before high Heaven I must declare it such. I think the old Spartans, who would have killed you instead, had shown more 'humanity,' more of manhood, than I thus do! More humanity, I say, more of *man*hood, and of sense for what the dignity of man demands imperatively of you and of me and of us all. We call it charity, beneficence, and other fine names, this brutish Workhouse Scheme of ours; and it is but sluggish heartlessness, and insincerity, and cowardly lowness of soul. Not 'humanity' or manhood, I think; perhaps *ape*hood rather,—paltry imitancy, from the teeth outward, of what our heart never felt nor *our* understanding ever saw; dim indolent adherence to extraneous hearsays and extinct traditions; traditions now really about extinct; not living now to almost any of us, and still haunting with their spectralities and gibbering *ghosts* (in a truly baleful manner) almost all of us! Making this our struggling 'Twelfth Hour of the Night' inexpressibly hideous!—

"But as for you, my indigent incompetent friends, I have to repeat with sorrow, but with perfect clearness, what is plainly undeniable, and is even clamorous to get itself admitted, that you are of the nature of *slaves*,—or if you prefer the word, of *nomadic, and now even vagrant and vagabond, servants that can find no master on those terms;* which seems to me a much uglier word. Emancipation? You have been 'emancipated' with a vengeance! Foolish souls, I say the whole world cannot emancipate you. Fealty to ignorant Unruliness, to gluttonous sluggish Improvidence, to the Beerpot and the Devil, who is there that can emancipate a man in that predicament? Not a whole Reform Bill, a whole French Revolution executed for his behoof alone: nothing but God the Maker can emancipate him, by making him anew.

"To forward which glorious consummation, will it not be well, O indigent friends, that you, fallen flat there, shall henceforth learn to take advice of others as to the methods of standing? Plainly I let you know, and all the world and the worlds know, that I for my part mean it so. Not as glorious unfortunate sons of freedom, but as recognised captives, as unfortunate fallen brothers requiring that I should command you, and if need were, control and compel you, can there henceforth be a relation between us. Ask me not for Indian meal; you shall be compelled to earn it first; know that on other terms I will not give you any. Before Heaven and Earth, and God the Maker of us all, I declare it is a scandal to see *such* a life kept in you, by the sweat and heart's-blood of your brothers; and that, if we cannot mend it, death were preferable! Go to, we must get out of this unutterable coil of nonsenses, constitutional, philanthropical, etc., in which (surely without mutual hatred, if with less of 'love' than is supposed) we are all strangling one another! Your want of wants, I say, is that you be *commanded* in this world, not being able to command yourselves. Know therefore that it shall be so with you. Nomadism, I give you notice, has ended; needful permanency, soldier-like obedience, and the opportunity and the necessity of hard steady labour for your living, have begun. Know that the Idle Workhouse is shut against you henceforth; you cannot enter there at will, nor leave at will;—you shall enter a quite other Refuge, under conditions strict as soldiering, and not leave till I have done with you. He that prefers the glorious (or perhaps even the rebellious *in*glorious) 'career of freedom,' let him prove that he can travel there, and be the master of himself; and right good speed to him. He who has proved that he cannot travel there or be the master of himself,—let him, in the name of all the gods, become a servant, and accept the just rules of servitude!

"Arise, enlist in my Irish, my Scotch and English 'Regiments of the New Era,'—which I have been concocting, day and night, during these three Grouse-seasons (taking earnest incessant counsel, with all manner of Industrial Notabilities and men of insight, on the matter), and have now brought to a kind of preparation for incipiency, thank Heaven! Enlist there, ye poor wandering banditti; obey, work, suffer, abstain, as all of us have had to do: so shall you be useful in God's creation, so shall you be helped to gain a manful living for yourselves; not otherwise than so. Industrial Regiments"—[*Here numerous persons, with big wigs many of them, and austere aspect, whom I take to be Professors of the Dismal Science, start up in an agitated vehement manner: but the Premier resolutely beckons them down again*]—"Regiments not to fight the French or others, who are peaceable enough towards us; but to fight the Bogs and Wildernesses at home and abroad, and to chain the Devils of the Pit which are walking too openly among us.

"Work, for you? Work, surely, is not quite undiscoverable in an Earth so wide as ours, if we will take the right methods for it! Indigent friends, we will adopt this new relation (which is *old* as the world); this will lead us towards such. Rigorous conditions, not to be violated on either side, lie in this relation; conditions planted there by God Himself; which woe will betide us if we do not discover, gradually more and more discover, and conform to! Industrial Colonels, Workmasters, Taskmasters, Life-commanders, equitable as Rhadamanthus and inflexible as he: such, I perceive, you do need; and such, you being once put under law as soldiers are, will be discoverable for you. I perceive, with boundless alarm, that I shall have to set about discovering such,—I, since I am at the top of affairs, with all men looking to me. Alas, it is my new task in this New Era; and God knows, I too, little other than a redtape Talking-machine, and unhappy Bag of Parliamentary Eloquence hitherto, am far behind with it! But street-barricades rise everywhere: the hour of Fate has come. In Connemara there has sprung a leak, since the potato died; Connaught, if it were not for Treasury-grants and rates-in-aid, would have to recur to Cannibalism even now, and Human Society would cease to pretend that it existed there. Done this thing must be. Alas, I perceive that if I cannot do it, then surely I shall die, and perhaps shall not have Christian burial! But I already raise near upon Ten Millions for feeding you in idleness, my nomadic friends; work, under due regulations, I really might try to get of"—[*Here arises indescribable uproar, no longer repressible, from all manner of Economists, Emancipationists, Constitutionalists, and miscellaneous Professors of the Dismal Science, pretty numerously scattered about; and cries of "Private Enterprise," "Rights of Capital," "Voluntary Principle," "Doctrines of the British Constitution," swollen by the general assenting hum of all the world, quite drown the Chief Minister for a while. He, with invincible resolution, persists; obtains hearing again:*]

"Respectable Professors of the Dismal Science, soft you a little. Alas, I know what you would say. For my sins, I have read much in those inimitable volumes of yours,—really I should think, some barrowfuls of them in my time,—and, in these last forty years of theory and practice, have pretty well seized what of Divine Message you were sent with to me. Perhaps as small a message, give me leave to say, as ever there was such a noise made about before.

Trust me, I have not forgotten it, shall never forget it. Those Laws of the Shop-till are indisputable to me; and practically useful in certain departments of the Universe, as the multiplication-table itself. Once I even tried to sail through the Immensities with them, and to front the big coming Eternities with them; but I found it would not do. As the Supreme Rule of Statesmanship, or Government of Men,—since this Universe is not wholly a Shop,—no. You rejoice in my improved tariffs, free-trade movements and the like, on every hand; for which be thankful, and even sing litanies if you choose. But here at last, in the Idle-Workhouse movement,—unexampled yet on Earth or in the waters under the Earth,—I am fairly brought to a stand; and have had to make reflections, of the most alarming, and indeed awful, and as it were religious nature! Professors of the Dismal Science, I perceive that the length of your tether is now pretty well run; and that I must request you to talk a little lower in future. By the side of the shop-till,—see, your small 'Law of God' is hung up, along with the multiplication-table itself. But beyond and above the shop-till, allow me to say, you shall as good as hold your peace. Respectable Professors, I perceive it is not now the Gigantic Hucksters, but it is the Immortal Gods, yes, they, in their terror and their beauty, in their wrath and their beneficence, that are coming into play in the affairs of this world! Soft you a little. Do not you interrupt me, but try to understand and help me!—

—"Work, was I saying? My indigent unguided friends, I should think some work might be discoverable for you. Enlist, stand drill; become, from a nomadic Banditti of Idleness, Soldiers of Industry! I will lead you to the Irish Bogs, to the vacant desolations of Connaught now falling into Cannibalism, to mistilled Connaught, to ditto Munster, Leinster, Ulster, I will lead you: to the English fox-covers, furze-grown Commons, New Forests, Salisbury Plains: likewise to the Scotch Hill-sides, and bare rushy slopes, which as yet feed only sheep,—moist uplands, thousands of square miles in extent, which are destined yet to grow green crops, and fresh butter and milk and beef without limit (wherein no 'Foreigner can compete with us'), were the Glasgow sewers once opened on them, and you with your Colonels carried thither. In the Three Kingdoms, or in the Forty Colonies, depend upon it, you shall be led to your work!

"To each of you I will then say: Here is work for you; strike into it with manlike, soldierlike obedience and heartiness, according to the methods here prescribed,—wages follow for you without difficulty; all manner of just remuneration, and at length emancipation itself follows. Refuse to strike into it; shirk the heavy labour, disobey the rules,—I will admonish and endeavour to incite you; if in vain, I will flog you; if still in vain, I will at last shoot you,—and make God's Earth, and the forlorn-hope in God's Battle, free of you. Understand it, I advise you! The Organisation of Labour"——[*Left speaking,* says our reporter.]

'Left speaking': alas, that he should have to 'speak' so much! There are things that should be done, not spoken; that till the doing of them is begun, cannot well be spoken. He may have to 'speak' seven years yet, before a spade be struck into the Bog of Allen; and then perhaps it will be too late!—

You perceive, my friends, we have actually got into the 'New Era' there has been such prophesying of: here we all are, arrived at last;—and it is by no means the land flowing with milk and honey we were led to expect! Very much the reverse. A terrible *new* country this: no neighbours in it yet, that I can see, but irrational flabby monsters (philanthropic and other) of the giant species; hyænas, laughing hyænas, predatory wolves; probably *devils,* blue (or perhaps blue-and-yellow) devils, as St. Guthlac found in Croyland long ago. A huge untrodden haggard country, the 'chaotic battle-field of Frost and Fire'; a country of savage glaciers, granite mountains, of foul jungles, unhewed forests, quaking bogs;—which we shall have our own ados to make arable and habitable, I think! We must stick by it, however;—of all enterprises the impossiblest is that of getting out of *it,* and shifting into another. To work, then, one and all; hands to work!

FROM *The Life of John Sterling*

1 8 5 1

[After Edward Irving, John Sterling (1806-1844) was probably Carlyle's closest friend, although there was a great difference in their ages and circumstances. Sterling was the son of the editor of the *London Times* and himself an Anglican priest. He was also a minor novelist and poet and he wrote the first valuable criticism of *Sartor Resartus*. Sterling died of consumption at the age of thirty-eight. Not until he had completed the caustic *Latter-Day Pamphlets* did Carlyle turn to the gentler task of writing Sterling's life. The *Life* itself paints an understanding picture of Sterling, but it is most memorable for the chapter depicting Coleridge in the years before his death in 1834 when he lived in Highgate and held court for the devoted and the curious. That chapter is printed below.]

PART I, CHAPTER VIII

COLERIDGE

Coleridge sat on the brow of Highgate Hill, in those years, looking down on London and its smoke-tumult, like a sage escaped from the inanity of life's battle; attracting towards him the thoughts of innumerable brave souls still engaged there. His express contributions to poetry, philosophy, or any specific province of human literature or enlightenment, had been small and sadly intermittent; but he had, especially among young inquiring men, a higher than literary, a kind of prophetic or magician character. He was thought to hold, he alone in England, the key of German and other Transcendentalisms; knew the sublime secret of believing by 'the reason' what 'the understanding' had been obliged to fling out as incredible; and could still, after Hume and Voltaire had done their best and worst with him, profess himself an orthodox Christian, and say and print to the Church of England, with its singular old rubrics and surplices at Allhallowtide, *Esto perpetua*. A sublime man; who, alone in those dark days, had saved his crown of spiritual manhood; escaping from the black materialisms, and revolutionary deluges, with 'God, Freedom, Immortality' still his: a king of men. The practical intellects of the world did not much heed him, or carelessly reckoned him a metaphysical dreamer: but to the rising spirits of the young generation he had this dusky sublime character; and sat there as a kind of *Magus,* girt in mystery and enigma; his Dodona oak-grove (Mr. Gilman's house at Highgate) whispering strange things, uncertain whether oracles or jargon.

The Gilmans did not encourage much company, or excitation of any sort, round their sage; nevertheless access to him, if a youth did reverently wish it, was not difficult. He would stroll about the pleasant garden with you, sit in the pleasant rooms of the place,—perhaps take you to his own peculiar room, high up, with a rearward view, which was the chief view of all. A really charming outlook, in fine weather. Close at hand, wide sweep of flowery leafy gardens, their few houses mostly hidden, the very chimney-pots veiled under blossomy umbrage, flowed gloriously down hill, gloriously issuing in wide-tufted undulating plain-country, rich in all charms of field and town. Waving blooming country of the brightest green; dotted all over with handsome villas, handsome groves; crossed by roads and human traffic, here inaudible or heard only as a musical hum: and behind all swam, under olive-tinted haze, the illimitable limitary ocean of London, with its domes and steeples definite in the sun, big Paul's and the many memories attached to it hanging high over all. Nowhere, of its kind, could you see a grander prospect on a bright summer day, with the set of the air going southward,—southward, and so draping with the city-smoke not *you* but the city. Here for hours would Coleridge talk, concerning all conceivable or inconceivable things; and liked nothing better than to have an intelligent, or failing that, even a silent and patient human listener. He distinguished himself to all that ever heard him as at least the most surprising talker extant in this world,—and to some small minority, by no means to all, as the most excellent.

The good man, he was now getting old, towards sixty perhaps; and gave you the idea of a life that had been full of sufferings; a life heavy-laden, half-vanquished, still swimming painfully in seas of manifold physical and other bewilderment. Brow and head were round, and of massive weight, but the face was flabby and irresolute. The deep eyes, of a light hazel, were as full of sorrow as of inspiration; confused pain looked mildly from them, as in a kind of mild astonishment. The whole figure and air, good and amiable otherwise, might be called flabby and irresolute; expressive of weakness under possibility of strength. He hung loosely on his limbs, with knees bent, and stooping attitude; in walking, he rather shuffled than decisively stept; and a lady once remarked, he never could fix which side of the garden walk would suit him best, but continually shifted, in corkscrew fashion, and kept trying both. A heavy-laden, high-aspiring and surely much-suffering man. His voice, naturally soft and good, had contracted itself into a plaintive snuffle and singsong; he spoke as if preaching,—you would have said, preaching earnestly and also hopelessly the weightiest things. I still recollect his 'object' and 'subject,' terms of continual recurrence in the Kantean province; and how he sang and snuffled them into 'om-m-mject' and 'sum-m-mject,' with a kind of solemn shake or quaver, as he rolled along. No talk, in his century or in any other, could be more surprising.

Sterling, who assiduously attended him, with profound reverence, and was often with him by himself, for a good many months, gives a record of their first colloquy.[1] Their colloquies were numerous, and he had taken note of many; but they are all gone to the fire, except this first, which Mr. Hare has printed,—unluckily without date. It contains a number of ingenious, true and half-true observations, and is of course a faithful epitome of the things said; but it gives small idea of Coleridge's way of talking;—this one feature is perhaps the most recognisable, 'Our interview lasted for three hours, during which he talked two hours and three quarters.' Nothing could be more copious than his talk; and furthermore it was always, virtually or literally, of the nature of a monologue; suffering no interruption, however reverent; hastily putting aside all foreign additions, annotations, or most ingenuous desires for elucidation, as well-meant superfluities which would never do. Besides, it was talk not flowing anywhither like a river, but spreading everywhither in inextricable currents and re-

[1] *Biography,* by Hare, pp. xvi-xxvi. [Carlyle's note.]

gurgitations like a lake or sea; terribly deficient in definite goal or aim, nay often in logical intelligibility; *what* you were to believe or do, on any earthly or heavenly thing, obstinately refusing to appear from it. So that, most times, you felt logically lost; swamped near to drowning in this tide of ingenious vocables, spreading out boundless as if to submerge the world.

To sit as a passive bucket and be pumped into, whether you consent or not, can in the long-run be exhilarating to no creature; how eloquent soever the flood of utterance that is descending. But if it be withal a confused unintelligible flood of utterance, threatening to submerge all known landmarks of thought, and drown the world and you!—I have heard Coleridge talk, with eager musical energy, two stricken hours, his face radiant and moist, and communicate no meaning whatsoever to any individual of his hearers,—certain of whom, I for one, still kept eagerly listening in hope; the most had long before given up, and formed (if the room were large enough) secondary humming groups of their own. He began anywhere: you put some question to him, made some suggestive observation: instead of answering this, or decidedly setting out towards answer of it, he would accumulate formidable apparatus, logical swim-bladders, transcendental life-preservers and other precautionary and vehiculatory gear, for setting out; perhaps did at last get under way,—but was swiftly solicited, turned aside by the glance of some radiant new game on this hand or that, into new courses; and ever into new; and before long into all the Universe, where it was uncertain what game you would catch, or whether any.

His talk, alas, was distinguished, like himself, by irresolution: it disliked to be troubled with conditions, abstinences, definite fulfilments;—loved to wander at its own sweet will, and make its auditor and his claims and humble wishes a mere passive bucket for itself! He had knowledge about many things and topics, much curious reading; but generally all topics led him, after a pass or two, into the high seas of theosophic philosophy, the hazy infinitude of Kantean transcendentalism, with its 'sum-m-mjects' and 'om-m-mjects.' Sad enough; for with such indolent impatience of the claims and ignorances of others, he had not the least talent for explaining this or anything unknown to them; and you swam and fluttered in the mistiest wide unintelligible deluge of things, for most part in a rather profitless uncomfortable manner.

Glorious islets, too, I have seen rise out of the haze; but they were few, and soon swallowed in the general element again. Balmy sunny islets, islets of the blest and the intelligible:——on which occasions those secondary humming groups would all cease humming, and hang breathless upon the eloquent words; till once your islet got wrapt in the mist again, and they could recommence humming. Eloquent artistically expressive words you always had; piercing radiances of a most subtle insight came at intervals; tones of noble pious sympathy, recognisable as pious though strangely coloured, were never wanting long: but in general you could not call this aimless, cloudcapt, cloud-based, lawlessly meandering human discourse of reason by the name of 'excellent talk,' but only of 'surprising'; and were reminded bitterly of Hazlitt's account of it: 'Excellent talker, very,—if you let him start from no premises and come to no conclusion.' Coleridge was not without what talkers call wit, and there were touches of prickly sarcasm in him, contemptuous enough of the world and its idols and popular dignitaries; he had traits even of poetic humour: but in general he seemed deficient in laughter; or indeed in sympathy for concrete human things either on the sunny or on the stormy side. One right peal of concrete laughter at some convicted flesh-and-blood absurdity, one burst of noble indignation at some injustice or depravity, rubbing elbows with us on this solid Earth, how strange would it have been in that Kantean haze-world, and how infinitely cheering amid its vacant air-castles and dim-melting ghosts and shadows! None such ever came. His life had been an abstract thinking and dreaming, idealistic, passed amid the ghosts of defunct bodies and of unborn ones. The moaning singsong of that theosophico-metaphysical monotony left on you, at last, a very dreary feeling.

In close colloquy, flowing within narrower banks, I suppose he was more definite and apprehensible; Sterling in aftertimes did not complain of his unintelligibility, or imputed it only to the abstruse high nature of the topics handled. Let us hope so, let us try to believe so! There is no doubt but Coleridge could speak plain words on things plain: his observations and responses on the trivial matters that occurred were as simple as the commonest man's, or were even distinguished by superior simplicity as well as pertinency. 'Ah, your tea is too cold, Mr. Coleridge!' mourned the good Mrs. Gilman once, in her kind, reverential and yet protective manner, handing him a very tolerable though belated cup.—'It's better than I deserve!' snuffled he, in a low hoarse murmur, partly courteous, chiefly pious, the tone of which still abides with me: 'It's better than I deserve!'

But indeed, to the young ardent mind, instinct with pious nobleness, yet driven to the grim deserts of Radicalism for a faith, his speculations had a charm much more than literary, a charm almost religious and prophetic. The constant gist of his discourse was lamentation over the sunk condition of the world; which he recognised to be given-up to Atheism and Materialism, full of mere sordid misbeliefs, mispursuits and misresults. All Science had become mechanical; the science not of men, but of a kind of human beavers. Churches themselves had died away into a godless mechanical condition; and stood there as mere Cases of Articles, mere Forms of Churches; like the dried carcasses of once-swift camels, which you find left withering in the thirst of the universal desert,—ghastly portents for the present, beneficent ships of the desert no more. Men's souls were blinded, hebetated; and sunk under the influence of Atheism and Materialism, and Hume and Voltaire: the world for the present was as an extinct world, deserted of God, and incapable of welldoing till it changed its heart and spirit. This, expressed I think with less of indignation and with more of long-drawn querulousness, was always recognisable as the ground-tone:—in which truly a pious young heart, driven into Radicalism and the opposition party, could not but recognise a too sorrowful truth; and ask of the Oracle, with all earnestness, What remedy, then?

The remedy, though Coleridge himself professed to see it as in sunbeams, could not, except by processes unspeakably difficult, be described to you at all. On the whole, those dead Churches, this dead English Church especially, must be brought to life again. Why not? It was not dead; the soul of it, in this parched-up body, was tragically asleep only. Atheistic Philosophy was true on its side, and Hume and Voltaire could on their own ground speak irrefragably for themselves against any Church: but lift the Church and them into a higher sphere of argument, *they* died into inanition, the Church revivified itself into pristine florid vigour,—became once more a living ship of the desert, and invincibly bore you over stock and stone. But how, but how! By attending to the 'reason' of man, said Coleridge, and duly chaining-up the 'understanding' of man: the *Vernunft* (Reason) and *Verstand* (Understanding) of the Germans, it all turned upon these, if you could well understand them,—which you couldn't. For the rest, Mr. Coleridge had on the anvil various Books, especially was about to write one grand Book *On the Logos,* which would help to bridge the chasm for us. So much appeared, however: Churches, though proved false (as you had imagined), were still true (as you were to imagine): here was an Artist who could burn you up an old Church, root and branch; and then as the Alchymists professed to do with organic substances in general, distil you an 'Astral Spirit' from the ashes, which was the very image of the old burnt article, its airdrawn counterpart,—this you still had, or might get, and draw uses from, if you could. Wait till the Book on the Logos were done;—alas, till your own terrene eyes, blind with conceit and the dust of logic, were purged, subtilised and spiritualised into the sharpness of vision requisite for discerning such an 'om-m-mject.'—The ingenuous young English head, of those days, stood strangely puzzled by such revelations; uncertain whether it were getting inspired, or getting infatuated into flat imbecility; and strange effulgence, of new day or else of deeper meteoric night, coloured the horizon of the future for it.

Let me not be unjust to this memorable man. Surely there was here, in his pious, ever-labouring, subtle mind, a precious truth, or prefigurement of truth; and yet a fatal delusion withal. Prefigurement that, in spite of beaver sciences and temporary spiritual hebetude and cecity, man and his Universe were eternally divine; and that no past nobleness, or revelation of the divine, could or would ever be lost to him. Most true, surely, and worthy of all acceptance. Good also to do what you can with old Churches and practical Symbols of the Noble: nay, quit not the burnt ruins of them while you find there is still gold to be dug there. But, on the whole, do not think you can, by logical alchymy, distil astral spirits from them; or if you

could, that said astral spirits, or defunct logical phantasms, could serve you in anything. What the light of your
mind, which is the direct inspiration of the Almighty, pro-
nounces incredible,—that, in God's name, leave uncredited;
at your peril do not try believing that. No subtlest hocus-
pocus of 'reason' *versus* 'understanding' will avail for that
feat;—and it is terribly perilous to try it in these provinces!

The truth is, I now see, Coleridge's talk and speculation
was the emblem of himself: in it, as in him, a ray of
heavenly inspiration struggled, in a tragically ineffectual
degree, with the weakness of flesh and blood. He says
once, he 'had skirted the howling deserts of Infidelity'; this
was evident enough: but he had not had the courage, in
defiance of pain and terror, to press resolutely across said
deserts to the new firm lands of Faith beyond; he pre-
ferred to create logical fatamorganas for himself on this
hither side, and laboriously solace himself with these.

To the man himself Nature had given, in high measure,
the seeds of a noble endowment; and to unfold it had been
forbidden him. A subtle lynx-eyed intellect, tremulous
pious sensibility to all good and all beautiful; truly a ray
of empyrean light;—but imbedded in such weak laxity of
character, in such indolences and esuriences as had made
strange work with it. Once more, the tragic story of a high
endowment with an insufficient will. An eye to discern the
divineness of the Heaven's splendours and lightnings, the
insatiable wish to revel in their godlike radiances and bril-
liances; but no heart to front the scathing terrors of them,
which is the first condition of your conquering an abiding
place there. The courage necessary for him, above all
things, had been denied this man. His life, with such ray
of the empyrean in it, was great and terrible to him; and
he had not valiantly grappled with it, he had fled from it;
sought refuge in vague daydreams, hollow compromises, in
opium, in theosophic metaphysics. Harsh pain, danger,
necessity, slavish harnessed toil, were of all things abhor-
rent to him. And so the empyrean element, lying smothered
under the terrene, and yet inextinguishable there, made
sad writhings. For pain, danger, difficulty, steady slaving
toil, and other highly disagreeable behests of destiny, shall
in no wise be shirked by any brightest mortal that will ap-
prove himself loyal to his mission in this world; nay, precisely the higher he is, the deeper will be the disagreeable-

ness, and the detestability to flesh and blood, of the tasks laid on him; and the heavier too, and more tragic, his penalties, if he neglect them.

For the old Eternal Powers do live forever; nor do their laws know any change, however we in our poor wigs and church-tippets may attempt to read their laws. To *steal* into Heaven,—by the modern method, of sticking ostrich-like your head into fallacies on Earth, equally as by the ancient and by all conceivable methods,—is forever forbidden. High-treason is the name of that attempt; and it continues to be punished as such. Strange enough: here once more was a kind of Heaven-scaling Ixion; and to him, as to the old one, the just gods were very stern! The ever-revolving, never-advancing Wheel (of a kind) was his, through life; and from his Cloud-Juno did not he too, procreate strange Centaurs, spectral Puseyisms, monstrous illusory Hybrids, and ecclesiastical Chimeras,—which now roam the earth in a very lamentable manner!

FROM *History of Friedrich II of Prussia, Called Frederick the Great*

1858-1865

[Carlyle's *History of Frederick the Great* was the most ambitious undertaking of his literary career, yet it has fared worse than any other work by Carlyle. For thirteen years, from 1852-1865, Carlyle researched and wrote *Frederick the Great,* the final work occupying six volumes. It was a great success when published and helped to redeem Carlyle in the eyes of the public that had reacted so unfavorably to *Latter-Day Pamphlets*; but it has been unjustly neglected since. Criticized today for its supposed exaltation of a tyrant, *Frederick* nevertheless exhibits tremendous literary power in battle scenes, in character portraits and caricatures, and in Carlyle's extraordinary grasp of the qualities of various ages and societies. The short selection printed below is taken from the beginning of the work where the author sets forth his intentions and offers some observations in the traditional Carlylean vein on Frederick's reputation and on the character of the eighteenth century.]

FROM BOOK I—BIRTH AND PARENTAGE / CHAPTER I

PROEM: FRIEDRICH'S HISTORY FROM THE DISTANCE WE ARE AT

1712

About fourscore years ago, there used to be seen sauntering on the terraces of Sans Souci, for a short time in the afternoon, or you might have met him elsewhere at an earlier hour, riding or driving in a rapid business manner on the open roads or through the scraggy woods and avenues of that intricate amphibious Potsdam region, a highly interesting lean little old man, of alert though slightly stooping figure; whose name among strangers was King *Friedrich the Second,* or Frederick the Great of Prussia, and at home among the common people, who much loved and esteemed him, was *Vater Fritz,*—Father Fred,—a name of familiarity which had not bred contempt in that instance. He is a King every inch of him, though without the trappings of a King. Presents himself in a Spartan simplicity of vesture: no crown but an old military cocked-hat,—generally old, or trampled and kneaded into absolute *softness,* if new;—no sceptre but one like Agamemnon's, a walking-stick cut from the woods, which serves also as a riding-stick (with which he hits the horse 'between the ears,' say authors); —and for royal robes, a mere soldier's blue coat with red facings, coat likely to be old, and sure to have a good deal of Spanish snuff on the breast of it; rest of the apparel dim, unobtrusive in colour or cut, ending in high over-knee military boots, which may be brushed (and, I hope, kept soft with an underhand suspicion of oil), but are not permitted to be blackened or varnished; Day and Martin with their soot-pots forbidden to approach.

The man is not of godlike physiognomy, any more than of imposing stature or costume: close-shut mouth with thin lips, prominent jaws and nose, receding brow, by no means of Olympian height; head, however, is of long form, and has superlative gray eyes in it. Not what is called a beautiful man; nor yet, by all appearance, what is called a happy. On the contrary, the face bears evidence of many sorrows, as they are termed, of much hard labour done in this world; and seems to anticipate nothing but more still coming. Quiet stoicism, capable enough of what joy there were, but not expecting any worth mention; great unconscious and some conscious pride, well tempered with a cheery mockery of humour,—are written on that old face; which carries its chin well forward, in spite of the slight stoop about the neck; snuffy nose rather flung into the air, under its old cocked-hat,—like an old snuffy lion on the watch; and such a pair of eyes as no man or lion or lynx of that Century bore elsewhere, according to all the testimony we have. 'Those eyes,' says Mirabeau, 'which, at the bidding of his great soul, fascinated you with seduction or with terror (*portaient, au gré de son âme héroïque, la séduc-*

tion ou la terreur).' [1] Most excellent potent brilliant eyes, swift-darting as the stars, steadfast as the sun; gray, we said, of the azure-gray colour; large enough, not of glaring size; the habitual expression of them vigilance and penetrating sense, rapidity resting on depth. Which is an excellent combination; and gives us the notion of a lambent outer radiance springing from some great inner sea of light and fire in the man. The voice, if he speak to you, is of similar physiognomy: clear, melodious and sonorous; all tones are in it, from that of ingenuous inquiry, graceful sociality, light-flowing banter (rather prickly for most part) up to definite word of command, up to desolating word of rebuke and reprobation; a voice 'the clearest and most agreeable in conversation I ever heard,' says witty Dr. Moore.[2] 'He speaks a great deal,' continues the doctor; 'yet those who hear him, regret that he does not speak a good deal more. His observations are always lively, very often just; and few men possess the talent of repartee in greater perfection.'

Just about threescore and ten years ago,[3] his speakings and his workings came to finis in this World of Time; and he vanished from all eyes into other worlds, leaving much inquiry about him in the minds of men;—which, as my readers and I may feel too well, is yet by no means satisfied. As to his speech, indeed, though it had the worth just ascribed to it and more, and though masses of it were deliberately put on paper by himself, in prose and verse, and continue to be printed and kept legible, what he spoke has pretty much vanished into the inane; and except as record or document of what he did, hardly now concerns mankind. But the things he did were extremely remarkable; and cannot be forgotten by mankind. Indeed, they bear such fruit to the present hour as all the Newspapers are obliged to be taking note of, sometimes to an unpleasant degree. Editors vaguely account this man the 'Creator of the Prussian Monarchy'; which has since grown so large in the world, and troublesome to the Editorial mind in this and other countries. He was indeed the first who, in a highly public manner, notified its creation; announced

[1] Mirabeau, *Histoire Secrète de la Cour de Berlin,* Lettre 28ᵐᵉ (24 Septembre 1786), p. 128 (in edition of Paris, 1821). [Carlyle's note.]
[2] Moore, *View of Society and Manners in France, Switzerland, and Germany* (London, 1779), ii. 246. [Carlyle's note.]
[3] A.D. 1856,—17th August 1786. [Carlyle's note.]

to all men that it was, in very deed, created; standing on its feet there, and would go a great way, on the impulse it had got from him and others. As it has accordingly done; and may still keep doing to lengths little dreamt of by the British Editor in our time; whose prophesyings upon Prussia, and insights into Prussia, in its past, or present or future, are truly as yet inconsiderable, in proportion to the noise he makes with them! The more is the pity for him, —and for myself in the Enterprise now on hand.

It is of this Figure, whom we see by the mind's eye in those Potsdam regions, visible for the last time seventy years ago, that we are now to treat, in the way of solacing ingenuous human curiosity. We are to try for some Historical Conception of this Man and King; some answer to the questions, 'What was he, then? Whence, how? And what did he achieve and suffer in the world?'—such answer as may prove admissible to ingenuous mankind, especially such as may correspond to the Fact (which stands there, abstruse indeed, but actual and unalterable), and so be sure of admissibility one day.

An Enterprise which turns out to be, the longer one looks at it, the more of a formidable, not to say unmanageable nature! Concerning which, on one or two points, it were good, if conveniently possible, to come to some preliminary understanding with the reader. Here, flying on loose leaves, are certain incidental utterances, of various date: these, as the topic is difficult, I will merely label and insert, instead of a formal Discourse, which were too apt to slide into something of a Lamentation, or otherwise take an unpleasant turn.

1. FRIEDRICH THEN, AND FRIEDRICH NOW

This was a man of infinite mark to his contemporaries; who had witnessed surprising feats from him in the world; very questionable notions and ways, which he had contrived to maintain against the world and its criticisms. As an original man has always to do; much more an original ruler of men. The world, in fact, had tried hard to put him down, as it does, unconsciously or consciously, with all such; and after the most conscious exertions, and at one time a dead-lift spasm of all its energies for Seven Years, had not been able. Principalities and powers, Imperial, Royal, Czarish, Papal, enemies innumerable as the sea-sand, had risen against him, only one helper left among the world's Potentates (and that one only while there should be help rendered in return); and he led them all such a dance as had astonished mankind and them.

No wonder they thought him worthy of notice. Every original man of any magnitude is;—nay, in the long-run, who or what else is? But how much more if your original man was a king over men; whose movements were polar, and carried from day to day those of the world along with them. The Samson Agonistes,—were his life passed like that of Samuel Johnson in dirty garrets, and the produce of it only some bits of written paper,—the Agonistes, and how he will comport himself in the Philistine mill; this is always a spectacle of truly epic and tragic nature. The rather, if your Samson, royal or other, is not yet blinded or subdued to the wheel; much more if he vanquish his enemies, *not* by suicidal methods, but march out at last flourishing his miraculous fighting implement, and leaving their mill and them in quite ruinous circumstances. As this King Friedrich fairly managed to do.

For he left the world all bankrupt, we may say; fallen into bottomless abysses of destruction; he still in a paying condition, and with footing capable to carry his affairs and him. When he died, in 1786, the enormous Phenomenon since called FRENCH REVOLUTION was already growling audibly in the depths of the world; meteoric-electric coruscations heralding it, all round the horizon. Strange enough to note, one of Friedrich's last visitors saw Gabriel Honoré Riquetti, Comte de Mirabeau. These two saw one another; twice, for half an hour each time. The last of the old Gods and the first of the modern Titans;—before Pelion leapt on Ossa; and the foul Earth taking fire at last, its vile mephitic elements went up in volcanic thunder. This also is one of the peculiarities of Friedrich, that he is hitherto the last of the Kings; that he ushers-in the French Revolution, and closes an Epoch of World-History. Finishing-off forever the trade of King, think many; who have grown profoundly dark as to Kingship and him.

The French Revolution may be said to have, for about half a century, quite submerged Friedrich, abolished him from the memories of men; and now on coming to light again, he is found defaced under strange mud-incrustations, and the eyes of mankind look at him from a singularly changed, what we must call oblique and perverse, point of vision. This is one of the difficulties in dealing with his History;—especially if you happen to believe both in the French Revolution and in him; that is to say, both that Real Kingship is eternally indispensable, and also that the destruction of Sham Kingship (a frightful process) is occasionally so.

On the breaking-out of that formidable Explosion, and Suicide of his Century, Friedrich sank into comparative obscurity; eclipsed amid the ruins of that universal earthquake, the very dust of which darkened all the air, and made of day a disastrous midnight. Black midnight, broken only by the blaze of conflagrations;—wherein, to our terrified imaginations, were seen, not men, French and other, but ghastly portents, stalking wrathful, and shapes of avenging gods. It must be owned the figure of Napoleon was titanic; especially to the generation that looked on him, and that waited shuddering to be devoured by him. In general, in that French Revolution, all was on a huge scale; if not greater than anything in human experience, at least more grandiose. All was recorded in bulletins, too, addressed to the shilling-gallery; and there were fellows on the stage with such a breadth of sabre, extent of whiskerage, strength of windpipe, and command of men and gunpowder, as had never been seen before. How they bellowed, stalked and flourished about; counterfeiting Jove's thunder to an amazing degree! Terrific Drawcansir figures, of enormous whiskerage, unlimited command of gunpowder; not without sufficient ferocity, and even a certain heroism, stage-heroism, in them; compared with whom, to the shilling-gallery, and frightened excited theatre at large, it seemed as if there had been no generals or sovereigns before; as if Friedrich, Gustavus, Cromwell, William Conqueror and Alexander the Great were not worth speaking of henceforth.

All this, however, in half a century is considerably altered. The Drawcansir equipments getting gradually torn off, the natural size is seen better; translated from the bulletin style into that of fact and history, miracles, even to the shilling-gallery, are not so miraculous. It begins to be apparent that there lived great men before the era of bulletins and Agamemnon. Austerlitz and Wagram shot away more gunpowder,—gunpowder probably in the proportion of ten to one, or a hundred to one; but neither of them was tenth-part such a beating to your enemy as that of Rossbach, brought about by strategic art, human ingenuity and intrepidity, and the loss of 165 men. Leuthen, too, the battle of Leuthen (though so few English readers ever heard of it) may very well hold up its head beside any victory gained by Napoleon or another. For the odds were not far from three to one; the soldiers were of not far from equal quality; and only the General was consummately superior, and the defeat a destruction. Napoleon did indeed, by immense expenditure of men and gunpowder, overrun Europe for a time: but Napoleon never, by husbanding and wisely expending his men and gunpowder, defended a little Prussia against all Europe, year after year for seven years long, till Europe had enough, and gave-up the enterprise as one it could not manage. So soon as the Drawcansir equipments are well torn off, and the shilling-gallery got to silence, it will be found that there were great kings before Napoleon,—and likewise an Art of War, grounded on veracity and human courage and insight, not upon Drawcansir, rodomontade, grandiose Dick-Turpinism, revolutionary madness, and unlimited expenditure of men and gunpowder. 'You may paint with a very big brush, and yet not be a great painter,' says a satirical friend of mine! This is becoming more and more apparent, as the dust-whirlwind, and huge uproar of the last generation, gradually dies away again.

2. EIGHTEENTH CENTURY

One of the grand difficulties in a History of Friedrich is, all along, this same, That he lived in a Century which has no History and can have little or none. A Century so opulent in accumulated falsities,—sad opulence descending on it by inheritance, always at compound interest, and always largely increased by fresh acquirement on such immensity of standing capital;—opulent in that bad way as never Century before was! Which had no longer the consciousness of being false, so false had it grown; and was so steeped in falsity, and impregnated with it to the very

bone, that—in fact the measure of the thing was full, and
a French Revolution had to end it. To maintain much
veracity in such an element, especially for a king, was
no doubt doubly remarkable. But now, how extricate the
man from his Century? How show the man, who is a Reality worthy of being seen, and yet keep his Century, as a
Hypocrisy worthy of being hidden and forgotten, in the
due abeyance?

To resuscitate the Eighteenth Century, or call into men's
view, beyond what is necessary, the poor and sordid personages and transactions of an epoch so related to us, can
be no purpose of mine on this occasion. The Eighteenth
Century, it is well known, does not figure to me as a lovely
one; needing to be kept in mind, or spoken of unneces-
sarily. To me the Eighteenth Century has nothing grand
in it, except that grand universal Suicide, named French
Revolution, by which it terminated its otherwise most
worthless existence with at least one worthy act;—setting
fire to its old home and self; and going up in flames and
volcanic explosions, in a truly memorable and important
manner. A very fit termination, as I thankfully feel, for
such a Century. Century spend-thrift, fraudulent-bankrupt;
gone at length utterly insolvent, without real *money* of
performance in its pocket, and the shops declining to take
hypocrisies and speciosities any farther:—what could
the poor Century do, but at length admit, 'Well, it is so.
I am a swindler-century, and have long been; having
learned the trick of it from my father and grandfather;
knowing hardly any trade but that in false bills, which I
thought foolishly might last forever, and still bring at least
beef and pudding to the favoured of mankind. And behold
it ends; and I am a detected swindler, and have nothing
even to eat. What remains but that I blow my brains out,
and do at length one true action?' Which the poor Century did; many thanks to it, in the circumstances.

For there was need once more of a Divine Revelation
to the torpid frivolous children of men, if they were not
to sink altogether into the ape condition. And in that whirlwind of the Universe,—lights obliterated, and the torn
wrecks of Earth and Hell hurled aloft into the Empyrean;
black whirlwind, which made even apes serious, and drove
most of them mad,—there was, to men, a voice audible;
voice from the heart of things once more, as if to say: 'Ly-

ing is not permitted in this Universe. The wages of lying, you behold, are death. Lying means damnation in this Universe; and Beelzebub, never so elaborately decked in crowns and mitres, is *not* God! This was a revelation truly to be named of the Eternal, in our poor Eighteenth Century; and has greatly altered the complexion of said Century to the Historian ever since.

Whereby, in short, that Century is quite confiscate, fallen bankrupt, given up to the auctioneers;—Jew-brokers sorting out of it at this moment, in a confused distressing manner, what is still valuable or saleable. And, in fact, it lies massed up in our minds as a disastrous wrecked inanity, not useful to dwell upon; a kind of dusky chaotic background, on which the figures that had some veracity in them,—a small company, and ever growing smaller as our demands rise in strictness,—are delineated for us.—'And yet it is the Century of our own Grand-fathers?' cries the reader. Yes, reader! truly. It is the ground out of which we ourselves have sprung; whereon now we have our immediate footing, and first of all strike down our roots for nourishment;—and, alas, in large sections of the practical world, it (what we specially mean by *it*) still continues flourishing all round us! to for-get it quite is not yet possible, nor would be profitable. What to do with it, and its forgotten fooleries and 'His-tories,' worthy only of forgetting?—Well: so much of it as by nature *adheres;* what of it cannot be disengaged from our Hero and his operations: approximately so much, and no more! Let that be our bargain in regard to it.

FROM *The Early Kings*
of Norway

1875

[Along with *The Portraits of John Knox*, *The Early Kings of Norway* was the last work published in Carlyle's lifetime. It was first published in *Fraser's* in January and March 1875. Because of the infirmities of age, Carlyle was obliged to dictate this work to an amanuensis, a method of writing he disliked. The work of a man of almost eighty, it still contains flashes of Carlyle's genius. Its subject returns him to the heroic and the Germanic and to the conflict of elemental powers, always congenial topics for Carlyle. The selection printed below, with a title supplied by the present editor, is taken from Chapter six, "Olaf Tryggveson," who ruled from 995-1000 and converted Norway, Iceland, and Greenland to Christianity. After his death Norway fell into disunity.]

FROM CHAPTER VI—OLAF TRYGGVESON

[DEATH OF OLAF TRYGGVESON]

Olaf Tryggveson, though his kingdom was the smallest of the Norse Three, had risen to a renown over all the Norse world, which neither he of Denmark nor he of Sweden could pretend to rival. A magnificent, far-shining man; more expert in all 'bodily exercises' as the Norse called them, than any man had ever been before him, or after was. Could keep five daggers in the air, always catching the proper fifth by its handle, and sending it aloft again; could shoot supremely, throw a javelin with either hand; and, in fact, in battle usually threw two together. These, with swimming, climbing, leaping, were the then admirable Fine Arts of the North; in all which Tryggveson appears to have been the Raphael and the Michael Angelo at once. Essentially definable, too, if we look well into him, as a wild bit of real heroism, in such rude guise and environment; a high, true, and great human soul. A jovial burst of laughter in him, withal; a bright, airy, wise way of speech; dressed beautifully and with care; a man admired and loved exceedingly by those he liked; dreaded as death by those he did not like. 'Hardly any king,' says Snorro, 'was ever so well obeyed; by one class out of zeal and love, by the rest out of dread.' His glorious course, however, was not to last long.

King Svein of the Double-Beard had not yet completed his conquest of England,—by no means yet, some thirteen horrid years of that still before him!—when, over in Denmark, he found that complaints against him and intricacies had arisen, on the part principally of one Burislav, King of the Wends (far up the Baltic), and in a less degree with the King of Sweden and other minor individuals. Svein earnestly applied himself to settle these, and have his hands free. Burislav, an aged heathen gentleman, proved reasonable and conciliatory; so, too, the King of Sweden, and Dowager Queen Sigrid, his managing mother. Bargain in both these cases got sealed and crowned by marriage. Svein, who had become a widower lately, now wedded Sigrid; and might think, possibly enough, he had got a proud bargain, though a heathen one. Burislav also insisted on marriage with Princess Thyri, the Double-Beard's sister. Thyri, inexpressibly disinclined to wed an aged heathen of that stamp, pleaded hard with her brother; but the Double-Bearded was inexorable; Thyri's wailings and entreaties went for nothing. With some guardian foster-brother, and a serving-maid or two, she had to go on this hated journey. Old Burislav, at sight of her, blazed out into marriage-feast of supreme magnificence, and was charmed to see her, but Thyri would not join the marriage party; refused to eat with it or sit with it at all. Day after day, for six days; flatly refused; and after nightfall of the sixth, glided out with her foster-brother into the woods, into by-paths and inconceivable wanderings; and, in effect, got home to Denmark. Brother Svein was not for the moment there; probably enough gone to England again. But Thyri knew too well he would not allow her to stay here, or anywhere that he could help, except with the old heathen she had just fled from.

Thyri, looking round the world, saw no likely road for her, but to Olaf Tryggveson in Norway; to beg protection from the most heroic man she knew of in the world. Olaf, except by renown, was not known to her; but by renown he well was. Olaf, at sight of her, promised protection and asylum against all mortals. Nay, in discoursing with Thyri Olaf perceived more and more clearly what a fine handsome being, soul and body, Thyri was; and in a short space of time winded up by proposing marriage to Thyri; who, humbly, and we may fancy with what secret joy, consented to say yes, and become Queen of Norway. In the due months they had a little son, Harald; who, it is credibly recorded, was the joy of both his parents; but who, to their inexpressible sorrow, in about a year died, and vanished from them. This, and one other fact now to be mentioned, is all the wedded history we have of Thyri.

The other fact is, that Thyri had, by inheritance or covenant, not depending on her marriage with old Burislav, considerable properties in Wendland; which, she often reflected, might be not a little behoveful to her here in Norway, where her civil-list was probably but straitened. She spoke of this to her husband; but her husband would take no hold, merely made her gifts, and said, "Pooh, pooh, can't we live without old Burislav and his Wendland properties?" So that the lady sank into ever deeper anxiety and eagerness about this Wendland object; took to weeping; sat weeping whole days; and when Olaf asked, "What ails thee, then?" would answer, or did answer once, "What a different man my father Harald Gormson was" (vulgarly called Blue-tooth), "compared with some that are now kings! For no King Svein in the world would Harald Gormson have given up his own or his wife's just rights!" Whereupon Tryggveson started up, exclaiming in some heat, "Of thy brother Svein I never was afraid; if Svein and I meet in contest, it will not be Svein, I believe, that conquers;" and went off in a towering fume. Consented, however, at last, had to consent, to get his fine fleet equipped and armed, and decide to sail with it to Wendland to have speech and settlement with King Burislav.

Tryggveson had already ships and navies that were the wonder of the North. Especially in building war ships,— the Crane, the Serpent, last of all the Long Serpent,[1]—he

[1] His Long Serpent, judged by some to be of the size of a frigate of forty-five guns (Laing). [Carlyle's note.]

had, for size, for outward beauty, and inward perfection of equipment, transcended all example.

This new sea expedition became an object of attention to all neighbours; especially Queen Sigrid the Proud and Svein Double-Beard, her now king, were attentive to it.

"This insolent Tryggveson," Queen Sigrid would often say, and had long been saying, to her Svein, "to marry thy sister without leave had or asked of thee; and now flaunting forth his war navies, as if he, king only of paltry Norway, were the big hero of the North! Why do you suffer it, you kings really great?"

By such persuasions and reiterations, King Svein of Denmark, King Olaf of Sweden, and Jarl Eric, now a great man there, grown rich by prosperous sea robbery and other good management, were brought to take the matter up, and combine strenuously for destruction of King Olaf Tryggveson on this grand Wendland expedition of his. Fleets and forces were with best diligence got ready; and, withal, a certain Jarl Sigwald, of Jomsburg, chieftain of the Jomsvikings, a powerful, plausible, and cunning man, was appointed to find means of joining himself to Tryggveson's grand voyage, of getting into Tryggveson's confidence, and keeping Svein Double-Beard, Eric, and the Swedish King aware of all his movements.

King Olaf Tryggveson, unacquainted with all this, sailed away in summer, with his splendid fleet; went through the Belts with prosperous winds, under bright skies, to the admiration of both shores. Such a fleet, with its shining Serpents, long and short, and perfection of equipment and appearance, the Baltic never saw before. Jarl Sigwald joined with new ships by the way: "Had," he too, "a visit to King Burislav to pay; how could he ever do it in better company?" and studiously and skilfully ingratiated himself with King Olaf. Old Burislav, when they arrived, proved altogether courteous, handsome, and amenable; agreed at once to Olaf's claims for his now queen, did the rites of hospitality with a generous plenitude to Olaf; who cheerily renewed acquaintance with that country, known to him in early days (the cradle of his fortunes in the viking line), and found old friends there still surviving, joyful to meet him again. Jarl Sigwald encouraged these delays, King Svein and Co. not being yet quite ready. "Get ready!" Sigwald directed them, and they diligently did. Olaf's men, their business now done, were impatient to be home; and grudged every day of loitering there; but, till Sigwald pleased, such his power of flattering and cajoling Tryggveson, they could not get away.

At length, Sigwald's secret messengers reporting all ready on the part of Svein and Co., Olaf took farewell of Burislav and Wendland, and all gladly sailed away. Svein, Eric, and the Swedish king, with their combined fleets, lay in wait behind some cape in a safe little bay of some island, then called Svolde, but not in our time to be found; the Baltic tumults in the fourteenth century having swallowed it, as some think, and leaving us uncertain whether it was in the neighbourhood of Rügen Island or in the Sound of Elsinore. There lay Svein, Eric, and Co. waiting till Tryggveson and his fleet came up, Sigwald's spy messengers daily reporting what progress he and it had made. At length, one bright summer morning, the fleet made appearance, sailing in loose order, Sigwald, as one acquainted with the shoal places, steering ahead, and showing them the way.

Snorro rises into one of his pictorial fits, seized with enthusiasm at the thought of such a fleet, and reports to us largely in what order Tryggveson's winged Coursers of the Deep, in long series, for perhaps an hour or more, came on, and what the three potentates, from their knoll of vantage, said of each as it hove in sight. Svein thrice over guessed this and the other noble vessel to be the Long Serpent; Eric always correcting him, "No, that is not the Long Serpent yet" (and *aside* always), "Nor shall you be lord of it, king, when it does come." The Long Serpent itself did make appearance. Eric, Svein, and the Swedish king hurried on board, and pushed out of their hiding-place into the open sea. Treacherous Sigwald, at the beginning of all this, had suddenly doubled that cape of theirs, and struck into the bay out of sight, leaving the foremost Tryggveson ships astonished, and uncertain what to do, if it were not simply to strike sail and wait till Olaf himself with the Long Serpent arrived.

Olaf's chief captains, seeing the enemy's huge fleet come out, and how the matter lay, strongly advised King Olaf to elude this stroke of treachery, and, with all sail, hold on his course, fight being now on so unequal terms. Snorro says, the king, high on the quarter-deck where he stood, replied, "Strike the sails; never shall men of mine think of flight. I never fled from battle. Let God dispose of my life; but flight I will never take." And so the battle arrangements immediately began, and the battle with all fury went loose; and lasted hour after hour, till almost sunset, if I well recollect. "Olaf stood on the Serpent's quarter-deck," says Snorro, "high over the others. He had a gilt shield and a helmet inlaid with gold; over his armour he had a short red coat, and was easily distinguished from other men." Snorro's account of the battle is altogether animated, graphic, and so minute that antiquaries gather from it, if so disposed (which we but little are), what the methods of Norse sea-fighting were; their shooting of arrows, casting of javelins, pitching of big stones, ultimately boarding, and mutual clashing and smashing, which it would not avail us to speak of here. Olaf stood conspicuous all day, throwing javelins, of deadly aim, with both hands at once; encouraging, fighting and commanding like a highest sea-king.

The Danish fleet, the Swedish fleet, were, both of them, quickly dealt with, and successively withdrew out of shot-range. And then Jarl Eric came up, and fiercely grappled with the Long Serpent, or, rather, with her surrounding comrades; and gradually, as they were beaten empty of men, with the Long Serpent herself. The fight grew ever fiercer, more furious. Eric was supplied with new men from the Swedes and Danes; Olaf had no such resource, except from the crews of his own beaten ships, and at length this also failed him; all his ships, except the Long Serpent, being beaten and emptied. Olaf fought on unyielding. Eric twice boarded him, was twice repulsed. Olaf kept his quarterdeck; unconquerable, though left now more and more hopeless, fatally short of help. A tall young man, called Einar Tamberskelver, very celebrated and important afterwards in Norway, and already the best archer known, kept busy with his bow. Twice he nearly shot Jarl Eric in his ship. "Shoot me that man," said Jarl Eric to a bowman near him; and, just as Tamberskelver was drawing his bow the third time, an arrow hit it in the middle and broke it in two. "What is this that has broken?" asked King Olaf. "Norway from thy hand, king," answered Tamberskelver. Tryggveson's men, he observed with surprise, were striking violently on Eric's; but to no purpose; nobody fell. "How is this?" asked Tryggveson. "Our swords are notched and blunted, king; they do not cut." Olaf stept down to his arm-chest; delivered out new swords; and it was observed as he did it, blood ran trickling from his wrist; but none knew where the wound was. Eric boarded a third time. Olaf, left with hardly more than one man, sprang overboard (one sees that red coat of his still glancing in the evening sun), and sank in the deep waters to his long rest.

Rumour ran among his people that he still was not dead; grounding on some movement by the ships of that traitorous Sigwald, they fancied Olaf had dived beneath the keels of his enemies, and got away with Sigwald, as Sigwald himself evidently did. 'Much was hoped, supposed, spoken,' says one old mourning Skald; 'but the truth was, Olaf Tryggveson was never seen in Norseland more.' Strangely he remains still a shining figure to us; the wildly beautifulest man, in body and in soul, that one has ever heard of in the North.

LETTER TO HIS SISTER

[The following letter to Carlyle's sister was written one week after the death of Jane Welsh Carlyle, who is the "she" referred to in the letter. Carlyle enclosed letters written to Mrs. Carlyle just before her death.]

LETTER TO MRS. AITKEN, *Dumfries*

Chelsea, 28 April 1866

Dear Sister—You will read these three Letters with a very melancholy interest;—especially the *one* of them I wrote from Scotsbrig the morning we left for Dumfries; and will regret with me to the end of your life that she did not see it; alas, no; it was *not* posted at Ecclefechan by 6 P.M. in time for the morning mail at London; would come about 2 P.M. by which time she was gone *out,* never to return more. Oh why didn't I post it myself at Blackburn as I rode past; why did I wait for anything,—why did Jamie [Carlyle] junior make any delay in posting! But alas what is the use of such reflexions!—was not her own death caused by the hurt toe of a miserable little scraping of a *dog* hardly even hers? That wretched animalcule has done *me* more mischief than all the men and animals that have ever lived in my time! We must take these paltrinesses to us, also; they are part of our bitter cup. The Letter she wrote, after that of Scotsbrig *should* have arrived, you will never forget reading with me last Sunday; after writing so, she lunched with the Forsters (old friends), was never seen more brilliantly cheerful, *well* beyond wont, and seemed to *eat* better than usual: "my Friend coming home to me, day after to-morrow!"—and within three-quarters of an hour, she sat dead. Oh, that Monday night, oh this week in general, the *black* week of my poor life.—But *she* died happy and victorious, in the way she had always wished to do.—No more; this is my first writing, and my hand is as you see.

In a few days I will write again. Day by day I am getting bits of order introduced into this great overturn of my past existence; that is the only thing *she* would have wished as a consolation to me. I saw her dead face twice: beautiful as Eternity, soft as an angel's or as a babe's. Put in these four Letters into the Miss Welsh's cover,—and dispatch them by *Monday's* mail, that you may have *time* for reading them (yourself only).—I will walk all day; my sleep only half come back: well otherwise. God bless you, dear Sister, and reward your sympathy and kindness for me.

Ever yours,

T.C.

FROM *Reminiscences*

1 8 6 6 , 1 8 8 1

[Carlyle's *Reminiscences,* published after his death in 1881, is a gathering of essays and recollections on persons and places Carlyle had known. Although some of the material (notably the essay on his father, James Carlyle) was written as early as 1832, most of it, including the selection that follows, was written in 1866 just after the death of Jane Welsh Carlyle. The elegiac tone of the *Reminiscences* (hardly surprising for a man of seventy who had just lost his wife) has occasioned some criticism as demonstrating a neurotic belated remorse over ill-treatment of Jane. Yet the tone is characteristic of Carlyle's acute awareness of the transitoriness of life and is consistent with many earlier writings. In the following selection, taken from the Reminiscence of Jane Welsh Carlyle, Carlyle recalls his and Jane's early years in London in the mid-1830s, the loss of the manuscript of *The French Revolution,* and acquaintanceship with prominent literary and political figures.]

FROM JANE WELSH CARLYLE

[EARLY YEARS IN LONDON]

. . . We proceeded all through Belgrave Square hither, with our Servant, our looser luggage, ourselves and a little canary bird ("Chico" which she had brought with her from Craigenputtock); one hackney coach rumbling on with us all. Chico, in Belgrave Square, burst into singing, which we took as a good omen. We were all of us striving to be cheerful (she needed no effort of striving): but we "had burnt our ships," and at bottom the case was grave. I don't remember our arriving at this door; but I do the cheerful Gypsy life we had here among the litter and carpenters, for three incipient days. Leigh Hunt was in the next street, sending kind *un*practical messages; in the evenings, I think, personally coming in; we had made acquaintance with him (properly he with us), just before leaving in Spring 1832. Huggermugger was the type of his Economics, in all respects, financial and other; but he was himself a pretty man, in clean cotton nightgown, and with the airiest kindly style of sparkling talk,—wanting only wisdom of a sound kind, and true insight into fact. A great want!

I remember going with my Dear One (and Eliza Miles, the "Daughter" of Ampton Street, as escort), to some dim ironmonger's shop, to buy kettles and pans, on the thriftiest of fair terms. How noble and more than royal is the look of that to me now, and of my Royal One then! California is dross and dirt to the experiences I have had.——A tinderbox with steel and flint was part of our outfit (incredible as it may seem at this date): I could myself burn rags into tinder; and I have groped my way to the kitchen, in sleepless nights, to strike a light, for my pipe, in that manner. . . . *Chico* got a Wife by and by (Oh the wit there was about that and its sequels), produced two bright yellow young ones, who, so soon as they were fledged, got out into the trees of the garden, and vanished towards swift destruction; upon which, villain Chico finding his poor wife fallen so tattery and ugly, took to pecking a hole in her head; pecked it, and killed her: by and by ending his own disreputable life. I had begun *The French Revolution* (trees at that time before our window—a tale by these too on her part): infinitesimal little matters of that kind hovered round me like bright fire-flies, irradiated by *her* light! Breakfast, early, was in the back part of this ground-floor room; details of gradual intentions etc. as to *French Revolution,* advices, approval or criticism, always beautifully wise, and so soft and loving had they even been foolish!

We were not at all unhappy during those three years of *French Revolution*; at least she was not; her health perhaps being better than mine, which latter was in a strangely painful, and as if conflagrated condition towards the end. She had made the house "a little Eden round her" (so neat and graceful in its simplicity and thrifty poverty); "little Paradise round you,"—those were Edward Irving's words to her, on his visit to us; short affectionate visit, the first and the last (October 1834); on horseback, just about setting off for Glasgow, where he died, December following: I watched him till at the corner of Cook's Grounds, he vanished, and we never saw him more. Much consulting about him we had already had: a *Letter* to Henry Drummond (about delivering him from the fools and fanatics that were agitating him to death, as I clearly saw) lay on the mantelpiece here for some days, in doubt, and was then burnt. Brother, Father, rational Friend, I could not think of, except Henry; and him I had seen only once, not without clear view of his unsoundness too. Practically we had long ago had to take leave of poor Irving: but we both knew him well, and all his *brotherhoods* to us first and last, and mourned him in our hearts as a lost Hero. Nobler men I have seen few if any, till the foul gulfs of London Pulpit-Popularity sucked him in, and tragically swallowed him.

We were beginning to find a "friend" or two here; that is, an eligible acquaintance,—none as yet very dear to us, though several brought a certain pleasure. Leigh Hunt was here almost nightly, three or four times a week, I should reckon;—he came always neatly dressed, was thoroughly courteous, friendly of spirit, and talked—like a singing bird. Good insight, plenty of a kind of humour too;—I remember little *warbles* in the turns of his fine voice which were full of fun and charm. We gave him Scotch Porridge to supper ("nothing in nature so interesting and delightful"): *she* played him Scotch tunes; a man he to understand and feel them well. His talk was often enough (perhaps at first oftenest) Literary-Biographical, Autobiographical, wandering into Criticism, *Reform of Society, Progress*, etc. etc.,—on which latter points he gradually found me very shocking (I believe,—so fatal to his rose-coloured visions on the subject). An innocent-hearted, but misguided, in fact rather foolish, *un*practical and often much-suffering man. John Mill was another steady visitor (had by this time introduced his Mrs. Taylor too,—a very Will-o'-wispish "Iridescence" of a creature; meaning nothing bad either). She at first considered my Jane to be a rustic spirit fit for rather tutoring and twirling about when the humour took her; but got taught better (to her lasting memory) before long. Mill was very useful about *French Revolution*; lent me all his Books, which were quite a Collection on that subject; gave me, frankly, clearly and with zeal, all his better knowledge than my own (which was pretty frequently of some use in this or the other detail): being full of eagerness for such an advocate in that cause as he felt I should be. His evenings here were sensibly agreeable for most part. Talk rather wintry (*"sawdust"*-ish, as old Sterling once called it); but always well-informed and sincere. The Mrs. Taylor business was becoming more and more of questionable benefit to him (we could see), but on that subject we were strictly silent; and he was very pretty still. For several years he came hither, and walked with me every Sunday,—Dialogues fallen all dim, except that they were never in the least genial to me, and that I took them as one would wine where no nectar is to be had,—or even thin ale where no wine. *Her* view of him was very kindly, though precisely to the same effect. How well do I still remember that night when he came to tell us, pale as Hector's ghost that my unfortunate First Volume was burnt! It was like *half* sentence of death to us both; and we had to pretend to take it lightly, so dismal and ghastly was *his* horror at it, and try to talk of other matters. He staid three mortal hours or so; his departure quite a relief to us. Oh the burst of sympathy my poor Darling then gave me; flinging her arms round my neck, and openly lamenting, condoling, and encouraging like a nobler second self! Under Heaven is nothing beautifuller. We sat talking till late; "*shall* be written again," my fixed word and resolution to her. Which proved to be such a task as I never tried before or since. I wrote out *Feast of Pikes* (vol. ii), and then went at it,—found it fairly *impossible* for about a fortnight; passed three weeks (reading Marryat's novels), tried, cautious-cautiously, as on ice paper-thin, once more; and in short had a job more like breaking my heart than any other in my experience. Jeannie, alone of beings, burnt like a steady lamp beside me. I forget how much of money we still had: I think there was at first something like £300; perhaps £280 to front London with. Nor can I in the least remember where we had gathered such a sum;—except that it was our own, no part of it borrowed or *given* us by anybody. "Fit to last till *French Revolution* is ready!"—and she had no misgivings at all. Mill was penitently liberal: sent me £200 (in a day or two), of which I kept £100 (actual cost of house while I had written burnt volume); upon which he bought me *Biographie Universelle*, which I got bound, and still have. Wish I could find a way of getting the now much macerated, changed, and fanaticised "John Stuart Mill" to take that £100 back; but I fear there is no way!

How my Incomparable One contrived to beat out these exiguous resources into covering the appointed space I cannot now see, nor did I then know: but in the like of that, as in her other tasks, she was silently successful always, and never, that I saw, had a misgiving about success. There would be some trifling increments from *Fraser's Magazine,* perhaps (*Diamond Necklace,* etc. were probably of those years); but the guess stated above is the nearest I can now come to, and I don't think is in defect of the actuality.—I was very diligent, very desperate ("desperate *hope!*"),—wrote my two (folio) pages (Perhaps four or five of print) day by day: then about two P.M. walked out; always heavy-laden, grim of mood; sometimes with a feeling not rebellious or impious against God Most High, but otherwise too similar to Satan's stepping the burning marle. Some conviction I had that the Book was worth something, —a pretty constant persuasion that it was not I that could make it better. Once or twice among the flood of equipages at Hyde-Park Corner, I recollect sternly thinking: "Yes; and perhaps none of you could do what I am at!" But generally my feeling was, "I will finish this Book, throw it at your feet; buy a rifle and spade, and withdraw to the Transatlantic Wilderness,—far from human beggaries and baseness!" This had a kind of comfort to me; yet I always knew too, in the background, that this would not practically do. In short, my nervous-system had got dreadfully irritated and inflamed before I quite ended; and my desire was *intense,* beyond words, to have done with it. The *last* paragraph I well remember writing: upstairs in the drawing-room that now is, which was then my writing-room; beside *her* there, in a gray evening (summer I suppose), soon after tea perhaps;—and thereupon, with her dear blessing on me, going out to walk. I had said before going out, "What they will do with this Book, none knows, my Jeannie, lass; but they have not had, for a two hundred years, any Book that came more truly from a man's very heart; and so let them trample it under foot and hoof as *they* see best!" "Pooh, pooh! they cannot trample that!" she would cheerily answer; for her own approval (I think she had read always regularly behind me), especially in vol. iii., was strong and decided.

We knew the Sterlings by this time, John, and all of them. Old Sterling very often here; knew Henry Taylor, etc., the Wilsons of Eccleston Street, Rev. Mr. Dunn, etc. etc.; and the waste wilderness of London was becoming a peopled garden to us, in some measure, especially to her, who had a frank welcome to every sort of worth and even kindly-singularity in her fellow-creatures, such as I could at no time rival.

Sprinklings of Foreigners, "Political Refugees," had already begun to come about us; to me seldom of any interest, except for the foreign instruction to be gathered from them (if any), and the curiosity attached to their foreign ways. Only two of them had the least charm to me as men: Mazzini whom, I remember, Mr. Taylor, Mrs. Taylor's (ultimately Mrs. Mill's) *then* Husband, an innocent dull good man, brought in to me one evening; and Godefroi Cavaignac, whom my Jane had met somewhere, and thought worth inviting. Mazzini I once or twice talked with; recognisably a most valiant, faithful, considerably gifted and noble soul; but hopelessly given up to his Republicanisms, his "Progress," and other Rousseau fanaticism, for which I had at no time the least credence, or any considerable respect amid my pity. We soon tired of one another, Mazzini and I; and he fell mainly to *her* share; off and on, for a good many years, yielding her the charm of a sincere mutual esteem, and withal a good deal of occasional amusement from his curious bits of Exile London- and Foreign-life, and his singular Italian-English modes of locution now and then. For example,—Petrucci having quenched his own fiery chimney one day, and escaped the fine (as he hoped), "there *came to pass* a Sweep," with finer nose in the solitary street, who involved him again, Or, *"Ma, mio caro, non v'è ci un morto!"* which, I see, she has copied into her poor little book of *notabilia.* Her reports of these things to me, as we sat at breakfast or otherwise, had a tinkle of the finest mirth in them, and in short a beauty and felicity I have never seen surpassed. Ah me, ah me, *whither* fled?

LETTER TO HIS SISTER

[The following letter was written at the request of Carlyle's sister that he report on his audience with Queen Victoria. It shows that at seventy-four Carlyle retained his gift for vivid description.]

LETTER TO MRS. AITKEN, *Dumfries*

Chelsea, 11 March 1869

Dear Jean— . . . "Interview" took place this day gone a week; nearly a week before that, the Dean and Dean*ess* (who is called Lady Augusta Stanley, once *Bruce,* an active hard and busy little woman) drove up here, and, in a solemnly mysterious, though half quizzical manner, invited me for Thursday, 4th, 5 P.M.:—Must come, a very "high or indeed highest person has long been desirous," etc., etc. I saw well enough it was the Queen incognita; and briefly agreed to come. "Half past 4 come *you!*" and then went their ways.

Walking up at the set time, I was there ushered into a long Drawing-room in their monastic edifice. I found no Stanley there; only at the farther end, a tall old *Gearpole* of a Mrs. Grote,—the most wooden woman I know in London or the world, who thinks herself very clever, etc.,—the sight of whom taught me to expect others; as accordingly, in a few minutes, fell out. Grote and Wife, Sir Charles Lyell and ditto, Browning and myself, these I saw were to be our party. "Better than bargain!" "These will take the edge off the thing, if edge it have!"—which it hadn't, nor threatened to have.

The Stanleys and we were all in a flow of talk, and some flunkies had done setting coffee-pots, tea-cups of sublime patterns, when Her Majesty, punctual to the minute, glided softly in, escorted by her Dame in waiting (a Dowager Duchess of Athol), and by the Princess Louise, decidedly a very pretty young lady, and *clever* too, as I found in speaking to her afterwards.

The Queen came softly forward, a kindly little smile on her face; gently shook hands with all three women, gently acknowledged with a nod the silent deep bow of us

493

male monsters; and directly in her presence everybody was as if at ease again. She is a comely little lady, with a pair of kind clear and intelligent grey eyes; still looks plump and almost young (in spite of one broad wrinkle that shows in each cheek *occasionally*); has a fine soft low voice; soft indeed her whole manner is and melodiously perfect; it is impossible to imagine a *politer* little woman. Nothing the least imperious; all gentle, all *sincere*-looking, unembarrassing, rather attractive even;— *makes* you feel too (if you have sense in you) that she is Queen.

After a little word to each of us in succession as we stood,—to me it was, "Sorry you did not see my Daughter," Princess of Prussia (or "she sorry," perhaps?), which led us into Potsdam, Berlin, etc., for an instant or two; to Sir Charles Lyell I heard her say, "Gold in Sutherland," but quickly and delicately cut him *short* in responding; to Browning, "Are you writing anything?" (he has just been publishing the absurdest of things!); to Grote I did not hear what she said: but it was touch-and-go with everybody; Majesty visibly *without* interest or nearly so of her *own*. This done, Coffee (very black and muddy) was handed round; Queen and Three women taking seats (Queen in the corner of a sofa, Lady Deaness in opposite corner, Mrs. Grote in a chair *intrusively close* to Majesty, Lady Lyell modestly at the *diagonal* corner); we others obliged to stand, and hover within call. Coffee fairly done, Lady Augusta called me gently to "come and speak with Her Majesty." I obeyed, first asking, as an old infirmish man, Majesty's permission to *sit*, which was graciously conceded. Nothing of the least significance was said, nor *needed*; however my bit of dialogue went very well. "What part of Scotland I came from?" Dumfriesshire (where Majesty might as well go some time); Carlisle, i.e., "Caer-Lewel, a place about the antiquity of King Solomon (according to Milton, whereat Majesty smiled); Border-Ballads (and even old Jamie Pool slightly alluded to,—not by name!); Glasgow, and even Grandfather's ride thither, —ending in mere *psalms* and streets *vacant* at half-past nine P.M.;—hard sound and genuine Presbyterian root of what has now shot up to be such a monstrously ugly Cabbage-tree and Hemlock-tree!" All which Her Majesty seemed to take rather well.

Whereupon Mrs. Grote rose, and good-naturedly brought forward her Husband to her own chair, *cheek by jowl* with Her Majesty, who evidently did not care a straw for him; but kindly asked, "Writing anything?" and one heard "Aristotle, now that I have done with Plato," etc., etc.—but only for a minimum of time. Majesty herself (I think àpropos of some question of my *shaking hand*) said something about her own difficulty in writing by dictation, which brought forward Lady Lyell and Husband, mutually used to the operation. After which, talk becoming trivial, Majesty gracefully retired,—Lady Augusta with her,—and in ten minutes more, returned to receive our farewell bows; which, too, she did very prettily; and sailed out as if moving on skates, and bending her head towards us with a smile. By the Underground Railway I was home before seven, and out of the adventure, with only a headache of little moment.

Froude tells me there are foolish *myths* about the poor business; especially about my share of it; but this is the real truth;—*worth* to me, in strict speech all but nothing; the *myths* even less than nothing. . . .

T. Carlyle.

LETTER TO HIS NEPHEW

[This is one of the latest of Carlyle's published letters. It depicts his reaction to the news of the death of his brother, Alexander Carlyle, who had emigrated to Canada.]

LETTER TO THOMAS CARLYLE, JR.,
Brantford, Canada

Chelsea, 4 May 1876

Dear Nephew Tom—Yesterday morning your sad Letter reached me; and to-day in spite of my weakness I must write you a word of sympathy and mournful affection. For a good many weeks past, ever since your Sister Maggie's Letter to me here, I had a sad and painful assurance in me, which was shared by all, that the fatal end could not be distant. We hoped, like you, that, the gloom of Winter being nearly over, the Spring with its sunshine might produce some temporary alleviation; but ever from that day your Father's sad image fixed itself in my mind, and a thousand thoughts and tender recollections of him were my continual companions. At last unexpectedly, on the 20th of April last your Brother Alick's Letter came to his Cousin Mary, with the news that all was now ended; and that the kindest and truest-hearted of Brothers was gone forever. For himself, so loaded with pain, one could only regard the event as a beneficent deliverance; but the shock we all had from it was heavy and sore. There never was a kinder Brother than he, from his earliest years and without break throughout life, was to me. True as steel he ever was, and with a fund of tenderness, strange in one of so fiery a temper; a man of infinite talent, too, had it ever been developed by friendly fortune; I never knew a more faithful, ingenious and valiant man. He was, withal, the first human being I ever came to friendship and familiarity with in this world; and our hearts were knit together by a thousand ties. Very beautiful, very sad and tender are the endless recollections I have of him, which must continue with me as companions while I live. No doubt similar thoughts dwelt in his mind about me, and it

496

seems were ever present with him. Nothing has affected me more than what Alick mentions in his Letter, that in the wanderings of mind in the last hours of his life your Father asked repeatedly "If Brother Tom were not coming from Edinburgh to-morrow." Ah me, ah me, can I ever forget these words? He always escorted me out to meet the Dumfries Coach near Moffat, and back again generally from Moffat, when I was returning, a right glad man on these latter occasions, a quietly sad but always helpful one on the former. . . .

I will beg you now further to send me some lucid account of family affairs at Bield and what new arrangements and settlements are made or contemplated in this great change. Make my loving regards to your poor Mother; be gentle and good to her, all of you,—I need not bid you. Your Sister Jane has not written to me for a long while. Tell her, too, I wish she would. With my best blessings on you all, and prayers that your lives may be worthy of him who has gone,

Ever your affectionate
T. Carlyle.